The Emergent African Union Law

The Emergent African Union Law

Conceptualization, Delimitation, and Application

Edited by

OLUFEMI AMAO
MICHÈLE OLIVIER
KONSTANTINOS D. MAGLIVERAS

OXFORD
UNIVERSITY PRESS

OXFORD
UNIVERSITY PRESS

Great Clarendon Street, Oxford, OX2 6DP,
United Kingdom

Oxford University Press is a department of the University of Oxford.
It furthers the University's objective of excellence in research, scholarship,
and education by publishing worldwide. Oxford is a registered trade mark of
Oxford University Press in the UK and in certain other countries

First Edition published in 2021

Impression: 1

Published in the United States of America by Oxford University Press
198 Madison Avenue, New York, NY 10016, United States of America

British Library Cataloguing in Publication Data

Data available

Library of Congress Control Number: 2021937970

ISBN 978–0–19–886215–4

DOI: 10.1093/oso/9780198862154.001.0001

Printed and bound by
CPI Group (UK) Ltd, Croydon, CR0 4YY

Contents

PART 3 ADDRESSING CIVIL AND POLITICAL CHALLENGES THROUGH AFRICAN UNION LAW: PERSPECTIVES

PART 4 ADDRESSING SOCIO-ECONOMIC CHALLENGES THROUGH AFRICAN UNION LAW: PERSPECTIVES

PART 5 ENFORCING AFRICAN UNION LAW: PERSPECTIVES

Contributors

Dr **Rhuks Ako**
(AUC, Addis-Ababa) rhuksako@gmail.com: Chapter 23 Propagation and Enforcement of AU Law: Perspectives from the Peace and Security Arena

Dr **Femi Amao**
(University of Sussex) o.amao@sussex.ac.uk: Road Map to the Emergent AU Law; Chapter 3 Framing AU Law through the Lenses of International Constitutionalization and Federalism; Chapter 24 AU Law and its Future: Reform and the Kagame Report

Aua Baldé
(University Institute of Lisbon (IUL)) auabalde@gmail.com: Chapter 16 The Right to Education in AU Law

Professor **Benedict Abrahamson Chigara**
(Qatar University): ben.chigara@qu.edu.qa: Chapter 13 The Quasi-Supranational AU and the International Criminal Court

Dr **Cristiano d'Orsi**
(SARCIL/University of Johannesburg) cristianod@uj.ac.za: Chapter 12 Combating Terrorism and Managing Asylum Seekers and Refugees under AU Law

Dr **Kamala Dawar**
(University of Sussex) K.Dawar@sussex.ac.uk: Chapter 4 Harmonization and Integration in Africa: The Case of Competition Law and Policy

Dr **Eghosa Ekhator**
(University of Derby) e.ekhator@derby.ac.uk: Chapter 18 Sustainable Development and the AU Legal Order

Rui Garrido
(University Institute of Lisbon (IUL) rui.a.garrido@gmail.com: Chapter 16 The Right to Education in AU Law

Professor **Robert Home**
(Anglia Ruskin University) robhome47@gmail.com: Chapter 15 Land, Property, and Human Rights in AU Law and Policy

Dr **Pablo Iglesias-Rodríguez**
(University of Sussex) p.iglesias-rodriguez@sussex.ac.uk: Chapter 5 The AU and Global Financial Standard-Setting

Dr **Ovo Imoedemhe**
(Dar Al-Hekma University, Jeddah, Saudi Arabia) ovocathy@yahoo.com: Chapter 21 The AU and Issues of Institutional Capacity and Enforcement

Dr **Emmanuel Kolawole Oke**
(University of Edinburgh) emmanuel.oke@ed.ac.uk: Chapter 8 The Statute of the Pan-African Intellectual Property Organisation: A Human Rights Perspective

Professor **Konstantinos D Magliveras**
(University of the Aegean, Rhodes) kmagliveras@aegean.gr: Chapter 2 The Implications of AU Law: Conceptual Analysis with Emphasis on the Institutional Consequences; Chapter 19 The Several Sanctioning Regimes in the AU: Analysis and Synthesis

Dr **Chidebe Matthew Nwankwo**
(University of Nigeria) 86mathieu@googlemail.com: Chapter 11 Human Rights, Statelessness, and The Right to Nationality (R2N) in Africa: What Can Vertical Structures Achieve?

Dr **Gino Naldi**
gnaldi@hotmail.com: Chapter 17 The Contribution of AU Human Rights Agreements to an Emergent AU Law

Dr **Adaeze Okoye**
(University of Brighton) a.okoye@brighton.ac.uk: Chapter 9 Is the AU Best Placed to Advance Cross-Cutting Gender Rights' Harmonization of Customary Laws?

Professor **Michèle Olivier**
(Dar Al-Hekma University, Jeddah, Saudi Arabia) molivier@dah.edu.sa: Chapter 1 Conceptualizing AU Law within the Constitutional Framework of the AU; Chapter 20 Enforcement Mechanisms in AU Human Rights Treaties: Lessons for the Wider AU law; Chapter 24 AU Law and its Future: Reform and the Kagame Report

Dr **Eki Yemisi Omorogbe**
eki.omorogbe@le.ac.uk: Chapter 10 The AU and Disputed Presidential Elections

Dr **Chisa Onyejekwe**
(Canterbury Christ Church University) chisa.onyejekwe@canterbury.ac.uk: Chapter 14 Development of AU Law: Tax Harmonization and Regional Integration towards Achieving Social Structures in Africa

Professor **Onyeka K Osuji**
(University of Essex) o.k.osuji@essex.ac.uk: Chapter 7 Contextual Centrality of Institutional Arbitration Framework for AU Legal Order

Dr **Iyare Otabor-Olubor**
(Aston University) i.otabor-olubor@aston.ac.uk: Chapter 6 The Evolution of the AU Private Business Structure

Dr **Regis Yann Simo**
(University of the Witwatersrand) regis.simo@wits.ac.za: Chapter 22 The (Domestic) Enforcement of AU International Economic Law Instruments: Exploring the Desirability of Direct Effect

Oluwafikunayo D Taiwo
(University of Essex) fikayo.taiwo@essex.ac.uk: Chapter 7 Contextual Centrality of Institutional Arbitration Framework for AU Legal Order

Road Map to the Emergent AU Law

Femi Amao

The novel concept of African Union law (AU law) is broadly defined in this book as the body of treaties, resolutions, decisions, and declarations that have direct and indirect application to the Member States of the African Union (AU). The concept is currently underdeveloped and underexplored in the discourse on legal systems created in the context of international organizations. However, it is contended that the concept has the potential to be groundbreaking and generate new understanding with far reaching implications. The contention of the contributions in this book is that the concept has important and potentially radical implications for the African continent, its constituent Member States and people in Africa, and in the diaspora. In addition, it is argued that the concept has the potential to address and provide normative solutions to some of the intractable problems on the continent. Furthermore, it is suggested that the concept would impact on the external relations of the AU and its Member States with third countries in the international community. Whilst exploring different theoretical perspectives, this book examines the emergence of AU law as a new legal order in the global community and its implications for existing legal orders. The idea of the AU and its organs as a standard-generating institution with its own unique features is novel and is gradually gaining traction. As noted in Chapter 2, notable scholars such as the eminent jurist, Abdulqawi Ahmed Yusuf, the president of the International Court of Justice, have recognized the emergence of a legal order at the continental level in Africa. The book examines how the AU legal order is evolving, its theoretical underpinnings, its legitimacy, the areas that it affects, and key implications.

Africa as a continent faces wide-ranging challenges which have impacted on its development over the years. The challenges are multifarious and include abuses of the rule of law, coups d'état, civil wars, human rights violations, child labour, modern slavery, corruption, racial and gender discrimination, and environmental degradation. It has historically been an ongoing challenge for individual states in Africa to successfully deal with these problems, hence, the need for collective or supranational solutions and support for Member States. The integration efforts that have been part of the continent's Pan-African vision since the end of colonialism is targeted at achieving that end. The overarching position of this book is that the concept of AU law could be the key driver to delivering the integration agenda and achieving collective solutions, faithful to the call for 'African solutions

Femi Amao, *Road Map to the Emergent AU Law* In: *The Emergent African Union Law*. Edited by: Olufemi Amao, Michèle Olivier and Konstantinos D. Magliveras, Oxford University Press. © Femi Amao 2021.
DOI: 10.1093/oso/9780198862154.003.0001

to African problems', and in pursuit of the much-cherished African renaissance. The concept provides a beyond state-level norm-generating mechanism that has the potential to be a creative tool in addressing these peculiar problems.

Though currently not as advanced as law-making in the EU, it is suggested that AU law is evolving slowly and exhibiting nascent traits similar to the development of EU law. It is acknowledged that the historical background and drivers for the two systems are different but there are important characteristics from which insights could be drawn. These traits require in-depth study, analysis, and nurturing to improve understanding of the AU legal system, its strengths, its pitfalls and its limitations, and its implications.

This book presents a timely collection of contributions on an emerging AU law by African scholars from different backgrounds, practising lawyers, and political commentators. The different contributions highlight how law stands at the heart of development and successful regional integration in Africa.

Contributions to this book, among other issues, also explore the extent to which AU law is impacting on domestic laws in Africa. This trend has been more particularly noticeable in the area of human rights, rule of law, democratic principles, and aspects of constitutional law.

Significantly, the book examines how the AU is engendering new norms from its legal order. Such norms include the non-indifference norm, the norm on unconstitutional change of government, the right to protect, free trade, free movement of people, economic approximation, and democratic constitutionalism. These and other emerging standards are covered extensively in this collection. In addition, the AU legal order has led to the emergence of a continental-level judicial system. The quasi-judicial system put in place under the African Charter on Human and Peoples' Rights and administered by the African Commission on Human and Peoples' Rights is now complemented by the African Court on Human and Peoples' Rights. The continental-level judicial system is playing a crucial role in the moulding of the emergent norms.

The chapters in this book are drawn from presentations at the series of workshops on AU law funded by the Arts & Humanities Research Council (AHRC)[1] over two years. The themes from the contributions also drew inspiration from the United Nation's programme, 'The International Decade for People of African Descent', established by General Assembly resolution 68/237 and running from 2015 to 2024. The book explores how new knowledge and new perspectives examined critically at the workshops are contributing to an in-depth understanding of AU law. The network has pioneered fresh ideas on the concept of AU law. Notable scholarship is now emerging on the subject.[2] This volume thus makes an original and significant contribution to the expanding scholarship on AU law.

[1] A UK public body that provides funding for research.

[2] O Amao, *African Union Law: The Emergence of a Sui Generis Legal Order* (Routledge, 2019); B Kabumba, 'The application of African Union (human rights) law in Uganda: trends and prospects

The contributions included in this book are structured around five key themes. Part 1 examines the scope of AU law *inter alia* as a driver for deeper regional integration. This Part provides the conceptual analysis of AU law and its scope. Similar to EU law, the expansive nature of the AU law allows for a multidimensional approach to its analysis. Part 1 thus examines AU law from several perspectives. Part 2 looks at harmonization and integration as drivers of AU law. This is exemplified by the developments in key areas including competition law, investment dispute resolution, consumer protection, and the financial institutions. Parts 3 and 4 examine some of the key challenges on the continent and how the AU law is responding or could respond to resolve them effectively for the benefit of all African peoples. Part 5 focuses on aspects of the enforcement of AU law, the challenges it faces, and offers some perspectives on the way forward.

In Chapter 1, Olivier focuses on the conceptualization of AU law. She approaches the conceptualization from the perspective of legal theory applicable to regional integration law in general and applied that to the African context. In addition, Olivier addresses the definitional framework and hierarchy of AU law and identifies broad spectrum of potential sources of AU law. She argues that the laudable Pan-African sentiments underpinning the AU needs to be backed by enforceable decision-making powers in order to make the AU and its legal order effective.

Complementing the previous chapter, in Chapter 2 Magliveras considers the implication of AU law from the perspective of the institutional architecture of the AU. Comparing the AU to the EU, the chapter argues that a revision of the AU Constitutive Act would be needed in order to effectively equip the AU and its institutions with sufficient capacity to deliver on AU law. This echoes the argument made by Olivier in Chapter 1.

In Chapter 3, Amao explores AU law as an emergent legal order in the context of international constitutionalization and federalism. He considers AU law as a new continental legal system and examines the interplay of that system with the idea of federalism and constitutionalization. The main contention of the chapter is that these concepts are useful for the understanding and analysis of the emerging AU law. It may also be useful in tracking the trajectory of the legal order as it develops.

The collection of chapters in Part 1 sets the stage for explorations of topical issues in norm and standard development at the AU level in the rest of the book.

Starting off Part 2, Dawar and Lipimile (Chapter 4) examine the process of harmonization of competition law and policy in Africa in the context of economic integration under the AU. The authors undertake a comparative examination of the various stages of development of competition laws and authorities with particular

from a comparative review' (2018) African Human Rights Yearbook / Annuaire Africain des Droits de l'Homme 90; E Ekhator, 'International Environmental Governance: A Case for Sub-regional Judiciaries in Africa' in M Addaney and A Jegede (eds) *Human Rights and the Environment under African Union Law* (Palgrave Macmillan, 2020) 209–31; ME Olivier 'The role of African Union law in integrating Africa' (2015) 22(4) South African Journal of International Affairs 513–33.

focus on the role of AU institutions. The authors assess various options and recommendations for harmonizing competition policy and integrating competition law across the continent.

In Chapter 5, Iglesias-Rodríguez examines the global financial standard setting as it applies in the African continent. Strengthening Africa's role in the global economy is one of the AU's core objectives in Article 3(i) of its Constitution and also emphasized in AU's Agenda 2063. The contribution is significant because there is scant research, at the time of writing on Africa's role and potential influence in this sphere. The chapter therefore focuses on the role of the African Financial Supervision Authorities, which participate in the International Networks of Financial Supervision Authorities (INFSAs). While acknowledging that INFSAs do not produce hard or mandatory laws, the authors argue that these play a central role in the financial architecture and influence standard setting globally.

On a similar theme, in Chapter 6 Otabor-Olubor notes the importance of harmonization of private business structures for a successful implementation of key trade and cross-border business agreements. By comparing data from eight jurisdictions, he explores the feasibility of such an endeavour and identifies key driving forces that could enable the realization of harmonization in this context. It is envisaged that the proposal in this chapter will address the key challenges facing cross-border business activities across the continent.

Underscoring the importance of a dispute resolution strategy to the AU's regional integration agenda, Osuji and Taiwo (Chapter 7) argue for an institutional framework for arbitration within the AU legal order. The authors propose an institutional framework that encompasses both investment and commercial arbitration, which is a significant departure from the exclusive focus on investment arbitration in current initiatives on the continent. The authors further argue that an African model of transborder arbitration is likely to be viable and also will gain widespread legitimacy and acceptability on the continent.

In the final chapter (Chapter 8) of the Part, Oke provides an analysis of the link between intellectual property and human rights in the African context, further underscoring the importance of human rights in the AU legal order. The chapter focuses on the Statute of the Pan-African Intellectual Property Organization (PAIPO Statute) and its implications for human rights. Oke argues in favour of incorporating a human rights perspective into the Statute by amending its provisions, especially Article 4. This, he contends, would make the Statute consistent with the African Charter on Human and Peoples' Rights.

The chapters in Part 3 provide some key perspectives on addressing civil and political challenges through AU law. In her contribution, Okoye (Chapter 9) examines the link between gender rights and customary law in the context of the harmonization agenda. She acknowledges the tension that exists between customary law and emerging standards at the continental level, especially in relation to human rights.

The chapter provides insights into how the divergence of customary law across the continent could be harmonized and made compatible with the core human rights instruments in the AU legal order.

Omorogbe (Chapter 10) tackles the long-standing challenges of political conflicts and illegal seizure of power prevalent on the continent. The author critically examines how the AU's response to coups d'état has evolved and particularly in relation to regimes that were originally democratically elected. Omorogbe contends that the AU has progressively expanded its policy and normative strategy to cover incumbent leaders who refuse to step down from office after losing elections. In addition, the strategy has been extended to address attempts by incumbents to increase the maximum permissible number of consecutive terms of office. The chapter showcases the impact of AU law on unconstitutional change of government.

In his contribution, Nwankwo (Chapter 11) addresses the critical issues of statelessness and citizenship. The chapter provides an analysis of the current legal framework on statelessness at the AU level. Taking a rights-based approach, it extends its coverage to nationality and citizenship. Noting the associated problems, such as an increase in refugee populations, terrorism, and insecurity, Nwankwo argues for a better focus on the issues especially in the application of the provisions of the African Charter on Human and Peoples' Rights. The author further argues that AU Member States need to work towards creating a definite framework for the protection of the right of the stateless to a nationality.

Following on from Nwankwo, d'Orsi (Chapter 12) focuses on the issues of terrorism, asylum, and refugee management in the AU legal order. Over the years, these issues have become major challenges to peace, security, and development in Africa. It is thus important to understand the current framework and how it could be improved to meet these ongoing challenges. The author makes credible suggestions on how the framework could be strengthened under the AU legal order.

As the AU legal order progresses, it is inevitable that there will be points of tension between it and other legal systems. It is therefore not surprising to detect such tension between AU law and general international law, considered by Chigara in Chapter 13. Focusing on the controversial issue of jurisdiction over international crimes, he looks at the ways in which the AU legal order on international crimes could be reconciled with current developments in international law.

Contributions in Part 4 highlight some of the key socio-economic challenges in Africa and how these could be impacted by the emerging AU law. In her contribution, Onyejekwe (Chapter 14) looks at how social structures could be improved through the harmonization of tax laws at the continental level. The aim of such an endeavour is the provision of sustainable revenue sources that could be utilized to achieve the goals of the AU and its Member States. The chapter looks at the critical role that Regional Economic Communities (RECs) could play in the harmonization process. Onyejekwe uses the Economic Community of West African States (ECOWAS) as an example for the purpose of analysing the underlying issues and offer pertinent solutions.

In Chapter 15, Home looks at issues relating to land and property in the context of the contest for land ownership within and between Member States. Home notes the importance that has been accorded to this issue within the AU policy and regulatory framework. He further examines the emerging jurisprudence of the African Court on Human and Peoples' Rights concerning land issues, which reinforces the evolving AU legal system. However, the author noted that there is limited progress in relation to implementation.

Garrido and Balde (Chapter 16) look at the issue of education, which is of critical importance to development and poverty alleviation. The authors analyse the positioning of education as a fundamental right in the AU legal order. They further examine the strategy and policies that the AU has adopted in advancing education as a right in Member States. The authors identify gaps in the current framework and offer some insights on the way forward.

Naldi, in his contribution in Chapter 17, examines the contribution of human rights agreements to the emergent AU law. Naldi notes that human rights form an integral part of the AU and because of the AU's distinctive approach it introduced a unique African conceptualization of human rights. According to the author, the unique perspective has influenced instruments and agreements on the continent. The author's contention is that the various human rights agreements paved the way for the emergent AU law.

Ekhator (Chapter 18) examines sustainable development in the context of the AU legal order. The author shows the growing importance of the concept on the continent and how the AU is contributing to developing countries' perspectives on sustainable development. The author examines key instruments and mechanisms of the AU that are central to promoting sustainable development. Ekhator argues that the AU and its agencies have a positive impact on the sustainable development discourse.

Given the importance of the normative frameworks highlighted by the contributions in Parts 1 to 4 on the various aspects of AU law, it leads to inevitable questions of effective implementation and enforcement strategy. This is an aspect of AU law that is widely acknowledged to be lacking in many respects. The chapters in Part 5 therefore focus on the challenges of enforcement and how improvements could be made to give teeth to AU law.

In Chapter 19, Magliveras focuses on the sanction powers of the AU in the enforcement process. These powers were introduced as a mechanism for ensuring compliance with AU-level obligations. Unlike Charter of the Organization of African Unity (OAU Charter), which did not contain provisions on sanctions, the

AU Constitutive Act contained various provisions on sanctions which has now been expanded by other instruments of the AU. The provisions cover a variety of infringements which, according to Magliveras, have led to several sanctions regimes. As Magliveras correctly argues, the existence of such a system for 'ordering punitive measures against recalcitrant parties is invariably a characteristic of the legal systems created by international organisations'. The chapter examines the various situations in which the sanctions regime may be applicable. The author also highlights key challenges facing the sanctions regime.

In her contribution, Olivier (Chapter 20) examines the enforcement mechanisms for AU human rights treaties with a view to providing some insights for wider AU law. She suggests that effective human rights enforcement in many ways presents a blueprint for good continental governance. The human rights system is currently the most developed aspect of the AU legal order. It therefore provides, to some extent, a work in progress template for other and less developed areas of AU law. The author focuses on AU human rights instruments and their application at both continental and national levels.

In Chapter 21, Imoehdemhe examines issues of institutional capacity and enforcement in AU law. She highlights some of the key challenges that AU law would need to overcome in relation to enforcement of laws. Focusing principally on the African Court on Human and Peoples' Rights, the author argues for what she describes as 'cultural and cognitive institutional reforms and transformation of the Court system'.

Simo (Chapter 22) looks at the principle of direct effect in EU law and explores the relevance of the principle in the African context. Focusing on the African Continental Free Trade Area (AfCFTA), Simo suggests that, even though the principle of direct effect is not a direct fit, there are ways in which it may play a role in the enforcement of AfCFTA norms and rules. Simo explores these possibilities and suggests amendments to the AfCFTA to accommodate them.

In Chapter 23, Ako looks at the issue of enforcement from the perspective of the peace and security agenda of AfCFTA. The author contends that the developments in the peace and security arena have been facilitating the emergence of new norms and standards that could be considered part of AU law. The author argues that these developments have an impact on RECs and on Member States.

Together, these contributions pull together clear and tangible evidence of the emergent AU law. The ambit of the contributions is wide because the legal order is manifested in different areas in the activities of the AU and its Member States. It is acknowledged that whilst the AU legal order is still in its formative years, to a limited extent it mirrors traits similar to those of the EU. It is therefore important that there should be further scholarly engagement with this development in order to understand its trajectory and potentials. This is particularly relevant because the AU legal order could be regarded as a tool for the advancement of the integrationist agenda that has been a cornerstone on the continent since independence. Indeed, the AU legal system has the potential to weave together various aspects of the integration agenda thereby increasing their coherence. As the chapters in this collection show, AU law is assisting in resolutely addressing some of the key challenges faced by Member States on the continent.

PART 1

SCOPING AFRICAN UNION LAW

1

Conceptualizing AU Law within the Constitutional Framework of the AU

Michèle Olivier

1. Introduction

Unlike European Union (EU) law, African Union (AU) law is not a widely established concept, leaving its content unmapped, open for contestation but also for development. Within the context of regional integration law and politics, the term AU law broadly refers to a society's response on how to self-regulate at a continental level through binding and legitimate decisions of the AU instead of being regulated by the other, powers or influences be it past colonial masters, Cold War puppeteers, or domestic despots.

The objective of this chapter is first to clarify the conceptual nature of AU law. This discussion has regard to legal theory applicable to regional integration law in general but specifically pertaining to the African context. Given the obvious link between African integration, AU governance, and AU law, it is suggested that Pan-African sentiments be backed up by enforceable decision-making in order to make the AU an effective institution.

The discussion then turns to establishing a definitional framework and hierarchy of AU law/laws. It is argued that an a priori constitutional framework within which AU institutions function should be the point of departure for any discussion on defining AU law. The 'constitutional law' of the AU, located in the various multilateral treaties establishing the AU and its institutions, is indicative of the institutional powers allocated and can as such be considered as the bedrock of an AU legal system. The nature of these powers, whether they are supranational, policy, or recommendations, will determine the level of African integration and whether an 'ever closer union' in Africa can incrementally evolve as has happened in Europe.

The discussion identifies a broad spectrum of potential sources of AU law. In addition to the constitutional instruments establishing the AU and its organs and binding decisions taken under these provisions, there are also a variety of other legal instruments and treaties adopted by the AU and its predecessor, the Organisation of African Unity (OAU), as well as soft law which influences the behaviour of AU members.

Michèle Olivier, *Conceptualizing AU Law within the Constitutional Framework of the AU* In: *The Emergent African Union Law*. Edited by: Olufemi Amao, Michèle Olivier and Konstantinos D. Magliveras, Oxford University Press.
DOI: 10.1093/oso/9780198862154.003.0002

Finally, the current initiative to reform AU institutions[1] provides an opportune moment to advance the development of AU law. It is suggested that the AU's limited capacity to take binding and enforceable decisions can be directly linked to the functional and legitimacy problems which confront the organization and prompted a quest for reform. Thus, AU law provides a valuable tool to help make the AU fit for purpose with the capacity to realize the socio-economic transformation envisaged by the AU's ambitious Agenda 2063.[2] AU reform will be explored more fully in the final chapter.

2. A Conceptual Framework of AU Law

The current lack of a clear definition of AU law opens possibilities for conceptual confusion where the term is used to refer to a wide variety of sources of law: African (national) legal systems, law establishing the AU, treaties, and binding and non-binding decisions adopted under auspices of the AU are often treated as falling under the wide umbrella of AU law.[3] To explore an accurate and useful description of AU law, the focus must be more concise.

Ostensibly AU law primarily refers to legal instruments establishing the AU (constitutional treaties) and the decisions taken by the AU's organs that will bind all Member States. AU law, furthermore, might refer to all legal instruments/treaties adopted by the AU and its predecessor, the OAU.[4] The latter can be supplemented by a plethora of soft law instruments that, despite not being legally binding, influence the behaviour of AU members. Application of treaties adopted by the OAU/AU, however, do not bind all Member States but only those who opted to become parties to the particular treaties.

Another way to describe AU law is with reference to supranationalism. In short, supranationalism would enable AU institutions to take binding decisions. State consent to individual decisions will not be required and the binding nature would derive from the sovereignty transfer through treaties establishing the AU and determining its mandate. As such, AU institutions can only bind Member States if they have agreed that the AU should possess certain powers and that such decisions would override rules of their own national legal systems. A third way would

[1] *Report on the Implementation of the Decision on the Institutional Reform of the African Union* (Paul Kagame, July 2017) available at <https://au.int/sites/default/files/documents/33272-doc-au_reform_implementation_report_july_2017_final_v2.pdf> accessed 25 October 2018.

[2] Agenda 2063 | African Union, 'A strategic framework for the socio-economic transformation of the continent over the next 50 years' (Agenda 2063 | African Union, 12 October 2014) available at <https://au.int/en/agenda2063> accessed 10 July 2019.

[3] The AU Law Research Network arranged four workshops to explore the emergence of AU law as a legal order between 2017 and 2019. The AU Research initiative received funding from the Arts and Humanities Research Council, United Kingdom.

[4] OAU/AU Treaties, Conventions, Protocols, and Charters are available at <https://au.int/en/treaties>.

be through the harmonization of African national legal systems as guided by AU model legislation. This approach has a wide but specific reach as it might relate to specific aspects of private, commercial, and criminal law.

All of this depends on what the concept of 'law' itself means in the present context. Does it refer to what states actually do or instead to what they are supposed to do? If actors give effect to a resolution or recommendation, is it law? A broad approach to law focuses on the outcome and downplays formalities. The downside of this approach is that it compromises legal certainty – where one cannot predict in advance what the law is. It also makes it difficult to distinguish law from non-law, the binding from the non-binding.

In order to establish a conceptual foundation of AU law, it should be understood in a broader normative context of the role and meaning of law in general. It should be accepted at the outset that AU law would fall under the broad category of positive regional international law,[5] not leaving aside its intended impact on divergent national legal systems of African states. (The latter will depend both on the status granted under national constitutions as well as the obligations created by the terms of each treaty.) The main theoretical thrusts that shaped the current understanding of international law and national law and the relationship between these legal orders apply to law universally. That said, there is recognition for the idea that any form of African law should be decoded from a socio-legal perspective[6] against a background of African thought, history, and with regard to Africa's unique identity. Different theories have shaped the evolving debate on the nature of law, often coinciding with prevailing schools of jurisprudence. Given Africa's history of colonialism, post-colonial responses, and current socio-political environment, certain theories resonated well with the African environment and understanding of the law.

The Austinian doctrine, following Hobbes and Bentham, suggests that law is the command of a sovereign backed up by a threat to enforce obedience. Such command theory does not accommodate international law which is largely consent based, whether such consent to be bound is expressly given in the case of treaties or by tacit approval in the case of customary law.[7] However, as argued by HLA Hart,[8] law does not always entail sanctions. It is suggested that international law is binding because it is accepted as law within a community – the international community.[9] The flipside of the command theory is echoed by Klabbers writing in the

[5] ME Olivier, 'The role of African Union law in integrating Africa' (2015) 22(4) South African Journal of International Affairs 513–33 available at <http://www.tandfonline.com/doi/full/10.1080/10220461.2015.1119718> accessed 1 July 2019.

[6] BZ Tamanaha, 'Social Theory of Law by Comparison to Legal Positivism' in BZ Tamanaha (ed), *Realistic Socio-Legal Theory: Pragmatism and a Social Theory of Law* (OUP, 1999) 129–52.

[7] H Triepel, *Volkerecht und Landesrecht* (Leipzig, C.L. Hirschfeld, 1899).

[8] HLA Hart, *The Concept of Law* (OUP, 1961).

[9] BA Boczek, *International Law: A Dictionary* (Scarecrow Press, 2005) 1.

context of law-making by international organizations, that law requires an a priori sense of obligation.[10]

Positivists, such as Jellinek,[11] argue for the binding nature of international law based on an auto limitation doctrine where states voluntarily create rules of international law which they may also unilaterally terminate. The following definition of international law, as suggested by the Permanent Court of International Justice in the *Lotus* case,[12] reflects such positivist thinking: 'rules of law binding on states ... emanate from their own free will as expressed in conventions or usages generally accepted as expressing principles of law'.[13] Another satisfactory response explaining the binding nature of international law is suggested by Frederick Pollock,[14] who requires the existence of a political community and the recognition of settled rules binding upon them by its members.

Early post-colonial international law scholars such as TO Elias relied on concepts traditionally associated with positivism such as sovereignty and non-interference[15] to acknowledge the status and role of newly independent states.[16] Although notions of sovereignty were used to legitimize and justify colonialism,[17] sovereignty continued to play a prominent role under the OAU and the AU. These notions echo in Third World Approaches to International Law (TWAIL).[18] TWAIL, in response to decolonization, challenges the legitimacy of international law because it largely reflects the intellectual, historical, and cultural experiences of Europe. International law, despite being postulated as universal, does not reflect the voices of former colonies. Historically, the Third World has viewed international law as a discourse of domination and subordination, reflecting what it collectively views as the hegemony of the West.[19] In accordance with TWAIL, AU law can thus be regarded as an African response to legitimize international law within a non-Western domain. Non-inclusive universality of international law is replaced with an all-inclusive regionality, where 'African-ness' prevails as dominant value. Ironically, a legitimacy crisis prevails in the AU because of an absence of an authentic democratic base. Critiquing colonialism thus shares foundational elements with the critique the AU currently faces.

[10] J Klabbers, *An Introduction to International Organisations Law* (3rd edn, CUP, 2015) 154–5.

[11] Georg Jellinek, *Die Lehre von den Staatenverbindungen* (A Hölder, 1882). For a discussion see Q Wight, 'The legal nature of treaties' ([1916)] 10(4) American Journal of International Law 706.

[12] *S.S. Lotus (Fr. v. Turk.)*, 1927 PCIJ (ser. A) No 10 (7 September).

[13] Boczek (n 9) 4.

[14] J Dugard, *International Law: A South African Perspective* (Juta, 2005) 27 fn 9.

[15] TO Elias, *Africa and the Development of International Law* (2nd revised edn, Martinus Nijhoff Publishers, 1988) 126–8.

[16] R Cryer, T Hervey, and others, *Research Methodologies in EU and International Law* (Hart Publishing, 2011) 38.

[17] A Antony, 'Finding the peripheries: sovereignty and colonialism in nineteenth-century international law' (1999) 40(1) Harvard International Law Journal 3..

[18] M Matua, 'What is TWAIL?' (Proceedings of 94th Annual meeting of the American Society of International Law, 5–8 April 2000) 31–40.

[19] ibid 37.

It is interesting to note that Elias, in a separate discussion on democracy and the rule of law, refers to the immediate relevance of Von Savigny and Roscoe Pound to African legal thinking. He states that African customary law, like customary international law, does not depend on any theory of sovereignty.[20] Elias thus views African legal thinking as being in line with and open to influences from non-African thinkers. He makes a convincing argument for supranational decision-making and AU law, arguing that:

> Sovereignty is clearly an inconvenient and unnecessary postulate introduced by analytical jurists to confuse the nature of law with its political presuppositions. Sovereignty has thus stood in the way not only of a universal acceptance of public international law and other customary bodies of law as law properly so called, but also of making it possible for Nation States of the world to accept a supranational authority as the cornerstone of a world government.[21]

In summary, African responses to international law did not develop in isolation from post-colonial Western trends and thinking. Since independence, there is clear evidence of a tempering influence by core ideas such as liberal political theory and feminism as reflected in acceptance of universal human rights, justice as fairness, equal citizenship, democracy, and challenging patriarchal structures.[22] Theoretically, therefore it appears that Africa is as much part of the world as it is distinct from other regions.

3. African Integration through Law

The sense of a shared African identity variously depicted as African fraternity or African unity has always been an important driver for African solidarity. There is strong 'we feeling' amongst African states, seeking to expunge Eurocentric influences from the continent and to own the solutions to African challenges as expressed by the now well-known call for African solutions to African problems.[23] When colonialism came to an end, leaders like Ghana's Kwame Nkrumah argued that Africa could only survive as a single united entity (Union of African States) when ridding itself of the scourges of slavery, colonialism, imperialism, and racism. A fully integrated United States of Africa was dreamed about under the flag

[20] Elias (n 15) 43–4.

[21] ibid 45.

[22] Cryer, Hervey, and others (n 16) 42–5.

[23] The term was first used by political economist George Ayittey in response to the behaviour of the international community in the crisis in Somalia. S Fiquremariam, 'African solutions to African problems' *ISS Today* (18 September 2008) available at <https://issafrica.org/iss-today/african-solutions-to-african-problems> accessed 19 November 2019.

of the OAU.[24] He argued for a balance between sovereignty and powers to be exercised at a continental level:

> [I]ntegration . . . need not infringe the essential sovereignty of the separate African States. These States would continue to exercise independent authority, except in the fields defined and reserved for common action in the interests of the security and orderly development of the whole continent.[25]

Contradicting this ideal, post-colonial Africa emerged as a Westphalian confederation of independent nations, manifesting particularly in the non-intervention dictum. The emergence of strong sovereign states complicated and stunted integration.[26] Colonial favouring of certain ethnic groups over others created lasting disparities in post-colonial independent African states, rendering sovereigntist territoriality as unsustainable.[27] As Deng observes in 2008, the sense of continental and ethnic identities of Africans are often more powerful than their identification at a national level.[28]

However, Pan-African sentiments, emphasizing the political and social union of people of African descent, operate mostly at an ideological level, leaving a wide gap between the ideal and the real. This notion is now being challenged to rise above the mythical historical narrative of bygone glory undisturbed by colonialism. AU law is suggested as a tool to bring Pan-Africanist ideals into the twenty-first century by giving greater practical effect to self-determination, integration, stability, prosperity, and development. The notion of AU law aims to fill a legal vacuum to serve the national self-interests of continental Africa within a decolonialist context informed by post-colonial discourse. At the same time, an integrated Africa with multilateral powers would enable Africa to compete better in a globalized context based on self-interest instead of being hamstrung by ideological constraints.

Roughly modelled on a more advanced European Union, the AU as vehicle for African integration was established in 2001,[29] replacing the dysfunctional OAU. AU law and African integration are closely linked. Accelerated regional integration is ostensibly a key priority of the AU with the objective of achieving peace, prosperity, and development and of strengthening Africa's role on the global stage.[30]

[24] K Nkrumah, *Africa Must Unite* (Frederick A Praeger Publisher, 1963).

[25] ibid 218.

[26] MN Barnett and E Solingen, *Designed to Fail or Failure of Design? The Origins and Legacy of the Arab League* (CUP, 2007); GC Olivier, 'Regionalism in Africa – cooperation without integration?' (2010) XXXII(2) Strategic Review for Southern Africa 17–43

[27] FM Deng, *Diversity and Constitutionalism in Africa* (United States Institute of Peace, 2008) 40.

[28] ibid 31.

[29] Constitutive Act of the African Union, adopted Lomé, Togo 11 July 2000 and entered into force 26 May 2001.

[30] Preamble of the Constitutive Act of the African Union. See also Key Pillars of Africa's Regional Integration, United Nations Economic Commission for Africa, available at <https://www.uneca.org/oria/pages/key-pillars-africa%E2%80%99s-regional-integration> where it is stated that '[t]he

Lamentably, other than advancing the symbolic importance of African unity, the OAU and the AU have not progressed far achieving these goals, largely due to weak institutional governance, political bias, and lack of enforcement. Intra-regional trade, crucial to development, has traditionally been low compared to other regions. In 2018, Africa had the lowest percentage of intra-regional trade as a share of total foreign trade at 18%, compared with 70% in Europe, 55% in North America, 45% in Asia, and 35% in Latin America.[31] In addition, it is widely acknowledged that regional fragmentation resulting from eight overlapping and competing Regional Economic Communities (RECs) hinder continental business activity.[32]

African leaders now recognize the urgency of accelerated political and economic integration to make Africa and the AU less reliant on foreign aid.[33] The African Continental Free Trade Agreement (AfCFTA) and the Protocol to the Treaty Establishing the African Economic Community relating to the Free Movement of Persons were adopted at the 10th Extraordinary Session of the AU on AfCFTA in March 2018. Entering into force on 30 May 2019 after 24 Member States deposited their instruments of ratification,[34] AfCFTA has the potential to boost intra-African trade by 52.3% by eliminating import duties and to double this trade if non-tariff barriers are reduced.[35] The Protocol on Free Movement of Persons seeks to establish a visa-less zone in Africa and support the creation of the AU Passport that is set to replace existing nationally issued AU Member State passports.[36] This flagship project of Agenda 2063 aims to transform Africa's laws.

In spite of recent progressive strides to establish a common market and free movement of people, goods, and services via AU treaties, AU institutions lack the required supranational powers to take decisions binding on Member States. National law prevails in all matters. Treaties adopted under auspices of the OAU and the AU suffer from various shortcomings including not imposing enforceable obligations, not being incorporated into domestic law of State Parties, or inadequately enforcement. The lack of political will by national politicians is frequently

Assembly of the African Union have adopted and are pursuing regional integration as an overarching continental development strategy'.

[31] S Akurede, 'How a single market would transform Africa's economy' *World Economic Forum* (28 February 2018) available at <https://www.weforum.org/agenda/2018/02/how-a-single-market-will-transform-africa-s-economy/> accessed 11 June 2019.

[32] UNCTADStat database (UN Conference on Trade and Development, 2018) available at <https://unctadstat.unctad.org/EN/> accessed 11 July 2019.

[33] *Seven Priorities for the African Union in 2018*, Crisis Group Africa Briefing No 135, Addis Ababa, Nairobi, Brussels, 17 January 2018.

[34] OAU/AU Treaties, Conventions, Protocols, and Charters, available at <https://au.int/en/treaties/agreement-establishing-african-continental-free-trade-area> accessed 21 July 2020.

[35] 'African Continental Free Trade Area' *Tralac, AfCFTA Legal Texts and Policy Documents* (July 2019) available at <https://www.tralac.org/resources/our-resources/6730-continental-free-trade-area-cfta.html> accessed 21 July 2020.

[36] The Protocol on Free Movement of Persons has not entered into force, it is available at <https://au.int/treaties accessed 22 July 2020>.

blamed for weak enforcement of international obligations. This is, however, a problematically vague and complex notion pointing to a variety of factors such as a lack of accountability and adversity to reform.

While absolute and formal sovereignty of Member States remain sacrosanct,[37] real integration is unattainable. The capacity to take binding decisions is limited and no provision is made for an AU law to give effect to the purposes of the institution. In fact, AU law as a nascent form of law is a term recently developed by legal academics rather than AU officials, Member States, or politicians.[38] What is found in practice is predominantly cooperation without integration.[39] At a geo-political level, territorial fragmentation provides a haven for bad governance and human insecurity. In the 2017 Kenyan elections, former South African president Thabo Mbeki, who headed the AU observer mission in Kenya, pointed out the obvious that the AU has no automatic right to investigate allegations of election rigging.[40] What is clear is that African integration will remain a mirage as long as its multilateral institutions cannot bind its Member States. To exercise such capacity, law-making powers are required. This capacity is indeed starting to evolve and there are a number of notable examples of supranational competence, as discussed elsewhere in this book. Examples of such capacity include, for instance, enabling AU sanctions, intervention in Member States' internal affairs under specific circumstances such as unconstitutional change of government and grave circumstances, namely war crimes, genocide, and crimes against humanity. The AU Passport planned to be rolled out will add another example.

The European Union can be singled out as the best developed example of regional integration globally.[41] The European Union follows an eclectic model of integration, comprising elements of multilateralism and state-centrism. EU law is based on supranational powers to take binding decisions on behalf of its Member States, as derived from its founding treaties. This law-making power of the European Union gives effect to European integration elevating it above a loose confederation of Member States.[42] In the landmark decision of *Flaminio Costa v*

[37] Article 3(b) of the Constitutive Act of the African Union identifies the defence of sovereignty, territorial integrity, and independence of Member States as an AU objective.

[38] See <https://en.wikipedia.org/wiki/African_Union_law> accessed 11 July 2019.

[39] Olivier (n 26) 17–43.

[40] C du Plessis, 'Mbeki: AU has no mandate to probe 'hacking' claims in Kenya polls … at least for now' *News24* (South Africa, 10 August 2017) available at <https://www.news24.com/Africa/News/mbeki-au-has-no-mandate-to-probe-hacking-claims-in-kenya-polls-at-least-for-now-20170810> accessed 15 August 2017.

[41] F Cameron, 'The European Union as a model for regional integration' *Council on Foreign Relations* (24 September 2010) available at <https://www.cfr.org/report/european-union-model-regional-integration> accessed 18 October 2019; GC Olivier and ME Olivier, 'Models of regional integration: the European Union and the African Union' (2004) 19(2) South African Public Law 351–64.

[42] G Tsebelis and G Barret, 'The institutional foundations of intergovernmentalism and supranationalism in the European Union' (2001) 55(2) International Organization 361–3.

ENEL,[43] the European Court of Justice established the primacy of EU law (then Community law) over the laws of its Member States:

> The precedence of Community law is confirmed by Article 189, whereby a regulation 'shall be binding' and 'directly applicable in all Member States.' This provision, which is subject to no reservation, would be quite meaningless if a State could unilaterally nullify its effects by means of a legislative measure which could prevail over community law.[44]

However, EU law as by-product of deeper integration is cumbersome and complex and not necessarily the best prototype to follow in all respects,[45] yet it underlines an important aspect, namely that the success of regional integration depends on the degree to which Member States are willing to transfer elements of national sovereignty to a central supranational body. Such delegation will endow the central body with supranational powers required to make legally binding decisions applicable to Member States and to move beyond symbolic gestures.[46]

For this to happen, a deep trust is required from both the governments of Member States and ordinary people to the effect that the centre can add more than it is taking away with regards to well-being, security, and prosperity. Self-interest and ideology as presented by Pan-Africanism and post-colonial struggle rhetoric are central in belonging to such a structure. However, a willingness amongst African states to shift loyalties and political activity to a new centre possessing political authority over national states is presently largely absent as evidenced by the low ratifications of various treaties, most notably the Protocol to the Constitutive Act of the African Union on the Pan-African Parliament (PAP) of 2014[47] that recorded 12 states in 2019. African leaders are loath to relinquish political power, in spite of their protestations otherwise.

4. Sources of AU Law

4.1 Constitutional Instruments as Primary Source of AU Law

The constitutional framework of the AU is taken as a starting point for a discussion on AU law.

[43] Case 6/64 *Flaminio Costa v ENEL* [1964] ECJ.
[44] ibid 257.
[45] U Schmalz, *Explaining Euro-Paralysis. Why Europe is Unable to Act in International Politics* (MacMillan Press, 1998).
[46] Tsebelis and Barret (n 42) 361, 365.
[47] Olivier (n 5) 513–33.

The AU was established by means of a multilateral treaty, the Constitutive Act of the AU, 2000/2001 agreed to by Member States of the OAU.[48] As the founding instrument, the Constitutive Act and amendments thereto[49] serve as constitution of the AU, establishing its structure and organs as well as the powers allocated to such organs, and is supplemented by various other constitutional treaties adopted under its provisions.[50] These treaties are jointly referred to as the primary sources of AU law, provided that they have achieved the required number of ratifications to enter into force. As foundational sources, such treaty provisions are not controversial but rather fixed in scope without the potential to expand much. Moreover, as treaties, they are recognized as sources of international law under Article 38 of the International Court of Justice (ICJ) Statute.

A constitutional approach to AU law, however, goes beyond the institutional structure and mandate of the organization's founding documents. It should rightly also include principles of constitutionalism such as the values, principles, and objectives of the organization.

4.2 Secondary Sources

The constitutional instruments determine the powers of the AU as an international organization and the decisions it is authorized to adopt under its constituent treaties. These would include binding decisions, policy, and recommendations, and can be classified as secondary sources. Secondary sources fall outside the scope of constitutional law as described above; however, their legality and scope depend on the latter. Jointly these sources determine the relationship between AU institutions, Member States, and individual citizens.

Where organs of the AU are vested with the power under constitutional instruments to take decisions that will bind Member States, such decisions are not treaties and will not qualify as a source of international law under Article 38 of the ICJ Statute. The ability to generate secondary sources depends on whether the organs are endowed with supranational powers. Members States will only be bound where there has been a prior delegation limiting national sovereignty in indicated respects.

48 Constitutive Act of the African Union (n 29).

49 Protocol on Amendments to the Constitutive Act of the African Union, adopted in Maputo, Mozambique, 2003. Ratified by a total of 29 out of a possible 55 Member States falling short of the required two-thirds ratification to enter into force. African Union (16 May 2019) available at <https://au.int/sites/default/files/treaties/35423-sl-PROTOCOL-3.pdf> accessed 15 July 2019.

50 Treaty establishing the African Economic Community (1991/1994); Protocol on the Pan-African Parliament (2001/2003); Protocols on the Peace and Security Council (2002/2003); Statutes of the Economic, Social and Cultural Council (2004); Protocol on the African Human Rights Court (1998/2004); and Protocol on the Statute of the African Court of Justice and Human Rights (2002/2003).

The best-known example where binding decision-making power is vested in a treaty body is the United Nations (UN) Security Council when acting under Article VII of the UN Charter.[51] Article 27 provides that UN Member States agree to carry out decisions of the Security Council in terms of the UN Charter. The constitutive treaties of the AU can therefore in principle provide for legally binding acts that will directly bind the Member States. This will then be a treaty-based power to generate binding law. The key lies in the enabling provisions of the AU constitutional treaties. Such decisions as secondary sources of AU law will be subject to the primacy of AU constitutional provisions. With a capacity for external engagement, secondary sources have the potential to relate directly to Member States and citizens, and it is here that there is vast potential for AU law to achieve the goals set out by the AU constitutive instruments. As will be discussed below, the AU Constitutive Act makes limited provision for taking decisions that will bind the Member States.

4.3 A Third Source

A third tier of sources refers to treaties negotiated under auspices of the AU and open for AU Member States to accede or ratify. The important point to recognize here is that states are not automatically bound to these treaties because they are AU Members but they need to express their consent or not independently. Member States prove to be tardy, often reluctant when it comes to ratification of treaties adopted by the AU, as evidenced by low levels of ratification. Once a state has become a party to a treaty, treaty provisions that require domestic application will need to be incorporated in domestic law in accordance with the State Party's relevant constitutional requirements. Where national legal systems of parties allow for self-executing treaties, such provisions will automatically form part of domestic law without the need for an act of transformation.[52]

Instruments of soft law are additional possible tertiary sources,[53] including the Declaration on Gender Equality in Africa; Guidelines and Measures for the Prohibition and Prevention of Torture, Cruel, Inhuman or Degrading Treatment or Punishment in Africa (The Robben Island Guidelines); Declaration of the Principles on Freedom of Expression in Africa; Ouagadougou Declaration and Plan of Action on Accelerating Prisons and Penal Reforms in Africa; Principles

[51] B Fassbender, 'The UN Charter as the constitution of the international community' (1998) 36 Columbia Journal of Transnational Law 529–616.

[52] J Paust, 'Self-executing Treaties' American Journal of International Law (1988) 82(4) 760–83.

[53] D Long and R Murray, 'The Role and Use of Soft Law Instruments in the African Human Rights System' in S Lagoutte, T Gammeltoft-Hansen, and others (eds), *Tracing the Roles of Soft Law in Human Rights* (OUP, 2016) 89–108, available at <http://www.oxfordscholarship.com/view/10.1093/acprof:oso/9780198791409.001.0001/acprof-9780198791409-chapter-6> accessed 10 May 2021.

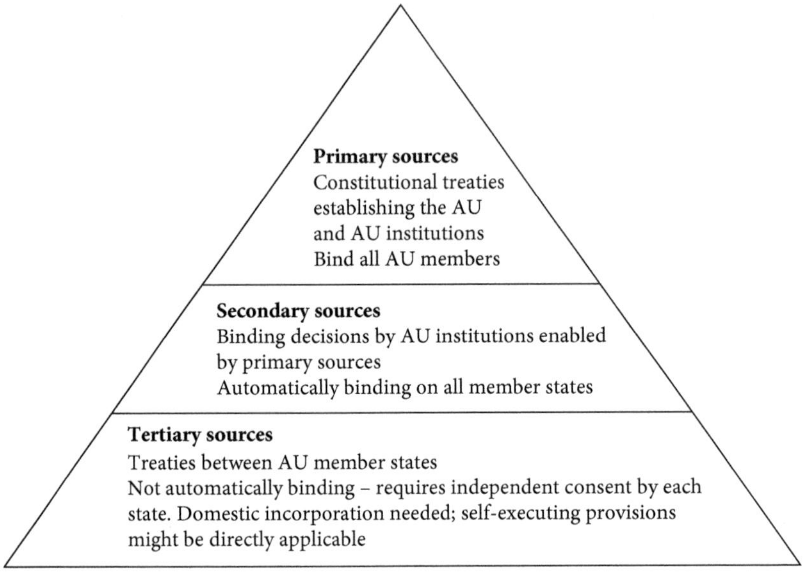

Figure 1.1 Hierarchy of sources of AU law

and Guidelines on the Implementation of Economic, Social and Cultural Rights in the African Charter on Human and Peoples' Rights; Guidelines for African Union Electoral Observations and Monitoring Missions; Pretoria Declaration on Economic, Social and Cultural Rights in Africa; Kigali Declaration; and Principles and Guidelines on the Right to a Fair Trial and Legal Assistance In Africa and Grand Bay (Mauritius) Declaration and Plan of Action.[54]

Under the present construction of AU law, it is suggested that such treaties generally carry a weaker imperative because of the fact that Member States can either opt in or out. Of course, within a wider context, AU treaties are relevant in the creation of norms and are supportive of AU policy and decisions.

4.4 A Hierarchy of AU Law

The diagram in Figure 1.1 suggests a hierarchy of sources of AU law determined by the supremacy of primary sources at the tip of the apex. Secondary sources flow from the enabling mechanisms provided for by the constitutional treaties and they differ from tertiary sources that are not automatically binding on all Member States.

[54] Available at <http://www.achpr.org>.

5. Constitutional Provisions to Take Binding Decisions

Engaging in a textual interpretation of the Constitutive Act and amendments, no reference to AU law *per se* is identified,[55] neither are AU organs provided with binding decision-making powers. When resorting to a teleological method of legal interpretation, however, it is necessary to consider the treaty as a whole to determine its object and purpose.[56] In this respect, the Preamble, 'objectives',[57] and 'principles'[58] provide guidance. The aspirational provisions of the Preamble calling for a united and strong Africa determined to promote and protect human rights, democratic institutions, good governance, and the rule of law create a presumption that these can only be achieved through law. Doing little to empower AU organs to take binding action in furtherance of these ideals, the body of the text is apparently out of sync with the organization's constitutionally proclaimed ideals. The objectives contained in Article 3 are furthermore aspirational and contextual. Words such as 'promoting', 'encouraging', and 'advancing' are used with reference to sovereignty, political and economic integration, peace and security, and democracy and human rights. The principles of the AU are equally aspirational, reflecting the positivist values of sovereignty and territorial integrity on which the OAU as a post-colonial institution was built. There are two possible exceptions: Sub-articles 4(h) and (j) provide for the right of the AU to intervene in Member States in grave circumstances and a similar right of Member States to request such intervention.

The Constitutive Act provides for executive, legislative, and judicial organs. These organs, however, lack the executive and regulatory powers of their EU counterparts. Whether they reflect supranational powers and create a legally binding constitutional framework must be considered with care. The AU Assembly, identified as supreme organ of the AU, is composed of heads of state and government and enjoys the most wide-ranging decision-making capacity.[59] However, it is doubtful whether internal administrative powers such as taking decisions on reports and recommendations of other AU organs,[60] appointing the Chairperson of the Commission,[61] and adopting the AU budget[62] will qualify. Other powers, such as establishing AU organs[63] and the delegation of power to any other organ are, without a doubt, binding based on supranational powers. Whether such decisions have a direct impact in Member States is debatable. The only power directly

[55] The Vienna Convention on the Law of Treaties (1969) Article 31(1) states as a general rule of interpretation that treaties shall be interpreted in accordance with the ordinary meaning given to terms of the treaty in their context and in the light of its object and purpose.

[56] ibid.

[57] Constitutive Act of the African Union (n 29) Article 3.

[58] ibid Article 4.

[59] ibid Articles 6, 7, 8, and 9.

[60] ibid Article 9(b).

[61] ibid Article 9(i).

[62] ibid Article 9(f).

[63] ibid Article 9(d).

referring to Member States is the power to monitor the implementation of AU policies and decisions as well as ensure compliance by all Member States.[64] This is backed up by a somewhat cautious provision on imposition of sanctions to be determined by the Assembly against Member States that default in payments of contributions to the AU budget and where Member States fail to comply with AU decisions and policies.[65] The latter category opens the possibility that 'decisions and policies of the Union' are potentially legally enforceable. No indication is provided on what the nature of such decisions and policies will be or the AU organ from which they should derive. Mentioning decisions and policies in the same breath creates confusion as to the distinct legal nature of each. For a start, policies are normally not binding, at most qualifying as soft law cementing the path for decisions to follow.

The Assembly is backed up by the Executive Council that has the power to take decisions on policy matters in a number of common interest areas,[66] but on its own lacks the power to take enforceable decisions. Both these organs function at an executive level and lack legislative powers. There are, however, indications that the Assembly might be given legislative capacity by endorsing model legislation developed by the PAP under the Protocol to the Constitutive Act on the AU on the Pan-African Parliament (Malabo Protocol).[67]

The obvious institution to exercise legislative powers will be the PAP, established by the Protocol to the Treaty Establishing the African Economic Community relating to the Pan-African Parliament.[68] The premise to establish a body with law-making powers, elected by universal adult suffrage representing all the peoples of Africa,[69] remains elusive in spite of the recent initiative by the Malabo Protocol to strengthen the PAP as the legislative organ of the AU and give a voice to African peoples and the diaspora.[70]

As is the case with many African instruments, there is a clear dichotomy between aspirations and concrete steps to which Member States are prepared to commit. While the Preamble of the Malabo Protocol clearly endorses the imperative and urgent need for African unity and the commitment to democratic principles and popular participation, it does not provide for any real legislative powers. Neither will Member States be directly elected. Each AU Member State shall be represented

[64] ibid Article 9(e).

[65] ibid Article 23.

[66] ibid Article 13.

[67] Protocol to the Constitutive Act on the African Union on the Pan-African Parliament, adopted 27 June 2014. Not yet in force. This protocol is not to be confused with the Protocol on Amendments to the Protocol on the Statute of the African Court of Justice and Human Rights also colloquially referred to as 'the Malabo Protocol' both adopted in the city of Malabo in 2014.

[68] Protocol to the Treaty Establishing the African Economic Community relating to the Pan-African Parliament, adopted March 2001, entered into force December 2003.

[69] ibid Article 2.

[70] Protocol to the Constitutive Act on the African Union on the Pan-African Parliament (n 67) Article 3(a).

by five Members elected by the respective national parliaments or other deliberative bodies from outside their membership.

The legislative powers provided for by the Malabo Protocol are severely qualified. The PAP is limited to propose model laws[71] on subject areas determined by the Assembly or on subjects/areas it would like to suggest for consideration and approval of by the Assembly. It will be a case where the supposedly democratic legislature is subordinate to the executive. No provision is made for executive accountability to the legislature. Despite the limited legislative powers granted by the Malabo Protocol, only 12 states have ratified the Protocol, falling short of the 28 ratifications needed to bring it into force.[72] Without real powers and not being directly elected by African citizens, it is difficult to see how the PAP will address the democratic legitimacy issues the AU faces. Proposing model legislation falls more within the framework of the work national law commissions normally perform within states. The difference is that such laws are presented to parliament and not the executive for approval. Before the Malabo Protocol comes into force the PAP remains largely advisory – an expensive gathering of national parliamentarians devoid of any real powers and representation. This is a status quo that most African leaders seem unprepared to change.[73] With an annual budget of US$22 million, the PAP is presently composed of 229 parliamentarians meeting twice a year and requiring 60 interpreters – a very expensive platform limited to discussion only.[74]

Understandably, African leaders are unwilling to cede sovereign powers to an outside parliament that would interfere with national parliaments under tight political control. A way out may be to grant the PAP legislative powers on specific areas of common concern. Commentators suggest terrorism, climate change, aspects of trade, and free movement of people as possibilities. Other areas would be reserved for states.[75] If such a balance could be agreed on, it might increase democratic

[71] ibid Article 8.

[72] (African Union, June 2021) <https://au.int/sites/default/files/treaties/7806-sl- protocol_to_the_constituti_act_of_the_african_union_relating_to_the_pan-african_parliament_5.pdf> accessed 30 June 2021.

[73] P Fabricius, 'Does Africa really want a continental Parliament?' *ISS Today* (24 October 2017) available at <https://issafrica.org/iss-today/does-africa-really-want-a-continental-parliament> accessed 11 July 2019.

[74] AFP, 'Pan-African Parliament in grip of existential crisis' *Mail Online* (17 October 2017) available at <https://www.dailymail.co.uk/wires/afp/article-4987450/Pan-African-parliament-grip-existential-crisis.html> accessed 11 July 2019.

[75] B Fagbayibo, 'Toothless Pan-African Parliament could have meaningful powers. Here's how' (The Conversation, 23 November 2017) available at <http://theconversation.com/toothless-pan-african-parliament-could-have-meaningful-powers-heres-how-87449 > accessed 12 July 2019; S Mpanyane, 'Transformation of the Pan-African Parliament A path to a legislative body?' Institute for Security Studies (March 2009) 181 available at <https://www.files.ethz.ch/isn/99267/PAPER181.pdf> accessed 12 July 2019; G Hugo, 'The Pan African Parliament: is the glass half-full or half-empty?' Institute for Security Studies (September 2008) 168 available at < https://www.files.ethz.ch/isn/98953/PAPER168.pdf> accessed 12 July 2019; P Mashele, 'The 3rd Pan-African Parliament Session: utility or futility?' (2005) 13(4) African Security Review 72–83.14;M Welz, 'A "culture of conservatism": how and why African Union members obstruct the deepening of integration' (2014) 36(1) Strategic Review for Southern Africa 4, 7–14; J Cilliers and P Mashele, 'The Pan-African Parliament: a plenary of parliamentarians' (2004) 13(4) African Security Review 72–83; B Fagbayibo, 'Nkrumahism, Agenda 2063, and

legitimacy of the AU whilst at the same time not trample on the core sovereignty of national governments.

6. Democracy and Legitimacy

Legitimacy is essential for successful regional integration. From recent experiences confronting the European Union, such as the Brexit referendum and negotiations and the rise of nationalism, the extent to which legitimacy problems hamper integration is clear. In Africa, closer integration will only be achieved if questions of legitimacy and democracy can be adequately addressed. It is suggested that current constitutional failures pointed out above are reflected by the AU's lack of legitimacy. Scholars of EU law have contemplated the legitimacy crisis within the European Union, which started as a result of change in public opinion at the end of the 1980s. These hold valuable lessons for Africa at the early stages of its own integration process. The European Union can no longer expect unconditional support of its citizens. Carter and Scott argue that an earlier era of popular consent, 'which had facilitated an elite-driven and ultimately successful period of European economic integration (involving intense trans-national co-operation, joint decision-making, and common institution building) across post-war Western Europe had come to an end'.[76] When EU governance ceased to command public support, integration sceptics focused on issues of national sovereignty and national identity.

Weiler argues that legitimacy has a formal (legal) and social element. The former requires an institutional governance according to acceptable structure and the rule of law, whilst the latter is founded on the democratic representation of society values.[77] Both these elements are lacking in the present AU configuration and must be addressed in order to accelerate integration. Similar to Europe, problems arose for the AU where legitimacy derives from Member States and not individual citizens. More tension is created where AU Member States do not all adhere to acceptable levels of democratic governance at national levels. A direct link between the institution and individual citizens is needed where the latter derive direct benefits from integration. Material benefits deriving from political and economic integration require strong

the role of intergovernmental institutions in fast-tracking continental unity' (2017) Journal of Asian and Africa Studies, available at <http://journals.sagepub.com/doi/abs/10.1177/0021909617709489> accessed 15 October 2018; GM Musila, 'United States of Africa: positioning the Pan-African Parliament and court in the political union debate' (2007) 142 Institute for Security Studies.

[76] C Carter and A Scott, 'Legitimacy and governance beyond the European nation state: conceptual governance of the European Union' (1998) 4(4) European Law Journal 430.

[77] JHH Weiler, After Maastricht: Community Legitimacy in Post-1992 Europe' in WJ Adams (ed), *Singular Europe: Economic and Polity in the EC after 1992* (Michigan University Press, 1992) 19–20.

supranational governance.[78] When these benefits cease, the social legitimacy of the institution is likely to diminish. The lack of direct public participation can likewise limit the formal legitimacy of the constitutional architecture which fails to deliver individual gains and limit losses.

The AU's constitutional architecture follows the top-down method developed by Monnet, widely regarded as the architect of the European Community.[79] According to the 'Monnet method', integration focused on national elites and made little provision for popular involvement.[80] Such inherent democratic deficit in the construction of African integration is a challenge that new governance arrangements within the AU need to address. A good starting point would be to empower the PAP with legislative authority exercised by Members directly elected by citizens of Member States.

Legitimacy concerns whether formal or social are crucial when contemplating the scope of AU law. This law should be seen to deliver and not encroach on national sovereignty over and above its bureaucratic remit.[81] Moreover, it should derive from accountable and transparent institutions. On the other hand, citizens should not regard it as remote but rather as a tool to deliver material benefits and uplift their standard of living. Africa is still waiting for an 'African Monnet' to develop a vision of Africa based on a legitimate constitutional blueprint. EU good practices provide material for reflection and Africa needs to heed to warnings where the European Union has failed. For example, Africa can ill afford to go down the spiral of a cumbersome and expensive bureaucracy, but neither can it afford an undemocratic, lame parliament.

7. Conclusion

The discussion around evolving AU law should be seen against the backdrop of the existential crisis which the AU and regional organizations face around the world. The tension between sovereignty and supranationalism is prevalent in Africa as much as it is in Europe, yet Africa has much to gain from deeper integration at levels of trade, good governance, and improved human security. Given the apparent quest for deeper integration and the low levels of formal and social legitimacy the AU enjoys, the need for both institutional reform and to step away from a top-down Monnet-inspired method have become imperative.

For integration to accelerate, political leaders and ordinary Africans need to commit to a deal accommodating the interests of states and individuals. Like

[78] Carter and Scott (n 76) 432.

[79] K Featherstone, 'Jean Monnet and the "democratic deficit" in the European Union' Journal of Common Market Studies)1994) 32, 150.

[80] ibid 165.

[81] Nkrumah (n 24) 218.

Europe, Africa must find a balance between regional and national powers that will meet African interests giving true effect to the drive for African self-determination. If that balance is not achieved, states will either fail to commit to an AU with supranational powers or will neglect to implement their obligations. AU Member States must get more out of the AU than they put in to make it advantageous.

Achieving the goals set by architects for reform will as always be difficult to achieve in the current context where African leaders rule the roost in an absolute fashion backed up by a plethora of ineffective AU institutions protecting vested interests. The AU has a history of aspirations and good intentions not translating to change. The soft obligations provided for by the present AU constitutional architecture have proven all but effective. Consequently, weak enforcement remains a reoccurring theme when assessing AU performance.

Against this background, it is necessary to set clear conceptual boundaries for an AU legal system. The obvious starting point to address the definitional uncertainty of AU law is to consider the institutional goals and functions of the AU set by its constitutional instruments and the powers of execution assigned to the organization. A core AU law will be crucial to introduce effective governance and accountability in a way that would serve African self-interest and benefit African citizens. It is suggested that constitutional sources and the binding decisions as enabled by the former should form the foundation of AU law at a primary and secondary level respectively, the latter being subject to the former. This calls for an amendment of relevant constitutional texts to allow for a closely defined range of binding decision-making powers directly applicable in Member States. A certain level of supranationalism is required to enable such decision-making power. Supranationalism should only make inroads into sovereignty in certain respects where there are distinct benefits to be derived.

Different layers of law will ultimately lead to the development of a hierarchy dovetailing with national law of Member States. Hierarchically, AU law flowing from those limited areas of supranational competence of AU institutions will override national law. It would add a next layer of decision-making over and above national parliaments. Through joining the AU constitutive treaties, Member States would delegate certain law-making powers to the AU and express their consent to be bound by specific AU laws. AU law will differ from treaties, where states can decide whether or not to sign/ratify and what the relationship with conflicting domestic law will be. The manner in which both sources are incorporated into domestic law will depend on the relevant provisions of state law. With such clarity, enforcement of decisions can be better managed as AU institutions and national governments will be accountable for outcomes within a particular sphere.

Academic contributions can do much to place AU law in the mainstream in a way that would provide a knowledge base that might support the AU in future reform endeavours. By promoting the idea at a non-political level, it might bolster reform and steer states in the right direction. African academics, including members of the African diaspora can do much to advance the establishment and credibility of AU law. One example would be the publication of a journal on AU law that would add to knowledge in this area. Similar efforts did much to advance an understanding of EU law and to develop the latter into a credible legal discipline.

2
The Implications of AU Law: Conceptual Analysis with Emphasis on the Institutional Consequences

Konstantinos D Magliveras

1. Introduction

Unlike other regional international organizations, the AU has not been endowed with a specific law-making mandate. Even though the Constitutive Act is silent on this question, this chapter argues that, over many years, which go back to the Organisation of African Unity (OAU) era, a certain 'AU law', namely a body of norms and rules, has come into existence and is constantly developing. The chapter begins with an overview of the distinct and autonomous legal order which has been created by the European Union. However, the EU law is referenced only as the best available paradigm globally and one from which other regional organizations can draw inspiration. However, the chapter does not suggest that the AU (AU) should follow or adhere to it. Thus, the chapter argues that the legal orders established by the Council of Europe (CoE) and the Organization of American States (OAS), two regional organizations sharing common characteristics with the AU, could serve as a better example for the evolutionary process of AU law. Based on this argument, the chapter focuses on how these two organizations have created legal orders through on the one hand, the conclusion of a large number of treaties, and on the other hand, the establishment of a regional system for the protection of human rights.

1.1 The European Union as the Paradigm of a Law-making Regional Organization

The European Union (EU) offers the best example of a regional international organization having created its own distinct legal system. EU law is understood as a specific body of rules which is made up of the following three categories of instruments. First, multilateral treaties (primarily the EU founding treaties, as amended and revised, but also the treaties of accession). Second, the legislative acts

Konstantinos D Magliveras, *The Implications of AU Law: Conceptual Analysis with Emphasis on the Institutional Consequences* In: *The Emergent African Union Law*. Edited by: Olufemi Amao, Michèle Olivier and Konstantinos D. Magliveras, Oxford University Press. © Konstantinos D Magliveras 2021. DOI: 10.1093/oso/9780198862154.003.0003

(regulations, directives, decisions) adopted by the competent organs (the Council of Ministers acting usually in conjunction with the European Parliament and, by delegated authority, the European Commission). Third, the judgments of the Court of Justice of the European Union (ECJ). A particular characteristic of EU law is that in cases of conflict with Member States' domestic law, it always takes precedence. Even though this is a fundamental principle of EU law, it has never been enshrined in the founding treaties. Rather, it is a judge-made rule laid down in 1964 in the famous case *Costa v Enel*. EU Member States have, overall, respected it. This shows that a regional organization's legal system could also comprise rules which have not emanated from traditional 'hard law' sources, namely the constitutive instrument. Thus, and this could prove important in the context of AU law, there might be indirect forms of law-making, allowing an international organization's legal system to adapt as it develops and to cater for the ever-changing circumstances.

EU law is binding. This is a strict rule disallowing Member States to promulgate conflicting rules in the areas where the European Union has exclusive competence. The obligatory nature of EU law stems from the fact that Member States have decided to transfer part of their sovereignty to it and have also consented to allow it to legislate on their behalf in the areas of competence. Moreover, EU law is based on uniformity: all Member States must always follow and apply the same rules. No deviation is tolerated, unless already agreed. It follows that Member States are not allowed to 'pick and choose' which rules to follow and which to ignore. They must adhere to exactly the same norms whether it suits them or not, whether it is politically expedient or not. Harmonization across the EU is not only a requirement but it is the name of the game. For this reason, an elaborate supervisory mechanism comprising two organs, the European Commission and the ECJ, has been implemented. However, just because a group of states in Europe has been willing (and able, for that matter) to adhere to a legal system which has been developed in the context of international organization, this neither means that it should or could be replicated in other parts of the world nor that it will be as successful as the European Union. To which extent states are willing to transfer their sovereignty to regional organizations differs considerably from region to region and this is especially true for African states.

2. The European Union and the African Economic Community: Why Sanctions and Coercion Are Not Always Necessary for Establishing Regional Economic Integration Organizations

The EU paradigm has led to a new category of intergovernmental institutions, the so-called regional economic integration organizations (REIOs), which are based on the understanding that these organizations will be very closely knit, a condition *sine qua non* for materializing economic integration. The establishment of REIOs has been attempted in other regions of the world,[1] and notably in Africa. In particular, the Treaty establishing the African Economic Community (AEC), was the continental attempt to gradually achieve economic integration.[2] However, it proved to be an ill-fated project and even though the AU Constitutive Act's Preamble[3] as well as the AU 50th Anniversary Solemn Declaration[4] reiterated the commitment to accelerate the materialization of AEC objectives, it has been left rather unceremoniously to perish. Arguably, the AU deserted the grand plan that was the AEC Treaty and opted for a less ambitious strategy.[5] Thus, the First Plan of Action of the Minimum Integration Programme (2012) asked Member States to speed up the integration process by initiating programmes promoting the integral parts of a common market (free movement of goods, services, persons, and capital).[6] However, subsequent events revealed that the AU was seriously contemplating the creation of a free trade area only. On 18 March 2018, the Agreement Establishing the African Continental Free Trade Area (ACFTA) was adopted, which entered into force on 7 July 2019. The Agreement was concluded as part of the Pan African Vision, 'An integrated, prosperous and peaceful Africa', which is enshrined in Aspiration 2 in the so-called Agenda 2063: The Africa we Want. As regards another component of a free trade area, namely the free movement of persons, the AU opted earlier in 2018 to revamp the AEC by concluding a Protocol to that effect.[7] However, Article 5 of the Protocol explicitly stipulates that it will be achieved progressively and no binding timetable was agreed.

The AEC was meant to establish its own legal order. Indeed, all contracting parties had undertaken the obligation to observe it.[8] Moreover, Article 99 of the

[1] Generally, see G Wignaraja, A Collins, and others, 'Opportunities and challenges for regional economic integration in the Indian Ocean' (2019) 1 Journal of Asian Economic Integration 129; M Rouis, Regional Economic Integration in the Middle East and North Africa (MENA Knowledge and Learning Quick Notes Series No 95, World Bank, 2013) available at <https://openknowledge.worldbank.org/handle/10986/20566> accessed 26 June 2021.

[2] Concluded in June 1991, entered into force in May 1994, currently 50 contracting parties. Integration was to be achieved in six stages of variable duration and over a transitional period not exceeding 34 years, Article 6 thereof. For analysis, see G Naldi and K. Magliveras, 'The African Economic Community: emancipation for African states or yet another glorious failure?' (1999) 24 North Carolina Journal of International Law and Commercial Regulation 601.

[3] It reads: '[c]onvinced of the need to accelerate the process of implementing the Treaty establishing the African Economic Community in order to promote the socio-economic development of Africa and to face more effectively the challenges posed by globalization'.

[4] AU Assembly, *Solemn Declaration on the 50th Anniversary of the OAU/AU*, Assembly/AU/Decl.3(XXI), 26 May 2013, para C.

[5] African Union, Agenda 2063 – The Africa We Want (AU Commission, Framework Document, September 2015) available at <https://au.int/sites/default/files/documents/33126-doc-framework_document_book.pdf> accessed 26 June 2021.

[6] AU Assembly, *Decision on African Integration*, Assembly/AU/Dec.392(XVIII), 30 January 2012.

[7] Protocol to the Treaty establishing the African Economic Community relating to Free Movement of Persons, Right of Residence and Right of Establishment, signed on 29 January 2018, not yet in force. Originally, the adoption of the Protocol was envisaged in Article 42(2) of the AEC Treaty.

[8] Article 3(e) of the AEC Treaty.

AEC Treaty stipulated that this legal order would form an integral part of the OAU Charter.[9] Therefore, for all intents and purposes, the AEC legal system should have been understood as part of OAU law.[10] Moreover, following the OAU's substitution by the AU in July 2002, the AEC law would have been regarded as part of AU law as well.[11] While 'the conspicuous absence in the [AEC] Treaty of an emphasis on legal issues in the integration process ... the word "law" appear[ing] only three times' has been noted,[12] it is also true that the AEC's operation would have led to a distinct legal system. All participating states would have to implement it and also refrain from any unilateral action having the potential of obstructing the AEC objectives.[13] Finally, it should be noted that the Pan-African Parliament (PAP), which was originally envisaged as an AEC organ,[14] was carried on in the AU's institutional architecture; when the instrument setting it up was concluded on 2 March 2001 it took the form of a Protocol to the AEC Treaty and not to the AU Constitutive Act.[15]

It has been argued that while sanctions and coercion are regarded as necessary futures of legal systems, they are not obligatory to explore the existence, the identity, and the structure of a particular legal order.[16] This submission appears to be true when one compares the EU legal system with the AEC legal system. Originally, the former did not envisage any sanctions for those Member States not fulfilling their obligations and/or violating them. It was only after the Common Market (or Internal Market or Single Market, in EU jargon) had been in full operation that the EU legal system was amended and sanctions against recalcitrant Member States were introduced. These changes materialized in two phases: first, by introducing punitive measures taking the form of monetary penalties for those states not executing ECJ judgments;[17] second, by introducing the sanction of suspending a Member State's membership rights when democratic values might be

[9] This followed from ibid Article 98(1) which made it an integral part of the OAU.

[10] That the AEC legal system would have become part of OAU/AU law raises the question if it were to be a legal order autonomous from its Member States, as is the case with EU law. Given that the AEC project never materialized, it remains a theoretical proposition.

[11] The AU neither replaced nor substituted the AEC, which was meant to continue existing subject to Article 33(2) of the Constitutive Act stipulating that its provisions take precedence over and supersede any inconsistent AEC Treaty provisions.

[12] See RF Oppong, *Legal Aspects of Economic Integration in Africa* (CUP, 2011) 83.

[13] Article 5 of the AEC Treaty.

[14] ibid Articles 7(1)(c) and 14.

[15] Protocol to the Treaty Establishing the African Economic Community Relating to the Pan-African Parliament, entered into force on 14 December 2003. PAP will become a proper AU organ when the Protocol to the Constitutive Act of the African Union Relating to the Pan-African Parliament, adopted on 17 June 2014, has entered into force. Presently, only 12 out of the 28 necessary instruments of ratifications have been deposited.

[16] See H Oberdieck, 'The role of sanctions and coercion in understanding law and legal systems' (1976) 21 American Journal of Jurisprudence 71. The central point of sanctions in transforming a social system into a legal system is best exemplified in HLA Hart, *The Concept of Law* (OUP, 1961). However, as has been observed, even Hart himself did not argue that there could be a legal system without sanctions, see AT Kronman, 'Hart, Austin, and the concept of legal sanctions' (1975) 84 Yale Law Journal 584, note 9 at 586.

[17] See Article 260 of the Treaty on the Functioning of the European Union (TFEU).

breached.[18] On the contrary, the AEC Treaty contained sanctions from the very beginning:

> Any Member State, which persistently fails to honour its general undertakings under this Treaty or fails to abide by the decisions or regulations of the [African Economic] Community, may be subjected to sanctions by the Assembly [of Heads of State and Government of the OAU] upon the recommendation of the Council [of Ministers of the OAU]. Such sanctions may include the suspension of the rights and privileges of membership and may be lifted by the Assembly upon the recommendation of the Council.[19]

On the basis of the above submissions, it would be incorrect to argue that, due to the lack of sanctions and coercion, no EU legal system existed while, precisely because of their presence, there was an AEC legal order. In the former case, there has always been a legal system in place, not least because this was the participating states' desire. Through the practice of Member States, it is evident that they accept the EU legal system to regulate their inter-state relations in the areas and fields of EU competence and of course their transactions with the European Union itself. Thus, that a legal system was established through the operation of an international organization does not presuppose that sanctions and coercion are necessary factors. It could very well be that the membership prefers the organization to develop a legal system featuring a 'light' form of regulation while, at the same time, accepting the mandatory nature of their obligations.

3. The CoE and the OAS: Examples of Regional Organizations with Distinct Legal Systems

Arguably, there are three necessary factors for an international organization to create its own legal system: (a) a certain process; (b) at least one organ to execute the process; and (c) the 'users' of the legal system. Taking the European Union as a paradigm, the process is set out in rather express terms in the founding treaties, an array of organs is involved in the process, while the 'users' are the Member States and their populations. The organs involved are the European Commission (it initiates the legislative acts), the Council of Ministers (the principal law maker usually acting in conjunction with), the European Parliament (where the population is directly represented), and the European Commission (this time as the legal system's guardian supervising Member States' behaviour and, in cases of alleged infractions, notifying) the ECJ (the final arbiter determining whether the legal system was

[18] Article 7 of the Treaty on European Union, as currently in force.
[19] Article 5(3) of the AEC Treaty.

breached).[20] The EU process is highly complex, but then Member States wanted it to mirror the traditional law-making process in a parliamentary democracy.

However, to create their own legal system, other regional international organizations have followed a different process. Two such examples are the CoE and the OAS, which will be examined in turn.

According to Article 1 of the CoE Statute (1949), one of its principal aims is to achieve 'a greater unity between its members' by means of, *inter alia*, 'agreements and common action in economic, social, cultural, scientific, legal and administrative matters and in the maintenance and further realisation of human rights'. Moreover, under Article 15 thereof, the required action to implement this aim is the conclusion of conventions and the adoption of common policies by Member States. So far, the CoE has concluded the very impressive number of 223 treaties[21] which, taken as a whole, should be construed as a law-making process leading to the creation of a legal system. Thus, since 1949, the CoE has consistently pursued the Statute-sanctioned strategy of preparing common norms to be presented to Member States in the form of conventions for adoption. Once they have ratified them in the required number to enter into force, they are bound by them and they should amend domestic legislation to be compliant. Finally, the population of Member States can 'use' these treaties to promote their own interests, to protect themselves from unlawful state acts, and so on.

That the CoE legal system's rules and norms may also be found in the legal orders of other international organizations, whether global (e.g. the United Nations) or regional (e.g. the EU), is of no consequence. This is because it has been developed as a distinct legal system meeting the aforementioned three factors, namely a certain process (laid down in the aforementioned Articles 1 and 15 of the Statute), carried out by the competent organs (the Committee if Ministers and, in a consultative capacity, the Parliamentary Assembly), and with the 47 Member States and their population being its 'users'. Thus, the domestic legal orders of those states which have accepted this or that convention will contain a commonality of rules and regulations to be found in the respective treaty and all conventions together constitute the CoE legal system.

The CoE has deliberately enlarged the scope of 'users' by allowing third states from all continents as well as regional organizations to become contracting parties to some of these conventions. Usually, it invites third states having an interest in a treaty's subject matter to participate in the deliberations and, if they so wish, to sign and ratify them. An excellent example is the Convention on Offences relating to

[20] Arguably, over the years, several ECJ judgments have led to 'judicial law-making'; for present purposes, this should be viewed as part and parcel with the overall process of developing the EU legal order. Generally, see F Wasserfallen, 'The judiciary as legislator? How the European Court of Justice shapes policy-making in the European Union' (2010) 17 Journal of European Public Policy 1128.

[21] See <https://www.coe.int/en/web/conventions/full-list≥ accessed 26 June 2021. This number includes revised conventions and amending/additional protocols to existing ones.

Cultural Property,[22] the only treaty on the international plane specifically dealing with criminalizing the illicit trafficking of cultural property, which is open to accession by any state.[23] The Explanatory Memorandum explained its potential global reach as follows:

> [t]he Convention was not only drafted with Council of Europe member States in mind, but was rather designed to be an open, globally-oriented Convention to protect the common cultural heritage of humanity. As the Convention was consciously drafted to operate in harmony with, and build upon, universal instruments, it is intended to further facilitate co-operation between all States willing and able to take concerted action to preserve precious art and antiquities for present and future generations.[24]

Another notable treaty is the Convention against Trafficking in Human Organs, which could be signed by five non-Member States as well as by the European Union.[25] Given that the European Union has its own, more advanced legal system, and has specific legislation covering this aspect of trafficking, it remains to be seen how the two systems will interact. Finally, it should be noted that African states may also accede to these treaties. Examples include Morocco which has become a party to the Convention on an Integrated Safety, Security and Service Approach at Football Matches and Other Sports Events (2016), to the Convention on the Manipulation of Sports Competitions (2014), and to the Convention on Laundering, Search, Seizure and Confiscation of the Proceeds from Crime and on the Financing of Terrorism (2005); Benin, Burkina Faso, Congo, Côte d'Ivoire, etc., to the Convention on the Counterfeiting of Medical Products and Similar Crimes Involving Threats to Public Health (2011); and Benin, Cabo Verde, Nigeria, Tunisia, etc., to the Convention on Cybercrime (2001).

As regards the OAS Charter,[26] it does not contain an express provision on law-making as the CoE Statute. But Article 2 thereof stipulates that it is an essential objective 'to seek the solution of political, juridical, and economic problems that may arise among [American states]' and authorizes the OAS to promote, by cooperative action, the membership's economic, social, and cultural development. Based on

[22] Opened for signature on 19 May 2017, not yet in force.

[23] Convention on Offences relating to Cultural Property Article 28(1) describing several conditions to be met for non-Member States to be invited to accede.

[24] Explanatory Report to the Council of Europe Convention on Offences relating to Cultural Property, 19 May 2017, para 13, available at <https://rm.coe.int/1680710437> accessed 26 June 2021. Only the Holy See, Japan, and Mexico participated in its drafting.

[25] Opened for signature on 25 March 2015, entered into force on 1 March 2018; A Pietrobon, 'Challenges in implementing the European Convention against Trafficking in Human Organs' (2016) 29 Leiden Journal of International Law 485; K Magliveras, 'A critical overview of the Council of Europe Convention against Trafficking in Human Organs' (2015) 31 International Enforcement Law Reporter 370.

[26] Signed on 30 April 1948, entered into force on 13 December 1951.

this law-making capacity, some 70 treaties (including amending protocols) have so far been negotiated and concluded.[27] The number might be much smaller compared to the CoE, but nevertheless an impressive one it is. Their ambit is similar to the CoE treaties (human rights, civil and criminal law matters, cultural affairs, etc.) and they cover conflict of laws issues as well

Neither the legal systems of the CoE nor of the OAS are exhaustive in the sense that they address only those areas where Member States have considered that regulation is required. On the contrary, the EU legal system regulates all areas where it exercises competence. However, the former should not be regarded as incomplete legal orders and the latter as complete because at the end of the day, they reflect the choices made by their memberships. What is of importance is that they do contain sets of rules and norms obliging contracting parties to give effect to them and disallowing any state action and behaviour which is in conflict. Thus, the decisive element in all cases is the development of a legal system pursuant to the wishes of the respective membership. Moreover, these legal systems have judicial organs in place which are mandated to rule authoritatively and with a binding force on whether State Parties are in breach of their obligations. State Parties must comply promptly with all decisions rendered against them in their entirety. Over and above the ECJ, such organs include the European Court of Human Rights (ECtHR) and the Inter-American Court of Human Rights (IACtHR), set up, respectively, by the Convention for the Protection of Human Rights and Fundamental Freedoms (ECHR) (1950) and by the American Convention on Human Rights (ACHR) (1969).

In this instance, the coercion to be imposed upon State Parties takes two forms. First, contracting parties are not allowed to disregard the judgments of the relevant court and have no option but to obey them.[28] Second, the execution of judgments is not left to the contracting parties themselves but is supervised to prevent non-compliance. In the European Union, this role is played by the Commission.[29] In the CoE, it is the Committee of Ministers (CM).[30] According to Article 46(4)–(5) of the ECHR, if the CM resolves that a state has not followed a judgment, it may ask the ECtHR to rule on the matter. If the ECtHR confirms it, the case shall be referred to the CM '[f]or consideration of the measures to be taken'.[31] Even though their

[27] Full list available at <http://www.oas.org/en/topics/treaties_agreements.asp> accessed 26 June 2021.

[28] Article 46(1) ECHR and Article 68(1) ACHR.

[29] Generally, see the European Commission annual Reports on monitoring the application of EU law, available at <https://ec.europa.eu/info/publications/annual-reports-monitoring-application-eu-law_en> accessed 26 June 2021.

[30] Article 46(2) ECHR. Further, see Supervision of the Execution of Judgments and Decisions of the European Court of Human Rights, 14th Annual Report of the Committee of Ministers (Council of Europe, 2021).

[31] Inserted to the ECHR under Protocol No 14, which entered into force in June 2010 and amended the control system.

nature is not laid down, the ECtHR and the CM should be considered as part of the CoE sanctioning regime.

In the OAS, the supervision of IACtHR judgments is stipulated in Article 65 of the ACHR: the IACtHR should record those states not in compliance in its annual reports to the OAS General Assembly and submit 'pertinent recommendations'. But the IACtHR has held that monitoring compliance is a power inherent in its jurisdictional functions.[32] This view is based on Article 67 of the ACHR (judgments are final and definitive), on Article 68(1) (contracting parties promise to comply with judgments), on *pacta sunt servanda* (a rule of peremptory international law embodied in Article 27 of the Vienna Convention on the Law of Treaties (1969) obliging states to give effect to their obligations),[33] and on the *effet utile* principle.[34] The IACtHR monitoring process culminates in Orders on supervision of compliance, which are issued after having taken into account (a) reports by respondent states informing it on compliance; (b) briefs by victims commenting on the respondent states' reports; (c) observations by the Inter-American Commission on Human Rights; and (d) *amicus curiae* briefs submitted by interested third parties. Apparently, OAS states have not disputed the IACtHR's ability to supervise itself the execution of judgments. As noted in the 2016 IACtHR Report to the General Assembly: 'Monitoring compliance … has become one of the most demanding activities of the Court, because each year there is a considerable increase in the number of cases at this stage … the Court monitors, rigorously and continually, prompt and cumulative compliance with every reparation ordered.'[35] While the General Assembly has thus far never discussed such infractions, it has confirmed that compliance with judgments is mandatory.[36]

In addition, the OAS legal system comprises model laws prepared for its 'users', the Member States, to assist them in adopting, in selected regulatory areas, domestic legislation which meets minimum standards and complies with applicable best practices. Examples of these instruments, some of which were approved by the General Assembly, include the Model Inter-American Law on Secured

[32] See, *inter alia*, IACtHR, *Case of Herrera Ulloa v Costa Rica*, Order of Supervision of Compliance with Judgment of 22 November 2010; *Case of Baena-Ricardo et al. v Panama*, Competence, Judgment of 28 November 2003, Series C No 104.

[33] IACtHR, *International Responsibility for the Promulgation and Enforcement of Laws in Violation of the Convention (Arts 1 and 2 of the American Convention on Human Rights)*, Advisory Opinion OC-14/94, 9 December 1994, Series A No 14, para 35.

[34] cf IACtHR, *Case of Ivcher Bronstein v Peru*, Competence, Judgment of 24 September 1999, Series C No 54, para 37.

[35] Annual Report of the Inter-American Court of Human Rights 2016 (San José, 2017) 72 noting that there were 182 cases at the stage of monitoring compliance which concerned 901 reparation measures. The Orders on compliance can be found at <http://www.corteidh.or.cr/cf/Jurisprudencia2/busqueda_supervision_cumplimiento.cfm?lang=en> accessed 26 June 2021.

[36] OAS General Assembly, 47th Regular Session, AG/RES.2908 (XLVII-O/17), 21 June 2017, item xiv (Observations and recommendations on the Annual Report of the Inter-American Court of Human Rights), OEA/Ser.P, AG/doc.5606/17 rev. 1 (22 September 2017) 101.

Transactions,[37] the Model Law Protecting Freedom of Expression Against Corruption,[38] the Model Inter-American Law on Access to Information,[39] the Model Law to Facilitate and Encourage the Reporting of Acts of Corruption and to Protect Whistleblowers and Witnesses,[40] and the Model Law on the Simplified Corporation.[41] The importance of these instruments lies in the fact that those Member States implementing them introduce common norms deriving from the OAS legal system in their own legal systems. Thus, in time, one could expect to find uniformity among the OAS membership in specific areas of law.

4. The Development of the AU Legal Order

From an institutional point of view, the AU shares characteristics with the CoE and the OAS. Importantly, it has also pursued a policy of negotiating and concluding treaties in a wide range of areas. While Member States are expected to become contracting parties to all of them,[42] in practice reception has varied: some treaties entered into force in a relatively short period of time and have been ratified by the majority of Member States, in other cases they have stood unratified and have not entered into force,[43] resulting in uncertainty as regards the legal system's development.

Naturally, not all OAU/AU treaties form part of AU law. One has to exclude those creating legal entities at continental level (e.g. the Convention establishing the African Centre for Fertilizer Development (1985); the Revised Constitution of the African Civil Aviation Commission (2009); the Statute of the Africa Sports Council (2016); the Treaty establishing the African Medicines Agency (2019)); those of a technical nature (e.g. the Phyto-Sanitary Convention (1967); the Revised Convention on the Conservation of Nature and Natural Resources (2017); the Convention establishing an African Technical Co-operation Programme (1975)) or those addressing specific matters (e.g. the Cultural Charter for Africa (1975); the Charter for African Cultural Renaissance (2006); and the Road Safety

[37] OEA/Ser.K/XXI.6/CIPID-VI/doc.24/02 rev. 3, 5 March 2002; SV Bazinas, 'The OAS and the UNCITRAL model laws on secured transactions compared' (2017) 22 Uniform Law Review 914.

[38] Adopted in 2002; RG Vaughn, T Devine, and others, contributor question: doesn't "others" imply more than one editor above and above the two named? 'The Whistleblower Statute prepared for the Organization of American States and the global legal revolution protecting whistleblowers' (2003) 35 George Washington International Law Review 857.

[39] AG/RES. 2607 (XL-O/10), 8 June 2010.

[40] SG/MESICIC/doc.345/12 rev. 2, 22 March 2013.

[41] AG/RES. 2906 (XLVII-O/17), 20 June 2017.

[42] Full list available at <https://au.int/en/treaties> accessed 26 June 2021.

[43] Suffice to mention the Protocol on the Statute of the African Court of Justice and Human Rights (2008), which, even though not in force, was revised by the Protocol on Amendments to the Protocol on the Statute of the African Court of Justice and Human Rights (2014); G Naldi and K Magliveras, 'The African Union's International Criminal Court: an appraisal' (2015) 21 African Yearbook of International Law 299.

Charter (2016)). The remaining treaties form the basis for the development of AU law. As in the case of the CoE and the OAS, they can be grouped together in two categories: those setting up a regional human rights system and those creating norms and rules common for Member States in areas relating to AU activities.

The first category comprises (a) the African Charter on Human and Peoples' Rights (concluded in 1981), the three Protocols on the Rights of Women (2003), the Rights of Older Persons (2016), and the Rights of Persons with Disabilities (2018) as well as the instruments pertaining to the African Court of Human and Peoples' Rights (ACtHPR); (b) the African Charter on the Rights and Welfare of the Child (1991); (c) the Convention Governing the Specific Aspects of Refugee Problems in Africa (1969); and (d) the Convention for the Protection and Assistance of Internally Displaced Persons in Africa (Kampala Convention) (2009). The second category covers the following four areas. First, democratic norms and good governance (the African Charter on Democracy, Elections and Governance (2007); the African Charter on Values and Principles of Public Service and Administration (2011); the African Charter on the Values and Principles of Decentralisation, Local Governance and Local Development (2014)). Second, protection of the environment (the Convention on the Ban of the Import into Africa and the Control of Transboundary Movement and Management of Hazardous Wastes within Africa (Bamako Convention) (1991); the African Nuclear-Weapon-Free Zone Treaty (Pelindaba Treaty) (1996)). Third, continental criminal law (the Convention on the Prevention and Combating of Terrorism (1999) and Protocol (2004); the Convention for the Elimination of Mercenarism in Africa (1977); the Convention on Preventing and Combating Corruption (2003); the Convention on Cyber Security and Personal Data Protection (2014); the AU Non-Aggression and Common Defence Pact (2005); the Charter on Maritime Security and Safety and Development in Africa (Lomé Charter) (2016)). Four, economic integration (the AEC Treaty (1991) and Protocol relating to Free Movement of Persons, Right of Residence and Right of Establishment (2018); the Convention on Cross-Border Cooperation (Niamey Convention) (2014); the Agreement Establishing the African Continental Free Trade Area (2018); the Regulatory and Institutional Texts for the Implementation of the Yamoussoukro Decision and Framework towards the Establishment of a Single African Air Transport Market (2018)).

It should be noted that not all these treaties are necessarily law-making instruments. However, taken as a whole, they have created a corpus of norms and rules which has been accepted by the 'users'. In their turn, they have agreed to make them the applicable law domestically. Some of these norms have had an impact going beyond the African continent and have influenced developments in international law and international relations. Suffice to mention: (a) the Convention on Mercenarism, concluded 12 years before the International Convention against the Recruitment, Use, Financing and Training of Mercenaries;[44] (b) the African

[44] Adopted under UN General Resolution 44/34, 4 December 1989.

Human Rights Charter which, *inter alia*, pioneered the environment as a human and justiciable right and mandated its protection from pollution,[45] and also made the equal enjoyment of the common heritage of humankind a right;[46] (c) the Bamako Convention, which consolidated the African position that the dumping of nuclear and industrial waste is a crime;[47] the Pelindaba Treaty, which has kept nuclear-weapon-free-zones alive as an issue on the international plane;[48] the Terrorism Convention, which defines the term 'terrorist acts';[49] the Kampala Convention, currently the only treaty on the protection of internally displaced persons (IDPs) globally;[50] and the Protocol on the Rights of Older People, concluded a year after the relevant OAS treaty.[51]

However, in several AU treaties there is a clear intention to augment the ambit of existing norms and/or to create new ones for the 'users' as well as to establish supervisory/compliance mechanisms, featuring coercion to ensure that the 'users' obey the rules. Thus, the Preamble to the aforementioned Cyber Security Convention explains that Member States need to harmonize their legislation to 'regulate a particularly evolving technological domain'.[52] The Convention aims at setting up an 'appropriate *normative framework* consistent with the African legal, cultural, economic and social environment and ... [a] *legal framework* for the emergence of the knowledge economy in Africa' (emphasis added). It creates new substantive law (contracting parties will have to adopt effective domestic legislative measures)[53] and new institutions taking the form of national regulatory authorities (NRAs), the so-called National Personal Data Protection Authorities.[54] Finally, Article 27 obliges parties to create national cyber security mentoring structures, while Article 32 sets up a mechanism at AU level to, *inter alia*, formulate harmonized codes of

[45] Article 24 of the African Charter; Grand Bay Declaration and Plan of Action (1999); African Commission on Human and Peoples' Rights, Comm No 155/96, *The Social and Economic Rights Action Center and the Center for Economic and Social Rights v Nigeria*, 15th Activity Report 2001–2002, para 52.

[46] Article 22 of the African Charter (n 45).

[47] Article 4 of the Convention; see also OAU Council of Ministers, *Resolution on Dumping of Nuclear and Industrial Waste in Africa*, CM/Res. 1153(XLVIII), 25 May 1988; Article 59 of the AEC Treaty; B Chaytor and KR Gray, *International Environmental Law and Policy in Africa* (Springer, 2003).

[48] K Magliveras, 'The African NWFZ, the African Commission on Nuclear Energy, and the Protection of the Environment' in J Black-Branch and D Fleck (eds), *Nuclear Non-Proliferation in International Law*, Volume IV (T.M.C. Asser/Springer, 2019) 189.

[49] Article (3) of the Convention, supplemented by the Algiers Plan of Action for the Prevention and Combating of Terrorism (September 2002).

[50] See further, International Conference on the Great Lakes Region, Protocol on the Protection and Assistance to Internally Displaced Persons (2006).

[51] Inter-American Convention on Protecting the Human Rights of Older Persons, adopted on 15 June 2015, entered into force 11 January 2017. At the UN level, the human rights of this category of people are thus far covered by political instruments (e.g. the Political Declaration and Madrid International Plan of Action on Ageing (2002)) and by Human Rights Council decisions (e.g. Resolution 33/5, 29 September 2016).

[52] Adopted on 27 June 2014, not yet in force (seven more ratifications are required).

[53] Article 25(1) of the Cyber Security Convention. For the criminal offences to be promulgated and the criminal sanctions to be inflicted, see Articles 29 et seq.

[54] Articles 11–12 and 25(2) of the Cyber Security Convention (n 53).

conduct for the use of public authorities.[55] In short, the Convention lays down minimum standards and procedures allowing Member States to share a common approach on security issues and, in the process, harmonize their legislation.

A second example is the aforementioned Charter on Maritime Security. According to Article 3, its objectives include the establishment of national, regional, and continental institutions and the implementation of appropriate policies promoting security and safety at sea. These are specified in Article 7 obliging contracting parties to set up national coordination structures and in Article 8 placing upon them the duty to harmonize domestic legislation to international law (principally to the UN Convention on the Law of the Sea (1982)). Under Article 40, parties agree to mutual judicial and legal cooperation (primarily in the criminal law domain), resulting in considerable complementarity among national measures on cooperation. Article 41 institutionalizes the participation of 'users' and creates a 15-member Committee of States Parties with its own rules of procedure responsible for monitoring the Convention's application and recommending follow-up action. The Committee meets international standards: members must be independent, have their own free volition, and not act as representatives of the party which appointed them. Monitoring will take the form of compulsory reports submitted by all parties on the measures taken to implement the Charter. Reports must be filed within two years of the Charter's entry into force and, thereafter, at five-year intervals. The Charter does not stipulate further on the reports' evaluation, presumably the Committee's rules of procedure will make provision for this. As the Committee will submit its own report on implementation to the AU Assembly every two years, there is ample opportunity to record infractions by contracting parties and propose the taking of appropriate measures.

The system for protecting and promoting human rights in Africa is another component of AU law. In terms of substantive law, it is considerably broader than both the CoE and the Inter-American systems. Thus, the aforementioned AU human rights instruments safeguard specific population groups and offer the added value of being lex specialis. In that respect, AU law has a distinctive advantage. However, its institutional aspects are wanting because the ACtHPR was not envisaged in the African Human Rights Charter but was set up under a Protocol concluded in 1998.[56] Currently, 25 Member States are not contracting parties to the Protocol and are not expected to ratify it in the foreseeable future (Chad was the last state that ratified it in January 2016). While this diminishes the AU law's value and validity in the area of fundamental freedoms, the African Commission on Human and Peoples' Rights is competent to hear complaints against all contracting parties

[55] Generally, see UJ Orji, 'The African Union Convention on Cybersecurity: a regional response towards cyber stability?' (2018) 12 Masaryk University Journal of Law and Technology 91.

[56] Protocol to the African Charter on Human and Peoples' Rights on the Establishment of an African Court on Human and Peoples' Rights, adopted on 10 June 1998, entered into force on 25 January 2004 (1998 Protocol).

to the African Human Rights Charter and, therefore, there is still room for supervision. Even though the African Commission, being a quasi-judicial treaty organ, issues 'recommendations' and not judgments, the former are not to be disrespected by respondent states.[57]

According to Article 30 of the 1998 Protocol, contracting parties undertake to comply with ACtHPR judgments within the stipulated time limit and guarantee their execution. Under Article 31, the ACtHPR must record instances of non-compliance in its yearly reports submitted to the AU Assembly.[58] A far stricter supervisory mechanism is stipulated in the Statute of the African Court of Justice and Human Rights (ACJHR),[59] the judicial organ emanating from merging the African Court of Justice[60] and the ACtHPR. Article 46 of the Statute provides that all decisions are binding, and judgments are final. Parties must comply with judgments and pledge their implementation. The coercive aspect is laid down in the fourth paragraph thereof, which stipulates that '[w]here a party has failed to comply with a judgment, the Court shall refer the matter to the Assembly, which shall decide upon measures to be taken to give effect to that judgment' as well as in the fifth paragraph allowing the AU Assembly to impose sanctions by virtue of Article 23(2) of the Constitutive Act.[61] While no other regional human rights system contains such a draconic and coercive provision, how the AU Assembly will apply Article 46(5) and whether it will actually impose sanctions against states found by the ACJHR to have breached their human rights obligations remains to be seen, if and when the ACJHR Statute becomes operative.

5. Conclusion

As has been mentioned, EU law-making is undertaken by specific organs which have been granted the competence to do so. Indeed, in certain areas of activities they have been given exclusive competence. This means that the European Union on its own may adopt legally binding acts to the exclusion of Member States.[62] The

57 D Inman, S Smis, and others, 'The (un)willingness to implement the recommendations of the African Commission on Human and Peoples' Rights: revisiting the Endorois and the Mamboleo decisions' (2018) 2 African Human Rights Yearbook 400.

58 See the Reports on the Activities of the African Court on Human and Peoples' Rights at <http://en.african-court.org/index.php/publications/activity-reports> accessed 26 June 2021.

59 Protocol on the Statute of the African Court of Justice and Human Rights, concluded on 1 July 2008, not yet in force. For analysis, see G Naldi and K Magliveras, 'The African Court of Justice and human rights: a judicial curate's egg' (2012) 9 International Organizations Law Review 387.

60 Protocol of the Court of Justice of the African Union, adopted on 1 July 2003, entered into force on 11 February 2009 (2003 Protocol). Generally, see K Magliveras and G Naldi, 'The African Court of Justice' (2006) 66 Zeitschrift fuer auslaendisches oeffentiches Recht und Voelkerrecht 187.

61 For analysis of Article 23(2) see Chapter 19. The imposition of such sanctions was first introduced in Article 52(2) of the 2003 Protocol.

62 See Articles 2(1) and 3 of the TFEU.

Constitutive Act has not granted such competence to AU organs. It could potentially be inferred from Articles 3 and 4 thereof, setting out, respectively, the AU objectives and principles, as well as from Articles 9 and 13, stipulating, respectively, the functions of the Assembly and the Executive Council. However, such an interpretation of the Constitutive Act does raise issues of considerable perplexity and no Member State should be prepared to accept it. However, there might be another avenue. Arguably, law-making could be undertaken by the AU Commission on International Law (AUCIL). It was set up under the authority of Article 5(2) of the Constitutive Act as an advisory organ with a mandate akin to the United Nations' International Law Commission (ILC), namely the codification and progressive development of international law in Africa. Article 4 of its Statute, which was approved in 2009,[63] cites as objectives, *inter alia*, conducting studies on legal matters of interest to the AU and its Member States, assisting in the revision of OAU/AU treaties, as well as proposing draft framework agreements and model regulations. Moreover, since 2012 it has held a Forum on International Law, which is described as follows: '[a] platform for discussing and interacting on matters of interest for Africa through the prism of international law and the *African Union Law* with the view of raising awareness on the necessity of accelerating regional integration, enlightening … on legal implications of regional integration, present the steps already achieved towards the African integration' (emphasis added).[64]

The further expansion of AU law and, more importantly, the realization by all 55 Member States that such a legal system does exist and that they are its 'users' should necessitate a revision of the Constitutive Act. The AU should be endowed with the mandate to legislate in those areas that Member States allow. Presently, this is a necessity given the aforementioned project to establish a Continental Free Trade Area and the decision to revitalize the AEC with the adoption of the Protocol on the Free Movement of Persons. These developments cannot but lead to the further consolidation of AU law and the need to have in place a sound law-making process.

[63] AU Assembly, *Decision on the Draft Statute of the African Union Commission on International Law*, Assembly/AU/Dec.209(XII), 3 February 2009.

[64] See <https://au.int/sw/node/32533> accessed 26 June 2021.

3
Framing AU Law through the Lenses of International Constitutionalization and Federalism

Femi Amao

1. Introduction

This chapter positions the African Union (AU) and its organs as norm 'entrepreneurs' or generators, standard setters and law-makers at the continental level facilitating the constitutionalization process. From this standpoint, the Constitutive Act of the AU could be seen as a social contract and a constitutional instrument governing distribution and allocation of powers. This could be contrasted with the predecessor to the AU, the Organisation of African Unity (OAU), which was not designed or conceived as a law- or norm-generating institution. However, it is arguable to contend that when the OAU started adopting treaties under its ambit, to some extent also in practice it exhibited some norm-generating capacities. It is suggested that international constitutionalization and federalism provide a useful way of analysing and understanding key aspects of the emergent legal order. The chapter starts by looking at the AU law as a legal system and its definition and sources. Thereafter it looks at regional integration and its legal consequences, drawing insights from the European Union (EU). It subsequently examines AU law from the perspective of federalism and constitutionalization. Finally, it examines the roles of two institutions of the AU as an expression of the concepts at the continental level.

2. AU Law as a Legal System

Perhaps an apposite preliminary question to ask is 'what is AU law'? This is because the concept itself is currently not in common usage in legal parlance and discourse. However, some African regional instruments made reference to the continental-level law without defining or explaining what it is, what it means, or its implications. For instance, in the AU statute establishing the African Union Commission on International Law, an independent advisory organ of the AU, references were

Femi Amao, *Framing AU Law through the Lenses of International Constitutionalization and Federalism* In: *The Emergent African Union Law.* Edited by: Olufemi Amao, Michèle Olivier and Konstantinos D. Magliveras, Oxford University Press.
 DOI: 10.1093/oso/9780198862154.003.0004

made to the 'laws of the Union'.[1] Furthermore, in the instrument expressing the AU's willingness to collaborate with the state of Tanzania's offer to establish an African Institute of International Law, reference was also made to an 'AU Law' but again without providing a definition.[2] In addition, in the Protocol on Amendments to the Protocol on the Statute of the African Court of Justice and Human Rights[3] passing reference was made to the 'laws of the African Union' in Article 28G.

It is also notable that the incumbent president of the International Court of Justice described the norms that have emerged at the continental level in Africa as the 'public law of Africa'.[4] According to him,

> [t]his public law of Africa provides a normative framework for the realization of the political, social and economic objectives of Pan-Africanism. It also corresponds to the present day needs and aspirations of the peoples of the continent. Some aspects of this public law possess, however, a universal vocation, in the sense that they may eventually influence the adoption of similar rules on the international plane.[5]

The author, Yusuf identified two categories of norms in this regard. According to him, the first category includes norms that 'are quite innovative and original as compared to universal international law norms in that they only exist within the public law of Africa as binding rules or principles'.[6] The second category are norms that supplement existing international law by widening their scope or adapting them to the African context. The two categories are components of what Yusuf described as the public law of Africa, broadly in line with the theme of this book, AU law. According to Yusuf, examples of the first category include norms emanating from the AU Constitutive Act such as the right of the AU to intervene in Member States in certain circumstances and norms emanating from conventions concluded at the continental level such as the Kampala Convention.[7] Examples of the second are norms derived from the African Charter on the Rights and Welfare of the Child which supplement the existing international law on the right of the child.[8]

[1] Article 4(a), (e) Statute of the African Union Commission on International Law, EX.CL/478 (XIV)a (2009). See also Article of the Constitutive Act of the AU. The Assembly of Heads of State and Government adopted the Statute in February 2009. Decision Assembly/AU/Dec.209(XII).

[2] Decision on the Establishment of an African Institute of International Law in Arusha, The United Republic of Tanzania, Assembly/AU/14(XVIII) Add.5 (2012).

[3] Protocol on Amendments to the Protocol on the Statute of the African Court of Justice and Human Rights, Assembly/AU/Dec.529(XXIII) (2014).

[4] AA Yusuf, *Pan-Africanism and International Law* (The Hague Academy of International Law, 2014) 185.

[5] ibid.

[6] ibid.

[7] *African Union Convention for the Protection and Assistance of Internally Displaced Persons in Africa.* African Union (2009) available at <https://au.int/en/treaties/african-union-convention-protection-and-assistance-internally-displaced-persons-africa> accessed 15 July 2021.

[8] African Charter on the Rights and Welfare of the Child (1990) available at <https://au.int/en/treaties/african-charter-rights-and-welfare-child> accessed 3 September 2020.

It is thus apparent that there is an understanding that a legal system has been developing alongside the AU institutions. The absence of a definition may not be too significant because the legal order may be seen as an organic and necessary corollary to the AU integration agenda. Nevertheless, for our purpose and preliminarily, AU law could be defined as the body of treaties, resolutions, and decisions under the auspices of the OAU/AU that have direct and indirect application to the Member States of the AU.[9] According to Ajulo, it could be regarded in a basic sense as a 'sub-regional international law' or, in the context of this chapter, regional law.[10] Though currently in a nascent state when compared to the laws of the European Union (EU), AU law is evolving slowly and exhibiting traits similar to the development of EU law. The establishment of the AU to replace the OAU was a significant step that has had the effect of piercing the once impenetrable national borders through transnational norms. These transnational norms form the basis for the evolvement or development of common legal rules, concepts, and principles applicable to all AU Member States without exception.[11]

3. Regional Integration and Legal Consequences

Like its predecessor the OAU, the AU has been the key driver for integration in Africa. Integration in this context would progress gradually from a free trade area, to a customs union, and ultimately to a political union. It is widely acknowledged that regional integration has legal consequences not only at the regional level but also at the international and the individual state's level. The EU model which greatly influenced the design of the AU is instructive.[12] The original idea behind the European Union or European Community (as it was previously known) was not to create a new legal order. Rather, the Treaties of Paris (1951)[13] and Rome (1957)[14] were accepted to be part of international law.[15] However, the European Court of Justice (ECJ) subsequently declared that the EU constituted 'a new legal order of international law'.[16] According to the Court, in contrast to ordinary international

[9] O Amao, *African Union Law: The Emergence of a Sui Generis Legal Order* (Routledge, 2019).

[10] SB Ajulo, 'Sources of African Law' (2001) 45(1) Journal of African Law 73, 74; ME Olivier, 'The role of African Union law in integrating Africa' (2015) 22 (4) South African Journal of International Affairs 513.

[11] See U Scheuner, Forward to CJ Mann, *The Function of Judicial Decision in European Integration* (Nijhoff, 1971).

[12] RK Edozie and K Gottschalk, *The African Union's Africa: New Pan-African Initiatives in Global Governance* (Michigan State University Press, 2014) xiii; T Maluwa 'The Transition from the Organisation of African Unity to the African Union' in AA Yusuf and F Ouguergouz (eds), *The African Union: Legal and Institutional Framework: A Manual on the Pan-African Organization* (Martinus Nijhoff, 2012) 25, 38.

[13] Treaty Establishing the European Coal and Steel Community, 18 April 1951, 261 UNTS 140.

[14] Treaty Establishing the European Economic Community, 25 March 1957, 298 UNTS 11.

[15] R Schutze, *From Dual to Cooperative Federalism: The Changing Structure of European Law* (OUP, 2013) 3.

[16] *Flaminio Costa v ENEL* [1964] ECR 585 (6/64) 593.

treaties, the treaties of the Union created its unique legal system, which became an integral part of the legal system of Member States and applicable by Member State courts. The ECJ concluded that,

> by creating a Community of unlimited duration, having its own institutions, its own personality and its own capacity in law, apart from having international standing and more particularly, real powers resulting from a limitation of competence or a transfer of powers from the States to the Community, the member-States, albeit within limited spheres, have restricted their sovereign rights and created a body of law applicable both to their nationals and to themselves.[17]

This, in Schutze's view, represents a 'middle ground' between international and national law, a system considered *sui generis* and which the EU thinkers labelled 'supranationalism'.[18] Similarly, the establishment of the AU underscores the advancement of the integration agenda in Africa, which has led to a wider level of intergovernmental cooperation and shows positive signs of supranationalism in some spheres. The predecessor organization of the AU, the OAU, started out as a treaty-based organization and thus was part of the international law architecture. However, the decision to create a Union to replace the OAU marked a significant shift. The legal order that was created and that is emerging from the AU is assuming greater importance in Africa with striking features compared to the OAU. There are strong indications that its structure and legal order will become increasingly *sui generis* in the same way the European Union has evolved.[19] For instance, Tieku has argued that the composition and competencies of the African Union Commission (AUC) under the Constitutive Act and the relative independence of the AUC underscores the supranational credentials of the AU. In support of this contention, he argued that the ability of the AUC to 'create regulations that are binding on member states' and the central role that the AUC played in the drafting of legal instruments 'reflect that of a supranational actor'.[20] This contention may be debatable but it increasingly shows the changing perception of the AU's capacity to act as a norm entrepreneur at the continental level.

The decision of the African Court on Human and Peoples' Rights (ACHPR) in *Femi Falana v The African Union*[21] underscores this point. It is significant that this was one of the first decisions of the AU Court. The African Court in that case, relying on the International Court of Justice's (ICJ) advisory opinion on 'Reparation for Injuries Suffered in the Service of the United Nations',[22] held that,

[17] ibid.
[18] Schutze (n 15) 3.
[19] Edozie and Gottschalk (n 12) 33.
[20] TK Tieku, *Governing Africa: 3D Analysis of the Africa Union's Performance* (Rowman & Littlefield, 2017) 38–44.
[21] *Femi Falana v The African Union* App No 001/2011.
[22] (Advisory Opinion) [1949] ICJ Reports 174.

as an international organization, the AU has a legal personality separate from the legal personality of its Member State.[23] It is an international person capable of possessing international rights and duties. It is notable that in defining the status of the AU, the African Court heavily relied on the precedent of the ICJ in reaching its decision. This enabled the Court to reach a decision in the case that is broadly consistent with the international legal order in this respect. It is also worth noting that having a legal personality and capacity in law were two of the factors that the ECJ considered in the *Costa v Enel*[24] judgment in holding that the European Union represents the creation of a new legal order.

In addition, to the absence of a definition in relation to AU law, it is observed that there was no attempt to state the sources of AU law in the AU Constitutive Act itself. However, the Statute establishing the African Union Commission on International Law (AUCIL) made reference to the 'laws of the Union'. In Article 4, the Statute, albeit indirectly and vaguely, did identify certain key sources of AU law and to some extent it echoes Article 38(1) of the ICJ mentioned below. A reading of the text shows an implicit recognition of particular sources of AU law in Article 4(a), which are, namely, Treaties of the African Union, decisions of the policy organs of the AU, and African customary international law arising from the practice of Member States. Though these legal sources were merely stated as the focus for the objectives of the AUCIL in its task of codification and the progressive development of international law, it is observed that they have immediate relevance as a statutory framework that impacts Member States. Significantly, the Protocol on the Statute of the African Court of Justice and Human Rights took a similar approach when it outlined the applicable law of the Court in Article 31 as follows.

> In carrying out its functions, the Court shall have regard to
>
> a) The Constitutive Act;
> b) International treaties, whether general or particular, ratified by the contesting States;
> c) International custom, as evidence of a general practice accepted as law;
> d) The general principles of law recognised universally or by African States;
> e) Subject to the provisions of paragraph 1, of Article 46 of the present Statute, judicial decisions and writings of the most highly qualified publicists of various nations as well as the regulations, directives and decisions of the Union, as subsidiary means for the determination of the rules of law;
> f) Any other law relevant to the determination of the case.[25]

23 *Femi Falana v The African Union* (n 21) para 68.
24 *Flaminio Costa v ENEL* (n 16).
25 Article 31(2). Reference should be made when and how the Protocol was concluded and signed.

Notably, Article 31(1) is similar to Articles 38(1)–(2) of the Statute of the ICJ, which has entrenched the generally accepted view that the Statute of the ICJ did not enumerate a formal hierarchy of sources. This view may be applicable to Article 31 in relation to the sources it outlined.[26] However, there are two significant differences due to the nature of the AU itself. In the first place, the AU Constitutive Act is a constitutional instrument, and it lies at the foundation of the AU legal order. Its provisions have constitutional status and thus will have supremacy within its legal order in the areas that it covers. Second, Article 31(d) specifically classified judicial decisions, writings by eminent experts, and regulations, directives of the AU as 'subsidiary' sources, which indicate that they may be lower in the hierarchy compared to the other sources in Article 31. The constitutional character of the AU Constitutive Act raises the pertinent question of the nature of such a 'constitution' at the continental level.

4. AU Law as International Constitutionalization

As an emergent legal order, the understanding of the norm emerging from the AU law may be approached from different perspectives. AU law is a development that is beyond state level and also has the ambition to unite separate states' systems within its order while respecting the integrity of those states. This makes constitutionalization and federalism compelling concepts for the understanding of AU law. Constitutionalization here refers to the international dimension as opposed to constitutionalism at the domestic level. Federalism provides the broad framework for allocation of powers while constitutionalization provides the principles and rules that govern the arrangement. In a constitutional legal order, 'power allocations are based upon divisions of constituted power' such as in a federalism.[27] However, as O'Donoghue noted, the extent of partition and the form it takes vary between legal orders.[28] In the context of the AU, the primary reference point would be the Constitutive Act. A written constitution is a feature of a constitutional legal order, albeit not in all cases.[29]

The traditions of federalism played a significant role in the discourse and the developments that led to the emergence of the AU and its legal order. As Tieku correctly argued, 'federal impulses drove the creation of the AU'[30] In his view, the AU 'lies close to the middle of a continuum between federalism and statistism' (sic).[31]

[26] KD Magliveras and GJ Naldi, 'The African Court of Justice' (2006) 66 *ZaoRV* 187–213.
[27] A O'Donoghue, *Constitutionalism in Global Constitutionalisation* (CUP, 2014) 17.
[28] ibid.
[29] ibid 8.
[30] TK Tieku, 'African Union: From Federalism to Fantasy Union' in J Kincaid and W Swenden (eds), *The Routledge Handbook of Regionalism and Federalism* (Routledge, 2013) 573.
[31] ibid.

In addition, Moller has described the AU as 'a federation *in statu nascendi*'.[32] While the relevance of the idea of federalism in the design and implementation of the AU has been acknowledged, no thorough analysis of its role, implications, and relevance to the future of the AU legal order has been undertaken.[33] It would be useful to consider how the philosophy of federalism and constitutionalization informs the AU legal order. This approach becomes even more significant because one of the key goals of the AU's fifty-year plan, Agenda 2063, is to achieve a political union within the continent and the formation of a continental government.[34]

Federalism has a notably long history in Africa, starting with the imperial-colonial federal legacies which employed the concept, although largely unsuccessfully, for administrative and political convenience.[35] Examples of these include the creation of the Central African Federation (1953–1963), the amalgamation of the regions that constituted Nigeria in 1914, and France's two-tiered federalism's Afrique Occidentale Francaise and the Equatoriale Francaise.[36] The federalism idea also manifested itself in the independence movement in the form of the concept of Pan-Africanism.[37] Historically, there were two strands to Pan-Africanism. The first strand and the earlier form was driven by the African diaspora with the aim of liberation from slavery and the unification of Africa. However, the second strand was focused on the anti-colonial struggle and, more significantly, on the political unification of the continent. These two strands influenced the establishment of the of the OAU and subsequently the AU as a unique Pan-African body.

The idea of federalism also led to the attempts to unite sovereign nation states post-independence. The examples of these attempts include the East African Federation, Senegambia Confederation, and the Union of African States – the first attempt to federate former colonies of the British and the French.[38] It is posited that these experiences contributed positively to the establishment of a continental legal order and its federal or quasi-federal features. It is therefore logical that constitutionalization at the continental level would exhibit federal characteristics to some extent.

Instructively, the pre-independence debate and the concomitant Pan-Africanism concept focused in the main on the question of federation versus

[32] B Moller, 'Pan-Africanism and federalism' (2010) 2(3) Perspectives on Federalism 38, 62.

[33] O Babarinde, 'The EU as a Model for the African Union: the Limits of Imitation' Jean Monnet/Robert Schuman Paper Series Vol 7 No 2 April 2007, p 5; Yusuf (n 4) 158–9.

[34] African Union, Agenda 2063 – The Africa We Want available at <https://au.int/en/Agenda2063/popular_version> accessed 20 August 2020.

[35] M Burgess, *Federalism in Africa: An Essay on the Impacts of Cultural Diversity, Development and Democracy* (The Federal Idea, 2012) 20.

[36] ibid 7.

[37] Moller (n 32) 55.

[38] A Hughes. 'The collapse of the Senegambian confederation' (1992) 30(2) Journal of Commonwealth & Comparative Politics 200–22.

statism conception at the heart of African continental integration.[39] Within the discourse about federalism was the sub-question as to whether an international or US tradition should shape the integration effort.[40] The reference to the US tradition is notable because of the influence of the tradition on Pan-Africanism and its proponents. A unique factor in the pre-independence debate in Africa is the historical fact that these ideas *sensu stricto* are not traditional in the continent where pre-colonial societies were structured around a mix of monarchical, religious, and collective modes of governance. However, what is common to the traditions across Africa in one form or another is the emphasis on the collective and on 'people' as a whole in the allocation of powers.[41] This emphasis has percolated into the emergent legal order, thus underpinning its foundational principles. Nonetheless, as the continent approached independence, the idea of federalism *prima facie* provided potential solutions to the challenges of independence, managing the legacies of colonialism and providing a level of unity in diversity.[42] The debate resulted in the compromise that led to the creation of the OAU, which is generally perceived to be an international organization, and the transformation of that institution into the AU with its somewhat supranational credentials.[43]

With regard to the concept of constitutionalization, it is recognized that constitutionalization has both a legal and political purpose.[44] De Wet has argued that, there is an 'emerging international constitutional order consisting of an international community, an international value system and the rudimentary structure for its enforcement'.[45] This reasoning is supported by major international constitutional law scholars such as Fassbender and Klabbers.[46] Notably, Fassbender has argued that the United Nations Charter has been confirmed and strengthened over the years to the extent that it must now be taken as the 'constitution of the international community'.[47] From this perspective global constitutionalization means

[39] See, for example, O Agyeman, 'Pan-Africanist Federalism' Center for Economic Research on Africa, Department of Economics, School of Business Administration, Montclair State College, 1991, 25–9.

[40] K Nkrumah, *Africa must Unite* (Praeger, 1963)214–15; Amao (n 9) 12–14; KO Kufuor, *African Unification: Law, Problems and Prospects* (Carolina Academic Press, 2016) 18.

[41] AN Allott, 'African Law' in JDM Derrett (ed), *An Introduction to Legal Systems* (Sweet & Maxwell, 1968) 131, 149–50.

[42] Edozie and Gottschalk (n 12) 17.

[43] Maluwa (n 12) 28; T Maluwa, 'The OAU/African Union and international law: mapping new boundaries or revisiting old terrain' (2004) 98 Proceedings of the Annual Meeting, American Society of International Law 232, 233.

[44] O'Donoghue (n 27) 16; A Peters, 'The merits of global constitutionalism' (2009) 16 Indiana Journal of Global Legal Studies 397.

[45] E De Wet, 'The international constitutional order' (2006) 55 International and Comparative Law Quarterly 51.

[46] B Fassbender, 'The United Nations Charter as constitution of the international community' (1998) 36 Columbia Journal of Transnational Law 529; J Klabbers, Anne Peters, and Geir Ulfstein, *The Constitutionalisation of International Law* (OUP, 2009) 10.

[47] B Fassbender, 'The United Nations Charter as constitution of the international community' (1998) 36 Columbia Journal of Transnational Law 529.

that key aspects of constitutionalism at the domestic level have been or are being transposed to the international plane and exhibited by beyond state-level institution such as the AU. It thus means that such an institution would increasingly display key features of constitutionalism such as a written constitution, division of powers, the rule of law, democratic legitimacy, and the protection of human rights.[48] According to Peters, the goal of global constitutionalization is the 'application of constitutionalist principles in the international legal sphere in order to improve the effectiveness and fairness of the international legal order'.[49] Similarly, O'Donoghue noted that constitutionalization 'is employed where a legal order is in a process, over a period of time, from a position not based upon constitutionalism to one taking upon its cloak'.[50] According to her, the EU model 'is an important example of how constitutionalization evolves particularly in the frame of subsidiarity'.[51] From the foregoing, it is thus compelling to describe the transitioning from the OAU to the AU and the structural and normative changes associated with this transitioning as the constitutionalization of the AU legal order.[52]

It is important to note that Fassbender put a caveat on the comparison between constitutionalism at the domestic level and constitutionalization at the international level. He argued that international constitutionalization does not replicate constitutionalism at the domestic level because the task and responsibility at the international level differs from the domestic level.[53] In support of this contention, Walker argued,

> The point is, that the concept of constitution changes its meaning when it is transferred and this change of meaning is reinforced by the current structural changes of the international system: the disaggregation of the state on the one hand, and the process of sectoralization within international law.[54]

While acknowledging the different approaches to the concept of constitutionalization, the Chapter adopts Peters' definition of constitutionalization as,

> the label for the evolution from an international order based on some organizing principles such as state sovereignty, territorial integrity, and consensualism to

48 O'Donoghue (n 27) 16.
49 Peters (n 44) 397.
50 O'Donoghue (n 27).
51 ibid 11.
52 See also M Olivier, 'The Emergence of a Right to Democracy – An African Perspective' in C Panara and G Wilson (eds), *The Arab Spring – New Patters of Democracy and International Law* (Martinus Nijhoff Publishers, 2013) 29–52.
53 B Fassbender, *Security Council Reform and the Right of Veto: A Constitutional Perspective* (Kluwer International Press, 1998).
54 C Walter, 'International Law in a Process of Constitutionalization' in JE Nijman and A Nollkaemper (eds), *New Perspectives on the Divide between National and International Law* (OUP, 2007).

> an international legal order which acknowledges and has creatively appropriated and – importantly – modified principles, institutions, and procedures of constitutionalism.[55]

Peters' definition is broadly consistent with definitions that have been put forward by other constitutional scholars. For instance, Loughlin describes the concept as 'the attempt to subject all governmental action within a designated field to the structures, processes, principles, and values of a 'constitution'.[56] As Loughlin correctly noted, constitutionalism is prominent at the international level today because of the realization that 'the activity of governing is increasingly being exercised through transnational or international arrangements that are not easily susceptible to the control of national constitutions'.[57]

It is that realization that informs the reform of the basis upon which supra or transitional bodies operate in ways that lead to constitutionalization.[58] As Loughlin argued, the subject of the constitutionalization of a treaty-based body is a major field of study in its own right.[59] To support this contention, he referenced major works that have been undertaken on conceiving the World Trade Organization (WTO) from the constitutionalization perspective and also on the question of whether the UN Charter could be considered as the constitution of the international community.[60] In that debate, 'international community' is seen as the surrogate for 'the people' in a constitutional order, while the legal framework or norms that govern the UN is perceived as its constitution.[61] Perhaps the UN Charter discourse is more apposite to the AU development. However, it must be acknowledged that what is meant by constitutionalization would also differ according to institutions such as with the UN, the European Union, and the WTO, or even the AU.[62]

Pertinently, Loughlin observed that the European Union is the most significant expression of supranational constitutionalism. According to him, the way in which the European Union has evolved incrementally in competence and transformed from an international organization 'to an entity which has established itself as a vertically integrated legal order is an important indicator of its constitutionalisation'.[63] It is noted that Loughlin conceded that the constitutionalization of the EU remains partial and incomplete[64] but this does not detract from the evidence that the

[55] A Peters, 'Constitutionalisation' in J d'Aspremont and S Singh (eds), *Concepts for International Law – Contributions to Disciplinary Thought* (Edward Elgar, 2017) 141.
[56] M Loughlin 'What is Constitutionalisation' in P Dobner and M Loughlin (eds), *The Twilight of Constitutionalism?* (OUP, 2010) 47.
[57] ibid.
[58] ibid 63.
[59] ibid 64.
[60] ibid.
[61] ibid 65.
[62] Peters (n 55) 3.
[63] Loughlin (n 56) 65.
[64] ibid 66.

constitutionalization process is entrenched in the European Union. This process of constitutionalization was aptly described as constitutionalization through integration. The constitutionalization process enabled the ECJ to hold that the founding treaties of the Community are its basic constitutional charter. The Court has further expounded on this by its creative interpretation of the treaties to create constitutional norms.[65]

The supranational credentials of the AU and its legal order is underscored by the modelling of the institution on the European Union and its legal order.[66] The developments surrounding the OAU and the AU and their institutions are a continuum that has heavily relied on a broad definition of the ideas of federalism and constitutionalization.[67] However, like the European Union, the federalism exhibited by the AU and its constitutionalization process are not directly comparable to federalism at the state level or confederation, hence the need to develop a unique understanding of these emergent phenomena.[68] The continental legal order at inception was dominated by a process that is akin to dual federalism which has shaped its existence to a large extent but its trajectory has moved largely in the direction of cooperative federalism with the creation of the AU.[69] This is exemplified by the ceding of aspects of sovereign powers to the centre as solutions to common problems in specific areas such as the regulation of unconstitutional change of government, human rights, judicial powers, sanction powers, trade, peace, and security. The concept of federalism and constitutionalization, especially in their supranational dimensions thus provide useful tools for the analysis of the discourse and its consequences.[70]

Such an understanding allows for the comparison of the emergent legal order to the influences that shaped its emergence: in the main, the colonial heritage (Westphalia state model) and the EU legal order. Such an understanding would also allow for a comprehensive analysis of the legal space that has emerged with the AU and reaching conclusions on the nature of AU law from that perspective. It would also allow for the prediction as to the legal trajectory that the AU legal order could take as the AU and its institutions evolve. In addition, it would allow for a

65 ibid 66. See *Parti écologiste 'Les Verts' v European Parliament* (1986) Case 294/83, [1986] ECR 1339; *Van Gend en Loos v Nederlandse Administratie der Belastingen* (1963) Case 26/62, [1963] ECR 1.

66 B Fagbayibo, 'Common problems affecting supranational attempts in Africa: an analytical overview' (2013) 16(1) Potchefstroom Electronic Law Journal/Potchefstroomse Elektroniese Regsblad 32; BO Fagbayigbo, A politico-legal framework for integration in Africa: Exploring the attainability of a supranational African Union (Thesis submitted to the University of Pretoria, 2010) 39; Edozie and Gottschalk (n 12) 33.

67 It is notable that just like the US Constitution, the AU Constitutive Act does not use explicitly the word 'federalism' but nevertheless evolves a federal system.

68 Fassbender (n 46) 529, 558.

69 Schutze (n 15) 3.

70 See also N Jain, Supranational federalism: a study of the European Union notes and comments (2002) 14 Student Bar Review 43–51.

critical examination of what aspects of constitutional federalism is shaping the development of the AU legal order as it develops.

5. African Commission on Human and Peoples' Rights and Cooperative Federalism

The emergence of the African Commission as a quasi-judicial body and the subsequent establishment of the African Court could be regarded as an expression of cooperative federalism at the continental level. This is because it represented a *de facto* ceding of aspects of judicial power to the continental level judicial system. The implication of this is that in the areas where the Commission and the Court have competence, cases that emanate from domestic jurisdiction could be dealt with at the continental level.

The African Commission was originally the main mechanism for ensuring compliance with the provisions of the African Charter. It was established under the Charter as a quasi-judicial body.[71] The Commission was modelled on the European Human Rights Commission (since abolished)[72] and the Inter-American Commission on Human Rights.[73] The Commission's functions are stated in Article 45 of the Charter and include the promotion of human rights, the protection of human rights under the African Charter, the interpretation of the African Charter, and any other functions assigned to the Commission by the Assembly of Heads of State. The Commission has both protective and promotional responsibilities. However, it is in connection with the exercise of its protective responsibility by its quasi-judicial powers that is more important in the context of this chapter. The Commission's responsibility in this regard involves receiving communications (cases) on violations of rights protected under the Charter, communicating them to states, and investigating them, with the ultimate goal of reconciling the parties. Its decisions on cases are also included in the Commission's activity report to the Assembly of the AU.

There has been a debate on the question of whether the decisions of the Commission are binding.[74] The African Commission itself has been ambiguous in stating the legal status of its decisions.[75] As noted by Murray and Long, the

[71] Article 30 of the African Charter.

[72] The European Commission on Human Rights was abolished by Protocol 11 to the European Convention for the Protection of Human Rights and Fundamental Freedoms (213 UNTS 222 as amended).

[73] The Inter-American Commission on Human Rights is an autonomous organ of the OAS. It was created in 1959 to promote and protect human rights in the Americas pursuant to the OAS Charter (119 UNT. 3 as amended) and the American Convention on Human Rights (OAS Treaty Series No 36, 1144 UNTS 123).

[74] R Murray and D Long, *The Implementation of the Findings of the African Commission on Human and Peoples' Rights* (CUP, 2015) 24, 50.

[75] ibid 50.

Commission has sometimes referred to its decisions as non-binding because of the quasi-judicial nature of its mandate.[76] Nevertheless, the Commission has also suggested that its decisions are authoritative interpretations of the Charter. Furthermore, it has been argued that since the Commission's recommendations are included in its activity report to the Assembly of the African Union, they should become binding upon adoption.[77] Relevant to this debate is the Commission's practice of granting interim or provisional measures to avoid irredeemable harm.[78] In *International PEN and others v Nigeria*, the Commission held that such provisional measures are binding and should be respected by Member States thus suggesting a level of bindingness.[79]

Irrespective of the debate as to whether the decision of the Commission is binding, the establishment and activities of the Commission shows that the Member States were willing to allow the Commission to exercise some jurisdiction over human rights cases emanating from domestic jurisdictions. These cases would have originated from Member States and gone through the domestic remediation process (in most cases) before being brought before the Commission. The Commission thus exercises its quasi-judicial power over Member States to the extent of its competence in the African Charter.

For instance, in *Egyptian Initiative for Personal Rights and INTERIGHTS v Egypt*,[80] a complaint was brought on behalf of four women who were part of a protest in Egypt. It was alleged that during the protest, the protesters were cornered by the riot police in such a way that allowed supporters of the government to attack them. In the circumstances, the women (complainants) were intimidated, insulted, and sexually harassed. All attempts to seek redress in the domestic jurisdiction was frustrated by the authorities. Unable to obtain redress at the local level, the women submitted a complaint to the African Commission. They were represented by Egyptian Initiative for Personal Rights and Interights. The complainants alleged violations of Articles 1 (respect for rights), 2 (non-discrimination), 3 (equality before law), 5 (cruel treatment), 9(2) (free expression), 16(1) (right to health), and 18(3) (discrimination against women), among others. The complainant included in their prayers, the payment of 57,000 Egyptian pounds to each complainant. The Commission found the Member State, Egypt, liable for the violation of several rights of the complainant protected in the African Charter. Even though the

[76] ibid 53.

[77] ibid 53.

[78] Rule 111 of the Rules of Procedures of the African Commission on Human and Peoples' Rights adopted on the 6 of October 1995 allows the Commission to grant interim provisional orders. See UO Umozorike, 'The African Charter on Human and Peoples' Rights: suggestions for more effectiveness' (2007) 13 Annual Survey of International & Comparative Law 179 at 186.

[79] See *International PEN and Others v Nigeria*, Comm Nos 137/94, 139/94, 154/96, and 161/97 (1998). See also R Wright, 'Finding an impetus for institutional change at the African Court on Human and Peoples' Rights' 24 Berkeley Journal of International Law 463 at 471.

[80] *Egyptian Initiative for Personal Rights and INTERIGHTS v Egypt, ACHPR*, Comm No 323/06 (2011).

Commission does not usually award compensation as it does not have a direct mandate to do so, it went further to request that Egypt compensate each of the complainants by paying each of them 57,000 Egyptian pounds for the physical and emotional damages and trauma they suffered. In that case, the Commission not only made a pronouncement on violation of rights in Egypt but also recommended specific monetary compensation.

6. The African Court on Human and Peoples' Rights

The need to strengthen the mechanism for the protection of human rights and to address the limitations and ambiguity surrounding the African Commission's procedure led to the establishment of the African Court on Human and Peoples' Rights (African Court).[81] The Court will be transformed into the African Court of Justice and Human Rights in the future,[82] once the protocol establishing the latter comes into force. The African Court itself was established by an additional protocol to the African Charter adopted by the Assembly of Heads of State and Governments of the OAU in 1998.[83] The Protocol came into force in 2004. The Court is empowered in the Protocol to exercise jurisdiction over all human rights instruments 'ratified by the States concerned'.[84] It has been contended that this may include regional, sub-regional, bilateral, and multilateral international treaties.[85] This means that where rights are not adequately protected under the African Charter, recourse could be had to other international treaties signed by Member States.[86]

The case of *Lohe Issa Konate v Burkina Faso*[87] exemplifies the role of the court in this context. The application in the case alleged the violations of the right to freedom of expression not only under the African Charter (Article 9) but also the International Covenant on Civil and Political Rights (ICCPR) (Article 19), and Article 66(2)(c) of the Economic Community of West African States (ECOWAS) Treaty. The complainant was an editor of a magazine. The complainant wrote and published articles alleging that the local prosecutor was involved in certain acts of

[81] African Union, Protocol to the African Charter on Human and Peoples' Rights on the Establishment of an African Court on Human and Peoples' Rights available at https://au.int/en/treaties/protocol-african-charter-human-and-peoples-rights-establishment-african-court-human-and accessed 15 July 2021.

[82] African Union, Protocol on the Statute of the African Court of Justice and Human Rights, 1 July 2008 available at <https://au.int/en/treaties/protocol-statute-african-court-justice-and-human-rights> accessed 15 July 2021.

[83] (n 81).

[84] ibid Article 3(1).

[85] RW Eno 'The jurisdiction of the African Court on Human and Peoples' Rights' (2002) 2(2) African Human Rights Law Journal 223 at 226; NJ Udombana, 'Towards the African Court on human and peoples' rights: better late than never' (2000) Yale Human Rights and Development Law Journal 45.

[86] ibid 226.

[87] App No 004/2013 (2014).

misconduct. Subsequently the complainant and another journalist were charged with defamation, public insult, and contempt of court. The High Court of the Member State sentenced the complainant to 12 months in prison and publication of his magazine was suspended for six months. He was also ordered to pay a fine and damages. The complaint contended that the laws under which he was prosecuted were inconsistent with the African Charter, the International Covenant on Civil and Political Rights, and the ECOWAS Treaty, especially the criminalization of defamation. At the preliminary stage, the complainant sought and was granted provisional measures to be released from custody and provided with adequate healthcare. In its opinion on the merit, the Court noted that the right to freedom of expression is not absolute. According to the Court, restrictions on the right may be provided by domestic law but must be consistent with applicable international norms. Furthermore, such restriction must be to achieve a legitimate aim and, importantly, it must be proportionate to that purpose. In this case the Court acknowledged that the restrictions were provided by law and were sufficiently clear. It further held that the restrictions were put in place to achieve a legitimate aim that was stated to be to protect the honour and reputation of magistrates, jurors, and assessors in the performance of their duties. However, the Court held that the restrictions were a disproportionate means to achieve the legitimate aim. According to the Court, proportionality requires a balancing of the interest of the society with the freedom of the individuals and any means of restriction imposed must be the least restrictive possible. Furthermore, in the Court's view, freedom of expression must be subject to a lesser degree of restriction when it relates to public debate relating to public figures. In particular, it stated that any punishment for the damaging of a public figure's reputation must not be more than the punishment for the damaging of the reputation of an ordinary citizen. Criminalizing the defamation of certain public figures under the law is therefore disproportionate and unjustifiable. The Court also held that the state failed to show that the suspension of the publication of the magazine was necessary and proportionate to protect the reputation of the prosecutor. The Court found a violation of Article 9 of the African Charter, Article 19 of ICCPR, and Article 66(2)(c) of the ECOWAS Treaty. Consequently, the Court ordered that the Member State amend its law to conform with the African Charter. According to the Court, the member State of Burkina Faso was required:

> to amend its legislation on defamation by repealing custodial sentences for acts of defamation, and by adapting its legislation to ensure that other sanctions for defamation meet the test of necessity and proportionality.[88]

[88] *Lohé Issa Konaté v Burkina Faso* App No 004/2013 (2014).

The order to the Member State to amend its law is a key example of the Court exercising jurisdiction that directly affect Member States. A similar order was made in the matter of *Actions Pour la Protection des droits de l'Homme (APDH) v Republic of Cote d'Ivoire* where after the finding of a violation of, *inter alia*, Article 26 ICCPR, the Court ordered the Member State, Cote d'Ivoire to make a specific domestic law consistent with the ICCPR.[89]

Another important feature of the African Court is that, unlike the Commission, it has a direct mandate to award compensation where there has been a violation of the rights protected under the African Charter. Article 27 of the African Court Protocol provides that 'if the Court finds that there has been violation of a human or peoples' rights, it shall make *appropriate* orders to remedy the violation, including the payment of fair compensation or reparation'. In the exercise of this function, the African Court appears to be directly performing functions usually reserved for courts at the domestic level.[90] The provision in relation to compensation has been further widened in respect to the African Court under the Malabo Protocol as follows:

> the Court shall establish in the Rules of Court principles relating to reparations to, or in respect of, victims, including restitution, compensation and rehabilitation. On this basis, in its decision the Court may, either upon request or on its own motion in exceptional circumstances, determine the scope and extent of any damage, loss or injury to, or in respect of, victims and will state the principles on which it is acting.[91]

It is important to emphasize that the AU law role in relation to Member States' legal order is limited. The Commission has generally refrained from considering and enforcing Member State laws itself. It has emphasized that its competence is confined to the interpretation and enforcement of the AU Charter. According to the AU Commission in *Groupe de Travail sur les Dossiers Judiciaires Stratégiques v Democratic Republic of Congo*,

> [r]egarding the national laws, the Commission notes that it is not competent to decide if the actions of the Respondent State are consistent with its national laws. The Commission is only competent to verify if the national laws and the Respondent State's actions are consistent with the African Charter.[92]

89 ibid para 153 (7).

90 G Pecorella, 'The African Court on Human and Peoples' rights and its case law: towards a Supreme Court for Africa?' available at <https://aninternationallawblog.wordpress.com/2015/06/22/the-african-court-on-human-and-peoples-rights-and-its-case-law-towards-a-supreme-court-for-africa/#_ftn5> accessed 15 July 21.

91 Article 45, Malabo Protocol.

92 *Groupe de Travail sur les Dossiers Judiciaires Stratégiques v Democratic Republic of Congo*, ACHPR, Comm No 259/2002 (2013) para 57.

However, as noted earlier, the jurisdiction of the African Court is wider and the evolving jurisprudence of the African Court may lead to a more interventionist role by the Court. Indeed, in *Onyachi and Njoka v Tanzania*,[93] the Court's competence to evaluate evidence presented to the Court of a Member State and the appropriateness of the penalty imposed was challenged on the ground that it required the Court to sit as a 'Supreme Appellate Court'. Responding to that contention, the African Court held that it was competent to do so because it has the power to examine whether the proceedings at the Member State's Court was in conformity with the fair trial provision in Article 7 of the African Charter. Nonetheless, the Court acknowledged that it does not directly apply a Member State's law or examine the constitutionality of domestic legislation.[94]

7. Conclusion

As a flexible and malleable concept, federalism is playing a pivotal role in the constitutionalization of not only international relations but also of regionalization. In the context of Africa, federalism provides an 'efficient institutional device for political integration, for ensuring the functioning of pluralistic societies, for protecting minorities, for solving ethnic, religious and national conflicts, and for answering the need for peace and international solidarity'.[95] International constitutionalization imports key elements of constitutional federalism to the international level. These include the rule of law, containment of political and potentially economic power through checks and balances, fundamental rights protection, accountability, democracy, and solidarity. The design of the AU has evolved another strand of federalism in its constitutionalization process that is peculiar to the African continent. This strand could be referred to as African federalism.[96] This underscores the necessity of also recognizing an African approach to federalism. The emerging tradition of African federalism is influenced by the history of the continent, its wide diversity of traditions and legal systems, and the multifarious challenges it has faced since independence. The size of the continent and the diversity of its Member States make federalism an attractive mechanism for governance. The concept of constitutional federalism underpinned the common value-based community created at the continental level in Africa.

The shift underpinned the increasing allocation of power to the centre and the impact the constitutional legal order is having or could have on Member States.

[93] App No 003/2015.

[94] *Onyachi and Njoka v Tanzania* App No 003/2015, paras 37–39. See also *Mohammed Abubakari v The United Republic of Tanzania*, App No 007/2013.

[95] Lucio Levi, 'Federalism: a way to govern globalization' (2018) 2 Glocalism: Journal of Culture, Politics and Innovation 1, 5.

[96] See for another perspective on this M Burgess (n 35) 20.

The shift also underpinned the emergence of new and significant norms under the AU. These norms include the non-indifference norm, the norm on unconstitutional change of government, human rights norms, the responsibility to protect, and democratic constitutionalism. The Constitutive Act of the African Union could be conceived as a continental-level social contract that manifests elements of cooperative federalism. Unlike global constitutionalism, which is fragmented and not united in any one document, the AU Constitutive Act brings a level of coherence to the AU legal order. The workings of the AU Commission and the African Court on Human and Peoples' Rights could also be explained as expressions of cooperative federalism in the AU legal order. Another recent expression of African federalism is the coming into effect of the AU's African Continental Free Trade Agreement (AfCFTA). This is the largest free trade agreement in the world and aims at creating a single market in Africa and facilitate free movement of businesses and people across the continent.[97]

[97] Agreement Establishing the African Continental Free Trade Area available at <https://au.int/en/treaties/agreement-establishing-african-continental-free-trade-area> accessed 15 July 2021. E Onyema, 'Reimagining the framework for resolving intra-African commercial disputes in the context of the African Continental Free Trade Area Agreement' (2020) 19(3)World Trade Review 446–468.

PART 2

HARMONIZATION AND INTEGRATION AS DRIVERS OF AU LAW

4

Harmonization and Integration in Africa: The Case of Competition Law and Policy

Kamala Dawar and George Lipimile

1. Introduction

Deeper integration under the African Union (AU), by reducing both tariff and non-tariff barriers across Africa, allows firms to transcend national borders and can serve as the foundation for developing regional value chains. In adopting the Agreement Establishing the African Continental Free Trade Area (AfCFTA),[1] the AU is seeking to boost intra-African trade by 52.3% through eliminating import duties – and if non-tariff barriers are also reduced, it could double the projected amount.[2]

However, cross-border trade also provides an opportunity for cross-border anti-competitive business practices in Africa. If competition rules lag behind the economic liberalization process, the benefits of integration can be undermined through the foreclosure of markets by private companies. It is widely recognized that market forces, when left unregulated during liberalization and privatization processes, do not automatically produce the desired efficiencies in the economy and, moreover, do not foster sustainable development. Firms can abuse their dominant market position through predatory behaviour to eliminate local competition or, through forming cartels, to fix higher prices and other market-sharing agreements. If no safeguards exist to prevent anti-competitive practices, no fundamental

The opinions expressed in this chapter are the authors' own. This chapter develops the arguments put forward in K Dawar and G Lipimile. *Africa: Harmonising Competition Policy under the AfCFTA*. Concurrences Review—International. 2020.

[1] Agreement Establishing the African Continental Free Trade Agreement, signed on 21 March 2018, entered into force 30 May 2019, available at <https://au.int/en/treaties/agreement-establishing-african-continental-free-trade-area> accessed 29 March 2020.

[2] The 2019 African Union Handbook. *A Guide for Those Working With and Within the African Union* (The African Union Commission and the New Zealand Ministry of Foreign Affairs and Trade/Manatū Aorere, 2019) 23.

Kamala Dawar and George Lipimile, *Harmonization and Integration in Africa: The Case of Competition Law and Policy* In: *The Emergent African Union Law*. Edited by: Olufemi Amao, Michèle Olivier and Konstantinos D. Magliveras, Oxford University Press. © Kamala Dawar and George Lipimile 2021. DOI: 10.1093/oso/9780198862154.003.0005

change will occur to incentivize firms to improve their overall behaviour and performance.[3]

There is therefore considerable merit in the AU developing modalities under the AfCFTA for continent-wide cooperation in relation to anti-competitive practices affecting the interests of several members.[4] A prerequisite set of competition rules is required to regulate firms' behaviour in commercial activities. Competition law is designed to enhance the economic welfare of people by, among other things, breaking down barriers to commerce and preventing the creation and misuse of corporate power through cartels and monopolistic strategies.[5] Within the European Union, for example, the contribution of competition policy transcends the realm of the purely economic.[6] Not only has it made essential contributions to the high standard of living enjoyed by European citizens but also to the policy and institutional infrastructure of Europe and to the creation of Europe itself.[7]

This chapter aims to assess the context of integration under the AU to identify pathways for promoting harmonized competition principles, which will complement the liberalization process. The chapter is set out as follows: section 2 looks at the process of economic integration under the AfCFTA. Section 3 sets out the issue of overlapping membership and variable geometry among the domestic competition regimes and within the various African Regional Economic Communities (RECs). Section 4 concludes with a critical analysis of the different options and recommendations for promoting harmonizing competition principles through AU institutions and law.

2. The Context of Economic Integration in Africa

Compared with norm development in the human rights sphere, development in the business and economic realm in Africa has been slow and has had lesser overall impact. In March 2018, the AU Assembly adopted the AfCFTA Agreement, the

[3] WTO Secretariat, *Synthesis Paper on the Relationship of Trade and Competition Policy to Development and Economic Growth* (Working Group on the Interaction between Trade and Competition Policy WT/WGTCP/W/80, 1998) 8.

[4] EM Fox and M Bakhoum, *Making Markets Work for Africa. Markets, Development and Competition Law in Sub-Saharan Africa* (OUP, 2018); T Hartzenberg. *Cooperation on Competition in the AfCFTA*, Trade Law Center (TRALAC) blog, 17 May 2019 available at <http://www.tralac.org/blog/article/14078-cooperation-on-competition-in-the-afcfta.html> accessed 29 March 2020.

[5] EM Fox, 'Toward world antitrust and market access' (1997) 91 American Journal of International Law 1.

[6] European Parliamentary Research Service. *EU competition policy; Key to a fair single market* (2019), 1, quoting European Court of Auditors, Enforcement of EU competition policy, Background Paper on Enforcement of EU competition policy, September 2018. Available at <http://www.europarl.europa.eu/RegData/etudes/IDAN/2019/642209/EPRS_IDA(2019)642209_EN.pdf> accessed 31 March 2020.

[7] RD Anderson and A Heimler, 'What Has Competition Done for Europe? An Inter-Disciplinary Answer' (2007) 62(4) Aussenwirtschaft, University of St. Gallen, School of Economics and Political Science, Swiss Institute for International Economics and Applied Economics Research 419–454.

Protocol on Trade in Goods, the Protocol on Trade in Services, and the Protocol on Rules and Procedures on the Settlement of Disputes.[8] For those states who are contracting parties, trading under the AfCFTA Agreement was delayed until January 2021, due to the pandemic. A draft Competition Protocol expected to be signed in January 2021,[9] has also been delayed. These legal instruments will all form a part of AU law.[10]

As per its Constitutive Act,[11] the AU is guided by the principle of sovereign equality and interdependence among its Member States, while the Protocol on Amendments to the Constitutive Act calls for the development and promotion of common policies on trade, defence, and foreign relations to ensure the security of the continent and the strengthening of its negotiating positions.[12] With the necessary political will, the AU is uniquely positioned to accommodate the sovereignty of the diverse State Parties while promoting the legal clarity and consistency to harmonize continent-wide competition law and enforcement principles under the umbrella framework of the AfCFTA. In this regard, Article 4(c) AfCFTA specifically calls for cooperation by the Member States on competition matters. The forthcoming Protocol on Competition will be the lynchpin of the AU harmonization strategy under the AfCFTA.

Supporting the objectives of AU law, the AfCFTA and its Protocols formally recognize the existing achievements of integration through free trade areas (FTAs) and customs unions. Within these legal instruments, the RECs are positioned as the building blocks that will lead to the establishment of a continental trading community.[13] The AfCFTA takes a two-tier approach: while AfCFTA law shall prevail in event of conflict or inconsistency with a regional agreement, State Parties that have attained a higher level of integration shall maintain such higher levels as they are seen to be more beneficial. Article 19 recognizes the possibility for 'variable geometry' among the RECs, which provides for differentiated integration. Variable geometry allows for progression in cooperation among groups within the AfCFTA, including wider integration schemes in various fields and at different speeds.[14]

[8] Agreement Establishing the African Continental Free Trade Agreement (n 1).

[9] In the Decision on the African Continental Free Trade Agreement, the AU Assembly requested the African Union Ministers to submit the draft legal texts to its January 2021 Session for adoption through the Specialised Technical Committee on Justice and Legal Affairs. See Key Decisions of the 32nd Ordinary Session of the Assembly of the African Union. February 2019 available at <https://au.int/pt/node/35794> accessed 29 March 2020.

[10] A Olufemi, *African Union Law: The Emergence of a Sui Generis Legal Order* (Routledge, 2018) 1.

[11] Constitutive Act of the African Union signed on 11 July 2000, entered into force on 26 May 2001, Article 4(a).

[12] Protocol on Amendments to the Constitutive Act of the African Union (2003), Article 3available at <https://au.int/sites/default/files/treaties/35423-treaty-0025-protocol_on_the_amendments_to_the_constitutive_act_of_the_african_union_e.pdf> accessed 31 March 2020. It should be noted that it has entered into force and there is no expectation that it will enter into force in the foreseeable future.

[13] Agreement Establishing the African Continental Free Trade Area (ACFTA), Article 1.

[14] J Gathii. *Variable Geometry: A Defining Aspect of African RTAs in African Regional Trade Agreements as Legal Regimes* (CUP, 2011) 34–64.

It is also a principle of some of the RECs, such as the Tripartite Free Trade Area Agreement (TFTA)[15] and the East African Community (EAC) Treaty.[16]

3. Variable Geometry and Overlapping Membership

The AU recognizes eight RECs, namely the Arab Maghreb Union (AMU), the Community of Sahel-Saharan States (CEN-SAD), the Common Market for Eastern and Southern Africa (COMESA), the East African Community (EAC), the Economic Community of Central African States (ECCAS), the Economic Community of West African States (ECOWAS), the Intergovernmental Authority on Development (IGAD), and the Southern African Development Community (SADC).[17] Although RECs are the designated building blocks under AfCFTA, State parties are individually responsible for implementing the AfCFTA obligations. The harmonization challenge here is not only in sovereignty pooling among the different states. This ambition requires national governments to bind themselves voluntarily by treaty to a supranational organization, such as the AU, in exchange for strengthening of national resources by combining them with those of partner countries.[18] An added legal difficulty lies in reconciling the overlapping membership of these diverse states in the different RECs. This has the potential to result in legal conflicts where there is also variable geometry between RECs. Maps 1 and 2 highlight the spread of national competition laws in Africa and the overlapping memberships within RECs.

Map 1 highlights the diversity in establishing competition legislation and competition authorities at the domestic level. Further, Map 2 indicates the multiplicity and overlapping memberships within the RECs. It suggests a potential for conflicts to emerge when implementing multiple competition rules should there be differences in the applicable regional competition laws for those states falling under more than one REC. For instance, the EAC regional competition rules contain provisions dealing with state aid and public procurement, neither of which are provided for under the COMESA or SADC regional competition rules. Substantive

[15] Agreement Establishing a Tripartite Free Trade Area among the Common Market for Eastern and Southern Africa, the East African Community and the Southern African Development Community. Article 6, signed 10 June 2015. It will enter into force after the deposit of the instrument of ratification by a majority of the Member/Partner States of COMESA, EAC, and SADC.

[16] East African Community Treaty, Article 7(1)(e), signed on 30 November 1999, entered into force on 7 July 2000 (amended on 14 December 2006 and on 20 August 2007).

[17] The recognized RECs are those which are signatory to the Protocol on Relations between the RECs and the AU (signed 28 January 2008) and the Arab Maghreb Union signed the 2018 Protocol on Relations between the RECs and the AU: CEN-SAD, AMU, COMESA, EAC, ECCAS, ECOWAS, IGAD, SADC.

[18] L Fioramonti and F Mattheis, 'Is Africa really following Europe? An integrated framework for comparative regionalism' (2016) 54(3) Journal of Common Market Studies 674–90.

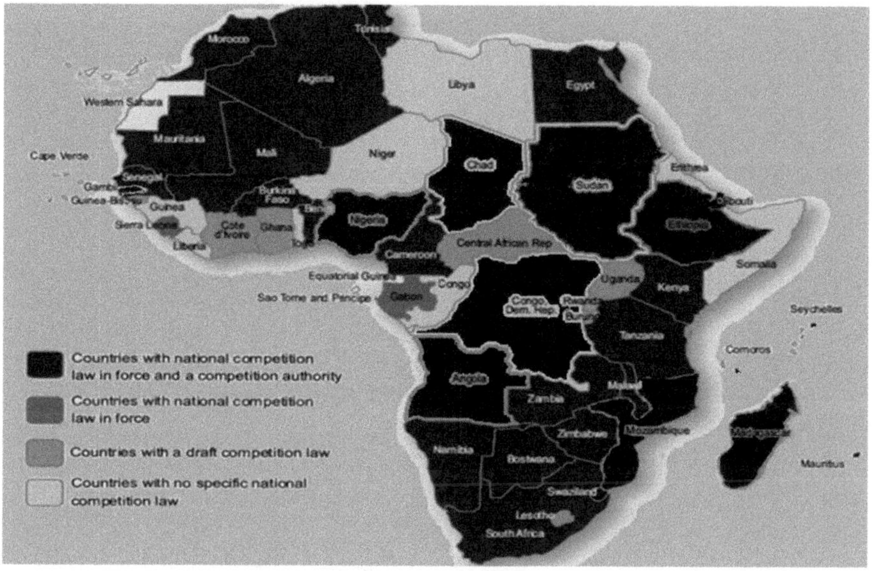

Map 1. Development of Competition Laws in Africa

divergences can also be found in terms of the three core elements of competition laws, namely restrictive agreements, mergers, and abuse of dominance. The multiple membership of some Member States (e.g. Rwanda is a member of both COMESA and EAC; Mauritius is a member of both SADC and COMESA) have created tensions among Member/Partner States and RECs in deciding which regional law should prevail.

To address cross-border anti-competitive practices effectively, individual states not only require a strong national competition law and an effective domestic competition authority but they must also cooperate with each other based on trust and shared competition principles. This is hindered at present because the states are at four broad different stages of competition law and policy implementation:

(1) 25 states have both a competition law in force and an operational competition authority;[19]
(2) eight states have enacted competition law but have not yet established a competition authority;[20]

[19] Algeria, Botswana, Burkina Faso, Cameroon, Democratic Republic of the Congo, Egypt, Ethiopia, Gambia, Ivory Coast, Kenya, Liberia, Madagascar, Malawi, Mauritius, Morocco, Namibia, Nigeria, Senegal, Seychelles, South Africa, eSwatini, Sudan, Tanzania, Zambia, and Zimbabwe.

[20] Angola, Burundi, Comoros, Cape Verde, Djibouti, Mali, Mozambique, and Rwanda.

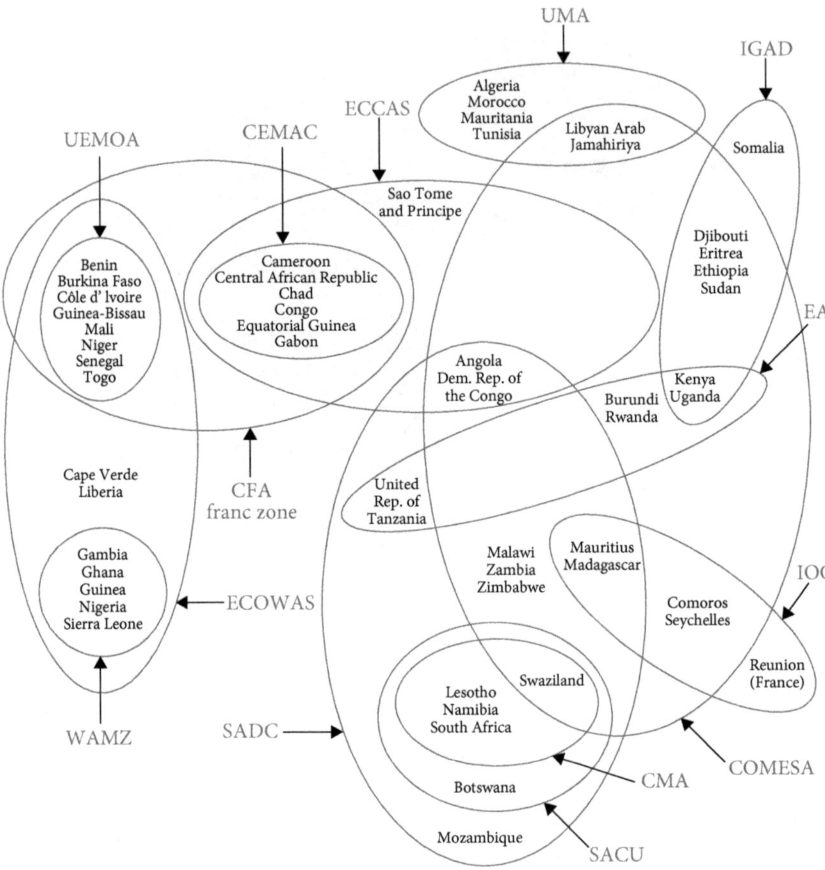

Map 2. Overlapping Membership to Different RECs in Africa

(3) four states where the preparation of competition legislation has reached a very advanced stage;[21] and
(4) 17 states which do not have a competition law or are still at early stages of preparation.[22]

As section 4 argues, this diversity has implications for an AfCFTA vision of a continental competition regime as well as how to achieve it.

[21] Lesotho, Niger, Togo, and Uganda.
[22] Benin, Central African Republic, Chad, Congo (Brazzaville), Equatorial Guinea, Eritrea, Gabon, Ghana, Guinea, Guinea Bissau, Libya, Mauritania, Sao Tomé and Principe, Sierra Leone, Somalia, South Sudan, and Western Sahara, also known as the Sahrawi Arab Democratic Republic.

3.1 Variable Geometry in REC Competition Regimes

There is also considerable variation across RECs in terms of level of ambition and institutional arrangements. The following subsection indicates that some RECs have established supreme regional competition authorities while others operate through a cooperation framework with few competition requirements for their Member States.

3.1.1 The Common Market for East and Southern Africa (COMESA)

COMESA[23] formally came into being in 1994.[24] Among all the regional trade agreements in Africa, COMESA has the largest membership with 21 members[25] and has the most established and developed regional competition authority in Africa. Seven of its members are also members of SADC,[26] one of the Southern African Customs Union (SACU),[27] and four of the EAC.[28]

The COMESA Treaty recognizes that competition rules are necessary to enhance economic integration by enabling action against business conduct that would jeopardize the benefits of an increasingly wide and open market within the COMESA region. Pursuant to Article 55 of the Treaty, any agreement between undertakings or any concerted practice, which has as its object or effect the prevention, restriction, or distortion of competition within the Common Market, shall be prohibited. The same article provides that such prohibition shall not apply to any agreement which improves production or distribution of goods or promotes technical or economic progress and has the effect of enabling consumers a fair share of the benefits provided that the agreement is not inconsistent with the attainment of the objectives of the Treaty or does not have the effect of eliminating competition. Article 55(3) empowers the Council of Minister to make regulations on competition.[29]

In 2004, the COMESA Competition Regulations and Competition Rules were adopted to prohibit anti-competitive practices within the Common Market, to establish a merger control regime for cross-border cases, and to address other

[23] The Common Market of Eastern and Southern Africa (COMESA) Treaty was signed on 5 November 1993 and ratified on 8 December 1994, as the successor to the 1981 Agreement on Preferential Trade Area for Eastern and Southern Africa.

[24] COMESA is a successor to the Preferential Trade Area for Eastern and Southern Africa, which had been established in 1981.

[25] Burundi, Comoros, Democratic Republic of the Congo, Djibouti, Egypt, Eritrea, Ethiopia, Kenya, Libya, Madagascar, Malawi, Mauritius, Rwanda, Seychelles, Somalia, Sudan, eSwatini (formerly Swaziland), Tunisia, Uganda, Zambia, and Zimbabwe.

[26] Democratic Republic of Congo, Madagascar, Malawi, Mauritius, eSwatini, Zambia, and Zimbabwe.

[27] eSwatini.

[28] Burundi, Kenya, Uganda, and Rwanda.

[29] The Treaty Establishing the Common Market for Eastern and Southern Africa available at <http://www.comesa.int/comesa-treaty/> accessed 29 March 2020.

competition law and consumer protection matters with a cross-border dimension.[30] The merger control regime was supplemented by two amendments to the Rules in 2014[31] and 2015,[32] along with the introduction of non-binding Merger Assessment Guidelines. Two competition bodies have been established for the purposes of enforcing competition law in the Common Market. The first is the COMESA Competition Commission (CCC), which became operational in January 2013. It is responsible for investigating anti-competitive practices and reviewing merger control filings. The second is the Board of Commissioners, with a mandate to make rulings, impose remedies, and hear appeals against decisions of the CCC. Appeals against the decisions made by the Board of Commissioners are made to the COMESA Court of Justice.[33]

Pursuant to Article 10 of the Treaty, the Regulations on cross-border competition and consumer matters are binding in their entirety on all the Member States. The Regulations take precedence over any conflicting national competition laws and are directly applicable in all Member States. The Treaty, Regulations, and Rules all impose obligations upon Member States. Article 5(2) of the Treaty provides that each Member State shall take steps to secure the enactment of and the continuation of such legislation to give effect to the Treaty and in particular to confer upon the regulations of Council the force of law and the necessary legal effect within its territory. This Treaty provision is echoed under Article 5 of the Regulations, which provides that pursuant to the aforementioned Article 5(2)(b), Member States shall take all appropriate measures, whether general or particular, to ensure fulfilment of the obligations arising out of the Regulations or resulting from action taken by the CCC under these Regulations.

These provisions are buttressed by Rule 5 of the Competition Rules, which states that CCC and Board of Commissioners decisions shall, pursuant to Article 5 of the Regulations, be binding on undertakings, the governments of the Member States, and domestic courts of justice. Where there is conflict between the Regulations and the national competition laws, the former shall always take precedence, and are directly applicable in all Member States. Pursuant to Article 6 of the Regulations, the CCC enjoys the status of international legal personality and has in the territory of each Member State the legal capacity required for the performance of its

[30] COMESA Competition Regulations as at December 2004. Official Gazette of the Common Market for Eastern and Southern Africa (COMESA) Vol 17, No 12, 20 November 2012 available at <http://www.comesacompetition.org/?page_id=64> accessed 29 March 2020.

[31] The COMESA Competition (Amendment) Rules, 2014 available at <http://www.comesacompetition.org/wp-content/uploads/2015/04/Amendement-to-COMESA-Competition-Rules-2004-Adopted-by-COM-26-March-2015.pdf> accessed 29 March 2020.

[32] COMESA Amendments to Merger Rules, 2015 available at <http://www.comesacompetition.org/wp-content/uploads/2015/04/Amendments-to-the-Rules-to-the-Determination-of-Merger-Thresholds-and-Method-of-Calculation-adopted-by-COM-26-March-2015.pdf> accessed 29 March 2020.

[33] Pursuant to Articles 7, 19–36 of the COMESA Treaty available at <https://comesacourt.org/jurisdiction-2/> accessed 29 March 2020.

functions under the Treaty. There is no conflict between national competition laws and the regional competition law as they apply to different types of conduct. The Regulations apply to cross-border conduct, whereas national competition laws do not ordinarily have such jurisdiction. As such this is a joint enforcement regime.[34]

The CCC has also entered into memoranda of understanding (MOU) with the national competition regulators of Kenya,[35] Malawi,[36] Mauritius,[37] Madagascar,[38] eSwatini (formerly Swaziland),[39] Seychelles,[40] Egypt,[41] Sudan,[42] and Zambia.[43] The majority of COMESA Member States now have operational national competition laws, and others are in the process of adopting and implementing such laws. The CCC has decided over 230 merger cases,[44] and has investigated more than 20 cases of restrictive business conduct, including restrictions to passive sales and the duration of non-compete clauses, while one case addressed harmful vertical restraints and fixed price and profit margins.[45] COMESA's joint enforcement approach is advanced and entrenched.

3.1.2 East African Community (EAC)

The Treaty for the Establishment of the EAC entered into force on 7 July 2000 following its ratification by the original three of the six Partner States – Kenya, Tanzania, and Uganda.[46]

Article 21 of the 2004 Protocol on the Establishment of an EAC Customs Union contains competition provisions similar to the COMESA Competition

[34] OECD Background note by the Secretariat. Regional Competition Agreements: Benefits and Challenges. Directorate for Financial and Enterprise Affairs Competition Committee. DAF/COMP/GF(2018)5. OECD, Paris, 8.

[35] <http://www.comesacompetition.org/wp-content/uploads/2016/06/MoU-with-CAK.pdf> accessed 29 March 2020.

[36] <http://www.comesacompetition.org/wp-content/uploads/2016/06/MOU-with-CFTC-Malawi.pdf> accessed 29 March 2020.

[37] <http://www.comesacompetition.org/wp-content/uploads/2017/04/CCC-and-CCM.pdf> accessed 29 March 2020.

[38] <http://www.comesacompetition.org/wp-content/uploads/2016/11/ENG-Cooperation-Agreement-with-MCC.pdf> accessed 29 March 2020.

[39] <http://www.comesacompetition.org/wp-content/uploads/2016/06/MOU-with-Swaziland-CC.pdf> accessed 29 March 2020.

[40] <http://www.comesacompetition.org/wp-content/uploads/2016/06/MoU-with-FTC-Seychelles.pdf> accessed 29 March 2020.

[41] <http://www.comesacompetition.org/wp-content/uploads/2016/08/Cooperation-Framework-Agreements-ECA-and-CCC.pdf> accessed 29 March 2020.

[42] <http://www.comesacompetition.org/wp-content/uploads/2020/01/EnglishSignedMOU-SudanCPMPC-CCC_compressed.pdf> accessed 29 March 2020.

[43] <http://www.comesacompetition.org/wp-content/uploads/2016/12/Cooperation-Agreement-with-CCPC1.pdf> accessed 29 March 2020.

[44] See COMESA Merger Cases, available at <http://www.comesacompetition.org/?page_id=639> accessed 29 March 2020.

[45] See COMESA Anti-Competitive Business Practices and Request for Authorisation – Cases available at <http://www.comesacompetition.org/?page_id=335> accessed 29 March 2020.

[46] Rwanda and Burundi acceded to the EAC Treaty on 18 June 2007 and became full Members with effect from 1 July 2007. South Sudan acceded on 15 April 2016 and become a full Member on 15 August 2016.

Regulations, both in content and coverage. EAC Partner States are required to prohibit any practice adversely affecting trade within the EAC, including agreements or concerted practices, which prevent, distort, or restrict competition.[47] The EAC Competition Act, enacted in 2006, promotes and protects fair competition, provides for consumer welfare, and establishes the EAC Competition Authority (EACCA).[48]

The EACCA was set up in 2016 and is the most recent regional competition authority in Africa. The EAC Competition Act provides that EACCA shall have all powers, express and implied, necessary for and conducive to the implementation and enforcement of the EAC Competition Law. Besides its powers to investigate and impose sanctions and remedies, the EACCA is also empowered to engage in competition advocacy and consultations as well as in cooperation with regional and international organizations and foreign competition authorities. The Authority is an independent organ of the EAC but its rulings are subject to judicial review by the East African Court of Justice,[49] while the CCC is subject to judicial review by the COMESA Court of Justice.[50]

The EAC Competition Act is in harmony with the COMESA Competition Regulations, both in content and coverage. Further, there has been cooperation between the EACCA and the CCC, demonstrating a willingness towards convergence and harmonization. From the outset, it is able to harmonize its legal and economic market analyses in line with a regional approach, with the necessary guidance and support from the AU level.

3.1.3 Southern African Development Community (SADC)

The Southern African Development Coordination Conference (SADCC), established in April 1980, was transformed into the Southern African Development Community (SADC) in August 1992. One of SADC's guiding principles is respect for the sovereign equality of all Member States, while promoting self-sustaining development on the basis of collective self-reliance, and the interdependence of Member States and achieving complementarity between national and regional strategies and programmes.[51]

Among the means to achieve SADC's objectives are the harmonization of the political and socio-economic policies aimed at the progressive elimination of

[47] The Protocol on the Establishment of an EAC Customs Union was enacted on 8 August 2004, entered into force 1 January 2005 available at <http://www.jus.uio.no/english/services/library/treaties/09/9-04/eac_establishment_protocol.xml> accessed 29 March 2020.

[48] The East African Community (EAC) Competition Act 2006 available at <http://www.industrialization.go.ke/images/downloads/policies/eac-competition-act-2006.pdf> accessed 29 March 2020.

[49] Sections 44 and 46 of the EAC Competition Act, 2006. ibid.

[50] Pursuant to Articles 7, and 19–36 of the Treaty establishing the Common Market for Eastern and Southern Africa available at <https://comesacourt.org/jurisdiction-2/> accessed 29 March 2020.

[51] Pursuant to Article 5 of the 1992 Declaration and Treaty of the Southern African Development Community (SADC Treaty), available at <http://www.sadc.int/documents publications/show/Declaration__Treaty_of_SADC.pdf> accessed 29 March 2020.

obstacles to free movement of goods and services, capital, labour, and people. The Protocol on Trade in the SADC Region[52] underlines cooperation in the areas of trade, industrialization, and cross-border investment promotion paving the way for the creation of a free trade area. Article 25 thereof (titled Competition Policy) requires Member States to implement measures prohibiting unfair business practices and promoting competition. Article 25 also binds Member States to the 2009 Declaration on Regional Cooperation and Consumer Policies,[53] which provides that to make cooperation effective, Member States shall take the necessary steps to adopt, strengthen, and implement the necessary competition and consumer protection laws domestically. Through the Declaration, Member States agree to converge their policies in order to preserve equity in trade and fair competition throughout the region, with the ultimate aim of regional policy harmonization. The Declaration also states the SADC Secretariat will establish a Competition and Consumer Policy and Law Committee to oversee cooperation on competition policies, and aid Member States in establishing competition authorities.

The national competition regulators of nine of the SADC Member States signed an MOU on Inter-Agency Cooperation in Competition Policy, Law and Enforcement to ensure cooperation between them and to strengthen the enforcement of competition law domestically.[54] While a non-binding soft law, it indicates their commitment to collaborate voluntarily on evidence gathering, remedy design, and implementation when conducting merger reviews. Thus, this decentralized approach is based on a cooperation framework, without regional law enforcement. Nevertheless, SADC is also a member of the Tripartite Free Trade Area (TFTA), with its own harmonizing dynamic.

3.1.4 The Tripartite Free Trade Area (TFTA)

The COMESA-EAC-SADC Tripartite Free Trade Area (TFTA) was officially launched at the Third Tripartite Summit on 10 June 2015, when the namesake Agreement was opened for signature.[55] The Treaties establishing the three RECs have various formulations of state commitment to the treaty. Article 5 of the COMESA Treaty, Article 8 of the EAC Treaty, and Article 6 of the SADC Treaty

52 The SADC Trade Protocol was signed 1 August 1996 and entered into force 25 January 2001, and is available at <http://www.sadc.int/documents-publications/show/Protocol%20on%20Trade%20> accessed 29 March 2020.

53 The SADC Declaration on Competition and Consumer Policies (2009) available at <http://www.sadc.int/documents-publications/show/825> accessed 29 March 2020.

54 The SADC MOU on Inter-Agency Cooperation in Competition Policy, Law and Enforcement was signed and came into effect on 26 May 2016, and is available at <http://www.sadc.int/news-events/news/competition-authorities-sadc-member-states-signed-memorandum/> accessed 29 March 2020.

55 The COMESA-EAC-SADC Tripartite Free Trade Area (TFTA) was officially launched at the Third Tripartite Summit on 10 June 2015. The Agreement covers 27 participating Member States across the three RECs. As at March 2020, eight countries have ratified the Agreement: Burundi, Kenya, Egypt, Rwanda, Uganda, South Africa, Namibia, and Botswana. The Agreement requires 14 ratifications to enter into force.

underscore the general obligations of Member States of RECs. As general treaties, there is no specific set of obligations requiring Member States to specify actions undertaken in respect of legislation subsidiary to the Treaties. However, Protocols or laws implementing specific segments of the Treaties state the obligations.

As noted, the TFTA Member/Partner States' competition frameworks comprise different enforcement methods varying from binding regional instruments, domestic laws, and institutions to those states with no laws and institutions. Even where there are laws, the record of implementation and enforcement remains minimal. The Tripartite Competition Protocol needs to address these gaps. This is feasible in the medium term because the three RECs and most Member/Partner States in the Tripartite region embrace competition policy and law. About 25 jurisdictions in the TFTA have competition laws, implying a competition regime has rapidly expanded in the region reflecting the growing role of competition policy and law on the development agenda.[56] If the TFTA can successfully bring diverse Member/Partner States together under one competition framework, sharing the same competition principles and approaches, it could serve as the springboard for harmonising competition framework at the AfCFTA level (see section 4).

3.1.5 Economic Community of West African States (ECOWAS)

ECOWAS is a regional grouping of 15 Member States founded in 1975 under the Treaty of Lagos[57] to promote economic integration and cooperation. ECOWAS introduced competition legislation in 2008 through the ECOWAS Supplementary Act on the Adoption of Community Competition Rules and the modalities of their application within ECOWAS.[58] The objectives of the Supplementary Act include prohibiting any anti-competitive business conduct that prevents, restricts, or distorts competition at regional level and ensuring consumers' welfare. It also provides for the establishment of the ECOWAS Competition Authority to implement Community-wide competition rules and regulations.[59]

While ECOWAS has a regional competition framework, there are several ECOWAS members that do not yet possess a competition law or authority, such as Guinea, Sierra Leone, and Niger. The variable geometry is particularly noticeable because ECOWAS also includes the eight members of the sub-regional bloc, the West African Economic and Monetary Union, which has a strong regional competition regime, enforcing a regional competition law through a supranational competition authority.

[56] Fox and Bakhoum (n 4).

[57] Economic Community of West African States (ECOWAS) Revised Treaty. (1993), originally signed 28 May 1975.

[58] ECOWAS Supplementary Act A/SA.1/06/08 of 19 December 2008.

[59] Article 11(2) of the Supplementary Act empowers the ECOWAS Regional Competition Authority to approve mergers, acquisitions, or other business combinations prohibited under Article 7 of the Supplementary Act, if such transaction is in the public interest.

3.1.6 West African Economic and Monetary Union (WAEMU)

The WAEMU was established in 1994 and now includes eight Member States holding a common currency,[60] who have concurrent membership with ECOWAS. However, WAEMU is a model of deep integration, unlike ECOWAS. Indeed, under Article 6 of the Treaty, the fundamental principles of WAEMU includes the primacy of community law over national law along with the direct and immediate applicability of community law.[61] Moreover, WAEMU has a common competition policy laid down in Articles 88 to 90 of the Treaty. While not unequivocally accepted, the WAEMU Court of Justice has stated that the competition authorities of Member States do not have the competence to regulate and monitor competition.[62] In 2002, WAEMU adopted regulations on anti-competitive practices, on procedures governing cartels and abuse of dominant position, and on State aid.[63] WAEMU also operates a voluntary merger filing regime In addition, a directive was adopted on cooperation between the Commission and the competition bodies of Member States for the application of the aforementioned Articles 88 to 90.[64]

While WAEMU's competition regime has developed along the lines of the COMESA and EAC approach, it is not well integrated with the other RECs, including in its membership of ECOWAS. Nevertheless, harmonization is strong within WAEMU's centralized competition regime, despite variations in competition among the members. For example, Benin and Guinea Bissau do not have national competition laws but they have approved the WAEMU Treaty and hence the competition provisions thereof.[65] WAEMU is a relevant model for the AfCFTA because those Member States without domestic competition regimes still address anti-competitive practices in a harmonized manner by reporting these cases to the WAEMU Commission.

[60] The Treaty Establishing the West African Economic and Monetary Union (WAEMU) was signed 10 January entered into force 1994, and is available at <http://www.uemoa.int/en/amended-treaty> accessed 29 March 2020.

[61] Article 6 of the Treaty Establishing the West African Economic and Monetary Union (WAEMU) 1994.

[62] Opinion 03/2000/CJ/UEMOA states that Articles 88, 89 and 90 of the WAEMU Treaty enshrine an exclusive competence of the Union. Member States are only entitled to take decisions pertaining to criminal law aimed at sanctioning anti-competitive practices, breaches of the laws on market transparency and competition regulation. See UNCTAD, *Voluntary Peer Review of Competition Policy: West African Economic and Monetary Union, Benin and Senegal Overview*, UNCTAD/DITC/CLP/2007/1(Overview) (UNCTAD, 2007) 11.

[63] Regulation No 2/2002/CM/UEMOA of 23 May 2002 (anti-competitive practices); Regulation No 3/2002/CM/UEMOA of 23 May 2002 (procedures applicable to restrictive agreements and abuse of dominant position); and Regulation No 4/2002/CM/UEMOA of 23 May 2002 (State Aid).

[64] Directive No 02/2002/CM/UEMOA of 23 May 2002 available at <http://www.uemoa.int/sites/default/files/bibliotheque/pages_-_directive_02_2002_cm.pdf> accessed 29 March 2020.

[65] In 2015, Niger validated a new Competition and Consumer Protection Law that replaced a 1992 law that was never fully operational. Togo's own competition law was replaced by the WAEMU community law on competition, which took effect on 1 January 2003. A National Competition and Consumption Commission became operational in Togo in 2006.

3.2 Challenges of Overlapping in REC Memberships: The Role of the AU

The Treaties of each REC generally require commitment that the Member States shall abstain from any activity or practice which could jeopardize the attainment of the objectives of the Treaty. However, this overview has indicated that despite a high-level consensus on the need for competition laws, its application and substantive rules often differ across the various RECs. Enforcement at national level is highly complex for those countries belonging to several RECs, and in parallel it increases the burden on the business community in terms of compliance costs. A consequence of such increased business costs can be reduced cross-border trade within or into the continent, thus impeding the objectives of continental integration.

This section identifies three areas to demonstrate that there is a role for AU institutions to establish legal instruments to harmonize competition regimes across the Member States.[66]

3.2.1 Abuse of Dominance

Despite considerable similarities in the practices which are considered as abuse of a dominant position at both national and regional levels, notably exclusionary conduct, predatory pricing, price discrimination, and refusal to deal, key differences can be found, however, in relation to what amounts to a dominant position. Different national laws employ different thresholds for identifying a dominant position. Among those that have adopted a market share threshold, differences can be found in the quantum considered. In Kenya, the Competition Act refers to 50% market share whereas in Zambia, a 30% share is considered when one enterprise is concerned (single dominance) and 60% where not more than three enterprises are concerned (collective dominance). The Egyptian law, on the other hand, incorporates a negative irrefutable presumption of the lack of dominance where the market shares of the undertaking is less than 25%. In Namibia, the Rules Made Under Competition Act, 2003 provide that an undertaking has, or two or more undertakings have, a dominant position in a market if (a) it has or they have at least 45% of that market; (b) it has or they have at least 35%, but less than 45%, of that market, unless it can show that it does not have market power; or (c) it has or they have less than 35% of that market, but it has or they have marker power. The Rules further provide that 'market power' means the power of an undertaking or undertakings to control prices, to exclude competition, or to behave to an appreciable extent independently of its competitors, customers, or suppliers.

[66] Other relevant issues include State aid/subsidy control, public procurement, intellectual property rights, and the digital economy.

The RECs (COMESA and EAC) have adopted qualitative criteria to describe a dominant position in their regional competition laws, referring to the position of economic strength that enables the undertakings concerned the ability or power to behave to a material extent independently of their competitors, customers, and consumers. The COMESA Guidelines on Abuse of Dominant Position nonetheless provides that the CCC will generally consider that an undertaking holding a market share of at least 30% of the relevant market is presumed to hold a dominant position.

The role of the AU law here is to use the AfCFTA's forthcoming Protocol on Competition to promulgate a continent-wide standard for assessing market dominance, including presumptions of abuse, based on the experience of RECs and the domestic competition authorities. These standards and norms can be set out in guidelines and supporting resources for domestic competition agencies to follow. As this standard becomes more widely used, the legal assessment of abuse of dominance can move from per se prohibitions to a rule of reason.

3.2.2 Merger Control

The merger control regime across the Tripartite Member/Partner States are considerably more varied as compared to the other types of conduct. It is noted that most laws consider both *de facto* and *de jure* control in establishing whether a merger transaction has occurred. However, differences exist among the countries on the type of transactions which may qualify as a merger; for instance, some jurisdictions do not expressly regulate joint ventures (e.g. Tanzania, Zimbabwe) or lease of assets (e.g. Malawi, Mauritius). Different tests also prevail in establishing 'control', with some laws referring to 'controlling interest', 'material influence', and 'decisive influence'.[67]

A distinction can also be made according to the type of merger control that exists, namely voluntary, mandatory suspensory, and mandatory non-suspensory. Most national competition laws seem to provide for a mandatory suspensory regime (such as Zambia, Zimbabwe, Kenya, Tanzania). Malawi and Mauritius are among the few with a voluntary regime. A few jurisdictions do not have an express form of merger control provided under their laws, such as Comoros and Egypt. The Egyptian Competition Authority, however, indicated that parties to merger transactions are required to notify their transactions to the authority who can intervene on an ex-ante basis via interim measures or an ex-post basis through the conduct provisions under the Egyptian Competition Act. These differences in the type of merger control regime also prevail at REC level, with COMESA operating a

[67] Assessing Regional Integration in Africa IX: Next Steps for the African Continental Free Trade Agreement. 2019. United Nations Economic Commission for Africa, African Union, African Development Bank and United Nations Conference on Trade and Development.

mandatory but non-suspensory regime whereas the EAC provides for a mandatory suspensory notification system.[68]

Most jurisdictions have in place turnover and asset value thresholds for purposes of determining whether a merger requires notification.[69] For example, in Zambia, mergers are notifiable where the merging parties achieve a combined turnover or asset base, whichever is higher, of at least 50 million fee units. In Zimbabwe, a merger is notifiable to the Competition and Tariffs Commission if the merging parties' combined annual turnover or assets, whichever is higher, exceed US$ 1,200,000. Mauritius is one of the few countries with market share thresholds for purposes of notification, whereas other jurisdictions have indicated that market shares are used for purposes of determining concentration during the assessment. In Botswana, merger review can be triggered through any of the three criteria: turnover, asset, or market share.[70] At REC level, the regional competition authorities also need to determine thresholds for merger notification. Otherwise, as with the EAC, all mergers meeting the regional dimension under the Act are required to be notified to the EAC. The AU could cooperate with the Member States to harmonize these thresholds on an AfCFTA level.

As with the issue of assessing abuse of dominance, these divergences are not fatal to the agenda of continental integration nor to the adoption of common principles for purposes of a continental competition protocol; on the contrary, a blanket one-size-fits-all competition policy would be hugely unsuccessful in the AfCFTA, given each country's distinct economic, social, and political needs. As long as the AU instruments set out sufficient convergence across the main types of conduct provisions, this will guide the drafting of common rules for the AfCFTA Protocol on Competition. However, one area where there are key divergences of particular relevant here is in the area of exceptions, exemptions, or 'public interest overrides' to competition rules.

3.2.3 The Role of the AU in Harmonizing Public Interest Overrides

The scope of competition assessments tends to vary. In some countries, the primary objective of the assessment is on maintaining the level of competition in a market, with emphasis being placed on the promotion of economic efficiency. However, in many jurisdictions, emphasis is also placed on 'public interest'. This is a broad concept and considered differently in various national and regional competition laws.

For example, under South African competition law, public interest factors can be used to approve an anti-competitive merger or to prohibit a pro-competitive one. The public interest test calls for an exhaustive list and involves an assessment

[68] ibid.

[69] Africa Guide – Competition. Bowmans. 2016 available at <http://www.bowmanslaw.com/wp-content/uploads/2016/12/Guide-Competition-3.pdf> accessed 29 March 2020.

[70] Assessing Regional Integration in Africa IX (n 67).

of impact on employment, regions, and sectors, the historically disadvantaged, small businesses, and industrial competitiveness.[71] In Botswana, public interest factors can be used to exempt certain mergers from review and also form a set of additional considerations in merger investigations, although the scope of public interest factors is not limited and can include any factor that bears on the broader public interest in the proposed merger.[72] In Zambia, public interest factors can be used to initiate an investigation into mergers that fall below the prescribed notification thresholds and also form a set of additional considerations in a merger review.[73] The scope of potential public interest factors for consideration is essentially unlimited, including socio-economic factors as may be appropriate, and any other factor that bears upon the public interest. A number of national Competition Acts do not specify the type of public interest factors which may be considered (e.g. Egypt, Mauritius) or provide a non-exhaustive list (e.g. Kenya, Zambia). This leaves the scope of application by the competition authorities fairly wide and may increase uncertainty with regard to the elements to be considered in the assessment carried out by the authorities.

The membership to several RECs further complicates this task given that differences also exist at REC level, which may result in countries adhering to the rules of one REC being in conflict with the rules of another REC. For example, while the EAC allows the Council to approve a merger on appeal if it believes it is to 'fulfil an overriding public interest', no public interest factors are described. Under the COMESA Competition Regulations, 'public interest grounds' can be used to justify an otherwise anti-competitive merger, although the listed factors generally overlap with a standard competition assessment. It is noted, however, that the concept of 'competition' under the COMESA Competition Regulations goes beyond the consideration of economic efficiency and incorporates, *inter alia*, the achievement of high economic growth, increasing employment opportunities.[74]

The challenge for the AU is to ensure the transparent use of these derogations and exemptions is necessary, proportionate, and consistently applied. Otherwise, they can be abused to the detriment of markets, citizens, and economic integration. In the European Union, many derogations and exemptions exist for the Member States to follow public policy interests, however they are carefully monitored and scrutinized for their ability to attain their stated objective at the least possible cost to competition within the Single Market.[75] As with the European Commission, the AU institutions need to be able to set out oversight instruments to promote good economic governance of public interest overrides without restricting the sovereign power of the Member States to define and implement public policies. This could,

[71] Competition Act, section 12A(1)(b) and 12A(3), and Amendments to Competition Act, 2019.
[72] The public interest considerations are stated under section 59(2) of the Act.
[73] Article 31. The Competition and Consumer Protection Act, 2010.
[74] COMESA Competition Regulations (n 30).
[75] P Ibáñez Colomo, *The Shaping of EU Competition Law* (CUP, 2018).

in the first instance, include notifying the AU on the use of these derogations and harmonizing impact assessment reporting.

4. Options for Harmonizing Competition Law in Africa under the AU

Given the challenges of overlapping membership, diverse competition laws, and variable geometry of RECs, it is useful to identify the main approaches to harmonizing domestic competition laws and policies. With regards to decision-making powers, one can distinguish the two-tier model followed by CEMAC, EAC, and ECOWAS, where both the regional competition authority and the national competition authorities can apply regional competition provisions concurrently.[76] There are two independently operating levels: for regional cases the regional competition authority has exclusive original jurisdiction and conducts the investigation and decides on the case, while for national cases the national competition authority has exclusive original jurisdiction and conducts the investigation and decides on the case. The national competition authority cannot enforce regional provisions.

The joint enforcement model is followed by COMESA, where national and regional authorities apply regional competition provisions in their respective competition cases (national and regional cases). WAEMU follows the single-tier model, where the regional competition authority investigates and takes decisions on national and regional competition cases, while the national competition authority cannot enforce regional provisions and perform a merely supportive role. SADC, on the other hand, takes a cooperation approach. Its regional body does not have a binding competition law and is based on inter-governmental cooperation. Competition law enforcement is situated at the national level, where those Member States have established a competition law and or authority.[77]

The strongest model for the AU to follow would involve full integration or unification of competition law under the AfCFTA, such as the WAEMU model. This would include the establishment of a nearly complete continental competition policy or code, along with a supranational enforcement agency that deals with cross-border anti-competitive practices. While attractive in providing for deep integration, at present, the institutional framework for variable geometry provided by the AfCFTA does not promulgate this option. Despite the advances made in some of the RECs, it does not correspond to the context of the African continent.

[76] OECD (n 34).
[77] ibid.

Member countries belonging to certain RECs, such as SADC, have not agreed to develop and enforce competition laws either regionally or domestically.

Indeed, the weakest approach for the AU to promulgate is the SADC cooperation model. It would entail no binding law at the continental level but a policy of harmonizing national competition laws incrementally through bottom-up convergence. This can be achieved through cross-fertilization or convergence of national law or enforcement agency cooperation, complemented by sectoral agreements. This approach produces a bilateral type of harmonization, based on shared principles. However, this approach is less relevant for integrating those countries with more developed competition norms and enforcement systems. It does not take advantage of the more advanced RECs in converging competition principles that can effectively underpin cross-border trade liberalization.

An alternative hybrid approach would entail AU institutions and legal instruments developing and integrating competition regimes through continental-wide minimum standard competition principles and enforcement guidelines, while strengthening cooperation between competition authorities. This approach produces tripartite-like arrangements that link principles of a constitutional dimension that prohibit anti-competitive blockages of market access and transnational cartels and provide a discipline for unjustified government trade-restraining acts. Under this hybrid approach, states would be required to prohibit only the few consensus wrongs domestically. This seems most appropriate for harmonising competition policy under the AfCFTA, given the variable geometry and overlapping membership in the RECs.

The Protocol on Competition will be pivotal to providing clear guidance on implementing these principles along common lines among the RECs and State Parties.[78] It could focus on those matters of principle in the State Parties or RECs that are currently incompatible or run contrary to AfCFTA trade policies. For example, the time periods for premerger notification filings can be harmonized. Countries and RECs can agree to accept pre-merger filings prepared for the first jurisdiction in which a filing is made, with supplements as necessary to cover different markets. Stronger cooperation can also be required among agencies when investigating anti-competitive conduct through market analysis, using guidelines to facilitate the convergence of legal and economic methodologies.

Under this approach, the RECs both support the Member States and the AU to implement AfCFTA-level guidelines on cross-border competition issues. This serves to ensure that the different competition strategies of individual states are identified and guided into alignment through the integrating role of the RECs. AfCFTA's two-tier system is compatible with this third approach, as well as the variable geometry in the RECs. AU institutions and instruments would be able to

[78] Assessing Regional Integration in Africa IX (n 67) 160.

provide direction on harmonizing minimum competition principles among RECs to reduce this variable geometry and integrate diverse countries with overlapping membership.

The AU harmonizing strategy could harness the work and reach of the African Competition Forum (ACF), a network membership of more than 30 national African competition authorities and five regional competition agencies. The ACF currently operates as an informal advocacy network to encourage and assist African states without a competition law to adopt one, and to build capacity of African competition agencies.[79] ACF activities have been organized primarily through the platform of the SADC Working Groups on Competition but could work through AU institutions with the support of the AU Secretariat. The ACF is well positioned to work on consensus policies towards new competition approaches to the digital economy, privacy, and intellectual property rights, for example.

One legal obstacle to this hybrid approach is that under Article 13(3) of the AfCFTA, the rights and duties of the Secretariat are not specified in the AfCFTA and there are no precedents to indicate the sort of independent legal powers the Secretariat will enjoy.[80] These require clarification through Council of Ministers' decisions adopted under Article 13. An effective AfCFTA Secretariat would provide an AU focal point for cooperating with RECs to find consensus on convergence towards similar competition principles and the minimum standards appropriate for individual Member States. Another challenge lies in the decision-making structure of AfCFTA institutions. Article 9 of the AfCFTA establishes the Assembly, the Council of Ministers, and the Committee of Senior Trade Officials, as well as the Secretariat. Although all AU Member States are represented in the AfCFTA Council of Ministers, there is no formal role for the RECs. Pursuant to Article 12 thereof, the Committee of Senior Trade Officials consists of officials designated by each State party to implement Council of Ministers decisions. Here the RECs are represented but only in an advisory capacity. This leaves open how strong this representational function will be.

In the area of competition, enforcement is often a greater problem than establishing laws. Without credible enforcement mechanisms, the incentives for governments and firms to prevent unfair business practices are reduced. In the event of disputes between the parties under the AfCFTA, the Protocol on Rules and Procedures on the Settlement of Disputes provides a detailed legal instrument to address disputes regarding the interpretation and/or application of the Agreement in relation to their rights and obligations.[81] However, the Protocol does

[79] The African Competition Forum available at <http://www.compcom.co.za/african-competition-forum/> accessed 29 March 2020.

[80] G Erasmus. *The AfCFTA Institutions: Could the Secretariat Hold the Key to Implementation* (2019) TRALAC Working Paper US19WP01, 6.

[81] (n 9), Article 1.

not provide jurisdiction over AU legal instruments, which includes the Protocol on Competition.

Evidently, the AU requires additional legal instruments to offer further clarity and guidance on competition law and enforcement issues. This entails establishing a legal committee specifically charged with the responsibility of drawing up legal texts for the several protocols under the treaty, or for advancing cooperation with within the community. However, this also needs to be addressed because it is not provided for under Article 25 of the Abuja Treaty dealing with the establishment of specialized technical committees.[82] Yet such a competition committee could provide the necessary harmonizing impetus by preparing studies and recommendations on the process of harmonization, promoting the codification and wider acceptance of common competition principles, and providing a platform for consulting Member States and the RECs when harmonizing and implementing competition policy under the AU.

5. Conclusion

This chapter has argued that the AU is well positioned to promulgate minimum requirement competition principles that build upon the achievements of established regional competition regimes, while harmonizing the actions of diverse State Parties. The African integration process, as the European experience indicates, requires a strong guiding role from the AU institutions and legal instruments to ensure that competition policy and trade liberalization complement each other in promoting efficiency, consumer welfare, growth, and development. The AU's regional integration policy needs to take account of the probability that liberalization and the removal of border barriers will fuel the incentives of both firms and governments to find other ways to re-erect barriers and protect their historical advantage, including through anti-competitive practices.[83]

With effective leadership, the AfCFTA can follow a hybrid approach, building on existing regional integration efforts, while facilitating policy convergence by resolving the implications of conflicting rules across the different trading regimes.[84] The successful grass-roots work and infrastructure of the ACF can be harnessed by the AU, while the Protocol on Competition could require the formal participation of the RECs and the State Parties within the various decision-making bodies

[82] Olufemi (n 10) 71.

[83] The World Bank Group, African Competition Forum. *Breaking Down Barriers: Unlocking Africa's Potential through Vigorous Competition Policy* (2016) World Bank, Nairobi, Kenya, 1 available at <https://openknowledge.worldbank.org/handle/10986/24688> accessed 30 March 2020.

[84] T Hartzenberg, 'The African Continental Free Trade Area Agreement – what is expected of LDCs in terms of trade liberalisation?' (2019) available at <http://www.un.org/ldcportal/afcfta-what-is-expected-of-ldcs-in-terms-of-trade-liberalisation-by-trudi-hartzenberg/> accessed 30 March 2020.

related to trade and competition issues. The political will of the AU to use its legal role and establish strong institutions and statutes is vital to this worthy endeavour. Implementing continent-wide trade liberalization policies without the necessary harmonized competition rules to address cross-border anti-competitive practices can frustrate the economic and social benefits to be reaped from African integration under the AU.

5

The AU and Global Financial Standard-Setting

Pablo Iglesias-Rodríguez

1. Introduction

African Union (AU) law[1] acknowledges the importance of strengthening the role of Africa in the international economic and financial arena. Notably, Article 3(i) of the Constitutive Act determines that one of the AU's objectives shall be to 'establish the necessary conditions which enable the continent to play its rightful role in the global economy and in international negotiations'. Likewise, one of the aspirations of the AU's Agenda 2063 is to enhance 'Africa's place in the global governance system'.[2]

Academic literature on Africa's role in global economic and financial governance is scant and has neglected the study of the role of African Financial Supervision Authorities (FSAs)[3] in International Networks of Financial Supervision Authorities (INFSAs)[4]. This topic is of major relevance for two main reasons.

First, although INFSAs do not produce hard, mandatory law, they are extremely influential and play a central role in the design of the global financial architecture. Indeed, many financial rules adopted at the domestic level by jurisdictions[5]

I am very grateful to Olufemi Amao and Konstantin Magliveras for extremely useful feedback on draft versions of this chapter. The usual disclaimer applies.

[1] This chapter applies the definition of AU law as 'the body of treaties, resolutions and decisions that have direct and indirect application to the Member States of the African Union', developed by O Amao, *African Union Law: The Emergence of a Sui Generis Legal Order* (Routledge, 2019) 21.

[2] African Union, *Agenda 2063 Framework Document – The Africa We Want* (African Union Commission, 2015) vi.

[3] There is no all-encompassing definition of the term 'financial supervision authority' but it generally refers to 'entities of a public nature with officially recognized authority to carry out regulation and [or] supervision of the financial sector – financial institutions, markets, and products – in a given jurisdiction', P Iglesias-Rodríguez, *The Accountability of Financial Regulators: a European and International Perspective* (Kluwer Law International, 2014) 5.

[4] INFSAs can be defined as 'institutional creatures within the general categories of "global administrative bodies", "transnational regulatory networks", "transgovernmental regulatory organizations" or "government networks", made of national regulators [FSAs] form different jurisdictions and aimed at exchanging information, coordinating supervision and enforcement, and reaching agreements about common regulatory standards, among their members' ibid 296–7.

[5] For consistency, this chapter uses the term 'jurisdiction' to refer to the place of operation of an FSA. However, the term 'jurisdiction' is not always interchangeable with 'country' or 'state'. There are cases

Pablo Iglesias-Rodríguez, *The AU and Global Financial Standard-Setting* In: *The Emergent African Union Law*. Edited by: Olufemi Amao, Michèle Olivier and Konstantinos D. Magliveras, Oxford University Press. © Pablo Iglesias-Rodríguez 2021. DOI: 10.1093/oso/9780198862154.003.0006

worldwide have their origins in the standards developed by INFSAs.[6] It has been suggested that African jurisdictions have strong incentives to adopt the INFSAs' standards, among other reasons, to signal sophistication and strong regulation, so as to attract investors, expand internationally, or even access funding from the International Monetary Fund (IMF).[7] An aspect that has been overlooked in this discussion is whether African FSAs play a relevant role in designing those standards and, more generally, in INFSAs. This has major potential implications, both in terms of input and output legitimacy.[8] From an input legitimacy perspective, it is important that African FSAs participate and are given due consideration in the development and adoption of INFSAs' standards so as to foster the latter's output legitimacy, namely that they embrace the features and needs of the African jurisdictions that may be affected by them.

Secondly, the analysis of the African FSAs' role in INFSAs, is instrumental to determine whether and to what extent (a) the model of economic and financial integration embraced by AU law relates to the power and influence of Africa in the global financial architecture; and (b) whether and how AU law, institutions, and policies may contribute to enhance such influence.

In order to address these important questions, the remainder of this chapter proceeds as follows. First, it analyses the role of African FSAs in INFSAs, focusing on the barriers they face for accessing, being effectively represented, and participating in the latter. The selected INFSAs are the Basel Committee on Banking Supervision (BCBS),[9] the International Organization of Securities Commissions (IOSCO),[10] and the International Association of Insurance Supervisors (IAIS),[11] which are the main global financial standard-setters. Secondly, it assesses how AU law and

where one country/state may have different jurisdictions, for the purposes of financial supervision, which are subject to the oversight of different FSAs. Conversely, there are cases where a single supranational FSA carries out exclusive supervision of the financial markets of a group of countries/states, which are collectively deemed as a single jurisdiction for supervisory purposes; these states will also be referred to as 'jurisdictions'.

[6] Iglesias-Rodríguez (n 3) 296.

[7] See, for example, T Beck, E Jones, and others, 'Basel standards and developing countries: a difficult relationship' *Vox* (London, 15 October 2018) – in relation to the Basel Committee on Banking Supervision standards.

[8] Input and output legitimacy are concepts developed within the field of democratic theory by F Scharpf, *Governing in Europe: Effective and Democratic?* (OUP, 1999). Input legitimacy relates to the idea of 'government by the people' (ibid 7) and whether the parties affected by a rule or policy have a say in their formulation. Output legitimacy is concerned with the idea of 'government for the people' (ibid 11) and whether a rule or policy matches the preferences and expectations of the parties affected by them.

[9] Its mandate is 'to strengthen the regulation, supervision and practices of banks worldwide with the purpose of enhancing financial stability', section 1 BCBS Charter.

[10] Its objective is 'to enable members to exchange information with a view to: (a) developing securities markets and improving their efficiency; (b) coordinating the enforcement of securities regulation; and (c) implementing common standards', section 1(2) IOSCO Bylaws.

[11] Its mission is 'to: (a) promote effective and globally consistent supervision of the insurance industry in order to develop and maintain fair, safe and stable insurance markets for the benefit and protection of policyholders; and to (b) contribute to global financial stability', Article 2(1) IAIS Bylaws.

institutions may contribute to enhance the position of Africa in global financial standard-setting.

2. Barriers to Africa's Access to INFSAs

A necessary condition for African FSAs to participate in and influence global financial standard-setting is to have access to the BCBS, the IOSCO, and the IAIS.

The BCBS does not have an open-membership policy and accession to it is by invitation only.[12] Decisions on new membership require consensus of existing members,[13] which, in making their determination, must give due regard to 'the importance of their national banking sectors to international financial stability'.[14] Indeed, whilst only 11 of the 28 jurisdictions represented at the BCBS through membership have Global Systemically Important Banks,[15] they generally consist of economies with large or relatively large banking sectors with an actual or potential relevant impact on global financial stability.[16]

The BCBS's restrictive approach to membership has substantially limited the presence of African FSAs. Indeed, as of September 2020, the only African jurisdiction represented at the BCBS was South Africa,[17] which has the largest banking sector on the continent.[18] With few exceptions, such as Morocco or Egypt, most African jurisdictions have relatively modest banking sectors[19] with little, if any, impact on global financial stability. Although the BCBS may invite observers,[20] who can influence the decision-making process at the level of discussions,[21] as of September 2020, no observer came from Africa.[22]

In addition, certain BCBS membership commitments could act as barriers. In this respect, the BCBS Charter requires members to 'work together to achieve the mandate of the BCBS'[23] and to 'implement and apply BCBS standards in their

[12] Section 4 BCBS Charter.
[13] ibid section 8(4).
[14] ibid section 4.
[15] These are: Canada, China, France, Germany, Italy, Japan, the Netherlands, Spain, Switzerland, the United Kingdom, and the United States of America, see '2018 list of global systemically important banks (G-SIBs)' (*Financial Stability Board*, 16 November 2018) available at <https://www.fsb.org/wp-content/uploads/P161118-1.pdf> accessed 29 May 2020.
[16] For instance, 20 of the 28 jurisdictions represented at the BCBS through membership are G-20 members – the G-20 membership is available at <https://g20.org/en/Pages/home.aspx> accessed 29 May 2020.
[17] See 'Basel Committee membership' (*BCBS*, 30 December 2016) available at <https://www.bis.org/bcbs/membership.htm?m=3%7C14%7C573%7C71> accessed 29 May 2020.
[18] See, for example, 'The Banker's Top 100 African Banks ranking 2019: a brighter picture' (*The Banker*, 1 May 2019) available at <https://www.thebanker.com> accessed 29 May 2020.
[19] ibid.
[20] Section 4 BCBS Charter.
[21] ibid sections 8(3) and 15(3).
[22] For a list of the BCBS's observers see BCBS (n 17).
[23] Section 5(a) BCBS Charter.

domestic jurisdictions'.[24] Making membership conditional on compliance with existing BCBS standards[25] may act as a disincentive to membership for several African jurisdictions. Some commentators have argued that Basel III[26] was developed by and tailored to the needs of economically developed jurisdictions[27] and that it may not suit all African banking systems.[28] Moreover, its implementation may be too complex, costly, and counterproductive for them.[29] Indeed, the degree of implementation of Basel III among African jurisdictions still remains very low.[30] This would suggest that the low levels of input legitimacy of the BCBS's standard-setting procedure, which are a consequence of its restrictive membership structure, have had an impact on the output legitimacy of its standards and, hence, their acceptance in Africa.

In contrast to the BCBS, the IOSCO and the IAIS have more inclusive membership policies. Membership in the latter is not by invitation but through application and is open to any organization that complies with the requisites corresponding to each membership category, which relate, primarily, to legal status, compliance with certain regulatory commitments, and the payment of annual fees.[31]

The IOSCO offers three types of membership, namely ordinary, associate, and affiliate.[32] Ordinary membership is generally reserved to national securities FSAs and is the only membership type with voting rights attached to it.[33] Associate membership includes, *inter alia*, supranational or subnational FSAs,[34] while affiliate membership applies to self-regulatory organizations and other entities with an interest in securities regulation.[35] Associate and affiliate

[24] ibid section 5(e).

[25] The BCBS standards address core aspects pertaining to the regulation and supervision of banks, particularly in terms of capital and liquidity, see BCBS, *The Basel Framework* (Bank for International Settlements, 2020).

[26] This comprises a series of standards of banking regulation and supervision developed by the BCBS in response to the global financial crisis, see BCBS, *Basel III: Finalising Post-Crisis Reforms* (Bank for International Settlements, 2017).

[27] See e.g. M Taylor, 'Basel III is bad news for emerging economies' *Financial Times* (London, 14 October 2010).

[28] See, for example, EB Nyantakyi and M Sy, 'The banking system in Africa: main facts and challenges' (2015) 6 Africa Economic Brief 1, 14.

[29] See, for example, ibid and African Development Bank, 'Forecasting the costs and benefits of implementing Basel III for North African emerging economies: an application to Egypt and Tunisia' (2012) Economic Brief 1, 20.

[30] A study published by the Financial Stability Institute in November 2018, examined the degree of implementation of Basel III among 15 African jurisdictions and found that only six had implemented it, see S Hohl, MC Sison, and others, *FSI Insights on policy implementation No 11: The Basel framework in 100 jurisdictions: implementation status and proportionality practices* (Bank for International Settlements, 2018) 8. According to PK Ozili, 'Basel III in Africa: Making It Work' (2019) Munich Personal RePEc Archive Paper No 94222, 3, among African jurisdictions, only South Africa has implemented Basel III fully.

[31] Sections 3–14(2) IOSCO Bylaws and Articles 6–8 IAIS Bylaws.

[32] Section 3 IOSCO Bylaws.

[33] ibid sections 6 and 27.

[34] ibid section 8(2).

[35] ibid section 9(1).

members enjoy some limited participation rights in IOSCO's decision-making activities.[36]

The IAIS distinguishes between voting and non-voting members.[37] Voting membership is open to insurance FSAs, which constitute the core of its membership.[38] Whilst non-voting membership is not open for applications, the IAIS Bylaws specify three such non-voting members, namely the National Association of Insurance Commissioners (NAIC),[39] the Federal Insurance Office (FIO), and the European Commission.[40] Moreover, the IAIS may recommend, for admission as non-voting members, international organizations that may further its mission.[41] Although non-voting members are deprived of voting rights, they are allowed to participate in the IAIS's affairs.[42]

Despite the greater openness and inclusiveness of the IOSCO's and the IAIS's membership policies, the representation of African FSAs remains limited. For instance, Africa is the continent with a lower percentage of voting members in the IOSCO, with only 17 voting FSAs, out of a total of 129, which represent 29 jurisdictions.[43] The IAIS has admitted 25 FSAs from Africa, out of a total of 152 member FSAs, which represent 38 jurisdictions.[44] This could be explained by the nature of the commitments with which voting members must abide. Whilst they are less burdensome than in the BCBS, they may, nevertheless, require important adaptation costs for African jurisdictions.

For instance, to become an IOSCO ordinary member, an FSA must be a signatory to the IOSCO Multilateral Memorandum of Understanding Concerning Consultation and Cooperation and the Exchange of Information (IOSCO MMoU),[45] a non-binding agreement aimed at facilitating supervisory cooperation between the signatory FSAs.[46] Before allowing an FSA to become a signatory of the IOSCO MMoU, the IOSCO assesses whether the applicable domestic law allows for compliance with the supervisory cooperation duties of the IOSCO MMoU, and may reject an application if it considers that this is not the case.[47] In 2015,

[36] For example, associate members may attend and speak at the Presidents Committee meetings and affiliate members may attend them, ibid sections 30 and 30(1).

[37] Article 6 IAIS Bylaws.

[38] ibid Article 6(2)(a).

[39] The NAIC is a standard-setting body that gathers insurance FSAs from 50 states, the District of Columbia, and five US territories, and is aimed at promoting the uniformity of insurance legislation throughout them, see Article 1 NAIC Bylaws, 'About The NAIC' (*NAIC*, 2020) available at <https://content.naic.org/index_about.htm> accessed 29 May 2020, and S Randall, 'Insurance regulation in the United States: Regulatory federalism and the National Association of Insurance Commissioners' (2014) 26 Florida State University Law Review 625, 626, 634–5.

[40] Articles 6(2)(b–d) and 6(4–5) IAIS Bylaws.

[41] ibid Article 6(2)(e).

[42] ibid Article 6(3).

[43] See IOSCO, *Annual Report 2018* (IOSCO, 2019) 66–8.

[44] See 'IAIS Organisation members' (*IAIS*, 2020) available at <https://www.iaisweb.org/page/about-the-iais/iais-members> accessed 29 May 2020.

[45] Section 6 IOSCO Bylaws.

[46] Article 6 IOSCO MMoU.

[47] ibid section I, Appendix B.

the IOSCO rejected the application for ordinary membership of the Securities and Exchange Commission of Zimbabwe on this ground.[48] Besides the costs of adapting domestic law to the IOSCO MMoU requirements, some African FSAs have been unable to become signatories owing to the lack of political support. For example, although the Securities and Exchange Commission of Ghana started working on adapting domestic law to the IOSCO MMoU in 2005,[49] because the Parliament of Ghana has subsequently failed to pass the relevant bills,[50] Ghana has not yet satisfied the conditions to become a signatory.[51]

IAIS members are required to pursue its mission and to carry out periodic self-assessments and peer reviews.[52] In addition, they must implement the IAIS's supervisory materials,[53] such as principles, standards, and guidance on insurance supervision;[54] however, the IAIS takes a flexible and holistic approach by allowing them to take into account 'specific market circumstances'.[55] For example, according to its Insurance Core Principles (ICPs) '[t]he framework described by the ICPs is general. Supervisors have flexibility in determining the specific methods for implementation which are tailored to their domestic context (e.g. legal and market structure).'[56] This allows African FSAs to apply IAIS's decisions in a way that better suits the conditions of their own insurance markets, hence mitigating transaction costs. This may also help explain the greater adherence of African FSAs to the IAIS than to the IOSCO.

3. Supranational African Financial Supervision and the Barriers to Africa's Effective Representation in INFSAs

The model of African economic integration, which is based on the African Regional Economic Communities (RECs),[57] is reflected in the continent's institutional system of financial regulation and supervision in which the oversight of the financial markets of a group of jurisdictions belonging to a given REC – or a sub-bloc of an REC or a combination of RECs – is often carried out by supranational

[48] Securities and Exchange Commission of Zimbabwe, *2018 Annual Report* (Securities and Exchange Commission of Zimbabwe, 2019) 4.

[49] Securities and Exchange Commission Ghana, *2005 Annual Report* (Securities and Exchange Commission Ghana, 2006) 8.

[50] See, for example, Securities and Exchange Commission Ghana, *2014 Annual Report* (Securities and Exchange Commission Ghana, 2015) 10.

[51] See '2013 List of Non-signatories to the MMoU' (*IOSCO*, 2019) available at <https://www.iosco.org/about/?subSection=mmou&subSection1=2013_list> accessed 29 May 2020.

[52] Article 6(6)(a), (c) IAIS Bylaws.

[53] ibid Article 6(6)(b).

[54] ibid Article 2(2).

[55] ibid Article 6(6)(b).

[56] IAIS, *Insurance Core Principles* (IAIS, 2018) 12.

[57] For an overview of economic integration in Africa and the role of RECs in such process see e.g. RF Oppong, *Legal Aspects of Economic Integration in Africa* (CUP, 2011) 6–29.

FSAs with a regional remit. Notable examples exist in West and Central Africa. The West African Monetary Union (UMOA)[58] has three supranational FSAs, namely the Central Bank of West African States (BCEAO),[59] the Banking Commission of the West African Monetary Union (CBUMOA),[60] and the Regional Council for Public Savings and Financial Markets (CREPMF)[61]. Likewise, the Central African Economic and Monetary Community (CEMAC)[62] also counts three supranational FSAs, namely the Bank of Central African States (BEAC),[63] the Banking Commission of Central Africa (COBAC),[64] and the Central African Securities Commission (COSUMAF)[65]. In addition, the Inter-African Conference on Insurance Markets (CIMA)[66] is the single insurance FSA of 14 jurisdictions in Central and West Africa.[67]

In this model, there is a full or very extensive delegation of regulatory, supervisory, and enforcement responsibilities from the national to the supranational level. This delegation is not only functional but also organic. Thus, the jurisdictions under the remit of these supranational regional FSAs do not have their own national FSAs and their representation in INFSAs is indirect, through supranational FSAs. For example, in the IOSCO, the UMOA and the CEMAC jurisdictions are represented by the CREPMF and the COSUMAF, respectively.[68] Likewise, in the IAIS, the jurisdictions under the CIMA supervision are all represented by CIMA.[69]

58 The UMOA (Union Monétaire Ouest Africaine) is a monetary union that comprises eight jurisdictions, see the Traité de l'Union Monétaire Ouest Africaine (signed on 20 January 2007, entered into force on 1 April 2010).

59 The BCEAO (Banque Centrale des États de l'Afrique de l'Ouest) is in charge of issuing currency, managing monetary policy, regulating and guaranteeing the supervision of the banking system in the UMOA, see Articles 11–34, Statuts de la Banque Centrale des États de l'Afrique de l'Ouest (these are annexed to, and constitute an integral part of the Traité de l'Union Monétaire Ouest Africaine).

60 The CBUMOA (Commission Bancaire de l'UMOA) is in charge of both banking supervision and resolution within the UMOA, see Article 2, Annexe à la Convention Régissant la Commission Bancaire de l'UMOA telle que Modifiée par la Décision N°010 du 29/09/2017/CM/ UMOA.

61 The CREPMF (Conseil Régional de l'Epargne Publique et des Marchés Financiers) supervises the UMOA's securities market, see Article 1, Convention Portant Création du Conseil Régional de l'Epargne Publique et des Marchés Financiers (signed on 3 July 1996).

62 The CEMAC (Communauté Économique et Monétaire de l'Afrique Centrale) is an economic and monetary community composed of six jurisdictions, see Preamble and Article 2, Traité Révisé de la Communauté Economique et Monétaire de l'Afrique Centrale (CEMAC) (signed on 30 January 2009).

63 The BEAC (Banque des États de l'Afrique Centrale) is one of the organs of the CEMAC – Article 10, Traité Révisé de la Communauté Economique et Monétaire de l'Afrique Centrale.

64 The COBAC (Commission Bancaire de l'Afrique Centrale) is one of the organs of the CEMAC – ibid Article 10 – and it is mandated to carry out banking supervision within it, see article 1 Annexe à la Convention portant création d'une Commission Bancaire de l'Afrique Centrale.

65 The COSUMAF (Commission de Surveillance du Marché Financier de l'Afrique Centrale) exercises regulation and supervision of the CEMAC securities market, see Article 2, Règlement 06/03-CEMAC-UMAC du 12 novembre 2003 portant Organisation, Fonctionnement et Surveillance du Marché Financier de l'Afrique Centrale.

66 CIMA stands for Conférence Interafricaine des Marchés d'assurance.

67 Article 1, Traité Instituant une Organisation Intégrée de l'industrie des Assurances dans les États Africains (signed on 10 July 1992, entered into force on 15 February 1995).

68 See, for example, IOSCO (n 43) 4.

69 See IAIS (n 44) 1.

This model of single representation has the advantage of allowing African jurisdictions under the scope of a given supranational FSA to have a single voice in INFSAs.[70] However, at the same time, the IOSCO and IAIS membership and voting rules put these African jurisdictions on a non-level playing field, in comparison with other jurisdictions, and, hence, they diminish the weight of Africa in decision-making processes.

As regards the IOSCO, its Bylaws determine that ordinary membership – the only membership with voting rights[71] – is reserved to national securities commissions, similar governmental bodies, or, in their absence, to provincial authorities with comparable powers[72] or even to self-regulatory organizations.[73] This membership model does not preclude a single jurisdiction from having various ordinary members.[74] At the same time, the IOSCO Bylaws generally embrace the principle of one member, one vote.[75] This gives jurisdictions with more than one ordinary member greater weight in the decision-making procedures at the IOSCO compared to jurisdictions with only one ordinary member. However, the IOSCO rules neither permit a supranational FSA to receive multiple seats nor plurality of votes, in proportion to the jurisdictions under its remit. For instance, UMOA and CEMAC jurisdictions are represented solely by the CREPMF and the COSUMAF, respectively,[76] and each of these FSAs has only one vote, even though they represent eight and six jurisdictions, respectively. Therefore, the representation of African jurisdictions under the remit of these supranational FSAs is hindered substantially.

The IOSCO's membership and voting rules put African jurisdictions under the supervision of the CREPMF and the COSUMAF in a detrimental position in comparison with other jurisdictions subject to supranational financial supervision arrangements but where there is a coexistence of both national and supranational FSAs.[77]

The IAIS's membership and voting rules are also detrimental for supranational FSAs with exclusive jurisdiction in insurance regulation and supervision, such as the CIMA. The IAIS Bylaws determine that voting membership is open to insurance FSAs,[78] not precluding the concurrent voting membership of various

[70] On the benefits of Africa acting with a single voice in the global arena see, for example, L Ndikumana, 'Why Africa needs a unified voice on the global stage' (*World Economic Forum*, 7 July 2015).

[71] Section 20(2) IOSCO Bylaws.

[72] ibid section 6.

[73] ibid section 7(1).

[74] For example, the United States has two ordinary members. Likewise, Canada, where there is no federal securities supervisor, is represented by four 'provincial' FSAs, see IOSCO (n 43) 66–8.

[75] Section 27 IOSCO Bylaws.

[76] See IOSCO (n 43) 66, 68.

[77] For example, in the European Union, Member State FSAs are ordinary members, and the European Securities and Markets Authority (ESMA) – the EU agency for securities supervision – has a separate seat as an associate member, see IOSCO (n 43) 66–8.

[78] Article 6(2)(a) IAIS Bylaws.

FSAs from the same jurisdiction; as a general rule, each member has one vote.[79] Consequently, jurisdictions represented by more than one member have greater voting power in the IAIS than the CIMA, which has only one vote.[80] This puts the CIMA Member States on a non-level playing field; for example, Australia, with two members,[81] has twice as much voting power in the IAIS than the 14 Member States of CIMA combined. The treatment of CIMA in the IAIS also contrasts with that given to the NAIC. Whilst the latter does not have voting rights,[82] it may designate up to 15 of its members, who can exercise them.[83] Both the CIMA and the NAIC are multilevel supervisory structures. Although the states represented by the NAIC have their own insurance FSAs – unlike the jurisdictions under the remit of CIMA – it is questionable whether this constitutes a fair rationale to justify such different treatment.

4. Elitist Governance as a Barrier to Africa's Effective Participation in INFSAs

The BCBS, IOSCO, and IAIS's governance structures determine the internal allocation of powers among their members. Therefore, their analysis is essential to understand the role that African FSAs play in global financial standard-setting. Such an analysis reveals an uneven treatment of FSAs, whereby those from Western jurisdictions are given control of internal structures that carry out the main standard-setting processes, whilst FSAs from 'emerging' jurisdictions are relegated to a more secondary role. This poses major problems for African FSAs to make their voices heard.

The BCBS's internal structure comprises a Committee, Groups, working groups, virtual networks and task forces, the Chair, and the Secretariat.[84] Standard-setting responsibilities fall under the remit of the Committee, which develops and adopts standards, guidelines, and sound practices.[85] The Chair plays a central role in the BCBS's internal governance, notably by directing the Committee's work.[86]

The BCBS Charter does not explicitly embrace an uneven treatment of members in the BCBS's internal governance structures as decisions are generally taken by consensus and all members have equal voting rights.[87] However, the differences

[79] ibid Article 6(3).
[80] IAIS (n 44) 1.
[81] ibid 1.
[82] Article 6(4)(a) IAIS Bylaws.
[83] ibid Article 6(4)(b).
[84] Section 7 BCBS Charter.
[85] ibid section 8(1)(b). All BCBS's members and observers have the right to appoint one representative to attend the Committee meetings but only the members have a right to vote, ibid sections 8(3)–(4).
[86] ibid section 10.
[87] ibid section 8(4).

in the number of members per jurisdiction result in some having greater voting power than others.[88] This may ultimately lead to an asymmetrical allocation of powers among jurisdictions. For example, data concerning the provenance of the BCBS's Chairs since its foundation, reveal a pre-eminence of chairs from Western economies with rather developed banking systems.[89] This suggests that jurisdictions with greater voting power may use it as a tool of control of the BCBS's internal decision-making structures.

Non-BCBS members may also engage with the BCBS through other channels. The BCBS Charter indeed embraces dialogues and consultations with non-member FSAs with a view to 'benefit from their input into the BCBS policy formulation process and to promote the implementation of BCBS standards, guidelines and sound practices beyond BCBS member countries'.[90] Non-member participation is channelled through a twofold system. On the one hand, the BCBS has instituted three ad hoc fora for debates and dialogues with non-member FSAs, namely the Basel Consultative Group (BCG),[91] the International Conferences of Banking Supervisors (ICBS),[92] and the Financial Stability Institute (FSI)[93]. On the other hand, the BCBS provides channels of cross-participation in decision-making; this is achieved through the engagement of non-member FSAs as observers in the BCBS's groups, working groups, virtual networks, and task forces[94] as well as through the involvement of the BCBS's staff in regional groups of banking supervisors.[95] Despite the BCBS Charter commitment to non-member engagement, the scope for input by African FSAs is limited, owing to two main reasons. First, two of the consultation and debate mechanisms, namely the FSI and the participation of the BCBS's staff in regional groups of banking supervisors, are primarily aimed at the provision of input by the BCBS to non-member jurisdictions on the implementation of its standards; therefore, they offer very little scope for non-member engagement with the BCBS's actual decision-making. Secondly, the presence of African jurisdictions in the other consultative mechanisms is very limited. For example, of the BCG's 43 members, only two are African, namely the

[88] The BCBS has 45 members from 28 jurisdictions. The following jurisdictions have two members: Australia, Canada, China, European Union, France, Germany, Indonesia, Japan, Korea, Mexico, Sweden, Switzerland, Turkey, and the United Kingdom. In addition, the United States has four members, see BCBS (n 17).

[89] See 'Basel Committee organisation and governance' (*BCBS*, 2020) available at <https://www.bis.org/bcbs/organ_and_gov.htm?m=3%7C14%7C573%7C73> accessed 29 May 2020.

[90] Section 2(f) and 15 BCBS Charter.

[91] According to section 15(1) of the BCBS Charter: 'The BCG ... facilitates broad supervisory dialogue with non-member authorities.'

[92] The ICBS take place every two years and are open to FSAs worldwide; they are aimed at discussing matters pertaining to banking supervision, ibid section 15(2).

[93] The FSI aims at, *inter alia*, assisting FSAs worldwide in the implementation of the BCBS's prudential standards of banking supervision, ibid section 15(4).

[94] ibid section 15(3).

[95] ibid section 15(5).

Central Bank of Tunisia and the Central Bank of West African States,[96] and whilst two other BCG members, namely the Arab Committee of Banking Supervisors and the Islamic Financial Services Board, also represent African jurisdictions, they do so in an indirect way only.[97]

The IOSCO's internal governance structure is made of the Presidents Committee, the Board, the Growth and Emerging Markets Committee, the General Secretariat, the Regional Committees, and the Consultative Committees.[98] The main standard-setting activities are carried out by the Board,[99] an organ with limited membership,[100] and subject to approval by the Presidents' Committee,[101] in which all ordinary members participate.[102]

The Board's rules give pre-eminence to jurisdictions with large securities markets. In this respect, 18 out of the 34 Board seats are reserved to 'jurisdictions with the largest markets (based on measures of equity market capitalization, debt market issuance, assets under management and derivatives trading)'.[103] Since the creation of the Board in 2012,[104] membership in this group of selected jurisdictions – termed 'nominated members'[105] – has remained almost unaltered and, due to the nature of its access criteria, which favours very large securities markets, it has never included African FSAs.[106] The remaining 16 members of the Board comprise both ex-officio members and other members appointed by the various IOSCO committees: the Chair and the two Vice Chairs of the Growth and Emerging Markets Committee (GEMC) (three seats), the Chairs and the Vice Chairs of each of the four Regional Committees (8 seats), one member elected by the GEMC among its members (one seat), and one member elected by each of the

[96] See 'Basel Committee groups' (*BCBS*, 2020) available at <https://www.bis.org/bcbs/mesc.htm?m=3%7C14%7C573%7C74> accessed 29 May 2020.

[97] ibid. Both the Arab Committee of Banking Supervisors and the Islamic Financial Services Board include members from African jurisdictions, see 'Members' (*Arab Monetary Fund, Council of Arab Central Banks Governors, Committee on Banking Supervision*, 2020) available at <https://www.amf.org.ae/en/page/members> accessed 29 May 2020; and 'List of Members: By Category' (*Islamic Financial Services Board*, 2020) available at <https://www.ifsb.org/membership.php> accessed 29 May 2020.

[98] Section 15 IOSCO Bylaws.

[99] ibid sections 40(1) and 1(2).

[100] The Board is made of 34 members and its composition is reviewed periodically, ibid section 37(1), and sections 2 and 4 of IOSCO, 'Resolution of the Presidents' Committee on the composition of the IOSCO Board' (Resolution 5/2013 as amended by Resolution 2/2015).

[101] Section 26(a) IOSCO Bylaws.

[102] ibid section 27.

[103] Section 2 Resolution 5/2013 as amended by Resolution 2/2015. For the criteria determining the largest markets see IOSCO, 'Resolution of the Presidents Committee Regarding the Framework to determine the Nominated Board Members' (Resolution 1/2019).

[104] Annex 1, IOSCO, 'Resolution of the Presidents Committee on Amendment to IOSCO's By-laws to reflect change in structure' (April 2011).

[105] Section 2, Resolution 5/2013 as amended by Resolution 2/2015.

[106] See IOSCO, 'Resolution of the Presidents' Committee on the composition of the IOSCO Board' (Resolution 5/2013); Resolution 5/2013 as amended by Resolution 2/2015; 'Resolution of the Presidents Committee on the composition of the IOSCO Board' (Resolution 1/2018); and 'Resolution of the Presidents Committee Regarding the Nominated Board Members 2019–2022' (Resolution 4/2019).

four Regional Committees among their members (four seats).[107] Both the GEMC and the Africa/Middle-East Regional Committee (AMERC) comprise African FSAs.[108] In addition, the IOSCO requires that when electing their representatives for the Board, both the GEMC and the Regional Committees 'give due consideration to ensuring representation on the Board from the largest transformative markets as well as regional and sub-regional balance', and also, that the seat elected by the GEMC is 'designated to the region that is most under-represented on the Board at the time the GEM Committee elects its representatives to the Board'.[109] Hence, the reservation of a number of seats to the members of the GEMC and the AMERC, allows African FSAs that would not in principle comply with the requirements of nominated membership, to become members of the Board. As of September 2020, the Board comprised three members from African jurisdictions, namely Egypt, Morocco, and Nigeria.[110] Despite the inclusion of members from 'emerging' jurisdictions, the latter's voting power is rather limited. Board decisions are taken by simple majority of members present;[111] as a result, the 18 nominated members, who hold a majority of seats, can exercise considerable control over decision-making.

Besides the Presidents Committee and the Board, African FSAs also participate in the AMERC, and the GEMC, which is the largest of the IOSCO's Committees, with a total of 90 voting member FSAs that represent circa 80% of the IOSCO's ordinary members.[112] The IOSCO describes the GEMC as an important element of inclusiveness that contributes to both its input and output legitimacy: 'IOSCO is the one of the few international standard-setters that has a committee dedicated to emerging market issues. This inclusiveness increases IOSCO's effectiveness and positions it to play a more significant role in shaping the global regulatory framework.'[113] In contrast with this characterization, and despite the calls for a stronger voice in the IOSCO made by emerging markets' FSAs,[114] the GEMC plays little

[107] Article 2 Resolution 5/2013 as amended by Resolution 2/2015.

[108] The GEMC includes member FSAs from Algeria, Angola, Botswana (non-voting), Cabo Verde, the COSUMAF, Egypt, Eswatini (non-voting), Ghana, Kenya, Malawi, Mauritius, Morocco, Namibia (non-voting), Nigeria, Rwanda (non-voting), Seychelles (non-voting), South Africa (one voting member and one non-voting member), Tanzania, Tunisia, Uganda, the WAMU, and Zambia, see 'Growth and Emerging Markets Committee' (*IOSCO*, 2020) available at <https://www.iosco.org/about/?subsection=display_committee&cmtid=8> accessed 29 May 2020. The presence of African jurisdictions in the AMERC is the same as in the GEMC, with the only difference that Mozambique is also a member (non-voting), see 'Africa / Middle-East Regional Committee' (*IOSCO*, 2020) available at <https://www.iosco.org/about/?subsection=display_committee&cmtid=7> accessed 29 May 2020.

[109] Article 7 Resolution 5/2013 as amended by Resolution 2/2015.

[110] 'IOSCO Board' (*IOSCO*, 2020) available at <https://www.iosco.org/about/?subsection=display_committee&cmtid=11> accessed 29 May 2020.

[111] Section 44(2) IOSCO Bylaws.

[112] IOSCO (n 43) 64 and IOSCO (n 108).

[113] IOSCO (n 43) 64.

[114] See, for example, IOSCO, 'IOSCO Emerging market regulators emphasised the need for stronger voice in shaping global regulatory reform to reflect emerging markets' position' Media Release IOSCO/MR/19/2013 (Madrid, 23 May 2013).

relevance in the IOSCO's core standard-setting activities. First, the GEMC's aim is to 'promote the development and greater efficiency of emerging securities and futures markets by establishing principles and minimum standards, providing training programs and technical assistance for members and facilitating the exchange of information and transfer of technology and expertise'.[115] This substantially limits the reach of the African FSAs' work because the GEMC's activities are directed, primarily, to its own members. In addition, the GEMC does not report to the Presidents Committee but to the Board,[116] which is largely controlled by FSAs from Western jurisdictions and has little representation from the GEMC in general and African FSAs in particular. Thus, rather than an instrument for inclusiveness in decision-making, the GEMC acts as 'a mechanism of exclusion of less sophisticated financial markets from the IOSCO's core decision-making'.[117] By means of this governance structure, the Board, dominated by a selected group of primarily Western jurisdictions, maintains control over the IOSCO's core decision-making through the development of standards of general application; at the same time, the GEMC is given a secondary role, consisting of carrying out marginal standard-setting activities of limited application – to its own members.

The limited representation of African FSAs in the IOSCO's core governance mechanisms contrasts with their readiness to assume increasing responsibilities within the organization and their active contribution to its core work. In this respect, over the years, African FSAs have expressed their concerns about their low visibility in the IOSCO and demanded greater influence and responsibilities.[118] The AMERC has played a critical role in giving voice to these concerns and in the adoption of actions aimed at fostering the representation of African FSAs in the IOSCO's work. This has been particularly the case since 2013, when Arunma Oteh, the Director General of the Securities Exchange Commission of Nigeria and then AMERC's Chair, sent a letter to the Board in which she demanded a more equitable representation of African and Middle-East FSAs within it.[119] This, indeed, became a central objective of the AMERC, whose demands played an important role in the expansion of the African FSAs' Board membership in 2014.[120] Also, Africa has taken a leadership position within the AMERC and, since 2010, all of its Chairs have come from African FSAs.[121] The willingness of African FSAs to

115 IOSCO (n 108).

116 Section 49 IOSCO Bylaws.

117 Iglesias-Rodríguez (n 3) 332–3.

118 See, for example, IOSCO, *Annual Report 2012* (IOSCO, 2013) 37; and IOSCO, *Annual Report 2013* (IOSCO, 2014) 38.

119 See, for example, IOSCO, *Annual Report 2012* (n 118) 39.

120 In 2014, Egypt and Kenya became members of the Board, see IOSCO, *Annual Report 2014* (IOSCO, 2015) 41.

121 During the period 2010–2020, the AMERC Chairs came from the Securities and Exchange Commission of Nigeria (2010–2016), the Capital Markets Authority of Kenya (2017–2020) and the Autorité Marocaine du Marché des Capitaux (since March 2020). Information on the AMERC and its chairs can be found at <https://www.iosco.org> accessed 29 May 2020.

assume greater responsibilities and exercise more influence in the IOSCO is also patent in their demands to that effect[122] and the changes in the scope of their work, which has increasingly focused on some of the IOSCO's core priority areas; for instance, in 2018, the AMERC was given responsibilities in and made important contributions to the fields of sustainable finance, fintech, and long-term market based finance, which were among the Board's main priorities.[123]

The IAIS's internal governance comprises the General Meeting of Members, the Executive Committee, with its committees and subcommittees, and the Secretariat.[124] The IAIS's approach to the allocation of responsibilities among its members is similar to that of the IOSCO. All of its standard-setting processes are led by the Executive Committee,[125] a body with limited membership[126] that comprises between 12 and 32 voting members as well as a number of non-voting members.[127] According to the IAIS Bylaws, the Executive Committee's voting members comprise two categories. One the one hand, there are members from 'standing jurisdictions',[128] which are jurisdictions with 'major global insurance markets'.[129] On the other hand, there are members chosen on the basis of regional criteria.[130] Both types of voting members are selected 'in accordance with procedures established by the Executive Committee'.[131] Although the IAIS does not disclose these procedures, the available information suggests that these may favour membership from jurisdictions with large insurance markets. First, the specific allocation of seats to members from 'standing jurisdictions' indicates a certain preference for the latter. Secondly, although the IAIS Bylaws stipulate that '[t]he Executive Committee shall be composed of an appropriate representation of the different geographic areas and different types of insurance markets, particularly in respect of the market sizes and development',[132] the IAIS's actions do not seem to embrace such diversity. For example, in 2018, the IAIS increased the number of seats of certain regions in the Executive Committee, based on 'market size and number of Members in the Region'.[133] This favoured jurisdictions with large insurance markets; for instance, whilst North America and Western Europe received two

[122] For instance, in 2017, under the Kenyan Chairmanship, the AMERC discussed with the Board on ways to foster its participation in the IOSCO's priority work, see IOSCO, *Annual Report 2017* (IOSCO, 2018) 43.

[123] IOSCO (n 43) 42.

[124] Article 9 IAIS Bylaws.

[125] Its tasks include the development of 'international principles, standards, guidance and other documents related to insurance supervision', ibid Article 14(3)(b).

[126] A member of the Executive Committee is 'a natural person who is wholly or principally employed by a Member [of the IAIS]', ibid Article 13(2).

[127] Ibid Article 13(1).

[128] Ibid Article 13(1)(a)(ii).

[129] IAIS, *The IAIS Strategic Plan 2020–2024* (IAIS, 2019) 19.

[130] Article 13(1)(a)(i) IAIS Bylaws.

[131] ibid Article 13(1)(a).

[132] ibid Article 13(5).

[133] IAIS (n 129) 19.

extra-seats each, the Sub-Saharan Africa received only one.[134] Thirdly, the analysis of the Executive Committee's composition in 2019 reveals a strong pre-eminence of major Western insurance markets. The only African insurance FSAs represented were the South African Reserve Bank–Prudential Authority (South Africa), the *Autorité de Contrôle des Assurances et de la Prévoyance Sociale* (Morocco), and the Insurance Regulatory Authority (Kenya).[135] Fourthly, whereas, as a general rule, in the Executive Committee there is only one voting member per IAIS member and per jurisdiction,[136] the special regime applicable to insurance FSAs from the United States, gives the latter, as a whole, a larger number of seats and voting power.[137] Lastly, the role of African FSAs in the IAIS's standard-making process is hindered by the default mechanism of approval of principles, standards, and guidance. In this respect, the IAIS Bylaws provide that these are adopted by the Executive Committee, unless it decides to forward such a decision to the General Meeting, or if, at least 10% of members with a right to vote at the General Meeting so request.[138] Although the adoption of principles, standards, and guidance requires the calling of a session open to all the members and a qualified majority of two-thirds of the Executive Committee's voting members,[139] African FSAs have very limited presence in the Executive Committee and an equally limited degree of influence in their adoption or in deferring the decision to the General Meeting. Whereas African FSAs represent 17% of the General Meeting's voting members,[140] and hence have the power collectively to defer the adoption of principles, standards, and guidance to it, their overall weight in the General Meeting is little. As a result, they would play a relatively marginal role in their eventual adoption by it.

As with the IOSCO, the limited representation of African FSAs in the IAIS's main governance mechanisms lies in stark contrast with their active contribution to the IAIS's core work. For example, the *Autorité de Contrôle des Assurances et de la Prévoyance Sociale* (ACAPS) from Morocco, is a member of two of the five IAIS's main committees,[141] namely the Audit and Risk Committee and the Implementation and Assessment Committee.[142] Also, in 2015, the ACAPS took the lead in holding the IAIS's annual conference in Marrakech.[143] Other African

[134] ibid.

[135] On the composition of the IAIS Executive Committee as of 28 February 2019 see 'Organisational Structure' (*IAIS*, 12 October 2019) available at <https://www.iaisweb.org/page/about-the-iais/organisational-structure> accessed 12 October 2019.

[136] Article 13(5) IAIS Bylaws.

[137] See IAIS (n 135).

[138] Article 14(6)(f) IAIS Bylaws.

[139] ibid Article 13(8).

[140] That is 26 out of 151 FSAs. See IAIS (n 44).

[141] These are committees set by the Executive Committee in accordance with Article 14(3) of the IAIS Bylaws.

[142] See 'Participation of the ACAPS in the IAIS committees and Global Seminar meetings' (*ACAPS*, 2020) available at <https://www.acaps.ma/en/l-acaps/notre-actualite/participation-acaps-iais-committees-and-global-seminar-meetings> accessed 29 May 2020.

[143] IAIS, *Newsletter 47* (IAIS, 2015).

FSAs have also played an important role in the direction of the IAIS's core work; for example, in the period 2012–2017, Jonathan Dixon – the deputy Executive Officer of the Financial Services Board of South Africa[144] – was the Implementation Committee's Chair[145] and one of the few persons in charge of the development of the IAIS's five-year strategic plan.[146] Likewise, between 2016 and 2018, Luc Noubissi – a CIMA representative – held the Vice-Chair (2016) and Chair (2017–2018)[147] positions of the Financial Inclusion Working Group.[148]

5. The AU and the Role of Africa in INFSAs

Sections 2–4 have shown that INFSAs have developed three sets of barriers aimed at maintaining the ascendancy of Western jurisdictions in global financial standard-setting, in detriment to, among others, African FSAs. These consist of barriers of access to membership, to effective representation, and to effective participation. The ascendancy of Western jurisdictions in the BCBS, the IOSCO, and the IAIS can be traced to the latter's origins; these INFSAs were created under the auspices and leadership of the Group of 10 (G-10),[149] the Securities and Exchange Commission (United States),[150] and the NAIC (United States),[151] respectively. By controlling INFSAs from the outset, Western FSAs have been able to shape their governance so as to guarantee their pre-eminence within them over time.[152] By exercising control over the INFSAs and their standard-setting processes, Western jurisdictions are able to promote global financial standards tailored to the interests of their own banking, securities, and insurance systems. At the same time, by linking membership in INFSAs to compliance with those very same standards, they encourage their adoption by African FSAs, even when this may be detrimental or burdensome for the latter.

[144] IAIS, *Newsletter 61* (IAIS, 2017) 6.

[145] The Implementation Committee is in charge of, *inter alia*, assisting in and monitoring the implementation of the IAIS's standards, see IAIS, *Annual Report 2016* (IAIS, 2017) 7.

[146] ibid.

[147] IAIS (n 145) 36; IAIS, *Annual Report 2017* (IAIS, 2018) 44; and IAIS, *Annual Report 2018* (IAIS, 2019) 37.

[148] The Financial Inclusion Working Group carries out work aimed at, amongst others, enhancing access to insurance for low income populations, see IAIS (n 145) 36.

[149] See, for example, 'History of the Basel Committee' (*BCBS*, 2020) available at <https://www.bis.org/bcbs/history.htm> accessed 29 May 2020.

[150] See, for example, AA Sommer, Jr, 'IOSCO: its mission and achievement' (1996) 17 Northwestern Journal of International Law & Business 15, 15; and European Parliament, 'The European Union's Role in International Economic Fora – Paper 6: The IOSCO' IP/A/ECON/2014-15 (2015) 9.

[151] See, for example, J Nakagawa, *International Harmonization of Economic Regulation* (OUP, 2011) 252.

[152] For a general discussion on the pre-eminence of Western jurisdictions in INFSAs and some measures adopted by the latter to enhance their legitimacy towards non-Western jurisdictions see MS Barr, 'Who's in charge of global finance?' (2014) 45 Georgetown Journal of International Law 971, 982–5.

From the point of view of African FSAs, this poses important input and output legitimacy problems. As regards input legitimacy, the burdens that they face in terms of access to and effective representation and participation in INFSAs result in standard-setting processes in which they often have little say, leading to low levels of input legitimacy. This, in turn, affects the output legitimacy of global financial standards and, consequently, their acceptance among African jurisdictions. This may, for instance, explain the low degrees of implementation of Basel III in Africa.

As was explained in the introduction, AU law acknowledges the importance of strengthening the role of Africa in global economic governance. Moreover, African FSAs have been demanding a more significant role in the work and governance of INFSAs and have shown a strong willingness to assume new tasks within them. Hence, an important question is whether and how AU law, institutions, and bodies can help to foster this goal.

First, the African Union Commission (AUC) recognizes the importance of African financial markets in the development of the continental economy and, more generally, the AU.[153] Indeed, the Agenda 2063 embraces various measures aimed at fostering the development and integration of African financial markets, such as the creation of an African Capital Market[154] which includes, *inter alia*, a Pan African stock exchange,[155] the African Investment Bank,[156] and the African Monetary Fund[157]. These measures may, in turn, have the effect of facilitating the compliance of African FSAs with the criteria to be members of INFSAs or, for existing members, to play a greater role in them.

Secondly, as regards financial regulation and supervision, the AU project embraces the creation of two supranational FSAs with a remit covering the whole African continent, namely the African Central Bank (ACB) and a Capital Markets Regulatory Authority (CMRA). The creation of the ACB is envisaged in Article 44 of the Abuja Treaty[158] and in Article 19 of the Constitutive Act. The CMRA, which is included in neither the Abuja Treaty nor the Constitutive Act, is succinctly referred to in the Agenda 2063 as part of the AU's plans for the development of African capital markets.[159] It is as yet unclear whether the ACB and the CMRA would take

[153] See, for example, African Union Commission, *Pan-African Financial Institutions. ART. 19 of the Constitutive Act of the African Union. The Founding Texts: The African Central Bank. The African Investment Bank. The African Monetary Fund* (African Union Commission Department of Economic Affairs, 2017) 22.

[154] African Union Commission (n 2) 16, 43.

[155] ibid 107, 171.

[156] ibid 96, 107. The African Investment Bank is one of the three AU Financial Institutions envisaged in Article 19 of the Constitutive Act. The other two are the African Monetary Fund and the African Central Bank.

[157] ibid 107. The African Monetary Fund is one of the three AU Financial Institutions envisaged in Article 19 of the Constitutive Act.

[158] Treaty Establishing the African Economic Community (signed on 3 June 1991, entered into force on 12 May 1994).

[159] African Union Commission (n 2) 158.

over all regulatory and supervisory responsibilities in their respective fields within the AU or if, on the contrary, they would operate under a co-regulatory/supervisory regime where FSAs of the AU Member States or of the RECs would keep certain responsibilities and maintain separate legal personality.[160] Under the current membership and voting arrangements at the BCBS, the IOSCO, and the IAIS, a supranational ACB or CMRA with exclusive competences would be treated as a single FSA. Therefore, in terms of representation in INFSAs, the AU would most likely benefit from a multilevel system of financial regulation and supervision that combines AU-level FSAs with AU Member States/RECs FSAs, as this would guarantee a multiplicity of seats and votes of African FSAs in INFSAs. However, both the ACB and the CMRA are long-term projects[161] and their impact on the position of African FSAs in global financial standard-setting, if any, will only be long-term. In the meantime, African FSAs may continue to experience the negative consequences of the BCBS's, IOSCO's, and IAIS's rules on membership, voting, and internal governance, which substantially limit their voice and power.

Thus, a reinforcement of the role of African FSAs in INFSAs would require a reform of the governance of the latter towards a more inclusive system, for example through the recognition of multiple voting rights for supranational FSAs, which are currently deemed as single jurisdictions and are given one vote only. However, ascendancy over the standard-setting processes of INFSAs brings important benefits for the controlling Western FSAs and their jurisdictions. Therefore, a change towards a more inclusive governance vis-à-vis African FSAs is unlikely to come spontaneously and may instead require the latter's coordinated activism and lobbying. Yet, besides the regional committees and working groups of INFSAs, the current institutional framework under which African FSAs operate offers limited support for coordinated action. In this respect, the only available ad hoc supranational FSAs' coordination fora are the Association of African Central Banks (AACB) and the Community of African Banking Supervisors (CABS), whose objectives include, respectively, to 'examine the effectiveness of international economic and financial institutions in which African countries have an interest and

[160] The strategy for the establishment of the ACB supports the coexistence of the ACB with Central Banks of the AU Member States and RECs, see African Union Commission and Association of African Central Banks, *Joint AUC-AACB Strategy on the Establishment of the African Central Bank (ACB)* (Joint AUC–AACB Committee Study Group, 2013) 44. When it comes to the CMRA, in addition to questions about its relationship with FSAs, it is unclear what legal mechanisms would be used to establish it and what its specific locus would be within the AU's institutional architecture, as the Agenda 2063 does not specify these matters.

[161] The ACB is to be established by 2045 and it will be preceded by the introduction of an African single currency in 2034, see African Union Commission, *Comments of Regional Economic Communities (RECs) on the Timelines for the Establishment of the African Central Bank (ACB) and AMCP Macroeconomic Convergence Criteria* (African Union Commission Department of Economic Affairs, 2020) 4, 6. The CMRA is a project that does not yet have a precise date, see African Union Commission (n 2) 98.

suggest ways of possible improvement'[162] and to 'promote the collective voice of African regulators in the international arena'.[163]

The AUC could play an important role in filling this gap through the development, within the AU's institutional framework, of a system of cooperation and coordination of African FSAs within and across financial sectors. The establishment of such a system would fall under the remit of the AUC, which includes, among others, the coordination of Member States' positions in international negotiations,[164] and the adoption of actions aimed at strengthening cooperation and coordination among them in areas of shared interest[165]. The AUC has valuable experience in coordinating African central banks through the Joint AUC–AACB Committee, which was set up in Tripoli in 2007 and whose target is to 'define a common strategy for the establishment of the African Central Bank'.[166] This Committee could serve as the basis for designing and establishing a system of African FSAs' cooperation and coordination, based on one or various committees, but with an expanded mandate that takes stock of their activities in INFSAs, and a broader scope that includes securities and insurance FSAs, as well the coordination across the three financial sectors. Such a system could bring about important benefits for both the strengthening of the position of African FSAs in INFSAs and the eventual construction of an AU market for financial services. First, as regards the former, it would offer an organized forum of debate where African FSAs could exchange views and reach common positions in areas of shared interest prior to INFSAs' meetings, including in matters regarding to their role, powers, and representation in the latter. Secondly, it could be useful for the AUC, which could benefit from specialized input by African FSAs on regulatory initiatives in the financial field and on the implementation of financial-sector aspects of the Agenda 2063, also those relating to the creation of pan-African FSAs, such as the CMRA. From the point of view of the AU, the involvement of the AUC in the setting up and running of the cooperation and coordination committee(s) – for example, through the participation of AUC representatives in their meetings – would allow the AUC to incorporate the AU's perspective into the committee(s)' discussions and, ultimately, into the international standard-setting activities in which African FSAs participate.

[162] Article 2.4 Statutes of the Association of African Central Banks (AACB) (Amended in Malabo, Equatorial Guinea on 14 August 2015).

[163] CABS, *Work Plan 2014–16* (CABS, 2014) 2.

[164] Article 3(2)(i) Statutes of the Commission of the African Union.

[165] ibid Article 3(2)(q).

[166] African Union Commission (n 153) 12. One of the main outcomes of the Joint AUC–AACB Committee was the Joint AUC–AACB Strategy on the Establishment of the African Central Bank (ACB), see African Union Commission and Association of African Central Banks (n 160).

6. Conclusion

This chapter has shown that African FSAs face important barriers to access and effectively engage in global financial standard-setting. From an African perspective, this substantially hinders the legitimacy of the standards issued by INFSAs. This chapter contends that AU law and institutions can play an important role in enhancing the position of Africa in global financial standard-setting, particularly through the development of the financial markets and institutions envisaged by the Agenda 2063, the establishment of an architecture of AU financial supervision where AU-level FSAs coexist with AU Member States' FSAs, and the creation, under the AU's institutional umbrella, of a system of organized cooperation and coordination of African FSAs.

6
The Evolution of the AU Private Business Structure

Iyare Otabor-Olubor

1. Introduction

While the mobility of natural persons and freedom of movement across Africa has engendered academic and policy debates over the years, the freedom of establishment of businesses and interconnectivity of business operations in Africa has not received much attention under African Union (AU) law.[1] A simplified and harmonized business registration framework in the AU can support a receptive business environment in its internal market, thus effectively facilitating business mobility in Africa. Article 3 of the Constitutive Act to the AU gives the Union a mandate to coordinate and harmonize policies for the attainment of AU objectives.

The Treaty Establishing the African Economic Community 1991 (Abuja Treaty) echoes the importance of trade liberalization initiatives by recommending cross-border coordination and harmonization of policies among Regional Economic Communities (RECs), while also mitigating non-tariff barriers to establishing a free trade area in Africa.[2] A transnational initiative of this nature can successfully enhance the competitiveness of African economies within the continent and globally, as laid down under the Article 3 of the Agreement Establishing the African Continental Free Trade Area (AfCFTA).[3] The AfCFTA is designed to create a single continental market for commodities and services, supported by the free movement of businesses and investment.[4] The availability of opportunities to expand and enter into new markets can become a reality under the AfCFTA regime as African

[1] Freedom of movement of persons is embodied under Article 12 of the African Charter on Human and Peoples' Rights 1982.

[2] Treaty Establishing the African Economic Community 1991 (Abuja Treaty), Article 4(1)(d) and Article 4(2)(d).

[3] Agreement Establishing the African Continental Free Trade Area (AfCFTA) 2018 available at <https://au.int/en/treaties/agreement-establishing-african-continental-free-trade-area> accessed 11 June 2020.

[4] CFTA – Continental Free Trade Area available at <https://au.int/en/ti/cfta/about> accessed 11 June 2020.

Iyare Otabor-Olubor, *The Evolution of the AU Private Business Structure* In: *The Emergent African Union Law.* Edited by: Olufemi Amao, Michèle Olivier and Konstantinos D. Magliveras, Oxford University Press.
DOI: 10.1093/oso/9780198862154.003.0007

countries take advantage of cross-border supply chains, while at the same time creating channels of employment in neighbouring countries.[5]

The AfCFTA will cover a market of 1.2 billion people and a gross domestic product (GDP) of US$ 2.5 trillion across all 55 Member States of the AU.[6] The AfCFTA will also be the world's largest free trade area since the formation of the World Trade Organization in 1995.[7] It will provide unprecedented opportunities to businesses, especially local businesses, which will enhance industrialization in Africa in line with Agenda 2063. With this consolidation, a single market offers excellent opportunities for companies, businesses, and consumers in Africa, with an estimate that the AfCFTA has the potential to boost intra-African trade by 52.3% by eliminating import duties and mitigating non-tariff barriers.[8]

The AfCFTA is dependent on intra-African business practices such as a standardized internal market process which invariably includes the mobility and registration of businesses. In September 2015, the AU launched the Agenda 2063 blueprint for the transformation of Africa through structural reforms and promotion of economic growth mechanisms.[9] This reforming ideology reinforces the spirit of Pan-Africanism for economic independence in Africa through an integrated, sovereign, independent, and self-reliant continent while promoting the management and connectivity of cross-border resources.[10] The AU and its RECs have been created to enhance sustainable economic development in the AU Member States. Their purpose reinforces the overarching aim of the AEC principles and objectives to facilitate the free movement of goods and services and the liberalization of trade. The harmonization of national policies to promote community activities, in this case the recognition and operation of private business entities across Africa, remains a primary objective of the Abuja Treaty.[11]

These priorities are aligned with the need to foster a standard trade policy that can govern the activities of African multi-national business enterprises,[12] and to meet the expectations of the AU Minimum Integration Programme (MIP) based on the level of integration activities of each REC.[13] The realization of the AU MIP

[5] L Abrego, MA Amado, and others, 'The African Continental Free Trade Agreement: Welfare Gains Estimates from a General Equilibrium Model' (IMF Working Paper WP/19/124, 2019) 4.

[6] African Continental Free Trade Area: Questions & Answers (African Trade Policy Centre of the Economic Commission for Africa) available at <https://www.uneca.org/sites/default/files/PublicationFiles/qa_cfta_en_230418.pdf> accessed 11 June 2020.

[7] ibid.

[8] Is the African Continental Free Trade Area a Game Changer for the Continent? (IMF Regional Economic Outlook: Sub Saharan Africa 2019) available at <https://www.imf.org/~/media/Files/Publications/REO/AFR/2019/April/English/ch3.ashx?la=en> accessed 11 June 2020.

[9] African Union, Agenda 2063 – The Africa We Want (African Union Commission, September 2015) available at <https://au.int/sites/default/files/documents/36204-doc-agenda2063_popular_version_en.pdf> accessed 11 June 2020.

[10] ibid Aspiration 2, p 4.

[11] Treaty Establishing the African Economic Community 1991 (Abuja Treaty), Article 4(2)(e).

[12] ibid Article 4(2).

[13] African Union, Minimum Integration Programme available at <https://au.int/en/ea/ric/mip> accessed 11 June 2020.

initiative, and the Abuja Treaty, in the advancement of regional economic development and integration in Africa, puts intra-African trade and elimination of non-tariff barriers as a priority sector for consideration.[14] The removal of non-tariff trade barriers and enhancement of ease of doing business in the RECs, such as the harmonization of registration processes, satisfies the objectives of the AU MIP.[15] These objectives may be met by Article 25 (1) of the Abuja Treaty which makes provisions for the establishment of technical committees, such as the committee on industry, and the committee on trade, customs, and migration matters. However, no committee was set up to support the development of legal texts or agreement with regards to the transnational harmonization of business laws in the AU.[16] The absence of a legal committee set up to draft a continental agreement on the harmonization and standardization of business law leads us to seek existing solutions elsewhere.

2. International and Continental Standards on the Harmonization and Recognition of Private Business Structures

The business environment is conditioned by a variety of legal institutions that directly affect how businesses are created.[17] In the last decades, coordinated efforts for economic liberation and policy implementation in Africa were designed to improve conditions for doing business.[18] The rules on business registration and formation vary in the AU.[19] Doing business can contribute to the improvement of quality of living because entrepreneurs in the market economy produce innovative goods and services that enhance the living standards of workers, consumers, and other key stakeholders in the society.[20] Acquiring information about these diverse national forms requires a concerted effort of time and expertise. Coupled with the unpredictability of the African courts, alleged corruption of the judicial systems, and challenges in the enforcement of rights,[21] the African business environment

[14] African Union, Minimum Integration Programme (May 2009) para 2.1.1 available at <https://au.int/en/ea/ric/mip> accessed 11 June 2020.

[15] ibid.

[16] F Amao, *African Union Law: The Emergence of a Sui Generis Legal Order* (Routledge, 2018) 71–2.

[17] PO Pederson and D McCormick, 'African business systems in a globalising world' (1999) 37 Journal of Modern African Studies 109.

[18] V Amavilah, S Asongu, and others, 'Effects of globalization on peace and stability: implications for governance and the knowledge economy of African Countries' (2017) 112 Technological Forecasting and Social Change 91.

[19] SA Asongu, 'Challenges of doing business in Africa: a systematic review' (2019) 2 Journal of African Business 259.

[20] SA Alvarez, JB Barney, and others, 'The poverty problem and the industrialization solution' (2015) 32 Asia Pacific Journal of Management 23.

[21] S Mancuso, 'The new African law: beyond the difference between common law and civil law' (2008) 14 Annual Survey of International and Comparative Law 39, 40.

appears to be a poisoned chalice for entrepreneurs in Africa and international investors. The key to understanding the types of businesses challenges in Africa may lie in the variety of economic, political, and socio-cultural institutions that influence the way businesses operate.[22]

Low regulatory barriers and harmonized business standards represent some of the nexus of international business laws. The production of cross-border business law is purportedly directed towards creating a transnational legal order. It is transnational as far as it facilitates a discernible legal pattern capable of transcending multiple nation states,[23] primarily when it represents an outcome socially fashioned by its domestic and regional actors.[24] In addition to local actors in Africa, international organizations are essential in the critical episodes of global business law-making encompassing law of e-commerce, franchise law, secured transactions law, international carriage of goods, commercial contracts, and many others.[25] It is upon these subject matters that successful campaigns of intergovernmental organizations generate global norms through a wide range of technical legal instruments from conventions to model laws, principles to legislative guides. These global norms can be substantive. They can take different forms to convey the norms they seek to establish. They are usually international instruments – hard law or soft law, or other sub-denominational frameworks such as best practice guidelines, and standards.[26]

Regional organizations such as the European Union[27] and the Association of Southeast Asian Nations (ASEAN)[28] have attempted to coordinate business registration standards and rules through the vehicle of their respective law-making organs. In Africa, the closest that has been achieved to an inter-regional reform of private business registration is the Organisation pour l'Harmonisation en Afrique du Droit des Affaires (OHADA) framework.[29] It established a partially

[22] Pederson and McCormick (n 17) 110.

[23] L Niklas, *A Sociological Theory of Law* (Routledge, 1985).

[24] B Moller, 'The African Union as a Security Actor: African Solutions to African Problems?' (LSE Crisis States Research Centre Working Paper 57, August 2009).

[25] WF Hanrieder, 'International organizations and international systems' (1966) 10 Journal of Conflict Resolution 3.

[26] S Block-Lieb and TC Halliday, *Global Lawmakers: International Organisations in the Crafting of World Markets* (CUP, 2017) 230.

[27] Small Business Act available at <https://ec.europa.eu/growth/smes/business-friendly-environment/small-business-act/> accessed 28 June 2020.

[28] ASEAN set up a Policy Blueprint for SME Development (2004–2014), which provides the overarching framework to facilitate small and medium-sized businesses (SMEs) development in South East Asia specifically to support simplification of business registration procedures and the adjustment of its policy and regulatory frameworks. This Blueprint was supported by the ASEAN Strategic Action Plan for SME Development (2016–2025) to further strengthen the establishment of businesses in the ASEAN region available at <https://asean.org/storage/2012/05/3-SAP-SMED-Final.pdf> accessed 28 June 2020.

[29] This initiative was as a result of OHADA adopting the Uniform Act relating to General Commercial Law (Acte Uniforme Sur le Droit Commercial General) available at <http://www.droit-afrique.com/upload/doc/ohada/Ohada-Acte-Uniforme-2010-droit-commercial.pdf> accessed 28 June 2020.

simplified statutory regime for small businesses managed by an entrepreneur (the 'entreprenant'). To effect valid registration of the 'entreprenant' business, the entrepreneur needs to submit a written declaration to the Trade and Personal Property Credit Register (Registre du Commerce et du Crédit Mobilier). Harmonized rules for simplification that pertain to SMEs are also included under article 13 of the Uniform Act Organising and Harmonising Undertakings' Accounting Systems in the Member States to the Treaty on the Harmonisation of Business Law in Africa (Acte uniforme portant organisation et harmonisation des comptabilités des enterprises).

Additionally, OHADA successfully adopted the Acte Uniforme Relatif au Droit des Sociétés Cooperatives, which designed special provisions for simplification of cooperatives ('sociétés cooperatives simplifiées').[30] Also, OHADA revised its Uniform Act Relating to Commercial Companies and Economic Interest Groups (Acte uniforme relatif au Droit des Sociétés Commerciales et du Groupement d'Intérêt Economique), which provides for different laws establishing and regulating multiple corporate enterprises.[31] The *travaux préparatoires* of the revised Act suggest reducing the minimal capital requirement and limiting the role of the notary in establishing a company as well as developing new company forms.[32]

Under Article 53 of the OHADA Treaty, the adoption of the Uniform Acts is open to any AU Member State and to states outside the AU who are invited to join by mutual agreement of State Parties. The generality of this framework is essential because, in the context of African unity, states may join OHADA even if they are not members of the AU. However, this comes with several challenges, as seen in the case of *Kevin Mgwanga Gunme et al. (on behalf of Southern Cameroons) v The Republic of Cameroon*.[33] This case concerned the purported violation of several provisions of the African Charter on Human and Peoples' Rights (ACHPR), including those that discriminated against Southern Cameroonian businesses from opening bank accounts where they were not registered under OHADA law and also where their company documents were not translated into French.[34] The African Charter of Human Rights (ACHR) recommended that the Republic of Cameroon abolishes all discriminatory practices against Southern Cameroonians, including those practices against businesses.[35]

[30] Acte Uniforme Relatif au Droit des Sociétés Cooperatives, Part II, Title 1 – Provisions specific to the different categories of cooperative societies.

[31] The Revised Act was adopted in Ouagadougou on the 30 January 2014.

[32] Laurence Boy, 'Les Limites du Formalisme du Droit de l'OHADA à la Sécurisation des Enterprises' (2002) 1 Revue de l'ERSUMA 1. See Selected Activities of International and Intergovernmental Organizations to Promote micro, Small and Medium-sized Enterprises (UNCITRAL Working Group I Twenty-second Session, 10–14 February 2014) 7.

[33] *Kevin Mgwanga Gunme and others (on behalf of Southern Cameroons) v. The Republic of Cameroon* Comm No 266/2003 (2009) ACHPR 99.

[34] ibid.

[35] ibid.

The significance of this decision gives priority to the AU institutions over OHADA institutions and laws where OHADA laws are inconsistent with the rights of persons in Africa, including juridical persons under AU instruments such as the ACHPR.[36] This decision demonstrates the superiority of AU law to OHADA law in the context of interpretation and application of regional laws in Africa. This decision contributes to this discussion that in the absence of an African legal order such as an AU legal committee to establish a uniform law applicable to business establishments and recognition of their right of abode in Africa, the creation of a uniform agreement to create an enabling business environment for the registration and recognition of private businesses in the AU is critical to the realization of the primary objectives of the Abuja Treaty and the AfCFTA.

Further, other AU instruments such as the Convention on Cross-Border Cooperation (Niamey Convention) 2014, inspired by the AU Constitutive Act 2000, sets forth a framework aimed at promoting and strengthening cross-border relations within the jurisdiction of two or more African states, including the conclusion of agreements and arrangements to facilitate cross border trade.[37] The Niamey Convention serves to promote cross-border cooperation, at a local, sub-regional, and regional level. Following the objectives of the Niamey Convention in the promotion of socio-economic development and the institutional development of projects and programmes in Africa,[38] harmonization of registration of private business structures fills a significant socio-economic void in the plight of African. Consequently, in the absence of a universal AU regional agreement to govern the creation and registration of businesses, international strategies on business registration and harmonization will be discussed.

It is based on these frameworks that harmonized rules in the registration of private businesses in the AU are recommended to promote transparency, predictability, and consistency. To this end, an AU Business Registration Agreement will be proposed to act as a reform toolkit and reference framework for national governments in Africa. Discussions will include existing business registration procedures, such as pre-registration, registration, and post-registration, in Africa, including the challenges that entrepreneurs face in multiple African countries. The World Bank Doing Business 2020 report provides secondary empirical data for analysing the current obstacles in the registration of private businesses. An analysis of these data is followed by a consideration of international best practices and reform of registration of private entities. The ongoing work of Working Group I of the United Nations Commission on International Trade Law (UNITRAL) is further discussed. Finally, a proposal for an AU Business Registration Agreement according to the objectives of the Niamey Convention and the AfCFTA to coordinate

[36] Amao (n 16) 81.
[37] Niamey Convention 2014, Article 1.
[38] ibid Article 3.

cross-border business registration in Africa will be critically analysed. The role of the World Bank and UNITRAL, as global actors, in the creation and modernization of international business laws will first be brought into consideration within the framework of an emerging AU law.

3. The World Bank Doing Business 2020 Report on African Countries

At the forefront of these inter-regional and global campaigns for business reform is the World Bank and its five associated institutions,[39] with bilateral donors and regional development banks acting as major participants.[40] The significant long-term goal of the World Bank is to end extreme poverty by decreasing the percentage of people throughout the world living on less than US$ 1.90 a day to no more than 3% and to promote collective prosperity by fostering the income growth of the bottom 40% of the population in every country.[41] It is clear from this that the World Bank is concerned with economic development and good governance reforms.[42] This ambition can be further reflected in the Doing Business report, a global initiative of the World Bank that seeks to encourage institutional reforms by providing objective benchmarks against these institutions to policy-makers and governments.[43] This report is arguably one of the most comprehensive sources of literature on a wide range of economic issues to encourage governments to undertake a broad degree of discretion in selecting the appropriate means of action to reforming their circumstances.[44] The World Bank emphasizes the relevance of economic freedom to do business that goes hand in hand with economic development and a thriving private sector, thereby capable of mitigating poverty and achieve shared prosperity.[45]

The latest edition of this report is Doing Business 2020, which, among other quantitative business indicators, recommends an efficient and inclusive ethos for

[39] The International Bank for Reconstruction and Development (IBRD), International Development Association (IDA), International Finance Corporation (IFC), Multilateral Investment Guarantee Agency (MIGA), International Centre for Settlement of Investment Disputes (ICSID).

[40] The regional development banks include the Inter-American Development Bank (IADB), the Asian Development Bank (the ADB), the African Development Bank (AfDB), the European Bank for Reconstruction and Development (EBRD), and the Asian Infrastructure Investment Bank (AIIB).

[41] World Bank Group, What We Do available at <https://www.worldbank.org/en/about/what-we-do> accessed 28 June 2020.

[42] L Tshuma, 'The political economy of the World Bank's legal framework for economic development' (1999) 8(1) Social & Legal Studies 75, 81.

[43] YS Tang, 'The international politics of legal reforms: hard bilateralism, soft multilateralism and the World Bank's 'doing business' indicators' (2017) 60(1) Revista Brasileira de Política Internacional 1, 5.

[44] ibid.

[45] World Bank, 'Doing Business 2020 – Sustaining the Pace of Reforms' (24 October 2019) available at <https://www.worldbank.org/en/news/feature/2019/10/24/doing-business-2020-sustaining-the-pace-of-reforms> accessed 28 June 2020.

entrepreneurship and business in the best interest of all societies.[46] Adopting efficient administrative procedures and less bureaucratic bottlenecks can facilitate entrepreneurship and enterprise innovation among businesses. This report may be overstretching the immediate possibilities in the context of Africa primarily since it represents one of the least developed regions in the world by an account of the Development Assistance Committee (DAC) list of Official Development Assistance (ODA) countries.[47] According to a recent Organisation for Economic Co-operation and Development (OECD) report, Africa receives the highest net ODA disbursements (52 USD million) based on the number of aid recipient countries, with Ethiopia, Nigeria, and Tanzania scoring the highest in African countries receiving international financial aid.[48] With economic challenges endemic to Africa, alleviating these problems through coordinated efforts to enhance entrepreneurship and innovative enterprise and make creating businesses in Africa as easy as possible is critical to the continent's long-term survival.

Several African countries continue to require the involvement of third-party professionals including lawyers, notaries, or accountants in the registration of a business to ensure regulatory compliance.[49] On average, the cost of third-party involvement in the registration process of businesses in Africa (including sub-Saharan African countries and African countries that comprise of the MENA region) equates to 15–20% of the average household income per capita.[50] On the other hand, third-party involvement represents up to 46% on the average of the overall cost of starting a business. The use of professional third parties correlates with a lack of transparency of business registration laws and complex and inconsistent registration processes which increase the cost of formalizing businesses, thus stifling opportunities for potential entrepreneurs to expand their businesses into other African markets. Also, in some jurisdictions in Africa, the minimum paid-in capital is mandatory, which represents the start-up financial obligation that entrepreneurs must deposit in a recognized financial institution or with a notary when registering a business.

[46] Doing Business 2020 is the 17th in a series of annual studies that progressively investigates the regulations that enhance and challenges that influence business activities. See complete Doing Business 2020 report available at <https://openknowledge.worldbank.org/handle/10986/32436> accessed 28 June 2020.

[47] E Mahembe and NM Odhiambo, 'Foreign aid, poverty and economic growth in developing countries: a dynamic panel data causality analysis' (2019) 7 Cogent Economics & Finance 1; see OECD DAC List of ODA Recipients: Effective for Reporting on 2020 Flows available at <http://www.oecd.org/dac/financing-sustainable-development/development-finance-standards/DAC-List-of-ODA-Recipients-for-reporting-2020-flows.pdf> accessed 28 June 2020.

[48] Development Aid at a Glance (OECD Statistics by Region, 2019) 2–3, see <https://www.oecd.org/dac/financing-sustainable-development/development-finance-data/Africa-Development-Aid-at-a-Glance-2019.pdf> accessed 28 June 2020.

[49] CM Coste, ML Delion, and others, 'The involvement of third-party professionals in business registration and property transfer' (World Bank Indicators Group Research Note, Research and Development Centre No. 2, October 2019) 1.

[50] ibid 2.

Evidence suggests that regulatory reforms lessening the burden to start a formal business are associated with increases in the number of newly registered businesses.[51] Easy and formal registration leads to higher levels of employment and productivity. Doing Business 2020 report data suggest that there is an apparent disparity that persists between low- and high-income economies on the ease of registering a business.[52] An entrepreneur in a low-income economy typically spends about 50% of income per capita to launch a company, compared to just 4.2% for an entrepreneur in a high-income economy.[53] With the majority of African countries being underdeveloped,[54] it is pertinent to discuss their business registration procedures.

4. World Bank Data on the Registration of Business in African Countries

Doing Business 2020 report lists 190 countries.[55] Among the top 100 countries, African countries accounted for just 10. Of the 10 countries, two are categorized under the Middle East and North African (MENA) region,[56] while eight are classified under the Sub-Saharan African Region.[57] The World Bank did not subcategorize African countries based on their membership of RECs.[58] To diversify the analysis, eight countries outside the top 100 globally ranked economies, drawn from the eight RECs in Africa, will be discussed accordingly. The study will be conducted under the two main regional categories of countries representing (or 'partly representing', in the case of the MENA region) Africa, as outlined by the World Bank. Essentially, the two regional categories that will be analysed are the MENA region comprising Libya, Egypt, and Djibouti; and Sub-Saharan region consisting of Zimbabwe, Burundi, Gabon, Lesotho, and Nigeria.

[51] M Motta, AM Oviedo Silva, and others, 'An Open Door for Firms: The Impact of Business Entry Reforms' (World Bank View Point Public Policy for the Private Sector, June 2010).

[52] Tracking Burdensome Regulation (World Bank Doing Business 2020 – Sustaining the Pace of Reforms, October 2019) 6.

[53] L Klapper and I Love, 'The Impact of Business Environment Reforms on New Firm Registration' (World Bank Policy Research Working Paper 5493, December 2010).

[54] DAC List (n 47).

[55] World Bank Doing Business 2020 available at <https://www.doingbusiness.org/en/rankings> accessed 28 June 2020.

[56] The 10 countries include Mauritius (Rank 13), Rwanda (Rank 38), Morocco (Rank 53), Kenya (Rank 56), Tunisia (Rank 78), South Africa (Rank 84), Zambia (Rank 85), Botswana (Rank 87), Togo (Rank 97), Seychelles (Rank 100). See Region Profile of Middle East and North Africa (MENA) (Doing Business 2020 Indicators) 4 available at <https://www.doingbusiness.org/content/dam/doingBusiness/media/Profiles/Regional/DB2020/MENA.pdf> accessed 28 June 2020.

[57] Region Profile of Sub-Saharan Africa (Doing Business 2020 Indicators) 4 available at <https://www.doingbusiness.org/content/dam/doingBusiness/media/Profiles/Regional/DB2020/SSA.pdf> accessed 28 June 2020.

[58] M Musah and PS Magai, 'Effects of regional economic community integration on regional trade in Africa: the case of regional economic communities' (2019) 22 Business Management Review 119.

5. The Middle East and North Africa (MENA) Regional Experience with Business Registration

The minimum capital requirement to start a formal business in Libya is 3,000 Dinars (1,600 GBP).[59] This fee represents 30% of the income per capita of Libyan workers. This requirement can be contrasted with other comparator AU MENA countries such as Algeria and Tunisia, where the minimum paid-in capital to form a business is nil.[60] The procedures, time, and cost to start a business in Libya are relatively cumbersome in that a third-party professional, a notary, is required to facilitate the formation of the business entity. The entire process may take up to 10 days to be completed after successful authorization from the relevant Ministry. Stamp duty is also payable, which may cost the founders up to 70 Dinars.

Egypt performed better than Libya in the Doing Business global ranking, where it scored 114.[61] Registration of a business 'Sharikat Zat Massouliyyah Mahdoodah', does not require a minimum capital requirement, which may be responsible for Egypt's higher global ranking score ahead of Libya. For the ease of starting a business section, Egypt ranked in the top 100 where it scored 90, eclipsing Libya at 164. However, the Egyptian legal system requires a married woman to seek the permission from her spouse before she can officially register a business.[62] While there is no minimum capital requirement to register a business in Egypt, there are several regulatory obligations and fees. They include fees with the submission of tax cards, payment of notary public fees and lawyer syndicate fees, chambers of commerce fees, and registration with the National Authority of Social Insurance.[63] To expedite the registration process, it costs EGP 7,500 (360 GBP). Value-added tax (VAT) registration is free in Egypt.

Djibouti is one of the smallest countries in Africa with a population of about 865,000 as of 2011.[64] Of its total population, 23% are living in extreme poverty.[65] There is no paid minimum capital requirement to start a formal business in Djibouti. The use of third-party professional, for example a notary or legal

[59] Libya is a member of the Arab Maghreb Union in the MENA region. Its Doing Business 2020 overall ranking is 186 out of 190 global economies.

[60] Economy Profile of Seychelles Doing Business 2020 Indicators available at <https://www.doingbusiness.org/content/dam/doingBusiness/country/a/algeria/DZA.pdf> accessed 27 June 2020. Economy Profile of Tunisia Doing Business 2020 Indicators available at <https://www.doingbusiness.org/content/dam/doingBusiness/country/t/tunisia/TUN.pdf> accessed 27 June 2020.

[61] Egypt is a member of the Community of Sahel-Saharan States (CEN-SAD) in the MENA region.

[62] Economy Profile of Egypt Arab Rep. Doing Business 2020 Indicators available at <https://www.doingbusiness.org/content/dam/doingBusiness/country/e/egypt/EGY.pdf> accessed 24 June 2020.

[63] See Economy Profile of Egypt, 8–9; see also D Vittas, 'The Role of Non-Bank Financial Intermediaries in Egypt and other MENA Countries' (Development Research Group World Bank, 1997).

[64] Djibouti is a country in the MENA region and a member of Intergovernmental Authority on Development (IGAD). Its Doing Business 2020 overall ranking is 112.

[65] Djibouti – Country Partnership Strategy for the Period FY2014–2017 (World Bank Country Partnership Framework Report No 83874, March 2013).

practitioner, is widespread, although it is not mandatory.[66] There is a five-step process for registering a private business in Djibouti which includes reserving the name with Registre du Commerce et des Sociétés (ODPIC), registering the business in the Companies Registry, the publication of notice of commencement of trading, registration of articles with the hôtel des impôts, and tax registration. The overall cost of income per capita needed to formalize a business amounts to about 39%,[67] and the period required to complete the registration process is approximately 14 days.

6. Sub-Saharan African Regional Experience with Business Registration

Economic growth in the entire Sub-Saharan African region was projected at 2.9% in 2019, up from 2.5% in 2018.[68] Nonetheless, Sub-Saharan Africa continues to underperform and remains one of the weakest performing regions on the World Bank Doing Business report with an average score of 51.8, ranking significantly below the OECD high-income economy average of 78.4 and the global average of 63.0.[69] Indeed, not all Sub-Saharan African countries have experienced economic growth. In Zimbabwe, abject poverty is estimated to have increased from 29% in 2018 to 34% in 2019, following an increase in population from 4.7 to 5.7 million people.[70] Zimbabwe is ranked 140 out of 190 comparator countries in the Doing Business 2020 report.[71] The financial cost of registering a business requires about 76% of an entrepreneur's income per capita; however, there is no minimum paid-in capital requirement to register a business.[72] There is a nine-step process for registering a business in Zimbabwe, including a workplace premises inspection, which needs to be completed by licensing officers.[73] This process means that where a

66 See Economy Profile of Djibouti Doing Business 2020 Indicators, available at <https://www.doingbusiness.org/content/dam/doingBusiness/country/d/djibouti/DJI.pdf> accessed 24 June 2020.

67 The cost to register is DJF 18,000 registration fees (immatriculation), DJF 5000 name reservation, DJF 1000 service fee of the Guichet Unique, DJF 10,000 for the registration of the articles of association, and DJF 1000 per page for the stamp duty, totalling 151 GPB.

68 *Global Economic Prospects: Heightened Tensions, Subdued Investments* (World Bank Group Flagship Report, June 2019) 121–2.

69 Doing Business 2020: Comparing Business Regulations in 190 Countries (World Bank, October 2020) 11 available at <https://russian.doingbusiness.org/content/dam/doingBusiness/pdf/db2020/Doing-Business-2020.pdf> accessed 24 June 2020.

70 *The World Bank in Zimbabwe* (World Bank Group, October 2019) available at <https://www.worldbank.org/en/country/zimbabwe/overview> accessed 24 June 2020.

71 Zimbabwe is a member of the Common Market for Eastern and Southern Africa (COMESA), an REC in Africa.

72 Economy Profile of Zimbabwe Doing Business 2020 Indicators available at <https://www.doingbusiness.org/content/dam/doingBusiness/country/z/zimbabwe/ZWE.pdf> accessed 28 June 2020.

73 ibid.

business intends to carry out commercial activities in more than one workplace, the various workplaces will have to be inspected individually.

Burundi is a low-income country of the Sub-Saharan African region, ranking at 166 out of 190 countries in the Doing Business 2020 report.[74] Its ease of starting a business score (92.9) exceeds the Sub-Saharan regional average (80.1).[75] Burundi possesses a one-stop-shop (OSS) formation process in the Investment Promotion Agency,[76] which significantly streamlines the registration of businesses, thus easing the procedural requirements for entrepreneurs. Registration fee payments can be paid to a designated representative of the Commercial Bank of Burundi (BANCOBU), and registration with the National Institute for Social Security. They are both located within the OSS. Documents required to be submitted include photographs of business partners (if any), identity documents of partners, and business formation document. While the OSS system is favourable to entrepreneurs, it may prove inaccessible to businesses in other parts of Burundi that need to register their business, since they will need to visit Bujumbura, the location of the OSS, to effect legal registration. This inaccessibility could ultimately prove to be expensive and time-consuming for a start-up business with relatively limited capital.

Gabon is another low-ranked country in the Doing Business 2020 report, at 169.[77] There is a paid-in minimum capital requirement to register a business in Gabon. However, the number of procedures needed to complete registration is not high, compared to the Sub-Saharan regional average. The founder of the business or notary public (a third-party professional) is required to carry out registration of the business with the Agence Nationale de Promotion des Investissements (ANPI-Gabon).[78]

In other parts of Sub-Saharan Africa, Lesotho and Nigeria were ranked at 122 and 131 respectively on the Doing Business score.[79] The Starting a Business global indicator ranks Lesotho at 84 while Nigeria is ranked at 86. The number of procedures necessary to start a business in both jurisdictions is relatively similar, however in Nigeria, registration of a business can be achieved electronically through the online system administered by the Corporate Affairs Commission (CAC).[80] Other requirements in Nigeria include preparation and submission of incorporation

[74] Burundi is a member of the East African Community (EAC), an REC in Africa.

[75] Economy Profile of Burundi Doing Business 2020 Indicators available at <https://www.doingbusiness.org/content/dam/doingBusiness/country/b/burundi/BDI.pdf> accessed 28 June 2020.

[76] K Karuretwa and A Marusic, 'The Curious Case of Business Registration Reforms in Burundi' (World Bank Group Report No 91280, June 2014) 1–2.

[77] Gabon is a member of the Economic Community of Central African States (ECCAS), an REC in Africa.

[78] Economy Profile of Gabon Doing Business 2020 Indicators available at <https://www.doingbusiness.org/content/dam/doingBusiness/country/g/gabon/GAB.pdf> accessed 28 June 2020.

[79] Lesotho is a member of the Southern African Development Community (SADC), while Nigeria is a member of the Economic Community of West African States (ECOWAS).

[80] OR Ola, 'Is Nigeria's Corporate Affairs Commission serious about online registration' (2019) 40 Company Lawyer 1.

(memorandum and articles of association), payment of stamp duties, a sworn declaration before a notary public or commissioner for oaths with the help of a legal practitioner, VAT registration, and registered proof of business premises.[81] There is no online filing in Lesotho but the procedures are mainly carried out at an OSS Business Facility Centre, which involves the application for an operational license and payment of the business registration fee at the Accounting Section.[82]

7. The Need for Reform

The above analyses demonstrate the need to harmonize business registration procedures in Africa. The Doing Business 2020 report measures these procedures, including time and cost for a small to a medium-size entity to establish and operate formally in their respective economies. While this Report reinforces the earlier presumptions that registration of businesses in African countries involves inconsistent procedures that may prevent the ease of doing business, the controversy is further magnified where businesses seek to carry out activities in other African market economies. The processes involved in business registration are conflicting and sometimes financially unfavourable to entrepreneurs wishing to expand into other markets. The impact of the inconsistencies of the diversified business registration laws will consequentially obstruct the free flow of cross-border trade across Africa.

A reform of this nature will reflect the ambitious initiatives of the AfCFTA, including the need for AU countries to cooperate in all trade-related areas.[83] Cooperation will require a significant effort from African leaders to coordinate an implementation plan while focusing on priority areas and realigning the AU structures, organs, and agencies to address the problems inherent in cross-border business creation and registration.

> Reform does not start with the Commission. It starts and ends with the leaders, who must set the right expectations and tempo. The effectiveness of the African Union, after all, is our business and responsibility.[84]

[81] Economy Profile of Nigeria Doing Business 2020 available at <https://www.doingbusiness.org/content/dam/doingBusiness/country/n/nigeria/NGA.pdf> accessed 28 June 2020.

[82] Economy Profile of Lesotho Doing Business 2020 available at <https://www.doingbusiness.org/content/dam/doingBusiness/country/l/lesotho/LSO.pdf> accessed 28 June 2020.

[83] AfCFTA, Article 4(d).

[84] HE Kagame, Imperative to Strengthen Our Union: Report on the Proposed Recommendations for the Institutional Reform of the African Union (29 January 2017) 7 available at <https://au.int/en/documents/20170129/report-proposed-recommendations-institutional-reform-african-union> accessed 6 June 2020.

Following the Kagame Report 2017, it has been recommended that the AU should prioritize the reform of institutions that impede on economic integration (including the Continental Free Trade Area) with effective collaboration between the AU, RECs, Member States, and other continental institutions.[85] Article 4 of the Niamey Convention 2014 also states that parties should endeavour to solve legal and administrative impediments that can hamper the functioning of cross-border cooperation in the AU region with an emphasis on the need for parties to coordinate with one another to ensure that integration is achieved.[86]

A piecemeal reform is being proposed to tackle this endemic problem in the form of an AU Agreement on Business Registration to harmonize legal business formation procedures in Africa. The Business Registration Agreement will not have a supranational authority but rather will act as a toolkit and reference framework for national governments to implement appropriate business reforms in their respective RECs. It will be an established set of principles based on international best practices for the registration of private business enterprises in Africa. It will carefully follow the recommendations of United Nations Commission on International Trade Law (UNCITRAL) Working Group I on Micro, Small and Medium-Sized Enterprises (MSMEs) (MSME Working Group).[87]

8. The UNCITRAL MSME Working Group

UNCITRAL states that a modern statutory regime for simplified business entities should begin with a focus on the commercial needs of the smallest business entities and avoid placing unnecessary legal and administrative burdens on them.[88] The MSME Working Group aims to promote inclusiveness of businesses by ensuring that entrepreneurs are included in a simple business registration regime, regardless of whether such entrepreneurs might be engaged in relatively simple commercial activities, including those transacting in the extra-legal economy.[89] Intelligently, the MSME Working Group has provided no standardized definition of an MSME.

[85] Kagame Report 2017, 11.

[86] Niamey Convention 2014, Article 4(1).

[87] United Nations Commission on International Trade Law available at <https://uncitral.un.org/en/working_groups/1/msmes> accessed 6 June 2020. The Working Group was created following the Commission's agreed mandate that work on international trade law aimed at reducing the legal obstacles faced by micro, small, and medium-sized businesses globally, especially in developing economies. The Commission also agreed that such work should commence with matters concerning the ease of incorporation and registration, see Report of the United Nations Commission on International Trade Law (A/68/17 Forty-sixth Session, 8–26 July 2013) 72.

[88] Draft Legislative Guide on an UNCITRAL Limited Liability Organization (Working Group I MSMEs Thirty-third Session, Vienna, 7–11 October 2019) para 5. The acronym 'UNLLO' is a temporary name given to a simplified business form during the Working Group's Twenty-seventh Session (para 43, A/CN.9/895).

[89] Report of Working Group I on the Work of its Twenty-second Session (New York, A/CN.9/800, 10–14 February 2014) para 24.

This is to allow countries and RECs to decide for themselves what an MSME should comprised, based on their economic parameters and national circumstances.[90]

Many small businesses in Africa predominantly operate within the informal sector (extra-legal economy), and they contribute a significant share to Africa's national income and employment.[91] However, informality could perpetuate non-compliance with business laws and weaken the rule of law, thus increasing the risk of tax avoidance, and sustain corruption, thereby constituting a hostile environment for investment and trade.[92] It has been indicated that MSMEs in the informal sector need a legal basis on which to engage in trade at the international level. The need for greater harmonization in the area of creating an enabling legal environment for such enterprises is vital.[93] The need for harmonization is apparent following the Report of the High-Level Panel of Eminent Persons on the Post-2015 Development Agenda where it revealed that businesses generally want a simplified regulatory framework, which makes it easy for entrepreneurs to set up, operate, and close a business.[94]

There are many commercial benefits for entrepreneurs to enter the formal economy. These benefits include wide visibility to the public and the internal market in Africa wherein registration of a business in the business registry can provide exposure to potential investors and clients, thus profiting from the international marketplace. Secondly, improved visibility to official banking systems can facilitate financial inclusion, for example access to bank accounts, loans, and revolving lines of credit. Thirdly, businesses can secure their innovations through market identity with a unique trading name and intangible personal property created in the course of doing business.[95]

Thus, the Business Registration Agreement will offer the AU Member States the choice to adapt their rules in line with best practice guidelines. This modern approach to business law reform would arguably achieve a greater level of harmonization capable of facilitating intra-African trade. As previously seen in the latest Doing Business report, many African states already have existing, but differing, formal legal business structures. These states could choose to implement, in a

[90] Reducing the Legal Obstacles Faced by Micro, Small and Medium-sized Enterprises (Working Group I MSMEs Thirtieth Session, New York, 12–16 March 2018) 5.

[91] L Medina, A Jonelis, and others, 'The Informal Economy in Sub-Saharan Africa: Size and Determinants' (IMF Working Paper WP/17/156, July 2017).

[92] AM Oviedo, MR Thomas, and others, 'Economic Informality: Causes, Costs, and Policies – A Literature Survey' (World Bank Working Paper 167, June 2009).

[93] United Nations General Assembly: Observations by the Government of Colombia (UNCITRAL Working Group I MSMEs, Twenty-second Session, New York, A/CN.9/WG.I/WP.83, 10–14 February 2014).

[94] A New Global Partnership: Eradicating Poverty and Transform Economies through Sustainable Development (The Report of the High-Level Panel of Eminent Persons on the Post-2015 Development Agenda, May 2013) available at <https://www.post2020hlp.org/wp-content/uploads/docs/UN-Report.pdf> accessed 28 June 2020.

[95] ibid.

piecemeal manner, the recommendations of the Business Registration Agreement by amending provisions of their existing laws to sustain modern business registration procedures based on international best practice guidelines.[96] Before embarking on analysing the business registration best practice guidelines provided by UNCITRAL, against this backdrop, the features of recent AU regulations as they affect cross-border business enterprises will be discussed.

9. AU Regulations on Harmonization of Business and Trade Practices (AfCFTA Trade in Services Protocol, and the Niamey Convention 2014)

The African RECs have identified trade liberalization as a priority area to facilitate business operation for economic integration.[97] However, the East African Community (EAC), in particular, has actively championed this objective to harmonize trade facilities in its sub-region.[98] The AfCFTA has taken the lead to implement a wholesale liberalization of trade in services to facilitate and coordinate the efforts undertaken by individual countries and their regional RECs.[99] To effect consistency and transparency in the reform of trade procedures, Article 16 of the AfCFTA outlines the need for AU countries to publicize promptly, through accessible mediums, domestic laws, regional laws, regulations, and procedures of general application for the need to promote transparency.[100] This information could be published through an official gazette, newsletter, or website in an official AU language. However, State Parties to the AfCFTA are not mandated to disclose confidential information that may be contrary to public interest or information which may interfere with the legitimate business interest of enterprises, whether private or public.[101]

Consistency and transparency in the creation of a harmonized Business Registration Agreement are further supported by the AfCFTA Protocol on Trade in Services (TIS Protocol). The TIS Protocol has been inspired by Article 4(2) of the Abuja Treaty that supports the gradual removal of obstacles to the free movement of persons, services, goods, and capital among the AU Member States. It promotes the right of residence and establishment.[102] The TIS Protocol seeks to create a

[96] Best Practices in Business Registration (UNCITRAL Working Group I Twenty-third Session, Vienna, 17–21 November 2014) available at <https://undocs.org/en/A/CN.9/WG.I/WP.85> accessed 28 June 2020.

[97] W Olayiwola, E Osabuohien, and others, 'Economic Integration, Trade Facilitation and Agricultural Exports Performance in ECOWAS Sub-Region' in M Ncube, I Faye, and others (eds), *Regional Integration and Trade in Africa* (Palgrave Macmillan, 2015).

[98] East African Community Trade Policy Review (WTO Doc WT/TPR/G/384, 13 February 2019).

[99] RY Simo, 'Trade in services in the African Continental Free Trade Area: prospects, challenges and WTO compatibility' (2020) 23 Journal of International Economic Law 65, 71.

[100] AfCFTA Article 16(1).

[101] ibid Article 16(2).

[102] Treaty Establishing the African Economic Community 1991 (Abuja Treaty), Article 4(2)(i).

transparent, inclusive, and integrated single market to liberalize trade in services to capitalize on the potential and capacities of business suppliers, at the micro, small, and medium scales, that can engage in African and global value chains.[103] Trade in services under the TIS Protocol means the supply of service – such as production, distribution, marketing, sales, and delivery of a service – from the location of a State Party into the territory of another State Party.[104] A significant barrier to the facilitation of trade in services is a restriction on freedom of establishment which could take the form of lack of market access to foreign businesses and limitations on the recognition of foreign businesses and their activities in regional markets.[105] The TIS Protocol provides little guidance on the recognition of divergent business practices that operate in the AU region, including those businesses participating in cross-border trade.

The treatment of divergent practices in cross-border trade and harmonization in the AU has been clarified under the Niamey Convention.[106] Article 7 prescribes that the AU Member States should harmonize their existing laws with the Convention and ensure that local authorities in the Member States are informed of the cross-border trade opportunities available to them. The mechanism through which cross-border cooperation between the Member States can be developed is by the creation of legal frameworks while taking into account the transplantation of the recommendations of the Convention into the development of domestic national policies and reform strategies.[107] An agreement will have the force of cross-border cooperation, capable of accelerating integration in Africa. Cross-border cooperation is defined as:

> any act or policy aimed at promoting and strengthening good neighbourly relations between border populations, territorial communities and administrations or other stakeholders within the jurisdiction of two or more states, including the conclusion of *agreements* and arrangements useful for this purpose.[108]

An AU Agreement on Business Registration represents an excellent legal framework to harmonize private business registration systems in Africa. Aligned with the provisions of the TIS Protocol and the Niamey Convention, recommendations for the creation of an AU legal framework on business registration is further discussed in the next section.

103 AfCFTA Protocol on Trade in Services.
104 ibid Article 1(o–p).
105 Simo (n 99) 72.
106 The Niamey Convention 2014 has been signed by 17 AU countries. Five signatories (Togo, Benin, Burkina Faso, Niger, Mali) have ratified the Convention.
107 Niamey Convention 2014, Article 8(1).
108 ibid Article 1.

10. Recommendations for an AU Agreement on Business Registration

In the Doing Business 2020 report, it was reported that business registration procedures across African countries could be inherently complex and they vary across these countries. As indicated, some states require a minimum paid-up capital before the commencement of trading, while others require the involvement of third-party professionals. UNCITRAL provides several best-practice benchmarks that modern business registries should consider implementing.[109] At the bare minimum, the AU should consider the implementation of these vital benchmarks which can be achieved through the proposed Business Registration Agreement, for respective law reform bodies and governments in African countries. Article 5 of the Niamey Convention requires the AU Member States to cooperate and share information and intelligence towards the harmonization of law. The following recommendations, following the UNCITRAL Working Group I best practice guidelines, and the Niamey Convention, should be considered in the drafting of an AU Business Registration Agreement.

Recommendation 1: *A Structured Regulation of Business Registration and Payable Fees*

Simplification and accessibility are prime characteristics of operating a business.[110] It is established that the registration of businesses in Africa entails some form of fees payable to the registries such as stamp duties, general registration fees, and value added tax. These processes can be unnecessarily complicated. The charges are collected for revenue generation, which can place a heavy financial burden on businesses. Countries that support best practice, such as Togo, take the opposite approach by admitting as many registered entities into the formal sector, thereby deriving revenue from the tax, with any fees set at a standardized level that encourages business registration.[111] Other reformed countries in Africa, such as Malawi, abolished registration fee requirements altogether, which is the recommended approach.[112] Fees that pertain to annual subscriptions in the company database registry can be counterproductive because they do not relate directly to

[109] Report of the United Nations Commission on International Trade Law (A/68/17 Forty-sixth Session, 8–26 July 2013) 71; Report of Working Group I on the work of its Twenty-second Session (New York, 10–14 February 2014) para 65.

[110] Draft Legislative Guide on an UNCITRAL Limited Liability Organization (Working Group I Thirty-third Session, 7–11 October 2019) para 11.

[111] See for example Togo which ranks first in Africa (15th worldwide) in Starting A Business benchmark under the Doing Business 2020 global ranking, Economy Profile of Togo Doing Business 2020 available at <https://www.doingbusiness.org/content/dam/doingBusiness/country/t/togo/TGO.pdf> accessed 26 May 2020.

[112] See Economy Profile of Mauritius Doing Business 2020 available at <https://www.doingbusiness.org/content/dam/doingBusiness/country/m/mauritius/MUS.pdf> accessed 27 May 2020.

the registration activities and they may affect the ability of the business to maintain its registered status. It is recommended that the Business Registration Agreement should provide a standardized fee structure, and where possible, advise against registration fee collection.

Recommendation 2: *Standardisation of Documents Required for Registration without Third-party Interference*

The Business Registration Agreement should provide a standard registration form for businesses to complete without the involvement of third-party professionals, for example a lawyer or notary public.[113] In the first instance, this form should be provided in the official languages of the AU – English, Arabic, French, Portuguese, Spanish, Kiswahili, and any other African language.[114] A standard form will cut down on administration errors, reduce workload at registries, and speed up the business registration process. Samples of correctly completed registration forms can be made available on the business registry websites of the AU Member States. Also, they may be uploaded from the AU website. Since the use of third-party professional services is expensive, it may constitute a very high percentage of the overall cost of registration.[115] A reformed system should eliminate the mandatory use of third-party professionals,[116] thereby leading to a standardized and predictable registration process. However, it is recommended that upon excluding the services of the notary or legal practitioner, supportive procedures to ensure the integrity of the registered information provided by the business should be established by a designated AU body.

Recommendation 3: *Reduce the Cost or Remove the Need for a Minimum Capital Requirement*

A minimum capital requirement represents a financial obligation in the pre-registration phase of a business. These costs are usually evidenced by a bank deposit instrument or with a notary before a business is legally registered.[117] For example, in Central African Republic (CAR), the cost associated with registration

[113] Draft Model Law on a Simplified Business Entity (UNCITRAL Working Group I Twenty-fourth Session, A/CN.9/WGI/WP.89, April 2015) para 20.

[114] Protocol on Amendments to The Constitutive Act of the African Union, Article 11. See available at <https://au.int/en/about/languages> accessed 26 May 2020.

[115] See Economy Profile of Somalia Doing Business 2020 available at <https://www.doingbusiness.org/content/dam/doingBusiness/country/s/somalia/SOM.pdf> accessed 26 May 2020.

[116] A Conrad, *International Encyclopedia of Comparative Law: Business and Private Organisations*, Vol. XIII (Detlev Vagts edn, Mohr Siebrek Ek, 1998) 2 and 13.

[117] A simple private business should function as flexibly as legally possible from the strict rules applicable to public companies including simpler registration procedures and nominal or no minimum capital requirement – see Legal Questions Surrounding the Simplification of Incorporation (UNCITRAL Working Group I Twenty-third Session, A/CN.9/WG.I/WP.86, November 2014) para 22.

of business include XAF 100,000 paid-in minimum capital requirement; XAF 1,000 towards procurement of resident certificate; XAF 50,000 towards registration with the chamber of commerce; and XAF 10,200 towards obtaining a business license.[118] In total, it could cost a new business up to XAF 162,000 (approximately 239 GBP) to register its entity in CAR. The is a financial burden for micro and small businesses, and more so for businesses in regional countries attempting to export their services into CAR. The function of the minimum capital requirement can work against poorer entrepreneurs, which may indirectly exacerbate poverty, thereby leading to delayed registration and, ultimately, loss of business opportunities. UNCITRAL acknowledges that while the minimum capital requirement may, at face value, protect creditors and investors, it does not truly fulfil any specific regulatory function to protect the stakeholders in the event of business failure.[119] Likewise, the requirement does not protect a business from suffering insolvency, and neither does it protect stakeholder investors from risky investments in new firms.[120] In light of this observation, it is recommended that the Business Registration Agreement should not make this requirement mandatory, but instead, urge creditors and investors to carry out due diligence either through forensic auditing or other corporate governance monitoring systems.[121]

Recommendation 4: *One-stop Shop (OSS) Single Interface, Electronic Registration and Interconnectivity of National Business Registries*

An OSS can eliminate the business registration processing time. This reform objective is inspired by the need to set up a single interface for entrepreneurs to receive the required procedures and submit the completed information to set up their business, rather than visiting several agencies that may not be in the same locality.[122] Unfortunately, one-stop shops are not prevalent in Africa; however, they serve a critical economic function by increasing the number of registered businesses, due to a speed-up in registration time. The view from UNCITRAL is that not all OSS have been successful, with some reforms creating more registration procedures instead of streamlining them.[123] To avoid this malaise, the relevant national business authorities in Africa need to set up coherent organizational improvements by the appointment of a standalone agency as their access point

[118] See Economy Profile of Central African Republic Doing Business 2020 available at <https://www.doingbusiness.org/content/dam/doingBusiness/country/c/central-african-republic/CAF.pdf> accessed 26 May 2020.
[119] UNCITRAL Best Practices in Business Registration (n 96) para 28.
[120] Why Are Minimum Capital Requirements a Concern for Entrepreneurs? (World Bank Doing Business 2014) available at <https://www.doingbusiness.org/en/reports/case-studies/2013/why-are-minimum-capital-requirements-a-concern-for-entrepreneurs> accessed 28 June 2020.
[121] UNCITRAL Best Practices in Business Registration (n 96) para 28.
[122] Reforming Business Registration: A Reform Toolkit for the Practitioners (World Bank 2013) 9.
[123] UNCITRAL Best Practices in Business Registration (n 96) para 40.

through which other appropriate governmental agencies may operate. For this to work effortlessly, an electronic registration solution will need to be adopted by the respective national OSS. The Business Registration Agreement will need to stress the importance of electronic registration because manual processes require physical space to store business data. It can be time-consuming to register if not conducted electronically and arguably more expensive in the long run. Electronic submission of registration particulars enhances information security, data integrity, transparency, and compliance.[124]

For a truly integrated and electronic business registration system to work in Africa, the use of a unique AU/REC business registration number is critical. Introduction of a unique business registration number can facilitate information sharing across national jurisdictions in Africa. This concept of business registration information sharing is not new. It was adopted by an EU Directive that requires the Member States to ensure that companies and their branches should have a unique identifier 'to be unequivocally identified' in the system to enhance communication between European business registries.[125] The adoption of unique identifiers for business registration in Africa will allow government agencies to track new and existing companies and to confirm the information submitted for registration. A reform of this scale can significantly improve the quality of the information provided in the registration particulars since the unique identifiers ensure the accuracy of the data submitted about the business.[126]

11. Implementing the AU Business Registration Agreement

The AU Member States should collaboratively apply the provisions of the Niamey Convention,[127] in particular they should set up cooperative agreements with authorities and policymakers in their respective RECs, in conformity with the domestic laws of their states.[128] To ensure the full participation of African policymakers in the economic integration of the continent, the Pan-African Parliament (PAP) has been given an overriding interest to facilitate and oversee the implementation of AU policies, objectives, and programmes (such as the Niamey

[124] Reforming Business Registration: A Reform Toolkit for the Practitioners (World Bank 2013) 10.

[125] Directive 2012/17/EU of the European Parliament and of the Council, 13 June 2012, amending Council Directive 89/666/EEC and Directives 2005/56/EC and 2009/101/EC of the European Parliament and of the Council as regards the interconnection of central, commercial, and companies registers.

[126] UNCITRAL Best Practices in Business Registration (n 96) paras 33–36.

[127] The Niamey Convention 2014 has been signed by seventeen AU countries and is available at <https://au.int/en/treaties/african-union-convention-cross-border-cooperation-niamey-convention> accessed 18 July 2020.

[128] Niamey Convention 2014, Article 8(3).

Convention).[129] The PAP is vested with possible legislative powers that may include working towards the harmonization and coordination of the laws of AU Member States,[130] as well as promote the coordination and harmonization of policies, measures, programmes, and activities of the RECs.[131]

The successful implementation of the Business Registration Agreement will depend on the legal environment to accommodate market access for businesses. Article 19 of the TIS Protocol to the AfCFTA specifies that each AfCFTA party will be able to conduct its business in any signatory Member State and should not be treated less favourably than other businesses operating in the country of establishment.[132] To implement the harmonization of a standardized business registration law and policy in the AU, the AU Commission would be required to promote the Business Registration Agreement through cooperative measures with the RECs using the AU Border Programme (AUBP) as a framework.[133] The primary goal of AUBP is to reinforce the integration process in the respective RECs,[134] including other large-scale cooperation initiatives such as the currently proposed Business Registration Agreement to harmonize business registration processes.

Also, AU Member States should be encouraged to sign and ratify the Niamey Convention,[135] which in turn would facilitate the swift adoption of the Business Registration Agreement. So far, 17 AU countries have signed the Niamey Convention,[136] which demonstrates long-term commitment of AU Member States to cooperate on cross-border matters. Through each REC, a Regional Border Consultative Committee should be established to develop the adoption of the Business Registration Agreement under Article 9 (2) of the Niamey Convention. Each committee will act in an advisory capacity to create stakeholder awareness about the need to adopt the Business Registration Agreement following international best-practice guidance and AU law. The committees will examine the business registration challenges faced by micro and small businesses in the facilitation of intra-African trade in the AU and suggest solutions, including the four recommendations already highlighted.[137] These suggestions can be referred to the PAP for consideration into final adoption.

[129] The PAP originated from the Abuja Treaty 1991, which was created to establish a parliament to ensure that African nationals are involved in the race for economic development and integration of Africa.

[130] Protocol to the Treaty Establishing the African Economic Community Relating to the Pan-African Parliament 2001, Article 11(3).

[131] ibid Article 11(7).

[132] See also TIS Protocol, Article 20.

[133] Niamey Convention, Article 9(1).

[134] African Union Border Programme (AUBP) available at <https://archives.au.int/handle/123456789/4982> accessed 29 June 2020.

[135] Niamey Convention, Article 9(1).

[136] The 17 countries that have signed the Niamey Convention are: Benin, Chad, Comoros, Congo, Gabon, Ghana, Guinea-Bissau, Guinea, Mali, Mozambique, Mauritania, Namibia, Nigeria, Niger, Sao Tome & Principe, Togo, and Zambia. See Status List available at <https://au.int/en/treaties/african-union-convention-cross-border-cooperation-niamey-convention> accessed 27 June 2020.

[137] Niamey Convention, Article 9(4)(e–f).

12. Conclusion

Harmonization of business registration procedures through the vehicle of an AU Business Registration Agreement will serve the purpose of achieving convergence towards a harmonized AU business registration process. The Business Registration Agreement will serve as a continuum of different formal legal business structures in Africa. It will operate as a reference framework and practical toolkit for national governments to reform existing rules that create regulatory and administrative burdens on micro and small businesses. Additionally, its adoption will contribute to the overall success and growth of micro and small businesses by freeing financial resources for innovation and entrepreneurship across African countries. The implementation of the Business Registration Agreement will act as a catalyst towards a favourable continental-wide intra-African trade policy and potentially a uniform business law regime.

7

Contextual Centrality of Institutional Arbitration Framework for AU Legal Order

Onyeka K Osuji and Oluwafikunayo D Taiwo

1. Introduction

One of the main objectives of the African Union (AU) is to 'accelerate the political and socio-economic integration of the continent' (Article 3(c) of AU Constitutive Act). With a number of small (landlocked) countries, economies, and markets combined with low per-capita income levels and insubstantial populations,[1] Africa's integration could increase cross-border trade, boost productivity and shape it into a global economic force.[2] The AU has pursued this objective in initiatives such as the African Continental Free Trade Agreement 2018 (AfCFTA) and draft Pan-African Investment Code (PAIC) 2016.[3] While the PAIC refers to the AU Constitutive Act's aim of 'fast tracking the political and socio-economic integration of' Africa, Article 3(a) of AfCFTA contains a general objective of deepening 'the economic integration of the African continent and in accordance with the Pan African Vision of "[a]n integrated, prosperous and peaceful Africa" enshrined in Agenda 2063'. To underscore the importance of regional integration, the AU has undertaken to establish an African Economic Community (AEC) by 2034[4] with AfCFTA as precursor.

Regional integration, though seen as a rational response to the difficulties faced by the continent, has largely failed to yield expected benefits. Regional trade agreements (RTAs) were initially targeted at facilitating Africa's post-colonial unity and subsequently graduated to promoting democracy, preventing regional conflicts, and, eventually, economic objectives.[5] An exponential increase in African

[1] United Nations Conference on Trade and Development, *UNCTAD Annual Report 2007: Thinking Development, Advancing Solutions* (UNCTAD/DOM/2007/3).

[2] P Brenton and I Gözde (eds), *De-Fragmenting Africa: Deepening Regional Trade Integration in Goods and Services* (World Bank, 2012).

[3] African Union Commission, Economic Affairs Department (2016). Draft Pan-African Investment Code, December 2016.

[4] Protocol to the Treaty establishing the African Economic Community relating to Free Movement of Persons, Rights of Residence and Right of Establishment 2018. Treaty Establishing the African Economic Community 1991.

[5] J de Melo and Y Tsikata, 'Regional Integration in Africa: Challenges and Prospects' (2014) 93(2) Document de traivail Politiques de Developpement 4.

Onyeka K Osuji and Oluwafikunayo D Taiwo, *Contextual Centrality of Institutional Arbitration Framework for AU Legal Order* In: *The Emergent African Union Law.* Edited by: Olufemi Amao, Michèle Olivier and Konstantinos D. Magliveras, Oxford University Press. DOI: 10.1093/oso/9780198862154.003.0008

RTAs[6] from the Lagos Plan of Action to the recent AfCFTA may suggest greater involvement in international trade. African countries, however, remain on the sidelines of the global economy, as evident from the continent's low level of intraregional trade and declining share in global production and trade. While the reasons may not be far-fetched, the role of dispute resolution to the success of Africa's integration has received little attention.

While it may be true that regional integration is 'a political project'[7] for the AU, some legal dimensions,[8] including alternative dispute resolution (ADR), are critical for the efficient operation of its legal order and achievements of its objectives. The need for a formal system, which resolves disputes arising from the interpretation and application of legal obligations and objectives, cannot be over-emphasized. The longer-term viability of an economic integration arrangement that promotes the existence of political institutions which allow Member States to reach decisions about how to implement treaty obligations and objectives without an effective dispute resolution mechanism is doubtful.[9]

Adeleke, for example, recently identified difficulties associated with investor–state dispute settlement in the African context[10] such as costs, exclusivity of compensatory damages remedy, inadequate consideration of multiple (including African-specific) public law issues, and even outright disregard of national laws and public policies. Adeleke's proposals include improving domestic legal systems to make African countries attractive to foreign investment, inter-state investment dispute settlement, political risk insurance to reduce disputes, and a role for regional human rights tribunals in investment disputes.[11] While PAIC appears to incorporate the first two proposals, AU law manifests legal infrastructure fragility for ADR. Contrary to the need for context-specific approaches as highlighted by the Third World Approaches to International Law (TWAIL),[12] there are no substantive

6 See T Hartzenberg, 'Regional Integration in Africa' (2011) available at <http://dx.doi.org/10.2139/ssrn.1941742> accessed 24 July 2020; SO Oloruntoba, *Regionalism and Integration in Africa: EU-ACP Economic Partnership Agreements and Euro-Nigeria Relations* (Palgrave Macmillan, 2016); T Chidede, 'The right to regulate in Africa's international investment law regime' (2019) 20 Oregon Review of International Law 437–68.

7 T Mkandawire, 'Political Will, Democracy: Imperatives for Regional Integration in Africa' (African Development Bank Group, 2013).

8 RF Oppong, *Legal Aspects of Economic Integration in Africa* (CUP, 2011); JT Gathii, *African Regional Trade Agreements as Legal Regimes* (CUP, 2011); JR Rudahindwa, *Regional Developmentalism through Law: Establishing an African Economic Community* (Routledge, 2018).

9 C O'Neal Taylor, 'Dispute resolution as a catalyst for economic integration and an agent for deepening integration: NAFTA and MERCOSUR?' (1996–1997) 17 Northwestern Journal of International Law and Business 850, 851.

10 F Adeleke, *International Investment Law and Policy in Africa: Exploring a Human Rights Based Approach to Investment Regulation and Dispute Settlement* (Routledge, 2018) 46–73.

11 ibid, 74–109.

12 MW Mutua and A Anghie, What is TWAIL? (2000) 94(5–8) Proceedings of the Annual Meeting (American Society of International Law 31–40; BS Chimni, Third world approaches to international law: a manifesto (2006) 8 International Community Law Review 3–27; U Natarajan, J Reynolds, and others, Introduction: TWAIL – on praxis and the intellectual (2016) 37(11) Third World Quarterly 1946–56.

and institutional provisions for ADR in the Constitutive Act or other instrument of the AU. It is potentially problematic to leave such matters to dispute resolution under the contemporary international economic law dominated by the more developed economies with neoliberalism at its core.[13] The United Nations Human Rights Council, for instance, has noted the 'inherently asymmetric nature'[14] of the dispute settlement system of international economic law, including the arbitration of investment disputes which features prominently in international instruments like the New York Convention,[15] the ICSID Convention,[16] and UNCITRAL Arbitration Rules[17].

Another difficulty is the adoption of international economic models that may be unsuited for Africa's regional integration. Existing bilateral investment treaties (BITs) are weighted against African countries, including their ability to regulate investors.[18] These BITs 'are distorted because they often reflect the agenda of a developed country treaty party'.[19] Even intra-African BITs lack critical African-specific 'public policy exceptions'[20] and regional investment treaties reflect neoliberal orientations that are alien to the continent.[21] The PAIC is an example. On the one hand, the PAIC shows that the AU is not simply relying on the global

[13] See H Chang, *Bad Samaritans: The Secret of Rich Nations and the Threat to Global Prosperity* (Random House, 2007); A Anghie, The evolution of international law: colonial and postcolonial realities (2006) 27(5) Third World Quarterly 739–53; BS Chimni, Capitalism, imperialism and international law in the twenty-first century (2012) 14(1) Oregon Review of International Law 17–45; K Miles, *The Origins of International Investment Law: Empire, Environment and the Safeguarding of Capital* (CUP, 2013); BS Chimni, *International Law and World Order: A Critique of Contemporary Approaches*, 2nd edn (CUP, 2017); J Linarelli, ME Salomon, and others, *The Misery of International Law: Confrontations with Global Injustice in the Global Economy* (OUP, 2018).

[14] United Nations Human Rights Council (2019), UN experts send a letter to the UNCITRAL Working Group III on Investor-State Dispute Settlement (ISDS) Reform, urging systemic changes to the ISDS system, 7 March 2019, OL ARM 1/2019, [1], available at <https://www.ohchr.org/Documents/Issues/Development/IEDebt/OL_ARM_07.03.19_1.2019.pdf> accessed 24 July 2020. See also United Nations Human Rights Council (2019), UN experts send a letter to the UNCITRAL Working Group III on Investor-State Dispute Settlement (ISDS) Reform, urging systemic changes to the ISDS system, 7 March 2019, OL ARM 1/2019, [2(b)] available at <https://www.ohchr.org/Documents/Issues/Development/IEDebt/OL_ARM_07.03.19_1.2019.pdf accessed 24 July 2020; UN Human Rights Council (2018), *Report of the Working Group III (Investor-State Dispute Settlement Reform) on the work of its Thirty-sixth Session* (Vienna, 29 October–2 November 2018) A/CN.9/964, [102].

[15] United Nations, *Convention on the Recognition and Enforcement of Foreign Arbitral Awards* adopted on 10 June 1958. United Nations Treaty Series (1959), Vol 330, 38, No 4739

[16] Convention establishing the International Centre for Settlement of Investments Disputes (ICSID), signed in Washington DC on 14 October 1966. Article 54(1).

[17] United Nations Commission on International Trade Law (2013), *UNCITRAL Arbitration Rules* Available at <https://uncitral.un.org/sites/uncitral.un.org/files/media-documents/uncitral/en/uncitral-arbitration-rules-2013-e.pdf> accessed 10 May 2021.

[18] DA Collins, 'A new role for the WTO in international investment law: public interest in the post-neoliberal period' (2010) 25(1) Connecticut Journal of International Law 1, 2; E Denters and T Gazzini, 'The role of African Regional Organizations in the promotion and protection of foreign investment' (2017) 18 Journal of World Investment and Trade 451, 481.

[19] Adeleke (n 10) 156.

[20] ibid.

[21] Rudahindwa (n 8) 27.

ICSID convention[22] and it reflects a trend towards 'Africanization'.[23] Its sustainable development objective is commended for highlighting 'Africa-specific and innovative features' and 'an attempt by African countries to shape an international investment treaty according to their own priorities'.[24] On the other, PAIC does not depart much from the neoliberal orientations[25] of prevailing international economic order, especially with regards to dispute settlement. While a precise global investment law is non-existent,[26] neoliberalism is the dominant approach.

The question, consequently, is whether a pan-African approach to investment arbitration and commercial arbitration can create a more conducive atmosphere for regional integration? The AU Constitutive Act implicitly acknowledges the importance of legal infrastructure for regional integration by also providing for the objectives of promoting 'democratic principles and institutions' (Article 3(g)) and establishing 'necessary conditions which enable the continent to play its rightful role in the global economy and in international negotiations' (Article 3(i)).

Accordingly, Article 4(f) of AfCFTA refers to a specific objective of establishing a dispute settlement mechanism (DSM) to be administered in accordance with a Protocol on Rules and Procedures on the Settlement of Disputes (DSM Protocol) (Article 20). The DSM Protocol is, however, limited to inter-state disputes going by the definitions of 'dispute' (Article 1(e)) and classes of party (Article 1(h)(i)(j)), making it inapplicable to investor–state and non-state commercial disputes. On the other hand, the PAIC's Preamble suggests 'the need for a comprehensive guiding instrument on investment for all' AU Member States. While the PAIC signals an emergent recognition of the role of arbitration and other ADR methods, its limited scope does not create an appropriate regional institutional framework the regional integration vision requires through the instrumentality of the AU. A well-designed dispute resolution system for regional integration needs to consider economic goals sought by Member States, their political constraints, and international institutions' perceptions.[27] A system that addresses these factors may contribute better to the achievement of goals than one that seeks to express the complexity of the situation and the parties' negotiating power.[28]

22 Convention on the Settlement of Investment Disputes Between States and Nationals of Other States, 14 October 1966, 575 UNTS 159.

23 M Mbengue, 'The quest for a Pan-African investment code to promote sustainable development' (2016) 5(5) Bridges Africa available at <https://www.ictsd.org/bridges-news/bridges-africa/news/the-quest-for-a-pan-african-investment-code-to-promote-sustainable> accessed 24 September 2019; MM Mbengue and S Schacherer, 'The "Africanisation" of international investment law: The Pan-African Investment Code and the reform of the international investment regime' (2017) 18 Journal of World Investment and Trade 414; Chidede (n 6) 448.

24 M Mbengue, (n 23).

25 Rudahindwa (n 8) 27.

26 OG Repousis, 'Multilateral investment treaties in Africa and the antagonistic narratives of bilateralism and regionalism' (2017) 52 Texas International Law Journal 313, 325

27 O'Neal Taylor (n 9) 851.

28 M Reisman and M Weidman, 'Contextual imperatives of dispute resolution mechanisms' (1995) 29(6) Journal of World Trade 5, 10

This chapter therefore proposes an institutional framework for arbitration within the AU legal order to facilitate its objectives of deepening regional integration and promoting Africa's development. The chapter demonstrates that the potentially costly and problematic nature of transnational disputes will hinder intra-Africa trade, interaction, and economic development, and other objectives in the AU Constitutive Act and pursued via AfCFTA, the PAIC, and other regional integration initiatives. The success of these initiatives depends, to a large extent, on the availability, legitimacy, and effectiveness of arbitration and other ADR mechanisms. We argue that the development of an African model of transborder arbitration is viable and more likely to gain widespread legitimacy and acceptability and will lead to robust and efficient resolution of horizontal and vertical disputes. The institutional framework developed here encompasses both investment and commercial arbitration, which is a departure from the exclusive focus on investment arbitration in existing RTAs and other initiatives.

This chapter makes several original contributions, including to the New Regionalism Approach[29] and emergent AU law. While it builds on previous studies on regional integration and development, the chapter frames transborder arbitration within AU law and its regional integration goal. Unlike existing works, it examines the need for formal institutional structures for arbitration within AU law, including its location within the AU's judicial and enforcement procedures. For example, while it highlights the importance of domestic investment regulation and regional investment agreements, Adeleke's work is limited to investor–state dispute settlement and even then, its focus is on promoting human rights, sustainable development, and public interests within international investment law.[30] Moreover, this chapter's unique outline of a pan-African arbitration model includes its application to investment and commercial disputes and provisions for arbitration rules, non-contractual arbitration, arbitration seat, and recognition and enforcement of arbitral awards.

The rest of this chapter is organized as follows. First, Africa's regional integration and dispute resolution initiatives are analysed in their historical and contemporary contexts and with insights from the European Union (EU). Secondly, we develop our argument that arbitration should be regarded as an essential component of AU regional integration. Third, we formulate original proposals for arbitration-focused AU regional legal infrastructure consisting of an overall pan-African approach, arbitration rules, non-contractual arbitration, application to investment and commercial arbitration, arbitral seat, and recognition and enforcement of arbitral awards. The final part is the conclusion.

[29] B Hettne and F Söderbaum, 'The new regionalism approach' (1998) 17(3) Politeia 6–21.
[30] Adeleke (n 10) 110–28.

2. Africa's Regional Integration and Dispute Resolution

In an attempt to create a free market, the AU's predecessor, the Organisation of AU (OAU) focused on encouraging political integration among Member States at the end of colonialism. The OAU was founded by 32 African States with the primary aims of intensifying cooperation among Africans to raise living standards, defend national sovereignty and territorial integrity, and settle inter-Member State disputes through peaceful and diplomatic negotiations.[31] The OAU Charter provided little details about economic integration beyond requiring Member States to 'coordinate and harmonize their general policies' in 'economic cooperation' (Article II).

Integration of the African continent gained significant momentum in the 1960s as part of efforts to rid it of colonialism. From 1963 when the OAU was established, the vision of a united Africa with a growing and prospering population began to take form. In 1979, the OAU released the Monrovia Declaration of Commitment of the Heads of State and Government of the OAU on Guidelines and Measures for National and Collective Self-Reliance in Social and Economic Development for the Establishment of a New International Economic Order (Monrovia Declaration). The Monrovia Declaration articulated the OAU's vision for economic cooperation and regional development with objectives that include promoting the:

- social and economic development and integration of African economies with a view to achieving an increasing measure of self-reliance and self-sustainment;
- economic integration of the African region in order to facilitate and reinforce social and economic interaction;
- establishment of national, sub-regional, and regional institutions to facilitate the attainment of self-reliance and self-sustainment objectives.[32]

In April 1980, the plans contained in the Monrovia Declaration were made concrete by the OAU in the Lagos Plan of Action (LPA), which the United Nations Economic Commission for Africa supported.[33] The LPA envisaged the establishment of a 'dynamic and interdependent African economy' via the AEC (Preamble paragraph 3(v)) while setting out a vision to integrate and develop Africa through import substitution industrialization by year 2000 (Annex I paragraph II(A)). In the 1991 Abuja Treaty Establishing the African Economic Community intended

[31] TO Elias, 'The Charter of the Organization of African Unity' (1965) 59(2) American Journal of International Law 243.

[32] Resolution AHG/ST. 3 (XVI) Rev. 1, Sixteenth Ordinary Session, Monrovia, Liberia, 17–20 July 1979.

[33] UNECA, 'Appraisal and Review of the Impact of the Lagos Plan of Action on the Development and Expansion of Intra-African Trade' E/ECA/TRADE/91/6, 8 March 1991) available at <http://repository.uneca.org/pdfpreview/bitstream/handle/10855/14129/Bib-55593.pdf?sequence=1> accessed 1 March 2020.

to come into force in 1994, OAU Heads of State reaffirmed their commitment to an integrated African economy by establishing the AEC with objectives including 'the integration of African economies in order to increase economic self-reliance and promote an endogenous and self-sustained development' (Article 4(1)). The Treaty provided for gradual integration of the African continent through the existing eight RECs ending in an economic union with a common currency, full mobility of factors of production, and free trade.[34] It was the genesis of RECs, which are seen as the building blocks of the AEC, that provided strong support for the African integration agenda and emphasized African solidarity and self-reliance through industrialization. However, the apparent political will signalled by the proliferation of integration agreements does not seem to correlate with the implementation measures put in place. African economic integration suffers from several problems ranging from overlapping memberships, institutional shortcomings, unfulfilled commitments, and unrealistic goals.[35] The RECs appear to have made some progress towards Africa's integration, particularly in infrastructure, trade liberalization and facilitation, free movement of people, and peace and security.[36]

Instructively, one of OAU's principal institutions, the Commission for Mediation, Conciliation and Arbitration, was responsible for peacefully settling disputes between Member States in line with the terms of reference set out in the 1964 Protocol of the Commission of Mediation, Conciliation and Arbitration. The Protocol made no reference to judicial means of settling disputes by organizations such as the International Court of Justice. While there are no specific references to investment and commercial disputes in the 1964 Protocol, these forms of dispute could arguably be addressed within the open-ended remit of the Commission to implement peace-making processes and procedures to ensure solidarity and maintenance of good relations among states. Nonetheless, no dispute was ever dealt with by the Commission.[37] Possible factors include African states' unwillingness to submit to formal judicial settlement unless they are absolutely sure of their legal position and reliance on their bargaining position due to uncertain customary international law rules.[38]

[34] United Nations Economic Commission for Africa, 'Assessing Regional Integration in Africa II: Rationalizing Regional Economic Communities' (UNECA and African Union, 2006)

[35] T Dinka and W Kennes, *Africa's Regional Integration Arrangements: History and Challenges* (European Centre for Development Policy Management Discussion Paper No 74, September 2007); P Draper, D Halleson, and others, 'SACU, regional integration and the overlap issue in Southern Africa: from spaghetti to cannelloni?' South African Institute of International Affairs, SAIIA Trade Policy Report No. 15, 2007).

[36] See RF Frimpong, 'The African Union, the African Economic Community and Africa's Regional Economic Communities: untangling a complex web' (2010) 18(1) African Journal of International and Comparative Law 92; CA Parker, 'The new African Union and its constitutive act' (2002) 96(2) American Journal of International Law 365.

[37] Z Červenka, 'The settlement of disputes among members of the Organization of African Unity' (1974) 7(2) Law and Politics in Africa, Asia and Latin America 117

[38] ibid 119–20.

Nevertheless, African states have drawn inspiration from the World Trade Organization (WTO) dispute settlement mechanism (WTO-DSM) for majority of RTAs despite not being active users of the mechanism.[39] The WTO-DSM seems the most active dispute resolution mechanism globally with over 500 dispute submissions and 350 rulings issued since 1995.[40] It is a multilateral multi-tiered system comprising, among others, consultations, panels, and appellate body that member countries agree to use for settling trade disputes. Member countries also agree to abide by procedures and respect judgments made by the Dispute Settlement Body (DSB), the WTO organ responsible for dispute adjudication.

The WTO-DSM approach is adopted by most African RECs. For example, the Southern African Development Community (SADC) Protocol on Trade Tribunal[41] and the Dispute Settlement Body under the Tripartite Free Trade Area (TFTA) Agreement between Common Market for Eastern and Southern Africa (COMESA), East African Community (EAC), and SADC[42] transplanted and are modelled after the WTO-DSM. Consequently, the attitude of African states towards the sub-regional DSMs is at best lukewarm[43] due to the inappropriateness of the DSM approach to the African context, including regional culture and priorities. For good reasons, TWAIL frown upon this type of wholesale transplantation of neoliberal approaches of current international economic law.

Moreover, there are no references to the apparent overarching supervisory jurisdiction of the AU court over all disputes within the AU and neither is there any express delimitation of the court's jurisdiction in the RECs. Notwithstanding the adoption of a more rules-based DSM, African states largely disfavour judicialization of disputes in formal regimes. This attitude seems prevalent across the continent even within sub-regional groupings with provisions for dispute settlement.[44] For instance, Zimbabwe's violations of its SADC and COMESA Trade Protocols obligations, as shown in *Campbell (Pvt) Ltd v Republic of Zimbabwe*,[45] highlight serious flaws in how the RECs regulate intra-African trade and resolve disputes.

[39] V Mosoti, 'Africa in the first decade of WTO dispute settlement' (2006) 9 Journal of International Economic Law 427; A Alavi, 'African countries and the WTO's Dispute Settlement Mechanism' (2007) 25(1) Development Policy Review 25

[40] World Trade Organization, 'Dispute Settlement' available at <https://www.wto.org/english/tratop_e/dispu_e/dispu_e.htm≥ accessed 24 September 2019.

[41] Articles 16 and 32, Declaration and Treaty of Southern African Development Community 1992; Article 32, Protocol on Trade in the Southern African Development Community (SADC) Region 1996; C Ng'ong'ola, 'Replication of WTO dispute settlement processes in SADC' (2011) 1 SADC Law Journal 35.

[42] Article 30, Agreement Establishing a Tripartite Free Trade Area among the Common Market for Eastern and Southern Africa, the East African Community and the Southern African Development Community 2015.

[43] KJ Alter, JT Gathii, and others, 'Backlash against international courts in West, East and Southern Africa: causes and consequences' (2016) 27(2) European Journal of International Law 293.

[44] ibid.

[45] (2/2007) [2008] SADCT 2 (28 November 2008).

In *Campbell*, the SADC Tribunal held that Zimbabwe violated the sub-regional treaty's human rights provisions in its land reforms programme. Zimbabwe national courts, which took a different view, refused to recognize and apply the decision of the tribunal. There were apparently no provisions in the sub-regional treaty and in Zimbabwe's law for the tribunal's supervisory or superior jurisdiction to compel the national courts to act otherwise. While there were some expectations to place political pressure on Zimbabwe to comply with the decision of the tribunal, the SADC Summit, which initially refrained from commenting on the case, ordered a review of the tribunal's role in 2010[46] with a view to its curtailment. The SADC Summit also failed to renew the tenure of the tribunal judges or appoint new ones in their place,[47] which is another signal of the low position judicialized processes hold in the sub-regional order. This is further reinforced by a 2014 Protocol which severely restricted the tribunal's jurisdiction to inter-state matters[48] and excluded human rights matters brought by individuals, businesses, and other non-governmental persons. The 2014 Protocol was arguably triggered by the claimants' success in South Africa's national courts[49] in their attempt to enforce the judgment of the tribunal. It is instructive that the Protocol was initiated despite a 2011 review[50] undertaken for the SADC Committee of Ministers of Justice/Attorneys-General which recommended that the tribunal be strengthened with superior jurisdiction like that of the Court of Justice of the European Union which, among other powers, adjudicates on matters between states and non-state actors when Member States are alleged to have violated their treaty obligations.

In 2002, the AU replaced the OAU for reasons including the need to divert attention from political independence, an aim which had more or less been achieved, to facilitating economic development devoid of reliance on former colonial powers.[51] Thereafter, the AU adopted a vision to create an 'integrated, prosperous

[46] *Communique of the 30th Jubilee Summit of the SADC Heads of State and Government*, 17 August 2010 available at <https://www.sadc.int/files/3613/5341/5517/SADC_Jubillee_Summit_Communique.pdf.pdf> accessed 24 July 2020.

[47] B Chigara, 'What should a re-constituted Southern African Development Community (SADC) tribunal be mindful of to succeed' (2012) 81 Nordic Journal of International Law 341–77; E de Wet, 'The rise and fall of the Tribunal of the Southern African Development Community: implications for dispute settlement in Southern Africa' (2013) 28 ICSID Review 45–63.

[48] F Cowell, 'The death of the Southern African Development Community Tribunal's human rights jurisdiction' (2013) 13 Human Rights Law Review 153–65; GJ Naldi and KD Magliveras, 'The new SADC Tribunal: or the emasculation of an international tribunal' (2016) 63(2) Netherlands International Law Review 133–59.

[49] *Government of Zimbabwe v Fick and others* (657/11) [2012] ZASCA 122 (South Africa's Court of Appeal); *Government of Zimbabwe v Fick and others* (CCT 101/12) [2013] ZACC 22 (South Africa's Constitutional Court). See also DF Cohen, 'A president, an international tribunal and a band of farmers walk into a constitutional court-the last laugh: Mike Campbell v. The Government of the Republic of Zimbabwe' (2014) 28 Emory International Law Review 29–41.

[50] L Bartels, 'Review of the role, responsibilities and terms of reference of the SADC Tribunal' (2011) WTI Advisors, Final Report.

[51] KO Kufuor, 'The collapse of the Organization of African Unity: lessons from economics and history' (2005) 49(2) Journal of African Law 132.

and peaceful Africa, driven by its own citizens and representing a dynamic force in global arena'. In furtherance this vision, the AU Constitutive Act provides for several organs including a regional court (Article 18)[52] having jurisdiction over the interpretation and application of the Act and 'all subsidiary legal instruments' adopted within the AU framework.[53] The reference to 'all subsidiary legal instruments' would appear to apply to all economic integration agreements executed by AU Member States but the continued existence of the RECs and their dispute settlement procedures show that this is not the case. The emergence of the AU and its apparent reference to a hierarchical system has therefore not addressed persisting concerns regarding the plurality of polyarchic dispute resolution procedures alongside the vision of a uniform regional legal order. The next section of this chapter consequently demonstrates the need for the AU to recognize a context-specific arbitration model for regional integration.

3. Arbitration and AU Regional Integration

Initially, the AU's goal was to achieve a continental economic integration scheme by 2028. This is implicit from the AU Constitutive Act, the Preamble of which refers to the need for 'economic emancipation' inspired by the 'determination to promote unity, solidarity, cohesion and cooperation among the peoples of Africa and African States'. This appears to have been extended by Agenda 2063, a strategic framework developed to further ensure the realization of Africa's long-term socio-economic and integrative transformation objectives. In conceptualizing AfCFTA, the AU aimed to bring together the largest number of countries within a free trade area in the world while promoting trade liberalization and improved interaction within the RECs. AfCFTA demonstrates a broad objective of creating a single continental market for goods and services, with free movement of businesspersons and investments, paving the way for accelerating the establishment of the Continental Customs Union. AfCFTA came into effect on 30 May 2019 with the promise of redefining trade relations among African states in accordance with the Agenda 2063 aspirations.

Nonetheless, the twin challenges of transplantation of the WTO-DSM approach and multiple integration forums which precede the AU remain. First, AfCFTA seems to have been designed with similar flaws affecting the RECs in terms of

[52] The African Court on Human and Peoples' Rights and the Court of Justice of the African Union were merged into the African Court of Justice and Human and Peoples' Rights (ACJHPR). African Union Protocol on the Statute of the African Court of Justice and Human Rights, adopted by the Eleventh Ordinary Session of the Assembly of the Union in Sharm El-Sheikh, Egypt, 1 July 2008; Protocol on Amendments to the Protocol on the Statute of the African Court of Justice and Human Rights, AU Doc. No STC/Legal/Min. 7(1) Rev. 1 (27 June 2014).

[53] Article 28 of the African Union Protocol on the Statute of the African Court of Justice and Human Rights (n 52).

dispute resolution. For example, AfCFTA (Article 20) and draft Protocol on Rules and Procedures on the Settlement of Disputes (Dispute Protocol) establish a DSB with a four-tiered DSM commencing with consultation. While AfCFTA's DSM may recognize the non-litigious nature of Africans and relational nature of trade,[54] it drew inspiration from the WTO-DSM and mirrored its procedures without consideration of African-specific circumstances. Gathii argued that while the wholesale adoption of the WTO-DSM in AfCFTA is premised on the desire to replicate a successful global system, its main challenge is the unwillingness of business actors to refer trade disputes to Africa's sub-regional trade courts,[55] such as the East African Court of Justice (EACJ) and the Economic Community of West African Community Court of Justice (ECCJ). Some of these tribunals have no record of issuing remedies that can be enforced as a result of the limited remedial powers they possess.[56] *Campbell (Pvt) Ltd v Republic of Zimbabwe*,[57] discussed in section 2, is an illustrative case. Akinkugbe also argued that while adopting the WTO-DSM may have been a step in the right direction towards a DSM that is 'Afro-centric in its norms',[58] the confidential nature of consultations may incentivize disputing parties to rely excessively on it thereby impeding the growth of relevant jurisprudence.

Secondly, a 'fragmented'[59] approach is unlikely to promote regional integration championed by the AU. For example, while it does not override existing investment agreements, the PAIC is expected to 'replace the intra-African [BITs] or investment chapters in intra-African trade agreements' at some point in the future (Article 3(2)). RECs are also required to avoid entering into future agreements that conflict with the PAIC (Article 3(3)), to cooperate with the AU Commission on investment-related matters (Article 47(1)), and to undertake investment-related programme design and development to assist AU Member States (Article 47(2)). The reality, however, is that the RECs are not going away any time soon as there are no concrete steps taken by the AU in that regard.

[54] B Faturoti, 'Institutionalised ADR and access to justice: the changing faces of the Nigerian judicial system' (2014) 1(1) Journal of Comparative Law in Africa 66, 72–3; OD Akinkugbe, (2019) 'Dispute settlement under the African continental free trade area agreement: a preliminary assessment' available at <http://dx.doi.org/10.2139/ssrn.3403745> accessed 24 July 2020.

[55] JT Gathii, 'Evaluating the Dispute Settlement Mechanism of the African Continental Free Trade Agreement' *Afronomics Law*, 10 April 2019 available at <http://www.afronomicslaw.org/2019/04/10/evaluating-the-dispute-settlement-mechanism-of-the-african-continental-free-trade-agreement/> accessed 16 September 2019.

[56] For example, the powers of the East African Court of Justice (EACJ) were analysed. The EACJ's jurisdiction is limited to declarations that governmental conduct is inconsistent with a treaty of the East African Community; the court cannot grant damages or exercise many of the powers national courts have. See JT Gathii, 'The Variation in the Use of Sub-Regional Integration Courts between Business and Human Rights Actors: The Case of the East African Court of Justice', Loyola University Chicago School of Law Public Law & Legal Theory Research Paper No 2015–007 available at <https://papers.ssrn.com/sol3/papers.cfm?abstract_id=2517040&download=yes> accessed 2 March 2020.

[57] Cohen (n 49).

[58] Akinkugbe (n 54).

[59] Adeleke (n 10) 7.

Prior to the pan-African vision of the PAIC, African countries addressed investment matters in two main ways.[60] First, they entered into BITs mostly between the mid-1990s and 2002. By the time the PAIC was initiated in 2016, these BITs constituted about a third of the global number of such treaties. Secondly, there was a proliferation of African RECs, hence the PAIC's Preamble acknowledges that it takes 'into account the various regional arrangements on investment across the continent'. RECs even have arbitral tribunals attached to them. An example is the arbitral tribunal set up and later dissolved by SADC Member States.[61] In addition to the PAIC, other African regional investment related instruments include the EAC Model Investment Code, the Protocol on the Establishment of the EAC Market Protocol, COMESA Common Investment Agreement 2007, SADC Protocol of Finance and Investment, the TFTA, and Economic Community of West African States (ECOWAS) Supplementary Act on the Common Investment Rules for the Community.

It is clear that the realization that increased economic activities and strategic investments provide the backdrop for promotion of transborder economic cooperation by African regional and sub-regional bodies.[62] The positive role of transborder trade and investment in economic growth is acknowledged generally,[63] and in the specific case of African countries.[64] For instance, a study of international trade and foreign direct investment in 45 African countries between 1990 and 2014 confirmed its correlation to economic growth.[65]

Nonetheless, unsuitable transplantation models and fragmented approaches will affect the ability of the AU to confront growing challenges to its regional integration and development agenda which arguably require a joined-up Africa-specific solution. As Burton noted, 'The continent of Africa is one of economic

[60] Mbengue (n 23).

[61] See *Swissbourgh Diamond Mines (Pty) Ltd v Kingdom of Lesotho*, PCA Case No 2013–29 (First Case); *Swissbourgh Diamond Mines (Pty) Ltd v Kingdom of Lesotho* [2018] SGCA 81.

[62] C Calderon, G Kambou, and others, 'An analysis of issues shaping Africa's economic future' *Africa's Pulse*, No 19 (International Bank for Reconstruction and Development/World Bank, 2019).

[63] J Bhagwati, 'The Theory of Immiserizing Growth: Further Applications' in MB Connolly and AK Swoboda (eds), *International Trade and Money* (UTP, 1973) 45–54; UNCTAD, 'The Role of International Trade in the Post-2015 Development Agenda' (United Nations, 2014); D Sakyi and J Egyir, 'Effects of trade and FDI on economic growth in Africa: an empirical investigation' (2017) 9(2) Transnational Corporations Review 66.

[64] L Ndikumana and S Verick 'The linkages between FDI and domestic investment: unravelling the developmental impact of foreign investment in Sub-SaharaAn Africa' (2008) 26(6) Development Policy Review 713; UNCTAD, *Economic Development in Africa, Export Performance following Trade Liberalization: Some Patterns and Policy Perspectives* (United Nations, 2008); S Adams, 'Can foreign direct investment (FDI) help to promote growth in Africa?' (2009) 3(5) African Journal of Business Management 178; J Sundaram, O Schwank, and others, 'Globalization and development in Sub-Saharan Africa' (Department of Economics and Social Affairs Working Paper (No. 102), United Nations, 2011); World Bank, 'An Analysis of Issues Shaping Africa's Economic Future' 2013 7 Africa's Pulse; S Adams, S and EE Osei Opoku, 'Foreign direct investment, regulations and growth in Sub-Saharan Africa' (2015) 47(C) Economic Analysis and Policy 48; UNECA, *Economic Report on Africa 2015: Industrializing through Trade* (United Nations Economic Commission for Africa, 201.

[65] Sakyi and Egyir (n 63).

paradox: Abundant natural resources lie within many of the states, yet despite their mineral wealth, these same states exhibit low levels of development and a poor standard of living.'[66] There has been a noticeable economic deceleration in recent times in both resource-intensive and non-resource-intensive African countries. The World Bank reported recently that low level of investment in African and other emerging and developing economies affected national and regional economic growth.[67] While a critical factor is the existence and quality of institutions,[68] especially in the African context,[69] there is fragility of transborder legal institutions where they even exist.

Much has been made of the unequal relationship between the developed countries and African nations, and adverse effects of unfavourable external environments on the continent, with little responsibility apportioned to Africa's leaders. As UNCTAD observed, 'even under a favourable external trading and financial environment, considerable domestic policy efforts would be needed to ensure that economies gradually become self-reliant in sustaining rapid growth'.[70] As arbitration is a widely used DSM, there is therefore the need for AU organs and Member States to display a political will to establish and implement an effective and Africa-sensitive arbitration mechanism. Section 4 outlines the components of an AU legal infrastructure for an African arbitration model we propose.

4. Context-specific AU Arbitration Legal Infrastructure

The key role that effective DSMs play in economic integration for predictable, fair, and prompt interpretation of rights and obligations cannot be over-emphasized. The corollary is that a regional integration project should have effective DSMs to

[66] EG Burton, 'Reverse the curse: creating a framework to mitigate the resource curse and promote human rights in mineral extraction industries in Africa' (2014) Emory International Law Review 425, 425.

[67] World Bank, *Global Economic Prospects* (World Bank, 2019).

[68] D Dollar and A Kraay 'Institutions, trade and growth (2003) 50(1) Journal of Monetary Economics. 133; D Rodrik, A Subramanian, and others, 'Institutions rule: the primacy of institutions over geography and integration in economic development' (2004) 9(2) Journal of Economic Growth, 131; S Bhattacharyya, S Dowrick, and others, 'Institutions and trade: competitors or complements in economic development?' (2009) 85(270) Economic Record 318; R Chang, L Kaltani, and others, 'Openness can be good for growth: the role of policy complementarities' (2009) 90 Journal of Development Economics 33; KP Biwott, DE Moyi, and others, 'Trade liberalization and economic growth: the role of regulatory policies' (2013) 2 Journal of World Economic Research 45; M Silberberger and J Königer 'Regulation, trade and economic growth' (2016) 40 Economic Systems 308.

[69] M Baliamoune-Lutz and L Ndikumana, L. 'The growth effects of openness to trade and the role of institutions: new evidence from African countries' Economics Department Working Paper Series (No 38), University of Massachusetts, 2007); JC Anyanwu, 'Factors affecting economic growth in Africa: are there any lessons from China?' (2014) 26 African Development Review 468; EK Agbloyor, A Gyeke-Dako, and others, 'Foreign direct investment and economic growth in SSA: The role of institutions' (2016) 7 Thunderbird International Business Review 479.

[70] UNCTAD, *Economic Development in Africa: Performance, Prospects and Policy Issues* (United Nations, 2001) 12.

attract and sustain the ability to encourage and secure direct and indirect investments and facilitate transborder transactions by providing mechanisms that give confidence in institutions designed to protect the rights and interests of Member States, investors, commercial parties, and other stakeholders. Consequently, we outline our proposed legal infrastructure for an African arbitration model in the AU legal order.

4.1 Pan-African perspective

In recognition of the fact that regional integration can accelerate the pace of economic growth by fostering efficient cross-border investment and trade flows, the role of legitimate, effective, and acceptable DSMs that Africans can identify with remains paramount. The emphasis should be on developing and implementing norms and values that suit the African context. Africa's pre-colonial economic history suggests aspects and norms[71] that are non-existent in transplanted models like the WTO-DSM. The argument lies primarily on the need for transplantation of laws to have regard to the socio-economic, political, historical, and heterogeneous nature of African societies without which their viability is questionable.

As demonstrated by TWAIL,[72] existing rules of international law may in fact reflect dominant national and regional perspectives,[73] especially the neoliberal approach. Furthermore, the global economic order is dominated by certain economically powerful states,[74] a class that excludes African countries. Accordingly, the ICSID Convention, the Arbitration Rules of the United Nations Commission on International Trade Law (UNCITRAL Rules, revised 2010), and International Chamber of Commerce (ICC) Arbitration Rules do not necessarily take African-specific issues into account. This raises questions regarding the continued transplantation and adoption of WTO-styled DSMs without adaptation to Africa-specific socio-political realities which have proven ineffective in addressing dispute resolution needs of regional trade and integration. WTO-style DSMs appear

[71] A Cohen, 'Cultural Strategies in the Organization of Trading Diasporas' in C Meillassoux (ed), *The Development of Indigenous Trade and Markets in West Africa* (Routledge, 1971) 266–81; PD Curtin, *Cross-Cultural Trade in World History* (CUP, 1984); G Austin, 'Reciprocal comparison and African history: tackling conceptual eurocentrism in the study of Africa's economic past' (2007) 50(3) African Studies Review 1.

[72] MW Mutua, 'What is TWAIL? Proceedings of the Annual Meeting ((2000) 94(5–8) American Society of International Law 31; BS Chimni, 'Third world approaches to international law: a manifesto' (2006) 8 International Community Law Review 3; Natarajan, Reynolds, and others (n 12) 1946.

[73] A Anghie, 'The evolution of international law: colonial and postcolonial realities' (2006) 27(5) Third World Quarterly 739; BS Chimni, 'Capitalism, imperialism and international law in the twenty-first century' (2012) 14 Oregon Review of International Law 17; BS Chimni, *International Law and World Order: A Critique of Contemporary Approaches*, 2nd edn (CUP, 2017).

[74] See H Chang, *Bad Samaritans: The Secret of Rich Nations and the Threat to Global Prosperity* (Random House, 2007).

more disadvantageous for Africa's regional integration especially since the WTO is currently struggling to survive,[75] despite some success at resolving trade disputes. While it may be true that '[t]he main purpose of all strategies of foreign economic policy is to make domestic policies compatible with the international political economy',[76] a regional regime like the AU can shape the transnational economy through a pan-African arbitration perspective and enhance its influence on the global economy.

4.2 Arbitration rules

An important dimension of the pan-African perspective is the determination and application of arbitration rules. While arbitrator neutrality is often touted,[77] in practice, however, a level of politicization of investor–state dispute settlement exists.[78] It is not unusual for arbitrators appointed by African governments to be in minority as against the duo appointed by investors and arbitral institutions.[79] This may also suggest that, in addition to the costs involved and despite statements confirming that domestic law determines property and contractual rights in investment disputes,[80] it is doubtful if African-specific norms, values and public interest issues receive the consideration they deserve in non-African forums.

It is instructive that regional integration is not a free-standing AU objective. In addition to regional integration, the AU Constitutive Act refers to the need to promote 'sustainable development at the economic, social and cultural levels as well as the integration of African economies' (Article 3(j)) and 'cooperation in all fields of human activity to raise living standards of African peoples' (Article 3(k)). A pan-African perspective will enable these objectives to be incorporated in arbitration rules. In this context, arbitration bodies need to recognize African peculiarities without neglecting the need for transparency and respect for the rule of law.

75 Akinkugbe (n 54).

76 PJ Katzenstein (ed), *Between Power and Plenty: Foreign Economic Policies of Advanced Industrial States* (University of Wisconsin Press, 1978) 4.

77 AF Lowenfeld, *Lowenfeld on International Arbitration, Collected Essays over Three Decades* (Juris, 2005) 101; J Paulsson, 'International Arbitration is not Arbitration' (2008) Stockholm International Arbitration Review 1, 2.

78 Adeleke (n 10) 18.

79 See *Process and Industrial Dev. Ltd. v The Ministry of Petroleum Resources of the Federal Republic of Nigeria*, Final Award (31 January 2017); *Swissbourgh* (First Case) (n 61).

80 *Emmis International Holding, BV v Hungary*, ICSID Case No ARB/12/2, Award, 16 April 2014; *Urbaser SA and Consorcio de Aguas Bilbao Bizkaia, Bilbao Biskaia Ur Partzuergoa v The Argentine Republic*, ICSID Case No ARB/07/26, Award, 8 December 2016, para 556; *Venezuela Holdings, BV and others v The Bolivarian Republic of Venezuela*, ICSID Case No ARB/07/27, Decision on Annulment, 9 March 2017, paras 168–170; A Newcombe and L Paradell, *Law and Practice of Investment Treaties: Standards of Treatment* (Kluwer, 2009) para 2.13; Z Douglas, *The International Law of Investment Claims* (CUP, 2009) paras 101, 102, 115, 121.

The PAIC is indicative of some initial steps in adopting the pan-African perspective by articulating the sole objective of fostering sustainable development (Article 1). This is a positive since investment is not always beneficial to receiving states[81] and the objective highlights a particularly serious concern for both the AU and African perspectives. The PAIC also contains specific provisions on human rights, labour standards, environment protection, sustainable development, and other issues of concern to African countries and peoples.

The PAIC, however, reflects a limited adoption of the pan-African perspective as exemplified by Article 42(1) which provides that dispute resolution should be as provided in specific investment agreements. If investor–state disputes are 'pursuant to' PAIC, parties are required to undertake 'consultations and negotiations, which may include the use of non-binding third-party mediation or other mechanism' and, when this fails, arbitration may be sought 'subject to the applicable laws of the host State and/or the mutual agreement of the disputing parties, and subject to exhaustion of local remedies'. Any such arbitration 'may be conducted at any established African public or African private alternative dispute resolution centre [and] shall be governed by the United Nations Commission on International Trade Law (UNCITRAL) rules' (Article 42(1)(d)).

Clearly, the rules are not African-specific. An advantage of pan-African substantive and procedural arbitration rulemaking is that the AU can provide a viable and trustworthy supranational alternative to legal infrastructural gaps in African countries. This will address concerns about the quality of African national adjudicative institutions.

4.3 Non-contractual arbitration

A pan-African perspective will enable the recognition of non-contractual forms of arbitration in addition to consent-based contractual models and provide them with appropriate legal framework. While the orthodoxy in international arbitration is contract-based despite its challenges,[82] non-contractual arbitration models[83] are a potentially viable alternative. The African arbitration model can provide for non-contractual arbitration, which exists in some African statutes[84] and customary

[81] LE Trakman, 'Foreign direct investment: hazard or opportunity' (2009) 41 George Washington International Law Review 1, 3; C Newman, J Rand, and others, 'Technology transfers, foreign investment and productivity spillovers' (2015) 76 European Economic Review 168.

[82] N Blackaby, C Partasides, and others, *Redfern and Hunter on International Commercial Arbitration*, 6th edn (OUP, 2015) 697.

[83] For example, G Cuniberti, 'The Proposed Model' in *Rethinking International Commercial Arbitration: Towards Default Arbitration* (Edward Elgar, 2017), 141–64.

[84] For example, Egyptian Law Concerning Arbitration in Civil and Commercial Matters No 27 1994 (Article 2): An arbitration is commercial 'when the dispute arises over a legal relationship of an economic nature, whether contractual or non-contractual'.

laws and practices.[85] This model can be based on the customary arbitration practice as recognized in jurisdictions like Nigeria where, based on the customs and way of life of communities, parties referred their disputes to 'wise men or chiefs'.[86] The recognition of arbitration and the Dispute Settlement Body (DSB) by Article 27 of the DSM Protocol as respective alternative contractual and non-contractual dispute resolution methods is a handy precedent for the AU for adopting a model which, as shown above, is not alien to African cultures. The lack of non-contractual dispute resolution for investment and commercial matters in the AU legal order could explain attempts by investors to frame them as human rights claims.[87] Non-contractual arbitration will enable stakeholders like host communities and civil society organizations who are not party to any underlying treaty, investment agreement, or other instrument, to have recourse to the dispute settlement procedures. In contrast, as the exclusion of host communities in the proceedings in *Bear Creek v Peru* suggests,[88] the contractual basis of dispute settlement in international economic law allows no room for stakeholder rights.

Another benefit of the recognition of non-contractual arbitration is with regard to the perceived attitudes of African leaders and people towards legalistic dispute resolution. Although contrary evidence exists,[89] Africans are acclaimed as non-litigious,[90] as evident from cases before the East African Court of Justice (EACJ).[91] Cases instituted before the EACJ suggest that businesspeople prefer non-judicial dispute resolution.[92] Even African governments prefer diplomatic channels to litigating against others. The PAIC hints at this by encouraging state–state disputes concerning the interpretation and application of its provisions to be resolved through 'consultations, negotiations or mediation' (Article 41).

Nonetheless, these attitudes may undermine the necessity for certainty and predictability of rights and obligations. A preference for informal[93] diplomatic

[85] *Okpuruwu v Okpokam* (1988) 4 NWLR (Pt 90) 554, 586–7; *Ohiaeri v Akabueze* (1992) 2 NWLR (Pt 221), 1, 7; *Eke v Okwaranyia* (2001) 12 NWLR (Pt 726) 181; VC Igbokwe, 'The law and practice of customary arbitration in Nigeria: Agu v. Ikewibe and applicable law issues revisited' (1007) 41(2) Journal of African Law 201; A Chukwuemerie, 'The internationalisation of African customary law arbitration' (2006) 14(2) African Journal of International and Comparative Law 143.

[86] *Agu v Ikewibe* (1991) 3 NWLR (pt 180) 385.

[87] For example, *Gombert Jean-Claude Roger v Republic of Côte d'Ivoire*, App No 038/2016, Judgment (23 March 2018); App No 006/2012. Judgment of 28/05/2017; *Kamdem Roger v Member States of the Inter-African Conference on Insurance Markets (CIMA)*, App No O21/2O15, Order striking out application.

[88] *Bear Creek Mining Corporation v Republic of Peru* (ICSID Case No ARB/14/21).

[89] Faturoti (n 54), 69–72.

[90] For example, a Yoruba proverb advises *Aa kii ti kootu de sore* (People who go to court never return as friends).

[91] JT Gathii, 'The variation in the use of sub-regional integration courts between business and human rights actors: the case of the East African Court of Justice' (2016) 79 Law and Contemporary Problems 37.

[92] JT Gathii, 'Variation in the Use of Subregional Integration Courts between Business and Human Rights Actors: The Case of the East African Court of Justice' (2016) 79 Law and Contemporary Problems 37.

[93] CC Nshimbi, 'Issues in African informality: what is the relevance for regional or continental integration?' (2018) 48(1) African Insight 41.

channels and negotiations in resolving trade disputes as opposed to recourse to institutions that can monitor compliance with the regional legal order negates the benefits associated with predictability of rights and obligations and finality of decisions. The dream of economic integration will enjoy limited success where informal or diplomatic dispute settlement continues to hold sway. In this context, non-contractual arbitration is a solution by precluding the need for the consent of all disputants and providing a formal and ascertainable method of determining rights and obligations. In any event, being that it is less formal and legalistic than judicial determination, African people and governments may view arbitration more favourably.

4.4 Expansive application

A pan-African arbitration approach needs a more expansive application in contrast to limited private sector roles in existing initiatives that focus on investor–state disputes. This proposal is twofold.

First, states should be allowed to institute claims against private parties. For example, the PAIC envisages only claims by investors against states investor–state disputes (Article 42) although Article 43 allows defendant states to bring counterclaims. This is a limitation especially in view of statements of investor obligations on matters like corporate governance (Article 19), socio-political obligations (Article 20), bribery (Article 21), corporate social responsibility (Article 22), use of natural resources (Article 23), business ethics and human rights (Article 24), technology transfer (Articles 29(2) and 30), labour standards (Article 34), environment protection (Article 37), and consumer protection (Article 40). These obligations are broadly in line with the wider roles and implications of investment acknowledged in UNCTAD Investment Policy Framework on Sustainable Development as a 'new generation of investment policies'.[94] In effect, however, defaulting investors can escape consequences in so far as they refrain from instituting claims against State Parties to investment agreements. Our proposal will enable states to approach a competent and independent arbitration body whose decisions can be enforced before the courts of investors' home state or another state. Even if investors' home states are unwilling to allow enforcement, decisions of a pan-African judicial body may have a sanctioning effect on an investor throughout the continent. In other words, defaulting investors will at least lose access to Africa's huge combined market.

[94] United Nations Conference on Trade and Development (2015) UNCTAD/DIAE/PCB/2015/5 available at <https://unctad.org/en/PublicationsLibrary/diaepcb2015d5>_en.pdf> accessed 24 September 2019.

Secondly, our proposition for arbitration as a central component of the AU regional integration project encompasses investment and commercial arbitration. Commercial arbitration should be included in the AU framework due to the important role the private sector has played elsewhere, including Europe, in promoting transborder trade and integration through dispute resolution initiatives.[95] Instructively, the failure of previous African regional integration projects is traced partly to the exclusion of the private sector.[96]

Nevertheless, the 2015 Addis Ababa Action Agenda adopted pursuant to the UN Third Financing for Development Conference[97] acknowledged the role of private sector investment in economic development. Similarly, the formation of the Pan-African Private Sector Trade and Investment Committee (PAFTRAC) in 2018 was an acknowledgment of the private sector's role in Africa's regional integration. As highlighted by the New Regionalism Approach[98] and the pioneer pan-Africanist, Edward Blyden,[99] private sector involvement is critical for regional integration. This position is, however, not reflected in existing regional integration initiatives despite some statements that suggest the contrary.

The PAIC's Preamble, for example, suggests that it seeks 'to achieve an overall balance of the rights and obligations between Member States and the investors' and highlights the important roles of 'investment and the private sector' in economic growth and sustainable development. The combined effect of the definitions of 'company or enterprise' (Article 4(1)) 'investor' (Article 4(5)), broad definition of 'investment' (Article 4(4)), and encouragement of public–private partnership (Article 27) is that the PAIC recognizes both vertical and horizontal investment activities involving states and public and private entities in so far as a company or enterprise is used as the investment vehicle. Chapter 6 in the PAIC, however, only provides for state to state (Article 41) and investor–state (Articles 42 and 43) dispute settlement.

Focusing on inter-state and investor–state disputes as exemplified by the PAIC may not reflect the reality that 'investment agreements' can be undertaken between private parties with or without the direct intervention or facilitation of host governments. Consequently, we propose that the AU arbitration regime should also encompass commercial arbitration. Transnational arbitration practice shows that it is not restricted to investor–state disputes. Moreover, while most investment treaties apply to 'investments territorially made within a host state',[100] aspects of

95 See PR Milgrom, DC North, and others, 'The role of institutions in the revival of trade: the law merchant, private judges, and the champagne fairs' (1990) 2(1) Economics and Politics 1.

96 Rudahindwa (n 8) 'The issue of harmonisation within the AU/AEC', 173–94.

97 Endorsed by the United Nations General Assembly Res. 69/313 of 27 July 2015.

98 Hettne and Söderbaum (n 29).

99 H Lynch, 'Edward W Blyden: pioneer West African nationalist' (1965) 6(3) Journal of African History 373, 380–4.

100 C McLachlan, L Shore, and others, *International Investment Arbitration: Substantive Principles*, 2nd edn (OUP, 2017), paras 6.88–6.89.

international investment law recognize its application where investments have territorial links with host states.[101] This suggests that, in some investment agreement cases, states are indirectly involved in what might potentially be regarded as commercial disputes in other contexts.

In either case of investment or commercial arbitration, the problem of not having an 'African' alternative exists. In commercial arbitration, for instance, African commercial parties should be able to point to an effective and cost-efficient supranational system. This understanding should be placed within the context of the fact that a greater proportion of interactions and transactions in free market economies is undertaken between private actors. This has even prompted suggestions for an international commercial court.[102]

4.5 Arbitration seat

The continued resolution by arbitration of trade, investment, and commercial disputes outside the region, even when they deal with African interests combined with award sums that are arguably questionable,[103] may suggest that dispute resolution is not an AU priority and reflect an endemic problem with its justice system. Years after African countries' independence and the creation of pan-African institutions, Africa-based investment and intra-African disputes are taken to arbitration and adjudication in non-African forums including London, Paris, and Singapore. For example, South African nationals and companies brought proceedings against Lesotho's government before the Permanent Court of Arbitration (PCA) seated in Singapore.[104] Lesotho's government had to apply to Singapore courts for the arbitration award to be set aside because of the PCA's lack of jurisdiction.[105]

The key point is that there should be an African forum for the arbitration of African disputes. If disputants are suspicious of African national courts and legal systems, a supranational body is not of the same class and should enjoy their trust and confidence. A critical dimension of a pan-African arbitration perspective is therefore the recognition of a specific arbitral body within the AU legal order to ensure that it is consistently adopted, especially within the continent. This is possible

[101] Douglas (n 80) para 349.

[102] See SD Franck, 'The legitimacy crisis in investment treaty arbitration: privatizing public international law through inconsistent decisions' (2005) 73 Fordham Law Review 1521, 1617; S Schwebel, 'The outlook for the continued vitality, or lack thereof, of investor–state arbitration' (2016) 32 Arbitration International 1.

[103] For example, in August 2019, the English High Court awarded US $6.6 billion plus interest as judgment sum for execution against Nigeria's assets in favour of an Irish firm for a failed gas project: *Process and Industrial Developments Limited v Federal Republic of Nigeria* [2018] EWHC 3714 (Comm).

[104] *Swissbourgh* (First Case) (n 60).

[105] *Swissbourgh Diamond Mines (Pty) Ltd v Kingdom of Lesotho* [2017] SGHCR 02, [2017] SGHC 104, [2017] SGHC 195 (Singapore High Court), [2018] SGCA 81.

with AU's Constitutive Act. While Article 19 confirms that the establishment of African Central Bank, African Monetary Fund, and African Investment Bank as regional integration institutions, Article 9(d) permits the Assembly to create more institutions.

Nonetheless, an emerging awareness of the need for arbitration seat is evident. For example, the PAIC provides that any arbitration agreed by Member States 'shall be conducted at any established African public or African alternative dispute resolution centre' (Article 41(1)). While Article 27 of the DSM Protocol refers to arbitration as an alternative to the DSB established by Article 5, the protocol demonstrates that the idea of a pan-African arbitration body is not far-fetched. Although limited to inter-state AfCFTA-related disputes, the outlines of DSB's procedures (Articles 6–28) reflect arbitration and other ADR methods in all but name.

A secretariat of a supranational arbitration body can be established to undertake responsibilities like DSM Protocol (Article 29) which are not unlike of typical arbitration institutions. The secretariat can be integrated within an established institution like the OHADA-based Common Court of Justice and Arbitration (CCJA)[106] with its own African professionals and systems. While addressing the need for a robust and efficient resolution of disputes, this step will eliminate the cost and bureaucracy associated with the establishment of an entirely new institution with relevant expertise. In contrast, Onyema,[107] who, while suggesting the endorsement of major arbitral centres as regional hubs for arbitration of intra-African commercial disputes, proposed the establishment of a continental level court for enforcing intra-African arbitral awards.

Arbitration panels may even sit at different AU sub-regions or Member States depending on proximity to the issues and parties, including language. This will help to reduce costs and increase accessibility to African and non-African parties. While some may argue that arbitration is cheaper to undertake than litigation, the reality is context-specific and neither dispute resolution method is inherently more cost effective.[108] For instance, African parties for arbitration conducted in Europe or Singapore will need legal representation before supervisory foreign courts in addition to other costs.

Another advantage of an AU arbitration body is the need to ensure consistency of decisions which is problematic with multiple bodies in international commercial

[106] Organisation pour l'harmonisation en Afrique du droit des affaires (Organization for the Harmonization of Business Law in Africa).

[107] E Onyema, 'Reimagining the framework for resolving Intra-African commercial disputes in the context of the African Continental Free Trade Area Agreement' 17, 19 available at <https://doi.org/10.1017/S1474745619000132> accessed 24 July 2020.

[108] GB Born, 'Planning for International Dispute Resolution' (2000) 17(3) Journal of International Arbitration 61, 66.

arbitration.[109] This requires that the DSMs of RECs, for instance, will have to give way to the AU arbitration body. Investors, commercial parties, and states will not be encumbered by the possible application of several national laws and rules of several RECs[110] or multiple jurisdictional forums within African countries and RECs. Providing an institutional framework for arbitration can therefore provide a one-stop shop for disputes and promote certainty.

4.6 Enforcement

In addition to subject-matter jurisdiction, specification of arbitration seat is important for enforcement.[111] The proposed arbitration body should be attached to the African Union as one of its institutions following the procedure in Article 9(d) of the Constitutive Act. An arbitration body attached to the AU will enjoy some advantages. First, its transnational status will afford the arbitral body a level of neutrality, an issue that is often raised[112] in relation to national courts and state control of adjudication. Since 'the neutrality advantage is a derivative of the enforceability advantage',[113] enforcement of the arbitral body's decisions is more likely to be favourably received within and outside AU Member States.

Secondly, while arbitral tribunals are limited in their remedies and powers over parties,[114] an arbitration body recognized as an AU organ may be able to refer to provisions for enforcement and remedies in AU law. However, this requires specific references in the arbitration framework to the AU's court's (ACJHPR) supervisory jurisdiction, when it comes into existence. This further opens up enforcement possibilities against Member States under the sanction regime of the AU Constitutive Act (Article 23) for enforcing the court's decisions. The PAIC seems to have acknowledged this approach by providing for ACJHPR's jurisdiction over inter-state disputes on its interpretation and application (Article 4(2)). In contrast, one of the drawbacks of AfCFTA's DSM is the lack of references to the AU in its enforcement procedures (Articles 24 and 25).

[109] Franck (n 102) 1617.
[110] Mbengue (n 23).
[111] See *Process v Nigeria* [2018] (n 103); *Process and Industrial Developments Limited v Federal Republic of Nigeria* No. 18-cv-00594-CRC; N Uwem, 'Process and Industrial Developments Limited v. Nigeria: exception under the FSIA when award has been set aside by a court of the country "under the law of which" the award was made' (2019) 26 University of Miami International and Comparative Law Review 437.
[112] See Lowenfeld (n 77).
[113] J Dammann and H Hansmann, 'Globalizing commercial litigation' (2008) 94 Cornell Law Review 1, 33.
[114] Cuniberti (n 83) 28–9.

5. Conclusion

This chapter examines the crucial role of arbitration in promoting and deepening AU regional integration. While it proposes a unique legal infrastructure for arbitration within the AU legal order, the chapter does not address its relative merits in comparison to other dispute resolution methods such as litigation.[115] Arbitration is focused on as a frequently applied ADR method in Africa's and international economic systems.

The chapter's content is contextualized in AU law as well as in existing international system for settlement of investment disputes and transborder arbitration. It examines successive initiatives aimed at Africa's regional integration before and after the AU's establishment with specific attention to DSMs they adopted. One insight from TWAIL is that neoliberal orientations of the existing international legal order may be unsuitable for the African context, including regional integration which the AU is designed by its Constitutive Act to champion and pursues through AfCFTA, the PAIC, and other initiatives. This chapter does not engage in the debate on the relative merits of possible alternatives[116] to regional integration as a development project but focuses squarely on the regional integrationist development model the AU has adopted as a political decision. Nonetheless, it demonstrates that regional integration has important legal elements, including ADR-like arbitration. In addition, the costly and problematic nature of transnational arbitration and dispute resolution hinders intra-Africa trade, economic development, and other AU objectives.

The chapter draws on African historical and contemporary political, legal, and economic experiences to demonstrate the need for a viable African ADR model centred around arbitration. It makes a case for the AU's active involvement in providing a comprehensive legal infrastructure for arbitration for the success of its regional integration project. The AU arbitration framework developed in this chapter includes provisions for a pan-African perspective, arbitration rules, non-contractual arbitration, expansive application to investment and commercial arbitration, arbitral seat, and institutional support for recognition and enforcement of arbitral awards. The proposed framework will promote legal certainty and robust and efficient resolution of investment and commercial disputes that are inevitable in transborder trade and regional integration schemes. This will guarantee a dispute resolution system that will enjoy widespread legitimacy and acceptability and attract the trust and confidence of AU Member States, investors, commercial contracting parties, and other stakeholders.

115 Born (n 108), 64; Blackaby, Partasides, and others (n 82), 28.

116 For example, 'Developmental regionalism': UNCTAD, *Intra-African Trade: Unlocking Private Sector Dynamism* UNCTAD/ALDC/AFRICA/2013 United Nations, 2013); Rudahindwa (n 8).

Africa needs a network of institutions with the AU's mandate to gain traction for, and sustain, a sense of African worth, and platforms to enable the propagation of African narratives and unique and innovative norms and values that are often neglected in global institutions. In making a case for rethinking Africa's place in existing international legal order, we argue that the AU should play a role in this regard generally and, in the context of this chapter, transborder investment and commercial disputes. We show that this is in line with the vision behind the AU as encapsulated in the Preamble to its Constitutive Act. The AU should be involved in private law and AU law should have an expansive application in the creation of an African identity, worth, and solidarity can help to deepen regional integration. An AU legal framework for arbitration could be a catalyst for Africa's economic integration.

8

The Statute of the Pan-African Intellectual Property Organisation: A Human Rights Perspective

Emmanuel Kolawole Oke

1. Introduction

In recent years, there have been two key initiatives aimed at the integration of intellectual property (IP) laws at the continental level in Africa. First, the creation of the Pan-African Intellectual Property Organisation (PAIPO) through the adoption of the Statute of the Pan African-Intellectual Property Organisation (PAIPO Statute) by the AU in January 2016.[1] Second, the plan to include IP in the next round of negotiations on the African Continental Free Trade Area (AfCFTA) Agreement.[2]

The focus of this chapter is on the former, the PAIPO, and, specifically, the PAIPO Statute. Article 2 thereof establishes PAIPO as an AU specialized agency. PAIPO's mandate entails responsibility for IP and the promotion of the effective use of the IP system as a tool for the economic, cultural, social, and technological development of Africa.[3] PAIPO's mandate equally includes setting intellectual property standards that reflect the needs of the AU, its Member States, the Regional Economic Communities in Africa (RECs), and the two other regional IP organizations currently in operation, the African Regional Intellectual Property Organisation (ARIPO) and the African Intellectual Property Organisation (OAPI).[4] At the time

[1] The PAIPO Statute was adopted at the 26th Ordinary Session of the Assembly of the AU Assembly on 30 January 2016. See, AU Assembly, *Decision on the Specialized Technical Committees*, Assembly/AU/Dec.589 (XXVI) (30 January 2016).

[2] The AfCFTA was launched in March 2018 at the AU Extraordinary Summit in Rwanda and it was signed by 44 AU Member States; it entered into force in July 2019. See, AU Assembly, *Decision on the Draft Agreement Establishing the African Continental Free Trade Area (AfCFTA)*, Ext/Assembly/AU/Dec.1(X) (21 March 2018). See also, ICTSD, 'Ratification of African Continental Free Trade Area gets underway' (24 May 2018) 22(18) Bridges Weekly 7–9 (noting that, according to officials, the second phase of negotiations on the AfCFTA 'would tackle other outstanding issues, such as investment and intellectual property rights'.). See also C Ncube, 'IP, PAIPO and the African Continental Free Trade Agreement' *Afro-IP* (23 March 2018) available at <http://afro-ip.blogspot.com/2018/03/ip-paipo-and-african-continental-free.html> accessed 11 May 2021.

[3] Article 3 of the PAIPO Statute.

[4] ibid.

Emmanuel Kolawole Oke, *The Statute of the Pan-African Intellectual Property Organisation: A Human Rights Perspective*
In: *The Emergent African Union Law.* Edited by: Olufemi Amao, Michèle Olivier and Konstantinos D. Magliveras, Oxford University Press. © Emmanuel Kolawole Oke 2021. DOI: 10.1093/oso/9780198862154.003.0009

of writing, the PAIPO Statute was not in force because it requires ratification by 15 Member States of the AU for it to enter into force.[5] As of October 2019, only six Member States had signed it and there was no single ratification.[6] It is unclear if and when it will enter into force.

This chapter does not seek to examine the merits or otherwise of the establishment of PAIPO. It takes the view that any plan to have a centralized intellectual property organization for Africa should not be done at the expense of the responsibility of African states to respect, protect, and fulfil human rights and fundamental freedoms. A critical examination of the PAIPO Statute reveals that the importance of securing human rights whilst seeking to protect IP was not appreciated by the drafters.

Crucially, in outlining the functions of PAIPO, the Statute, among other things, mandates it to take measures to promote the harmonization, protection, and exploitation of IP rights among AU Member States.[7] However, the Statute makes no reference to human rights while outlining the functions of PAIPO. This chapter contends that the failure to incorporate a human rights perspective reflects the narrow conception of IP adopted by the drafters and it seems to confirm the criticisms made prior to its adoption that its drafting was driven by an IP-maximalist ideology.[8] This failure equally contradicts one of the key AU objectives, to promote and protect human rights in accordance with the African Charter on Human and Peoples' Rights (ACHPR) and other relevant human rights instruments.[9]

This chapter will examine the PAIPO Statute in light of the potential impact that it could have on the human rights to health and education (which are both recognized in Articles 16 and 17 respectively of the ACHPR). The focus here is on these two specific socio-economic rights because they relate to the ability of states to regulate in the public interest. That is not to say that IP rights do not affect other human rights, such as the right to freedom of expression. However, an exhaustive treatment of the interface between IP and human rights is impossible here due to constraints of space. This chapter will contend that there is a need to incorporate a human rights perspective into the Statute by amending its provisions (particularly Article 4 which outlines the functions of PAIPO) in order to avoid an incoherence between it and the ACHPR. Incorporating a human rights perspective into

5 PAIPO Statute Article 24(1).

6 See AU, 'List of Countries that Which Have Signed, Ratified/Acceded to the Statute of the Pan African Intellectual Property Organization (PAIPO)' (28 June 2019) available at <https://au.int/sites/default/files/treaties/32549-sl-STATUTE%20OF%20THE%20PAN%20AFRICAN%20INTELLECTUAL%20PROPERTY%20ORGANIZATION%20%28PAIPO%29%20%281%29.pdf> accessed 11 May 2021.

7 Article 4 of the PAIPO Statute.

8 B Baker, 'Intellectual property policy incoherence at the African Union threatens access to medicines' *Infojustice* (28 September 2012) available at <http://infojustice.org/archives/27392> accessed 11 May 2021.

9 See Article 3(h) of the AU Constitutive Act (2000).

the PAIPO Statute will equally ensure congruence between the functions of PAIPO and the AU objectives.

The chapter is structured into three sections. Section 2 provides a brief historical and legal analysis of the PAIPO Statute. Section 3 examines the PAIPO Statute from a human rights perspective. Section 4 provides some suggestions for its amendment.

2. A Historical and Legal Analysis of the PAIPO Statute

The emergence of PAIPO is traceable to the African Ministerial Council on Science and Technology (AMCOST) which was set up in 2003.[10] AMCOST formally proposed the creation of PAIPO in 2012.[11] Thereafter, the AU Assembly agreed to establish it at its 20th Ordinary Summit in Addis Ababa in 2013.[12] The Statute establishing PAIPO was subsequently adopted in 2016.[13]

It should be noted that the World Intellectual Property Organization (WIPO) also played a role in the creation of PAIPO and it has been suggested that its Statute reflects WIPO's vision of development through the strong protection of IP rights.[14] It is also worth noting that the creation of PAIPO is connected to the AU's goal of regional integration.[15] As stated in Article 3(c) of the Constitutive Act, one of the AU objectives is to 'accelerate the political and socio-economic integration of the continent'.

[10] C Ncube and E Laltaika, 'A new intellectual property organization for Africa?' (2013) 8(2) Journal of Intellectual Property Law and Practice 114, 115. However, it should be noted that one of the early proponents of a centralized IP organization for Africa is Tshimanga Kongolo, see T Kongolo, 'The African Intellectual Property Organizations: the necessity of adopting one uniform system for all Africa' (2000) 3(2) Journal of World Intellectual Property 265, 284, proposing the establishment of the 'Folklore and Intellectual Property Organization of Africa'.

[11] AU Executive Council, *Decision on the Report of the Fifth Ordinary Session of the African Union Conference of Ministers in Charge of Science and Technology*, EX.CL/Dec.746(XXII) (21–25 January 2013).

[12] AU Assembly, *Decision on the Creation of the Pan-African Intellectual Property Organization (PAIPO)*, Assembly/AU/Dec.453 (XX) (28 January 2013).

[13] AU Assembly, *Decision on the Specialized Technical Committees*, Assembly/AU/Dec.589 (XXVI) (30 January 2016). See generally, GA Aneme and U Lamikanra, 'Introduction to the norms and institutions of the African Union' (2018) available at <https://www.nyulawglobal.org/globalex/African_Union1.html> accessed 11 May 2021.

[14] SI Štrba, 'Intellectual Property Pluralism in African Development Agendas: Food Security, Plant Variety Protection and the role of the WIPO' in S Frankel (ed), *Is Intellectual Property Pluralism Functional?* (Edward Elgar, 2019) 43–4. On WIPO's role in the creation of PAIPO, see WIPO, 'Technical Assistance Database: Experts Group Meeting on Pan African IP Organization (PAIPO), Addis Ababa, Ethiopia' (18 May 2009) available at <https://www.wipo.int/tad/en/activitydetails.jsp?id=787> accessed 11 May 2021. See also C Ncube, *Intellectual Property Policy, Law and Administration in Africa: Exploring Continental and Sub-regional Co-operation* (Routledge, 2016) 127; SI Štrba, 'Legal and institutional considerations for plant variety protection and food security in African development agendas: solutions from WIPO?' (2017) 12(3) Journal of Intellectual Property Law and Practice 191, 194–5.

[15] Y Mupangavanhu, 'African Union rising to the need for continental IP protection? the establishment of the Pan-African Intellectual Property Organization' (2015) 59(1) Journal of African Law 1, 3.

As noted in the introduction, PAIPO is intended to operate as a specialized agency of the AU[16] with a mandate to promote the effective use of the IP system as a tool for the economic, cultural, social, and technological development of Africa.[17] PAIPO is composed of four organs, namely the Conference of States Parties, the Council of Ministers, the Secretariat, and the Board of Appeal.[18] The Conference of States Parties is the supreme policy-making organ.[19] Importantly, it is tasked with overseeing the implementation of the PAIPO Statute.[20] The Council of Ministers is the highest decision-making organ and the general assembly.[21] It is composed of Ministers in charge of IP in the contracting parties[22] and it is tasked with, *inter alia*, giving policy direction to PAIPO and electing the Director General.[23] The Council of Ministers also has the duty of deciding and prioritizing the activities of the Organization with regard to IP.[24]

The Secretariat is tasked with, *inter alia*, drafting policies and objectives aimed at fulfilling PAIPO's objectives for adoption by the Council of Ministers, taking necessary actions to ensure the protection of IP rights in Africa, and the daily management of PAIPO.[25] The Board of Appeal has the sole task of hearing disputes and litigation arising from the activities of the Organization.[26]

Prior to the creation of PAIPO, there had been two regional IP organizations operating in Africa, the African Regional Intellectual Property Organization (ARIPO) and the African Intellectual Property Organization or, as it is known in French, Organization Africaine de la Propriete Intellectuelle (OAPI). ARIPO was established pursuant to the Lusaka Agreement of 1976 and it caters mainly to English-speaking African countries. OAPI was established pursuant to the Bangui Agreement of 1977 and it caters mainly to French-speaking African countries.

Currently, ARIPO has 19 Member States,[27] while OAPI currently has 17 Member States.[28] One key difference between them concerns the level of autonomy that they grant to their Member States with regard to the administration of IP rights. For its own part, OAPI assumes the role of a central intellectual property office

[16] Article 2 of the PAIPO Statute. This can be compared with WIPO's status as a specialized agency of the United Nations as recognized in Article 1 of the Agreement between the United Nations and WIPO of 1974.

[17] Article 3 of the PAIPO Statute.

[18] ibid Article 9.

[19] ibid Article 10(1).

[20] ibid Article 10(3)(a).

[21] ibid Article 11(1).

[22] ibid Article 11(2).

[23] ibid Article 11(6)(a) and (c).

[24] ibid Article 11(6)(e).

[25] ibid Article 13(2)(b), (d), and (h).

[26] ibid Article 14(2).

[27] ARIPO, 'Member States' available at <https://www.aripo.org/member-states/> accessed 11 May 2021.

[28] OAPI, 'États Membres' available at <http://www.oapi.int/index.php/en/aipo/presentation/member-countries> accessed 11 May 2021.

and it harmonizes both the substantive and procedural aspects of IP law and administration of its Member States.[29] The situation is, however, different with regard to ARIPO: it receives applications for patents and trademarks and it may decide to grant these applications.[30] Nevertheless, individual Member States of ARIPO can still decide to reject such applications in their respective jurisdictions.[31] Thus, ARIPO only deals with procedural matters but largely leaves substantive aspects of IP law to its Member States.[32] With the emphasis on the harmonization of IP standards and laws as stated in Article 4 of the PAIPO Statute, it appears that its drafters have opted to follow the OAPI system of harmonizing both the substantive and procedural aspects of IP law and administration.

The PAIPO Statute is quite ambiguous regarding the nature of the relationship between PAIPO and the two existing organizations (i.e. ARIPO and OAPI). There are some provisions in the PAIPO Statute that suggest that both ARIPO and OAPI will remain functional and will coexist with PAIPO. There are other provisions in the PAIPO Statute that indicate that PAIPO will eventually replace both ARIPO and OAPI, if and when the Statute enters into force.

Concerning the provisions of the PAIPO Statute that suggest coexistence with both ARIPO and OAPI, the following provisions are worth highlighting. The Preamble contains a number of statements that suggest coexistence rather than replacement. For instance, the Preamble takes note of the autonomy of both ARIPO and OAPI and it recognizes their role as building blocks for the creation of PAIPO. Furthermore, in spelling out the mandate of PAIPO in Article 3 of the Statute, PAIPO has a mandate to set IP standards that reflect the needs of, *inter alia*, ARIPO and OAPI. Moreover, the first function of PAIPO is to harmonize IP standards in a manner that reflects the needs of, among others, ARIPO and OAPI.[33]

Crucially, Article 4(f) of the Statute empowers PAIPO to 'strengthen existing regional organizations or such other organisations as may be necessary'. While there is no explicit reference to either ARIPO or OAPI in this provision, one could argue that they are both included within its scope. In addition, Article 15 provides that PAIPO may invite, among others, regional organizations to attend any of its meetings. Moreover, Article 16 empowers PAIPO to establish and maintain working relationships with organizations that may help to achieve its objectives, such as regional organizations. This provision envisages that PAIPO can maintain a working relationship with both ARIPO and OAPI. Furthermore, Article 22(1) clarifies that no provision in the Statute shall be interpreted as derogating from the principles and values in other relevant instruments for the promotion of IP development in

[29] Mupangavanhu (n 15) 19–21.
[30] ibid.
[31] ibid.
[32] ibid.
[33] Article 4(a) of the PAIPO Statute.

Africa. The precise scope and implications of this provision is unclear but it could be argued that it applies to the instruments establishing both ARIPO and OAPI.

In relation to the provisions of the PAIPO Statute that indicate that ARIPO and OAPI would eventually be replaced by PAIPO, Article 4(b) empowers PAIPO to facilitate the harmonization of national laws and regional treaties with continental IP standards. In this regard, the Statute does not envisage any role for both ARIPO and OAPI. Importantly, Article 4(l) empowers PAIPO to promote the harmonization of the IP systems of its Member States with particular regard to the protection, exploitation, commercialization, and enforcement of IP rights. This provision essentially usurps the current role being played by both ARIPO and OAPI on behalf of their Member States. If PAIPO assumes this function, then both ARIPO and OAPI might be rendered redundant.

Moreover, Article 4(m) of the Statute envisages that PAIPO may perform administrative tasks provided in IP treaties adopted by the Conference of States Parties. If PAIPO begins to perform administrative tasks at the continental level, then the continued relevance of both ARIPO and OAPI would be called into question. This becomes especially true if, for instance, the Conference of States Parties were to adopt treaties that empower PAIPO to receive applications for and grant trademarks and patent rights. Besides, PAIPO is also empowered to take the lead with regard to Africa's negotiations on issues relating to international IP law and to ensure the attainment of common African positions.[34] PAIPO equally has responsibility for the conclusion of bilateral and multilateral agreements.[35]

Although this chapter does not intend to examine the merits or otherwise of the establishment of PAIPO, it should be noted that various reasons have been adduced for its creation. For instance, it has been noted that the existence of two separate regional IP offices (i.e. ARIPO and OAPI) will not facilitate greater integration and unification, hence the need for a single continental IP office.[36] Furthermore, it is possible to argue that PAIPO can increase economies of scale in the coordination of scientific and technological resources for development.[37] PAIPO is also regarded as a step towards greater cooperation and singularity of position by African countries on issues relating to international IP law.[38] However, the centralization of IP administration on a continental level also has its disadvantages. In a continent as diverse as Africa, it might be difficult for countries with different problems and economic challenges to harmonize their IP laws.[39] Besides, as Drahos points out,

[34] ibid Article 4(q).
[35] ibid Article 4(h).
[36] Mupangavanhu (n 15) 3–4.
[37] Ncube and Laltaika (n 10) 115; Mupangavanhu (n 15) 4.
[38] Ncube and Laltaika (n 10) 115; Mupangavanhu (n 15) 4. See also, UNECA, AU, and AfDB, 'Innovation, Competitiveness and Regional Integration' Assessing Regional Integration in Africa VII (2016) x.
[39] See P Drahos, *The Global Governance of Knowledge: Patent Offices and their Clients* (CUP, 2010) 325.

regulatory capture becomes easier and cheaper when corporate actors have to deal with only one office.[40]

Another serious concern with PAIPO is the risk that it could lead to a recalibration of IP standards across the continent in a manner that is not suitable to the needs and economic challenges facing some of the countries on the continent.[41] Importantly, in its present form, there is a potential risk that the PAIPO Statute can negatively impact the ability of states to discharge their human rights obligations especially with regard to the rights to health and education. This issue will now be discussed.

3. The PAIPO Statute and Human Rights

There has been a lot of debate on the interface between IP and human rights.[42] This chapter will not address these debates exhaustively but a few salient points will be made regarding the status of IP in international human rights law. A good starting point in this regard is the Universal Declaration of Human Rights (UDHR) of 1948.[43] Article 27(1) of the UDHR recognizes the right of everyone 'to participate in the cultural life of the community, to enjoy the arts and to share in scientific advancement and its benefits'. Article 27(2) further recognizes the right of everyone to benefit from 'the protection of the moral and material interests resulting from any scientific, literary or artistic production of which he is the author'. Thus, it could be argued that Article 27 reflects an attempt by the UDHR drafters to find a balance between protecting the interests of members of the society in enjoying the arts and sharing in the gains produced through scientific advancements on one hand and protecting the interests of creators and inventors on the other hand. Article 27 (later incorporated into Article 15 of the International Covenant on Economic,

[40] ibid.

[41] A number of African countries have problems with regard to providing access to affordable medicines for their citizens. See T Pheage, 'Dying from lack of medicines' *African Renewal* (December 2016–March 2017) available at <https://www.un.org/africarenewal/magazine/december-2016-march-2017/dying-lack-medicines> accessed 11 May 2021. Access to learning materials is also a problem in Africa. See, S Bashir, M Lockheed, and others, *Facing Forward: Schooling for Learning in Africa* (Africa Development Forum Series, World Bank, 2018).

[42] There is an extensive literature on the interface between IP and human rights. See generally P Drahos, 'Intellectual property and human rights' (1999) 3 Intellectual Property Quarterly 349; L Helfer, 'Human rights and intellectual property: conflict or coexistence?' (2003) 5(1) Minnesota Intellectual Property Review 47; P Yu, 'Reconceptualizing intellectual property interests in a human rights framework' (2007) 40 University of California Davis Law Review 1039; P Torremans (ed), *Intellectual Property and Human Rights* (Kluwer Law International, 2008); L Helfer and G Austin, *Human Rights and Intellectual Property: Mapping the Global Interface* (CUP, 2011); A Plomer, 'The human rights paradox: intellectual property rights and rights of access to science' (2013) 35(1) Human Rights Quarterly 143; C Geiger (ed), *Research Handbook on Human Rights and Intellectual Property* (Edward Elgar, 2015).

[43] UN General Assembly, Universal Declaration of Human Rights, 10 December 1948, 217 A (III).

Social and Cultural Rights (ICESCR))[44] does not make any direct reference to IP rights.[45] The provision therefore does not elevate IP rights to the status of human rights.[46]

Nevertheless, IP can be (and is being) used by states as a tool to protect the moral and material interests of creators. Moreover, states ought to equally structure IP laws in a manner that ensures that there is no interference with the right of their citizens to participate in the cultural life of the community and to enjoy the benefits of scientific advancements. It is thus contended here that in designing and implementing their national IP laws, states need to be mindful of their responsibility to respect, protect, and fulfil a number of human rights, especially the right to health[47] and the right to education.[48] Crucially, both the right to health and the right to education are intrinsically connected to the right to participate in the cultural life of the community and to share in the benefits of scientific advancements. Thus, protecting the right to education will enable individuals to participate meaningfully in the cultural life of the community. Likewise, sharing in the benefits of scientific advancements can contribute towards the health of individuals.

In other words, states need to incorporate a human rights perspective into their national IP laws.[49] It has even been argued that from a human rights perspective, states have an obligation to use the flexibilities available to them under international

[44] UN General Assembly, International Covenant on Economic, Social and Cultural Rights, 16 December 1966, UNTS, vol 993, p 3.

[45] Indeed, it has been suggested that one of the drafters' aims was to secure the interests of creators as 'intellectual workers'. This is apparent from a speech by the Mexican delegate in support of the inclusion of a provision to protect the 'material interests' of creators during the negotiations on the UDHR. According to the Mexican delegate, 'The Committee had already recognized the rights of the wage earner, the family, the mother and the child; if it did not wish there to be a serious omission in the text it was drawing up it must now proclaim the rights of the individual as an intellectual worker, scientist or writer.' UN GAOR, 'Draft International Declaration on Human Rights, Hundred and Fiftieth Meeting', 3d Sess., UN Doc. A/C.3/SR. 150 (1948) 617.

[46] The UN Committee on Economic, Social and Cultural Rights (UN CESCR) in its General Comment No 17 on Article 15(1)(c) of the ICESCR has cautioned against equating intellectual property rights with the human right to the protection of the moral and material interests of creators. CESCR, 'General Comment No 17, The Right of Everyone to Benefit from the Protection of the Moral and Material Interests Resulting from any Scientific, Literary or Artistic Production of which He or She is the Author (Article 15, Paragraph 1(c) of the Covenant)' E/C.12/GC/17 (2006) para 3. See also, L Shaver, 'The right to science and culture' (2010) 1 Wisconsin Law Review 121, 150.

[47] The right to health is recognized in Article 25 of the UDHR, Article 12 of the ICESCR, and Article 16 of the ACHPR.

[48] The right to education is recognized in Article 26 of the UDHR, Article 13 of the ICESCR, and Article 17 of the ACHPR.

[49] For instance, in a line of cases, the Court of Justice of the European Union has emphasized the importance of striking a fair balance between the protection of IP and other human rights. In this regard see *Scarlet Extended SA v SABAM*, Case C-70/10 (24 November 2011) para 53 (holding that, 'in adopting the injunction requiring the ISP to install the contested filtering system, the national court concerned would not be respecting the requirement that a fair balance be struck between the right to intellectual property, on the one hand, and the freedom to conduct business, the right to protection of personal data and the freedom to receive or impart information, on the other'.). See also, *SABAM v Netlog NV*, Case C-360/10 (15 February 2012); *UPC Telekabel Wien GmbH v Constantin Film Verleih GmbH*, Case C-314/12 (27 March 2014).

intellectual property law such as the World Trade Organization (WTO) Agreement on Trade Related Aspects of Intellectual Property Rights (TRIPS Agreement).[50] It should be noted that incorporating a human rights perspective into a country's IP laws does not mean that the protection of IP rights will be abolished or diminished in importance. It merely means that the protection of human rights should not be ignored in the design, implementation, revision, and interpretation of IP laws. Indeed, some national courts in Africa have had some experience with regard to incorporating a human rights perspective into the interpretation and application of national IP laws.[51] Furthermore, the ruling of a WTO Panel upholding the tobacco plain packaging law of Australia suggests that the framework of the TRIPS Agreement permits states to incorporate a human rights perspective into their national IP laws.[52]

It is against this backdrop that the PAIPO Statute needs to be critically examined. Its Preamble acknowledges, *inter alia*, 'international human rights laws and international agreements on sustainable development'. However, a critical examination of the Statute reveals that it merely pays lip service to human rights. This is apparent from the provisions of Article 4 which lists the functions of PAIPO. Indeed, there is no single reference to human rights or to the interface between IP and human rights in Article 4 of the Statute.

There is an undue emphasis on the promotion and protection of IP rights in Article 4 of the Statute. For instance, Article 4(e) empowers PAIPO to '[i]nitiate and facilitate strategies that shall promote and develop the intellectual property system'. Furthermore, Article 4(h) empowers PAIPO to '[t]ake deliberate measures to promote the protection and exploitation of intellectual property rights within the Member States, including conclusion of bilateral and multilateral agreements'. Moreover, Article 4(l) mandates PAIPO to '[p]romote the harmonization of intellectual property systems of its Member States, with particular regard to protection, exploitation, commercialization and enforcement of intellectual property rights'.

50 See Report of the Special Rapporteur in the field of cultural rights, Farida Shaheed, 'Patent policy and the right to science and culture' UN Doc. A/70/279 (2015) para 72. Shaheed's statement obviously only applies to the WTO Member States. It should be noted that except for a few countries that are currently observers seeking accession (i.e. Algeria, Libya, Sudan, Equatorial Guinea, South Sudan, Ethiopia, and Somalia), and Eritrea which is not a Member, all other African countries are Member States of the WTO. See WTO, 'Members and Observers' (2019) available at <https://www.wto.org/english/thewto_e/whatis_e/tif_e/org6_e.htm> accessed 11 May 2021.

51 See, for example,, Constitutional Court of South Africa, *Laugh It Off Promotions CC v South African Breweries International*, Case CCT 42/04, Judgment of 27 May 2005, [2005] ZACC 7, 2006 (1) SA 144 (CC) (making some pronouncements on the interface between trademarks and the right to freedom of expression). See also High Court of Kenya at Nairobi, *Patricia Asero Ochieng et al. v Attorney General*, Petition No. 409 of 2009, Judgment of 20 April 2012 (making some pronouncements on the interface between IP rights and the right to health).

52 WTO, *Australia – Certain Measures Concerning Trademarks, Geographical Indications and Other Plain Packaging Requirements Applicable to Tobacco Products and Packaging*, WT/DS435/R, WT/DS441/R, WT/DS458/R, WT/DS467/R Report of the Panels of 28 June 2018.

Importantly, although there is a general reference to the role of PAIPO in contributing to the accelerated achievement of the AU objectives as stated in the Constitutive Act,[53] there is no specific reference to the ACHPR in the PAIPO Statute. The drafting of the Statute rather suggests a lack of awareness of the impact that IP rights can have on the enjoyment of certain human rights such as the right to health and the right to education. Patent rights can have an impact on access to affordable medicines, and access to medicines is a component of the right to health[54] which is guaranteed in Article 16 of the ACHPR. Ironically, African countries played a major role in the process[55] that led to the adoption of the Doha Declaration on the TRIPS Agreement and Public Health which affirmed that the TRIPS Agreement should be interpreted in a manner supportive of the right of states to protect public health and promote access to medicines.[56] Moreover, as part of measures to protect public health, individual African countries might also need to regulate the use of trademarks in the sale of tobacco products in order to reduce the harmful effects of tobacco consumption.[57] In addition, copyright laws can have an impact on access to learning materials, and access to learning materials is a component of the right to education[58] which is guaranteed in Article 17 of the ACHPR.

It is therefore contended here that the PAIPO Statute does not really cohere with Article 3(h) of the Constitutive Act which provides that one of the objectives of the AU is to promote and protect human rights. PAIPO was created as a specialized agency of the Union, it is therefore crucial that its functions and activities correspond with the objectives of the AU. It would be odd if the Union can create

[53] Article 4(k) of the PAIPO Statute.

[54] See generally, UN CESCR 'General Comment No.14 on the right to the highest attainable standard of health, Article 12 of the International Covenant on Economic, Social and Cultural Rights', UN Doc. E/C.12/2000/4 (2000); UN Human Rights Council, 'Access to Medicines and Vaccines in the Context of the Right of Everyone to the Enjoyment of the Highest Attainable Standard of Physical and Mental Health', A/HRC/RES/41/10 (11 July 2019); H Hestermeyer, *Human Rights and the WTO: The Case of Patents and Access to Medicines* (OUP, 2007). Access to medicines also has implications with regard to the right to life.

[55] WTO Council for TRIPS, Proposal by the African Group, Bangladesh, Barbados, Bolivia, Brazil, Cuba, Dominican Republic, Ecuador, Haiti, Honduras, India, Indonesia, Jamaica, Pakistan, Paraguay, Philippines, Peru, Sri Lanka, Thailand, and Venezuela, 'Ministerial Declaration on the TRIPS Agreement and Public Health' IP/C/W/312; WT/GC/W/450, (4 October 2001).

[56] WTO, 'Declaration on the TRIPS Agreement and Public Health' adopted on 14 November 2001, WT/MIN(01)/DEC/2 (2001) para 4.

[57] For instance, in May 2018, the South African Department of Health published the Control of Tobacco Products and Electronic Delivery Systems Bill of 2018 which would introduce plain packaging measures in South Africa if passed into law. At the time of writing, the status of this Bill was unclear.

[58] L Helfer and G Austin, *Human Rights and Intellectual Property: Mapping the Global Interface* (CUP, 2011). See also UN CESCR, 'General Comment No. 13: The Right to Education (Art. 13)' E/C.12/1999/10 (1999); F Coomans, 'Content and Scope of the Right to Education as Human Right and Obstacles to its Realization' in Y Donders and V Volodin (eds), *Human Rights in Education, Science and Culture: Legal Developments and Challenges* (UNESCO/Ashgate, 2007) 183–230; S Foster, 'The Conflict between the Human Right to Education and Copyright' in P Torremans (ed), *Intellectual Property and Human Rights* (Kluwer Law International, 2008) 287–306; C Armstrong, J de Beer, and others (eds), *Access to Knowledge in Africa: The Role of Copyright* (UCT Press, 2010).

specialized agencies whose functions do not correspond with its objectives. There is really no reason why a human rights perspective cannot be incorporated into PAIPO's functions and overall mandate.

Besides, it is worth emphasizing here that PAIPO is not designed to function like a typical IP office that merely receives, examines, and grants applications for patents and trademarks (such as the US Patent and Trademark Office and the European Patent Office). As noted above in section 2, the Statute empowers PAIPO to harmonize the IP laws of its Member States and, consequently, it would not only be administering IP laws but it would also have law-making powers. It is crucial that these law-making powers are exercised in a manner that is compatible with human rights. Considering the impact that IP rights can have on human rights, such as the rights to health and education, it is suggested here that the Statute (specifically, Article 4) be amended to incorporate a human rights perspective and bring it in line with both the objectives of the AU and the relevant provisions of the ACHPR.

4. Suggestions for Revising the PAIPO Statute

In thinking about the revision of the PAIPO Statute, two key principles need to be borne in mind. One, the importance of a balanced approach to the protection of IP rights as enshrined, for instance, in Articles 7 and 8 of the TRIPS Agreement. Two, as argued in section 3 above, the importance of incorporating a human rights perspective into the design and implementation of IP laws.

In relation to the importance of a balanced approach to the protection of IP rights, it is pertinent to consider the object and purpose of IP protection as laid out in a preeminent treaty on IP rights, the TRIPS Agreement. The object and purpose of the TRIPS Agreement is laid out in its Articles 7 and 8 thereof, which read as follows:

> Article 7 The protection and enforcement of intellectual property rights should contribute to the promotion of technological innovation and to the transfer and dissemination of technology, to the mutual advantage of producers and users of technological knowledge and in a manner conducive to social and economic welfare, and to a balance of rights and obligations.
>
> Article 8(1) Members may, in formulating or amending their laws and regulations, adopt measures necessary to protect public health and nutrition, and to promote the public interest in sectors of vital importance to their socio-economic and technological development, provided that such measures are consistent with the provisions of this Agreement.
>
> Article 8(2) Appropriate measures, provided that they are consistent with the provisions of this Agreement, may be needed to prevent the abuse of intellectual

property rights by right holders or the resort to practices which unreasonably restrain trade or adversely affect the international transfer of technology.

The goal of both Articles 7 and 8 can be summed up in one word, balance.[59] Thus, the TRIPS Agreement permits states to adopt a balanced approach to the protection and enforcement of IP rights. Crucially, IP laws should not simply be focused on securing the rights and interests of those who own IP rights but the needs and interests of the society as a whole also need to be taken into consideration. It is thus surprising that the PAIPO Statute fails to adopt this balanced approach. The emphasis of the PAIPO Statute is overwhelmingly on securing the rights and interests of those who own IP rights. This is encapsulated in the provisions of Article 4(l) of the PAIPO Statute which tasks PAIPO with the duty to promote the harmonization of IP systems in Africa and with further instructions that this should be done 'with particular regard to protection, exploitation, commercialization and enforcement of intellectual property rights'. It is contended here that this is not a balanced approach to the protection of IP rights. In order to address this gap in the PAIPO Statute, Ncube and Laltaika have rightly recommended that 'the text of the Preamble be revised to emphasize such perspectives as is done by Articles 7 and 8(1)' of the TRIPS Agreement.[60]

Concerning the importance of incorporating a human rights perspective into the design and implementation of IP laws, it is worth noting that a balanced approach to the protection and enforcement of IP rights also entails the need to consider other rights and obligations that exist outside of the IP system such as human rights. In other words, the incorporation of a human rights perspective as outlined in section 3 above is compatible with a balanced approach to the protection of IP rights.[61] Thus, a balanced approach to the protection of IP rights would give due consideration to human rights such as the rights to health and education.

In light of the analysis above, this chapter suggests that Article 4 of the PAIPO Statute should be revised to include the following two provisions:

> The PAIPO shall:
> Promote and facilitate the protection and enforcement of intellectual property in a manner that promotes and respects human rights and fundamental freedoms as recognized in the African Charter on Human and Peoples' Rights and in any other relevant treaty that Member States have ratified.

[59] See S Frankel, 'WTO application of the customary rules of interpretation of public international law to intellectual property' (2006) 46 Virginia Journal of International Law 365, 393. See also P Yu, 'The objectives and principles of the TRIPS Agreement' (2009) 46 Houston Law Review 979.

[60] Ncube and Laltaika (n 10) 116.

[61] See A Slade, 'The objectives and principles of the WTO TRIPS Agreement: a detailed anatomy' (2016) 53 Osgoode Hall Law Journal 948, 971–2.

> Promote and facilitate the protection and enforcement of intellectual property in a manner that is appropriate to and in accordance with the level of technological and economic development of each of the member states, in a manner conducive to social and economic welfare, and to a balance of rights and obligations.

The inclusion of these two provisions will help to align the functions of PAIPO with the objective of the AU to promote and protect human rights. It will also help to avoid an incoherence between the functions of PAIPO and the ACHPR. Furthermore, it will help to prevent a situation where African countries will be unable to discharge their human rights responsibilities as enshrined in their national constitutions and other relevant international treaties to which they are parties. Importantly, the provisions will help to ensure a balanced approach to the protection of IP rights at the continental level in Africa. Moreover, these two provisions will help to secure the IP policy space of African countries and this will help them to tailor their national IP laws to suit their respective needs and challenges.

5. Conclusion

Notwithstanding the merits or otherwise of the creation of a centralized IP organization in Africa, one cannot help but wonder whether such an organization should be a priority for Africa at this point in time. In order to spur technological and economic development in Africa, it is suggested that greater investment in human capital development (especially education) should be the priority.

This line of reasoning is also reflected in a report jointly published by the UN Economic Commission for Africa, the AU, and the African Development Bank.[62] While not opposed to the creation of PAIPO, the joint report notes that, with regard to regional integration, innovation and competitiveness, policy-makers in Africa should 'start with crafting and then effectively implementing policies anchored on human capital development, with special attention to higher education'.[63] Interestingly, the report also stresses the importance of using the flexibilities contained in the global IP regime to preserve the policy space of African countries in order to ensure that IP laws are designed in a manner that is suitable to their changing development needs.[64]

Instructively, and contrary to the mandate of PAIPO which stresses the harmonization of IP standards, the joint report recommends that African countries 'should consider adopting differential standards of intellectual property protection within

[62] UNECA, AU, and AfDB, 'Innovation, competitiveness and regional integration' Assessing Regional Integration in Africa VII (2016).

[63] ibid ix. The report goes on to note that '[i[ntellectual property rights cannot boost innovation if the required conditions – skills, information, capital, market prospects – do not exist'. ibid 60.

[64] ibid.

the flexibilities of the TRIPS Agreement'.[65] It is also noteworthy that, according to this report, one of the challenges flowing from the current two regional IP offices in Africa, i.e. ARIPO and OAPI, is that they 'tend to take a "one size fits all" approach in attempting to harmonize rather than coordinate' and this further reduces the policy space available to African countries with regard to IP.[66] It is suggested here that the coordination of IP laws in Africa is preferable to harmonization because the countries in Africa are at different levels of technological and economic development. Thus, what may be an appropriate level of IP protection in one African country may not be suitable to the technological, educational, and health needs of another. The 'one-size-fits-all' approach of the current regional IP offices (particularly OAPI) is thus quite problematic. With its current mandate, it seems that PAIPO will only reinforce, rather than attenuate, this particular challenge.

Preserving a country's IP policy space is critical to ensuring that its IP system does not have a negative impact on the protection and promotion of relevant human rights. Thus, with its current mandate to harmonize IP standards across Africa, PAIPO might make it more difficult for African countries to design their IP laws in a manner that respects the human rights of their citizens. While IP rights are important, they should be seen as a means to an end and not an end in themselves. Importantly, they should be conceptualized as tools that can be used to promote and facilitate the enjoyment of human rights.

[65] ibid 9.

[66] ibid 74. See also C Ncube, T Schonwetter, and others, 'Intellectual Property Rights and Innovation: Assessing Regional Integration in Africa (ARIA VIII)' *Open AIR*, Working Paper 5 (5 May 2017) 9.

PART 3

ADDRESSING CIVIL AND POLITICAL CHALLENGES THROUGH AFRICAN UNION LAW: PERSPECTIVES

9
Is the AU Best Placed to Advance Cross-Cutting Gender Rights' Harmonization of Customary Laws?

Adaeze Okoye

1. Introduction

The advent of the AU is seen as the resurgence of Pan-Africanism which holds the potential to tackle huge socio-economic development challenges collectively.[1] The AU has adopted robust international human rights protections covered amongst others by the African Charter on Human and Peoples' Rights[2] (the African Charter) and the Protocol to the African Charter on Human and Peoples Rights on the Rights of Women in Africa (the Maputo Protocol),[3] backed up by the AU's African Court of Human and People's Rights (AfCtHPR). The AfCtHPR is a result of the 1998 Protocol to the African Charter that came into force in 2004.[4]

And yet, the African context presents a unique challenge in the implementation and actualization of the rights narrative because of the plurality of legal systems and key questions about the relationship between context and human rights.[5] The questions touch on the 'universality' and the dominance of the Western tradition in the conceptualization of human rights.[6] Flowing from this, the issue is whether

[1] GJ Naldi and KD Magliveras, 'The African Court of Justice and Human Rights: a judicial curate's egg' (2012) 9 International Organisations Law Review 383–449.

[2] African Charter on Human and Peoples Rights. This is also referred to as the Banjul Charter. Adopted 27 June 1981, OAU Doc. CAB/LEG/67/3 rev. 5, 21 ILM 58 (1982), entered into force 21 October 1986, see <https://www.achpr.org/legalinstruments/detail?id=49> accessed 24 July 2020.

[3] Date of Adoption 11 July 2003, entered into Force 25 November 2005, see <https://au.int/en/treaties/protocol-african-charter-human-and-peoples-rights-rights-women-africa> accessed 24 July 2020.

[4] Protocol to the African Charter on Human and People's Rights on the Establishment of an African Court on Human and People's Rights. Date of Adoption 10 January 1998, entered into Force: 25 January 2004, see <https://au.int/en/treaties/protocol-african-charter-human-and-peoples-rights-establishment-african-court-human-and> accessed 24 July 2020.

[5] L Ramina, 'Third world approaches to international law and human rights: some considerations' (2018) 5(1) Journal of Consitutional Research (Revista de investigacoes constitucionais) 261–72; M Mutua 'Savages, victims and saviors. The metaphor of human rights.' (2001) 42(1) Harvard International Law Journal 201–45.

[6] B Rajagopal, *International Law from Below: Development, Social Movements and Third World Resistance* (CUP, 2003). Amao also discusses this in relation to conceptions of African law in Chapter 2 of F Amao *African Union Law: The Emergence of a Sui Generis Legal Order* (Routledge, 2018).

Adaeze Okoye, *Is the AU Best Placed to Advance Cross-Cutting Gender Rights' Harmonization of Customary Laws?* In: *The Emergent African Union Law.* Edited by: Olufemi Amao, Michèle Olivier and Konstantinos D. Magliveras, Oxford University Press. © Adaeze Okoye 2021. DOI: 10.1093/oso/9780198862154.003.0010

customary law, often perceived as mere customary practices, should be considered as culturally discriminatory towards women. This issue is recognized in the joint AU/UN report released on women's rights in Africa in 2017.[7] The report identified that a number of countries had reservations about the Maputo Protocol on the grounds that certain articles are incompatible with 'national law, tradition, religion and culture'.[8] It also identified the problem of 'contestation' between the 'universality' of human rights and particular African values relating to women.[9]

Therefore, customary law and human rights are often presented as opposing forces either to be balanced or subjugated in a hierarchical format. Bennett points out that some human rights narratives can be seen as a resonance of the past because 'the present talk about human rights has an echo of the 1960s ... when it was believed that customary law was primitive and backward and should be swept aside to make way for a brave new legal order imported from the West'.[10] Nonetheless, the resilience of customary law can be seen as a challenge to an overriding Western-based human rights narrative.[11] Lagoutte suggests instead the need for the balancing approach from West African studies including Benin, Senegal, Niger, and Mali. She proposes 'a balance between acknowledging the practices that the population in its vast majority still follows and the requirements of international and regional human rights law which also applies in these countries'.[12]

Furthermore, the notion of subjugation of customary law entrenches the colonial narrative of outdated and repugnant customs and practices as a dominant aspect of customary law and therefore denies to customary laws the ongoing examination to which 'proper' laws are globally subjected. Such examination could result in reform, development, and evolution. Furthermore, when attempts are made to reconcile customary law with received laws from this subjugated outlook, it results in a lack of effectiveness, where the laws written in texts differ from the law observed in the daily lives of persons in their communities.[13] It does not accurately

[7] See AU/UN Women Rights in Africa Report available at <https://www.ohchr.org/Documents/Issues/Women/WRGS/WomensRightsinAfrica_singlepages.pdf> accessed 24 July 2020.

[8] ibid 13.

[9] ibid 19; see also VO Ayeni (ed) *The Impact of the African Charter and the Maputo Protocol in Selected African States* (Pretoria University Law Press, 2016).

[10] TW Bennett, 'The compatibility of African customary law and human rights' (1991) Acta Juridica 18–35, 32.

[11] ibid.

[12] S Lagoutte, 'Law makers ignore real life family issues in West Africa' 19 December 2014. The conference was supported by the Danish institute for Human Rights in Cotonou, Benin December 10–12 see <https://www.humanrights.dk/news/law-makers-ignore-real-life-family-issues-west-africa> accessed 24 July 2020.

[13] Some studies have explored these differences: see J Sarich, M Olivier, and others, 'Forced marriage, slavery and plural legal systems: an African example' (2016) 38(2) Human Rights Quarterly 450–76; see also F Von Benda-Beckmann and K Von Benda-Beckmann 'The dynamics of change and continuity in plural legal orders' 38 The Journal of Legal Pluralism and Unofficial Law 1–44.

depict women's experiences, and solutions proffered from this point of view yield a lack of effective outcomes.[14]

This lack of effectiveness is recognized by the Women's Gender & Development Directorate (WGDD) of the AU which accepts that 'many challenges still persist that hinder women and girls from attaining their full rights ... (including) ... entrenched cultural and religious practices, exclusionary economic systems ... as well as women's inability to own or inherit land'.[15] These challenges are linked to areas in many African countries which are regulated by customary laws such as laws that govern family life, marriage, leadership, and ownership of land and property.

This chapter proposes that the question of customary law's own evolution is essential and that this has the potential to contribute to the African human rights narrative from a bottom-up approach. This is urgent especially as the post-colonial African societies which make up the AU cannot afford to replicate within AU law the dominant narratives of international law without reflecting the rich traditions of the African continent itself. The proposal is that the legal transplantation of laws and rights at national or international level should take into account contextual contributions of evolved customary law because this has the potential to enhance effective implementation and development.

Article 2 of the Maputo Protocol, which provides for the elimination of all forms of discrimination against women, enshrines a top-down approach to social and cultural practices by imposing the obligation on states to eliminate, through legislation, and to modify social and cultural patterns through education, information, and so on.[16] The aim is that the state, as party to the treaty, bears responsibility for the effective implementation of these objectives. While state centrism is the traditional international law approach, this chapter advocates that the AU should also embrace alternative processes in international law which allow bottom-up law-making. It is suggested that an emerging AU law, as is suggested by various chapters in this book, will only enjoy the broad legitimacy needed if it reflects the life experiences and views of African communities and ordinary Africans.

This contextual bottom-up approach to AU law may have more success in embedding gender rights issues in customary laws across the AU states. The

[14] AS Manji ' Imagining women's 'legal world': towards a feminist theory of legal pluralism in Africa' (1999) 8(4) Social and Legal Studies 435–55 Manji points out that 'an exclusive focus on state law, which is the approach of a study located within the legal centralist paradigm, is inadequate to explain the law as it is experienced by women' 450.

[15] WGDD of the AU (2016), Maputo Protocol on Women's Rights: A living document for Women's Human Rights in Africa see <https://au.int/sites/default/files/documents/31520-doc-maputo_protocol_on_womens_rights_a_living_document_for_womens_human_rights_in_africa_submitted_by_the_women_gender_and_development_directorate_wgdd_of_the_african_union_commission.pdf> accessed 24 July 2020.

[16] Protocol to the African Charter on Human and People's Rights on the Rights of Women. Adopted 7 November 2003, entered into Force 25 November 2005 (Maputo Protocol) see <https://www.achpr.org/legalinstruments/>; <https://www.un.org/en/africa/osaa/pdf/au/protocol_rights_women_africa_2003.pdf> accessed 24 July 2020.

bottom-up approach will involve engagement with narratives, philosophies, and emblems of change from the grassroots and reflect this in AU law, implementation, and decisions. Levit points out this difference:

> In the traditional top-down approach, state elites enact rules (typically formal, treaty-based rules) that govern the practices and behaviour of those who are subject to the rules. In contrast, in the bottom-up approach, the practices and behaviours of various actors inform and constitute the rules, which, in turn, govern the practices and behaviours of those very same actors. The drama in these bottom-up cases is how the informal, practice-based rules become law.[17]

Whilst this approach acknowledges the plurality of African laws, it simultaneously recognizes their ability to contribute to new narratives of international law and regional law such as AU law.

The chapter begins with an analysis of the contextual background of legal pluralism in Africa, followed by an examination of the rights framework and the AfCtHPR case of *APDR & IHRDA v Republic of Mali* as an exemplar of a top-down approach. Section 3 illustrates what a bottom-up approach could look like by examining customary justice systems and domestic cases. The conclusion suggests that AU law could attempt to understand the nature of customary law and its development from below, to enable the effective implementation of rights of all genders including women. This is especially important in the areas effectively governed by customary law in many African societies.

2. Contextual Background: Legal Pluralism

The unique nature of African societies, its rich cultural heritage, and its colonial history have resulted in domestic legal systems which pose a conundrum to the traditional understandings of law. This is why African societies have been referred to as 'probably today's largest living laboratory of effective legal pluralism'.[18]

Legal pluralism can be seen in the operation of 'more than one legal system in a single political unit'.[19] In one sense, legal pluralism can be traced to colonialism. In this respect, Griffiths identifies the date, 1772, and the East India Company document devolving matters of inheritance, marriage, and caste to the local laws.[20] In

[17] JK Levit, 'A bottom-up approach to international law making: the tale of three trade finance instruments' (2005) 30(1) Yale Journal of International law 126–209, 126–7.

[18] J Fremont, 'Legal pluralism, customary law and human rights in Francophone African countries' (2009) 40(1) Victoria University of Wellington Law Review 149.

[19] D Pimentel, 'Legal pluralism in post-colonial Africa: linking statutory and customary adjudication in Mozambique' (2011) 14 Yale Human Rights and Development Law Journal 59–104.

[20] J Griffiths, 'What is legal pluralism?' (1986) 24 Journal of Legal Pluralism and Unofficial Law 1–56, 6.

more general terms, the British and the French imposed their laws on to customary laws, incorporating customary law only to the extent that it was not 'repugnant to natural justice, equity and good conscience' or 'inconsistent with any written law'.[21] Thus, customary law, which was unwritten and intertwined with the culture as the way of life of a people,[22] became subjugated to written law.

This resulted in a surfacing distinction between the 'law in action' and the 'law in books'.[23] These circumstances are apparent in the African context. Banda further points out that the dynamic nature of customary laws as 'living law' where the day-to-day practice differs from the fossilized customary law, evolved from this assimilation process.[24] She exemplified this by examining the diversity of unions and relationships viewed as marriage, within and outside the purview of the law in Tanzania, Botswana, South Africa, Namibia, Zambia, and Zimbabwe.[25]

Similarly, a West African family conference also recognized the gap between the letter of the law and the real life experiences in areas such as civil registration, access to court, experiences of unmarried women, and children born out of wedlock.[26] This is again reflected by further examples of marriages in East Africa,[27] and in the differences between the law and the social treatment of divorced women in Tunisia and the guardianship family law in Egypt (both in North Africa).[28]

To assert commonality of customary law to African legal systems does not mean that it is the same substantive customary law in each case. Customary laws are often community-specific and not country-specific. Due to the artificial demarcation of colonial borders, most modern African states are not homogeneous but instead composed of a plurality of peoples and cultures. There are not only customary law

[21] SE Merry, 'Legal pluralism' (1988) 22(5) Law and Society Review 869–96, 870. Demian also discusses the link between repugnancy clauses and power of disgust and shame on the one hand and a device to make external connections on the other. See M Demian, 'On the repugnance of customary law' (2014) 56(2) Comparative Studies in Social History 508–36.

[22] ibid.

[23] These are phrases coined by Roscoe Pound in advocacy for legal realism, see R Pound 'Law in books law in action' (1910) 44(1) American Law Review 12–36. See also the notion of living law, E Ehlirch 'The sociology of law' (1922) 36(2) Harvard Law Review 130–45, 141.

[24] F Banda 'Women, law and human rights in Southern Africa' 32(1) Journal of Southern African Studies 13–27; see also T Ranger 'The Invention of Tradition in Colonial Africa' in E Hobsbawm and T Ranger (eds), *The Invention of Tradition* (CUP, 1983) 211–62. Ranger analyses the extent of creativity that went into the assimilation and governance process.

[25] ibid 14–15.

[26] Lagoutte (n 12).

[27] B Bwire, 'Integration of African customary legal concepts into modern law: restorative justice: a Kenyan example' 9(1) Societies 17–25, 18, examining dowry (bride price) and polygamy.

[28] M Kimani, 'Women in North Africa secure more rights' July 2008 UN Africa Renewal magazine available at <https://www.un.org/africarenewal/magazine/july-2008/women-north-africa-secure-more-rights> accessed 24 July 2020. 'Ms. Moghadam notes that the countries of North Africa continue to be marked by social practices that not only discriminate against women and are inconsistent with international treaties, but also contravene their own national laws.' See also R Bendermel, 'Why do Tunisian women divorce more and more often?' see <http://eng.babelmed.net/article/7717-why-do-the-tunisian-women-divorce-more-and-more-often/> E Jobrane, 'Bridging the rights between women's right and practice in Tunisia' *Arab Weekly* (30 March 2019) available at <https://thearabweekly.com/bridging-gap-between-womens-rights-and-practice-tunisia> accessed 24 July 2020.

differences within the same domestic legal system for example in countries with large and diverse populations like Nigeria[29] but also and across different regions such as West, East, Central, Southern, and North Africa.[30] There are patrilineal and matrilineal societies as well as agricultural, nomadic, and trading communities which impact on the content of substantive law adhered to by those societies.[31]

To gain a fuller picture of the African legal landscape, one must add a further layer of national laws framed after independence on to a mix of received laws and post-independence law-making as well as regional and international laws. These regional and international laws will include United Nations treaties, treaties and decisions of the AU, and the eight Regional Economic Communities (REC).[32]

Legal pluralism within the national legal systems means that any supranational process adds a further layer of legal regulation. Yet, there is a role for such legal pluralism to feed into AU law and for the one system to complement the other. In this instance, customary law has the potential to evolve within the analysis of the body of work which should constitute AU law. This is important for three reasons. First, it will contribute to engagement with profound questions about decolonization of thought and legal processes and the necessity for the specific contribution of the 'third world' to human rights discourse. It will challenge the perception that developing countries, such as those within Africa, are the 'principal arena of deployment of human rights'[33] but with little input in the 'origins and evolution of human rights discourse'.[34]

Secondly, it will help address the notorious implementation gap, especially the limitations that law can have in changing behaviour and practices within African communities.[35] The customary form of law represents a bridging law that takes socio-cultural factors into account. Given the participatory informal law-making process of customary law, a sole emphasis on top-down regulation may demoralize

[29] AA Oba, 'Religious and customary laws in Nigeria' 25(2) Emory International Law Review (2011) 881–95.

[30] See the J Fenrich, P Galizzi, and others (eds.) *The Future of African Customary law* (CUP, 2011). Stewart wrote on the paucity of information concerning customary law in North Africa. See FH Stewart, 'Customary law in North Africa and the Arab East' (2006) 13 Islamic Law and Society 1–5.

[31] J Goody and J Buckley, 'Inheritance and women's labour in Africa' (1973) 43(2) Africa Journal of International African Institute 108–21; A Sheikh-Mohammed and JP Velema, 'Where health has no access: the nomadic populations of sub-Saharan Africa' (1999) 4(10) Tropical Medicine & International Health 695–707; D Northrup, 'The growth of trade among the Igbo before 1800' (1972) 13(2) The Journal of African History 217–36.

[32] The Arab Maghreb Union (North), the Economic Community of West African States (West), the East African Community (East), the South African Development Community (South), the Common Market for Eastern and Southern Africa (South-East), the Economic Community of Central African states (Central), the Community of Central Sahel-Saharan States (North), the Intergovernmental Authority on Development (East). For details on the RECs see the UN Office of the Special Adviser on Africa (OSAA) The Regional Economic Communities of the African Union available at <https://www.un.org/en/africa/osaa/peace/recs.shtml> accessed 24 July 2020.

[33] B Rajagopal, *International Law from Below: Development, Social Movements and Third World Resistance* (CUP, 2003) 172.

[34] ibid.

[35] See Banda (n 24).

and silence the voices of evolution and law reform in customary settings and within the traditional justice systems. This is especially the case when it results in the simplification of narrative that places the local customs within the full scope of the legacy of repugnancy tests yet stultifies it with very little change to everyday practice.

The final argument is about the wider contextualization of human rights in the African community. It has been pointed out that 'the development of the state in Africa is so radically different from its European equivalent that the traditional liberal conception of the relationship between state and individuals is of limited utility in imagining a viable regime of human rights'.[36] In the case of women, it is important to note that historically, women have not always been passive recipients and that the cultural historic rules for women have not always been a single delineated story. There have been strong roles for women in African agriculture, economics, and politics. For example, this is evidenced by the Aba women's war against the British colonial government in 1920s south-east Nigeria.[37] The necessity for African voices to speak and be heard in any evolution of rights discourse is essential to the survival and success of the transplantation of rights in the African setting. Furthermore, the role of traditional justice systems and their ability to evolve solutions can be seen in old systems such as woman-to-woman marriage[38] or the 'oil-ekpe' custom.[39] While these were not always egalitarian solutions, they revealed the innate ability of customary law as responsive law. In the case of these examples, traditional methods devised by women to circumvent the male inheritance rule are clearly illustrated.[40]

Section 3 now examines the current framework for gender rights within AU law.

3. Gender Rights within the AU Law Framework

AU law is seen as 'a body of treaties, resolutions and decisions that have direct or indirect application to the member states of the AU'[41] and as such presents form of international regulation at the regional level. The Organisation of African Unity (OAU) was created in 1963 and by 1965 was granted UN observer status in the

[36] M Mutua, 'Conflicting conceptions of human rights: rethinking the post-colonial state' (1995) 89 Proceedings of the Annual Meeting (American Society of International Law) 487–90, 489.

[37] F I Abaraonye 'The Women's War of 1929 in South-Eastern Nigeria' in MJ Diamond (ed) *Women and Revolution: Global Expressions* (Springer, 1998).

[38] CO Akpamgbo 'A "woman to woman" marriage and the repugnancy clause: a case of putting new wine into old bottles' (1977) 9 (14) The Journal of Legal Pluralism and Unofficial Law 87–95.

[39] AC Diala 'A critique of the judicial attitude towards matrimonial property rights under customary law in Nigeria's southern states' (2018) 18(1) African Human Rights Law Journal 100–22.

[40] NU Nzegwu, *Family Matters: Feminist Concepts in African Philosophy of Culture* (State University of New York Press Albany, 2006) 136.

[41] See Chapter 1, M Olivier.

spirit of cooperation between the two international organizations to indicate that the former is recognized as a subject of international law.[42]

When the AU was established in 2002 as a successor to the OAU, the Constitutive Act of the AU[43] identified (among other things) the objective to 'promote and protect human and peoples' rights in accordance with the African Charter on Human and Peoples' Rights and other relevant human rights instruments'[44] and 'promote sustainable development at the economic, social and cultural levels as well as the integration of African economies'.[45] The Protocol on Amendments to the Constitutive Act of the African Union adds the inclusion of other objectives, such as to 'ensure to ensure the effective participation of women in decision-making particularly in the political, economic and socio-cultural areas'.[46]

Thus, a key principle enshrined in the Constitutive Act is the promotion of gender equality.[47] In line with this the AU published a gender policy in 2009.[48] This is based on the two main human rights documents of the AU, namely the African Charter[49] and the Maputo Protocol.[50] The historical background to the promotion of gender equality also draws on the UN Convention for the Elimination of All Forms of Discrimination Against Women (CEDAW).[51] The African Commission on Human and Peoples Right established by the African Charter[52] is encouraged to draw on inspiration from international law on human and people's rights.[53]

The key document on women's rights in Africa is the Maputo Protocol, signed in 2003 and entered into force in 2005. It enshrines an extensive number of women's rights such as elimination of discrimination;[54] dignity;[55] life, integrity, and security;[56] elimination of harmful practices;[57] marriage;[58] access to justice and equal

[42] UNGA 20th Session A/RES/ 2011 (XX) see <https://undocs.org/en/A/RES/2011(XX)>accessed 24 July 2020.

[43] The Constitutive Act Adopted 11th July 2000 (36th Ordinary Session of the assembly of heads of state and government, Lome, Togo) available at <https://au.int/en/constitutive-act> accessed 24 July 2020.

[44] ibid Article 3h.

[45] ibid Article 3j.

[46] Article 3i, The Protocol on Amendments to the Constitutive Act, adopted 11 July 2003 available at <https://au.int/en/treaties/protocol-amendments-constitutive-act-african-union> accessed 24 July 2020.

[47] Article 4L, the Constitutive Act (n 43).

[48] AU Gender Policy available at <https://www.un.org/en/africa/osaa/pdf/au/gender_policy_2009.pdf> accessed 24 July 2020.

[49] African Charter (n 2).

[50] Maputo Protocol (n 16).

[51] CEDAW, adopted 18 December 1979, entry into force 3 September 1981 available at <https://www.ohchr.org/Documents/ProfessionalInterest/cedaw.pdf> accessed 24 July 2020.

[52] See Article 30 of the African Charter (n 2) and Article 45 of the African Charter (n 2) for the Mandate of the African Commission.

[53] See Article 60 of the African Charter (n 2).

[54] Article 2 Maputo Protocol (n 16).

[55] ibid Article 3.

[56] ibid Article 4.

[57] ibid Article 5.

[58] ibid Article 6, Article 7 covers Separation, Divorce and Annulment.

protection;[59] participation in the political and decision-making process;[60] protection of women in armed conflicts;[61] peace;[62] education and training;[63] economic social welfare rights;[64] health and reproductive rights;[65] food security;[66] adequate housing;[67] positive cultural context;[68] healthy and sustainable environment;[69] sustainable development;[70] widow's rights;[71] inheritance;[72] and special protections of the elderly women, women with disabilities, and women in distress[73].

The implementation mechanisms rely on the traditional top-down enforcement mechanisms found in international treaties which include adoption of legislation implementing treaties and protocols at national level; national government plans and policies promoting gender equality and women's rights; and decisions of the African Commission and potentially domestic courts enforcing both international and national provisions implementing women's rights, depending on the nature of each individual national legal system.[74] Furthermore, unlike other regional human rights instruments such as the European Convention on Human Rights (ECHR), the American Convention on Human Rights (ACHR) and the International Covenant on Civil and Political Rights, the African Charter contains no derogation clause.[75] Therefore, there is also limited application of the 'margin of appreciation' doctrine which is present in the ECHR jurisprudence.[76] However the charter does contain specific clawback clauses which have been seen as a weakness in the system.[77]

[59] ibid Article 8.
[60] ibid Article 9.
[61] ibid Article 11.
[62] ibid Article 10.
[63] ibid Article 12.
[64] ibid Article 13.
[65] ibid Article 14.
[66] ibid Article 15.
[67] ibid Article 16.
[68] ibid Article 17.
[69] ibid Article 18.
[70] ibid Article 19.
[71] ibid Article 20.
[72] ibid Article 21.
[73] ibid Articles 22–24.
[74] Article 25 of the Maputo Protocol provides for remedies which are state responsibility: 'States Parties shall undertake to: a) provide for appropriate remedies to any woman whose rights or freedoms, as herein recognised, have been violated; b) ensure that such remedies are determined by competent judicial, administrative or legislative authorities, or by any other competent authority provided for by law', and Article 26 'States Parties shall ensure the implementation of this Protocol at national level, and in their periodic reports submitted in accordance with Article 62 of the African Charter, indicate the legislative and other measures undertaken for the full realisation of the rights herein recognised'. S Omondi, E Waweru, and others, *Breathing life into the Maputo Protocol: jurisprudence on the rights of women and girls in Africa* (Equality Now, 2018).
[75] See for an analysis: MA Toledo 'Absence of a derogation clause under the African Charter: The position of the African Commission' (2014) 4(2) Bahir Dar University Journal of Law 229–83.
[76] S Singh 'The impact of clawback clauses on human rights and people's rights in Africa (2009) 18(4) African Security Studies 95–104.
[77] ibid; see also: AO Enabulele Incompatibility of national law with African Charter on human and peoples' rights: does the African Court on Human and Peoples' Rights have the final say? (2016)

An exemplar of the top-down approach can be seen in the case *APDF & IHRD v Republic of Mali* (2018).[78] This was a case before the African Court of |Human Rights on the Mali Family Code. The AfCtHPR which operates from Arusha Tanzania is distinct and complementary to the African Commission. Article 3 of the Protocol provides that the jurisdiction of the court shall extend to all cases and disputes submitted to it concerning the interpretation and application of the Charter, this Protocol, and any of the relevant human rights instrument ratified by the states concerned.[79] The Court also has jurisdiction to decide any disputes about the jurisdiction of the court. Article 5 of the Protocol gives access rights to the commission, State Parties, and the African intergovernmental organizations. It also allows relevant non-governmental organizations with observer status before the Commission and individuals to institute cases directly before it in accordance with Article 34(6) of this Protocol.[80] This section also requires a state declaration of competence of the Court.[81]

In the case of *APDF & IHRDA v Republic of Mali* (2018), the Court had jurisdiction over the dispute regarding the Mali Family Code which was alleged to have infringed the human rights provisions of the Charter. Mali became a party to the African Charter in 1986, a party to the Protocol establishing the Court in 2004, and to the Maputo Protocol in 2005. The state had deposited the required declaration prescribed by Article 34(6). The case took place in the context of the government of Mali trying to qualify the rights of individuals and the family via modification legislation and to bring such rights in line with international human rights law. The reform process was marked by agitations and protests which resulted in further modifications and a new family code promulgated by the head of state on 30 December 2011.[82]

The non-governmental organizations (NGOs) Association pour le progrés et la défense des droits des femmes maliennes (APDF) and The institute for human rights and development in Africa (IHRDA) brought the case alleging violations

16(1) African Human Rights Law Journal available at <http://dx.doi.org/10.17159/1996-2096/2016/v16n1a1> accessed 23 July 2020. He points out that the African commission has set limits in its decisions to claw back legislation.

[78] *Association Pour Le Progres et la Defense Des Driot Des Femmes Maliennes (APDF) and The Institute for Human Rights and Development in Africa (IHRDA) V Republic of Mali* App. No 046/2016, Judgment: 11 May 2018. For a copy see <http://www.african-court.org/en/index.php/56-pending-cases-details/942-app-no-046-2016-apdf-ihrda-v-republic-of-mali-details> accessed 23 July 2020.

[79] Article 3 Protocol to the African Charter of Human and people's Rights on the establishment of the African Court on Human and people's rights (Court Protocol), adopted 10 June 1998, entry into force 25 January 2004 and available at <https://au.int/en/treaties/protocol-african-charter-human-and-peoples-rights-establishment-african-court-human-and> accessed 23 July 2020.

[80] Article 5(3) Court Protocol.

[81] Article 34(6) Court Protocol states that 'at the time of the ratification of this protocol or at any time thereafter the state shall make a declaration accepting the competence of the court to receive cases under article 5(3) of this protocol'.

[82] See the judgment: *APDF & anor. V Mali* (046/2016) [2018] AFCHPR 15

of relevant sections of international human rights instruments which protect the minimum age of marriage for girls, the right of consent to marriage, the right to inheritance, and the obligation to eliminate traditional practice and conduct harmful to the rights of women and children.[83] The Court established its jurisdiction with reference to the provisions of Articles 3(1) and 34(6) of the Protocol establishing the AfCtHPR.

With regard to the right to inheritance, which is enshrined in the Maputo Protocol, the Court examined Article 751 of the Family Code. This article applied the provisions of the new Family Code: 'when religion or custom has not been established in writing, by testimony, experience or by common knowledge or where deceased, in his lifetime has not manifested in writing or before witnesses his wish that his inheritance should be distributed otherwise'.[84] The NGO argued that this provision installs religious or traditional law as the default in matters of inheritance. They alleged therefore this meant that Islamic law which would give the woman half of what the man receives would violate Article 21 of the Maputo Protocol.

Article 21 requires that widows have an *equitable* share in the inheritance of the property of their husbands and that women and men to have the right to inherit in *equitable shares* from their parents' estates. The NGOs also alleged a violation of the Convention on the Elimination of Discrimination against Women (CEDAW)[85] if the practice did not give women the same share as men. They also noted that the Children's Charter[86] does not discriminate between children born in wedlock or out of wedlock, as is the case in Islamic law which they argued would only grant an equal share to children born out of wedlock on discretion.

The NGOs contended that although the new code provides for an equal share of the inheritance, the right would be rendered illusory if the application of customary or religious regimes are applicable in the absence of a will to the contrary. The state as respondent submitted that the initial code of 2009 had enshrined an equal share for men and women but that under pressure and the fear of social unrest, the state had agreed to redraft the text to acknowledge situations where citizens may want to determine succession to be arranged through customary or religious rules. It argued that the legislation had just simplified the mode of expression of this choice which can be made even by testimony.

However, the court found that Islamic law currently applicable in Mali in matters of inheritance and the customary practices are not in conformity with the

[83] ibid. Each of these issues were dealt with separately but our focus is on the right of inheritance as exemplar.
[84] See the judgment (n 82) at para 96, 21.
[85] CEDAW (n 51).
[86] African Charter on the Rights and Welfare of the Child, adopted 1 January 1990, entry into force 29 November 1999 available at <https://au.int/en/treaties/african-charter-rights-and-welfare-child> accessed 23 July 2020.

instruments ratified by the respondent state.[87] Therefore, it found the respondent state in violation of Article 21(2) of the Maputo Protocol and Articles 3 and 4 of the Children's Charter. The Court requested that the state comply with the obligation in Article 25 of the African Charter with respect to information, teaching, education, and public awareness of the populations. It also ordered the respondent state to submit a report on measures taken to address the amendment of the impugning law and harmonization as well as information on teaching, education, and public awareness within a period of two years from the date of the judgment.[88]

This is an interesting case because it represents the attempt of a government to modernize its existing framework which indicated gaps and lack of protection but also the intent of the government to bridge the gap between the international obligations and standards and the dominant practice of the people within the country. Pecorella noted that the derogation provided for in Article 15 of the ECHR would have sufficiently covered this scenario and that the African Charter does not have any clause of this kind, thereby resulting in a more stringent top-down application than in other regions.[89]

The question posed by the state in permitting for the expression of the will of the testator in inheritance matters to be in an unwritten form is one that needs to be explored in the context of customary law, especially in view of the literacy levels and chosen ways of expression of the local populations in African communities. The necessity for a will to be written is a dominant Western requirement which is not widely practised in African countries, resulting in a gap between applicable customary law and international human rights practice.

An underlying thrust of the arguments is the distrust of the flexibility allowed for by unwritten wills such as those suggested by the relevant provision of the Code. It is feared that the establishment of such intention or will by testimony or evidence at a traditional level could be abused and manipulated. These are not unwarranted concerns as there is anecdotal evidence of dominant patriarchal views at that level which may lead to exploitation of such exceptions enshrined in law.[90] However, to ignore the choice of the customary law or religious law totally may not yield to the desired effectiveness either.[91] If the intention is for law to have some impact

[87] See the judgment (n 76) at para 114, 24.

[88] See the judgment (n 82).

[89] The arguments for force majeure failed as the socio-economic circumstances could be foreseen, see G Pecorella, 'A commentary on the African Court's decision in the case APDF and IHRDA v Republic of Mali: why socio-cultural endemic factors of a society could support arguments based on force majeure' available at <https://internationallaw.blog/2019/01/14/a-commentary-on-the-african-courts-decision-in-the-case-apdf-and-ihrda-v-republic-of-mali-why-socio-cultural-endemic-factors-of-a-society-could-never-support-arguments-based-on-force-majeure/> accessed 23 July 2020.

[90] *The Guardian* report. ST Diarra, 'Women's rights in Mali set back "50 years" by new "Family code" law' available at <https://www.theguardian.com/global-development/2012/may/01/womens-rights-mali-50-years> accessed 23 July 2020.

[91] Paragraph 66 of the judgment (n 82). Mali asserts as follows: 'With regard to the allegation of violation of the minimum age of marriage, the Respondent State maintains that the established rules must not eclipse social, cultural and religious realities; that the distinction contained in Article 2g1 of the

on social practice, then the adoption of a different approach towards disputes of this nature may be necessary. Section 4 examines the potential for a bottom-up approach by examining traditional justice systems and cases in the domestic context highlighting contrasting approaches. Approaches are indicated which could feed into the international level and facilitate an expansion of rights at grassroots level.

4. The Potential Benefits of a Bottom-up Approach?

The International Development Law Organisation (IDLO) study on Mali 'estimates that 80% of family and land conflicts in poor and rural communities are handled by customary justice systems'.[92] Interviews conducted by the Clingendael Institute into customary systems in Northern Mali reveal the drivers of this high level of use are cost, accessibility, and efficiency.[93]

This is in line with the UN report on Human Rights and Traditional Justice Systems in Africa which also points to the scope of justice claims handled through the traditional system. It estimates that in some African countries, this could cover 80–90% of the total caseload.[94] The report highlights noticeable features of traditional justice systems that include a distinctive process and philosophy plus the importance of trust and familiarity in making this a forum which is used by the local populations. The context specific reasons for choosing such alternative forums include social cohesion, familiarity with the processes, and being an essential part of the relevant traditional culture and beliefs system. This underlines the importance of customary laws and justice systems in responding to community needs in an understanding and accessible manner.

The report also identifies divergence between legal models that are reflected in ex-colonies of Italy and the United Kingdom on the one hand, which acknowledge the existence of the customary law and run side by side with the official state systems versus ex-French colonies, where such legal plurality is less tolerated, with

Family Code should not be seen as a lowering of the marriage age or a discrimination against girls, but should rather be regarded as a provision that is more in line with the realities in Mali; that it would serve no purpose to enact a legislation which would never be implemented or would be difficult to implement to say the least; that the law should be in harmony with sociocultural realities; that it would serve no useful purpose creating a gap between the two realities.'

[92] IDLO, *Journeys to Justice; Exploring Customary Systems of Justice in Mali* (April 2018) available at <https://www.idlo.int/news/highlights/journeys-justice-exploring-customary-systems-mali> accessed 23 July 2020.

[93] D Goff, M Diallo, and others, *Under the Microscope: Customary Justice Systems in Northern Mali* (Clingendael, July 2017) available at <https://www.clingendael.org/sites/default/files/pdfs/under_the_microscope_customary_justice_systems_in_northern_mali.pdf> accessed 23 July 2020.

[94] See the UN and TJR in Africa report available at <https://www.ohchr.org/Documents/Publications/HR_PUB_16_2_HR_and_Traditional_Justice_Systems_in_Africa.pdf> accessed 23 July 2020.

limited legal recognition of customary justice in these states.[95] And yet, irrespective of the level of formality, recognition, and level of state regulation, such customary justice systems remain resilient across Africa because of links to the cultural and daily practices of the communities involved.

Accordingly, the IDLO confirms, 'there are three different systems of law at play in Mali that produce multifaceted legal dynamics: the legal legacy of French colonization; Islamic law, generally applied in the northern regions; and customary law, inspired by local practices and traditions'.[96] While such continued legal pluralism caters for parallel community needs, it may challenge government efforts to advance legal certainty and secure the rule of formal law at the same time.

Integration of legal systems across African communities can take on different forms as the report summarizes:

> Traditional forums were integrated into the official system and became the lowest levels of the official system (e.g., Mozambique, Malawi and the Sudan); traditional forums served as a parallel forum over which the formal courts would have appellate jurisdiction (e.g., Zimbabwe, Uganda and South Africa); or the formal court system recognized and incorporated aspects of the traditional system's customary substantive or procedural law (e.g., the Niger). In some countries, the disputants have a choice of going to the traditional justice system or the formal court system. In others, the traditional justice mechanism is the sole forum initially available.[97]

In Nigeria, for example, customary courts and sharia courts are both constitutionally recognized. The customary court of appeal and the Sharia court of appeal are specified in the constitution. Section 240 of the 1999 Constitution provides:[98]

> Subject to the provisions of this Constitution, the Court of Appeal shall have jurisdiction to the exclusion of any other court of law in Nigeria, to hear and determine appeals from the Federal High Court, the High Court of the Federation Capital Territory, Abuja, High Court of a state, Sharia Court of Appeal of the Federal Capital Territory, Abuja, Sharia Court of Appeal of a state, Customary Court of Appeal of a state and from decisions of a court martial or other tribunals as may be prescribed by an Act of the National Assembly.

However, the Constitution does not state a hierarchy of laws which means that the resolution of conflicts could be undertaken by reference to relevant constitutional

[95] ibid.
[96] See IDLO (n 92).
[97] UN and TJR in Africa (n 94) at 23.
[98] Constitution of the Federal Republic of Nigeria 1999 available at <https://publicofficialsfinancialdisclosure.worldbank.org/sites/fdl/files/assets/law-library-files/Nigeria_Constitution_1999_en.pdf> accessed 23 July 2020.

principles, international human rights treaties such as those within AU law or through repugnancy tests.[99] Regardless of how reconciliation takes place between customary law and state law, courts would need to engage with the philosophy of the customary law which they seek to change in order to give a persuasive judgment which would reform the traditional justice system in question.[100]

The position of women in traditional customary justice systems is varied. For example, Clingendael reporting on Northern Mali observes a varied response which ranged from marginalization in leadership roles in some parts to functional positions for older respected women in others.[101] However, the limitations with regards to leadership do not in themselves justify the subjugation of the role of such traditional justice systems as the judicial systems appeals to diverse users. These challenges for a representative judiciary (leadership/judges) are also faced in Western justice systems.[102]

Anekwe v Nzekwe,[103] a case before the Nigerian Supreme Court, is indicative of the dominant subjugation approach, yet there are aspects of the case which allow the exploration of a potential bottom-up approach. The respondent in this case put forward an assertion to her right to inheritance from her husband's estate under Awka customary law, irrespective of whether she had a male child or not. In confirmation of the foregoing assertion, she also relied on the final arbitration made by the highest level of chiefs in her society (Ozo Awka society) on this issue.[104]

The Court's judgment recognized the testimony of Ozo Nwogbo Okafor, which confirmed the respondent's assertion[105] but then proceeded to give a decision

[99] A Diala 'Reform of customary law of inheritance in Nigeria: lessons from South Africa' (2014) 14 African Human Rights Law Journal 633–54. For the explicit approach see Section 211 Constitution of the Republic of South Africa Act No 108 of 1996, which provides 'Recognition. (1) The institution, status and role of traditional leadership, according to customary law, are recognised, subject to the Constitution. (2) A traditional authority that observes a system of customary law may function subject to any applicable legislation and customs, which includes amendments to, or repeal of, that legislation or those customs. (3) The courts must apply customary law when that law is applicable, subject to the Constitution and any legislation that specifically deals with customary law. Section 212. Role of traditional leaders. (I) National legislation may provide for a role for traditional leadership as an institution at local level on matters affecting local communities. (2) To deal with matters relating to traditional leadership, the role of traditional leaders, customary law and the customs of communities observing a system of customary law (a) national or provincial legislation may provide for the establishment of houses of traditional leaders; and (b) national legislation may establish a council of traditional leaders.' This is available at <https://www.justice.gov.za/legislation/constitution/SAConstitution-web-eng-12.pdf> accessed 24 July 2020. However, the formalization of hierarchy and subjugation of customary law is not the only potential solution to reconciling the two legal systems.

[100] This is indicated to some extent in the cases of *Bhe & Others v Magistrate, Khayelitsha, & Others* (Commission for Gender Equality as amicus curiae); *Shibi v Sithole & Others*; *South African Human Rights Commission & Another v President of the Republic of South Africa & Another* 2005 (1) SA 580 (CC) (Bhe).

[101] See UN and TJR in Africa (n 94) 28–9.

[102] E Rackley, *Women Judging and the Judiciary: From Difference to Diversity* (Routledge, 2013). This examines the judiciary in England and Wales.

[103] See *Anekwe v Nweke* (2014) 9 NWLR 393–428, (SC129/2013) 11 April 2014.

[104] See ibid 395.

[105] This testimony said that the society deliberated on the matter and concluded by saying that the plaintiff is entitled to live in our husband's compound, and that under Awka custom even when a man

based on the repugnancy test. Notably, the Court did not refer upwards to national or international human rights instruments nor rely wholly downwards on the arbitral award of the customary law of the Ozo Awka society,[106] but instead focused on notions of repugnancy with comments stating that the culture was 'barbaric' and 'takes the Awka community to the era of the caveman'.[107] These proclamations did not permit the interrogation of the philosophy behind the evolved customary practice in order to encourage aspects of change emerging within its current practice. For example, it may have been necessary to establish if this customary decision was for the widow's possessory rights or for full inheritance rights, thereby building this judgment on change which was evidently taking place as evidenced by the *Ozo Awka* arbitral decision. This lack of interrogation of customary rules and focus on written law may be seen as a limitation of top-down legal centrism in general.[108]

Ironically this divergent approach was recognized in the colonial decision of *Eshugbaye Eleko v Government of Nigeria.* (1931),[109] where Lord Atkins suggested that:

> their Lordships entertain no doubt that the more barbarous customs of earlier days may under the influence of civilisation become milder without losing their essential character of custom. It would, however, appear to be *necessary to show that in their milder form they are still recognised in the native community as custom, so as in that form to regulate the relations of the native community inter se*. In other words, the Court cannot itself transform a barbarous custom into a milder one. If it still stands in its barbarous character it must be rejected as repugnant to 'natural justice, equity and good conscience.' It is the assent of the native community that gives a custom its validity, and, therefore, barbarous or mild, it must be shown to be recognised by the native community whose conduct it is supposed to regulate.

dies without a male child, the wife will not be driven away from her husband's compound; see Anekwe (n 103) 413.

[106] Nigeria has a dualist system and has domesticated the African Charter of Human Rights in the African Charter on Human and Peoples' Right (Ratification and Enforcement) Act. It is also bound by the Maputo Protocol as applied against it in the ECOWAS judgment, *Njemanze and others v Federal Government of Nigeria* (2017), Judgment no ECW/CCJ/JUD/08/17 available at <http://prod.courtecowas.org/wp-content/uploads/2019/01/ECW_CCJ_JUD_08_17-1.pdf> accessed 23 July 2020.

[107] See judgment (n 103) 399–401 and specifically the judgment of Ogubiyi JSC 421–22, Ngwuta JSC 425.

[108] Anthropological and philosophical investigations into customary property systems have found community-based systems or systems which seek to consolidate wealth and property through primogeniture. For example, the Succession to the Crown Act (UK) changed succession to the throne from male primogeniture to absolute primogeniture. The availability of alternative systems which allow for trusts or companies as a way of preserving the name and wealth within families will need to be critically and jurisprudentially observed.

[109] AC 662.

Engagement with and the evolution of customary law and justice systems are necessary to ensure the impact of AU law rights at a community level in Africa.[110] This must be done from a point which recognizes the validity of both systems of law whilst recognizing the need for reform in certain aspects of customary law. AU law has an opportunity to do things differently and add a democratic dimension to international law in the face of this strong presence of customary justice systems. This could begin with a different conversation between AU law and customary law. Levit points that[111]

> [t]his improvisational, practice-driven route to formal law stands in stark contrast to the familiar top-down, treaty-based story, with state diplomats and policymakers who are often quite removed from on-the-ground practice proclaiming the law. Bottom-up international law making does not replace or supplant traditional top-down accounts; within the international legal system, they operate side-by-side. Yet because international legal scholars have largely overlooked bottom-up law making in favor of more traditional stories, bottom-up law making has not yet played a significant role in international legal theory.

Therefore, within the African context, this engagement is a necessity if AU law is to have an impact. It could take the lead in exploring jurisprudential methodologies that allow for better interaction with customary justice systems across Africa. It could explore the issue of bottom-up law-making in AU law. This could begin with a legal contextual assessment undertaken directly or indirectly through the state which could allow for derogation with an implementation plan or, in the reverse, infer the possibility that good practice in customary law could find its way into state law or even AU treaties.

5. Conclusion

Customary law is often viewed as a static and outmoded type of informal law but its presence throughout African states presents a general platform for analysis about its potential contribution to AU law. Although such customary law displays a diversity within and between states and communities, exploring different contexts using a bottom-up approach to the harmonization of customary law and human rights could help develop a legitimate and effective AU law on gender rights.

To achieve this, conversations between customary law and international human rights instruments will have to take place. Existing national and regional case law,

[110] 'Customary justice is not a luxury – it's a necessity.' See IDLO (n 92).

[111] Levit (n 17) 173. Although she focuses on international trade and finance, the analogy exists because as she rightly identifies bottom-up law-making is rooted in custom.

which reflects both upwards and downwards, has an important role to play in enabling customary law's evolution and contribution to the narratives of rights.

Furthermore, human rights need to be contextualized for impact. Contextualization may yield contributions to the African narrative of human rights. The AU currently practises the top-down regional international law approach to issues of women rights and gender rights and this has proven to have limited impact. The suggestion is that there is potential to engage more actively with living customary laws and the traditional justice systems within which they operate. Such an approach will recognize the prevailing legal pluralism which is dominant in African countries while enhancing the impact of these rights in a way that ensures African ownership and contribution to such narratives.

There is also room for further detailed empirical research into traditional justice systems and customary law across Africa. Such studies could be explored at a continental level of AU law and thus contribute to a much needed bank of information for the progressive evolution of customary law. This is suggested as a necessary step in pushing for unique context-relevant, bottom-up methodologies and approaches to AU law.

10

The AU and Disputed Presidential Elections

Eki Yemisi Omorogbe

1. Introduction

The African Union (AU) like its predecessor organization, the Organisation of African Unity (OAU), holds that credible elections and democratic governance are crucial for peace, security, and development in African states.[1] Under the AU/OAU Declaration on the Principles Governing Democratic Elections in Africa (2002), elections in African states 'should be' conducted according to the wider democratic values and civil liberties.[2] That would include free and fair elections at regular intervals by impartial and competent electoral institutions under a system of governance in which the rights of opposition parties are respected and in which election results announced by competent national authorities are respected.[3] The majority of African states regularly hold multiparty elections. However, many of these elections are deeply flawed – as of 2019 only 10 of 55 Member States conducted elections according to wider democratic values.[4] A critical challenge is the reluctance of some heads of African states to cede power. Certainly, at mid-December 2019, eight serving heads of African states have been in power for more than 20 years.[5] The knock-on effect is that the peaceful transfer of executive power remains unusual in most African states.[6]

[1] OAU/African Union (AU), 'Declaration on the Principles Governing Democratic Elections in Africa' OAU/AU Doc. AHG/Decl.1 (XXXVIII) (8 July 2002), Articles II (3) and III (f).

[2] ibid sections II, III, and IV.

[3] ibid and section IV (13).

[4] Fully Democratic (10 states) (Benin, Botswana, Cape Verde, Ghana, Mauritius, Namibia, Sao Tome and Principe, Senegal, South Africa, and Tunisia). Partly democratic (23 states): Burkina Faso, Cameroon, Cote d'Ivoire, Comoros, Gambia, Guinea, Guinea Bissau, Kenya, Lesotho, Liberia, Madagascar, Malawi, Mali, Morocco, Mozambique, Niger, Nigeria, Seychelles, Sierra Leone, Tanzania, Togo, Zambia, and Zimbabwe. The remaining 22 states are authoritarian. Freedom House, 'Freedom in the World 2019 Countries' available at <https://freedomhouse.org/report/countries-world-freedom-2019> accessed 11 May 2021.

[5] Incumbent heads of African states at 18 December 2019: Teodoro Obiang Nguema (Equatorial Guinea) 40 years (since 3 August 1979); Paul Biya (Cameroon) 37 years as President (since 6 November 1982) and 5 years as Prime Minister 30 June 1975–76 November 1982; Yoweri Museveni (Uganda) 33 years (since 29 January 1986); Mswati III (Swaziland) 33 years (since 25 April 1986); Idriss Deby (Chad) 29 years (since 2 December 1990); Letsie III (Lesotho) 27 years in total (12 November 1990–15 January 1995 and since 7 February 1996); Isaias Afwerki (Eritrea] 26 years (since 27 April 1993); Ismail Omar Guelleh (Djibouti) 20 years (since 8 May 1999).

[6] KO Kufuor, 'The OAU and the recognition of governments in Africa: analyzing its practice and proposals for the future' (2002) 17(2) American University International Law Review 369–400, 369–70.

Eki Yemisi Omorogbe, *The AU and Disputed Presidential Elections* In: *The Emergent African Union Law*. Edited by: Olufemi Amao, Michèle Olivier and Konstantinos D. Magliveras, Oxford University Press.
DOI: 10.1093/oso/9780198862154.003.0011

This chapter considers the law, policy, and practice of the AU on unconstitutional changes of government. Section 2 of this chapter traces the development of the regional opposition to unconstitutional change and provides an overview of the AU's legal framework and policies against perpetrators. It argues that the AU's definition of unconstitutional change refers to the failure to cede office and other significant violations of democratic standards including fraudulent results obtained through rigged elections and the violent intimidation of the political opposition. Section 3 of this chapter considers the enforcement of AU law in practice. It focuses on fraudulent electoral practices (Kenya 2007 and Zimbabwe 2008) and the refusal of incumbents to transfer power following electoral defeat (Cote d'Ivoire 2010 and Gambia 2016). It shows that the AU generally supports negotiated settlements which allow the illegal incumbent to retain power, and that has led African Regional Economic Communities (RECs) and the United Nations (UN) to take the lead in resolving some crises. The exception is the Gambia where the AU led threats to use force to unseat an illegal incumbent, but ultimately supported a soft exit. The chapter concludes that AU practice, though improving, continues to undermine the deterrent effect of AU law and policy.

2. Instruments, Policies, and Responses on Unconstitutional Change

2.1 The OAU Framework: Sanctions and Negotiated Solutions

The OAU traditionally did not respond to unconstitutional changes in Member States. Nevertheless, in the post-Cold War era (1989 onwards), the OAU began to shift its focus on to how governments come to power. That is reflected in its promotion of democratic principles, in particular political pluralism, democratic elections, democratic institutions, human rights, and good governance, and its prohibition of unconstitutional change.[7] While the OAU's shift is open to criticism that it infringes on the non-interference principles in international law as recognized by the 1963 OAU Charter, the Member States supported this change in the light of the urgent peace, security, and socio-economic development challenges occurring in the African region.[8]

[7] See OAU Assembly, 'Declaration of the Political and Socio-economic Situation in Africa and the Fundamental Changes Taking Place in the World' (Addis Ababa, Ethiopia, 11 July 1990) OAU Doc. AHG/Decl.1 (XXVI) [6]; 'Decision' (Algiers, Algeria 12–14 July 1999) OAU Docs. AHG/Dec 141 (XXXV) and AHG/Dec 142 (XXXV) [1]; OAU, 'Decision on Unconstitutional Changes of Government in Africa' OAU Doc. AHG/Dec. 150 (XXXVI) (10–12 July 2000) [4](2]; OAU Council of Ministers, 'Sierra Leone' (Harare, Zimbabwe, 28–31 May 1997) OAU Doc. CM/356(LXVI)(c).

[8] Charter of the Organization of African Unity (entered into force 13 September 1963) 479 UNTS 39, Articles III(3) and III(2); OAU Assembly, 'Declaration of the Political and Socio-economic Situation' (n 7) [10]–[12]. Much has been written on the development of a right to democracy under international law and international interference in cases of human rights abuses. See, for example, M Olivier, 'The

A significant turning point came in 2000 when the OAU Assembly adopted the Declaration on a Framework for Response to Unconstitutional Changes of Government (the Lomé Declaration), providing definitions of situations which constitute an unconstitutional change of government:

- a military *coup d'état* against a democratically elected government;
- intervention by mercenaries to replace a democratically elected government;
- replacement of a democratically elected government by armed dissident groups and rebel movements;
- the refusal by an incumbent government to relinquish power to the winning party after free, fair, and regular elections.[9]

In the Lomé Declaration, the OAU adopted a policy of non-recognition of such unconstitutional governments and sanctions against these.[10] Sanctions, which were to be used incrementally in response to unconstitutional change within the first six months of the occurrence, range from immediate public condemnation and warning that such action will not be tolerated or recognized, to 'discreet moral pressure' to return the country to constitutional rule, and suspension from participating in OAU policy organs. Notably, it stopped short of suspension from OAU membership or financial obligations to the OAU. In the event of continued failure to return the country to constitutional rule, limited and targeted sanctions were also to be directed against the regime including visa denials, restriction of government-to-government contacts, and trade restrictions (in addition to the other OAU polices).[11]

It is not clear what would happen in the event the regime failed to regulate its behaviour. However, the Assembly prioritized negotiated solutions over the use of military force. That was made clear in the Solemn Declaration on Security, Stability, Development and Cooperation (CSSDA, adopted in the same session as the Lomé Declaration).[12] As will be illustrated, that softer approach when not backed by the threat of firmer action can undermine quick responses to constitutional crises in African states.

Emergence of a Right to Democracy – An African Perspective' in C Panara and G Wilson (eds), *The Arab Spring – New Patters of Democracy and International Law* (Martinus Nijhoff Publishers, 2013) 29–52.

[9] OAU, 'Declaration on the Framework for an OAU Response to Unconstitutional Changes of Government' OAU Doc. AHG/Decl.5 (XXXVI) (10–12 July 2000).

[10] ibid.

[11] ibid.

[12] CSSDCA Solemn Declaration OAU Doc. AHG/Decl.4 (XXXVI) 2000, Article 14(b) and 14(e), in relation to stability.

2.2 The AU: Powers and Procedure

Crucially, the OAU Assembly also adopted the Constitutive Act of the AU at the Lomé meeting.[13] The Constitutive Act entered into force on 26 May 2001, after ratification by two-thirds of the Member States of the OAU, and replaced the OAU Charter.[14] By 7 July 2003, all of the 53 OAU Member States – every state in Africa other than Morocco – had ratified the Constitutive Act.[15] By 20 January 2017, all 55 states in Africa have ratified it. Key provisions of the AU Constitutive Act place democratization at the heart of the AU's agenda. The list of 'objectives' set out in Article 3 of the Constitutive Act which the AU is to promote include 'democratic principles and institutions, popular participation and good governance' and 'human and peoples' rights in accordance with the African Charter Human and Peoples' [Banjul Charter] and other relevant human rights instruments'.[16] That includes the right to participate freely in public affairs either directly or through freely chosen representatives as provided under Article 13 of the Banjul Charter.[17] The list of 'principles', set out in Article 4 of the Constitutive Act includes 'respect for democratic principles, human rights, the rule of law and good governance' and the 'condemnation and rejection of unconstitutional changes of governments'.[18]

The Constitutive Act specifically prohibits unconstitutional change in providing that the AU may impose sanctions against an AU state whose government has come to power by unconstitutional means. Under Article 30, the AU may suspend the state from AU activities. No time limit is placed on the suspension. However, it is assumed that the suspension is to be lifted once the state returns to constitutional order. The AU's practice in respect of governments that come to power through coup d'états support this conclusion.[19] More generally, the AU can impose sanctions on a Member State that fails to comply with AU decisions and policies (Article 23(1)–(2)).

The Constitutive Act also opens up the possibility of AU military action against a regime that has come to power by unconstitutional means. Under Article 4(j) of the Constitutive Act, Member States may request intervention 'in order to restore

[13] OAU, 'Decision on the establishment of the African Union and the Pan-African Parliament' (10–12 July 2000) OAU doc. AHG/Dec.144 (XXXVI).

[14] Constitutive Act of the African Union 2158 UNTS 3, Article 33(1).

[15] Morocco ratified the AU Constitutive Act on 20 January 2017. It had withdrawn from the OAU in 1985 after the admission of Western Sahara (Sahrawi Arab Democratic Republic), which Morocco regards as part of its territory.

[16] Article 3(g) and 3(h).

[17] African Charter on Human and Peoples' Rights (adopted 27 June 1981, entered into force 21 October 1986) OAU Doc. CAB/LEG/67/3 rev. 5, 21 ILM 58 (1982). By 14 January 1999, 54 states have ratified the Banjul Charter. Morocco remains outside the treaty. Status List available at <https://au.int/sites/default/files/treaties/36390-sl-african_charter_on_human_and_peoples_rights_2.pdf> accessed 11 May 2021.

[18] AU Constitutive Act (n 14) Articles 4(m), 4(o), and 4(p) respectively.

[19] See EY Omorogbe, 'A club of incumbents? the African Union and coups d'état' (2011) 44(1) Vanderbilt Journal of Transnational Law 123–54.

peace and security'. In parallel, Article 4(h) gives the AU the right of intervention on the occurrence of core international crimes (war crimes, genocide, and crimes against humanity). Significantly, under a proposed amendment to Article 4(h) of the AU Constitutive Act, intervention would be expanded to include situations of threats to legitimate order. No definition is given as to what would be included, but the failure of an incumbent to transfer power to the winner of an election would pose such a threat.

In line with Article 5(2) of the Constitutive Act, the AU Peace and Security Council (PSC) is established as a standing decision-making organ of the AU. That was done under the 2002 Protocol Relating to the Establishment of the AU Peace and Security Council (PSC Protocol, in force 26 December 2003).[20] At the time of writing (mid-December 2019), 52 of 55 African states have ratified it.[21] In cases where unconstitutional change as defined under the Lomé Declaration has occurred in a Member State, the PSC has the power to respond through sanctions or a range of other options.[22] While the AU Assembly has final decision-making powers on the use of force in response, the PSC can recommend action under Article 4(h) of the Constitutive Act and approve the mode of intervention including under Article 4(j).[23] It is the PSC which provides the mandates for troops.[24] The PSC acts on behalf of all AU Member States and these are obliged to implement its decisions.[25] The African sub-regional economic communities (RECs) form part of the AU framework for peace and security.[26] RECs are bound by the PSC's decisions on unconstitutional change and, in particular, cannot admit a state which the AU has suspended.[27] In turn, the PSC must consider the capacities of the RECs for response.[28]

For present purposes, three RECs are relevant. These are the East African Community (EAC, established in 2000) which has 6 members, the Southern African Development Community (SADC, established in 1980) which has 16 Member States, and ECOWAS (established in 1975) which has 15 Member States.[29]

[20] PSC Protocol (adopted 9 July 2002).

[21] The exceptions are Cape Verde, Democratic Republic of the Congo (DRC) and South Sudan. See Status List available at <https://au.int/sites/default/files/treaties/37293-sl-protocol_relating_to_the_establishment_of_the_peace_and_security_council_of_the_african_union_1.pdf> accessed 11 May 2021.

[22] PSC Protocol, Articles 7(1)(g) and 9.

[23] ibid Article 7(1)(e) and 7(1)(f).

[24] ibid Article 7(1)(c) and 7(1)(d).

[25] ibid Article 7(2)–7(4).

[26] ibid Article 16.

[27] AU, 'Decision on the Prevention of Unconstitutional Changes of Government and Strengthening the Capacity of the African Region to Manage Such Situations' AU Doc. Assembly/AU/Dec.269(XIV) Rev.1 (2 February 2010) [6](iii)(a).

[28] ibid.

[29] Member States of EAC: Burundi, Kenya, Rwanda, Tanzania, South Sudan, and Uganda. SADC: Angola, Botswana, Comoros, DRC, Lesotho, Madagascar, Malawi, Mauritius, Mozambique, Namibia, Seychelles, South Africa, Swaziland, Tanzania, Zambia, and Zimbabwe. ECOWAS: Benin, Burkina Faso, Cape Verde, Cote d'Ivoire, Gambia, Ghana, Guinea, Guinea Bissau, Liberia, Mali, Niger, Nigeria, Senegal, Sierra Leone, and Togo.

Each REC recognizes the importance of democracy, democratic institutions and practices, human rights, the rule of law, and peace and security to socio-economic development.[30] Each REC provides for sanctions against Member States for failing to fulfil treaty obligations.[31] However, the EAC has no provision for intervention in its Member States on the occurrence of unconstitutional change. SADC's framework can be read to allow for intervention in last resort where unconstitutional change and undemocratic practices lead to instability, armed conflict, and the breakdown of law and order.[32] ECOWAS' legal framework provides clear powers.[33] That is the result of necessity: post-2003 all coups in Africa except in Madagascar have taken place in that sub-region.[34] It can impose sanctions where democracy is abruptly brought to an end by any means.[35] It has the power to intervene in a Member State to assist a democratically elected government against a coup or attempted coup, and can act through the ECOWAS Ceasefire Monitoring Group (ECOMOG) as a standby force.[36] Notably, ECOWAS has a mandatory zero-tolerance policy against unconstitutional change and governments which are maintained through unconstitutional means.[37] In its practice, ECOWAS has deployed ECOMOG in support of democratically elected governments against a coup in Sierra Leone (1997) and the refusal of an incumbent to relinquish power in Gambia (2016–2017, discussed in sub-section 3.2.2).

The AU and its RECs have, however, sometimes struggled to provide a collective and coordinated response when unconstitutional change has occurred as discussed in section 3.

[30] See, as example, EAC treaty (signed 30 November 1999, in force 7 July 2000, as amended on 14 December 2006 and 20 August 2007) Articles 6(d) and 124; Consolidated Text of the Treaty of the SADC (21 October 2015) Articles 4 (c), 5(1)(a) and 5(c); ECOWAS Revised Treaty (24 July 1995) Articles 4 (g) and 4(j).

[31] EAC treaty Articles 29, 143, 146, and 147; Treaty of the SADC Article 33 (1); ECOWAS Revised Treaty Article 77.

[32] SADC Protocol on Politics, Defence and Security Cooperation (adopted 2001, in force 2004) Article 2(a), 2(g), and 2(f).

[33] See AM Mangu, 'Unconstitutional Changes of Governments' and limitations to African Union/ Regional Economic Communities' Responses' in G Masterson and M Meirotti (eds), *Checks and Balance: African Constitutions and Democracy in the 21st century* (EISA, 2017) 77–88, 79.

[34] O Bamidele and B Ayodele, 'In the service of democratic governance: the African Union Normative Framework on Unconstitutional Change of Government and ECOWAS Protocol on Good Governance and Democracy in the Post-Arab Spring' (2018) 53(1) Journal of Asian and African Studies 132–46.

[35] ECOWAS Protocol on Democracy and Good Governance (21 December 2001) (PDGG) Articles 45(1), 45(2), and 45(4).

[36] ECOWAS Protocol Relating to the Mechanism for Conflict Prevention, Management, Resolution, Peacekeeping and Security 1999 (ECOWAS Mechanism) arts 21, 22, 25–26, and definitions section.

[37] ECOWAS (n 35) Article 1(c).

2.3 The African Charter on Democracy, Elections and Good Governance (2007) and the Malabo Protocol (2014)

A second critical juncture came with the adoption of the AU's African Charter on Democracy, Elections and Good Governance (Democracy Charter) on 30 January 2007. The Democracy Charter came into effect in February 2012 after 15 Member States deposited instruments of ratification. At mid-December 2019, 34 African states have ratified the treaty, meaning 21 states remain outside it. The Democracy Charter builds on and develops previous OAU/AU treaties on unconstitutional change. Article 2 of the Democracy Charter states as objectives, *inter alia*, 'the promotion of the holding of regular free and fair elections to institutionalize the legitimate authority of representative government as well as democratic change of governments'. This Treaty gives effect to the Lomé Declaration. It also expands that Declaration in several respects. For present purposes, what is important is that Article 23(5) of the Democracy Charter provides a new definition of circumstances that are 'illegal means of accessing or maintaining power'. It includes all of the unconstitutional scenarios listed in the Lomé Declaration. It also includes a new scenario: 'Any amendment or revision of the constitution or legal instruments, which is an infringement on the principles of democratic change of government'. Alongside that, Article 23(4) prohibits '[a]ny refusal by an incumbent government to relinquish power to the winning party or candidate after free and fair elections'.

The definition of unconstitutional change may have been widened to include other violations. Article 24 of the Democracy Charter requires the PSC to exercise its responsibilities to maintain constitutional order in State Parties where situations arise which 'may affect its democratic political institutional arrangements or the legitimate exercise of power'.[38] It is possible to argue that under this provision, the PSC has a duty to act to protect democratic political arrangements and legitimate governments against fraudulent electoral practices. That conclusion is supported by the Assembly's 2010 'Decision on the Prevention of Unconstitutional Changes of Government' in which the AU agreed:

> the need for a comprehensive approach to the issue of unconstitutional change based on a zero tolerance policy for coups d'État but also for violations of democratic standards, the persistence and reoccurrence of which could result in unconstitutional changes.[39]

The Democracy Charter imposes new sanctions thus expanding the possible range of binding AU law. Article 25 prohibits perpetrators of unconstitutional change from participating in elections held to restore the democratic order and from

[38] See Omorogbe (n 19) 135.
[39] AU, (n 27) [5].

holding high political office. Alongside that, the AU Assembly may impose punitive economic measures against them. Further, sanctions are to be applied against AU states which fail to comply with AU decisions and policies by instigating or supporting unconstitutional change.[40]

The Democracy Charter opens up the possibility of criminal proceedings against perpetrators of unconstitutional change. Under Articles 25(8) and 25(9) of the Democracy Charter respectively, AU Member States cannot harbour or give sanctuary to perpetrators of unconstitutional change and have an obligation to try or extradite them to states that can prosecute. Perpetrators of unconstitutional change instead 'may . . . be tried before a competent court' of the AU (Article 25(5)). The Democracy Charter, however, fails to specify the offence that perpetrators of unconstitutional change would be charged with. Another challenge is that there is no regional court with competency over criminal matters. The African Court on Human and Peoples' Rights (Human Rights Court) established under a 1998 Protocol to protect and interpret Banjul Charter rights has heard disputes on violations of the right to democratic participation in national government, but it has no jurisdiction over criminal matters.[41]

The AU Assembly has addressed this gap by proposing that a specialist chamber for international crimes be established within the Human Rights Court, with the AU Assembly and PSC eligible to submit cases to the court. That proposal is to be found under the Protocol on Amendments to the Protocol on the Statute of the African Court of Justice and Human Rights (the Malabo Protocol), which the AU Assembly adopted on 27 June 2014.[42] Most significant is that the Malabo Protocol list of 14 crimes which could be tried at the regional chamber includes unconstitutional change (Article 28).[43] The crime of unconstitutional change is novel and region-specific – it does not exist elsewhere. But, like the other 13 crimes listed in the Malabo Protocol, it is included because it is deemed most detrimental to the security and socio-economic interests of the African region.

The Malabo Protocol also develops the AU position on unconstitutional change in other ways. The Protocol includes all of the unconstitutional scenarios listed in the Democracy Charter definition, and it adds two new scenarios: 'Any amendment or revision of the constitution or legal instruments, which is an infringement on the principles of democratic change of government or is inconsistent with the

[40] Articles 25(4)–25(7) of the Democracy Charter. See also AU (n 27) [6](i)(b)(a), [6](i)(b)(b), and [6](i)(c).

[41] See, for example, *Rev R Christopher Mtikila v United Republic of Tanzania* App. No 011/2011, Judgment on Merits (14 June 2013) in which the Human Rights Court held that the ban on independent electoral candidates from contesting elections under an amendment in the Tanzania national Constitution breached the African Charter on Human and Peoples Rights Articles 13 and 10 (right to participate in national government and right to freedom of association respectively).

[42] Articles 16, 17, 19 *bis*, and 29.

[43] The others are genocide, crimes against humanity, war crimes, piracy, terrorism, mercenarism, corruption, money laundering, trafficking in persons, trafficking in drugs, trafficking in hazardous waste, illicit exploitation of natural resources, and the crime of aggression.

Constitution', and 'Any substantial modification to electoral laws in the last six (6) months before elections without the consent of the majority of the political actors' (Articles 28E(e) and 28E(f) respectively).

One remaining challenge is that the Malabo Protocol grants incumbent leaders and senior state officials immunity from prosecution in regional courts while in office. That is reflected in the immunity provided under Article 46A *bis*:

> No Charges shall be commenced or continued before the Court against any serving Head of State or government, or anybody acting or entitled to act in such capacity, or other senior state officials based on their functions, during their tenure of office.

This provision is controversial. The AU has explained its rationale – the removal of a sitting head of state could destabilize the state.[44] But that argument lacks force where an incumbent is preventing a democratic transition.

A second challenge is that AU Member States have proved reluctant to ratify the Malabo Protocol. The Malabo Protocol will enter into force after 30 AU states have ratified it. However, at mid-December 2019, no state has ratified it[45] leading to the criticism that 'African leaders are not serious about constitutionalism and democracy'.[46]

3. The AU's Practice

This section considers the enforcement of AU law through treaties and policies on unconstitutional change in a number of disputed presidential elections. The focus is on fraudulent electoral practices and the failure of incumbents to transfer power after losing democratic elections.

3.1 Fraudulent Electoral Practices

3.1.1 Kenya (2007–2008)

Kenya's presidential elections took place on 27 December 2007. The two major political actors in that election were Mwai Kibaki, the President of Kenya since 2002, as candidate for the Party of National Unity (PNU), and Raila Odinga, the candidate

[44] See, for example, AU, 'Communique' (21 July 2008) PSC/MIN/Comm(CXLII) [9].

[45] AU, Status List available at <https://au.int/sites/default/files/treaties/36398-sl-PROTOCOL%20ON%20AMENDMENTS%20TO%20THE%20PROTOCOL%20ON%20THE%20STATUTE%20OF%20THE%20AFRICAN%20COURT%20OF%20JUSTICE%20AND%20HUMAN%20RIGHTS.pdf> accessed 11 May 2021.

[46] Mangu (n 33) 87.

for the Orange Democratic Movement (ODM). Widespread fraud by all parties, including vote buying, ballot stuffing, and intimidation of political opponents, was carried out with impunity.[47] Observers from the East African Communities (EAC) also reported that the voting and tallying process was flawed.[48]

The critical point came on 30 December 2007 when Samuel Kivuitu, the Chairman of the Electoral Commission of Kenya, declared that Kibaki had won with 46.4% of the votes cast and Odinga had 44.1%.[49] Although the opposition immediately rejected the result as fraudulent, Kibaki was sworn into office that day.[50] Kivuitu subsequently denounced the result and stated that his declaration had been made under pressure from the PNU.[51] The dispute over the election led to riots and inter-ethnic violence and by February 2008, over 1,000 people had been killed and an estimated 500,000 displaced.[52]

The AU's preference was for a political solution to the crisis. On 21 January 2008, the AU PSC issued a Press Statement in which it asked all parties and their supporters to refrain from violence. In that statement, the PSC gave its support to the EAC mediation led by then EAC Chair, President Yoweri Museveni of Uganda.[53] From 24 January 2008, the AU ran parallel mediation through the PSC's Panel of Eminent African Personalities led by Kofi Annan, the ex-UN Secretary General.[54] That ultimately led the parties to sign the National Accord and Reconciliation Act and the Agreement on the Principles of Partnership of the Coalition Government on 28 February 2008, a power-sharing agreement under which Kibaki would be the President and Odinga would be the Prime Minister.[55] In line with that, amendments were required to Kenya's constitution to provide for, *inter alia*, the post of Prime Minister.[56] Nevertheless, the AU PSC and Assembly supported these strategies, and the AU Commission and the Panel worked with the Kenyan parties

[47] Republic of Kenya, *Report of the Independent Review Commission on the General Elections held on 27 December 2007* (17 September 2008, IREC) X, 8–9, 24, available at <http://aceproject.org/regions-en/countries-and-territories/KE/reports/independent-review-commission-on-the-general/view> accessed 11 May 2021.

[48] EAC Secretariat, *The East African Community Observer Mission Report, Kenya General Elections December 2007* (Arusha, January 2008).

[49] EU Election Observation Mission, *Kenya Final Report: General Elections 27 December 2007* (3 April 2008) 32–3, available at <http://eeas.europa.eu/archives/docs/eueom/pdf/missions/final_report_kenya_2007.pdf> accessed 11 May 2021.

[50] IREC (n 47) 59.

[51] D Mugonyi, 'Kenya: Yes, Vote Tallying Had Problems, Admits Kivuitu' *Daily Nation* (3 January 2008) available at <https://allafrica.com/stories/200801030025.html> accessed 11 May 2021.

[52] Human Rights Watch, 'Kenya: Ballots to Bullets' (16 March 2008) 5.

[53] AU PSC, Press Statement, AU Doc. PSC/PR/BR(CIX) (21 January 2008).

[54] Other members of the panel included ex-President of Tanzania, Benjamin Mkapa, and Graca Machel. AU Assembly, 'Decision on the Activities of the Peace and Security Council of the African Union and the State of Peace and Security in Africa' (Addis Ababa, Ethiopia 31 January-2 February 2008) Assembly/AU/Dec.177 (X) [14].

[55] Agreement on the Principles of Partnership of the Coalition Government (signed at Nairobi, Kenya on 28 February 2008).

[56] Laws of Kenya: The Constitution of Kenya (Revised edition 2008 (2001)) National Council for Law Reporting, sections 15A and 17.

in implementing the agreements.[57] As a result, Odinga was sworn in as Prime Minister on 17 April 2008.[58] Kibaki remained President until 2013 when he lost the election to Uhuru Kenyatta.

It is accepted that the AU responded quickly to the Kenyan crisis and a peaceful transition was ultimately effected.[59] The challenge is in the AU's response. Several other options were open to the Union. It could have demanded a recount of the votes or ordered a rerun of the elections under AU supervision. Instead, and perhaps rather predictably, the AU supported a power-sharing agreement and constitutional amendments which enabled an incumbent to remain in office following manipulation of the election results. The AU is therefore open to the criticism that its action in Kenya undermines the importance of democratic principles and elections as a reflection of the popular will and the legitimacy of the government.

3.1.2 Zimbabwe (2008–2009)

The African regional support for Robert Mugabe, Prime Minister of Zimbabwe (1980–1987) and President (1987–2017) can perhaps be explained: he was widely seen as a hero across Africa for his significant role in the armed struggle for national independence from colonial rule in his state. Certainly, the AU and SADC proved reluctant to criticize him, including during the 2002 election in which fraud was evident (through intimidation, violence, and vote rigging) and the 2013 elections (in which aspects of the election process lacked integrity).[60] Alongside that, the Assemblies of SADC and the AU respectively elected Mugabe as Chairperson of SADC in 2004 and Chairperson of the AU in 2015.[61]

The question of the AU's commitment to democracy was again tested. In May 2008, the Zimbabwe Electoral Commission (ZEC) declared that Morgan Tsvangirai the candidate for the Movement for Democratic Change (MDC) party led the polls with 47.9% of the vote against 43.2% of the vote for Mugabe, the candidate for ZANU-PF.[62] Because neither party had won outright, a run-off election was scheduled for 27 June 2008.[63] However, Tsvangirai withdrew from the race on

[57] AU PSC, 'Communique', AU Doc. PSC/PR/Comm(CXV) (14 March 2008 [10]; AU Assembly, 'Decision on the Report of the Peace and Security Council on its Activities and the State of Peace and Security in Africa', AU Doc. Assembly/AU/Dec.193 (XI) (1 July 2008) [7].

[58] 'Odinga Sworn in as Kenyan Premier' *BBC News* (17 April 2008) available at <http://news.bbc.co.uk/1/hi/world/africa/7351842.stm> accessed 11 May 2021.

[59] T Murithi, *The African Union's Transition from Non-Intervention to Non-Indifference: An Ad Hoc Approach to the Responsibility to Protect* (IPG I, 2009) 90–107, 94 and 97.

[60] R Bate, 'Mugabe Calls Africa's Bluff', *National Review* (2 July 2008) available at <https://www.nationalreview.com/2008/07/mugabe-calls-africas-bluff-roger-bate/> accessed 11 May 2021.

[61] S Jones, 'Robert Mugabe assumes African Union helm with familiar rallying cry' *Guardian* (30 January 2015) available at <https://www.theguardian.com/global-development/2015/jan/30/robert-mugabe-african-union-chairman-familiar-rallying-cry> accessed 11 May 2021.

[62] C McGreal, 'Election body confirms Mugabe lost the vote' *The Guardian* (3 May 2008) 28.

[63] SADC Election Observer Mission (SEOM), 'Preliminary Statement' (27 June 2008), 5.

the grounds of escalating political attacks and intimidation against him and his supporters, and Mugabe was returned to office.[64]

The African election observation missions quickly criticized the legitimacy of the election. The AU Observer Mission in Zimbabwe concluded that the run-off election fell short of AU standards governing democratic elections because of violence in the run-up to elections and because that deterred political participation.[65] Alongside that, the SADC Election Observer Mission in Zimbabwe (SEOM) reported that the conditions in the pre-election period and in the lead up to the run-off undermined the credibility of the electoral process.[66] Most damning is the report of the Election Observer Mission of the Pan-African Parliament which found that state-sponsored violence' including hate speech and 'high levels of intimidation, violence, displacement of people, abductions, and loss of life' were present, that the police and security forces openly favoured the ruling party, and the independence of the ZEC was in doubt.[67]

However, the AU remained reluctant to criticize or sanction Mugabe. Instead, the AU Assembly encouraged Mugabe and Tsvangirai to establish a power-sharing government.[68] The Assembly justified its position on the grounds of 'the need to create an environment conducive to democracy', the complexity of the situation, the potential spread of conflict, and consequent negative effects in Zimbabwe and in the sub-region.[69] The AU and SADC facilitated the intra-Zimbabwean talks which ultimately led to the signing of the Global Political Agreement (GPA) on 15 September 2008, providing for a national unitary government by ZANU-PF (Mugabe) and two formations of the MDC (Tsvangirai and Arthur Mutambara).[70] Under the terms of the GPA, Mugabe would remain President and appoint a Prime Minister (Tsvangirai) and two Deputy Prime Ministers (one each from the MDC formations) – those appointments would require an amendment to the national constitution.[71]

The AU remained unwilling to act when Mugabe proved reluctant to share power. That was reflected in his unilateral allocation of key ministries to ZANU-PF in contravention of the GPA.[72] It was SADC which set deadlines for the formation

[64] ibid.

[65] AU Office of the Observer Mission to the Presidential Run-off and House of Assembly By-Elections in Zimbabwe, 'Preliminary Statement of the African Union Observer Mission' (29 June 2008).

[66] SEOM (n 63) 6.

[67] Pan African Parliament, *The Pan-African Parliament Election Observer Mission to the Presidential Run-Off and Parliamentary By-Elections in Zimbabwe: Interim Statement* (29 June 2008) 1–3.

[68] AU Assembly, 'Resolution on Zimbabwe' (Sharm El-Sheikh, Egypt, 30 June–1 July 2008) AU Doc. Assembly/AU/Res.1 (XI) (1 July 2008) [3].

[69] ibid Preamble.

[70] ibid; Zimbabwe Global Political Agreement 2008 (GPA), Article 6, available at <http://www.mbeki.org/2019/10/02/zimbabwe-global-political-agreement-2009/> accessed 11 May 2021.

[71] ibid Article 20.1.6.

[72] Zimbabwe GPA Articles 20.1.3–20.1.4, and 20.1.6; Dumisani Muleya and Hopewell Radebe, 'Zimbabwe: SADC 'Deal' Puts MDC`s Tsvangirai on the Spot' (28 January 2009) available at <https://palapye.wordpress.com/2009/01/28/zimbabwe-sadc-deal-puts-mdcs-tsvangirai-on-the-spot/> accessed 11 May 2021.

of the government, with Tsvangirai and Mutambara to be sworn in as Prime Minister and Deputy Prime Minister respectively by 11 February 2009.[73] Those demands, which the AU supported, were met.[74]

Murithi argues that the AU's involvement in Zimbabwe in 2008–2009, though in a supporting role, demonstrates that the Union is taking responsibility for the behaviour of its members.[75] That conclusion is difficult to support. More fitting is de Wet's conclusion that the AU condones the unconstitutional retention of power through fraudulent elections.[76] Certainly, the AU's support for the 2009 negotiated settlement enabled Mugabe to remain in power and endorsed his continued subversion of the electoral process and the use of violence to achieve power. Significantly, Mugabe remained in office until November 2017 when he was deposed by the military in a popular coup. That followed his attempt to establish his wife, Grace, as his successor. The AU and SADC, after initial hesitation, allowed the coup to stand in recognition of the will of the people 'to secure the democratic future of the country'.[77] That acceptance ran counter to the AU's blanket opposition to military coups in Africa.[78] What is clear is that throughout the actions of the AU in Zimbabwe undermined AU law and policy on democratic and constitutional change and the legitimate exercise of state power in Africa.

3.2 The Refusal of Incumbents to Step Down after Election Defeat

3.2.1 Cote d'Ivoire (2010–2011)

Cote d'Ivoire was a fragile post-conflict state at the time of the 2010 election crisis. Prior to that, on 4 March 2007, the government of President Laurent Gbagbo and

[73] SADC Heads of State and Government Extraordinary Summit, Communiqué (Pretoria, South Africa 27 January 2009) available at <https://www.sadc.int/files/4613/5292/8386/SADC_ExtraordinarySummit_Communique-Jan_2009.pdf> accessed 11 May 2021.

[74] AU Assembly, 'Decision on Zimbabwe' (Addis Ababa, Ethiopia 1–3 February 2009) AU Doc Assembly/AU/Dec.219(XII) [2]; C McGreal, 'Mugabe swears in rival Tsvangirai as Zimbabwe PM,' *The Guardian* (11 February 2009) available at <https://www.theguardian.com/world/2009/feb/11/tsvangirai-zimbabwe-prime-minister-mugabe> accessed 11 May 2021.

[75] Murithi (n 59), 96.

[76] E de Wet, 'The role of democratic legitimacy in the recognition of governments in Africa since the end of the Cold War' (2019) 17(2) International Journal of Constitutional Law 470–8, 474.

[77] See African Union, 'Statement by the Chairperson of the African Union Commission on the situation in Zimbabwe' (15 November 2017) available at <https://au.int/sites/default/files/pressreleases/33377-pr-statement_by_the_chairperson_of_auc_on_zimbabwe_ff.pdf>; African Union, 'Statement by the Chairperson of the African Union Commission on the situation in Zimbabwe' (21 November 2017) available at <https://au.int/sites/default/files/pressreleases/33382-pr-statement_of_the_chairperson_of_the_commission_of_the_african_union_on_the_situation_in_zimbabwe_.pdf>, accessed 11 May 2021. 'SADC Organ Troika plus Council Chairperson Ministerial Meeting held to discuss the Political Situation in Zimbabwe' Press Statement (16 November 2017); SADC Secretariat, *Inside SADC*, Monthly Newsletter Issue 11, November 2017, 1–3.

[78] See Omorogbe (n 19).

the Forces Nouvelles rebel group led by Guilllaume Kigbafori Soro agreed to a ceasefire under the Ouagadougou Political Agreement (OPA) to end a civil conflict which began in 2002. The then Chairperson of ECOWAS, Blaise Campaore the President of Burkina Faso facilitated that agreement, and the AU and the UN endorsed it.[79] The peace agreements were supported by France's Force Licorne and the UN Mission in Cote d'Ivoire (UNOCI), which previously had absorbed ECOWAS Forces in Cote d'Ivoire (ECOMICI); all had initially been deployed under previous (failed) ceasefire agreements..[80] A crucial commitment in the Supplementary treaty to the OPA (7 March 2007) was that presidential elections were to take place in the Ivory Coast in the first half of 2008, but Gbagbo delayed these.[81] The elections were finally held on 31 October 2010, and with no candidate winning outright, a run-off was held on 28 November.[82]

The political crisis followed the declaration of the result of the run-off. On 2 December 2010 Youssouf Bakayoko, head of the Independent Electoral Commission (CIE) declared that Ouattara had provisionally won the election with 54.1% of the vote and that the incumbent President Gbagbo had received 45.9% of the vote. In line with responsibilities assumed under an agreement with the conflict parties, the Special Representative of the UN Secretary-General in Cote d'Ivoire (Choi Young-Jin, SRSG) certified the result.[83] However, on 3 December 2010, Paul Yao N'Dre, the president of the Constitutional Council declared Gbagbo winner, on the grounds that 10% of the ballots were fraudulent. Both candidates claimed victory. During the post-electoral violence which followed both sides committed grave abuses and more than 3,000 people were killed, 800,000 were displaced and another 180,000 fled to neighbouring states.[84]

The AU PSC responded quickly to events in Cote d'Ivoire. On 4 December 2010, it demanded that Gbagbo transfer power to Ouattara and declared the 'AU's total rejection of any attempt to create a *fait accompli* to undermine the electoral process and the will of the people' as expressed in the ballot and the possible consequences

[79] AU PSC, 'Communiqué', AU doc. PSC/PR/COMM(CCXXXIV) (28 June 2010) [1]; 'Communique', AU doc. PSC/PR/Comm.1(CCXLVI) (28 October 2010) [3].

[80] Section 6.2. Ceasefire: Ouagadougou Political Agreement (OPA). See UNSC Resolution 1528 (February 2004) and ibid [5]. See also M Malan, 'Africa: Building Institutions on the Run' in DCF Daniel, P Taft, and others (ed), *Peace Operations: Trends, Progress, and Prospects* (Georgetown University Press, 2008) 93–5.

[81] *Report on the Evolution of the Crisis Exit Process in Cote D'Iviore since the beginning of the Ouagadougou Political Agreement*, AU Doc. PSC/PR/2 (CCXXXIV) (28 June 2010) [8].

[82] ibid [10]–[12].

[83] See Resolution 1795 (2008) (15 January 2008) [9]–[10]; UNSC, *Twenty-ninth progress report of the Secretary-General on the United Nations Operation in Cote d'Ivoire*, UN Doc. S/2011/807 (29 December 2011) [21].

[84] The number of those killed is from Human Rights Watch, '"They Killed Them Like It Was Nothing": The Need for Justice for Cote d'Ivoire's Post-Election Crimes' (5 October 2011) available at <https://www.hrw.org/report/2011/10/05/they-killed-them-it-was-nothing/need-justice-cote-divoires-post-election-crimes> accessed 11 May 2021; other figures are from UN Office for the Coordination of Humanitarian Affairs, 'Cote d'Ivoire: Humanitarian Crisis Situation Report No 21' (15 April 2011) 1.

including a civil conflict in the state.[85] A few days later, the PSC suspended Cote d'Ivoire from all AU activities until the transfer of power took place.[86] That suspension would stay in place until 21 April 2011, after Ouattara had assumed power.[87]

Regrettably, AU organs were undecided as to the appropriate way forward. Jean Ping, the Chair of the AU Commission (Secretariat) opened up the possibility of a power-sharing government in which Gbagbo would be a key part when he said:

> The winner of the election is clearly Ouattara but we need to find a peaceful negotiated solution ... Non-Africans only think of democracy ... Africans are concerned about democracy and peace, their continent being afflicted by conflict and civil war.[88]

In contrast, the PSC's High-Level Panel of five Heads of States led by President Mohamed Ould Abdel Aziz of Mauritania (then head of the AU PSC) recommended that Gbagbo step down from office and be granted safe passage and Ouattara be sworn in by the Constitutional Court. It also recommended that a government of national unity and reconciliation be established.[89] That would leave allies of Gbagbo in government. The PSC adopted those recommendations under its binding powers but it proved reluctant to enforce its decisions when Gbagbo failed to comply.[90]

A common regional response proved challenging. While ECOWAS supported the use of peaceful measures to resolve the matter, it was also willing to use 'legitimate force' as a last resort to ensure the transition. It adopted that position in December 2010 and later confirmed that in March 2011 when it declared the situation in Cote d'Ivoire a regional humanitarian emergency and requested UNSC authorization for ECOWAS intervention.[91] It also requested that the UN authorise UNOCI to use force, *inter alia*, to ensure an immediate transition.[92] That demand would provide regional legitimization for UN action.

85 AU PSC, 'Press Statement', AU Doc. PSC/PR/BR.(CCLI) (4 December 2010).

86 AU PSC, Communique, AU Doc. PSC/PR/COMM.1(CCLII) (9 December 2010) [4]–[5].

87 ibid; AU PSC, *Report of the Chairperson of the Commission on the situation in Cote D'Ivoire*, AU Doc. PSC/PR/2 (CCLXXIII) (21 April 2011) [18]].

88 P Bernard, 'African Union seeks negotiated solution for Ivory Coast' *The Guardian* (1 February 2011) available at <https://www.theguardian.com/global/2011/feb/01/ivory-coast> accessed 11 May 2021.

89 Other members of the Panel were Presidents Jacob Zuma of South Africa, Blaise Compaore of Burkina Faso, Idriss Deby of Chad, and Jakaya Kikwete Tanzania. AU PSC, 'Communique', AU. Doc PSC/PR/COMM(CCLXIII (28 February 2011) [3].

90 AU PSC, 'Press Statement', AU Doc. PSC/PR/BR.1(CCLXX) (5 April 2011) 2.

91 ECOWAS, 'Final Communique On the Extraordinary Session of the Authority of Heads of State And Government On Cote d'Ivoire', Press Release (7 December 2010) [7]–[9]; 'Extraordinary Session of the Authority of Heads of State and Government on Cote D'Ivoire: Final Communique' (24 December 2010) ECOWAS Doc. ECW/CEG/ABJ/EXT/FR./Rev. 0 [7]–[10]; Resolution A/RES.1/03/11 of the Authority of the Heads of State and Government of ECOWAS on the situation in Cote d'Ivoire (24 March 2011).

92 Resolution A/RES.1/03/11 of the Authority of the Heads of State and Government of ECOWAS on the situation in Cote d'Ivoire (24 March 2011).

It was external actors that resolved the crisis. On 30 March 2011, the UNSC unanimously adopted Resolution 1975 in which it gave support to the AU and ECOWAS's peaceful initiatives, condemned Gbagbo's decision not to accept the AU's solution, urged him to step down immediately, and imposed targeted sanctions against Gbagbo and his closest advisors. UNOCI and Force Licorne troops then assisted Ouattara's Forces Republicaines du Cote d'Iviore (formerly Force Nouvelles) in military operations in Abidjan and played a decisive role in arresting Gbagbo on 11 April 2011.[93] Following that, N'Dre swore Ouattara into office.[94]

In Cote d'Ivoire, the AU failed to uphold its zero-tolerance policy against unconstitutional change. Its prioritization of peaceful initiatives and the protection of incumbents undermine AU law and is not conducive to the development of a strong AU capable of supranational decision-making. It seemed willing to allow an incumbent to remain in office after losing elections and flouting PSC edicts. As Vijay Nambiar, chief of staff to UN Secretary-General Ban Ki-moon has put it, that sets 'a dangerous precedent for the continent and undermine[s] the principles of democracy'.[95]

3.2.2 The Gambia (2016–2017)

Yahya Jammeh came to power in Gambia in 1994 through a coup which ousted the democratically elected president, Dawda Jawara. Since then, Jammeh had won a series of presidential elections (1996, 2001, 2006, and 2011), all of which are hard to describe as free and fair. Alongside that, the Jammeh government's record of human rights was problematic.[96]

The crisis in Gambia began after the result of the election was declared. On 6 December 2016, Gambia's Electoral Commission declared that Adama Barrow, an independent candidate, had won the presidential election which had been held five days prior with 45.5% of the votes while Jammeh, a candidate for the APRC in the election, received 36.7% of the votes. Jammeh initially acknowledged defeat and congratulated Barrow. But on 9 December 2016 Jammeh announced that he disputed the result and would not step down.[97] In line with the state constitution, power was to be transferred to Barrow on 19 January 2017. However, on 17 January 2017, Jammeh declared a state of emergency in the state for 90 days and banned 'acts of disobedience ... incitement of violence and acts intended to disturb public

[93] See AU PSC (n 87) [9]–[10].

[94] A Nossiter, 'In Belated Inauguration, Ivory Coast's President Urges Unity' *New York Times* (22 May 2011) 14.

[95] V Nambiar, 'Dear President Mbeki: The United Nations Helped Save Ivory Coast', *Foreign Policy* (17 August 2011) available at <https://foreignpolicy.com/2011/08/17/dear-president-mbeki-the-united-nations-helped-save-the-ivory-coast/> accessed 11 May 2021.

[96] Human Rights Watch, 'More Fear than Fair: Gambia's 2016 Presidential Election' available at <https://www.hrw.org/report/2016/11/02/more-fear-fair/gambias-2016-presidential-election> accessed 11 May 2021.

[97] AU, 'The AU Calls for Orderly and Peaceful Transition and Transfer of Power to the New Authorities in the Gambia', Press Release (10 December 2016).

order and peace' and he instructed the security forces to 'maintain absolute peace, law and order'.[98] The Gambian National Assembly, which was dominated by APRC members, sanctioned the term extension.[99]

The response of the AU signalled a change in approach. Throughout, AU organs demanded that Jammeh transfer power.[100] The AU PSC on 12 December 2010 declared the election results to be inviolable.[101] It authorized AU mediation through a high-level delegation to the Gambia led by the AUC Chair and comprising heads of state from each of Africa's regions, while supporting ECOWAS' mediation led by President Muhammad Buhari of Nigeria.[102] Critically, the AU adopted a policy of non-recognition of Jammeh from 19 January 2017, when his legal mandate would expire.[103] It also threatened to use force against him. That threat was first seen in mid-December 2016 when the PSC 'stresse[d] the determination of the AU to take all necessary measures, in line with the relevant AU Instruments, with a view to ensuring full respect and compliance with the will and desire expressed by the people of The Gambia on 1 December 2016'.[104] It was also reflected in the PSC's warning to 'outgoing President Yahya Jammeh of serious consequences in the event that his action causes any crisis that could lead to political disorder, humanitarian and human rights disaster, including loss of innocent lives and destruction of properties'.[105] The PSC did not state what those consequences would entail. But that could include intervention under Articles 4(h) and 4(j) of the AU Constitutive Act. The AU may have also been open to using criminal proceedings. Certainly, the PSC referred to the AU Constitutive Act and Article 25 of the African Charter on Democracy in its decision, even though Gambia had signed but not yet ratified that treaty.

ECOWAS and the UN were similarly robust in their opposition to Jammeh's actions. Following the AU's threat of force, the ECOWAS Authority made known it too would consider 'all necessary means' to ensure that the will of the people was met in the Gambia. ECOWAS also arranged for Barrow to be inaugurated as President of the Gambia on 19 January in Dakar Senegal within the premises of the Gambian embassy.[106] ECOWAS then deployed 7,000 troops in the Gambia ensure the transition (ECOMIG, Operation Restore Democracy). That followed

[98] 'Gambian President Jammeh declares state of emergency' *Reuters* (17 January 2017) available at <https://www.reuters.com/article/us-gambia-politics-idUSKBN15119P> accessed 11 May 2021.

[99] 'Gambia votes to extend President's term of office for three months' *The Independent* (19 January 2017) 34.

[100] AU PSC (n 97); AU PSC, 'Communique', AU Doc. PSC/PR/COMM. (DCXLVII) (13 January 2017) [4]–[5]; AU PSC, 'Communique', AU Doc. PSC/PR/COMM. (DCLIV) (20 January 2017) [2].

[101] AU PSC, 'Communiqué' AU Doc. PSC/PR/COMM. (DCXLIV) (12 December 2016) [3]–[7].

[102] ibid [10]–[11].

[103] AU PSC (n 100) (13 January 2017) [2], [4] and [5](ii).

[104] AU PSC (n 101) [12].

[105] AU PSC (13 January 2017) [5](iii).

[106] J Starkey, 'Foreign forces enter Gambia to drive out beaten president' *Financial Times* (London, 20 January 2017) 30.

Barrow's request for ECOWAS, AU, and UN intervention.[107] ECOWAS also set a deadline for Jammeh to leave office (20 January 2017). Similarly, under resolution 2337 (19 January 2017), the UNSC gave 'its full support to ECOWAS in its commitment to ensure, by political means first, the respect of the will of the people of the Gambia as expressed in the results of 1st December elections'.[108] That left open the use of force in last resort. The AU PSC gave its support to the ECOWAS and UN position.[109]

Providing a cohesive and credible regional and international response, isolated Jammeh and enabled quick resolution of the crisis.[110] Jammeh left Gambia on 21 January 2017.[111] He now lives in Equatorial Guinea having been granted political asylum by President Teodoro Obiang who, having come to power through a military coup, has remained in office for more than 40 years.[112]

A remaining concern is the extremely favourable terms for Jammeh's exit – the AU along with ECOWAS and the UN had guaranteed his safety and assets in return for his departure from the country with immediate effect.[113] Those assets include US$ 11 million and a fleet of 13 luxury vehicles.[114] It is not known how Jammeh amassed such wealth but the Barrow government has accused Jammeh of stealing from the state.[115] What is clear is that excessively soft exits undermine the deterrent effect of AU law and policy and AU practice should not support this.

4. Conclusion

Unconstitutional change of government undermines the OAU/AU's promotion of peace, security, and development in the African region. The AU has adopted

[107] ibid.

[108] UN resolution 2337 (19 January 2017) [6].

[109] AU PSC (n 100) (20 January 17) [7]–[9].

[110] See generally A Schuit, 'Recognition of governments in international law and the recent conflict in Libya' (2012) 14(4) International Community Law Review 381–402, 383.

[111] R Maclean, 'The Gambia: defeated president backs down and agrees to go into exile' *The Guardian* (21 January 2017) available at <https://www.theguardian.com/world/2017/jan/20/the-gambia-jammeh-has-agreed-to-leave-new-president-tweets> accessed 11 May 2021.

[112] C Freeman, 'Gambia's ousted dictator is living the good life in a palace in Guinea', *Foreign Policy* (3 April 2017) available at <https://foreignpolicy.com/2017/04/03/gambias-ousted-dictator-is-living-the-good-life-in-a-palace-in-equatorial-guinea> accessed 11 May 2021.

[113] 'Joint Declaration by the Economic Community of West African States, the African Union and the United Nations on the Political Situation of the Islamic Republic of the Gambia' (21 January 2017) [4]–[8], and [11]–[13].

[114] 'Gambia's Yahya Jammeh 'allowed to keep' luxury car collection' *AFP* (25 January 2017) available at <https://www.nation.co.ke/news/africa/Jammeh-to-keep-luxury-car-collection/1066-3786006-b7wjf7z/index.html> accessed 11 May 2021.

[115] 'Gambia's Yahya Jammeh "stole $50 million", assets frozen, says Minister' *Daily Nation* (23 May 2017) available at <https://www.nation.co.ke/news/africa/Gambias-Jammeh-stole-50m-assets-frozen/1066-3937788-7dsa14z/index.html> accessed 11 May 2021.

key treaties and a regime of zero tolerance towards such behaviour. Alongside these, the AU has put forward a novel regional crime of unconstitutional change and a regional court to try perpetrators. These measures are conducive in cementing a progressive AU legal system that will support decisive and enforceable action.

The AU's progressive agenda is undermined by the conservative use of AU laws and powers in practice. There are several reasons for this. The first is that the democratic credentials of many African states are open to question, and that affects the will to act against perpetrators. A second is that while the failure to transfer power following electoral defeat is clearly established in AU law as unconstitutional, retaining power via fraud and subverting democratic norms is debatable. The final factor is the lack of ratification by AU states of key treaties in this area. As things stand neither the crime of unconstitutional change nor a standing regional criminal chamber is likely to be established. As a result, the AU's range of responses is limited to the diplomatic and the military when such situations occur.

As seen in Kenya and Zimbabwe, the AU's response to fraudulent electoral practices is weak. It has supported power-sharing agreements enabling the incumbent to retain presidential office and forcing those who have won elections to take subsidiary roles in the government. The AU may be moving towards firmer action against incumbents who refuse to effect a democratic transition after losing elections. In contrast to its ambivalent position in Cote d'Ivoire, the AU led threats to remove the illegal incumbent by force in Gambia and, coupled with a credible threat of force by ECOWAS, enabled quick transition. Nevertheless, the regional support for an exit strategy which greatly benefits a serial perpetrator of unconstitutional change (and serious human rights abuses) is at odds with emerging AU law.

Looking towards the future, the AU is likely to benefit from revising the definition of unconstitutional change in its treaties to specifically include governments which are maintained through undemocratic means.[116] That redefinition could lead to a strengthening of AU practice in line with AU law. The prosecution of incumbents which perpetrate unconstitutional change and undemocratic practices for crimes against humanity when large-scale loss of life or gross violations of human rights result from their actions is likely to have a deterrent effect. Such prosecution could be carried out by AU states on the basis of national or territorial jurisdiction (where applicable) or under universal jurisdiction principles. Alternatively, the AU could establish a regional ad hoc tribunal for this purpose. The AU has used this route before. The Extraordinary African Chambers within

[116] Mangu (n 33) 86.

the Senegalese court system was established under agreement between the AU and Senegal to prosecute, on behalf of Africa, ex-President Hissene Habre of Chad for torture, war crimes, and crimes against humanity during his period of office (1982–1990).[117] Taken together, these changes could advance the AU's objective of democratic principles, democratic institutions, and peace in Africa.

[117] See M Fall, 'The Extraordinary African Chambers: The Case of *Hissene Habre*' in G Werle, L Fernandez, and others (eds), *Africa and the International Criminal Court* (2014, Asser Press) 117–31. That court convicted Habre in 2016.

11

Human Rights, Statelessness, and the Right to Nationality (R2N) in Africa: What Can Vertical Structures Achieve?

Chidebe Matthew Nwankwo

1. Introduction

The United Nations High Commissioner for Refugees (UNHCR) estimates place the figure of stateless individuals around the world at about 10 million. Africa contributes a substantial percentage to the global population of stateless people. Groups most affected by statelessness in Africa include descendants of colonial-era migrants, nomadic pastoralists, populations separated by arbitrary colonial borders or affected by nascent states, and internally displaced persons. These groups are increased by the rise in climate change induced migration and Africa's continuous ethnic conflicts. These persons are denied the right to nationality by a combination of systematic discrimination through bad policies, weak administrative systems, and laws that effectually provide limited rights based on nationality through *jus soli*,[1]and restrict nationality through *jus sanguinis*[2] on discriminatory grounds. Reverberations around regional institutions suggest an increasing appreciation of the fatal potentialities of this menace to African states. The African Commission on Human and Peoples' Rights and the African Committee of Experts on the Rights and Welfare of the Child have passed decisions and resolutions affirming the right to nationality.

On this evidence, this chapter examines the current legal framework for addressing statelessness in the African region. It takes a rights approach by covering

[1] The principle of *jus soli* literally means law or right of the soil. It is a concept whereby an individual obtains citizenship because he or she was born in a particular country. A legal system where the exclusive *jus soli* rule applies prevents individuals from claiming the citizenship of their parents if they had moved away from their 'historical' home but is more favourable to actual residents of a particular territory.

[2] *Jus sanguinis* or law or right of blood, applies to citizenship based on descent from parents who themselves are citizens. In general, a law based on *jus sanguinis* will tend to exclude from citizenship residents of a country who are descended from individuals who have migrated from one place to another. common law concept of *jus soli* and the civil law model *jus sanguinis* are applied in Africa and combine the two basic concepts.

Chidebe Matthew Nwankwo, *Human Rights, Statelessness, and the Right to Nationality (R2N) in Africa: What Can Vertical Structures Achieve?* In: *The Emergent African Union Law.* Edited by: Olufemi Amao, Michèle Olivier and Konstantinos D. Magliveras, Oxford University Press.
DOI: 10.1093/oso/9780198862154.003.0012

the right to nationality in the African human rights system. It argues that there is a lack of sufficient coverage in the *lex scripta* of the African Union (AU) and provisions of the African Charter on Human and Peoples' Rights (The African Charter), if any, on the right to nationality are weak. With the increase in refugee populations and stateless individuals within the territories of African states, the attendant problems of terrorism, insecurity, and looming humanitarian crisis can only worsen. It becomes imperative that AU Member States work decisively to create a definite framework for the protection of the right of the stateless individual to a nationality and by implication stem the potential usurpation of sovereign powers.

2. The Human Rights Conundrum and the Problem of Statelessness

Presently, there appears to be a crisis in the efficacy of human rights as the widely accepted ideal in the measurement of our collective moral bearing in this age. Human rights are often thought of as the metaphysical framing – something 'which we possess independently of membership in a political community'.[3] Liberal contentions of a world relatively safe and secure under human rights law and its institutions suffer credibility when the prevalence of challenges such as statelessness is discussed.[4] Staples, for instance, in his critique of Rorty's argument that an expansion of liberal human rights values such as sentimentalism and solidarity furthers the interest of the individual in society, argues that human rights are limited and do not necessarily culminate in the protection of those stripped of their dignity.[5]

Staples further contends that there is a substantial mismatch between Rorty's dependence on both liberal norms and international political practice, and his hopes for the human rights culture to include those stripped of human dignity. This he believes is so because of the prevalence of stateless communities and the constant perception of a universalism that is shared by all as members of one global community. According to him, Rorty's thesis suffers because he is unable, in spite of his attempt to break the link between territory and moral justification, to move beyond an overtly sentimental universalism, which is powerless against the norms of the international community, and against the norms of the liberal community. Finally, Staples argues that liberal thought generally offers no means for the actualization

[3] P Hayden, 'From exclusion to containment: Arendt, sovereign power and statelessness' (2008) 3 Societies Without Borders 248 at 266.

[4] For a critique of liberalist views of human rights as a tool for societal ordering and its limitations vis-a-vis statelessness see KL Staples, 'Statelessness, sentimentality and human rights: a critique of Rorty's liberal human rights culture' (2011) 37 Philosophy and Social Criticism, 1011; see also G Calder, *Rorty's Politics of Redescription* (Chicago University Press, 2007).

[5] ibid. See generally R Rorty, 'Universality and Truth' in RR Brandom (ed), *Rorty and His Critics* (Blackwell, 2000); R Rorty, *Truth and Progress: Philosophical Papers*, Vol 3 (CUP, 1998);

of the protection necessary for the avoidance of the indignity and harm of real-world stateless places.[6]

But Staples is not alone in his criticism of the abstract reality of human rights in times of emergency and the popular acceptance of the norms undergirding human rights as currently constituted. Arendt offers critical insights which are useful in understanding the continuing legal and political exclusion of stateless people. Her critique of the modern conception of human rights also repudiates naturalist metaphysics and liberal subjectivism as the bases for human rights, arguing that the weakness of such foundations is demonstrated by the lack of progress on eradicating the problem of stateless persons in the last century.[7] Arendt pinpoints the abject status of those who have been excluded from belonging to any state thus:

> No paradox of contemporary politics is filled with poignant irony than the discrepancy between the efforts of well-meaning idealists who stubbornly insist in regarding as 'inalienable' those human rights, which are enjoyed only by citizens of the most prosperous and civilized countries, and the situation of the rightless themselves.[8]

Arendt's argument draws from the fact that human rights were first realized only in the particular contexts of the American and French Revolutions. Thus, inherent in the concept of human rights is the contradiction that the sovereignty of each individual had to be reconciled with that of the group which constitutes the body politic.[9] Furthermore, this entails a fundamental devaluation of the importance of the vaunted inalienable rights of the individual vis-a-vis the national will and the collective right to self-determination. It therefore follows that the rights deemed to solely depend on the human being's natural life in reality presupposed the existence of the polity and also the sovereignty of the collective will of the people. As Arendt effectively argues, this impractical coupling of individual sovereignty as the expression of subjective inalienable rights and national sovereignty as the expression of the collective rights of the people to self-government are suppositions upon which the modern nation state emerged. This entails that 'man had hardly appeared as a completely emancipated, completely isolated being who carried his dignity within himself without reference to some larger encompassing order, when he disappeared again into a member of a people;.[10] This idealization of human rights as an infallible metaphysical notion ultimately of benefit to a sovereign subject elevated the abstract individual above the nation state, while simultaneously the affirmation of the supremacy of national sovereignty idealized as the 'nebulous

[6] Staples (n 4) 1021.
[7] H Arendt, *The Origins of Totalitarianism* (Schocken Books, 2004) 353.
[8] ibid 355.
[9] Arendt (n 7) 77–99.
[10] ibid 369.

representative of a "national soul"' meant that 'human rights were protected and enforced only as national rights'.[11]

The contradiction between human rights and national sovereignty also throws the legitimacy of the Westphalian state into question. The ascendancy of the strict territorial boundaries of statehood transformed the sovereign from an entity whose supreme function was the protection of the human rights of all inhabitants in its territory regardless of their nationality 'into one whose function was to distinguish between nationals and non-nationals on the basis to grant full civil and political rights only to those who belonged to the national community by right of origin and fact of birth'.[12] The defeat of the rule of law by popular nationalist sentiment, abstract national interest took priority over the interest of the individual – a phenomenon which Arendt referred to as the 'conquest of the state by the nation'. By description, non-nationals within a given state were immediately subject to the potential for exclusion from the polity and its supposed functions of providing equal rights. This decline of the state signifies that its legal institutions no longer served all its inhabitants equally but left non-nationals outside the protection of the law and on the margins of society.

By implication, the association of human rights to nationality meant that these rights existed solely within domestic law and belonged only to recognized citizens of particular nation states. Seen from another perspective, it may be argued that the changing nature of international institutions[13] and the emergence of regimes such as the International Criminal Court (ICC), the regional human rights systems, and other entities responsible for ensuring peace and stability around the world suggests that human rights is no longer best guaranteed within the confines of the nation state. However, the problem of statelessness is fundamental and goes to the very essence of human rights. In practice, the identification of citizenship with nationality rather than humanity remains the precondition for the effective possession of human rights.[14] Thus, human rights are mainly delimited to the domain of a specific state and placed under the protection of a single government. This leaves critics of the current system no choice than to argue, and they may be forgiven, that the Rights of Man have been divested of their supposedly universal and inalienable character, exposing them as entirely contingent and social.[15] For the stateless, only

[11] ibid 279.

[12] ibid 296.

[13] International institutions continue to expand into issue areas formerly considered the exclusive preserve of sovereign states. This has prompted inward-looking by states evidenced by the recent Brexit conundrum in the United Kingdom, Trump's withdrawal from the Paris Accord, and other acts of states intended to assume greater independence from supranational organizations. See J Klabbers, 'Transforming institutions: autonomous international organisations in institutional theory' (2018) 6 International Organizations 105.

[14] In this chapter the term nationality and citizenship are used conjointly to refer to individuals who are without any form of legal identification within the boundaries of a sovereign state.

[15] Hayden (n 3) 253.

membership within a particular nation state could guarantee them rights derivable from their legal status.

It is noteworthy that Arendt's analysis of statelessness transcends the narrow juridical definition that distinguishes between the stateless persons and refugee populations fleeing from disaster. As a solution, Arendt emphasizes the need to recognize both the *de jure* stateless, or 'a person who is not considered as a national by any state under the operation of its law',[16] and the *de facto* stateless, such as refugees, internally displaced persons (IDPs), resident aliens, and immigrants threatened by denationalization, ineffective nationality, or who are able to prove neither their nationality nor that they are legally stateless.[17] Flowing from this, it then becomes clear that the loss of membership in a political community expressed as citizenship or nationality becomes tantamount to the loss of all human rights and dignity. This state of complete rightlessness or being 'merely human' means that the person is effectively excluded from all states and thrust out of legality altogether.[18] It is for this reason that Arendt maintains that the most basic right of the individual, prior to the enjoyment of any of the rights proclaimed in various domestic and international instruments, is the right to have rights, that is the right to be legally and politically included in a community that guarantees the equal status of all persons residing there, citizens and non-citizens inclusive, irrespective of their nationality.[19]

Arendt's prognosis of the modern conception of human rights is far reaching and various actions of states in the past arguably lend credence to her arguments.[20] However, it may be claimed that the impact of the current conception of human rights, particularly in international law, has been profound. So far, human rights has developed the role of the individual as a subject of international law; claims of title of territory cannot be made without some consideration of the rights of the inhabitants of that territory; and it has meant that a state's sovereignty is not entirely absolute, as the treatment of an individual by a state is a matter of international concern and not a matter purely for national jurisdiction.[21] Thus, the forecast of human rights law is not entirely gloomy although the chink in its armour is the prevalence of enduring conditions such as statelessness which reduces some persons into physical objects totally devoid of human dignity. This notwithstanding, there remains potential in the emerging norms and institutions under international law which may serve as catalysts for the gradual eradication of this

[16] Article 1, 1954 Convention Relating to the Status of Stateless Persons.

[17] Arendt (n 7) 365.

[18] ibid 375–6.

[19] ibid at 377.

[20] The implications of the sovereign power to exclude persons from political community has in the past played out in the denationalization of large segments of the European population in the wake of the First World War; the persecution of the Rohingya and other populations around the world that lack governmental representation of any form.

[21] M Dixon, R McCorquodale, and others, *Cases and Materials on International Law* (OUP, 2011) 175.

menace. The following sections examine the mechanisms under regional law in Africa.

3. An African Perspective on Statelessness

The African continent contributes significantly to the population of stateless persons around the world. Across the region, citizenship is being manipulated and restricted to deny rights to those whom states wish to exclude for political reasons. An example of note is the period 1998–2002 where Ethiopia and Eritrea expelled an estimated 150,000 people. These individuals were arbitrarily stripped of their legal rights, their property, and, most importantly, their nationality. This only tells the story of a particular case in East Africa. In Southern Africa and Western Africa the story of statelessness remains rife. The major causes of statelessness include:

- Gaps in nationality laws are a major cause of statelessness. Every country has laws which establish under what circumstances someone acquires nationality or can have it withdrawn. If these laws are not carefully written and correctly applied, some people can be excluded and left stateless. An example is children who are of unknown parentage in a country where nationality is acquired based on descent from a national. Fortunately, most nationality laws recognize them as nationals of the state in which they are found.
- Another factor that can make matters complicated is when people move from the countries where they were born. A child born in a foreign country can risk becoming stateless if that country does not permit nationality based on birth alone and if the country of origin does not allow a parent to pass on nationality through family ties. Additionally, the rules setting out who can and who cannot pass on their nationality are sometimes discriminatory.
- Another important reason is the emergence of new states and changes in borders. In many cases, specific groups can be left without a nationality as a result and, even where new countries allow nationality for all, ethnic, racial, and religious minorities frequently have trouble proving their link to the country. In countries where nationality is only acquired by descent from a national, statelessness will be passed on to the next generation.
- Finally, statelessness can also be caused by loss or deprivation of nationality. In some countries, citizens can lose their nationality simply from having lived outside their country for a long period of time. States can also deprive citizens of their nationality through changes in law that leave whole populations stateless, using discriminatory criteria like ethnicity or race.

In a nutshell, the problem persists due to failure to integrate historical and contemporary migrants (whether forced or voluntary) and their descendants, and discrimination in law or in fact on the basis of gender, race, or ethnicity (whether against migrants, or people who have never moved). These causes are intertwined and must be seen within the historical context of the region, and the way in which post-colonial African states emerged.[22] In addition to the main causative factors already outlined, the existential challenge of climate change and the attendant fallout from it such as movement of nomadic populations across borders in search of scarce resources to feed cattle has exacerbated the already tenuous political structures of African states leading to an increase in the population of IDPs.[23] This adds an extra dimension to an already portentous phenomenon.

It is critical at this juncture to properly contextualize the concept of nationality in the African sense. A critical study of the concept involves tracing the notion from the time of its initial appearance as a concept of law towards the end of the 18th century. A historical analysis of the concept from this timeline will help to aid appreciation of its true significance in Africa and above all to help grasp the content of African national legislation on the subject.[24] It is common knowledge that the etymological root of 'nationality' is derived from the word 'nation'. This suggests that nationality *simplicter* is a political notion reflecting a person's origin from a particular nation. But the real nature or meaning of this bond between the person and the state has evolved throughout history and the concept has been expanded to also include a legal bond between an individual and the population of a state that further comprises an 'ideological dimension (effective solidarity of interests, reciprocity of rights and duties), an emotional dimension (feelings of solidarity) and a cultural dimension (social bonds)'.[25]

As highlighted above, nationality overlaps with citizenship which has prompted its almost indistinguishable connotation due to interchangeable use in contemporary times.[26] Traditionally, they serve distinctively different purposes under civil and common law traditions. Thus, both concepts are understood differently in Anglophone, Francophone, and other countries in the region. The use of the word citizenship connotes participation and the exercise of civil and political rights that are not implied in the word nationality. However, the purpose for which

[22] B Manby, 'Statelessness in Southern Africa', Briefing Paper for UNHCR Regional Conference on Statelessness in Southern Africa, 1–3 November 2011 available at <https://www.refworld.org/pdfid/50c1f9562.pdf> accessed 3 November 2019.

[23] For an extensive insight into the national security challenge of herders/farmers clashes in Africa see CM Nwankwo, 'National Security, Property Rights and Development in Nigeria: How Should the Leviathan Resolve Herder-Farmer Conflict?' (2020) African Journal of Legal Studies, doi: https://doi.org/10.1163/17087384-12340068.

[24] African Commission on Human and Peoples' Rights, 'The Right to Nationality in Africa' Study undertaken by the Special Rapporteur on the Rights of Refugees, Asylum Seekers and Internally Displaced Persons available at <https://www.refworld.org/pdfid/54cb3c8f4.pdf> accessed 3 November 2019.

[25] ibid. See also C Goasguen, Report on the Right on The Law of Nationality in France, No 3605, French National Assembly, 29 June 2011, at 142.

[26] See J Salmon, *Dictionnaire de droit International Public* (Bruylant, 2001) 175, wherein the author states that the term citizenship is synonymous with nationality.

both terms are used synonymously in contemporary international law is to describe the legal relationship between an individual and a state.[27] The lack of scholarly material on the subject of nationality in pre-colonial African communities has somewhat dimmed the understanding of the relationship between Africans and the post-colonial state. Few authors who had ventured into this area by studying pre-colonial societal formations such as clans or lineage, kingdoms, and empires suggest that the types of community solidarities that were developed in that era gave citizenship an entirely different context.[28]

In pre-colonial African societies, Africans claimed several types of citizenship, each of which had 'its own framework, territory, and management and self-management groups'.[29] For example, the case of the Mandé is very illustrative of the unique nature of citizenship on the continent to the extent that

> all those who belonged to the Kingdom of Mali possessed a sort of Malian citizenship. When people travelled, they were viewed as nationals of Mali. After the last village belonging to Mali, people from elsewhere were thought of as belonging to other entities. Malian nationals were Mandinka. The term designated both people from Mandinka land and nationals of the Empire of Mali.[30]Everywhere in Africa, references to extended families, villages, neighbourhoods, and cantons [were] highly significant.[31]

In pre-colonial African societies, despite the frictions that may have existed between them, African people constantly moved around 'in a state of osmosis and symbiotic exchanges, in terms of social uses, languages, dances, ideologies, religions'. This inter-ethnic solidarity, of which border fluidity represented one of the most highly perfected forms, explains why foreigners were granted special protection in many pre-colonial states.[32] With the advent of colonialism and the arbitrary demarcation of African ethnicities into states, the laws and practices of the new administration changed the situation and imposed a new philosophy of nationality whose roots were fundamentally tethered to the common law and civil law traditions of nationality or citizenship.

The transfer of legal concepts from Western European powers through colonialism permeated every aspect of national life of the erstwhile colonial territories in

[27] PF Gonidec, 'La nationalité dans les États de la Communauté et dans les États marginaux' in *Annuaire Français de Droit International* (AFDI, Vol 7, 1961) 814–35.

[28] See, on this subject, DT Niane, 'Introduction' in *General History of Africa IV: Africa from the Twelfth to the Sixteenth Century* (UNESCO/NEA, 1985) 33.

[29] J Ki-Zerbo, *À quand l'Afrique: entretien avec René Holenstein* (Éditions de l'Aube, 2003) 79.

[30] African Commission on Human and Peoples' Rights (n 23) 9.

[31] Ki-Zerbo (n 28).

[32] The Mandé people for instance operated a strict code which instructed the indigenes to 'never do harm to foreigners'. See Énoncé 24 of the Charte de Kurukan Fuga in Celhto, *La Charte de Kurukan Fuga, Aux sources d'une pensée politique en Afrique* (L'Harmattan, 2008) 51, cited in African Commission on Human and Peoples' Rights (n 23) 9.

Africa. Thus, not only has inclusive pre-colonial conceptions of nationality been overtaken but there has also been a variation in the contemporary frameworks for the implementation of the right to nationality in African states. This lacuna necessitated the drive for more inclusive legal and institutional frameworks at regional level under the auspices of the AU and the Regional Economic Communities (RECs) to raise the standards for national institutions to adopt. This is arguably most achievable within the African human rights system which so far represents the strongest thread connecting regional institutions with national structures. The following sections of this chapter examine the extant frameworks that are obtainable in the region.

4. Legal Framework for Statelessness in Africa

It is important to outline the key provisions under international law and AU law[33] which addresses statelessness. International law stipulates that '(1) Everyone has the right to a nationality', and that '(2) No one shall be arbitrarily deprived of his nationality nor denied the right to change his nationality'.[34] This right has found its way into subsequent treaties in various forms. Subsequently, the 1961 UN Convention on the Reduction of Statelessness,[35] places a duty on states to prevent statelessness in nationality laws and practices. Article 1 of the Convention provides that 'a Contracting State shall grant its nationality to a person born in its territory who would otherwise be stateless'. Such nationality may be granted by birth, by operation of law, or upon application, including at a date after birth (e.g. at majority). The more preferred option would be for the nationality to be granted at birth by operation of law. Also, the 1954 Convention relating to the Status of Stateless Persons, binds State Parties to facilitate the assimilation and naturalization of stateless persons to the fullest extent possible.[36]

As at the time of writing this chapter, 20 African states are contracting parties to the 1961 UN Convention on the Reduction of Statelessness. However, all African states, with the exception of Somalia, have ratified the UN Convention on the Rights of the Child (CRC), which provides in Article 7 for every child to have 'the right to acquire a nationality', and for states to ensure the implementation of these rights, in particular where the child would otherwise be stateless. The CRC mirrors

[33] AU law consists of the body of laws that apply to the African Union as the continental superstructure and other laws that emanate from the RECs as well as national legal systems. As a subject under international law, this burgeoning field analyses the ebb and flow of a continent-wide legal order.

[34] Universal Declaration of Human Rights, G.A res. 217A (III), U.N Doc A/810 at 71 (1948), Article 15.

[35] UNTS, 989, at 175.

[36] UNTS, 360, at 117, Article 32.

the provision of Article 24 of the International Covenant on Civil and Political Rights (ICCPR),[37] which has been ratified or acceded to by a host of African states.

Under the body of laws that constitute AU law, the African Charter on the Rights and Welfare of the Child (ACRWC)[38] also enshrines, in Article 6, the right to acquire a nationality. The ACRWC further improves on the CRC by providing that 'state parties shall undertake to ensure that their constitutional legislation recognizes the principles according to which a child shall acquire the nationality of the State in the territory of which he has been born if, at the time of the child's birth, he is not granted a nationality by any other state in accordance with its laws'.[39] State Parties are under the principle of *pacta sunt servanda*[40] legally obliged under international law not to take actions against the 'object and purpose' of the ACRWC.

One key factor responsible for the number of stateless people in the region are national registration systems that systematically discriminate against populations based on gender and other grounds. AU Member States are parties to a number of international conventions that prohibit discrimination in any form. Chief among these treaties is the 1979 UN Convention on the Elimination of All Forms of Discrimination Against Women (CEDAW).[41] CEDAW provides in its Article 9 that women be granted equal rights with men in respect of citizenship. In addition to this, the African Charter on Human and Peoples' Rights (the African Charter)[42] prohibits discrimination by providing for equality before the law in general, although it is silent on the right to nationality. In addition to this, the Protocol to the African Charter on Human and Peoples' Rights on the Rights of Women in Africa[43] (the Protocol) contains provisions that prescribe strong anti-discrimination measures. The provisions of the Protocol also reflect the unease present among some AU Member States about gender inequality in exercise of the right to nationality. Its provisions also contradict the provisions of the African Charter itself and CEDAW in some respect. For example, the Protocol allows national law to override the non-discrimination presumptions of the treaty in relation to passing citizenship to children and fails to recognize the right of a woman to confer citizenship on her husband.[44]

[37] International Covenant on Civil and Political Rights, G.A res. 2200A (XXI), 21 UN GAOR Supp. (No 16) at 52.

[38] *African Charter on the Rights and Welfare of the Child*, 11 July 1990. CAB/LEG/24.9/49 (1990). Forty-four African countries have signed the charter and 47 have ratified.

[39] Article 6 of the ACRWC.

[40] *Pacta sunt servanda* is a principle of international law which provides that agreements must be kept. See *Vienna Convention on the Law of Treaties*, UNTS 1155, Article 26.

[41] UNTS, 249, 13.

[42] African Charter on Human and Peoples' Rights (Banjul Charter), 27 June 1981, CAB/LEG/67/3 rev. 5, 21 ILM.

[43] Protocol to the African Charter on Human and Peoples' Rights on the Rights of Women in Africa, adopted 1 July 2003 available at <https://au.int/en/treaties/protocol-african-charter-human-and-peoples-rights-rights-women-africa> accessed 25 July 2020.

[44] See Article 6(g) which provides that a woman shall have the right to retain her nationality or to acquire the nationality of her husband; and Article 6(h) a woman and a man shall have equal rights with

It also worthy to note that discrimination on grounds of race and ethnicity in the process of registration of citizens is also a contributing factor to statelessness. African states have complex historical pasts, which through colonialism have emerged in the multi-ethnic states with populations of ethnic minorities scattered around. Hence, the systematic exclusion of these minorities in the citizenship registration process in some states is a cause for concern. However, African states are party to a range of conventions which prohibits discrimination on grounds of race. The UN Convention on the Elimination of All Forms of Racial Discrimination (CERD)[45] is the most important document in this respect. Article 5 of CERD provides that State Parties undertake to eliminate racial discrimination in the enjoyment of other rights, including the right to nationality. It is noteworthy that racial discrimination is fully entrenched in customary international law which elevates it to the status of *jus cogens*.[46]

These instruments have been reflected in the resolutions of the African Commission on Human and Peoples' Rights (the Commission) on the right to nationality. At one of its Ordinary Sessions[47] the Commission, amongst other things, expressed 'its deep concern at the arbitrary denial or deprivation of the nationality of persons or group of persons by African States, especially as a result of discrimination on grounds of race, ethnic group, colour, sex, language, religion, political or any other opinion, national and social origin, fortune, birth or other status'.[48] The communication expressed regret over the failure of African states to ensure that all children are registered at birth. But the communication also expressed conviction that it is in the general interest of Africa for all African states to recognize, guarantee, and facilitate the right to nationality of every person on the continent and to ensure that no-one is exposed to statelessness. It also reaffirmed the right to nationality of every human person as a fundamental human right implied within the provisions of Article 5 of the African Charter and essential to the enjoyment of other fundamental rights and freedoms under the Charter.

The resolution of the Commission above underscores the importance of the right to nationality to the enjoyment of other fundamental human rights. Consequently, it has gone on to take concrete steps to enhance the right to nationality in Member States and at the regional level. One such step is the Draft Protocol on the African

respect to the nationality of their children, except where this is contrary to a provision in national legislation or is contrary to national security interests.

[45] UNTS 1249, 13.

[46] *Jus cogens* norms are peremptory norms from which no derogation is permitted under international law.

[47] See the African Commission on Human and Peoples' Rights, meeting at its 53rd Ordinary Session held 9–23 April 2013 in Banjul, Gambia.

[48] ibid.

Charter on Human and Peoples' Rights on the Right to Nationality.[49] The provisions of this document are instructive. In its Preamble, it affirms that statelessness is a violation of the right to human dignity and to legal status which is guaranteed in Article 5 of the African Charter. It also references the history of the African continent, especially the initial establishment of borders of colonial powers, which has given questions of nationality and statelessness particular characteristics in African states that are not sufficiently taken into account by the existing African and international instruments. The Preamble further recognizes the need to establish, by voluntary agreement, standards and procedures for settling questions relating to the specific aspects of the right to a nationality and the eradication of statelessness in Africa. The draft protocol sets as its main objective to establish the obligations and responsibilities of states relative to the specific aspects of the right to a nationality in Africa and to ensure that statelessness is eradicated.

The said draft protocol, while yet to be operative, is commendable in that it aims to create a regional normative standard for the fight against statelessness. If Arendt's criticism about the inadequacies of the concept of human rights in the implementation of the right to nationality all those years ago is still to be considered, the approach of the Commission and the admission that statelessness is a grave injustice deserving of the strictest standards of rules at all levels is commendable.

5. Jurisprudence of Regional Human Rights Bodies on the Right to Nationality

The African Commission as a quasi-judicial body has contributed immensely to the advancement of the African human rights system. Its decisions mostly serve the purpose of directing the discourse of human rights on the continent. Pertaining to statelessness, the African Commission has made a few notable pronouncements on the right to nationality in Africa. These key decisions of the Commission deserve mention and can aid a better understanding of the concept in Africa. Although the African Charter does not explicitly provide for the right to nationality, the Commission has ruled that the provision of Article 5 of the Charter which provides that 'every individual shall have the right to the respect of the dignity inherent in a human being and to the recognition of his legal status' applies specifically to attempts to denationalize individuals and render them stateless, in light of the consequences that flow from statelessness.

[49] Draft Protocol on the African Charter on Human and Peoples' Rights on the Right to Nationality available at <https://www.achpr.org/public/Document/file/English/draft_citizenship_protocol_en_sept2015_achpr.pdf> accessed 25 July 2020.

In *Modise v Botswana*[50] the applicant had spent years confined either to the South African 'homeland' of Bophuthatswana or the no-man's land between South Africa and Botswana because of the respondent government's refusal to recognize his nationality from birth, the Commission found against the Botswanan government and held, *inter alia*, that Modise's 'personal suffering and indignity' violated Article 5 of the African Charter.[51]Similarly, in *Amnesty International v Zambia*,[52] the Commission considered an application brought by Amnesty International on behalf of deportees William Banda and John Chinula from Zambia to Malawi. It found for the applicants and held that '[b]y forcing [the complainants] to live as stateless persons under degrading conditions, the [Zambian] government . . . [had] deprived them of their family and [was] depriving their families of the men's support, and this constitutes a violation of the dignity of a human being, thereby violating Article 5'.[53]

In addition to decisions that emphasize the right to a nationality through the interpretation of provisions of the African Charter, the Commission has also sought to invalidate constitutional provisions of AU Member States that exclude certain groups from enjoying the right to a nationality. In *Legal Resources Foundation v Zambia*[54] the Commission entertained an application which bordered on a constitutional amendment in Zambia that required any presidential aspirant to prove that both parents were Zambians from birth. The Commission ruled that Article 2 (non-discrimination), Article 3 (equality before the law), and Article 13 (participation in public life) of the African Charter were being violated by such law. The Commission further noted that freedom of movement in what was previously the Central African Federation meant that it would be an injustice to suggest that only a person who himself was born in and whose parents were born in what later became the sovereign territory of the state of Zambia could be considered an indigenous Zambian. The Commission found that the retroactive application of such a law could not be justified under the African Charter.

Similarly, in *Mouvement ivoirien des droits humains (MIDH) v Côte d'Ivoire*[55] the Commission considered a constitutional provision of Côte d'Ivoire which required a presidential candidate to be both Ivorian from birth and for both parents to also be Ivorian from birth. The Commission held that such provisions were 'unreasonable and unjustifiable and . . . an unnecessary restriction on the right to participate in government' as well as 'discriminatory because it applies varying standards

50 Comm No 97/93, *Modise v Botswana*, African Commission on Human and Peoples' Rights (ACHPR) 2000.

51 ibid para 91.

52 Comm No 212/98, *Amnesty International v Zambia*, ACHPR 1999.

53 ibid para 50.

54 Comm No 211/98, *Legal Resources Foundation v Zambia* (2001) AHRLR 84 (ACHPR 2001).

55 Comm No 246/02, *Mouvement ivoirien des droits humains (MIDH) v Côte d'Ivoire* (ACHPR 25th activity report 2008).

to the same categories of persons, that is persons born in Côte d'Ivoire, are now treated based on the places of origin of their parents'.[56]

More recently, the African Court on Human and Peoples Rights (the African Court) delivered its first judgment on the right to nationality. In *Anudo Ochieng v Tanzania*[57] the applicant a citizen of Tanzania by birth had his citizenship revoked by the Tanzanian government. He had applied to register his marriage, but his passport was retained on the grounds that there were doubts about his citizenship.[58] After he lodged an official complaint to Tanzanian authorities, a letter from the Minister of Home Affairs and Immigration informed the applicant that his passport had been confiscated on the ground that he was not a citizen. He was escorted to the Kenyan border and compelled to sign a notice of deportation and a document attesting that he was a Kenyan citizen.[59] After being rejected by the Kenyan government, the applicant lived in no-man's land between Kenya and Tanzania for three years. The applicant had no right of appeal due to the bar placed by the Tanzania Citizenship Act 1995 which provides that the Minister's decision in relation to any application under the Act 'shall not be subject to appeal or review in any court'.[60] The Immigration Act 1995 similarly provides that in decisions relating to matters contained in the act, the Minister's 'decision shall be final'.[61]

The African Court held that the deprivation of the applicant's nationality was arbitrary under Article 15 of the Universal Declaration of Human Rights (UDHR), and Articles 12 of the African Charter and 13 of the ICCPR. The Court further held that the applicant's right to due process protections had been violated including the right to be heard before an impartial tribunal, under Article 7 of the African Charter and Article 14 of the ICCPR.[62] The African Court ordered Tanzania to amend its legislation to provide individuals with judicial remedies in the event of a dispute over citizenship, and to take all necessary steps to restore the applicant's rights, including readmission to the country.[63]

While the African Court noted that there is no general provision on nationality in the ICCPR and the African Charter, it relied on the provisions of article 15(2) of the UDHR which states that '[n]o one shall be arbitrarily deprived of his nationality'. By this, the African Court asserted (without discussion) that the UDHR is part of customary international law, noting also a reference to the UDHR in article 9(f) of the Constitution of Tanzania.[64] Thus, while the African Court affirmed that

[56] ibid.
[57] App No 012/2015, 22 March 2018.
[58] ibid 3 [8].
[59] ibid 3 [9].
[60] *Tanzania Citizenship Act* 1995, Article 23.
[61] *Immigration Act* 1995 (Tanzania), Article 10(f).
[62] *Anudo Case* (n 56) 20[88]; 21[96]–[97]; 23[106]; 24–25 [110]–[115].
[63] ibid 17 [76]. See also B Manby, 'Anudo Ochieng Anudo v Tanzania (Judgment)' (2019) 1 Statelessness & Citizenship Review 170, 174.
[64] ibid, 17 [76], citing Constitution of Tanzania (Tanzania) Article 9(f).

the conferral of nationality is the sovereign right of states, it states that international law permits loss of nationality only in 'very exceptional situations'.[65] This particular admission of the court has been fodder for the critique of human rights by proponents of Arendt's school of thought. However, as this chapter made clear earlier, international law may be limited, but it offers a fairly effective route to eradicating the problem. For this reason, human rights may not be considered toothless. The African Court has taken a step in changing the narrative from a judicial point of view. The African Commission has accumulated a number of decisions that helped advance the discourse on the complicity of AU Member States in the exclusion of citizens within a state. It is left for the African Court to build on the decisions of the Commission to further impress on AU Member States the importance of creating systems that protect the right to nationality domestically.[66]

The African Court deserves plaudits for its contribution to international law in this field on how it interpreted the burden of proof in matters of this nature. In the vast majority of cases in Africa where citizenship of an individual is in contention, governments mostly do not invoke formal deprivation procedures under the relevant law but rather assert that the individual acquired nationality illegitimately.[67] From the governments' perspective, the advantage of this approach is that it masks its lack of due process protections which usually apply. In the *Anudo case* the African Court outlaws this approach to circumventing the individual's rights by its holding that if a person already holds official documents attesting citizenship, the onus then lies on the state to prove (to the satisfaction of an independent tribunal) that the person in question is not a citizen.[68]

Another very important decision of a principal human rights body in Africa is the decision on the merits of a communication to the African Committee of Experts on the Rights and Welfare of the Child regarding the nationality of children of Nubian descent born in Kenya.[69] The Committee of Experts in its first decision, found Kenya guilty of the violation of her obligations under Article 6 of the ACRWC, despite the reforms in the 2010 Kenyan Constitution, by failing to provide for the children of stateless parents born in Kenya.[70] The Committee emphasized the devastating consequences of statelessness for children in relation to their socio-economic rights.[71]

[65] ibid 17 [18].

[66] Manby argues that the court appears to have missed a trick by failing to read the right to nationality into the African Charter and also to rely on the rich jurisprudence of the African Commission. See Manby (n 62) 175.

[67] See generally B Manby, *Citizenship in Africa: The Law of Belonging* (Hart Publishing, 2018).

[68] *Anudo case*, (n 56) 18 [80].

[69] Comm No 002/2009, *Institute for Human Rights and Development in Africa and Open Society Justice Initiative on behalf of Children of Nubian Descent in Kenya*, African Committee of Expert on the Rights and Welfare of the Child, 22 March 2011.

[70] ibid para 53.

[71] ibid paras 42 and 46.

6. Sub-regional Frameworks for Tackling Statelessness

There is general consensus that the advancement of international law has been crucial to the process that led to the separation of the right to nationality from the exclusive purview of the state. Up until the early 20th century, it was generally agreed that determining rules relating to nationality was the prerogative of sovereign states.[72]Two advisory opinions of the Permanent Court of International Justice (PCIJ) handed down in 1923 challenged that status of exclusivity which states enjoyed.[73] Here the predecessor to the International Court of Justice (ICJ) laid down the principle that laws on nationality must comply with treaties, stipulating that 'though, generally speaking, it is true that a sovereign State has the right to decide what persons shall be regarded as its nationals, it is no less true that this principle is applicable only subject to the Treaty obligations (of said State)'.[74]

What followed after this was a flurry of international conventions which encapsulated the spirit of that opinion. The Hague Convention of 1930 adopted this condition and consolidated it with two other sources, namely customary international law and generally recognized principles of law with regard to nationality – which was novel at the time.[75] Since then, international law has evolved, recognizing the individual right to nationality in a two-stage process:

- The first phase, which extended from the end of the Second World War to the early 1970s, which can be seen as a period of advocacy by the UN for an international right to nationality, which was materialized through drafting, under its aegis, of a great number of treaties containing principles on nationality.
- The second phase, when the states began to undertake to follow in the footsteps of the UN, was marked by the adoption of a large number of binding regional instruments on nationality.[76]

A possible third stage to be considered under international law scholarship should be the establishment of regional laws and policies to influence national policies on the right to nationality. In Africa, as earlier indicated, there appears to be an awakening on the severity of the challenge of statelessness. Under the aegis of the AU, Regional Economic Communities (RECs) in Africa are taking steps to

[72] See, for example, Convention on Certain Questions relating to the Conflict of Nationality Laws, signed at The Hague, on 12 April 1930. It provides that '[i]t is for each State to determine under its own law who its nationals are'.

[73] See PCIJ, Advisory opinion of 7 February 1923 on Nationality Decrees Issued in Tunis and Morocco (French Zone), Rec Series B, No 4 and Advisory opinion of 15 September 1923 on Acquisition of Polish Nationality. Series B, No 7.

[74] See PCIJ, Advisory opinion of 15 September on the Acquisition of Polish Nationality. Series B, No 7, at 16.

[75] See Article 1 of the Convention on Certain Questions relating to the Conflict of Nationality Laws.

[76] African Commission on Human and Peoples' Rights (n 23) 15.

strengthen further the normative foundations of the right to nationality in Africa. These attempts to tackle the menace of statelessness will be discussed in the following paragraphs. This analysis is even more important when it is recalled that RECs are considered the building blocs[77] of the AU and as such are strategically positioned to make laws and policies that are peculiar to their community, given the transboundary nature of statelessness in the region.

Most treaties of RECs in Africa have as their main objective the establishment of regional communities with free movement of persons, goods, and services. This is in tandem with the goal of market integration or an African Economic Community. But other ancillary instruments attempt to enhance the protection of the right to nationality in different ways. In 1982 ECOWAS adopted its Protocol Relating to the Definition of a Community Citizen.[78] The Protocol provides an important recognition of the common rights and obligations among the nationals of West African States. However, the provisions of this Protocol are not quite clear in its definition and what particular purpose it serves millions of stateless people in the sub-region.

Article 1 of the said Protocol, 'on the acquisition of community citizenship', provides for four ways of becoming a community citizen; by descent, by place of birth (providing one parent is a national), by adoption, and by naturalization. Article 2(1) provides for loss of community citizenship on the following grounds: (a) permanent settlement in a state outside the Community; (b) voluntary acquisition of the nationality of a state outside the Community; (c) a *de facto* acquisition of the nationality of a state outside the Community; (d) loss of one's nationality of country of origin; (e) on his express request. Article 2(2) provides for deprivation of community citizenship from a naturalized citizen if he or she is involved in 'activities incompatible with the status of Community citizen, and/or prejudicial to the fundamental interests of one or more Member States of the Community'. It also adds, 'The situation is the same when such a crime is committed against a citizen of the Community'. Article 2(3) provides for loss of citizenship in cases of fraud or if it becomes apparent that the person did not fulfil the conditions to acquire citizenship.

The provisions regarding who is responsible for the recognition or deprivation of community citizenship, and what the content of community citizenship beyond the rights of citizenship derived from a state's constitution should be, have a certain degree of ambiguity to them. While the primary responsibility of Member States to guarantee citizenship to every individual is clear, the wording about the role of

[77] On the relationship between the RECs and the African Continental Free Trade Area (AfCFTA) Agreement see CC Ajibo, CM Nwankwo, and EO Ekhator, 'Regional Economic Communities as the Building Blocs of the African Continental Free Trade Area Agreement' (2021) 18(4) Transnational Dispute Management 1–16.

[78] Protocol A/P.3/5/82 Relating to the Definition of Community Citizen available at <https://documentation.ecowas.int/download/en/legal_documents/protocols/Protocol%20Relating%20to%20the%20Definition%20of%20Community%20Citizen.pdf> accessed 25 July 2020.

the ECOWAS Council of Ministers or other community organs implies that the Community bodies have a direct function to fulfil in the process. However, no procedures have ever been adopted to provide for ECOWAS to recognize community citizenship independent of the recognized procedures under municipal law. There is also no requirement on Member States to reduce statelessness among people who have always lived within West Africa. Finally, the protocol omits to prescribe a harmonization of Member States' own nationality in a way that would give effect to the Protocol.[79]

Programmes of ECOWAS in combating causative factors of statelessness in the region are worthy of mention. Amongst them are the 2001 Political Declaration and 2002-2003 Initial Plan of Action to Combat Trafficking in Persons in West Africa.[80] In 2005 a dedicated anti-trafficking ECOWAS unit was created. This is in addition to numerous bilateral agreements to counter trafficking in persons in the region.[81] In addition ECOWAS have attempted to tackle issues related to cross-border pastoralism, with bilateral and multi-lateral agreements to facilitate cross-border movement. From 2000 ECOWAS commenced the issuance of explicit sets of livestock passports, international transhumant certificates (ITC), and the handbooks for travel to pastoralists.[82] Furthermore, the AU adopted a *Policy Framework for Pastoralism in Africa* in 2010 which endorses the ECOWAS framework and creates strategic objectives relating to the recognition of pastoralism in development. It is however important to note that cross-border migrations have accelerated communal clashes in some ECOWAS Member States due to competition for green land to feed cattle. The drought in the Sahel which is caused by climate change has led to an increase in southward movement by nomadic people.

In the East African Community (EAC) efforts are also being made to protect the right to nationality. The EAC realizes that market integration is best achieved through free movement of persons and that the right to nationality further enhances the movement of persons from one member state to another to trade. Article 1 of the Protocol for the Establishment of the East African Common Market defines a national of a Partner State as a natural or legal person who is a national in accordance with the laws of the Partner State. But in comparison to the ECOWAS Protocol for the Definition of Community Citizens, it fails to define who a citizen of the EAC is. This is understandable considering that the EAC considers itself to be far from a political federation.[83] But like the ECOWAS Trade Liberalization

[79] B Manby, 'Nationality, Migration and Statelessness in West Africa', Study prepared for the UNHCR Regional Office for Africa, June 2015 available at <https://www.unhcr.org/ecowas2015/Nationality-Migration-and-Statelessness-in-West-Africa-REPORT-EN.pdf> accessed 25 July 2020.

[80] Joint ECOWAS/ECCAS Plan of Action 2006–2009, and the ECOWAS Plan of Action against trafficking in human beings 2008-2011.

[81] Some include Burkina Faso and Mali (2004), Mali and Senegal (2004), Mali and Guinea (2005), Benin and Nigeria (2005), and Benin and Congo Brazzaville (2011).

[82] Manby (n 77) 85.

[83] This was one of the reasons adduced by a principal officer of the EAC on why there is no provision for community citizenship under EAC Law. See, 'Right to Nationality (R2N) in East African

Scheme (TLS), the EAC Common Market Protocol provides for free movement of persons without any discrimination based on nationality. The right to free movement of persons includes the right to enter the territory of a Partner State without a visa; the right to move freely within the territory of a Partner State; the right to stay in the territory of a Partner State; the right to exist without restrictions; and the right to full protection by the laws of a Partner State. However, implementation of the scheme is far from certain.

One institutional feature which the EAC enjoys over ECOWAS and sister RECs is the operation of the East African Legislative Assembly (EALA)[84] which enjoys full legislative powers. With the EALA, it will be easier for community laws and policies protecting the right to a nationality to be implemented. As it stands, the EAC is yet to adopt a framework of its own specifically focusing on the right to nationality beyond domestic institutional frameworks on nationality. However, all EAC partner states also belong to the International Conference on the Great Lakes Region (ICGLR).[85] The ICGLR has recognized, from its first meeting in 2004, the contribution that issues relating to contested nationality have made to conflict in the Great Lakes region. For instance, the 2004 Dar es Salaam Declaration that established the Conference enjoined states to:

> adopt a common approach for the ratification and implementation of the UN Convention on Statelessness, harmonise related national laws and standards, and provide refugees and displaced persons with identification documents enabling them to have access to basic services and exercise their rights.[86]

More recently in 2017, ICGLR Member States strengthened these commitments by adopting a Declaration and Regional Action Plan on the Eradication of Statelessness (2017–2019).[87] The Declaration and Plan of Action commit ICGLR

Community', Conference in Tanzania, 26 November 2015 available at <http://citizenshiprightsafrica.org/right-to-nationality-r2n-in-the-east-african-community/> accessed 25 July 2020.

[84] The East African Legislative Assembly was established under Article 9 of the EAC Treaty. The EALA is vested with the power to make laws binding on EAC partner states.

[85] The ICGLR held its first meeting in 2004 and was established in 2006 with the signing of a Pact on Security, Stability and Development in the Great Lakes Region. The original signatories were Angola, Burundi, Central African Republic, Congo, DRC, Kenya, Rwanda, Sudan, Tanzania, Uganda, and Zambia; South Sudan acceded in 2012 after it gained its independence.

[86] Dar-es-Salaam Declaration on Peace, Security, Democracy and Development in the Great Lakes Region, ICGLR, adopted by the First Summit of Heads of State and Government, Dar-es-Salaam, 19–20 November 2004, para 68 available at <https://ungreatlakes.unmissions.org/sites/default/files/icglr_dar_es_salaam_declaration_on_peace_security_democracy_and_development_in_glr.pdf> accessed 25 July 2020.

[87] Declaration on the Eradication of Statelessness, adopted by Ministers of Foreign Affairs of ICGLR Member States, June 2017 available at <http://www.refworld.org/docid/59e9cb8c4.html>; Action Plan of the ICGLR on the Eradication of Statelessness 2017-2019 available at <http://www.refworld.org/docid/5a7c16aa4.html> both accessed 25 July 2020. Both documents were endorsed by the ICGLR 7th Ordinary Summit of Heads of State and Government in Brazzaville, Republic of Congo, 19 October 2017.

Member States to ratification of the UN Conventions on statelessness, reform of nationality laws to bring them into line with international standards on nationality and statelessness, adoption of national action plan to end statelessness, and nomination of government focal points on statelessness. By April 2018, focal points had been nominated in all 12 Member States and trained with the support of the UNHCR.[88]

It is noteworthy that sub-regional courts have been mute on the issue of the right to nationality. Perhaps this is due to a scarcity of litigants approaching the courts on this issue. This notwithstanding, the jurisprudence of the African Commission, and more recently the African Court, provides enough backing for litigants who wish to subject Member States to domestic enforcement of the judgment of sub-regional courts in this area. Given the growing impact of sub-regional courts in the region, this is certainly another route worth exploring to eradicate statelessness in Africa.

7. A Step Forward?

The legal landscape on the right to nationality in African states is fraught with problems. Nationality is a touchy subject because considerations surrounding it are mostly political and this feature has delayed focused reforms of national laws on the right to nationality. The first problem is the recognition by individuals that statelessness is a social handicap requiring urgent reforms. For instance, a very large number of people in West Africa have no means of identity mainly because they do not see the point of having documents, and because they are costly in time and money to obtain.[89] Thus an important next step for states to take is to create a transparent and predictable system which is reliant on proper documentation and which people appreciate and realize as indispensable.

To achieve effective nationality laws and administration systems it is imperative that government functions, that have important roles to play in the process of establishing a person's nationality, are harmonized. For instance, civil registration, judicial confirmation of nationality, national identity card systems, issuing of passports and other travel documents, refugee protection agencies, child protection units, electoral registration, border management and immigration control, and census bodies all have a part to play in nationality administration. There is no gainsaying that these bodies must work together to ensure effective administration.

88 B Manby, 'Citizenship and Statelessness in the East African Community', Report prepared for the UNHCR, September 2018 available at <https://www.refworld.org/docid/5bee966d4.html> accessed 3 November 2019.

89 Manby (n 77) 88.

It is often the case that African states lack cooperation to resolve cases where nationality is in doubt.[90] As it stands, there is no positive system to establish nationality and documents for a person where it is clear that he or she can only lay claim to the nationality of two possible states, where both states are currently disputing that claim.[91] Consular authorities, courts, and immigration and nationality officials of states only prioritize policing of boundaries without setting up platforms to harmonize attempts to attend to nationality claims. Under the current legal systems in West Africa for instance, there is no requirement on officials to ensure that individuals do not lose their right to nationality. Hence, it is vital that national authorities do not parochially focus on ensuring that individuals that lay claim to a particular nationality receive citizenship. There should be mechanisms set in place to ensure that authorities ensure that millions of West African citizens who do not belong to any particular nationality are absorbed by the respective states they claim after verification.

At the vertical level, it is important that African states accede wholesale to the 1954 Convention relating to the Status of Stateless Persons and the 1961 Convention on the Reduction of Statelessness while also reviewing national law and practice to ensure its compliance with the requirements and standards of these international human rights instruments based on the Guidelines on Statelessness published by the UNHCR. In the same vein, African states must ensure the strict application of the ACRWC which deals with birth registration and the right to a name and nationality, providing for every child to have the right to acquire a nationality, and in particular to 'acquire the nationality of the State in the territory of which he has been born if at the time of the child's birth, he is not granted nationality with any other state in accordance with its laws'.[92]

8. Conclusion

In conclusion, the menace of statelessness may be enduring in Africa but that stems from a number of factors already highlighted above. However, there exist within regional systems mechanisms which can serve as catalysts for greater enforcement of the right to nationality and the reduction of statelessness. These standards contained in these instruments must be matched by the political will of AU Member States to have any real impact. Furthermore, African states must be made to see the connection between statelessness and the realization of human rights obligations

[90] A case in point is the case of Ethiopia and Eritrea who while formerly being part of one territory have refused to include cross-border asylum seekers who belonged to the old territory. See JR Campbell, 'The enduring problem of statelessness in the Horn of Africa: how nation-states and western courts (re) define nationality' (2011) 23 International Journal of Refugee Law 656.

[91] Manby (n 77) 94.

[92] ibid.

contained in regional and international instruments. This is also tied to the actualization of a unified continental market represented by the newly signed African Continental Free Trade Agreement (AfCFTA), the Sustainable Development Goals (SDGs), and the new continental blueprint –Agenda 2063 which seeks resurgence in the Pan-African vision of an integrated, peaceful, and prosperous Africa. As a whole, these ideals are connected and it is apparent that one cannot be achieved independent of the other. Consequently, national structures should be improved and synchronized with regional and international standards.

Furthermore, while statelessness may appear insurmountable, this does not invalidate the usefulness of the modern conception of human rights as a system for protecting the individual. A lot of progress has been made over the years and the emergence of regional human rights systems may be the best advised path to follow. In Africa, the regional human rights system has borne fruit in defining the normative and institutional standards for protecting the rights of the citizen. What could be more desirable than a regional system upon which domestic laws and policies are built? This in fact seems to be the case as the AU and its organs appear keen to display by establishing a protocol for the right to nationality.

12
Combating Terrorism and Managing Asylum Seekers and Refugees under AU Law

Cristiano d'Orsi

1. Introduction: Causes of Terrorism in Africa

Over recent years, terrorism has become a key challenge to peace, security, and development in Africa. Terror activities have grown exponentially on the continent, not only in terms of the number of attacks but also in terms of the number of countries affected due to the proliferation of terrorist groups.[1]

As highlighted in 2014 by the Chairperson of the Commission on Terrorism and Violent Extremism in Africa, several factors influence the rise of terrorism in Africa. These involve radicalization and violent extremism, transnational organized crime, kidnapping for ransom, the proliferation of arms, weapons and ammunitions, and mercenarism, as well as the consequences of political instability in Northern Africa.[2] Several weaknesses, common to most Member States of the African Union (AU), have also contributed to the threat of terrorism. Among these is the presence of vast, sparsely populated and poorly administered territories, which are found in all the countries affected by terrorism, particularly in the Sahel. Such enormous tracts of land provide the perfect ground for hidden training camps for terrorists, some of which have a broad financial base to tailor the desert according to their specific needs. Moreover, widespread conflict and poverty, marginalization, human rights violations, ethnic, national, and religious-based discrimination, and lack of employment and opportunities for youth create

[1] The most famous groups currently acting in Africa are Boko Haram in Nigeria, Al-Shabaab, Al-Qaeda in the Sahel (AQIS), and Al-Qaeda in the Maghreb (AQIM). In this regard, see A Caro de Beer, *Peremptory Norms? of General International Law (Jus Cogens) and the Prohibition of Terrorism* (Brill/Nijhoff, 2019) 15: 'The rise of terrorism in Africa has seen the Islamist militant group Boko Haram carry out attacks on civilians as well as suicide bomb attacks in Nigeria. There were further attacks in 2017 by the Al-Qaeda affiliated Al-Shabaab terrorist group in Southern Somalia, including an attack on an African Union ... convoy in July 2017.'

[2] AU, *Report of the Chairperson of the Commission on Terrorism and Violent Extremism in Africa*, PSC/AHG/2(CDLV) (2 September 2014) para 17 available at <https://au.int/sites/default/files/speeches/25397-sp-psc-rpt-terrorism-nairobi-2-09-2014-pdf_0.pdf> accessed 1 February 2020.

Cristiano d'Orsi, *Combating Terrorism and Managing Asylum Seekers and Refugees under AU Law* In: *The Emergent African Union Law*. Edited by: Olufemi Amao, Michèle Olivier and Konstantinos D. Magliveras, Oxford University Press.
 DOI: 10.1093/oso/9780198862154.003.0013

a favourable ground for alienation and radicalization, rendering segments of the population vulnerable to terrorists, who offer financial reward and a sense of belonging.[3]

Another difficulty experienced in Africa is the reluctance by affected African states to embrace anti-terrorism legislation. This would give far-reaching powers to the executive arm of governments in an environment where democratic traditions and the principles of the rule of law are not well established.[4]

This chapter analyses the legal and policy framework for combatting terrorism in Africa. The chapter argues that the prohibition of terrorism has become accepted as a norm of *jus cogens*[5] and examines how this norm has challenged the status quo of asylum seekers and refugees in Africa. Finally, suggestions are made on how to strengthen the legal and policy framework under an emerging AU law which will bind AU members.

The discussion first considers the various initiatives adopted within the AU framework to counter terrorist activities on the continent. The focus then turns to the key provisions in the main international and regional legislation protecting refugees in Africa against the threat of terrorism. The chapter concludes with a final assessment of the situation and recommendations for relevant stakeholders.

2. OAU/AU Efforts to Protect Asylum Seekers and Refugees from Terrorism

As an initial step towards combating terrorism, the Organisation of African Unity (OAU) adopted the 1994 Declaration on a Code of Conduct for Inter-African Relations to reject all forms of terrorism and extremism based on religion, ethnicity, or sectarianism. The criminalization and condemnation of acts, methods, and practices of insurgency were further confirmed by the now defunct organization.[6]

[3] ibid paras 27–28.

[4] A Thomashausen, 'The War on Terror in Africa in International Law and State Practice', [2007] 32 South Africa Yearbook of International Law 85, 94. With regard to Guinea, Monica K Juma and Peter M Kagwanja contend: '[T]here is a marked gap between what refugee jurisprudence guarantees in the Guinean context and what actually happens in the daily life of refugees and asylum-seekers. In this particular case, the concern is not about the adaptation of international refugee law. It is about the lack of implementation, application and efficient monitoring of it from within the domestic domain, as well as the barring of international organizations from intervening in cases of malpractice.' See: MK Juma and PM Kagwanja, 'Securing Refuge from Terror: Refugee Protection in East Africa after September 11' in N Steiner, M Gibney, and others (eds), *Problems of Protection: The UNHCR, Refugees and Human Rights* (Routledge, 2003) 234.

[5] Caro de Beer (n 1) 102: '[T]he prohibition of terrorism reflects the core characteristics of *jus cogens* norms. The prohibition protects the fundamental values of the international community, is hierarchically superior to other norms of international law and is universally applicable.'

[6] OAU (Assembly of Heads of State and Government), *Declaration on a Code of Conduct for Inter-African Relations* AHG/Decl.2 (XXX) (13th Ordinary Session, 13–15 June 1994) Preamble available at <https://au.int/sites/default/files/decisions/9539-1994_ahg_res_228-233_xxx_e.pdf> accessed 1 February 2020.

'Condemnation (of the acts) and cooperation (among Member States)' is the repeated refrain often used in Africa when it comes to deal with issues such as terrorism and the 1994 Declaration is no exception.[7] This falls significantly short of the requirements for a continental legal system built on commitments with tangible legal implications as foreseen by the emerging AU law discussed and developed in this book. At the OAU's 28th Ordinary Summit held in Dakar in 1992, a resolution was adopted to enhance cooperation, and in this case again, 'coordination' among Member States to fight all forms of extremism. Such calls for cooperation and coordination, however, remain meaningless unless backed up by specific action and facilitated in order to ensure the stability and territorial integrity of African states.[8]

In October 2001, representatives of 27 African states convened in Dakar and adopted a declaration calling for zero tolerance of all acts of terrorism and the need to strengthen, yet again, inter-state cooperation and coordination in the fight against all forms of terrorism.[9] In effect, the declaration of a terrorism-free continent sounds redundant because no other continent would admit the presence of terrorists on its territory.

An important breakthrough came when AU institutions succeeded in addressing the lack of universal agreement on what constitutes a 'terrorist act'. This was achieved in 1999 through the definition contained in Article 1(3) and Article 3 of the 1999 OAU Convention on the Prevention and Combating of Terrorism (1999 Convention).[10]

> In essence, article 1(3) stipulates:
> 'Terrorist act' means: a) any act which is a violation of the criminal laws of a State Party and which may endanger the life, physical integrity or freedom of, or cause serious injury or death to, any person, any number or group of persons or causes or may cause damage to public or private property, natural resources, environmental or cultural heritage … b) any promotion, sponsoring, contribution to, command, aid, incitement, encouragement, attempt, threat, conspiracy, organizing, or procurement of any person.

Affirming the spirit of self-determination that pervades in other AU legal instruments, Article 3(1), points out:

[7] ibid para 10.

[8] OAU (Assembly of Heads of State and Government), *Resolution on the Strengthening of Cooperation and Coordination among African States* AHG/Res. 213 (XXVIII) (28th Ordinary Session, 29 June–1 July 1992) para 2 available at <https://au.int/sites/default/files/decisions/9537-1992_ahg_res_206-217_xxviii_e.pdf> accessed 1 February 2020.

[9] OAU, *Dakar Declaration against Terrorism* (17 October 2001) available at <https://www.refworld.org/docid/3deb22b14.html> accessed 1 February 2020.

[10] OAU, *Convention on the Prevention and Combating of Terrorism (with Annex)* (14 July 1999) UNTS vol 2219, No 39464, 179 available at <https://au.int/sites/default/files/treaties/7779-treaty-0020_-_oau_convention_on_the_prevention_and_combating_of_terrorism_e.pdf> accessed 1 February 2020.

> Notwithstanding the provisions of article 1, the struggle waged by peoples in accordance with the principles of international law for their liberation or self-determination, including armed struggle against colonialism, occupation, aggression and domination by foreign forces shall not be considered as terrorist acts.

In addition, Article 4(2)(g) of the 1999 Convention clarifies that State Parties should 'ascertain, when granting asylum, that the asylum seeker is not involved in any terrorist act'. The definition of the term 'terrorist act' in the 1999 Convention is confirmed by Article 1(1) of its 2004 Protocol (2004 Protocol),[11] whose main purpose is explained in Article 2(2):

> To enhance the effective implementation of the Convention and to give effect to Art. 3(d) of the Protocol Relating to the Establishment of the Peace and Security Council (PSC) of the African Union, on the need to coordinate and harmonize continental efforts in the prevention and combating of terrorism is all its aspects,[12] as well as the implementation of other relevant international instruments.

This additional protocol addresses a major weakness of the 1999 Convention – its failure to include an implementation mechanism. The 2004 Protocol mandates the AU's PSC to monitor and facilitate implementation. It also encourages the African Regional Economic Communities (RECs: eight in Africa, among them AMU, ECOWAS, IGAD, and SADC) to take a more active role.[13] In this regard, the 2004 Protocol enhances coordination and harmonization of counter-terrorism activities in Africa[14]

To date,[15] 43 countries have ratified the 1999 Convention, which entered into force on 26 December 2002, after the deposit of the instrument of ratification by South Africa. In contrast, only 21 states have ratified the 2004 Protocol, which entered into force on 26 February 2014, after the deposit of the instrument of ratification by the Sahrawi Arab Democratic Republic.[16]

[11] AU, *Protocol to the OAU Convention on the Prevention and Combating of Terrorism* (8 July 2004) 1 No UNTS available at <https://treaties.un.org/doc/Publication/UNTS/No%20Volume/39464/A-39464-0800000280526e0a.pdf >accessed 1 February 2020.

[12] AU, *Protocol Relating to the Establishment of the Peace and Security Council of the African Union* (9 July 2002) available at <https://www.refworld.org/docid/3f4b1d374.html> accessed 1 February 2020

[13] SA Good, *Talk, not enough action: The AU's counter-terrorism architecture, and why it matters*, ISS Policy Brief 66 (March 2015) 5 <issafrica.s3.amazonaws.com/site/uploads/PolBrief66.pdf> accessed 1 February 2020.

[14] Martin Ewi, *Regional integration in an age of terrorism: A critical study of pan-African responses to terrorism*, Institute of Security Studies (2015) 49 available at <https://www.researchgate.net/publication/284189017_Regional_integration_in_an_age_of_terrorism_A_critical_study_of_pan-African_responses_to_terrorism> accessed 1 February 2020.

[15] 1 February 2020.

[16] Table of ratifications of the Convention available at <https://au.int/sites/default/files/treaties/7779-sl-oau_convention_on_the_prevention_and_combating_of_terrorism_1.pdf> accessed 1 February 2020. Table of ratifications of the Protocol available at <https://au.int/sites/default/files/

The legal developments in this very topical field – as reflected in the adoption of a regional convention and its relative protocol – clearly represent progress on human rights. The AU should be able to maintain this impetus, in accordance with international standards,[17] based on evidence that international terrorism also has roots in Africa.[18] However, the United Nations High Commissioner for Refugees (UNHCR) cautioned that a failed *coup d'état* should not be mistaken for a terrorist act: 'In Africa, a coup is often the only means through which a change in the political regime can be effected… As a result, fear of persecution arising from an unsuccessful coup attempt may be regarded as grounded upon political opinion/activities and within the ambit of the 1951 Convention.'[19]

The AU also toughened its stance on terrorism and insurgency by adopting the 2002 Algiers Plan of Action on the Prevention and Combating of Terrorism in Africa (2002 Plan).[20] Paragraph 11(n) of the 2002 Plan specifically provides for Member States 'to ensure that an asylum seeker is not involved, directly or indirectly, in terrorism-related activities prior to granting asylum to the concerned person'. However, in general, the classification of acts of terrorism in the 1999 Convention raises a number of concerns, including the question of intent and the failure of states to distinguish terrorism from ordinary crimes.[21]

In 2004, as part of the implementation of the 2002 Plan, AU Member States established, according to its Section H, the African Centre for the Study and Research on Terrorism (ACSRT). One of the aims of the Centre is to develop counter-terrorism capacity-building programmes.[22] In the same year, the AU Heads of

treaties/7787-sl-protocol_to_the_oau_convention_on_the_prevention_and_combating_of_terror.pdf> accessed 1 February 2020.

[17] For a general panorama on this feature see R Murray, *Human Rights in Africa: From the OAU to the African Union* (CUP, 2004) 239.

[18] E Pan (Council on Foreign Relations), *Africa: Terror Havens* (3 February 2005) available at <https://www.cfr.org/backgrounder/africa-terror-havens> accessed 1 February 2020.

[19] Letter from UNHCR to Bradford Smith Esq, quoted in M Zagor, 'Persecutor or persecuted: exclusions under article 1F(a) and (b) of the Refugees Convention' (2000) 23 University of New South Wales Journal 164, 181.

[20] AU, *Plan of Action of the African Union High-Level Inter-Governmental Meeting on the Prevention and Combating of Terrorism in Africa*, Mtg/HLIG/Conv.Terror/Plan.(I) (11–14 September 2002) available at <http://www.peaceau.org/uploads/au-anti-terrorism-plan-of-action.pdf> accessed 1 February 2020. In this regard, see also AU, *Declaration of the Second High-Level Intergovernmental Meeting on the Prevention and Combating of Terrorism in Africa*, Mtg/HLIG/Conv.Terror/Decl. (II) Rev. 2 (13-14 October 2004) 5: '[We, the representatives of the Member States of the African Union] emphasize the fact that the Plan of Action provides the most viable and comprehensive strategies for the prevention and combating of terrorism in Africa, particularly in the areas of police and border control, legislative and judicial measures, suppression of the financing of terrorism, exchange of information, and coordination at the regional, continental and international levels. However, we note that Member States have not fully exploited its provisions and recommendations.' available at <http://www.iri.edu.ar/publicaciones_iri/anuario/CD%20Anuario%202005/Africa/00B-au_2%20high%20level%20meeting%20prevention%20terrorism.pdf> accessed 1 February 2020.

[21] N J Udombana, 'Battling Rights: International Law and Africa's War on Terrorism' (2005) 13 African Yearbook of International Law 67, 96.

[22] In detail, see para 20 of the Plan of Action.

State and Government adopted a Declaration on a Common African Defence and Security Policy (CADSP). While recognizing the security implications of forced migration, this Declaration demonstrates African states' intention to harmonize the various refugee policies on the continent.[23]

The 2002 Plan mandated the Commission for Peace and Security to provide advice on counter-terrorism initiatives.[24] As a result, the Commission developed the African Anti-Terrorism Model Law (Model Law).[25] This law intends to assist Member States in implementing the provisions contained in both the continental and international counter-terrorism instruments, including the 1999 Convention and as such provides an important vehicle for establishing AU law. In addition, the Model Law reaffirms that the fight against terrorism must be carried out in accordance with refugee law.[26]

In its 2014 resolution on Terrorist Acts in Africa, the African Commission on Human and Peoples' Rights (ACHPR) invited 'all African States to take the necessary measures to combat terrorism particularly by initiating joint actions aimed at preventing all activities relating to the financing, sale and transfer of weapons to terrorist groups'.[27] Although terrorist prevention activities are highlighted, these are not explained in any detail, nor, specifically, is any explanation offered regarding what these activities should comprise.

While much good progress has been made, significant challenges remain. Historically, counter-terrorism initiatives have sometimes been poorly resourced because terrorism is not always a high priority for some AU Member States when compared to more immediately pressing environmental, developmental, and poverty-eradication issues. Additionally, there are also difficulties associated with securing the requisite levels of accompanying political will of AU Member States on some issues. That is also, perhaps, why the ACHPR remains vague when it comes to define counter-terrorism measures to be adopted on the continent.

As indicated in the 1981 African Charter on Human and Peoples' Rights (Banjul Charter),[28] the role of the ACHPR is to formulate principles aimed at solving legal

[23] AU Heads of State and Government, *Solemn Declaration on a Common African Defence and Security Policy* (28 February 2004) para 42 available at <http://www.peaceau.org/uploads/declaration-cadsp-en.pdf> accessed 1 February 2020.

[24] In detail, see para 18(c) of the Plan of Action.

[25] The Model Law which was endorsed by the decision of the AU Assembly in AU, *Decision on the Report of the Peace and Security Council on its Activities and the State of Peace and Security in Africa* (AU/Dec.369(XVII) (30 June–1 July 2011) para 30 available at <https://au.int/sites/default/files/decisions/9647-assembly_au_dec_363-390_xvii_e.pdf> accessed 1 February 2020.

[26] AU, *The African Model Anti-Terrorism Law. Final Draft as Endorsed by the 17th Ordinary Session of the Assembly of the Union* (30 June–1 July 2011) Preamble available at <http://www.peaceau.org/uploads/african-model-law-on-counter-terrorsim-final-version-as-endorsed-by-the-17th-session-english.pdf> accessed 1 February 2020.

[27] ACHPR, *Resolution on Terrorist Acts in Africa* No 276 (28 April–12 May 2014) available at <https://www.achpr.org/sessions/resolutions?id=323> accessed 1 February 2020.

[28] OAU, *African Charter on Human and Peoples' Rights* (27 June 1981) UNTS vol 1520, No 26363, 217 available at <https://au.int/sites/default/files/treaties/36390-treaty-0011_-_african_charter_on_human_and_peoples_rights_e.pdf> accessed 1 February 2020.

problems relating to human and peoples' rights on the continent.[29] Thus, in 2015, the ACHPR adopted the Principles and Guidelines on Human and Peoples' Rights while Countering Terrorism in Africa.[30] The Banjul Charter, in its Article 23(2)(b), has already stipulated that the territories of Member States 'shall not be used as bases for subversive or terrorist activities against the people of any other state party to the present Charter'.[31] Oddly enough, however, the 2015 Principles do not refer to Article 23,[32] which gives rise to the impression that if the principles prove to be simply expressions of continental sentiment not followed by concrete steps, the AU is a 'toothless lion', lacking the strength to impact national and regional law and practice for a more secure future for Africa.[33]

The 2015 Principles refer to the link between terrorism and refugees in Africa. They contend that the obligation to refrain from and prevent terrorism on the continent must be carried out in accordance with a state's obligations under refugee law.[34] More importantly, however, these principles highlight the paramount refugee law principle of *non-refoulement*. According to the ACHPR, in the case of terrorism, this means that '[n]o State shall, for any reason, transfer ... any individual to the custody of another State where there are substantial grounds for believing that there is a real risk of serious human rights violations. States shall place no restrictions on this rule.'[35]

Despite the regional efforts referred to above to counter-terrorism across Africa, terrorist networks have proliferated, especially but not exclusively in East Africa and the Horn of Africa (HoA), exacerbated by local indigenous conflicts that have served to increase refugee flows.[36] With the multiplication of various extremist groups throughout the continent, the activities and threat levels have remained constant, thus challenging one of the main objectives of the AU which is to safeguard the sovereignty and territorial integrity of Member States.[37]

29 Article 45(1) (b) of the Banjul Charter.

30 ACHPR, *Principles and Guidelines on Human and Peoples' Rights while Countering Terrorism in Africa*. Adopted by the African Commission on Human and Peoples' Rights during its 56th Ordinary Session in Banjul, Gambia (21 April–7 May 2015) available at <https://www.achpr.org/legalinstruments/detail?id=9> accessed 1 February 2020.

31 Article 23(2)(b) of the Banjul Charter.

32 R Murray, *The African Charter on Human and Peoples' Rights* (OUP, 2019) 545.

33 Z Yihdego, 'African Union: Founding Principles, Frameworks and Prospects [The]' (2011) 17 European Law Journal, 568, 594.

34 ACHPR (n 30) 12.

35 ibid 26. For the African definition of *non-refoulement*: OAU *Convention Governing the Specific Aspects of Refugee Problems in Africa* (10 September 1969) UNTS vol 1001, No 14691, 45 available at <https://au.int/sites/default/files/treaties/36400-treaty-0005_-_oau_convention_governing_the_specific_aspects_of_refugee_problems_in_africa_e.pdf> accessed 1 February 2020. See Article II(3) of the 1969 OAU Convention. For the universal definition of *non-refoulement*: UNGA *Convention Relating to the Status of Refugees* (28 July 1951) UNTS vol 189, No 2545, 150 available at <https://www.unhcr.org/3b66c2aa10> accessed 1 February 2020. For details, see Article 33(1).

36 DH Shinn, 'Terrorism in East Africa and the Horn: An Overview' (2003) 23 The Journal of Conflict Studies 79, 80–.

37 OAU *Constitutive Act of the African Union* (11 July 2000) UNTS vol 2158, No 3733, 328 available at <https://au.int/sites/default/files/pages/34873-file-constitutiveact_en.pdf> accessed 1 February 2020. The abovementioned objective is listed at Article 3(b).

As for the plight of refugees, this is briefly mentioned by the 2015 Principles also within the strategic priority on 'strategic security issues'. This is a specific section on 'counter-terrorism measures' in the African Peace and Security Architecture (APSA) Roadmap of the AU Commission (Peace and Security Department) for the period 2016–2020.[38] In addition, the Peace and Security Council (PSC) has also repeatedly stressed the relationship between terrorism and protection of refugees. In 2016, the PSC requested the AU Commission to provide support to Kenya, Somalia, and the UNHCR in their efforts to achieve a 'balanced and realistic solution' to the attacks against refugee camps in Kenya by the Al-Shabaab terrorist group.[39] This communication followed the one issued in 2015 on the same subject in which the PSC stressed the need for all stakeholders to extend support and cooperation to prevent the use of refugee camps to plan and launch terrorist attacks that may destabilize and threaten the humanitarian role of the camps.[40] However, despite the numerous initiatives launched at AU level, there seems to be no end in sight to the wave of terrorist activity sweeping the continent.[41] Terrorism in Africa is a manifestation of the so-called new wars. Unknown individuals or entity financers, who operate outside the control of state authorities, finance these wars privately. Terror activities are often youth-led; young people join these organizations for economic gain as most African youth have little to no prospect of gainful employment. This ties in with the reality of Boko Haram and al-Shabaab; young people joining as extremists, fleeing poverty, insecurity, and injustice which are still widespread throughout the continent, have largely, sustained these terrorist groups.[42]

In this regard, Shinn contends, '[p]overty is not and never has been the cause of terrorism in sub-Saharan Africa. On the other hand, it is one of a dozen or more factors that have contributed to an environment that has enabled terrorist organizations to draw support.'[43]

[38] AU Commission, *APSA Roadmap 2016–2020* (2015) 60 available at <http://www.peaceau.org/uploads/2015-en-apsa-roadmap-final.pdf> accessed 1 February 2020.

[39] AU Peace and Security Council, *Communique on the situation of Dadaab Refugee camps in Kenya* (590th Meeting, 14 April 2016) para 14 available at <http://www.peaceau.org/uploads/psc-comm-590th-dadaab-en.pdf> accessed 1 February 2020.

[40] AU Peace and Security Council, *Communique on the situation of Dadaab Refugee camps in Kenya* (554th Meeting, 3 November 2015) para 4 available at <http://www.peaceau.org/uploads/psc-554-com-kenya-dadaab-3-11-2015-en.pdf> accessed 1 February 2020.

[41] SO Ehiane, 'Strengthening the African Union (AU) counter terrorism strategy in Africa: a re-awakened order' (2018) 7 *Journal of African Union Studies* 109, 111.

[42] L Kambela *Terrorism in Africa: A Manifestation of New Wars* African Centre for the Constructive Resolutions of Disputes (24 June 2019) available at <https://www.accord.org.za/conflict-trends/terrorism-in-africa/> accessed 1 February 2020.

[43] D Shinn, 'Poverty and Terrorism in Africa: The Debate Continues' (2016) 17 Georgetown Journal of International Affairs 16, 21.

3. Protection of Refugees: An Analysis of the Exclusion Clauses in the Geneva Convention of Refugees and the 1969 OAU Convention on the Protection of Refugees in Africa

In the African doctrine, there continues to be a lack of consensus as to whether or not 'terrorist acts' should be included[44] in the 'subversive activities' indicated in Article III of the 1969 Convention Governing the Specific Aspects of Refugee Problems in Africa (1969 OAU Convention) and Article 23(2) of the 1981 Banjul Charter. A critique of the latter article would exclude 'terrorist acts' from the 'subversive activities' given that Article 23(2)(b) mentions both activities separately. Murray notes that the term 'subversive activities' indicates a threat from outside the continent which is perceived by Member States to be particularly relevant, with support for refugees being necessary, particularly in the context of the decolonization and liberation struggles as well as in the broader context of African unity.[45] In contrast, Ouguergouz questions the current meaning of the term 'subversive activities' contained in the 1969 OAU Convention, suggesting a stricter definition which should expressly include armed or terrorist actions. In his scholarly opinion, this could be the better way to eradicate the dangers of arbitrariness concerning the implementation by the refugee of his/her rights.[46]

Snyman disagrees, asserting that terrorism is a more serious crime than subversion. As such, he contends that it was not the intention of the drafters of the 1969 OAU Convention to consider terrorism as a 'subversive activity'. As an example, the author affirms that the death penalty may be carried out for terrorism but not for subversion.[47] At present, scholars in Africa continue to debate the inclusion of 'terrorist acts' in 'subversive activities'. 'Terrorist acts' can be analysed within the context of the 'serious non-political crimes' mentioned as an exclusion clause from the status of refugee by the 1969 OAU Convention in Article I(5)(b).[48]

Article I(5)(b) of the 1969 OAU Convention is similar to Article 1(F)(b) of the 1951 Convention Relating to the Status of Refugees (1951 Geneva Convention), since the 1969 OAU Convention can be regarded as a 'complement' to the 1951 Geneva Convention.[49] To date, the latter convention has been ratified by 49 African

[44] See Article III of the 1969 OAU Convention.

[45] Murray (n 32) 544.

[46] F Ouguergouz, *The African Charter on Human and Peoples' Rights* (Martinus Nijhoff Publishers, 2003) 351–2.

[47] CR Snyman, '*Dolus eventualis* in the offences of terrorism, subversion and sabotage' (1990) 107 South African Law Journal 365, 375.

[48] In full, Article 1(5)(b) stipulates: 'The provisions of this Convention shall not apply to any person with respect to whom the country of asylum has serious reasons for considering that: ... b) he committed a serious non-political crime outside the country of refuge prior to his admission to that country as a refugee.'

[49] According to its Article VIII(2) '[t]he present [OAU] Convention shall be the effective regional complement in Africa of the 1951 United Nations Convention on the Status of Refugees'. See also H Strydom, and others (eds), *International Law* (OUP, 2016) 306.

countries.[50] Thus, the analysis of Article 1(F)(b) of the 1951 Geneva Convention can be considered as it is also contained in the said African convention. Article 1(F)(b) of the 1951 Geneva Convention stipulates that:

> [t]he provisions of this Convention shall not apply to any person with respect to whom there are serious reasons for considering that: ... (b) he has committed a serious non-political crime outside the country of refuge prior to his admission to that country as a refugee.

Since 2003, the UNHCR contends that acts considered as 'terrorist' should fall within the exclusion clauses; Article 1F is not merely a simple anti-terrorism provision. The UNHCR underscores the importance of individual responsibility, and that simple affiliation with a terrorist organization is not in itself sufficient to withdraw refugee status under Article 1F of the 1951 Geneva Convention.[51] The UNHCR adds that consideration of the exclusion clause is often unnecessary given that suspected terrorists may not be eligible for refugee status in the first place, their fear being legitimate prosecution as opposed to persecution for reasons mentioned in the 1951 Geneva Convention.[52] Finally, UNHCR highlights that Article 1F(b) is particularly appropriate because acts of terrorist violence are often disproportionate to any declared political objective. That is why each case requires individual consideration. The mere fact that an individual is associated with a terrorist organization, although this should trigger consideration of the exclusion clauses, will not, however, in itself constitute sufficient proof to justify exclusion.[53]

Hitherto, historically there have been difficulties in applying the exclusion clause mentioned in Article 1(F)(b) of the 1951 Geneva Convention as well as the relative Article I(5)(b) of the 1969 OAU Convention to an individual who has committed an act of terrorism. This is because for many years, there was no universal consensus on the definition of 'terrorism' established within doctrine.[54]

[50] 1 February 2020. On the same date, the 1969 OAU Convention has been ratified by 46 countries. Tables of ratifications for the 1951 Geneva Convention available at <https://treaties.un.org/Pages/ViewDetailsII.aspx?src=TREATY&mtdsg_no=V-2&chapter=5&Temp=mtdsg2&clang=_en#EndDec>; for the 1969 OAU Convention available at <https://au.int/sites/default/files/treaties/36400-sl-OAU%20Convention%20Governing%20the%20Specific%20Aspects%20of%20Refugee%20Problems%20in%20Africa.pdf> both accessed 1 February 2020.

[51] UNHCR, *Guidelines on International Protection: Application of the Exclusion Clauses: Article 1F of the 1951 Convention relating to the Status of Refugees* HCR/GIP/03/05 (4 September 2003) paras 18–19.

[52] ibid para 25.

[53] ibid para 26. In this regard, see also: S Singh, 'Will acceptance of a universally approved definition of terrorism make article 1 F of the 1951 Refugee Convention more effective in excluding terrorists?' (2006) 2 Journal of Migration & Refugee Issues 91, 111–12.

[54] GS Gilbert, 'Current Issues in the Application of the Exclusion Clauses' in E Feller, V Türk, and others (eds), *Refugee Protection in International Law: UNHCR's Global Consultations on International Protection* (CUP & UNHCR, 2003) 443. In addition, James J Lambert adds: '[a]lthough there seems to be general agreement that terrorism involves the threat or use of violence ... differences in definition range from semantic to the conceptual'. See JJ Lambert, 'The Problem of International Terrorism and the Response of International Organizations' in PJ Van Krieken (ed), *Refugee Law in Context: The Exclusion Clause* (TMC Asser Press, 1999) 177 and 179.

In this regard, Brumar contends that it is not definitively agreed in doctrine and practice concerning the qualification of the terrorist acts, if they would fall under the notion of 'serious non-political crime' or the 'acts contrary to the purposes and objectives of the United Nations'. She stresses, however, that the UNHCR seems to prefer inclusion in the first category because the methods and consequences are those of a serious non-political crime. The author concludes that this position is also more favourable to the individual because usually, the perpetration of a serious non-political crime is proved by the initiation of criminal proceedings, prosecution applications, and judicial decisions.[55]

I share this position because since the term 'terrorism' in Africa as elsewhere often lacks the legal accuracy needed for its virtuous application, the use of Article 1F(b) helps to ensure that the terrorist label is not used for political goals, for example barring legitimate activities of political dissidents.[56] Nonetheless, it appears that the text of the 1951 Geneva Convention implicitly refers to anterior jurisprudence and it gives a certain margin of appreciation in its application to states.[57]

In returning to the definition of 'non-political' crime in the 1951 Geneva Convention, 'serious' crimes have exclusively been taken into consideration. The majority of the doctrine affirms that crimes that form part of multilateral conventions on terrorism are to be qualified as 'serious'. When evaluating whether a crime is 'serious' or not, the country of refuge may take into consideration what the sentence would be if the applicant were to be tried by his/her national courts.[58] Nevertheless, circumstances need to be assessed on a case-by-case basis, maintaining a degree of flexibility given the developments following the 1951 Geneva Convention.[59]

This begs the question whether the drafters of the 1951 Geneva Convention intended for the exclusion clause to play a key role in the process of extradition. This question remains unanswered. It would appear that the role of the paragraph in question is not just limited to extradition,[60] although scholars do not entirely

[55] C Brumar, 'The asylum, between humanitarian response and political instrument' (2012) 19 Lex et Scientia International Journal 52, 57.

[56] N Djordjevic, 'Exclusion under Article 1F(b) of the Refugee Convention' (2014) 12 Journal of International Criminal Justice 1057, 1060.

[57] G Guillaume, 'Terrorisme et droit international' in *Recueil des Cours de l'Académie de La Haye/ The Hague Academy Collected Courses*, vol 215 (Brill, 1989) 287, 362.

[58] SD Amarasinha and M Isenbecker, 'Terrorism and the right to asylum under the 1951 Convention and the 1967 Protocol Relating to the Status of Refugees – a contradiction in terms or do opposites attract?' (1996) 65 Nordic Journal of International Law 223, 228.

[59] R Higgins, *Problems and Process: International Law and How We Use It* (Clarendon Press, 1994). In particular, see Chapter 1, 'The Nature and Function of International Law' 1–16 and Chapter 11, 'The United Nations', 169–85.

[60] UNHCR, *Handbook on Procedures and Criteria for Determining Refugee Status under the 1951 Convention and the 1967 Protocol Relating to the Status of Refugees*, 2nd edn (UNHCR, 1992) paras 157, 26. See also ExCom, 'Problem of extradition affecting refugees' (1980) *Conclusion No 17 (XXXI)*. Sections (f) and (g) read: '[The ExCom] f) stressed that nothing in the present conclusions should be considered as affecting the necessity for States to ensure, on the basis of national legislation and international instruments, punishment for serious offences, such as the unlawful seizure of aircraft, the taking of hostages and murder; g) stressed that protection in regard to extradition applies to persons

agree on this subject. James C Hathaway affirms in this regard: '[This exclusion clause] is simply a means of bringing refugee law into line with the basic principles of extradition law, by ensuring that important fugitives from justice are not able to avoid the jurisdiction of a state in which they may lawfully face punishment'.[61] Nevertheless, the dominant position seems to be in the sense of not according the extradition of the refugee to the country of origin.[62]

An investigation of the nature, gravity, and context of a criminal offence ascribed to an individual in the context of an extradition request, and its assessment in light of the criteria under international refugee law, is necessary where the acts in question are considered terrorist in nature. However, even if a particular conduct is considered as 'terrorist' according to the definition provided in Africa, an extradition request does not per se justify the application of an exclusion clause of the 1951 Geneva Convention, although an examination of the applicability of exclusion will normally be necessary in such cases.[63]

Once it is established, the proposed African Court of Justice and Human Rights (ACJHR) will become an institution adjudicating on the relation between terrorism and the protection of refugees. This is in accordance with the stipulations of Article 28(G) of the 2014 AU Protocol on Amendments to the Protocol on the Statute of the African Court of Justice and Human Rights (2014 Malabo Protocol).[64] There are possible legal implications of the exclusion of political or other motives under the Malabo Protocol (Article 28(G)(E): '[p]olitical, philosophical, ideological, racial, ethnic, religious or other motives shall not be a justifiable defence against a terrorist act'. This provision could have a bearing on whether an offence is treated as a 'serious non-political crime' when considering whether or not to exclude a person from refugee protection under Article 1(F)(b) of the 1951 Geneva Convention. The 2014 Malabo Protocol does not expressly intend to exclude all terrorists from refugee status. The exclusion of political reasons as a criminal defence, although an important factor, is not decisive.[65]

Analysing Article IV(o) of the 2000 AU Constitutive Act ('The Union shall function in accordance with the following principles: ... o) respect for the sanctity of

who fulfil the criteria of the refugee definition and who are not excluded from refugee status by virtue of Article 1(F)(b) of the 1951 United Nations Convention relating to the Status of Refugees'.

[61] JC Hathaway, *The Law of Refugees Status* (Butterworths, 1991) 221.

[62] D Alland and C Teitgen-Colly, *Traité du droit d'asile* (PUF, 2002) 635

[63] UNHCR, *Guidance Note on Extradition and International Refugee Protection* (April 2008) para 83 available at <https://www.refworld.org/docid/481ec7d92.html> accessed 1 February 2020.

[64] AU, *Protocol on Amendments to the Protocol on the Statute of the African Court of Justice and Human Rights* (June 2014) available at <https://au.int/sites/default/files/treaties/36398-treaty-0045_-_protocol_on_amendments_to_the_protocol_on_the_statute_of_the_african_court_of_justice_and_human_rights_e-compressed.pdf> accessed 1 February 2020. To date, however, the Protocol has not been ratified by any country.

[65] B Saul, 'The Crime of Terrorism within the Jurisdiction of the African Court of Justice and Human and Peoples' Rights' in CC Jalloh, KM Clarke, and others (eds), *The African Court of Justice and Human and Peoples' Rights in Context* (CUP, 2019) 409, 446–7.

human life, condemnation and rejection of impunity and political assassination, acts of terrorism and subversive activities'), there is clearly an evident link with the exclusion clause contained in Article I(5)(c) of the 1969 OAU Convention. The latter stipulates that '[t]he provisions of this Convention shall not apply to any person with respect to whom the country of asylum has serious reasons for considering that: ... c) he has been guilty of acts contrary to the purposes and principles of the Organisation of African Unity'.

In effect, the latter article excludes an individual having acted in contrast with the principles of the AU from refugee status and according to Article IV(o) of its 2000 Constitutive Act, among the principles of the AU there is also the condemnation and the rejection of 'acts of terrorism'.

Moreover, Article I(5)(c) of the 1969 OAU Convention is very similar to Article 1(F)(c) of the 1951 Geneva Convention which envisages the exclusion of refugee status for each individual guilty of acts contrary to the goals and principles of the UN.[66] UNHCR agrees that this clause should be invoked only in residual cases when the other clauses contained in the same article, Article 1(F)(b), cannot be invoked. In this regard, the UNHCR affirms that Article 1(F)(c) is only triggered in extreme circumstances, by activity which must have attacked the very basis of the international community's coexistence. Such activity must have an international dimension and should affect international peace, security, and peaceful relations between states, as well as serious and sustained violations of human rights. In cases involving a terrorist act, the correct application of Article 1(F)(c) involves an assessment of the extent to which the activity impinges on the international plane, in terms of its gravity, international impact, and implications for international peace and security.[67] The vagueness of the expression 'acts contrary to purposes and principles of' is reflected in the fact that there are no international

[66] For the purposes and the principles of the UN, see Articles 1 and 2 of the UN Charter. UN, *Charter of the United Nations* (24 October 1945) 1 UNTS XVI available at <https://www.refworld.org/docid/3ae6b3930.html> accessed 1 February 2020. UNHCR underlines that the preparatory works of the 1951 Geneva Convention have been vague relating this provision. In this regard, as UNHCR affirms: 'The last exclusion provision, Article 1(F)(c), refers to acts contrary to the purposes and principles of the United Nations... The *travaux préparatoires* reflect a lack of clarity with respect to the use of this provision. Comments by delegates suggest that the drafters viewed the provision as one that would be rarely invoked, and applicable only to individuals who were in a position of power or influence in a State and instrumental in the State's infringement of the UN purposes and principles. There may be overlap with Article 1(F)(a), in that crimes against peace and crimes against humanity also are acts against the purposes and principles of the United.' See UNHCR, *Interpreting Article 1 of the 1951 Convention relating to the Status of Refugees* (1 April 2001) para 50 available at <https://www.refworld.org/docid/3b20a3914.html> accessed 1 February 2020.

[67] UNHCR(n 51) para 17. For a similar position in the doctrine see E Kwakwa, 'Article 1(F)(c): acts contrary to the purposes and principles of the United Nations' (2000) 12 (special supplementary issue) International Journal of Refugee Law 79, 91. At ibid 84, Kwakwa makes two further observations on Article 1(F)(c). First, it appears patent that while paragraph (b) of the same article requires the commission of very specific crimes, paragraph (c) does not entail actual 'crimes' but simply refers to 'acts'. Second, paragraph (c)'s use of the phrase 'has been guilty' would seem to suggest a higher threshold for the establishment of culpability. It is certainly worth questioning whether paragraph (c) requires a pronouncement of guilty by a competent body, a requirement that is evidently missing in paragraph (b).

instruments that clearly define or elaborate this concept. However, terrorist suspects will be excluded from this provision only when the impact of their acts is felt at the international level and has implications for international peace and security.[68] In effect, this point was updated after 11 September 2001, as it was clearly affirmed by the United Nations Security Council (UNSC) that acts of international terrorism constituting a threat to international peace and security are contrary to UN principles.[69]

Kenya provides a case in point, in so far as it has expressed concerns at the spillover effect of conflict from neighbouring states and the mass movement of people fleeing from terrorist activities. Because of the connection between Islamic fundamentalism, the lack of central authority in Somalia, and a long history of irredentism within its own ethnic population, the government of Kenya now views Somali refugees on its territory almost exclusively as a security threat.[70] However, prior to 1991, Kenya pursued an open asylum policy, recognizing various benefits of hosting refugees. Refugees enjoyed freedom of movement, access to labour markets, and the benefits of many of the social rights enunciated in the 1951 Geneva Convention.[71] 1991 has been a turning point in Kenya's refugee policy mainly because of the Somali emergency that increased the rate of arrival of refugees from 16,000 in March 1991 to 92,200 by December of the same year.[72]

Somali refugees, however, have also been the victims of repressive legislation, introduced in the aftermath of 9/11 as the country clamped down on terrorist incursions. These anti-terrorist laws have failed to strike a balance between the security imperatives of combating terrorism and the need to protect human rights. This made Somali refugees in Kenya easy targets for illegal arrests and prolonged detention on grounds of suspicion, in violation of both universal and regional refugee conventions.[73] Refugees also became targets of a special counter-terrorist unit formed in Kenya in early 2003.[74] Despite the activities of this counter-terrorism unit[75] and contrary to expectations, the mass influx of displaced persons

[68] Singh (n 53) 116–17.

[69] UNSC, *Threats to international peace and security caused by terrorist acts*, No 1368, S/RES/1368 (12 September 2001)para 1.

[70] G Loescher and JHS Milner, 'Understanding the Problem of Protracted Refugee Situations' in G Loescher, J Milner, E Newman, and G Troeller (eds), *Protracted Refugee Situations: Political, Human Rights and Security Implications* (United Nations University Press 2008) 35.

[71] James HS Milner, *Refugees, the State and the Politics of Asylum in Africa* (Palgrave/Macmillan 2009) 86.

[72] ibid 86–8.

[73] See the Operation Usalama Watch illustrated in Human Rights Watch (HRW), 'Kenya: End Abusive Round-Ups' (12 May 2014) available at <https://www.hrw.org/news/2014/05/12/kenya-end-abusive-round-ups> accessed 1 February 2020.

[74] Peter M. Kagwanja, Monica K. Juma, 'Somali Refugees: Protracted Exile and Shifting Security Frontiers' in Loescher, and others (eds) (n 70) 225.

[75] A Lindley 'Between a protracted and a crisis situation: policy responses to Somali refugees in Kenya' (2011) 30 Refugee Survey Quarterly 14, 22.

from Somalia to Kenya continues unabated, although Somalia is still believed to host terrorist organizations on its soil.[76]

4. Conclusion: What Does the Future Hold for Africa's Fight against Terrorism?

Unfortunately, and despite the 1999 OAU Convention on Terrorism, African states have often extended and applied their domestic definition of terrorism in a way that is inconsistent with the 1999 OAU Convention. This has been ongoing even though, as stated by Gilbert, the 1969 OAU Convention gives greater recognition to terrorist acts as grounds for seeking asylum than the 1951 Geneva Convention. This is largely due to the expression 'events seriously disturbing public order in either part or the whole of his country of origin or nationality' contained in the refugee definition of the 1969 OAU Convention (Article I(2)).[77]

Intra-African organizations and African countries have several available options to curb terrorism. First, they should conduct screening that is more thorough in order to distinguish criminals from genuine asylum seekers and refugees. They should also direct the military to end the unlawful and indiscriminate forced return of asylum seekers and refugees from the border areas.

Secondly, they should investigate allegations of soldiers' abuse, extortion, and sexual exploitation of asylum seekers and refugees, and prosecute those against whom there is evidence of having committed crimes against genuine, forcibly displaced persons.

Thirdly, local authorities should also swiftly register all asylum seekers and recognize as refugees those who pass security screening. Alternatively, after screening, the UNHCR should be allowed to register and recognize the asylum seekers. At the same time, they should allow asylum seekers and refugees to live in local communities, expand the congested camps, or establish additional camps where they could receive adequate assistance while respecting their right to freedom of movement, none of which can be denied to all just to punish a few. This should be done while remaining cognizant of the fact that refugee camps in Africa can still represent a breeding ground for terrorists.[78]

[76] International Crisis Group, 'Somalia's Al-Shabaab Down but Far from Out' (27 June 2016) available at <https://www.crisisgroup.org/africa/horn-africa/somalia/somalia-s-al-shabaab-down-far-out> accessed 1 February 2020.

[77] G Gilbert 'Terrorism and International Refugee Law' in B Saul (ed), *Research Handbook on International Law and Terrorism* (Edward Elgar, 2014) 473.

[78] Xinhua, 'Kenyan police arrest 12 terror suspects at refugee camp' (29 January 2019) available at <http://www.xinhuanet.com/english/2019-01/29/c_137784414.htm> accessed 1 February 2020; IOL, 'Kenya terror attack suspects traced to Dadaab refugee camp' (4 February 2019) available at <https://www.iol.co.za/news/africa/kenya-terror-attack-suspects-traced-to-dadaab-refugee-camp-19120342> accessed 1 February 2020.

The APSA suggests other important strategies to address the causes of the problem, the first of which indicates legislative support available to Member States in ratifying and domesticating regional and international anti-crime and counter-terrorism instruments. Furthermore, special training and capacity-building support should be given to judges, prosecutors, and law enforcement agencies. These initiatives would contribute to the effective domestication of legal counter-terrorism instruments and the strengthening of criminal justice systems.[79]

However, some challenges remain, such as the need for greater cooperation and harmonization of continent-wide efforts to counter terrorism, and the establishment of continental frameworks and strategies as well as an effective and appropriate system of follow-up mechanisms.[80]

Within the AU counter-terrorism context, the AU Commission has also taken steps to implement UNSC Resolution 1540 (2004) in Africa.[81] The resolution requires states to refrain from providing any form of support to non-state actors, including terrorist groups that attempt to develop, acquire, manufacture, possess, transport, transfer, or use nuclear, chemical, or biological weapons and their means of delivery. The resolution also requires states to adopt and enforce appropriate effective laws in this respect.[82]

Most AU Member States are financially unable to combat terrorism alone. The AU should assist Member States in this regard not just by urging them to cooperate or offer legal assistance to one another but, as proposed by Okpala, by combating terrorism through a universal court.[83]

In the end, whatever anti-terrorism strategies Africa adopts, a just balance must be struck between national security and individual freedom, and between genuine terrorists and non-combatants. This balancing act will continue to be a significant challenge to governments and courts in Africa and for the developing AU law.[84] Against this backdrop, however, the enforcement of policies aimed at protecting legitimate national security concerns should not prevent asylum seekers from entering any potential country of asylum.

Despite these positive initiatives, terrorism continues to be on the rise, threatening peace and security on the continent. It is therefore no surprise that the AU has been obliged to condemn repeatedly the recent terrorist attacks

[79] AU Commission (n 38) 49.

[80] ibid 20.

[81] AU (n 2) para 64.

[82] UNSCR, *Non-proliferation of weapons of mass destruction*, S/RES/1540 (2004) para 2 available at <https://undocs.org/S/RES/1540> accessed 1 February 2020.

[83] CC Okpala, *A Re-Assessment [sic] of the Effectiveness of OAU (AU) Conventions on Preventing and Combating Terrorism* (Golden Gate School of Law SJD Dissertation, August 2014) 218–19.

[84] Udombana (n 21) 130.

against refugees such as the suicide bombing at a refugee camp in northern Cameroon on June 2017,[85] the attack on a refugee camp in Niger in October 2016,[86] and the terrorist acts in Kenya in 2015, the ACHPR adopting a specific resolution (no 302) on this subject where refugees were considered more victims than criminals.[87]

85 AU, 'The African Union strongly condemns the suicide bombing at a refugee camp in northern Cameroon' (2 June 2017) available at <http://www.peaceau.org/en/article/the-african-union-strongly-condemns-the-suicide-bombing-at-a-refugee-camp-in-northern-cameroon> accessed 1 February 2020.

86 AU, 'The African Union strongly condemns the attack on a refugee camp in Niger' (11 October 2016) available at <http://www.peaceau.org/en/article/the-african-union-strongly-condemns-the-attack-on-a-refugee-camp-in-niger> accessed 1 February 2020.

87 AHCPR, Resolution on terrorist acts in the Republic of Kenya – ACHPR/Res.302(LVI) 2015 (56th Ordinary Session, 21 April–7 May 2015). In paragraph 3(IV) of the resolution, the ACHPR calls upon the Republic of Kenya to '[t]ake all necessary measures to protect refugees in conformity with regional and international commitments that Kenya has entered into'.

13

The Quasi-Supranational AU and the International Criminal Court

Benedict Abrahamson Chigara

1. Introduction

Gibbs' reflective cycle[1] gives structure to learning from past experiences. It is premised on the view that by reflecting on their experiences in a specific situation, people can generate new or revised and more appropriate frameworks for engaging with repeated or cyclic or similar experiences.

The cyclic nature of the routines of public international institutions and of public international organizations on the one hand, and on the other, the need for each state to be strategically prepared for the next round of proceedings in the annual international calendar strongly suggests that the dynamics of international relations are generally cyclic in nature. Therefore, states can individually or as a regional or other collective evaluate their performances in previous cycles to make themselves better prepared for the next cycle and so on. According to Henkin, to make sense of state behaviour requires recognition of the fact that in their relations with one another, states are characteristically motivated by strategizing with their own best interests in mind.[2]

The purpose of reflection is to '*make sense*' of an experience.[3] It enables the reflector(s) to both learn and plan 'from things that went well or, didn't go well'[4] by going through specific stages of reflection. This process can start from any of the stages in the sequence but must follow through all six stages to complete the reflection.

Stage 1 involves describing the experience accurately. For instance, appropriately characterizing the Second World War, the Balkans War of the mid-1990s, or the Herero and Nama massacres, colonialism, or the Rwanda genocide.

[1] G Gibbs, *Learning by Doing: A Guide to Teaching and Learning Methods* (Oxford Polytechnic, 1998) 1.

[2] L Henkin, *How Nations Behave*, 2nd edn (Columbia University Press, 1979) 31–2.

[3] Edinburgh University, Reflection Toolkit available at <https://www.ed.ac.uk/reflection/reflectors-toolkit/reflecting-on-experience/gibbs-reflective-cycle> accessed 9 October 2020.

[4] ibid.

Benedict Abrahamson Chigara, *The Quasi-Supranational AU and the International Criminal Court* In: *The Emergent African Union Law.* Edited by: Olufemi Amao, Michèle Olivier and Konstantinos D. Magliveras, Oxford University Press.
 DOI: 10.1093/oso/9780198862154.003.0014

Stage 2 requires identification and recording of feelings or emotions evoked or generated by that experience. Stage 3 requires a holistic evaluation of the experience, encapsulating both positive and negative observations. Stage 4 requires an analysis that informs understanding of the dynamics involved or underlying the experience. What were the drivers and goals/outcomes of the experience, and who controlled them, and what was the reflector's role – malicious or benevolent contribution? The analysis can be deep or ephemeral, depending on the type, quality, and value of the experience under review and the significance of the experience for the future.

The conclusion, stage 5, leads to lessons learnt regarding what could and should have been done differently by the reflector in order to ensure a better experience and improved outcomes in similar situations. Africans did not emerge from their experiences of slavery or colonialism, or more recently International Criminal Court's (ICC) targeting of African situations for prosecution while the Court ignored similar events elsewhere, feeling dignified, confident, or even hopeful about the impartiality of the ICC.

The Organisation of African Unity (OAU) years of fumbling with international diplomacy and juvenile engagement with international institutions, particularly the Bretton Woods financial institutions, must have provided sufficient material for deep reflection that led African states to transform the regional organization from a toothless body to an agile quasi-supranational African Union (AU). Stage 6 involves drawing up a plan of how the reflector would deal with similar occurrences in the future should they arise by identifying, listing, and describing the general changes that would be required in order to ensure a more positive outcome.

2. The European Union: A Result of Reflective Cycle Approach to the Second World War?

By the end of the Second World War more than 50 countries had suffered casualties. Around 24 million military personnel had been killed and around 45 million civilians had been killed.[5] The paramount issue for Europe and indeed for the rest of the world was how to ensure that European countries would not start another world war. The *reflective decision* taken in Europe was to control production of coal and steel so that no state could alone outstrip others in the production of armaments for war.

[5] See also the National WWII Museum, Research Starters: Worldwide Deaths in World War II, available at <https://www.nationalww2museum.org/students-teachers/student-resources/research-starters/research-starters-worldwide-deaths-world-war> accessed 9 October 2020.

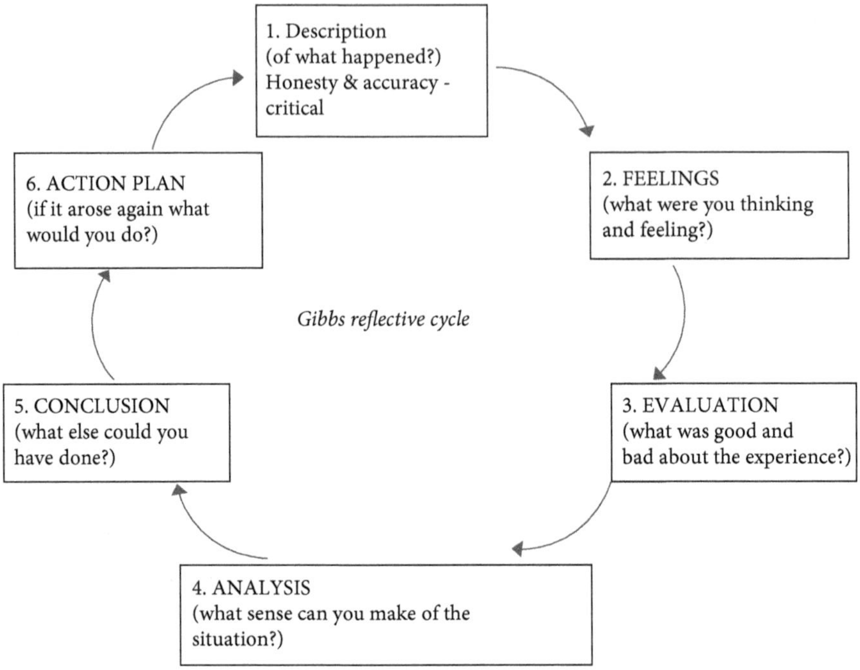

Figure 13.1 Gibbs' reflective cycle
Source: Graham Gibbs, Learning by Doing: A Guide to Teaching and Learning Methods, 1998

Petzina Dietmar[6] writes that just before the opening of the London Conference of the Foreign Ministers of the three Western Powers on 9 May 1950, the French Foreign Minister, Robert Schuman, submitted his plan for the comprehensive organization of the 'totality of Franco-German coal and steel production under a common High Authority' to an international audience. The proposal put an end to a discussion which had proceeded for several years as to the possible aims and content of a political and economic unification of Western Europe.

The Schuman plan was premised on the view that such a political and economic framework would extinguish mistrust that had precipitated previous Franco-German conflicts, leading to the catastrophe of world war. If the Schuman plan was achievable, then not only would war become unthinkable but materially impossible. The consequence of these reflections and conclusions (Gibbs' reflective cycle stage 5) was the establishment of the European Coal and Steel Community (ECSC)

[6] See also D Petzina, and others, 'The Origin of the European Coal and Steel Community: Economic Forces and Political Interests' (1981) 137(3) Zeitschrift Für Die Gesamte Staatswissenschaft / Journal of Institutional and Theoretical Economics 450–68.

by the Treaty of Paris (1951) concluded between France, West Germany, Italy, the Netherlands, and Luxembourg[7] – (Gibbs' reflective cycle stage 6).

The treaty establishing the European Atomic Energy Community (EAEC) followed on 25 March 1957. Its purpose was to create and regulate a specialist nuclear power market in Europe. Thus began the establishment of what is now the supranational European Union (EU). From these strategic developments based on the reflective cycle, Europe averted the embryonic repetition of war and peace, followed again by war, on its shores. In fact, these two treaties are the bedrock upon which later European agreements evolved and crystallized to establish the EU.

Alter and Steinberg have summed up Europe's outcomes of its post-Second World War reflections and action plans thus:

> The Schuman Plan was designed to alleviate concerns that Germany's dominance in coal and steel could be used to harm European reconstruction efforts or to build another war machine. Jean Monnet, the Plan's chief architect, also wanted to shore up the French planning process for reconstruction by Europeanizing the technocratic planning approach. Most supporters of the ECSC project expected integration to expand beyond Coal and Steel, and hoped that it would serve as a first step toward deeper European integration.[8]

3. Africa Region's experiments with Reflective Cycle Approach to Inferiorization Narratives in International Relations

Assa Okoth[9] accurately chronicles the rapid creation of the quasi-supranational AU that replaced the OAU as the regional international organization. In July 2000, in Lome, Togo, 53 African leaders agreed a text on the Constitutive Act that launched the Charter of the AU. On 26 May 2001, a Constitutive Act of the AU was signed in Lusaka, Zambia, and a committee appointed to look into all aspects of the organization that needed restructuring. On 9 July 2002, in Durban, South Africa, 53 African leaders inaugurated with a fanfare the AU as their new regional organization, replacing the OAU.

The AU has three main goals. First, it is intended to ensure continental unity in the pursuit of common goals by bringing together the plethora of sub-regional institutions (ECOWAS, SADC, EAC, and others) in order to pursue continent-wide

[7] See also *Fairhurst's Law of the European Union* 12th edn (Pearson, 2018) 4–49.

[8] See also KJ Alter and D Steinberg, 'The theory and reality of the European Coal and Steel Community' Researchgate publication available at <https://www.researchgate.net/publication/228187047_The_Theory_and_Reality_of_the_European_Coal_and_Steel_Community> accessed 9 October 2020.

[9] *A History of Africa Volume 2: African Nationalism and the De-colonisation Process* (East African Educational Publishers, 2006) 321–30.

cooperation and integration amongst African states – Articles 3(c), (j), and (k). Secondly, it is intended to facilitate African states' engagement in social, economic, and political relations in a way that will make war between them unthinkable or unlikely – Articles 3(a), (b), (f), and (e). Thirdly, it is intended as a tool for presenting an African position in international relations with other entities, including in international finance and trade – Articles 3(d); 4(a), (b), (g), and (e).

Thomas Kwasu Tieku[10] appropriately distinguishes the AU from its predecessor, the OAU, by contrasting their powers. Whereas the OAU Charter prioritized and made the principle of juridical sovereignty an inviolable artefact, the Constitutive Act of the AU creates room for the continental organization to interfere with some sovereign prerogatives of African states. By Article 4(h) the AU is empowered to intervene, without consent, for the purpose of restoring peace and stability; preventing war crimes, genocide, and crimes against humanity; and in response to a serious threat to legitimate order in a Member State.

This is a seismic escalation of powers from those of an OAU that was incapable of stopping civil wars on the African continent primarily because it lacked authority to compel its membership into action. Consequently, it could not to uphold its values. For instance, it was completely helpless over the Nigerian Biafra War (1967–70), and in the Ogaden War between Ethiopia and Somalia (1977–78), and in Libya's intervention in Chad (1980–87).

Moreover, the OAU appeared ill-suited for the modern challenges that African states faced six decades after its establishment. It was criticized for numerous inherent weaknesses that rendered it ineffective. Assa Okoth writes that the OAU had no institution, similar to the UN Security Council, to enforce its decisions. It relied on persuasion rather than compulsion. Consequently, many of its recommendations went unheeded by its Member States. The non-intervention in internal affairs of Member States clause shortened the OAU's arm from settling wars, imposing sanctions, etc.[11]

Thus, the transformation from OAU to AU has been described as representing 'the most significant political change in inter-state relations in Africa in almost 40 years … The new authority delegated to the AU has not only given teeth to the continental organization, but also marked a radical overhaul of co-operation among African states.'[12] This points to deep-reflection-led learning by a new African leadership that is determined to transform African states' roles and their fortunes in international relations by compelling a new and dignified international relations narrative on Africa. One that shows them as co-sovereign equals with other states, and not as mere objects of international institutions and their rules.

[10] TK Tieku, "Explaining the Clash and Accommodation of Interests of Major Actors in the Creation of the African Union" (2004) 103(411) African Affairs 249–67.

[11] Alter and Steinberg (n 8) 324.

[12] Supra (n 11) 250.

The ICC's early practice on the prosecution of Article 5 crimes under the Rome Statute (1998) made the ICC the first test ground for the AU's resolve to transform the international relations narrative on Africa. UN Security Council indifference to referrals of the ICC regarding African States Parties' failure/refusal to surrender indicted persons to the Court[13] when requested by the Court to do so is a high watermark in the stalemate between an international legal bureaucracy that appears puzzled by AU reaction to the ICC on the one hand and, on the other, the AU's determination to wipe away perceived inferiorization practices of international practices against its membership and its interests.

3.1 Deep-reflective Cycle-led Transformation of Africa's Regional Entity from Compliant OAU to Reactive AU

Emergent tensions between African States Parties to the ICC and the ICC itself appear to be rooted in lessons learnt from African states' own collective deep reflections on their experience with international law's historical inferiorization of Africa, generally through the narrative of international institutions. This inferiorization narrative appears to have been nurtured through particular phases in the evolution of international law,[14] and aided by wilful compliance of Africans themselves who, particularly during the OAU years, appeared to offer their own backs to others that gladly used them as trampolines for bouncing into the clouds of their dreamlands.

The colonial phase,[15] which was characterized by the scramble for, and partitioning of Africa into Western zones of control, could have been a consideration in this reflection on Africa and the narrative of international relations. The narrative of colonialism is an insufficiently told account of barbaric subjugation and dehumanization of native Africans by their colonizers, in some cases for almost a century.[16] Throughout, international law recognized and sanctioned the aim and effects of colonialism.

Another consideration in African states' reflections on Africa and the narrative of international relations was the post-colonial pedagogic phase,[17] where juvenile

[13] See also BA Chigara, 'Towards a *nemo judex in parte sua* critique of the International Criminal Court?' (2019) 19 International Criminal Law Review 412.

[14] See also A Roberts, *Is International Law International?* (OUP, 2017); T-H Cheng, 'Making international law without agreeing what it is' (2011) 10 Washington University Global Studies Law Review 1; KT Gaubatz and M MacArthur, 'How international is international law?' (2001) 22 Michigan Journal of International Law 239.

[15] See D Judd, *Empire: The British Imperial Experience, from 1765 to the Present* (Fontana Press, 1997); International Labour Office, *African Labour Survey* (Studies and Reports, New Series No 48, 1958).

[16] See also B Chigara 'Latecomers to the ILO and the authorship and ownership of the International Labour Code' (2007) 29 Human Rights Quarterly 706.

[17] See also 'About the African Union' (African Union) available at <https://au.int/en/overview> accessed 9 October 2020; M Gassama, *From the OAU to the AU: The Odyssey of a Continental Organization* (L'Harmattan RASD, 2015).

black majority rule governments that emerged from decolonization suffered immensely from their inept dealings with an international legal system (ILS) that required a thorough knowledge and understanding which they severely lacked, particularly on the uses and misuses of the dynamics of international law.

The current impasse between the AU and the ICC over non-compliance with ICC and related UN Security Council orders may be directly linked on the one hand, to the history of international law's ambivalence towards Western states' historic abuses of Africa generally, and on the other, to the AU's pedagogy during and after the OAU years (1963–2002).

Looking from the current AU/ICC impasse, it is arguable that the main lesson learnt by African states under the OAU years is twofold. One is about the need to establish regional institutions fit for purpose – which the OAU was not, particularly in relation to the modern challenges faced by African states in international relations (Gibbs' reflective cycle stages 5 and 6).

The other, and equally important lesson learnt is clearly on the potential uses and misuses of international law, both in its creation and in its implementation. From this lesson, African states appear determined to transform themselves from continuing as mere objects of international law throughout slavery, colonization, and political independence for years under the OAU, to making themselves proper subjects of international law – if Western states will allow it (Gibbs' reflective cycle stages 5 and 6). This is because law is the primary tool for translating the morality and the aspirations of any community or organization into rules that bind the political, social, and economic relations of all subjects of the legal system.

Party election manifestos normally reflect political and social preferences as well as their moral views on a range of issues. Once elected, these viewpoints and morals are translated into the force of the law, usually by legislating to establish the rights and responsibilities for the relevant subjects under their jurisdiction.[18] International law is no different in this regard. Its regulations, norms, and standards reflect the desires and aspirations of those that championed it. They continue to maintain their own influence through its powerful institutions and dynamic, including the UN Security Council and its special veto power that is held by each of the permanent five members only: China, Russia, France, the United States, and the United Kingdom.

Nonetheless, the scope of international regulation is continuing to increase at a rapid pace, one that threatens African states' desire to achieve a place in the law of nations, a law which has hitherto, and for the most part, appears to have regarded African states merely as objects of the ILS and not equal members to it.

From finance, trade, aviation, the environment, migration, intellectual property, and dispute resolution to warfare and movement of goods, services, and

[18] See also *Lloyd's Introduction to Jurisprudence*, 9th edn (Sweet & Maxwell, 2014) I–015.

people, international law has always been initiated and developed by and therefore championed pro-Western state interests.[19] A recent and notable exception is the International Labour Organization's (ILO) international labour code, which has recently been deliberately revised by the ILO Working Party on Policy Regarding the Revision of Standards (1994–2002) to make it truly representative of its diverse membership.[20] It may well be that the inclusive approach taken by the ILO is more conducive to compliance than the approach taken by the ICC, which seems to stigmatize African states as theatres of the worst crimes in the world.

4. AU Reaction to Perceived ICC Bias: A Challenge to International Law's Western-centric Nature

Western states have always controlled international organizations and their institutions and they still retain enormous influence over decision-making within them.[21] Other regions of the world are permitted only minimal, transient, or, relative influence, if they are allowed any at all. Secondly, international law is yet to become a law inspired by truly global aspirations, values, and needs. Judge Crawford writes that:

> [i]n terms of intellectual history, international law was thus European in origin, although the Europe in question was large, expanding to the whole Mediterranean, to Russia and the Near East; thence international law travelled with the colonizers to the Americas, to Asia, to Africa and eventually to Oceania.[22]

In fact, Koskenniemi[23] rightly opines that Europeans are hypocritical and self-centred in their regard for international law which, in their view must uphold the strictures of EU law or not apply to any state or matter at all. The EU is '[s]olipsistic in the sense of capable of seeing nothing other than [its] own legal system; [and] ... imperialistic because everything taking place in the world is judged from its perspective'.[24] The recent decision of the Court of Justice of the European Union (CJEU) in the *Mox Plant case*[25] illustrates this loudly and clearly.

[19] See also M Koskenniemi, 'International law: constitutionalism, managerialism and the ethos of legal education' (2007) 1 European Journal of Legal Studies 8, 8–9.

[20] See B Chigara 'Latecomers to the ILO and the authorship and ownership of the International Labour Code' (2007) 29 Human Rights Quarterly 706.

[21] Regarding the abuse of the 'veto power' conferred on the five permanent members of the UN Security Council under Article 27(3) of the UN Charter (1945), see also Security Council Report, 'The Veto' (No 3, 19 October 2015); R Butler, 'Reform of the United Nations Security Council' (2012) 1 Penn State Journal of Law and International Affairs 23; see also the United Nations Evaluation Group, *Norms and Standards for Evaluation* (UN, 2016).

[22] J Crawford, *Brownlie's Principles of Public International Law*, 7th edn (OUP, 2008) 4

[23] Koskenniemi (n 19) 9.

[24] ibid.

[25] Case C-459/03 *Commission of the European Communities v Ireland* [2006] ECJ I–4657.

Thirdly, there might be a strategic weakness in Western states' claim that what is essentially Western law is intrinsically international. Membership of the UN for all former colonies was conditional on their consent to be bound by all norms of customary international law (CIL), and they played no part in the formation of these norms, which may contradict their particular realities or their aspirations – uti possidetis being a clear but not the only example.

5. AU Push-back on International Law's Inferiorization Narrative on Africa's Situations

Claire Lauterbach writes that immediately following the ICC's indictment of Sudan's President at the time, Al Bashir, for Article 5 crimes, both detractors and supporters of the ICC began speculating on how:

> the ICC might shape and be shaped by the domestic politics of Africa. African states are likely to be what Finnemore and Sikkink term 'critical states' to the evolution of the ICC. Yet the Court's relationship with modern Africa contains a fundamental tension. While accused of 'targeting' only African politicians for special condemnation, the ICC has also been positively welcomed among African human rights groups as legitimizing their domestic attempts to seek redress for crimes.[26]

Through the quasi-supranational AU, African states appear now to be resolute in their attempt to push back on international law's ambivalence towards them generally. Hence, the current impasse of continual supranational AU legislation that prohibits African states that are also parties to the Rome Statute (1998) from fulfilling their obligations to cooperate with ICC and UN Security Council orders. The ICC has jurisdiction over the most serious crimes of concern to the international community as a whole, namely the crime of genocide, crimes against humanity, war crimes, and the crime of aggression.

If the AU's current objection to ICC intrusions on situations in Africa is indicative of African states' new approach to international institutions, which comes as a consequence of lessons learnt from the 60-year OAU learning phase, then we might conclude that African states are perhaps tired of being treated as mere objects of a legal system that requires only their compliance with its edicts, without ever recognizing their equality with other Member States under the law of nations.

The current and ongoing AU stance that ICC orders directed at certain African individuals are unacceptable to them as long as the ICC ignores similar

[26] C Lauterbach, 'Commitment to the International Criminal Court among Sub-Saharan African States' (2008) 5 Eyes on the ICC 85, 85.

circumstances in other parts of the world points to a new awareness and clear intent of African states to sanitize international law's attitude towards them. This would be a clear policy departure from the OAU's placid, inexperienced unquestioning collaborative approach to international relations.

6. A Symbiotic Coincidence: From OAU to AU at the Establishment of the ICC?

In the colonial phase[27] Africa's experience of 'international law' is characterized largely by treaties between European states partitioning of Africa into Western zones of control, followed by an insufficiently told and often, marginalization of subjugation and dehumanization of natives by their colonial masters. The international laws developed by European states for African colonies at that time sanctioned gross abuse of Africans through practices that included, *assimilado*, servitude, and forced labour. Modern international law now prohibits and criminalizes some of these practices through its most potent standards – norms *jus cogens*.[28]

In the post-colonial, neo liberal, learning phase,[29] African majority-rule governments that were complete novices and 'freshmen' to international law's orchestrated pro-Western practices under the UN's Bretton Woods institutions,[30] the global trading system,[31] the world foreign investment system,[32] and the like suffered badly as they were outwitted by their colonial masters in the game they were required to play.[33]

[27] See Judd (n 15); International Labour Office (n 16).

[28] See also International Convention on the Suppression and Punishment of the Crime of Apartheid (adopted 30 November 1973, entered into force 18 July 1976) 1015 UNTS 243; International Convention against Apartheid in Sports (adopted 10 December 1985, entered into force 3 April 1988) 1500 UNTS 161.

[29] See also B Fagbayibo, 'From OAU to AU: Rethinking Supranational Governance in Africa' in S Oloruntoba and T Falola (eds), *The Palgrave Handbook of African Politics, Governance and Development* (Palgrave Macmillan) 771–82. See also African Union (n 17); Gassama (n 17).

[30] The Bretton Woods Institutions are the World Bank and the International Monetary Fund (IMF). They were set up at a meeting of 43 countries in Bretton Woods, New Hampshire, United States in July 1944. Their aims were to help rebuild the shattered postwar economy and to promote international economic cooperation. See also 'What are the Bretton Woods Institutions?' (*Bretton Woods Project*, 1 January 2019) available at <https://www.brettonwoodsproject.org/2019/01/art-320747/> accessed 3 October 2020.

[31] See also the General Agreement on Tariffs and Trade (adopted 30 October 1947, entered into force 1 January 1948) 55 UNTS 187 (GATT) that was superseded in 1994 by the Marrakesh Agreement establishing the World Trade Organization (adopted 15 April 1994, entered into force 1 January 1995) 1867 UNTS 3.

[32] See also B Chigara, 'Trade liberalization: savior or scourge of SADC economies?' (2001) 10 University of Miami International and Comparative Law Review 7; B Chigara, 'European/Southern African Development Community (SADC) States' Bilateral Investment Agreements (BITs) for the Promotion and Protection of Foreign Investments vs post-apartheid SADC economic and social reconstruction policy' (2011) 10 Journal of International Trade Law and Policy 213.

[33] L Henkin, *How Nations Behave*, 2nd edn (Columbia University Press, 1979) 49–87

As new hands to the practice of international law, African states suffered miserably because their former colonial masters exploited all their mistakes, whether in aid negotiations or trade agreements, etc. For instance, not a single African state has achieved any meaningful benefit from participating in International Monetary Fund (IMF) conditional financial lending schemes that are commonly known as economic structural adjustment programmes (ESAP). And yet, almost every African state has been subjected to periodic bouts of IMF or World Bank ESAP of one form or another and left in a worse-off condition at the end of the five-year cycle that the programmes are normally designed to run.[34]

Therefore, the significance of the transformation from the OAU dynamic that began in 1963 into the supranational-inclined, even supranational-incubated[35] AU (2002) that is showing all the signs of a strong, dynamic, and reactionary stance against the dominance of Western interests in international relations is only now beginning to manifest as a strategic and post-reflection modality (Gibbs' reflective cycle stages 5 and 6).

Through AU-directed rejection of ICC requests and orders, and even the challenge to the UN Security Council orders to arrest and surrender former President Al Bashir to The Hague-based ICC for alleged torture, crimes against humanity, and war crimes, the AU's dynamic shows a no-nonsense approach. Such an approach has shocked everyone else except African states themselves. How could AU member states that comprised the biggest regional grouping of the founding membership of the ICC when it came into force on 1 July 2002[36] have turned against the Court they decisively helped to found? Perhaps it would have been more logical to anticipate that African states would be the most cooperative members of the ICC. Thus, 'business as usual with Africans' would have made perfect sense.

Notwithstanding, African states' tensions with the ICC herald a major setback to the widely acclaimed era of constitutionalization in international relations.[37] Constitutionalism was meant to diminish power politics in international relations by increasing the number and range of international institutions with capacity to implement international policies – from the World Trade Organization (WTO), World Intellectual Property Organization (WIPO), International Centre for

[34] See also B Sadasivam, 'The impact of structural adjustment on women: a governance and human rights agenda' (1997) 19 Human Rights Quarterly 630; JK Mapulanga-Hulston, 'The implementation of structural adjustment programmes in Sub-Saharan Africa: an infringement of state sovereignty' (2003) 35 Zambia Law Journal 1.

[35] See especially BA Chigara 'The administration of international law in national courts and the legitimacy of international law' (2017) 17 International Criminal Law Review 909; BA Chigara, 'National courts and the integrity of international Law' (2018) 48 California Western International Law Journal 189.

[36] 'United Nations Diplomatic Conference of Plenipotentiaries on the Establishment of an International Criminal Court' (17 July 1998) UN Doc A/CONF.183/9.

[37] See especially M-S Kuo, 'Taming governance with legality? critical reflections upon global administrative law as small-C global constitutionalism' (2011) 44 New York University Journal of International Law and Politics 55.

Settlement of Investment Disputes (ICSID), International Arbitration Act (IAA), International Tribunal for the Law of the Sea (ITLOS), International Maritime Organization (IMO) regimes to that of the ICC, so that the prevalence of such institutions would minimize the space previously navigated by powerful or recalcitrant states that preferred to go it alone without risking the justifiable condemnation of others.

7. AU Challenge of ICC: A Setback on Constitutionalization in International Relations?

One presumed benefit of constitutionalism, as explained below, is its potential to transform the legitimacy of international law positively.[38] Von Bogdandy writes that constitutionalism entails a reconfiguration of international law in pursuit of 'a global legal community that frames and directs political power in light of common values and a common good'.[39] Proponents include German scholars Christian Tomuschat, Wilhelm Wengler, and others. Similarly, the global governance paradigm argues for legal reform projects based on 'some form of political ordering that transcends nation states' and pointed towards ensuring the rule of law in inter-state relations.[40]

This chapter pursues the current impasse between what is probably the strongest human rights enforcement institution established consequent to the constitutionalization drive in international relations, the ICC, on the one hand, and on the other, the traditional 'objects' of international law, African states. This impasse points to AU rejection of the status-quo in international relations. This is backed up by the increasing reflective awareness of an AU driven Africa. The AU will no longer contend with the status of 'mere object' or 'law taker' in international relations. Rather, by legislating regionally that its Member States Parties should not cooperate with ICC and with UN Security Council Orders, the AU has declared a new era where its Member States Parties' relationship with international institutions shall proceed only on the basis of equal treatment, co-authorship, and co-membership under international law.

By escalating its challenge to both ICC authority and to UN Security Council arrest warrants against African leadership, the AU has either called a bluff by establishing explicit counter-ICC legislation and practice in defiance of international arrest warrants for Al Bashir,[41] or shown a 'maturity' generated under AU

[38] TM Franck, 'Legitimacy in the international legal system' (1988) 82 American Journal of International Law 705.

[39] A von Bogdandy, 'Constitutionalism in international law: comment on a proposal from Germany' (2006) 47 Harvard International Law Journal 223.

[40] Kuo (n 37) 56–7.

[41] See 'Situation in Darfur, Sudan: ICC-02/05' (*International Criminal Court*) available at <https://www.icc-cpi.int/darfur> accessed 3 October 2020.

pedagogy of international law as being ambivalent to the aspirations of equal dignity among nation states. If the latter, then the Eurocentric legal framework that has been masquerading as the law of nations may no longer be sustainable.

Moreover, in the *Kadi case*, the CJEU appeared to challenge the spirit of international constitutionalism by insisting that the UN Counter-Terrorism Committee had encroached upon the foremost principle of EU integrity by violating the requirements of the principle of the rule of law, including the right to be heard, the right to judicial review,[42] the right to natural justice,[43] and the requirement that justice must be seen to be done.[44]

AU Member States Parties' claim that ICC practice lacks the watermark of legitimacy, including the duty of fair treatment owed by decision-makers[45] to those that they preside over, may eventually serve as a trigger to tensions elsewhere in the international legal system regarding cases of apparent bias of international law against African or developing states.

8. AU Approach to International Relations: Reflective and Declaratory or Mere Bluff?

The reflective phase in African leaders' engagement with an international order that has been authored, instituted, and controlled by Western states has coincided with the strengthening of constitutionalization of international law. In part, constitutionalism is intended to weaken power-based international relations by strengthening institutions for a rule of law-based global governance. One of the

[42] Joined Cases C-402/05 P and C-415/05 P *P Yassin Abdullah Kadi and Al Barakaat International Foundation v Council of the European Union and Commission of the European Communities* [2008] ECR I-06351.

[43] See also *R (on the application of Hill) v Institute of Chartered Accountants in England and Wales* [2013] EWCA Civ 555, [2014] 1 WLR 86, para 14: 'The first rule of natural justice that no judge should be a judge in his own cause or, as it is now more popularly known, the rule against bias is an elementary but highly important component of any developed system of justice. So is the second rule that each party must be heard, sometimes expressed in Latin as "*audi alteram partem*". It is sometimes also expressed in the form "he who decides must hear".'

[44] See also *Broadview Energy Developments Limited v The Secretary of State for Communities and Local Government* [2016] EWCA Civ 562 2016, [2016] 6 WLUK 517, para 31: '[T]he principle that justice must not only be done but must manifestly and undoubtedly be seen to be done *R v Sussex Justices ex parte McCarthy [1924] 1 KB 256*, 259 per Lord Hewart C.J. and the principle that once it is established that a decision-maker has received representations from one side behind the back of the other, the court will not enquire into the likelihood of prejudice, *Kanda v Government of the Federation of Malaya [1962] A.C. 322*, 337 per Lord Denning. These are, of course, salutary principles when the decision-maker receives evidence or arguments raising matters unknown to the complainant. Kanda is itself a good example. A police constable was dismissed without being shown a board of inquiry report into his conduct (available to the dismissing body) which decided (page 336) that he had fabricated evidence at a criminal trial and that he had suborned witnesses to commit perjury. These were allegations which he had no opportunity to contradict or comment on. It is not surprising that the Privy Council was not prepared to inquire whether the police constable was actually prejudiced, and said that it was sufficient that he might have been.'

[45] See also ibid.

most powerful institutions established in this phase is the ICC, which came into force in July 2002. It is this institution that African states' frustration with power brokered international organization has targeted because of its perceived bias against African nations.

The 13th AU Summit held on 6 July 2009 ordered Member States Parties 'not co-operate pursuant to the provisions of Article 98 of the Rome Statute of the ICC relating to immunities for the arrest and surrender of Sudanese President Omar al Bashir to the ICC'.[46] South Africa's President declared: 'There is an African stance on this and we are not different from it.... the United Nations Security Council should have listened to Africa before issuing the interdict'.[47] Thus, regional anti-ICC customary international law[48] began to emerge.

Further, the outcomes of the *lex specialis* AU Extraordinary Summit on Africa–ICC Relationship held by the highest decision-making organ of the AU, the Assembly, on 12 October 2013[49] declared that:

i. No International Court or Tribunal has capacity to commence or to continue charges against any serving AU Head of State or Government or anybody acting or entitled to act in such capacity during their term of office.
ii. That the trials by the ICC of President Uhuru Kenyatta and Deputy President William Samoei Ruto, who are the current serving leaders of the Republic of Kenya, should be suspended until they complete their terms of office; and
iii. To fast track the establishment of the criminal jurisdiction of the African Court on Human and Peoples' Rights and to table for discussion at the Assembly of State Parties of the ICC, amendments to the ICC on immunity of heads of state and government among other matters.[50]

Even without the passage of much time,[51] the *lex specialis* outcomes of this AU Extraordinary Summit probably point to the emergence of sudden or wild

46 B Mbola, 'AU leaders will not extradite Al Bashir' (*South African Government News Agency*, 6 July 2009) available at <http://www.sanews.gov.za/south-africa/au-leaders-will-not-extradite-al-bashir> accessed 4 October 2020.

47 Ibid.

48 See especially the *Asylum Case (Columbia v Peru)* (Merits) [1950] ICJ Rep 266; See also B Cheng, 'United Nations Resolutions on outer space: "instant" customary international law' (1965) 3 Indian Journal of International Law 23.

49 Assembly of the African Union, 'Decision on Africa's Relationship with the International Criminal Court (ICC)' (12 October 2013) Ext/Assembly/AU/Dec.1(Oct.2013); see also SA Dersso, 'The AU's Extraordinary Summit Decisions on Africa–ICC Relationship' (*EJIL: Talk*, 28 October 2013) available at <http://www.ejiltalk.org/the-aus-extraordinary-summit-decisions-on-africa-icc-relationship/> accessed 4 October 2020.

50 ibid.

51 *North Sea Continental Shelf Cases (Federal Republic of Germany v Denmark; Federal Republic of Germany v Netherlands)* (Merits) [1969] ICJ Rep 3, 43. The Court ruled that although the passage of only a short period of time is not necessarily, or of itself a bar to the formation of a new rule of customary international law on the basis of what was originally a purely conventional rule, an indispensable requirement would be that within the period in question, short though it might be, state practice, including that of states whose interests are specially affected, should have been both extensive and

customary international law[52] requiring none of custom's gradual crystallizing elements, including the passage of time, to observe a consistent and uniform practice.[53] Prost and Clarke write that:

> the emergence of the hypothesis of 'instant' customs, whereby custom is essentially based on the recognition, formally expressed in certain international instruments, of a 'need for law'. Admittedly, solemn resolutions such as those emanating from the United Nations, have a decisive influence in the genesis of 'instant' or 'wild' customs. They are often regarded as their means of expression par excellence.[54]

African states have solidified their opposition to and distrust of the ICC by producing regional anti-ICC customary international laws. These laws are evident also in:

(1) The unequivocal outcomes of the *lex specialis* AU Extraordinary Summit on Africa–ICC Relationship held by the highest decision making organ of the AU, the Assembly on 12 October 2013.[55] The Assembly has authority to pass binding directives under Article 9(e) and (g) of the Constitutive Act of the African Union (2000).[56]
(2) The refusal of Uganda, Chad, Kenya, Djibouti, Malawi, Congo, South Africa, and Egypt to be involved in detaining and surrendering President Al Bashir to the ICC.
   (i) The crux of AU / ICC confrontation

The dispute concerns, *inter alia*,

(1) The competence of the office of the ICC Prosecutor (OTP) and of the UN Security Council to order the surrender of serving African heads of

virtually uniform in the sense of the provision invoked, and should moreover have occurred in such a way as to show a general recognition that a rule of law or legal obligation is involved.

[52] M Prost and P Kingsley Clark 'Unity, diversity and the fragmentation of international law: how much does the multiplication of international organizations really matter?' (2006) 5 Chinese Journal of International Law 341.
[53] *North Sea Continental Shelf Cases* (n 51) 42: 'Even without the passage of any considerable period of time, a very widespread and representative participation in the Convention might suffice of itself, provided it included that of states whose interests were specifically affected.'
[54] Prost and Kingsley Clark (n 52).
[55] Assembly of the African Union (n 49).
[56] Constitutive Act of the African Union (adopted 11 July 2000, entered into force 26 May 2001) 2158 UNTS 3.

government/states to the ICC once they have been charged in their individual capacity with offences that properly fall under the jurisdiction of the ICC.

(2) The legality under international law of the AU's refusal to cooperate with the ICC by ordering its Member States Parties not to arrest or surrender persons against whom the ICC has issued international arrest warrants.[57]

(3) The status under international law of AU Member States Parties that comply with the AU directive not to cooperate with the ICC regardless of their obligations under UN Charter Law and under the *lex specialis* of international criminal law.

(4) Rejection by the AU of *lex specialis* obligations under international criminal law and the AU's preferred interpretations of both universal jurisdiction, and sovereign immunity.

Prolongation of this dispute threatens the legitimacy of the young and only permanent international criminal tribunal. It also risks trumping human rights with impunity, which may disillusion many who had pinned enormous hope on the advancement of human rights protection everywhere on the establishment of the ICC. Further, it risks obfuscating the scope of the notions of universal jurisdiction and sovereign immunity in international law. It would also deepen further the question about the supremacy/limits of UN law over posterior regional supranational laws of the AU and of the EU – a point raised by the CJEU's Grand Chamber decision in the *Kadi case*.[58]

The AU was adamant that the ICC warrant of arrest in the *Al Bashir case* was void as its object was a serving head of state. This position introduces a clear conflict of interests between the ICC and the AU. The AU remains adamant that ICC arrest warrants against serving heads of states trump the well-established principle of sovereign immunity.[59] But the OTP at the ICC perceives no such link between sovereign immunity guarantees and personal crimes, the order of which could not be described as acts of a sovereign. Further, the AU insists that the ICC warrants

[57] Assembly of the African Union, 'AU Decision on the Implementation of the Decisions of the International Criminal Court (ICC) Doc. EX.CL/731 (XXI)' (15–16 July 2012) Assembly/AU/Dec.419(XIX).

[58] *Yassin Abdullah Kadi and Al Barakaat International Foundation v Council of the European Union and Commission of the European Communities* (n 42); see also A Posch 'The Kadi case: rethinking the relationship between EU Law and international law?' (2009) 15 Colombia Journal of European Law 1; J Kokott and C Sobotta 'The *Kadi* case – constitutional core values and international law – finding the balance?' (2012) 23 European Journal of International Law 1015.

[59] A point repeated by the Assembly of the African Union, 'Decision on the Progress Report of the Commission on the Implementation of Previous Decisions on the International Criminal Court (ICC) Doc. Assembly/AU/18(XXIV)' (30–31 January 2015) Assembly/AU/Dec.547(XXIV); and also by Mokhari, State Counsel in *Southern Africa Litigation Centre v Minister of Justice And Constitutional Development and Others* [2015] ZAGPPHC 402, Case No 27740/2015; See also 'Failure to Arrest Al Bashir 'Unconstitutional'' (*News 24*, 15 June 015) available at <http://www.news24.com/SouthAfrica/News/LIVE-Court-to-hear-Al-Bashir-arrest-application-20150615> accessed 5 October 2020.

of arrest against serving African heads of state/ government constitute a threat to local peace initiatives and risk a return to or an escalation of violence, while the ICC insists that such warrants are compelled by the pursuit of international justice for the most serious international human rights crimes.

9. Conclusion

Because all legal systems reflect the morality of those in control – the ruling classes[60] – the question of the *function* of other regions of the world in an international legal system founded by Western states has never been more acute than in the current constitutionalization phase in the development of international law.

Western states remain adamant that the structure of the UN Security Council shall not be changed. Moreover, newer institutions such as the ICC and the UN Counter Terrorism Committee with powers that target individuals directly by requiring states to comply with Security Council Resolutions that may require the arrest, detention, and surrender of nationals to UN institutions abroad, or freeze their financial assets and bank accounts, are the high watermark in the recognition of the individual as a subject of international law. No less significant are those international institutions that have institutionalized the power of investors to take foreign governments to arbitration. Developing states are continually being frog-marched to arbitration, which usually results in crippling awards against their national policies.

The agenda to constitutionalize international criminal law appears to have coincided with African states' own crystallization of lessons learnt from their evaluation of OAU performance during and after decolonization. Implementation of lessons learnt about the uses and misuses of international law in international relations generally shows a new awareness by African states that rejects international law's enduring ambivalence towards those states' self-interest and towards their dignity.

The confrontation between African states that are dual members of both the AU and the ICC over Al Bashir arrest warrants issued in 2009 and 2010 by the Security Council and the ICC respectively probably points to the zeitgeist of African states' determination to implement lessons that they have learnt about the nature and the practice of international law particularly during the OAU (1963–2002) period. They include the realization that they have a role to play in transforming Eurocentric international law from its ambivalence or tolerance of African states to their full recognition by UN Charter Article 2 as equals.

[60] See also S Shavell, 'Law versus morality as regulators of conduct' (2002) 4 American Law and Economics Review 227.

This is because joining a pre-formed club does not entitle one to ownership of the club until one can show that one has also acquired co-ownership of the right to determine what the club does, when and why, and what it should not attempt and why. To make it one's own club, one must upon taking up membership also become a co-controller and co-umpire of the club's routines and issues and its general and specific direction of travel. This is the lesson that African states appear to have learnt in the 25–60 years of post-colonial experience of engaging with the international legal system.

For this reason, they discontinued the collaborative OAU in July 2002 and replaced it with the more than quasi-supranational AU, just as the ICC came into force. This coincidence set up the scene for the extreme tensions currently playing out between African states that have dual membership in both the AU and the ICC, and within the ICC itself.

This situation informs the view that to carry any legitimacy in the 21st century, international law must shake off its Eurocentric tendencies and transform into a genuine law of all nations. That would probably ensure that other regions that are proximately placed close to African states in terms of their relationship with international law do not take up similar positions against other international institutions that may be perceived to be in breach of the *pacta sunt servant* rule. Were that to happen, the agenda to institutionalize international law would be severely weakened, and the legitimacy of international law severely tested and probably crippled.

PART 4

ADDRESSING SOCIO-ECONOMIC CHALLENGES THROUGH AFRICAN UNION LAW: PERSPECTIVES

14

Development of AU Law: Tax Harmonization and Regional Integration towards Achieving Social Structures in Africa

Chisa Onyejekwe

1. Introduction

As is evidenced by Agenda 2063, the AU is currently undergoing systematic reform, its focus being to achieve sustainable development goals. Agenda 2063 is both a vision and an action plan with the objective of a socially and economically developed Africa. It is a call for action to all segments of African society to 'work together to build a prosperous and united Africa based on shared values and a common destiny'.[1] Its aspirations regarding social development echo the definition of a domestic welfare state by Barr, which reflects

> 'a series of institutions which provide poverty relief, redistribute income and wealth and seek to reduce social exclusion ... a series of institutions which provide insurance and offer a mechanism for redistribution over the life-cycle'.[2]

Agenda 2063 enables the AU to become an integrated, prosperous, and peaceful continent, enriched by its own population, not reliant on exterior sources of finances to represent a dynamic force in the world. Over the next 50 years, the strategic framework for the socio-economic transformation is to build upon

[1] African Union, Agenda 2063 – The Africa We Want (Framework Document, September 2015) available at <https://au.int/sites/default/files/documents/33126-doc-framework_document_book.pdf> accessed 27 March 2020. The Aspirations of Agenda 2063 are: (a) A prosperous Africa based on inclusive growth and sustainable development; (b) an integrated continent, politically united, and based on the ideals of Pan-Africanism and the vision of Africa's Renaissance; (c) an Africa of good governance, democracy, respect for human rights, justice, and the rule of law; (d) a peaceful and secure Africa; (e) an Africa with a strong cultural identity, common heritage, shared values and ethics; (f) an Africa whose development is people-driven, relying on the potential of African people, especially its women and youth, and caring for children; and (g) Africa as a strong, united, and influential global player and partner.

[2] N Barr, *Economics of the Welfare State*, 5th edn (OUP, 2012) 3.

Chisa Onyejekwe, *Development of AU Law: Tax Harmonization and Regional Integration towards Achieving Social Structures in Africa* In: *The Emergent African Union Law*. Edited by: Olufemi Amao, Michèle Olivier and Konstantinos D. Magliveras, Oxford University Press. © Chisa Onyejekwe 2021. DOI: 10.1093/oso/9780198862154.003.0015

and accelerate the implementation of past and existing continental initiatives for growth and sustainable development.[3] The aim is to educate the entire population, with an underlining focus on science, technology, and innovation. In so doing, cities can become hubs of cultural and economic activities. For these goals to be achieved, it requires a greater focus on inclusive growth and sustainable development, in addition to sustainable tax revenue schemes, amongst other matters.

Accordingly, this chapter argues that to achieve 'a high standard of living, quality of life and well-being for all citizens', a sustainable source of revenue in the form of direct taxation (corporation tax to be precise) must be achieved.[4]

Section 2 discusses the background of these issues that surround sustainable social structures in Africa and how taxation can be harnessed towards developing and maintaining them. It identifies the AU's position towards achieving social structures using tax revenue and surrounding issues. Section 3 analyses tax harmonization in the ECOWAS and WAEMU – a regional political and economic union of 15 states located in West Africa. This analysis of tax harmonization demonstrates how the AU can not only achieve sustainable social structures but also become funded specifically through tax revenue. Furthermore, the section demonstrates the challenges that will affect successful harmonization before reaching a circumspect conclusion. The crux of the chapter leads to supporting the strong foundation already laid, arguing for the development of an AU Model Law on taxation whilst proffering policy recommendations.

2. Background

Social-economic development and its impact on poverty reduction in Africa hinges on structural transformation, invariably begging the question of how this will be achieved. This chapter suggests that growth and development can be actualized through regional integration and corporate tax harmonization that bears directive of AU law continent-wide. It is submitted that Regional Economic Communities (RECs) are the best vehicles to achieve this. RECs are closely integrated with the AU's work and serve as its building blocks by facilitating regional economic integration between members of the individual regions and through the wider African Economic Community (AEC).[5] RECs have also been involved in coordinating AU Member States' interests in wider areas such as peace and security, development,

[3] ibid.

[4] African Union, 'Goals & Priority Areas of Agenda 2063' (African Union Commission, 2013) available at <https://au.int/agenda2063/goals> accessed 27 March 2020.

[5] AU, 'Regional Economic Communities' (African Union Commission, 2013) available at <https://au.int/en/organs/recs> accessed 27 March 2020. Although RECs are not created by the AU, the relationship between them is mandated by the Abuja Treaty and the AU Constitutive Act and guided by the 2008 Protocol on Relations between the RECs and the AU.

and governance.[6] Tax harmonization can be viewed as a means by which to consolidate policies in order to form a driving force for investment and trade; its goal is to generate revenue for the Member States of integrated regions whilst deterring excessive competition.[7] According to Kopits, tax harmonization is a process of adjusting the tax systems of different jurisdictions to achieve some common fiscal policy objectives.[8] Harmonization in this case would be any situation in which differences between the tax systems of states are reduced, either by cooperation between public authorities, or by the implementation of government policy measures.[9] However, Faria argues that tax harmonization implies a high level of intergovernmental cooperation, which may materialize through regional economic agreements based on factors other than economic development that are common to the contracting states.[10] These factors include culture, geographical grouping affecting cross-border transactions, common or similar needs, etc. Tax harmonization aims at establishing and regularly maintaining an online tax database that provides comprehensive information about the tax structures of different countries.[11] It offers collaboration for tax incentives that encourage investment rather than those that reduce transparency or act purely as vehicles for tax minimization. Additionally, it creates a clear and transparent system of taxation that harmonizes policies to prevent investment barriers and to avoid double taxation. Of importance is that tax harmonization mitigates the harmful consequences of tax competition through the application of regulatory mechanisms or policies.[12] Successful integration requires harmonization and an underlying need and wish amongst Member States to improve the economic circumstances of their population. An important factor in integration and harmonization invariably rests on relinquishing parts or segments of sovereignty to an international or supranational organization. This implies that AU Member States, through their RECs, would ideally have the same tax system to protect themselves against multinational corporations (MNCS) whose majority shareholders are foreign investors or African MNCS.

[6] ibid; see also the 2008 Memorandum of Understanding (MoU) on Cooperation around Peace and Security between the AU, RECs and the Coordinating Mechanisms of the Regional Standby Brigades of Eastern and Northern Africa.

[7] AI Azuka, 'Achieving sustainable development through tax harmonisation: potentials, paradoxes and policy imperatives' (2015) 6(1) International Journal of Sustainable Development Law and Policy 274–96.

[8] George Kopits, 'Overview', in *Tax Harmonization in the European Community: Policy Issues and Analysis*' (International Monetary Fund:IMF Washington, 1992) 3.

[9] TA Rounds, 'Tax harmonization and tax competition: contrasting views and policy issues in three federal countries' (1992) 22 Journal of Public Administration Research and Theory 24.

[10] A Faria, *Tax Coordination and Harmonization* in Parthasarathi Shome (ed) *Tax Policy Handbook* (IMF, 1995) 228–30.

[11] IMF, 'Tax Coordination, Tax Competition and Revenue Mobilization in the West African Economic and Monetary Union' (IMF Working Paper, WP/13/163, 2013).

[12] A Podviezko, L Parfenova, and others, 'Tax competitiveness of the new EU Member States' (2019) 12(1) Risk Financial Management 2.

There are, however, legitimate challenges to integration and harmonization. First, African states may not be prepared to relinquish sovereignty to such an extent. It may represent a form of subjugation by fellow states, whilst they are in the process of overcoming the scars of colonialism. Nonetheless, harmonization of legislation will ensure that AU Member States will be in a better position to achieve Agenda 2063 goals through revenue generated from tax. However, harmonization cannot be complete without states surrendering some of their sovereignty to the relevant international organization. Another challenge of regional integration centres is to ensure that community law is recognized and accepted as being superior to national law. This chapter examines tax harmonization and integration in West Africa through ECOWAS. RECs in Southern and Eastern Africa have already taken major steps in harmonizing tax policies. Moreover, ECOWAS can be considered to have achieved a considerable development in this area with the backing of its Founding Treaty and regulations. Accordingly, Nwauche argues that ECOWAS norms and rules can apply in Member States through the doctrine of direct effect, as it applies in the European Union (EU), once the ECOWAS Treaty has been domesticated into national law.[13]

Where regional law has been domesticated and, in some cases, takes precedence over national law, such regional rules and norms entrenched in a treaty could be likened to law or perhaps to a specific legal system. Applying this to RECs sets a foundation for the development of AU law where the AU integrates regional treaties as part of its legal system. This will be accomplished when an AU law, through an amendment of the Constitutive Act, grants the Assembly the mandate to regulate RECs. Possible challenges are recognized as the Preamble of the revised ECOWAS Treaty points to Member States having a collective political will:

> 'Convinced that the integration of the Member States into a viable regional Community may demand the partial and gradual pooling of national sovereignties to the Community within the context of a collective political will'.[14]

In this case, regarding corporate taxation and trade levies in favour of an REC, true integration will certainly develop when Member States have the political will to give up their sovereign rights.

[13] ES Nwauche, 'Enforcing ECOWAS Law in West African National Courts' (2011) 2 Journal of African Law 181–202. The principle of direct effect was a result of the judgment by the European Court of Justice (ECJ), which held that the provisions of the Treaty Establishing the European Economic Community (EU Treaty) can create legal rights which could be enforced by both natural and legal persons before the courts of Member States, see *NV Algemene Transport-Expedite Onderneming Van Gend en Loos v Nederlandse Administratie der Belastingen* (1963) Case 26/62.

[14] ECOWAS, 'Revised Treaty of The Economic Community of West African States' (ECOWAS, 2015) available at <https://www.ecowas.int/wp-content/uploads/2015/01/Revised-treaty.pdf> accessed 29 June 2020.

To use taxation in order to create better social structures in Africa, one must explore the relationship between taxation and social structures, especially the extent to which tax revenues can create these social structures. This chapter advocates for raising revenue from taxation on the basis that tax can be viewed as a social 'value' or 'ethic' enshrined in law and potentially channelled towards sustainable social structures and systems. An example of such tax is corporate tax as it can be argued that the corporation is a wealth-generating entity, and its taxation is one of the tools through which it can contribute to society.[15] To achieve this, it is argued that there is a need for harmonizing and integrating tax policies with the aim of achieving structural economic transformation and inclusive growth in Africa where there is poverty, lack of basic infrastructure, and underemployment, amongst other disadvantages. Such law can be accomplished by the development of AU law with the goal of engaging binding RECs to achieve this.

3. Social Structures and the Influence of Tax Revenue in Africa

3.1 Africa's Need for Sustainable Social Structures

Despite its vast natural and human resources as well as great cultural, ecological, and economic diversity, Africa remains underdeveloped. Poverty, social structure, and wealth distributional concerns have taken centre-stage in almost every developmental effort. This has become a priority for the AU – its foundation rests on the need for the AU to revise and adapt its development agenda. Africa is determined to eradicate poverty within a single generation's lifetime and build prosperity through its social and economic transformation.

To build up social structures, development must take root in all spheres of the AU and this includes infrastructure. A World Bank study published in 2017 found that the poor state of infrastructure in many African countries reduced national economic growth by two percentage points despite the enormous natural resources many of these nations possess.[16] Evidently, there are gaps in both the national and regional policies governing the activities of MNCs and more should be done to enhance social structures through economic development. Although most of the MNCs investing in Africa are based abroad, investment

[15] A Okoye and C Onyejekwe, 'Law's Ethics and Sustainability: Corporate Tax and Sustainable Social Structures' in L Filho W and A Consorte McCrea (eds), *Sustainability and the Humanities*. (Springer, 2018) 525–38.

[16] World Bank, 'Africa's Pulse: An analysis of issues shaping Africa's economic future' (World Bank Group, 2017) available at <http://documents.worldbank.org/curated/en/348741492463112162/pdf/114375-REVISED-4-18-PMWB-AfricasPulse-Sping2017-vol15-ENGLISH-FINAL-web.pdf> accessed 29 June 2020.

and transparency would be encouraged by specific and uniform regional policies targeted at both foreign and domestic MNCs. Therefore, it is suggested that infrastructure development will assist with economic transformation, leading to sustainable social structures.[17]

3.2 Taxes and Development

It has long been accepted that a clearly defined and sustainable revenue stream is indispensable for a government to meet its responsibilities towards its citizens. To achieve this, attention must be paid to establishing an effective tax system backed by law; this plays a fundamental role in the development of national economies. Certainty and sustainability in revenue generation is essential because they foster economic growth, and, as such, governments should pursue the objective to find avenues through which they can generate revenue. A tax system offers itself as one of the most effective means of mobilizing a nation's internal resources and it lends itself to creating an environment of economic growth.[18] Ideally, the optimal tax system for all economies will be one that raises essential revenue to counter the excessive government borrowing that is persistent in developing and less-developed African states.[19] This should be achieved either without discouraging economic activity or without deviating too much from the tax systems in other countries.[20] According to Moore, the formation of accountability and the effectiveness of states are closely linked with tax systems.[21] Taxes underwrite the capacity of states to achieve their goals. Without the ability to generate revenue, states are limited as to what extent they can provide social structures for their population and, in particular, foster economic development.

The importance of the tax system to individuals and to society at large cannot be undermined as it benefits both a government and its populace. As such, a poor

[17] I Mayaki, 'Why Infrastructure Development in Africa Matters' (UN Africa Renewal, July 2014) available at <https://www.un.org/africarenewal/web-features/why-infrastructure-development-africa-matters> accessed 2 July 2020.

[18] AJ Ayuba, 'Impact of non-oil tax revenue on economic growth: the Nigerian perspective' (2014) 3(5) International Journal of Finance and Accounting 303–9.

[19] V Tanzi and H Zee, 'Tax Policy for Developing Countries' (IMF, 2001) available at <http://www.imf.org/external/pubs/ft/issues/issues27/> accessed 20 March 2020. See also R Dom and M Miller, 'Reforming tax systems in the developing world. What can we learn from the past?' (Overseas Development Institute, June 2018) available at https://www.odi.org/sites/odi.org.uk/files/resource-documents/12280.pdf > accessed 4 July 2020; M Keen and J Slemrod, 'Optimal tax administration' (2017) 152 Journal of Public Economics 133–42.

[20] ibid.

[21] M Moore, 'How Does Taxation Affect the Quality of Governance?' (IDS Working Paper 280, April 2007) available at <https://opendocs.ids.ac.uk/opendocs/handle/20.500.12413/4044> accessed 4 July 2020.

system will disadvantage individuals and discourage business, which, unsurprisingly, negatively impacts both government and populace. The effects of economic challenges have brought about considerable competition between both developed and developing economies to attract foreign investment, and the use of tax laws and tax systems has become a significant player in this struggle. Revenue generation for governments, especially since the financial crises in the 1980s and the oil price crash, has become paramount, more so for countries who rely heavily on revenue from oil. Furthermore, the oil price plunge from the mid-2014 to the early 2016 had long-lasting effects on economic activity in oil-exporting states, which led to a decline in growth and development.[22] Many of Africa's oil-producing and oil-exporting states, which rely heavily on hydrocarbon revenues, undertook severe fiscal consolidation in order to realign spending with revenues despite rising economic slack and diminishing long-term growth prospects.[23] The population of affected AU Member States felt the impact of this in currency depreciation and rising inflation, which led to loss of income and the inability to provide the basic needs of their populations. Thus, the use of taxation and tax structures is fundamental because until a better idea emerges, taxation remains the most sustainable means of raising revenue to finance government spending.[24]

In exploring the relationship between taxation and economic growth, Kuznets defines economic growth as a 'long-term rise in capacity by a government to supply increasingly diverse economic goods to its population'.[25] Considering that a state's ability to increase the supply of products and services does not portray growth, if sustainable economic growth and development occur, the majority of the population should be able to provide certain amenities for themselves. In this case, the government will only have to cater for a certain or reduced number of its population especially those who cannot afford to provide these amenities for themselves. Thus, the government will not be heavily burdened and will be left to provide the necessary basic social structures.[26] Governments should be determined to create and maintain avenues through which they can reasonably expect an optimal rate of economic growth. Consequently, they structure economic growth programmes in the form of policies and legislation that are geared towards raising the standard of living for their population through the improvement of economic and social

[22] World Bank, 'With the Benefit of Hindsight: The Impact of the 2014–16 Oil Price Collapse' (Special Focus, 2018) available at <http://pubdocs.worldbank.org/en/910311512412250749/Global-Economic-Prospects-Jan-2018-Topical-Issue-oil-price-collapse.pdf> accessed 4 July 2020.

[23] ibid 59. With increased need for funding, Nigeria, Angola, and Algeria, among others, sought to diversify their revenue sources by increasing taxation on businesses.

[24] ibid 24.

[25] S Kuznets, 'Economic Growth and Income Inequality' (1955) 1 American Economic Review 45.

[26] These include roads, water, schools, health facilities protection, and most of the others listed as part of Agenda 2063.

conditions. Chigbu maintains that for both developed and developing countries, taxes play a vital role in their economic history. He explains that taxation creates fiscal goals that influence the direction of investment while at the same time taming the production of certain goods and services.[27] Furthermore, taxes are imposed to regulate the production of certain goods and services, to protect small businesses, to control business and commerce, to curb inflation, and to reduce income inequalities.[28] All these result in economic growth. However, this does not represent the reality of tax systems in the African context. The AU has recently launched the operation of the African Continental Free Trade Area (AfCFTA) with the aim to accelerate intra-continent trade to boost investment. Consequently, this could also be an opportunity for tax harmonization amongst Member States.

To use tax revenue successfully as a means by which to create social structures in Africa, Member States of RECs will need to harmonize their tax policies and laws. Legislation and policy instruments that regulate taxation are an important factor in the relationship between taxes and economic growth and can create effective social structures. Essentially, these instruments form the guide that foreign investors use within the business environment of the country in which they seek to invest. Finally, the effects of tax on economic growth and development are varied and are largely positive, which can be evidenced in different ways. First, there is a positive financial impact. Considering tax as one of the indicators for the location of foreign direct investment (FDI), an effective and predictable tax system provides a fiscal platform that encourages FDI whilst promoting regional and international trade as well as healthy competition amongst states. With such a tax system, investors will bring in capital and technology; subsequently, this will simultaneously create social structures and employment, all of which will improve the economy. Secondly, taxes also promote an equitable relationship between developed and developing economies to ensure that the latter get a fair allocation of taxing rights in bilateral relations using tax treaties. When this is properly applied, both economies benefit through the quantity and quality of investment, through either tax receipts, or information technology transfers and infrastructure investment. Without a functioning tax regime, the governments' ability to achieve and enhance sustainable development goals is limited. For developing economies, a well-structured and corruption-free tax regime eases the burden of the constant need for borrowing funds to fund economic activities.

[27] EE Chigbu, LE Akujuobi, and others, 'An empirical study on the causality between economic growth and taxation in Nigeria' (2012) 4(2) Current Research Journal of Economic Theory 29.

[28] For more detailed reading and empirical literature on the effects of tax on economic growth, see E Ferede and B Dahlby, 'The impact of tax cuts on economic growth: evidence from the Canadian provinces' (2012) 65 National Tax Journal 563; K Mertens and M Ravn, 'The dynamic effects of personal and corporate income tax changes in the United States' (2012) 103 American Economic Review 1212; J Arnold, B Brys, and others, 'Tax policy for economic recovery and growth' (2011) 121 Economic Journal 59; N Gemmell, R Kneller, and others, 'The timing and persistence of fiscal policy impacts on growth: evidence from OECD countries' (2011) 121(550) The Economic Journal, F33–F58; L Young and R Gordon, 'Tax structure and economic growth' (2005) 89 Journal of Public Economics 1027.

3.3 Challenges of Achieving Social Structures in Africa

The challenge of establishing sustainable social structures in Africa hinges on lack of sustainable flows of revenue. It has been argued that this is because of corruption, illicit financial flows, and, above all, tax evasion. Anderson states that lost revenue from tax evasion is damaging to African states:

> 'In total, the continent lost about $850 bn between 1970 and 2008.[29] An estimated $217.7 bn was illegally transferred out of Nigeria over that period, while Egypt lost $105.2 bn and South Africa more than $81.8 bn.'[30]

This revenue had the potential to make significant changes over time for some of the states and has now been lost due to lack of tax compliance by MNCs. This lack of compliance and its substantial impact on Africa has allowed for a new umbrella term to arise. This gathers the large-scale of tax evasion into a definitive term, thus creating a more consistent and reliable view on what are now regarded as illicit financial flows (IFFs). In Africa, tax avoidance and evasion, in addition to IFFs, have seen the developing and emerging economies of the continent losing more than $50 billion every year.[31] This is due to illicit financial outflows as MNCs engage in fraudulent schemes aimed at avoiding tax payments,[32] thereby causing a significant drain on government resources across the continent.[33] The World Bank has set out an early definition of this label:

> 'In the international development community, the concept of IFFs is emerging as a powerful and constructive umbrella to bring together previously disconnected issues'.[34]

Although IFFs were initially associated with capital flight, they now generally refer to cross-border movement of capital associated with illegal activity. More explicitly, this is illegally earned money that is transferred or used across borders. IFFs are grouped into the acts which are in themselves illegal (e.g. corruption, tax evasion); funds from illegal acts (e.g. smuggling and trafficking in minerals, wildlife,

[29] SA Igbatayo, 'Combating illicit financial flows from Africa's extractive industries and implications for good governance: a multi-country study of Angola, the Democratic Republic of Congo and Nigeria' (2019) 44(3) Africa Development / Afrique Et Développemen 55–86 available at <http://www.jstor.org/stable/26873436> accessed 5 July 2020.

[30] C Abugre, A Cobham, and others, 'Vulnerability and exposure to illicit financial flows risk in Africa' (*Tax Justice Network*, 20 August 2019) available at <https://www.taxjustice.net/2019/08/20/vulnerability-and-exposure-to-illicit-financial-flows-risk-in-africa/> accessed 3 October 2020..

[31] ibid.

[32] ibid.

[33] ibid.

[34] P Reuter, 'Illicit Financial Flows and Governance – The Importance Of Disaggregation' (World Bank Report, 2017).

drugs, and people); or funds used for illegal purposes (e.g. financing of organized crime).

Considering the impact of this problem in Africa, the AU has called for reforms to be made in the international tax system amongst others which now enables IFFs from Africa to tax havens or offshore accounts.[35] The AU Commission lists remedies that are likely to deter IFFs, amongst which are legal reforms covering taxation, banking and capital markets, and tax harmonization.[36]

Additionally, there are challenges concerning the sheer size of Africa and the amount of work that must be implemented in order to achieve tax harmonization. Africa as a continent is home to a vast number of people indicating a workforce and market with should create a strong economy, thus making their economic status an issue that relates to social developments. Considering Africa's size and its dire financial situation and the various challenges which include providing social amenities for its people. This is even more so as the AU is not supranational in nature and hence cannot superimpose laws and directives to solve developmental issues. It should be noted, however, that policies adopted by the Assembly are binding and sanctions may be imposed on defaulting Member States.[37] In line with Model Laws already adopted, the AU Commission could negotiate a model law on taxation. Model laws include the Model Law on Access to Information for Africa, which was adopted in February 2013 by the African Commission on Human and Peoples' Rights to assist African states in the development and amendment of existing access to information laws.[38] Despite not being binding on Member States, since its publication there has not only been an increase in access to information between Member States but also an increase of participating Member States towards reflecting the normative content of the Model law.[39]

Arguably, the best way forward to achieve integration and harmonization is by having the AU Member States, acting through the different RECs, implement Model Laws on Taxation. Given that most RECs Member States share similar socio-economic problems, it therefore makes sense to agree to a similar approach to implementation. Such regional implementation would require extensive supervision by the AU with the possibility of sanctions for non-conforming Member States. However, the use of sanction is limited by two factors. First, Model Laws are

35 AU, 'Domestic Resource Mobilization: Fighting Against Corruption and Illicit Financial Flows' (African Union Commission, 2019) available at <https://au.int/sites/default/files/documents/37326-doc-k-15353_au_illicit_financial_flows_devv10_electronic.pdf> accessed 3 July 2020.

36 ibid.

37 Article 23(2) of Constitutive Act of the African Union adopted 11 July 2000, OAU Doc. CAB/LEG/23.15 (entered into force 26 May 2001).

38 O Shyllon (ed), *Model Law on Access to Information for Africa and Other Regional Instruments: Soft Law and Human Rights in Africa* (Pretoria University Law Press, 2018). See also the Model Law for the Implementation of the African Union Convention for the Protection of and Assistance to Internally Displaced Persons in Africa (IDP Model Law), approved by the AU Assembly in January 2018 available at <https://www.refworld.org/pdfid/5afc3a494.pdf> accessed 2 July 2020.

39 (n 38).

generally non-binding, which makes it difficult to mandate the membership to implement and enforce them. The AU Constitutive Act does not expressly delineate between binding and non-binding decisions, which makes it difficult to enforce or ensure the implementation of the Model Law on Taxation. Secondly, only the violation of legally binding instruments or decisions can warrant AU intervention to impose sanctions or punitive measures on Member States. This is supported by Article 23 of the Draft Protocol between the AU and RECs which permits either the Assembly or Executive Council to impose sanctions on defaulting Member States. This applies in cases where the measures and programmes pursued by the RECs are deemed incompatible with the AU treaties and plans.[40] However, if the AEC can be viewed or recognized as having features of a supranational organization like the EU,[41] the Model Laws can then, perhaps, have a legal binding status to achieve its objectives.

4. Regional Integration and Tax Harmonization

4.1 Sub-regional Integration in Africa

Integration and regionalism in Africa have gone through various stages depending on the prevailing socio-economic and ideological conditions both at domestic and international level.[42] Various efforts have been made towards building regionalism in West Africa, especially within the context of the neoliberal economic paradigm in which the removal of barriers to market access and the creation of social and economic development have been the driving force.[43] Despite some successes, the effectiveness of ECOWAS has been hampered by both domestic and external factors. In 1991, the OAU Assembly through the Lagos Plan of Action adopted regional integration as an overarching continental development strategy; it led to the signing of the African Economic Community (AEC) Treaty.[44] Amongst the AEC several objectives is the goal for integration, through the harmonization of

[40] ISS Africa Report, 'Defining AU–REC relations is still a work in progress' available at <https://issafrica.org/pscreport/psc-insights/defining-aurec-relations-is-still-a-work-in-progress> accessed 2 July 2020.

[41] KD Magliveras and GJ Naldi, *The African Union: History, Institutions, and Activities* (Kluwer Law International, 2018) 394.

[42] SO Oloruntoba, ECOWAS and Regional Integration in West Africa: From State to Emerging Private Authority (History Compass Wiley Online, 2016) available at <https://doi.org/10.1111/hic3.12317> accessed 5 July 2020.

[43] ibid 3.

[44] Treaty Establishing the African Economic Community 12 May 1994 available at <https://au.int/en/treaties/treaty-establishing-african-economic-community> accessed 15 July 2020. See also OAU, Lagos Plan of Action for the Economic Development of Africa 1980–2000 (International government publication, 2nd ed, Athlone Pr, 1982).

KP Apuuli, 'The African Union and Regional Integration in Africa' in DH Levine and D Nagar (eds), *Region-Building in Africa* (Palgrave Macmillan, 2016) 143–56.

sectoral policies.[45] The foundation of this objective centres on having harmonized policies in place which would generate a common ground where the rules of the game for the stakeholders are both evident and predictable. Common policies and expanded cooperation allow for economies to reap the full benefit of regional integration, therefore resulting enabling sustainable economic development. The AEC Treaty has been described as a framework treaty setting down general policies with much of the detail to be provided in subsequent protocols,[46] thereby setting a foundation for the relationship between the AU and RECs.

Through RECs, the AU has sought to bring about integration and development.[47] Regional integration creates unique opportunities to bring about transformation and development by communities working together irrespective of cultural or traditional differences and enmities. The goal is to bring development and unity to a region, especially for countries torn apart by a history of colonialization and war. The expectation is that through integration and by Member States supporting each other, especially by removing trade barriers and other constraints, transformation of social structures will be achieved. However, as recognized in the African Regional Integration Report, RECs presently face challenges including underfunding, overlapping memberships, weak implementation of key regional integration programmes and projects, as well as insecurity and infrastructure bottlenecks, all of which deter deeper integration.[48] Importantly, the Report recognized the ever-important need to devise innovative mechanisms for funding of RECs. This may be achieved through revenue generated from corporate taxation and levies on inter-REC transactions.

Furthermore, a coordination meeting between the AU and RECs held in 2019 highlighted the need to streamline and strengthen the work of the RECs as an important measure for realizing the objectives the AEC and AU in general.[49] Evidently, the AU understands the need for RECs to drive this agenda as they are better situated to understand the needs and aspirations of African states in their regions. This confirms the chapter's argument of using RECs to drive and actualize AU law. However, as will be discussed shortly, there are several challenges that deter or affect a successful integration plan within the regions, no matter the dedication and effort put into it.

[45] Article 4(c) and (d) Treaty Establishing the African Economic Community 12 May 1994 available at <https://au.int/en/treaties/treaty-establishing-african-economic-community> accessed 15 July 2020.

[46] See KD Magliveras, and GJ Naldi, 'The African Union: History, Institutions, and Activities' in J Wouters (ed), *International Encyclopaedia of Laws: Intergovernmental Organizations* (Kluwer Law International, 2018) 394..

[47] ibid.

[48] AU Commission, '2019 African Regional Integration Report: Towards an integrated and prosperous and peaceful Africa' available at <https://au.int/sites/default/files/documents/38176-doc-african_integration_report-eng_final.pdf> accessed 3 July 2020.

[49] ibid.

4.2 Actualizing Regional Integration in West Africa through Tax Harmonization

West Africa has two regional economic institutions, ECOWAS and the West African Economic and Monetary Union (WAEMU), both of which have been involved in coordination and harmonization of tax rates and tax policy. WAEMU has a long history in these areas.[50] It was established in 1994 by the WAEMU treaty signed in Dakar[51] which aimed at promoting economic integration amongst a group of states sharing the same currency; initially it was pegged to the French franc (the so-called CFA Franc), but in 2019 WAEMU and France unanimously changed it to the Eco.[52] Article 4 of the 1994 Treaty can be interpreted to call for the harmonization of Member States' tax legislation to the extent that it refers to economic and financial activities to support its goals in the areas of economic integration and harmonization, thus achieving Member States' growth.[53] On the other hand, ECOWAS, in which all eight WAEMU Member States participate together with the English-speaking countries of the region, has had less of a history of tax coordination and harmonization and does not explicitly mention this in its founding Treaty.[54] Since its formation in 1975 as a 15-member regional group, ECOWAS has been shaping the evolution of regional integration in West Africa. With the mandate to promote economic integration in all fields of activity, amongst its achievements include better crisis prevention and management and financial and macroeconomic integration to free movement of people.[55] A basis for its establishment was to foster the ideal of collective self-sufficiency for Member States. As a trading union, it is also meant to create a single, large trading bloc through economic cooperation. Integrated economic activities in ECOWAS revolve around, but are not limited to,

[50] UK Department for International Development, E-J Quak, 'Tax Coordination and Tax Harmonisation within the Regional Economic Communities in Africa' (K4D Helpdesk Report, 2018) available at <https://assets.publishing.service.gov.uk/media/5b18f76c40f0b634cfb505ce/Tax_Coordination_within_Regional_Economic_Communities_Africa.pdf> accessed 7 July 2020. WEAMU Member States share a single currency, form a customs union, and have had extensive tax coordination and tax harmonization experience.

[51] The Treaty was signed on 10 January 1994 and entered into force on 1 August 1994. In May 1997, Guinea Bissau joined it as the eighth Member State.

[52] K Georgieva, 'Statement by the IMF Managing Director on the Reform of West Africa's CFA Franc' (IMF website, 21 December 2019) available at <https://www.imf.org/en/News/Articles/2019/12/21/pr19487-md-statement-on-the-reform-of-west-africa-cfa-franc> accessed 2 July 2020.

[53] It reads: 'Without prejudice to the objectives defined in the WAEMU Treaty, the Union shall, in conditions established by this Treaty, the achievement of the following objectives: (a) enhancing the competitiveness of the economic and financial activities of the Member States in an open and competitive market and a legal environment streamlined and harmonized'.

[54] WAEMU, 'The Amended Treaty of the West African Economic and Monetary Union' available at <http://www.uemoa.int/en/amended-treaty> accessed 7 July 2020.

[55] ECOWAS available at <https://www.ecowas.int/about-ecowas/basic-information/> accessed 27 June 2020. See also Preamble of the Revised Treaty of the Economic Community of West African States available at <https://www.ecowas.int/wp-content/uploads/2015/01/Revised-treaty.pdf> accessed 27 June 2020.

industry, transport, telecommunications, energy, agriculture, natural resources, commerce, monetary and financial issues, as well as social issues.[56]

Tax harmonization in ECOWAS can be categorized under uniform standardization in different Member States, mainly where there are comparable taxes on similar tax handles or burdens. The idea is to remove barriers to the free movement of goods and ensure compatibility by adjusting the tax structure or the rate of taxes. Likewise, Member States agree on certain taxes or structures in many instances for economic integration and coordination.[57] Tax cooperation is used when a group of states is endogenously determined and is based on situations where only some countries cooperate on tax policy and issues.[58] According to Kouba, coordination is a process where participating States maintain more control of their laws and policies, whilst harmonization leads to a full unification or centralization of their policies.[59] The harmonization process could be initiated at the request of a Member State or by the ECOWAS Council of Ministers.[60] It needs to be clearly stated the Treaty will act as the legal basis for enforcing the harmonization process, despite the fact that this request is not explicit in the Treaty. The harmonization of a sector in a specific area must go through a legislative process with various stages, each estimated by the ECOWAS Commission to last between four to five years. First, the Commission undertakes a detailed study of the targeted sector. Then, a draft harmonized regulation is presented during a meeting of experts from government ministries as well as representatives from the private sector and the civil society.[61]

With a view to stimulate the lengthy harmonization process, ECOWAS has adopted a new regime for Community acts which allows acceleration of the legal texts' entry into force. Its legal framework encompasses supplementary acts, protocols, regulations, directives, decisions, recommendations, and opinions. At the highest level stands the ECOWAS Treaty which can be complemented by supplementary acts. Equally important are protocols, namely instruments implementing the Treaty and having the same legal status, which are binding on both the Member States and its organs. Therefore, each Member State is obliged to carry out the

[56] ES Nwauche, 'Enforcing ECOWAS law in West African national courts' (2011) 55(2) Journal of African Law 181–202; MA Yusuf, 'ECOWAS agenda and regional integration development in West Africa: any role for all-inclusive education?' (2019) 10(1) International Journal of Education Economics and Development 76–93; J Ogbuabor, OA Orji, and others, 'Regional integration and growth: New empirical evidence from WAEMU' (2019) 19(2) Progress in Development Studies 123–43; S Ouedraogo and D Drabo, 'Dynamics of integration and economic growth of the West African Economic and Monetary Union (WAEMU)' (2019) 10 Modern Economy, 10, 1121–33.

[57] S Ouedraogo and D Drabo, 'Dynamics of integration and economic growth of the West African Economic and Monetary Union (WAEMU)' (2019) 10 Modern Economy, 10, 1121–33.

[58] M Mansour and G Rota-Graziosi, 'Tax Coordination, Tax Competition and Revenue Mobilization in the West African Economic and Monetary Union' (IMF Working Paper WP/13/163, July 2013).

[59] L Kouba, M Mádr, and others, 'Policy autonomy, coordination or harmonization in the persistently heterogeneous European Union' (2016) 7 Law and Economics Review 57.

[60] ibid.

[61] ibid 4.

functions prescribed therein and to introduce or bring the necessary changes to its domestic legislation.

Bringing this to the African context, when RECs harmonize the tax policies of their Member States it presents them as a reckoning force for trade and investment. This signals to the international community the readiness of RECs for business by creating a safe and transparent business environment. This is exemplified through the AfCFTA, which aims at bolstering trade cooperation at a continental level.[62] Africa has been recipient of FDI by both Western and Asian economies, including France, the Netherlands, the United States, China, India, and the United Kingdom.[63]

At the time of writing, there is no continental or model taxation law for African states to adhere to, but states have their own domestic tax laws. However, the need for trade and investment has seen harmonization of taxes amongst Member States through regional integration.

WAEMU has moved further in terms of direct taxation such as corporate tax, unlike ECOWAS which has concentrated on indirect taxation.[64] It can be argued that ECOWAS Member States have a protectionist attitude towards their control of direct taxation especially with regards to corporate tax, which is driven by the need to promote national interests and revenue. Most developing countries in Africa depend heavily on revenue from corporate tax and therefore would like to control setting tax rates and perhaps granting incentives and tax credits to MNCs. For instance, Nigeria runs a tax regime where tax incentives such as tax credits, reduced tax rates, and tax holidays appear to favour MNCs more than domestic corporations, thereby creating an imbalance in the system.[65] The harmonization of tax policies especially on corporate tax will eliminate a lot of the issues that arise with national tax policies.

WAEMU has adopted directives on tax coordination and harmonization,[66] but the same cannot be said for ECOWAS. However, it is recognized that ECOWAS

[62] AU Commission, 'General Objectives of the Agreement Establishing the African Continental Free Trade Agreement' (AfCFTA, 2018) available at <https://www.tralac.org/documents/resources/african-union/2162-afcfta-agreement-legally-scrubbed-version-signed-16-may-2018/file.html> accessed 7 July 2020.

[63] UN Conference on Trade and Development, 'Foreign direct investment to Africa defies global slump, rises 11%' (UNCTAD, 12 June 2019) available at <https://unctad.org/en/pages/newsdetails.aspx?OriginalVersionID=2109> accessed 7 July 2020.

[64] WAEMU covers corporate income tax coordination (CIT): Directive 01/2008/CM/UEMOA (adopted 28 March 2008) defines a common corporate tax base; and Directive 08/2008/CM/UEMOA (adopted September 2008) specifies the range for a single rate between 25% and 30%. The harmonization of tax rates and tax base have been implemented in all Member States.

[65] M Ndajiwo, 'Are tax incentives in Nigeria attracting investment or giving away revenue?' (*Tax Justice Network*, 14 August 2018) available at <https://www.taxjustice.net/2018/08/14/are-tax-incentives-in-nigeria-attracting-investment-or-giving-away-revenue/> accessed 30 June 2020.

[66] M Diakite, J-F Brun, and others, 'The effects of tax coordination on the tax revenue mobilization in West African Economic and Monetary Union (WAEMU)', Études et Documents, No 12, 2017 Centre d'Études et de Recherches sur le Développement International available at <http://cerdi.org/production/show/id/1881/type_production_id/1> accessed 30 June 2020.

Member States have adopted the Common External Tariff (CET) with the goal of achieving economic integration.[67] The idea is to set the same customs duties, import quotas, preferences, and other non-tariff barriers to trade applicable to all goods entering the territory of the group, regardless of which state within the group they are entering.[68] With the advent of AfCFTA, ECOWAS Member States are considering possible reviews which should rightly reflect the ideas and measures of the AfCFTA.[69] As mentioned previously, this begs the question regarding whether it is time for ECOWAS to take on WAEMU's tax directives, which will potentially ease crossovers of the AfCFTA and directives of both bodies. The argument for this could be that ECOWAS is the more dominant REC and may have the legal basis backed by its founding Treaty and authority to achieve integration and harmonization. On the other hand, WAEMU might be more successful considering that Member States share the same currency and language thus leading to having a sense of kinship compared to ECOWAS.

Ultimately, in order to achieve integration there must be an underlying need for a successful achievement of both the AU and RECs agendas at the heart of Member States.

4.4 Challenges towards Harmonization

Despite a successful integration process, tax harmonization in any part of the world comes with certain challenges. Harmonization puts a spotlight on challenging political economy issues. This includes the lack of commitment by Member States to coordinate their tax policies effectively. Such challenges are not peculiar to Africa or its regions.[70] Furthermore, tax harmonization reflects the weakness of states' ability in terms of proper infrastructure to build, maintain, and finance the necessary institutions that will coordinate the process. Tax harmonization is viewed by some economists as a strong factor undermining state sovereignty, a betrayal of national interests.[71] Every state guards its sovereignty carefully and in particular, the ability to make its own legislation without external interferences and to maintain all powers over its resources and revenue. Giving up these rights is never easy.

[67] E von Uexkull and L Shui, 'Implementing the ECOWAS Common External Tariff Challenges and Opportunities for Nigeria' (Africa Trade Practice Working Paper Series, June 2014) available at <https://openknowledge.worldbank.org/bitstream/handle/10986/18935/888430REPLACEM0Box385245B00PUBLIC0.pdf?sequence=1&isAllowed=y> accessed 30 June 2020.

[68] ibid.

[69] ECOWAS Website, 'Directors General of Customs in the region hold meeting on Common External Tariff'(22 November 2019) available at <https://www.ecowas.int/directors-general-of-customs-in-the-region-hold-meeting-on-common-external-tariff/> accessed 30 June 2020.

[70] ibid (n 40).

[71] A Podveizko, L Parfenova, and others, 'Tax competitiveness of the new EU Member States' (2019) 12(1) Journal of Risk Financial Management 34.

This is considering that taxation is among the few areas where states still enjoy an absolute right of regulation especially as direct taxes are more easily utilized for economic integration as they are paid directly by the individual or taxable entity to the state coffers.[72] Hence, surrendering the right to set tax rates and polices or even tax incentives will be very difficult for ECOWAS Member States. Tax policy transformation has remained limited in most African countries because there continues to be a common setback with domestic legislation and policy-making processes towards harmonization.

Fundamentally therefore, this chapter posits that WAEMU's success with its harmonization agenda could lie in the sharing this demography in language and perhaps the previous colonial government with which they may still be existing relationships. Despite their independence, WAEMU Member States still have strong ties with France. This is not the same for ECOWAS, but despite the fact that some of the Member States do not share the same colonial antecedents, this should not deter harmonization or integration. A paramount challenge lies with the state governments' political will to improve tax policies, especially as it is governments which are ultimately responsible for transforming tax policies by creating a conducive environment and by addressing inherent governance challenges. Furthermore, the instability of the current political regimes in Africa has continually affected the continuation of policies and this persistent outcome certainly has diverse implications for reform in different contexts, especially in the future.

4.5 Beyond Social Structures to Funding the AU

As identified, the chapter's argument is for sustainable social structures and development. However, the chapter submits that revenue generated by the RECs through tax harmonization can also be used to fund the AU itself. Presently, the AU relies on the annual contributions from its 55 Member States and funding from outside Africa, including foreign donor aid.[73] These contributions are calculated based on a triennial assessment and are meant to be paid in advance at the start of each budget year (it runs from 1 January to 31 December). Currently, there have been significant difficulties in funding the AU and this has created a dire need for more reliance on funding from beyond Africa. Therefore, in a bid to tackle excessive dependence on external funding, the AU Assembly has aimed at having

72 ibid.

73 K Pharatlhatlhe and J Vanheukelom, 'Financing the African Union on mindsets and money', Discussion Paper No 240, Political Economy Dynamics of Regional Organisations in Africa (European Centre for Development Policy Management, 2019) available at <https://ecdpm.org/wp-content/uploads/DP240-Financing-the-African-Union-on-mindsets-and-money.pdf> accessed 22 June 2020.

Member States contributing more in order to cover a larger part of its operational budget.[74]

For instance, the President of Rwanda, Paul Kagame has argued that achieving this is means more than simply having the funding; rather it is about Member States having the right mindset whereby the states will be committed to developing the AU for themselves and by themselves.[75] This Decision argued for internal and sustainable financing of the Union with a lesser reliance on external funding.[76] This was accompanied by recommendations, *inter alia*, to implement the Kigali Financing Decision to ensure the AU's financial sustainability and to develop and set a number of rules setting out clear financial management and accountability targets, embedded within AU law.[77]

The underling agenda is one where an improvement in the AU's financial systems as well as harmonization within the continent, the policy agenda may become more prioritised. In this way, there will be less dependence on foreign donors. Thus, supporting the argument for a sustainable source of revenue as proffered in this chapter.

5. Conclusion

The welfare of the present and future African generations is a central concern of the AU and RECs. This is the opportunity to establish the utilization of African Union Law on taxation which will solidify the notion that integration and harmonization can only be backed by the authority of law. This way, the AU law on taxation has social sustainability via the vehicle of public purpose as its central concern. By consolidating the taxation policies of RECs where possible and by building on the success of RECs such as WAEMU, a Model Law on Taxation for the AU can be created and thus will set a foundation to achieve not only the goals of Agenda 2063 but also to finance the AU itself. The Model Taxation Law should act as a vehicle to solidify the integration agenda and set the continent towards a path of sustainable growth and development. This will be achieved by drawing from the success and failure of adopted and existing Model Laws as mentioned earlier. However, there are challenges which will threaten the success of such a law, despite ongoing integration

[74] The African Union, Decision on the Outcome of the Retreat of the Assembly of the African Union, Assembly/AU/Dec.605 (XXVII) adopted July 2016 available at <https://au.int/sites/default/files/pages/31953-file-assembly_au_dec_605_financing_the_au.pdf> accessed 27 June 2020.

[75] K Pharatlhatlhe and J Vanheukelom, 'Financing the African Union. On mindsets and money' PEDRO Discussion Paper No 240 (Maastricht 2019) available at <https://ecdpm.org/wp-content/uploads/DP240-Financing-the-African-Union-on-mindsets-and-money.pdf> accessed 31 June 2020.

[76] P Kagame, 'The Imperative to Strengthen our Union Report on the Proposed Recommendations for the Institutional Reform of the African Union' January 2017 available at <https://www.tralac.org/images/docs/11191/report-on-the-proposed-recommendations-for-the-institutional-reform-of-the-au-kagame-29-january-2017.pdf> accessed 27 June 2020.

[77] ibid.

process. Where tax harmonization is not possible, the AU, through its own institutions and through RECs, can influence Member States to adopt social sustainability as a goal in designing their tax system. It should be noted that mind that tax harmonization is not in itself the goal but rather a means towards creating social infrastructure several areas, including health, education, and transportation. The goal is towards the amelioration of living conditions and higher living standards, and of course towards achieving eventually the goals of Agenda 2063.

Additionally, the chapter has provided some policy recommendations. First, the AU, in strengthening its coordination with RECs, should consider prioritizing the development of an AU law on taxation which will, *inter alia*, achieve the aims of the draft protocol which importantly will impose sanctions on non-compliance. This law will be coordinated between the Assembly and RECs and will be uniform to all RECs but have some flexibility for each REC or region, taking into consideration their different societal and economic needs.

Finally, revenue generated from tax proceeds as a result of the AU will be the vehicle towards achieving one of the AU's most pressing needs, the need for adequate and sustainable funding to ensure its own survival by being financed by the Member States themselves. This is essential towards reducing the dependence on foreign funding, thereby solving Africa's problems by African means.

15

Land, Property, and Human Rights in AU Law and Policy

Robert Home

1. Introduction

Nation states possess two essential attributes: sovereignty over territory and sovereignty over its citizens. This implies both duties and responsibilities, including the laws governing social relations in land and those guaranteeing human rights. While historically international law mostly concerned state sovereignty over territory, human rights law since the 1948 Universal Declaration of Human Rights has advanced the rights of citizens and groups within states and may challenge existing national legal orders. Human rights law has expanded from civil and political rights into wider social and economic rights but has been less concerned with land, except as immovable property. This chapter explores the relationship of land to human rights, relating to property, natural resources, and development, and the changing policy and juridical environment, both within the AU and the wider development community.[1] The human rights jurisprudence of the AU is relatively young (since 1986), and operates in a rapidly evolving international environment of institutional structures and legal instruments. Recent theoretical development in critical legal geography has widened the traditional model of property as absolute, exclusive and private ownership, into relational approaches that include 'non-owner', especially collective or communal, interests, and challenge the idea of landed property as a tradable commodity.[2] This chapter draws from theories of historic institutionalism and actor network theory to distinguish between the different institutional and political structures involved, each with distinct origins, aims, and path dependencies.[3] It then examines the AU case law relating to land and property, with particular attention to Indigenous peoples' rights, and

[1] D Shelton (ed) *Commitment and Compliance: The Role of Non-binding Norms in the International Legal System* (OUP, 2000); AE Boyle, 'Soft Law in International Law Making' in M Evans (ed) *International Law* (OUP, 2010) 122–40.

[2] N Graham, *Lawscape: Property, Environment, Law* (Routledge-Cavendish, 2010); E van Wagner 'Seeing the place makes it real' (2017) 34 *Environmental and Planning Law Journal* 522.

[3] J Mahoney and K Thelen (eds), *Explaining Institutional Change: Agency, Ambiguity and Power* (CUP, 2010); A Sorensen, 'Taking path dependence seriously: a historical institutionalist research agenda in planning history' (2014) 30(1) Planning Perspectives 1–22.

Robert Home, *Land, Property, and Human Rights in AU Law and Policy* In: *The Emergent African Union Law.* Edited by: Olufemi Amao, Michèle Olivier and Konstantinos D. Magliveras, Oxford University Press.
DOI: 10.1093/oso/9780198862154.003.0016

discusses problems of implementation and enforcement of such judgments at nation state level.

2. Land and Human Rights Law in Africa

2.1 Land and Property

The word 'land' does not appear in the African Charter on Human and People's Rights (the Banjul Charter), yet, in the years since the Charter was adopted in 1981, land has come to assume greater importance in international soft law and development policy. Africa's development prospects depend upon how its states accommodate rapid population growth and climate change, and conflicts over land and natural resources manifest themselves in wars and displacement of people from their land in growing numbers.[4] Arguably, the question which should be put but is not asked is whether there is a right to land and how it ties up to the right to property

The right to property is regarded as a fundamental right in democratic societies, reflected in such international instruments as the First Protocol of the European Convention for the Protection of Human Rights and Fundamental Freedoms, and in national constitutions.[5] The Banjul Charter (Article 14) states:

> The right to property shall be guaranteed. It may only be encroached upon in the interest of public need or in the general interest of the community and in accordance with the provisions of appropriate laws.

Thus, this right can be overturned in national legislation. English common law identifies real or immovable property as land which belongs to some person, and all structures integrated with or affixed to the land. Hernando de Soto argued that a framework of secure, transparent, and enforceable property rights is a critical precondition for poverty reduction and economic growth.[6] States have the right to control the use of property in accordance with the public or general interest, usually under planning laws and regulations, but there remains scope for dispute over who should have property rights protected (human beings, communities,

[4] B Derman, R Odgaard, and others (eds), *Conflicts over Land and Water in Africa* (James Currey, 2007); S Evers, M Spierenberg, and others (eds), *Competing Jurisdictions: Settling Land Claims in Africa* (Brill, 2007). Habitat, *Forced Evictions: Towards Solutions?* (2007) available at <http://hlrn.org/img/violation/Forced%20Evictions%20Towards%20Solutions%202005.pdf> accessed 12 October 20; Habitat, *Scoping and Status Study on Land and Conflict* available at <https://unhabitat.org/scoping-and-status-study-on-land-and-conflict-english-2016> accessed 12 October 2020.

[5] T Allen, *The Right to Property in Commonwealth Jurisdictions* (CUP, 2000).

[6] H de Soto, *The Mystery of Capital* (Black Swan, 2000); R Home and H Lim, *Demystifying the Mystery of Capital* (Cavendish, 2004).

corporations, or other legal entities, and even *biota*), and the reasons for which property rights can be restricted in the public interest. Who can be registered title bearers varies between different national legal systems.

2.2 Right to Development and Natural Resources

The Banjul Charter was also the first international human rights instrument to recognize a right to development (RTD), in Article 8:

> (1) States should undertake, at the national level, all necessary measures for the realisation of the right to development and shall ensure, inter alia, equality of opportunity for all in their access to basic resources, education, health services, food, housing, employment and the fair distribution of income . . .
> (2) States should encourage popular participation in all spheres as an important factor in development and in the full realisation of all human rights.[7]

The RTD has been described as a composite or collective right, although its legitimacy and justiciability is still debated, and is linked to peoples' rights in the Banjul Charter.[8] The subsequent 1986 UN RTD Declaration is now included within the mandate of several UN institutions and various national constitutions, but again does not mention land specifically. The Preamble to the Banjul Charter defines 'development' as:

> a comprehensive economic, social, cultural and political process, which aims at the constant improvement of the well-being of the entire population and of all individuals on the basis of their active, free and meaningful participation in development and in the fair distribution of benefits resulting therefrom.[9]

Since land is the basic resource upon which any physical act of development takes place, the RTD is necessarily closely related to how land is secured, used, and managed. Indeed, British law on land use planning (transferred and still applied in its former African colonies, which collectively covered more African territory than other European colonial interventions) defines 'development' differently, as 'building, engineering and other operations in, on, over or under land, or the making of any material change in the use of any building or other land'.[10]

[7] Banjul Charter (OAU Doc AB/LEG/67/3, 1981) section 22(2).
[8] R Home, 'Land and the Right to Development in Africa' in CC Ngang, S Kamga, and others (eds), *Perspectives on the Right to Development* (Pretoria University Law Press, 2019).
[9] *Declaration on the Right to Development* (United Nations General Assembly, A/RES/41/128, 1986).
[10] Town and Country Planning Act 1947, section 55 (England and Wales).

The Banjul Charter in Article 21 also guarantees '[a]ll peoples' right to their wealth and natural resource'. The African Convention on Conservation of Nature and Natural Resources, expects states 'to ensure that traditional rights and intellectual property rights of local communities' are protected,[11] and give them equal standing with government representatives in joint management approaches of such common land resources. The relationship between peoples' rights and traditional rights is emerging as a contested area.

2.3 The Urban Connection

While policy on land and natural resources has been largely concerned with food security and agriculture, and thus primarily with rural areas, there is a growing international recognition that the majority of the world's human populations are urban, with the continent of Africa experiencing the most rapid urbanization. The New Urban Agenda (NUA) as agreed at the Habitat III Conference in 2016 is now driving policy agendas alongside Sustainable Development Goal (SDG) 11.[12] The state has responsibility for managing conversion of land to urban uses, in order to lend confidence to investment, economic performance, and wealth creation. Basic and enforceable laws can support sustainable urban development, with development rights, building, and planning codes and standards for street and plot layouts.[13] Urban law change is, however, a slow and complex process which has to be undertaken at national level.

In 2009 the AU adopted a Land Declaration, and subsequently created new institutional structures for its implementation in the form of the African Land Policy Centre, a joint programme of the African Union Commission (AUC), African Development Bank (AfDB), and United Nations Economic Commission for Africa (UNECA).[14] This policy centre has published various reports reflecting the increasing importance of land on the global development agenda.[15] Its Land Policy Guidelines state that they are neither a normative framework intended to be binding upon Member States, nor a draft land policy to be adopted by them, nor instructions for specific country situations. The document does, however, use some remarkably prescriptive language such as '[t]he overwhelming presence of the state

[11] *African Convention on Conservation of Nature and Natural Resources* (Maputo, 2003) Article XVII (1).

[12] New Urban Agenda, *Habitat III* (UN, A/RES/71/256, 2017).

[13] Habitat, *Effectiveness of Planning Law in Sub-Saharan Africa*, available at <https://unhabitat.org/sites/default/files/documents/2019-06/effectiveness_of_planning_law_in_sub_sahara_bookweb-un_habitat.pdf> accessed 12 October 2020.

[14] *Declaration on Land Issues and Challenges in Africa* (AU Assembly/AU/Decl.l (XIII) Rev.I 2009).

[15] *Tracking Progress in Land Policy Formulation And Implementation in Africa* (AUC-ECA-AfDB, Addis Ababa, 2012); *Guiding Principles on Large-Scale Land-Based Investments in Africa* (AUC-ECA-AfDB, Addis Ababa, 2014).

in land matters must change'.[16] While state sovereignty means non-interference in domestic affairs, declarations adopted by AU organs should be treated as part of AU law, even if they are not legally binding. The AU Constitutive Act acknowledges the sovereignty and sovereign equality of its Member States (now 55 in number), who are mostly former colonies of European states, with a great diversity of legal systems, geography, and population, and retained their colonial boundaries under the *uti possedetis* principle. Some 20 of them are small, with populations of fewer than 5 million people, but they all claim the right to decide their own land laws and policies and defend their sovereignty under the Westphalia state model. Human rights instruments devised in an era of decolonization struggle are applicable to successor states inheriting colonial legal machinery, holding them accountable to their own populations, but the AU's deference to state sovereignty allows states effectively to ignore legal judgments and treaty obligations.

Approaches to land reform vary widely between states. Land reform is not only a complex legal challenge but also highly political, especially when it attempts to redress historic inequalities in land ownership. In Africa, the so-called land question usually refers to the exclusion of much of the African population from access to land, whether by a white settler minority, postcolonial elites, or foreign investors. Systems of control and exclusion, often legacies of colonial rule, allow powerful vested interests to maintain extreme inequalities of land ownerships.[17] Elites may prefer an environment of insecure land rights, titling programmes for the poor move slowly, and corruption in the allocation of land advantages those with political connections. The African Union Convention on Preventing and Combating Corruption (2003) is part of AU law but lacks a serious and effective mechanism for holding states accountable. Also, the link between corruption and violation of human rights is not sufficiently emphasized in the Convention, which could be amended to become a protocol to the African Charter on Human and Peoples' Rights.[18]

State regulation of social relationships in land involves a potentially wide and costly array of agencies, professions, and bureaucracies, for which land governance is a convenient overarching term. Their tasks include confirming rights to ownership and use, surveying, and subdividing land, valuing and managing property, handling disputes, and reviewing laws and regulations. State or public lands include defence estates, railways, and other infrastructure, forestry, national and wildlife parks, heritage sites, and environmental protection. Such institutional

16 *Framework and Guidelines on Land Policy in Africa* (AUC, 2010), section 2.1.

17 C Boone, *Property and Political Order in Africa: Land Rights and the Structure of Politics* (CUP, 2014); A Onoma, *The Politics of Property Rights Institutions in Africa* (CUP, 2010). A Manji, 'The grabbed state: lawyers, politics and public land in Kenya' (2012) 50(3) Journal of Modern African Studies 467; P Kantai, 'In the grip of the vampire state: Maasai land struggles in Kenyan politics' (2007) 1 Journal of Eastern African Studies 107.

18 K Olaniyan, 'The African Union Convention on Preventing and Combating Corruption: a critical appraisal' (2004) 4 African Human Rights Law Journal 74.

frameworks are potentially state responsibilities everywhere but may be weak and ineffective in much of Africa because of resource and political constraints.

Applying the *terra nullius* principle the colonial state (the 'colonial masters') could take land it considered vacant and ownerless for its own use (in British colonies designated as 'Crown land', with similar state interventions elsewhere), and then transfer it through grant, sale, or lease to white settlers and private or public bodies (such as mines and railways), overriding pre-existing communal rights. Outside the towns and white settler lands, 'native reserves' or 'tribal trust lands' remained under customary tenure. An evolutionary theory of land rights regarded such tenure as a vestige of the past, in an inevitable historical process that meant a greater concentration of rights in the individual and a corresponding loss of control by the community as a whole.[19] Action by colonial administrations to gazette customary land for some public purpose as forestry or wildlife would have the effect of extinguishing customary tenure.

Some AU Member States have in recent years overridden communal or customary land rights by allowing in the name of development what has been called 'land grabbing' and a second 'scramble for Africa'. Large-scale land-based foreign investments, for biofuel, agriculture, and forestry were often facilitated by a legal provision inherited from colonial times to 'set aside' customary land according to the state's interpretation of the 'public interest', with little or no consultation or compensation. The AU Land Policy Guidelines advocate equal legal status for both customary and 'modern' property rights, but they are often in contestation on the ground. Customary land tenure has also discriminated against women and children by entrenching patriarchal privilege, notwithstanding paper guarantees of women's property rights in African constitutions. While the proportion of female-headed households is growing, property settlements under customary tenure systems often disinherit and impoverish women, for example after divorce or the death of a spouse, and consider them as only 'secondary' holders of property rights.

International policy agendas are changing in the 21st century, with the eight Millennium Development Goals agreed in 2000 for achievement by the 2015, *now* superseded by the 2030, UN Agenda for Sustainable Development, adopted by the UN General Assembly in 2015. This set 17 SDGs with 169 targets and 232 indicators, but with no binding legal force. Five of the 17 goals (1, 2, 5, 11, and 15) refer specifically to land in sustainable development, while indicator 1.4.2 tracks progress in strengthening tenure security. SDG 11 commits to the concept of 'inclusive, safe, resilient and sustainable cities', and UN-Habitat through its GLTN and Urban Legislation Unit is promoting innovative urban planning tools such as land

[19] J-P Platteau, 'The evolutionary theory of land rights as applied to Sub-Saharan Africa: a critical assessment' (1996) 27 Development and Change 29.

readjustment and participatory mapping.[20] Another relevant SDG for law is 16 ('Peace, Justice and Strong Institutions').

The AU adopted its own Agenda 2063 at its 24th Assembly Session in January 2015, before the UN SDGs, as a 'collective vision and roadmap', but also without binding legal force. Relevant to land and the RTD were aspirations for the following:

> People-centred development, gender equality and youth empowerment, which place the African people at the centre of all continental efforts, to ensure their participation in the transformation of the continent,
>
> Opportunities for all Africans to have decent and affordable housing in clean, secure and well planned environments by:
>
> Providing access to affordable and decent housing to all in sustainable human settlements;
>
> Ensuring effective and territorial planning and land tenure, use and management systems;
>
> Ensuring balanced development of all human settlements while embracing a rural urban continuum; and
>
> Improving the livelihoods of the great percentage of the people working and living in slums and informal settlements.[21]

Agenda 2063's first 10-year implementation plan additionally included 7 Aspirations, 20 Goals, 13 Fast-Track Projects, 39 Priority Areas, and 255 targets, creating major resource and capability challenges.

While a healthy scepticism is appropriate for such broad, aspirational documents, they do provide a context for the constantly expanding law and policy of AU institutions in relation to land and the right to development.

3. Land under the Banjul Charter

The AU's legal instrument for human rights is the Banjul Charter, which was originally approved unanimously by its precursor body, the Organisation of African Unity (OAU) in 1981 and came into effect in 1986. It reflected OAU aims to free Africans of colonialism, sought to confirm a distinctive African approach to human rights, and gave more emphasis to economic, social, and cultural rights than other such instruments. 'Peoples' had the right of self-determination, and Article 19 stated that '[n]othing shall justify the domination of a people by another', although 'peoples' were not defined and this domination referred to external

[20] Habitat, *Remaking the Urban Mosaic: Participatory and Inclusive Land Readjustment* (Habitat, 2012).

[21] African Union Commission, *The Africa We Want* (AUC, 2015).

colonial interventions. The Charter laid the foundations for what has been called a new or *sui generis* African human rights legal order, and the AU expanded its provisions through instruments such as the Maputo Protocol on the rights of women, which included economic and social rights (Article 13), the RTD (Article 19), and property inheritance (Article 21).[22] The Kampala Convention (formally, the African Union Convention for the Protection and Assistance of Internally Displaced Persons in Africa), ratified in 2012, is becoming more relevant as the numbers of displaced persons increase year by year.

Justiciability was initially provided by the processes of the African Commission on Human and Peoples' Rights, created in 1986 (and not to be confused with the African Union Commission). Its judgments were only advisory and were often criticized for lack of depth, but it did expand the Charter's jurisprudence in some areas. The African Court of Human and Peoples' Rights was subsequently established to complement the Commission's work and provide a more binding judicial process, although it has encountered difficulties with compliance and enforcement of its judgments.[23]

Another, but short-lived, judicial institution was the Southern African Development Community's own tribunal, which made a highly contentious judgment relating to land. Established on paper in 1992, its members were only sworn in 2005, and it was disbanded in 2012 after its determination that the Zimbabwean government of Robert Mugabe had denied access to the courts for, and discriminated against, white farmers whose lands had been confiscated. This judgment might have followed human rights law on the right to property, but the Zimbabwe government did not comply, challenged the tribunal's legitimacy, and proceeded with further confiscations. When the South African government cleared the way for seized Zimbabwean government assets to be sold by auction to compensate the white farmers, it was probably the first ruling in international legal history that a country's assets should be sold to provide compensation for human rights violations.[24]

Various cases brought before the African Commission and Court relate to land as property. The *Mbiankeu* case confirmed the role of the state as a guarantor of private property title.[25] A Cameroonian citizen with French nationality living in France had bought land in Cameroon with title, but was prevented from building,

[22] Protocol on the rights of women in Africa (CAB/LEG/66.6 (2003)); O Amao, *Union Law: The Emergence of a Sui Generis Legal Order* (Routledge, 2019)

[23] EA Ankumah, *African Commission on Human and Peoples' Rights* (Kluwer, 1996); A Bösl and J Diescho, *Human Rights in Africa. Legal Perspectives on their Protection and Promotion* (Macmillan, 2009); RH Murray, *Human Rights in Africa: From the OAU to the African Union* (CUP, 2004); MD Evans and RH Murray (eds), *The African Charter on Human and Peoples' Rights: The System in Practice 1986–2006* (CUP, 2008)

[24] *Mike Campbell (Pvt) Ltd and others v Republic of Zimbabwe* (SADC Case 2/2007). See also B Chigara, 'The *humwe* principle: a social-ordering *grundnorm* for Zimbabwe and Africa?' in R Home (ed), *Essays in African Land Law* (Pretoria University Law Press, 2011) 113–34.

[25] *Mbiankeu Genevieve v Cameroon Commission*, Comm No 389/10 (2015).

the title certificate annulled, and the land transferred fraudulently to a new owner, with no adequate public interest justification. The Commission determined against the Cameroon government. Since the state was held at fault, financial compensation was awarded corresponding to the market value of the property, including material damages, loss of income, travel and other expenses, deprivation of enjoyment, and use of property, as well as feelings of uncertainty and frustration. The Commission found a violation of the right to property, which included land, a plot, and right to build, and a valid land certificate was regarded as proof of property ownership. As the appellant's intent was to build a family home, the Commission held that the state's action also violated the associated and interdependent right to housing. In The Commission also introduced the principles of peaceful enjoyment of property, and the state's right to control the use of property in accordance with the public or general interest.[26] In another case a right to property was included in finding forced expulsion and dispersal of families as a violation of family rights under Article 18.[27] Even a female judge of the Court had personally experienced loss of her late husband's property, sold off by a relative without her knowledge or consent, and she secured new legislation against the practice in Malawi through the Deceased Estates (Wills, Inheritance and Protection Act) Act 2011.

The Banjul Charter (Articles 19–22) allowed for group or collective rights to a greater extent than other human rights instruments but made no specific mention of Indigenous peoples. Article 19 (that '[n]othing shall justify the domination of a people by another') conferred a right of self-determination, reflecting OAU aims to free Africans of colonialism. In the *Ogoni* case, where the Nigerian federal government controlled mineral extraction rights, the Commission found a violation of multiple articles of the Banjul Charter, and urged the government to stop attacking Ogoni communities, investigate violations, compensate victims, and clean up environmental damage.[28] It also held that rights to housing, affirmed by the UN Committee on Economic, Social and Cultural Rights in 1992, were implied in the Charter even when not made explicit.[29] In Cameroon the Commission found that the *Bakweri Land Claims Committee* case had a rich historical and legal foundation, and recommended the parties to seek an 'amicable settlement' through its good offices, but was effectively ignored by the government.[30] In the *Cabinda* case the Commission found that a community of Indigenous people could own property,

[26] *Interights v Mauritania*, Comm. 373/2009, 28th ACHPR Annex (November 2009–May 2010)

[27] *Amnesty International v Zambia*, Comm No 212/98 (1999) ACHPR 1, 5 May 1999.

[28] *The Social and Economic Rights Action Center and the Center for Economic and Social Rights (SERAC) v Nigeria*, Commission Comm No 155/96 (2001–02); D Shelton, 'Decision regarding Communication 155/96' (2002) 96(4) American Society of International Law 937.

[29] UN-Habitat, *Rights to Adequate Housing* (2009), available at <https://www.ohchr.org/documents/publications/fs21_rev_1_housing_en.pdf> accessed 12 October 2020.

[30] N Kofele-Kale 'Asserting permanent sovereignty over ancestral lands: the Bakweri land litigation against Cameroon' 2007 (1) *Annual Survey of International and Comparative Law* 13; A Njoh, 'Indigenous Peoples and Ancestral Lands: Implications of the Bakweri Case in Cameroon' in R Home (ed), *Essays in African Land Law* (Pretoria University Law Press, 2010) 69–90.

subject to the same limitation as individual right to property, provided they could prove a strong traditional attachment to their land.[31] The Nubian Community in Kenya, who were not indigenous to Kenya but descended from soldiers of the former colonial power, successfully claimed the Nairobi neighbourhood of Kibera as their ancestral homeland, the place where they have buried their dead for generations, having no other homeland to go to; the government had routinely evicted them with no notice, alternative property, or compensation, and no satisfactory public interest argument.[32]

Article 14 allows states the right to expropriate land in the public interest, but Member States have often abused that right, failing to identify or justify that interest, follow due process, or pay appropriate compensation. Forced evictions are frequent, especially of informal settlements in urban areas, as evidenced through the work of the Centre on Housing Rights and Evictions (COHRE), an international non-governmental organization that operated between 1994 and 2014.[33] Cases coming before the African Commission and Court included Sudan's forced displacement from land of black African peoples tribes in the Darfur region, which was held to be a gross, massive, and systematic violation of human rights.[34] The confiscation and looting of property of black Mauritanians between 1986 and 1992, and expropriation or destruction of their land and houses before forcing them to go abroad, was held to be a violation of the right to property under Article 14.[35] In Zambia, the forced expulsion and dispersal of families was held to be a violation of family rights under Article 18.[36] Unfortunately such judgments have not deterred states from continuing to undertake forced evictions, and the situation has been further complicated when Indigenous peoples' rights were introduced into the mix.

4. The 'Wicked' Problem of Indigenous Peoples' Ancestral Lands

Indigenous peoples' rights in Africa can be seen as a 'wicked' problem: 'wicked' not in the sense of evil but difficult or impossible to solve because of complexity and incomplete, contradictory, or changing requirements.[37] It has certainly been so in

[31] Front for Liberation of the State of Cabinda v Republic of Angola, Commission Comm No 328/06 (2013).

[32] *Nubian Community in Kenya v Republic of Kenya*, ACHPR Comm No 317/06 (2016).

[33] *Second Report of the Advisory Group on Forced Evictions to the Executive Director of UN-HABITAT* HS/932/07E, 2006.

[34] *Sudan Human Rights Organisation & Centre on Housing Rights and Evictions (COHRE) v Sudan*, Comm No 279/03-296/05 (2009).

[35] *Malawi African Association and Others v Mauretania*, Commission Comm No 54/91, 61/91, 98/93, 164/97, 196/97, and 210/98 (2000).

[36] *Amnesty International v Zambia*, Commission Comm No 212/98 (2009).

[37] J Conklin, *Dialogue Mapping: Building Shared Understanding of Wicked Problems* (Wiley, 2005).

the two long-running cases eventually heard by the African Court and discussed shortly: the *Endorois* case in 2010 and the *Ogiek* case in 2017.

Globally an estimated 370 million people in over 70 countries claim to be Indigenous peoples, and the influential *Mabo* case in 1992, which confirmed that Australian Indigenous peoples' concepts of land tenure pre-dating the British conquest were legitimate, was followed by many Indigenous land cases in different countries.[38] The UN Declaration on the Rights of Indigenous Peoples (UNDRIP), adopted in 2007, set a framework of minimum standards, but was not a legally binding instrument.[39] African states had an ambivalent attitude to it: 33 states voted in favour, three abstained (Burundi, Kenya, and Nigeria), and the rest were absent. Some African states (notably Cameroon and Uganda) argued that the meaning of 'Indigenous' in their constitutions differs from the UNDRIP definition, and the Banjul Charter, pre-dating UNDRIP by nearly three decades, made no mention of Indigenous peoples, but frequent reference to 'peoples'. Africa has been accepted as the 'cradle of humankind', and most African peoples can claim to be Indigenous. The continent is now largely occupied by sedentary agriculturalists, but its diverse ethnic groups include some pastoralist or hunter–gatherer peoples, marginalized by a variety of historical and environmental circumstances.

The AUC working group on the subject reported in 2005 that:

> The land alienation and dispossession and dismissal of their customary rights to land and other natural resources has led to an undermining of the knowledge systems through which indigenous peoples have sustained life for centuries and it has led to a negation of their livelihood systems and deprivation of their means. This is seriously threatening the continued existence of indigenous peoples and is rapidly turning them into the most destitute and poverty stricken. This is a serious violation of the African Charter (Article 20, 21 and 22), which states clearly that all peoples have the right to existence, the right to their natural resources and property, and the right to their economic, social and cultural development.[40]

Some African national courts have been determining Indigenous people cases in their favour. The *Richtersveld* case in South Africa (2003) transferred from Australia the concept of Indigenous customary land rights for nomadic hunter–gatherers.[41]

[38] *Mabo v Queensland* (No 2) (1992) 175 CLR 1; K Engle, *The Elusive Promise of Indigenous Development: Rights, Culture, Strategy* (Duke University Press, 2010); J Gilbert, 'Historical indigenous peoples' land claims: a comparative and international approach to the common law doctrine on indigenous title' (2007) 56 International and Comparative Law Quarterly 583–611; C Tennant, 'Indigenous peoples, international institutions, and the international legal literature from 1945–1993' (1994) 16(1) Human Rights Quarterly 1.

[39] UN General Assembly, United Nations Declaration on the Rights of Indigenous Peoples: resolution adopted by the General Assembly, 2 October 2007, A/RES/61/295.

[40] *Report of Working Group of Experts on Indigenous Populations/Communities* (AUC, 2005) 108.

[41] TM Chan, 'The Richtersveld Challenge: South Africa Finally Adopts Aboriginal Title' in R Hitchcock and D Vinding (eds) *Indigenous People's Rights in Southern Africa* (IWGIA, 2004) 114.

The Botswana High Court found that denying the San community entry to their ancestral lands in the Kalahari deprived them of their rightful property, and was thus unlawful and unconstitutional.[42] Another celebrated dispossession dating back over a century relates to the Maasai of Kenya, an iconic ethnic group much photographed by tourists, who laid claim to much of the country's best land, the former white Highlands.[43]

The Banjul Charter's reference to 'peoples' without defining them offered an opening for Indigenous groups to assert their collective rights. Kenya had abstained from voting on UNDRIP, but the African Court's judgments in the *Endorois* and *Ogiek* cases effectively mapped articles in the UNDRIP declaration across to those in the Banjul Charter, and thereby expanded their scope. When the *Endorois* case came to the African Court, on referral from the Commission, a quarter of its lengthy 80-page judgment related to Article 14 rights to property. The Endorois claimed that after the Kenya government gazetted their ancestral lands around Lake Bogoria as a game reserve, it failed to consult them, and displaced families with minimal compensation. In 1997 the Kenya High Court had held that the government's act of gazetting the game reserve extinguished any Endorois claim to the land, but in 2003 the Commission found in favour of the Endorois. The newly constituted African Court considered the case on referral in 2009 and confirmed multiple violations of the Banjul Charter. It considered that Kenya as the 'Respondent State has a higher duty in terms of taking positive steps to protect groups and communities like the Endorois' and required Kenya to restore Endorois ancestral land with unrestricted access, pay compensation and royalties for losses suffered, and engage with the Endorois Welfare Committee over implementation.[44] The Court subsequently determined another Kenyan Indigenous peoples case on referral from the Commission. The Ogiek claimed as ancestral land much of the extensive Mau forest, and the Court in 2017 again ruled that the Kenya government had violated multiple rights, including to property, natural resources, and development, although the government subsequently continued with its evictions.[45]

Ancestral lands lie at the heart of Indigenous peoples' cases and raise particular difficulties in moving from judgment in a far-away international court to the facts on the ground. Colonial powers treated land, if not being cultivated or otherwise in obvious occupation, as *terra nullius*, disregarding movements of pastoralists and

[42] L Nyati-Ramahobo, *Minority Tribes in Botswana: The Politics of Recognition* (Minority Rights Group International, 2006).

[43] L Hughes, *Moving the Maasai: A Colonial Misadventure* (Palgrave, 2006); Y Ghai and J Cottrell (eds), *Marginalized Communities and Access to Justice* (Routledge, 2010).

[44] *Centre for Minority Rights Development (Kenya) and Minority Rights Group International on behalf of Endorois Welfare Council v Kenya*, Complaint No 276/2003, decision endorsed by the AU Assembly 2010. G Lynch, 'Becoming indigenous in the pursuit of justice: the African Commission on human and people's rights and the Endorois' (2012) 111 African Affairs 24.

[45] African Court App No 006/2012, *African Commission on Human and Peoples' Rights v Republic of Kenya*, Judgment, 2017.

hunter–gatherers who are now increasingly litigating. In practice it is questionable whether ancestral lands can even be defined by boundaries on a map, within which legitimately titled private ownerships are likely to exist. A complex history may need disentangling and local disputes adjudicated, perhaps involving different state agencies' claims of ownership or management rights. Property owners with title granted by the state (individual or group) may have to share access with 'non-owners' such as Indigenous peoples. Joint management agreements can work. Australia has involved Indigenous citizens in the management of national parks through community land councils and joint management plans.[46] The judges in the Commission and Court, however, were not concerned with the complex land issues arising, and the roles of professionals in land matters, who may have legitimate contributions to make, such as property registrars, surveying and mapping experts, land use planners, valuers, and ethnographers.

5. Implementation and Enforcement

The determinations by the Commission and Court referred to above presume effective compliance and enforcement. The AU Assembly mandates its Executive Council to oversee the implementation of judgment but the Commission has formally complained of difficulties in effectively discharging its mandate, and the Court of poor implementation of decisions.[47] Different legal instruments and a growing number of soft law documents have to be interpreted through jurisprudence. The Banjul Charter (Article 7) provides for remedies by an appropriate forum at national level, yet the separation of powers in African states is weak, with a colonial legacy of overlap and merging of legislative, executive, and judiciary powers. The Bakweri in Cameroon, for instance, complained to the Commission that there was no national tribunal to hear their case, while the judiciary was not independent, being made up of appointees of the head of state. The Kenyan government created a Truth, Justice and Reconciliation Commission and a National Commission for Human Rights to investigate human rights violations by the state since independence in 1963 but, when they reported in 2013 decades of state discrimination against minority and Indigenous communities, the government did little, undermining confidence in the justice system.[48] The Kenya government was

[46] K Davis, 'Aboriginal involvement in the management of Queensland national parks and other protected areas' 6 (1999) James Cook University Law Review 29.

[47] AU Executive Council, 2016 Activity Report of the African Court of Human and Peoples' Rights (2017), section (i). EX.CL/999(XXX).

C Okoloise 'Circumventing obstacles to the implementation of recommendations by the African Commission on Human and Peoples' Rights' (2018) 18 African Human Rights Law Journal 27; CM Fombad 'An overview of the crisis of the rule of law in Africa' (2018) 18 African Human Rights Law Journal 213.

[48] Kenya Truth Justice and Reconciliation Report (2013); Kenyan National Human Rights Commission, *Fourth State of Human Rights Report Post-Promulgation 2010–2014*.

reluctant to allow minority rights against the majority, the Endorois and Ogiek comprising at the most (demographic data being approximate) 200,000 people out of a total Kenyan population of over 50 million in 2018. Indigenous peoples' ancestral lands claims potentially challenge the territorial integrity and sovereignty of the nation state, and the Kenya government failed in its argument that it was seeking to protect the wider public interest (in the *Endorois* case a national game reserve, in the *Ogiek* case the Mau national forest and water catchment area).

Compliance with judgments in these human rights cases also raises issues of consultation and free, prior, and informed consent for those communities affected.[49] African governments have consistently been reluctant to consult or seek consent from them, whether before or after the event, and also opposed their right to select who represents them (Article 18 of UNDRIP). SDG16 ('Peace, justice and strong institutions') supports better access to justice, yet in 2017 the Institute for Human Rights and Development in Africa petitioned the Commission to express its 'concern and alarm at the shrinking of the civic society space' in many African countries.[50] UNDRIP (Article 28) also refers to Indigenous peoples' right to return to or be compensated when their lands, territories, or resources have been wrongly taken away, occupied, used, or damaged without their consent, and international legal guidelines continue to impose restitution obligations upon states after human rights violations and displacements.[51] African non-civil society organizations continue to lobby their governments for better representation and participation in decision-making, notably in the recent Kilimanjaro initiative by rural women for progress with land titling.[52]

6. Conclusion

Land is not mentioned in the Banjul Charter, but the Commission and the Court have determined a number of land-related cases in favour of applicants and against Member States, sometimes finding multiple violations of Charter rights. The rights violated include the right to property, the right to natural resources, the right to development, and the right to family, involving sometimes individuals and sometimes groups. States were found to have abused their own land titling systems and guarantees of private property title: in the *Mbiankeu* case fraudulent annulment

[49] UN Committee on the Elimination of Racial Discrimination, General Recommendation XXIII (51) concerning Indigenous Peoples (1997).

[50] IHRDA statement to African Commission, Banjul, 5 November 2017.

[51] Basic Principles and Guidelines on the Right to a Remedy and Reparation for Victims of Gross Violations of International Human Rights Law and Serious Violations of International Humanitarian Law (UN resolution 60/147 of 2005); P Pinheiro, *Housing and Property Restitution for Refugees and Displaced Persons: Implementing the 'Pinheiro Principles* (joint FAO, IDMC, OCHA, Habitat, UNHCR, 2007).

[52] *Charter of Demands: Actualizing Women's Land Rights in Africa* (Women to Kilimanjaro, 2016).

of its own land certificates, and in the *Mike Campbell* case large-scale land expropriation without due process or rights of redress. Cases of arbitrary displacement or eviction from land have exposed abuses of power by states against their own people, continuing a colonial tradition. The claims of Indigenous peoples added a further complication. The much-discussed *Endorois* and *Ogiek* cases had the effect of mapping UNDRIP rights onto the similar rights already guaranteed under the Banjul Charter, even though the UNDRIP declaration had a lesser legal status, and the status of particular Indigenous peoples may be contested by governments.

Such cases also exposed the toxic legacy of exclusionary laws derived from past colonial regimes, especially white settler colonialism in East, Central, and Southern Africa. In Zimbabwe the best land was dubiously acquired by white settlers whose private property was constitutionally protected in the post-independence constitution and set the SADC tribunal against the Mugabe government in the *Mike Campbell* case. In Kenya colonial laws passed on after independence allowed the government to take and set lands under customary tenure, but the Endorois and Ogiek in the African Court defeated the government's argument that gazetting of land for forestry or wildlife use extinguished their group property rights. Meanwhile, state organs in the land sector have been complicit in corrupt land sector transactions and practices, with the collusion of land professionals (surveyors and lawyers particularly).

So-called ancestral lands in Indigenous rights cases raise particular difficulties in moving from the judgment given by an international court, which is located in Africa but remote from the in-country facts on the ground. Such interpretation necessarily involves the messy complexity of land use relationships and an often tangled sequence of legal events, with the judges having little direct knowledge of the land affected, and even the language of court judgments may be inaccessible to the litigants. Existing landowners with protected property rights may or may not be members of the group claiming ancestral land rights. Compensation may have already been paid for previous land takings, the status of beneficiaries may need to be established, and retrospective valuation of land may be needed. The status of current and potential land uses may need to be established, for instance logging uses in forest areas, both legal and illegal. These contentious issues are being illuminated by recent development of scholarship in critical legal geography. That has widened the pure model of property as absolute, exclusive, and private ownership, to accepting relational approaches that include 'non-owners', especially collective or communal, interests, and challenge the idea of landed property as a tradable commodity.

Determining the extent of ancestral lands, whether for Indigenous peoples or for other groups (as in the *Nubian community* case), is thus fraught with difficulties. Restoring them to community control requires at least some joint management arrangement between the different interests. Such community claims to ancestral lands could potentially challenge the territorial integrity and sovereignty of the nation state, and shared management arrangements that balance the needs of the different stakeholders are difficult to negotiate even when undertaken with good will. The state may defend its own interests in opposition to the legitimate human rights claims of its own citizens.

Compliance by Member States with Commission and Court determinations has been poor in complex land cases, as evidenced in the progress reports of the African Court. Each Member State is responsible for its own land laws, and compliance may require unwelcome changes in national law and policy and have resource implications which are difficult to manage. Requirements for consultation with communities, and for reparation or compensation for past abuses, may be unwelcome, and local dispute resolution mechanisms may be inadequate. Alongside the role of the AU's human rights judiciary, supranational guidance on land policy and legislative is increasingly being provided by institutions such as the African Land Policy Centre and international development agencies. Interpreted in the context of theories of historic institutionalism and path dependency, such institutions have their various starting points, narrative trajectories over time, and organizational structures, as do the individual AU Member States and civil society groups.

As well as struggling with issues of land and human rights, AU juridical bodies operate within a complex and shifting legal environment. The Banjul Charter and subsequent protocols are binding treaties, if imperfectly implemented, but they have to be interpreted against various less binding international declarations and policy agendas, such as the UN declarations on RTD and UNDRIP and the AU Land Declaration. States may sign these declarations but be reluctant to adhere to the obligations in them. AU law is indeed, as Amao wrote in his path-breaking book on the subject, a 'work in progress'. 'Fine words butter no parsnips', as the saying goes.

16

The Right to Education in AU Law

Rui Garrido and Aua Baldé

1. Introduction

This chapter analyses the protection of the right to education bearing in mind African Union (AU) law and its policies. AU law has been defined as 'body of treaties, resolutions and decisions that have direct and indirect application to the Member States of the African Union'.[1] It is our understanding AU law encompasses the legal framework adopted by AU and its predecessor, the Organisation of African Unity (OAU), as well as the resolutions, guidelines, and jurisprudence by the AU human rights treaty bodies. Further, it suggests how the AU can contribute to expanding the scope of education not only as a human right but as a fundamental key to the development of AU Member States through the design and implementation of several structural policies on education.

Education is considered an 'empowerment right'[2] or a 'development right'[3] that enables the enjoyment of fundamental civil and political rights as well as social, economic, and cultural rights.[4] While this holds true for other human rights given their interconnectedness and indivisibility, the right to education is particularly transformative as it plays a central role in the development of a child and allows a child to unleash his or her full potential as a citizen. In fact, through education it is possible to participate in one's community life and make informed choices, as

[1] F Amao, *African Union Law* (Routledge, 2019) 21; ME Olivier, 'The role of African Union law in integrating Africa' (2015) 22(4) South African Journal of International Affairs 513–33 available at <http://www.tandfonline.com/doi/full/10.1080/10220461.2015.1119718>; accessed 13 May 2021. Also see Part I of this book.

[2] KD Beiter, *The Protection of Right to Education by International Law: Including a Systematic Analysis of Article 13 of the International Covenant on Economic, Social and Cultural* (Martinus Nijhoff Publishers, 2005) 2. Donnelly and Howard define empowerment rights as those that 'provide the individual with control over the course of his or her life, and in particular, control over (not merely protection against) the state' in J Donnelly and RE Howard, 'Assessing nations human rights performance: a theoretical framework' (1988) 10 Human Rights Quarterly 215.

[3] O Ekundayo, 'Does the African Charter on the Rights and Welfare if the Child (ACERWC) only underline and repeat the Convention on the Rights of the Child (CRC)'s provisions? examining the similarities and the differences between the AWRWC and the CRC' (2015) 7(1) International Journal of Humanities and Social Science 150 available at <http://www.ijhssnet.com/journals/Vol_5_No_7_1_July_2015/17.pdf> accessed 08 October 2019.

[4] See generally Beiter (n 2); CESCR General Comment 13, The Right to Education E/C.12/1999/10 para 1.

Rui Garrido and Aua Baldé, *The Right to Education in AU Law* In: *The Emergent African Union Law.* Edited by: Olufemi Amao, Michèle Olivier and Konstantinos D. Magliveras, Oxford University Press. © Rui Garrido and Aua Baldé 2021.
DOI: 10.1093/oso/9780198862154.003.0017

well as fully engage in activities with the potential for socio-economic growth. As summarized by Bieter, the right to education enables 'the enjoyment of many civil and political rights as well as economic, social and cultural rights', highlighting the 'interdependence and indivisibility of all human rights'.[5]

The centrality of education is recognized in several AU instruments (treaties, soft law, and policies) that will be discussed in this chapter. The right to education was enshrined in the African Charter on Human and Peoples' Rights (African Charter) and in other regional human rights treaties and protocols, as well as clarified in soft law instruments. The African Charter was reaffirmed in the Constitutive Act of the African Union as one of the commitments of the organization,[6] changing the regional human rights approach from the one adopted by OAU.

In addition to the AU legal framework concerning education, the organization has adopted and sought to implement several educational policies with a view to encouraging positive action on a continental scale and promoting better education standards within the AU Member States. Indeed, the Organisation of African Unity (OAU) in its final years laid the foundation for this by designing the first educational policy, the First Decade of Education for Africa (1997–2006).[7] While the First Decade policy was not fully implemented, due the lack of political engagement, it nonetheless paved the way for the AU to correct flaws and move ahead in the implementation of political measures regarding education. Since 2016 there has been a new educational policy in place: the Continental Education Strategy for Africa (2016–2025),[8] and Agenda 2063 – The Africa We Want.[9] Both enshrine an aspiration of social, cultural, and economic development for the 21st century, and position education as a key engine to achieving these goals.

2. The Right to Education within AU Law

2.1 The Protection of the Right to Education in AU Treaties

The right to education in AU law is protected and regulated in two ways. The African Charter was the first African regional human rights treaty to formulate the right to education, albeit through a general and vague formulation. Subsequently,

5 Beiter (n 2) 30.

6 Article 3(h) of the Constitutive Act of the African Union.

7 There is a specific webpage about this strategy in the AU main website, but no further information is giving, including the official document of the strategy. See AU, *First Decade of Education for Africa (1997–2006)* available at <https://www.edu-au.org/strategies/first-decade-of-education-for-africa> accessed 6 October 2019.

8 AU, *Continental Education Strategy for Africa (2016–2055)* available at <https://au.int/sites/default/files/documents/29958-doc-cesa_-_english-v9.pdf> accessed 12 September 2019.

9 AU, Agenda 2063 – The African We Want available at <https://au.int/sites/default/files/documents/36204-doc-agenda2063_popular_version_en.pdf> accessed 22 September 2019.

additional protocols to the African Charter and other treaties have provided a detailed layer of protection to vulnerable groups such as children, youth, women, the elderly, and people living with disabilities.

The African Charter, establishes that 'every individual shall have the right to education'.[10] The framing of this article is succinct but vague, a characteristic common to all economic, social, and cultural rights in the African Charter.[11] The right to education in the African Charter does not specify any content or meaning of education, and it is unclear what the precise obligations of Member States are.[12]

Despite these shortcomings, this right was further developed in some of the African Charter protocols and other AU treaties which contributed to the expansion and consolidation of its scope. The right to education was included in the African Charter on the Rights and Welfare of the Child[13] (African Children´s Charter), the African Youth Charter,[14] the Protocol on the African Charter on Human and Peoples´ Rights on the Rights of Women in Africa[15] (African Women's Protocol), the Protocol to the African Charter on Human and Peoples' Rights on the Rights of Older Persons in Africa[16] (African Older Person´s Protocol), and the Protocol to the African Charter on Human and Peoples' Rights on the Rights of Persons with Disabilities in Africa[17] (African Disability Protocol).

The African Women´s Protocol,[18] adopted to complement the African Charter on the promotion and protection of women in Africa, establishes women´s rights to education as a way of ensuring both 'gender equality and parity'.[19] Brown and Oder stress that education has 'an enormous transformative potential for the realization of gender equality and the promotion of human dignity at the individual, communal, and national levels.'[20] The elimination of obstacles that can hinder women's access to education is the core of the right to education in the African Women's Protocol. The treaty imposes on state parties the obligation to take appropriate measures to 'eliminate all forms of discrimination against women and

10 Article 17(1) of the African Charter on Human and Peoples' Rights.

11 Amao (n 1) 132.

12 F Ouguergouz, *The African Charter on Human and Peoples´ Rights: a Comprehensive Agenda for Human Dignity and Sustainable Democracy in Africa* (Martinus Nijhoff Publishers, 2003) 190.

13 OAU/LEG/153/Rev.2 adopted 1 July 1990 and entered into force 29 November 1999.

14 African Youth Charter, adopted 2 July 2006, entered into force 8 August 2009 available at <https://au.int/en/treaties/african-youth-charter> accessed 28 July 2020.

15 AU DOC CAB/LEG/66.6 adopted 11 July 2003 and entered into force 25 November 2005.

16 Adopted 31 January 2016, The Protocol has not yet entered into force. At the time of the writing, only Angola and Lesotho had ratified it. Available at <https://au.int/en/treaties/protocol-african-charter-human-and-peoples%E2%80%99-rights-rights-older-persons> accessed 28 July 2020.

17 Adopted on 29 January 2018. The Protocol has not yet entered into force. Available at <https://au.int/en/treaties/protocol-african-charter-human-and-peoples-rights-rights-persons-disabilities-africa> accessed 28 July 2020.

18 Article 12, African Women's Protocol.

19 cf Ouguergouz (n 12) 132.

20 R Brown and J Oder, 'The Protection of Women´s Economic, Social and Cultural Rights in Africa' in D Mzikenge Chirwa and L Chenwi (eds), *The Protection of Economic, Social and Cultural Rights in Africa: International, Regional and National Perspectives* (CUP, 2016) 121–154, 131.

guarantee equal opportunity and access in the space of education and training'.[21] States are also expected to take specific action to promote women's literacy as well as to fight them dropping out of the education system.[22]

The African Children's Charter[23] is unique in the sense that it provides a distinctive promotion and protection of the rights of the children while bearing in mind the specific context and needs of African children.[24] The protection of children in the African regional system has been labelled 'the most progressive achievement of all the regional systems',[25] given its comprehensive mechanism that includes not only the substantive rights enshrined in the African Children's Charter but also the establishment of the African Committee of Experts on the Rights and Welfare of the Child (ACERWC), responsible for monitoring compliance of Member States with the African Children's Charter.[26] The Committee forms part of AU institutions[27] and is responsible for the implementation within the AU of African children's rights demonstrating the protection imperative of children for the AU human rights system.

One of the substantive rights protected in the African Children's Charter is the right to education. Compared to the provision contained in the African Charter itself, the right to education in the African Children's Charter was inspired by the needs of the African child and provides for a comprehensive and detailed concept of education as a right of the child and a central tool of its development. The article states that '[e]very child shall have the right to an education',[28] specifying that such education shall promote the child's development and potential,[29] 'fostering respect for human rights and fundamental freedoms',[30] the preservation of positive African morals and values,[31] and 'the preparation of the child for responsible life in a free society' in the spirit of tolerance and respect.[32] Education is also perceived as a

[21] Article 12(1)(a) of the African Women's Protocol.

[22] ibid Article 12(2).

[23] It is interesting to note that, even prior to the adoption of the African Children's Charter, the OAU adopted the Declaration on the Rights and Welfare of the African Child which urged OAU members to formulate and implement programmes in the field of education, as well as to ensure alternative strategies for cases where formal education services were not available. See OAU Doc. AHG/ST.4 (XIV) Rev.1(1979) paras 6 and 7.

[24] T Kaime, *The African Charter on the Rights and the Welfare of the Child: A Socio-legal Perspective* (Pretoria University Law Press, 2009), 143.

[25] A Lloyd, 'The African Regional System for the Protection of Children's Rights' in J Sloth-Nielsen (ed), *Children's Rights in Africa: A Legal Perspective* (Ashgate, 2008) 33–52, 33.

[26] The Committee was created by Article 32 of the African Children's Charter and has a broad mandate of promotion, protection, and interpretation of the rights of children, as well other tasks of supervision, of gathering information, organizing meetings, and engaging with other African institutions. Article 42 of the African Children's Charter.

[27] A Lloyd and R Murray, 'Institutions with Responsibility for Human Rights Protection under the African Union' (2004) 48 Journal of African Law 165, 175.

[28] Article 11(1) of the African Children's Charter.

[29] ibid Article 11(2)(a).

[30] ibid Article 11(2)(b).

[31] ibid Article 11(2)(c).

[32] ibid Article 11(2)(d).

tool for the child to become an active citizen and play a prominent role in the preservation of African unity, environment, and resources.[33] The African Children's Charter goes far beyond this, as it consecrates several duties of the Member States, such as to take all measures to provide a free, compulsory, and inclusive education at all levels that allow every children, regardless of their socio-economic status, gender, or other disadvantages, to be able to attend school.[34]

The African Youth Charter provides a framework for the protection of youth and addresses key challenges that the African youth face including education-related issues. The African Youth Charter recognizes the right of African youth to good quality education in its multiple forms, 'including formal, non-formal, informal, distance learning'.[35] The Charter further calls on states to take appropriate measures to provide free and compulsory basic education and emphasizes the need to encourage youth to engage in the fields of science and technology. This Charter also places on youth the responsibility for their own development, and in the case of education, young people are expected to 'engage in peer-to-peer education to promote youth development in areas such as literacy, use of information and communication technology, HIV/AIDS prevention, violence prevention and peace building'.[36]

The African Disability Protocol provides for the protection of the right to education at the AU level for persons with disabilities. This is particularly relevant in the African context, where there is not only a high percentage of children with disabilities but also only a handful of African states which protect in their constitutions the educational rights of children with disabilities.[37] Article 16(1) of the African Disability Protocol recognises that 'every person with a disability has the right to education'. Furthermore, the African Disability Protocol provides specifically for the right to 'inclusive quality education',[38] therefore challenging 'the view that it is acceptable to segregate and to exclude some children on the basis of their disability'.[39] It does not, however, impose an absolute duty to attend inclusive schools; on the contrary, it reserves the right of a person with disabilities to choose to attend a special school.[40]

The African Older Persons' Protocol provides a normative framework for the protection of the elderly in the African continent.[41] Instead of a comprehensive

[33] ibid Article 11(2)(e),(f),(g).
[34] ibid Article 11(3).
[35] Article 13(2) of the African Youth Charter.
[36] ibid Article 26(e).
[37] J Biegon, 'The Scope of Recognition and Protection of the Right to Inclusive Education in the African Human Rights System' in G Beco, S Quinlivan, and others (eds), *The Right to Inclusive Education in International Human Rights Law* (CUP, 2019) 473–494.
[38] Article 16(3) of the African Disability Protocol.
[39] G de Beco, S Quinlivan, and JE Lord, 'Introduction' in Beco, Quinlivan, and others (eds) (n 37) 2.
[40] Biegon (n 37) 494.
[41] DM Chirwa and CI Rushwaya, 'Guarding the guardians: a critical appraisal of the Protocol to the African Charter on the Rights of Older Persons in Africa' (2019) 19(1) Human Rights Law Review 53.

list of substantive rights, the African Older Persons Protocol focuses on rights considered particularly relevant to older persons in Africa.[42] One such right concerns the access to education, guaranteed in Article 16, which stipulates that 'State Parties shall provide opportunities for Older Persons to have access to education and to acquire ICT skills'. Bearing in mind the relevance of technology in today's world and the likelihood of limited access to such training by older persons, the article places emphasis on their right to receive training in information, communication, and technology skills.

The AU legal framework concerning education highlights two important features. First, the AU legislator's has broadened the scope and content of education, as well as further clarified the goals and obligations of states to realize the right to education. Second, with the exception of the African Charter and its protocols and Children's Charter, the remaining legal instruments suffer from a lack of specific implementation mechanisms which may undermine their compliance.[43] Regarding state obligations under the African Children's Charter, the ACERWC has underscored that states have the duty to prevent human rights violations and investigate them in case of the occurrence. States are therefore, obliged to demonstrate their compliance with human rights commitments 'assessed against the backdrop of the efficacy and adequacy of the implementation measures it has undertaken to enforce laws and administrative and other measures'.[44] This points to the ineffectiveness of mechanisms of the AU organs to compel states to take all necessary steps to implement domestically their human rights commitments. Despite the duty of comply with decisions and policies of the AU, imposed by Article 23(2) of the Constitutive Act the Assembly lacks a more robust and assertive approach regarding the states that fails their human rights commitments. The inefficiency is also underlined in the decisions taken by the supervision bodies, especially the ACERWC. Despite several rulings on the violation of the right to education by Member States,[45] the Committee's decisions themselves are non-binding recommendations, and as such depend on states' willingness to comply with them.

[42] ibid 61.

[43] Regarding implementation, the African Committee on the Rights and Welfare of the Child defines it as the 'process whereby governments take the necessary legal, policy, budgetary, administrative and other appropriate measures to ensure the full realization of all children's rights stipulated in the CRC, the African Children's Charter and other relevant national, regional and international human rights laws and instruments pertaining to children to ensure the wellbeing of all children'. cf ACERWC, 'General Comment No 5 on "State Party obligation under the African Charter on the Rights and Welfare of the Child (Article 1) and systems strengthening for Child protection"' (2018) 4.

[44] ibid 15.

[45] See, for example, *Institute for Human Rights and Development in Africa (IHRDA) and Open Society Justice Initiative on behalf of children of Nubian descent Kenya v The Government of Kenia*, African Committee of Experts on the Rights and Welfare of the Child (ACERWC), Comm No 002/Com/002/2009 (2011); *African Centre of Justice and Peace Studies (ACJPS) and People's Legal Aid Centre (PLACE) v The Government of Republic of Sudan*, ACERWC, Comm No 005/Com/01/2015 (2018); *Minority Rights Group International and SOS-Esclaves on behalf of Said Ould Salem and Yarg Ould Salem v The Government of the Republic of Mauritania*, ACERWC, Comm No 007/Com/003/2015 (2017).

2.2 The Protection of Right to Education in AU Soft Law

In addition to the human rights treaties which provides a comprehensive framework for the protection of the right to education in the AU, the African Commission on Human and Peoples' Rights (African Commission) has played a significant role in the promotion and protection of the right to education within the African continent. In fact, the African Commission has contributed over the years towards further clarification of the normative content of the right to education through the adoption of documents that can be regarded as soft law due to their non-binding nature.[46]

The African Commission has adopted three non-binding instruments relevant to the right to education: the Pretoria Declaration on Economic, Social and Cultural Rights in Africa[47] (Pretoria Declaration); the Principles and Guidelines on the Implementation of Economic, Social and Cultural Rights in the African Charter on Human and Peoples' Rights[48] (the Nairobi Principles); and the State Party Reporting Guidelines for Economic, Social and Cultural Rights in the African Charter on Human and Peoples' Rights[49] (the Tunis Guidelines).

The Pretoria Declaration clarified the core content of socio-economic rights contained in the African Charter, including the right to education. Paragraph 8 of the declaration specifically addresses the normative content of the right to education under Article 17 of the African Charter, elucidating that it entails, *inter alia*, the right to free and compulsory basic education, as well as accessible and affordable secondary and higher education. It further ensures the freedom of parents and legal guardians to select schools.

The Nairobi Principles, which provide for an extensive catalogue of socio-economic rights,[50] confirm the previous construction of the right to education under Article 17 of the African Charter. The Principles reinforce the idea of free and compulsory basic education while stressing that states are expected to make secondary education 'generally available and accessible to all by appropriate means, and in particular by the progressive introduction of free education'.[51]

[46] In addition, the African Commission has also adopted a number of resolutions on the right to education attesting to its growing relevance within the AU framework: Resolution on Human Rights Education – ACHPR/Res.6 (XIV) 93; Resolution on the Right to education in Africa – ACPR/Res. 346 (LVIII) 2016 and Resolution on States′ Obligation to Regulate Private Actors Involved in the Provision of Health and education Services – ACHPR/Res. 420 (LXIV) 2019.

[47] Adopted during the 36th Ordinary Session held in Dakar in December 2004. It is worth noting that this Declaration was the result of a seminar held in Pretoria in September 2004. For details on the discussion in Pretoria see S Khoza, 'Promoting economic, social and cultural rights in Africa: the African Commission holds a seminar in Pretoria' (2005) 4 African Human Rights Law Journal 34.

[48] Adopted during the 48th Ordinary Session on 4 November 2011 held in Banjul.

[49] Adopted at the 49th Ordinary Session of the African Commission, held in Banjul, The Gambia, April 28–May 11, 2011.

[50] Beyond the rights enshrined in the African Charter.

[51] Nairobi Principles and Guidelines, para 71.

The Tunis Guidelines stress that the right to education should be considered as one of the priorities in the initial and periodic reports and require states to indicate the measures taken to secure this right.

These three instruments reinforce education as a fundamental right that demands positive actions from states for its realization. States are invited to grant free and compulsory education to all children, as well as to provide conditions for parents and legal guardians to choose their children's school freely, granting not only their education but other fundamental rights, and the promotion of the cultural values of the community.

3. AU Policies on Education

Alongside this treaty law, the AU has developed a number of strategies and guidelines to put into practice the legal protection of education as a right in the AU's normative framework. For this purpose, the AU has adopted the Continental Education Strategy for Africa, which enshrines the major guidelines for Member States to improve their national education at all levels, because education is understood as the core for the development of the continent. These policies and their impact are assessed below as efforts to put law into practice.

Education in Africa has a strong link with the struggle for human rights. During the decade 1960 to 1970, education played an important role in the struggle for independence from colonial rule, nation building and decolonization.[52] From 1980 to the end of the 20th century, education played a central role in regional integration of Africa, conflict resolution, and post-conflict reconstruction.[53] With the dawn of the AU and the new Millennium, educational goals in Africa shifted towards an education for sustainable development.[54]

The roots of education as a key for development in Africa are found in Article II(2)(c) of the Charter of the Organisation of African Union (OAU Charter) of 25 May 1963, which postulated the necessity of states to coordinate educational cooperation. The OAU Charter stipulated that the Assembly shall establish specialised commissions, for example the 'Educational, Scientific, Cultural and Health Commission'.[55] This commission was replaced, in the new AU architecture, by a specialized technical committee on education, science and technology.[56] This

[52] KK Tsegaye, 'The place of private higher education in regional institutions in Africa: the case of the OAU/AU and the Intergovernmental Authority on Development' (2015) 8(7) The Journal of Pan African Studies, 80 available at <https://www.jpanafrican.org/docs/vol8no7/8.7-7-Tsegaye.pdf> accessed 5 September 2019.

[53] cf ibid (n 52).

[54] cf ibid (n 52).

[55] Article XX (2) of the OAU Charter (1963).

[56] 'Specialised Technical Committees' (African Union) available at <https://au.int/en/stc> accessed 25 July 2020.

approach was expanded and further developed in the human rights framework of OAU/AU, as discussed earlier. The OAU focused on education as a development tool of recently freed states but faced the cruel reality of the massive illiteracy of Africans. Illiteracy remained one of the major challenges for education in Africa at the start of the 1990s, along with gender inequality, lack of training for teachers, and poor facilities.[57]

In 1991, under the auspices of the OAU, the Treaty Establishing the African Economic Community (Abuja Treaty), which created a Committee on Education, Culture and Human Resources (Article 25 (1)(g)) and exhorted states to cooperate in the revision of educational systems for a better development in Africa, was adopted. Article 68 states that:

> Member States shall strengthen co-operation among themselves in the field of education and training and coordinate and harmonize their policies in this field for the purpose of training persons capable of fostering the changes necessary for enhancing social progress and the development of the Continent.[58]

The process of regional integration proposed by the Abuja Treaty is ambitious and has a strong pillar for its implementation in the Regional Economic Communities (RECs). Regarding the goals for education, the Abuja Treaty required OAU Member States to develop policies and actions oriented towards the efficiency of educational systems; to empower trainers, design strategies at a regional level, and stop the brain-drain out of Africa. The Abuja Treaty places education as the driving force of development of Africa and, in that sense, it shifts the paradigm of education as a domestic national affair of the states.

With the dawn of the AU and the inception of the New Partnership for Africa's Development (NEPAD), the right to education was placed under a new framework. Higher education, for example, was the subject of a renewed strategy entrenched in the concept of the knowledge economy.[59] This approach was reflected in the institutional arrangement of the AU and resulted in the creation of a specialized division in the administrative apparatus of the organization; the Education Division of the Department of Human Resources, Science and Technology. The AU Education Division has the ambitious mission of:

> [contributing] towards revitalized, quality, relevant, and harmonized education systems responsive to the needs of Africa, taking into account Africa's aspiration

[57] K Namuddu, 'Educational Research Priorities in Sub-Saharan Africa' in G Morin and K Sorensen (eds), *Strengthening Educational Research in Developing Countries* (UNESCO, 1991) 41.

[58] Article 68 (1) of the Treaty Establishing the African Economic Community (1991).

[59] ET Woldegiorgis, 'Historical and Political Perspectives on Regionalization of African Higher Education' in J Jbight and ET Wordegiorgis (eds), *Regionalization of African Higher Education. Progress and Prospects* (Sense Publishers, 2017) 29–46, 40.

and capacity in terms of human and material resources; systems that produce Africans with appropriate attitudes, values, knowledge and skills to facilitate attainment of the AU vision; systems that generate applied and new knowledge and contribute towards its harnessing for meeting Africa's challenges as well as placing Africa firmly within the core of the global knowledge economy.[60]

The Education Division is an umbrella division that accommodates specialized education agencies and is responsible for the design and implementation of educational strategies and it is responsible for the education, science, and technology strategies for the continent. The strategies are soft law instruments, but they reflect guidelines for states to implement domestically and complement the AU law framework.[61] Several states have domestic policies with national goals regarding education, but it is not clear if states engage with public policies emanating from the AU. South Africa presented a report on the implementation of the Second Decade of Education for Africa[62] – a policy that was in place between 2006 and 2015 – which demonstrates some compliance with AU policies. More recently, and with a new policy in place – the Continental Education Strategy for Africa (2016–2025) – a meeting was held in June 2016 to evaluate the engagement of stakeholders and measures already in place.[63] The coordination of regular meetings, as milestones of the policy, denotes that the AU is making efforts to operate a real transformation at a national level through the implementation of the measures provided by the AU's policies.

3.1 The First Decade of Education for Africa Policy (1997–2006)

The First Decade of Education for Africa Policy (First Decade Policy) was a landmark document in the field of education in Africa and a clear sign that the OAU was assuming a decisive role in African affairs. It sought to reinforce the Abuja Treaty and launch a wide educational policy for the continent. A plan of action for this policy was adopted in March 1999, during the first conference of African

[60] AU, The Education Division available at <https://www.edu-au.org/about/au-education-division> accessed 2 August 2019.

[61] The Education Division is composed by three main agencies – African Union International Centre for Girls and Women Education in Africa (AU/CIEFFA); Pan African Institute of Education for Development (IPED); Pan African University (PAU) – and it is responsible for the education, science, and technology strategies for the continent – Technical and vocational Education Training Strategy (TVET Strategy); Science, Technology and Innovation Strategy for Africa (STISA–2024); First Decade of Education for Africa (1997–2006); Second Decade for Education for Africa (2006–15); and the Continental Educations Strategy for Africa (CESA).

[62] See <https://www.gov.za/sites/default/files/gcis_document/201409/dobesadc-au-draft-report0.pdf> accessed 2 August 2019.

[63] See <http://www.adeanet.org/youth-skills-forum/en/news/implementation-of-the-continental-education-strategy-for-africa-cesa> accessed 10 October 2019.

Ministers of Education, which took place in Harare.[64] The plan of action was anchored on the following points: (a) equity and access to basic education; (b) the quality, relevance and effectiveness of education; (c) complementary learning modalities; (d) capacity building.[65]

Although this policy was a result of considerable effort of the OAU to improve education in Africa and contribute to the awareness of Africans of their basic rights and the possibility of a better life, several authors stress the failure of the implementation of the First Decade Policy[66] and the inefficiency of its action plan.[67] Kassa Tsegaye, for example, highlights the lack of ownership of stakeholders, insufficient publicity of the policy, the lack of engagement of development partners, and inefficient domestication of the policy.[68] This policy also suffered from the transition from the OAU to the AU, in which political efforts were centred on the establishment and implementation of the new Pan-African organization. Official information about the First Decade Policy is absent in any of the official AU websites. There is only a reference to it in the subsequent policy, but neither the official policy nor other related documents are available, denoting some lack of interest in this policy.

3.2 The Second Decade of Education for Africa Policy (2006–2015)

In 2006, and after the experience gained during the First Decade of Education for Africa, the AU designed a new policy for the coming decade. The Second Decade of Education for Africa Policy (2006–2015)[69] was adopted in January 2006. The new policy goes far beyond its predecessor in terms of focus and goals.[70]

The failures and weaknesses in the implementation of the First Decade Policy were taken into consideration as the AU endowed the Second Decade with several mechanisms to manage and control the process of implementation. A Plan of Action was designed granting a multi-layered strategy of communication and management. The Plan was composed of multiple layers – continental, regional, and national level, respectively, the AU Commission, the RECs, and the Member States national authorities.[71] The engagement of all political entities in the process

64 OA Touray, *The African Union: The First Ten Years* (Rowman & Littlefield, 2016) 95.

65 NB Pityana, *A Decade of Development and Education in Africa: The Promise of Open and Distance Learning* (University of South Africa, 2008) 5.

66 cf Tsegaye (n 52).

67 cf Touray (n 64) 95.

68 cf Tsegaye (n 52) 79.

69 Assembly/AU/Dec. 92 (VI).

70 AU, *Second Decade of Education for Africa (2006–2015). Plan of Action*, at 4 available at <http://www.unesco.org/new/fileadmin/MULTIMEDIA/FIELD/Dakar/pdf/AU%20SECOND%20DECADE%20ON%20EDUCTAION%202006-2015.pdf> accessed 7 September 2019.

71 ibid.

of implementing and monitoring the application of the Second Decade Policy was important to the success of the policy.[72]

The Second Decade Policy had a strong human rights-oriented perspective and was considered a core step for the economic growth and development Africa.[73] The policy not only sought to guarantee the elimination of gender disparities between men and women through the promotion of the qualified jobs of girls and women but also to improve the quality of life of other vulnerable and disadvantaged groups through education. The outcome was a new design for all education policies having a strong human rights foundation including respect for the rights of the most vulnerable persons.[74] The results pertaining to access to primary education are impressive: a report states that in 2012, nearly 149 million of African children were in primary school, more than double the numbers of 1990s during which 62 million children had access to primary school.[75] However, as the level of education gets higher, the reality changes: only 49 million African youth were able to attend secondary school.[76]

The policy aimed also to ensure that education 'is used as an effective tool for entrenching peace, justice and equity' and 'contributes to re-establishing the dignity of Africans'.[77] Priority areas included the promotion of the correct application and enforcement of human rights, the universal access to basic and secondary education, and the reduction of the rates of out-of-school children and youth, in line with provision of the African Youth Charter.[78] The policies during the Second Decade reflect the general trends of detailed protection of vulnerable groups, as identified in the first part of this chapter.

3.3 The Continental Education Strategy for Africa (2016–2025)

After the period of implementation of the Second Decade Policy, which ended in 2015, the AU discussed and adopted a new holistic policy for education. The

72 Tsegaye (n 52) 80.

73 Woldegiorgis (n 59) 44.

74 The policy enumerates, non-exhaustively, 'girls, persons with disabilities and children affected by HIV and AIDS'. In 2011, the African Commission on Human and Peoples' Rights expanded this notion to 'vulnerable and disadvantaged groups' to those 'who have faced and/or continue to face significant impediments to their enjoyment of economic, social and cultural rights'. African Commission on Human and Peoples' Rights, *Guidelines and Principles on Economic, Social and Cultural Rights in the African Charter on Human and Peoples' Rights* (2011) 8.

75 The Africa-America Institute, State of Education in Africa Report 2015, at 7 available at <http://www.aaionline.org/wp-content/uploads/2015/09/AAI-SOE-report-2015-final.pdf> accessed 10 September 2019.

76 ibid 8.

77 AU (n 70) 5.

78 AU, *African Youth Decade 2009–2018. Accelerating Youth Empowerment for Sustainable Development* available at <https://www.un.org/en/africa/osaa/pdf/au/african_youth_decade_2009-2018.pdf> accessed 12 September 2019.

Continental Education Strategy for Africa (hereafter CESA) is much more ambitious than its predecessors and proposes a revolution in education as a transformative force for Africa and Africans. The CESA is part of Agenda 2063 and was designed after consultation with several stakeholders, such as NEPAD, the RECs, and other regional actors.[79]

The CESA aims to create a 'new African citizen'[80] who will be the key sustainable development promoter. In fact, development is the guiding force of the CESA as it is central in its guiding principles, pillars, and strategic objectives. Similarly, it presents a holistic approach to human rights and a concern to improve education as the basis for a better way of life where Africans are empowered as citizens to embrace their rights and duties in full. This idea is central throughout the document, despite the fact that the words 'human rights' are never mentioned in the text. In line with previous AU education policies, CESA endeavours to eliminate gender disparities and empower women and girls.

The CESA has a concrete goal of reducing school dropout rates and the number of unschooled children and youth. It proposes measures for all levels of education, from pre-primary to tertiary education and non-traditional methods of education, such as informal and non-formal education. CESA has a connection with other AU education policies, such as the Technical and Vocational Education Training Strategy and Science, Technology and Innovation Strategy for Africa – 2024 that might assist in this regard. Harmonization of educational systems is a requirement for the development of an intra-Africa cooperation programme, which aims to allow the mobility of people and knowledge in Africa. A good example of that is the *Intra-África Pax Lusófona*, an academic mobility programme coordinated by the Law Faculty of Agostinho Neto University (Angola) and developed by the AU in cooperation with EU. The programme offers mobility for post-graduate studies in law between African Lusophone Universities and through it the recognition of studies and the portability of competences.[81] These kinds of programmes not only improve the education level in less developed countries and supply highly qualified people but they also enhance the bonds between African citizens and promote peace and good relationships.

3.4 Education in Agenda 2063

Agenda 2063: The African We Want[82] is a holistic policy for the development of the African continent for the 21st century. Agenda 2063 was proclaimed in 2013

[79] AU (n 8).
[80] AU (n 8) 7.
[81] See <http://www.intraafricapaxlusofona.org/index.php> accessed 20 September 2019.
[82] AU, Agenda 2063 – The African We Want available at <https://au.int/sites/default/files/documents/36204-doc-agenda2063_popular_version_en.pdf> accessed 22 September 2019.

and enshrines the main development goals and aspirations for the next 50 years. Regarding education, Agenda 2063 enshrines some of the objectives (Article 3(j), (k), and (m)) and principles (Article 4(l) and n)) proclaimed in the Constitutive Act of the African Union. Education plays a crucial role in this policy, as it is a cornerstone for the economic, cultural, and social revolution that Agenda 2063 proclaims. Although no specific reference is made to education, its implementation sheds light on the vital role of education in the realization of the human rights of African citizens.

The Plan of Action for the first decade (2014–2023) of Agenda 2063 gives special attention to strategies that foster education in the continent. The plan of action defines the flagship programme as the establishment of an African Virtual and E-University, which will allow students from around the continent to pursue higher education and acquire technical and soft skills.[83] Aspiration 1 (a prosperous Africa based on inclusive and sustainable development) aims to fight several inequalities that pose actual challenges to the enjoyment of human rights. It proposes to:

> [end] poverty, inequalities of income and opportunity; job creation, especially addressing youth unemployment; facing up to the challenges of rapid population growth and urbanization, improvement of habitats and access to basic necessities of life –water, sanitation, electricity; providing social security and protection; developing Africa's human and social capital (through an education and skills revolution emphasizing science and technology) and expanding access to quality health care services, particularly for women and girls.[84]

Education remains crucial for the realization of these aspirational goals. The expected outcomes in 2063 are an increase in the number of children with access to childhood education, compulsory education from primary to secondary levels, with special focus on science, technology, and innovation, leveraging economic growth for the continent, and a better life for Africans. In 2016 the ACERWC adopted 'Agenda 2040, Africa's Agenda for Children: Fostering an Africa Fit for All',[85] inspired by the Agenda 2063, and with a specific aspiration for education, and its goal is to ensure that every child benefits fully from quality education.[86] Agenda 2040 reinforces the dispositions of CESA and Agenda 2063 regarding education as a central tool for the development of the child, society and Africa.

83 AU, First Ten-year Implementation Plan 2014–2023, at 16 available at <https://www.un.org/en/africa/osaa/pdf/au/agenda2063-first10yearimplementation.pdf> accessed 22 September 2019.

84 AU (n 82) 36.

85 AU, Agenda 2040, Africa's Agenda for Children: Fostering an Africa Fit for All available at <https://au.int/sites/default/files/documents/36204-doc-agenda2063_popular_version_en.pdf> accessed 12 October 2019.

86 ibid 13.

4. Conclusion

The AU is changing the role of education in Africa. Education is not seen only as a human right imposing positive obligation on states towards their citizens and foreigners under its jurisdiction but also as a way to realizing higher social mobility, better living standards, better health services, and creating jobs for which higher qualifications are required.

As this chapter has highlighted, the right to education is enshrined in several AU treaties, from a vague protection formulation in the African Charter towards a comprehensive and more detailed protection of specific groups, such as women, children, youth, and older persons. The protection of the right to education in the African Charter has largely been complemented by subsequent additional treaties and soft law instruments. However, the main issue that arises from this multiplicity of treaties is that while the African Charter has full ratification by AU Member States, the subsequent treaties are at a different level of ratification and as such create uneven treatment of African citizens concerning the right to education. This inconsistency could be addressed through a comprehensive review of the African Charter to incorporate the protection developed in subsequent treaties, not only concerning the right to education but other human rights as well. There is a necessity to guarantee full compliance of future decisions adopted by the AU human rights mechanisms as a crucial condition for the implementation of measures to education at a domestic level. A measure of supranationalism as foreseen by an AU law system as discussed in earlier chapters of this book will do much to assist in the enforcement of these core rights by undercutting the option of opting out of unwanted obligations.

In addition to the multiplicity of AU treaties granting the right to education, the AU has moved forward and designed policies that place education as a means towards economic development and prosperity as well as a prerequisite for the enjoyment of other human rights. The First and Second Decades of Education for Africa policies were part of an effort that started with the OAU and leveraged education as a centrepiece for the development and economic growth of the continent. The AU is currently implementing the Continental Education Strategy for Africa, complemented by other policies including Agenda 2063, the major aspirational policy for Africa. All these policies, in partnership with the AU treaties, are part of the AU's positive action which perceives education as a transformative force to develop African societies and start an economic, social, and cultural revolution.

17

The Contribution of AU Human Rights Agreements to an Emergent AU Law

Gino Naldi

1. Introduction

The Organisation of African Unity (OAU) did not have the advancement of human rights amongst its core objectives.[1] The OAU Charter was silent on the subject save for a passing reference to the Universal Declaration on Human Rights (UDHR).[2] Rather, the OAU was founded on the ideals of continental unity and solidarity and provided for cooperation across a range of areas, with an emphasis on the liberation struggle.[3] Nevertheless, in time the OAU took measures to promote and protect human rights through the adoption of various treaties and other initiatives that laid the foundations for a regional human rights system. Included in this system was machinery for their protection which has made, and continues to make, a distinctive contribution to human rights law.[4] This was a gradual, measured, evolutionary process similar to the road travelled by the Organization of American States (OAS)[5] and the European Community/European Union (EU).[6] The most significant achievements of the OAU in this field arguably were the adoption of the African Charter on Human and Peoples' Rights (Charter)[7] and the Protocol on the African Court on Human and Peoples' Rights (Court Protocol)[8].

[1] K Mbaye, 'Keynote Address on the African Charter on Human and Peoples' Rights' in International Commission of Jurists (ed), *Human and Peoples' Rights in Africa and the African Charter* (International Commission of Jurists, 1986) 20–1.

[2] Charter of the Organization of African Unity (adopted 25 May 1963, entered into force 13 September 1963) 479 UNTS 39 Article 2(1)(e).

[3] 50th Anniversary Solemn Declaration, AU Doc Assembly/AU/Decl. 3 (XXI) (adopted 26 May 2013) para I; P Sands and P Klein, *Bowett's Law of International Institutions*, 6th edn (Sweet & Maxwell, 2009) 248–9, who consider freeing Africa from colonialism and apartheid the OAU's greatest achievement.

[4] R Murray, *Human Rights in Africa: From the OAU to the African Union* (CUP, 2004) 7–30.

[5] JM Pasqualucci, *The Practice and Procedure of the Inter-American Court of Human Rights* (CUP, 2003) 2–6.

[6] It was only with the Treaty on European Union (Maastricht Treaty) Article 6(2) in 1992 that the EU undertook a treaty obligation to respect fundamental rights.

[7] African Charter on Human and Peoples' Rights (adopted 17 June 1981, entered into force 21 October 1986) 1520 UNTS 217.

[8] Protocol on the Establishment of an African Court on Human and Peoples' Rights (adopted 10 June 1998, entered into force 25 January 2004) reprinted in C Heyns and M Killander (eds), *Compendium of Key Human Rights Documents of the African Union*, 6th edn (Pretoria University Law Press, 2016) 41.

Gino Naldi, *The Contribution of AU Human Rights Agreements to an Emergent AU Law* In: *The Emergent African Union Law.* Edited by: Olufemi Amao, Michèle Olivier and Konstantinos D. Magliveras, Oxford University Press.
DOI: 10.1093/oso/9780198862154.003.0018

In accordance with these treaties the African Commission on Human and Peoples' Rights (Commission) and the African Court on Human and Peoples' Rights (Court) were assigned the role of monitoring the observance of the rights enshrined in the Charter and other relevant treaties.[9] By the time of the adoption of the Court Protocol in 1998 human rights was assuming a higher priority for the OAU, reflected in the Grand Bay Declaration which, *inter alia*, called for human rights issues to be integrated into all OAU activities.[10] These treaties were supplemented by initiatives such as New Partnership for Africa's Development (NEPAD) adopted in 2001 and the African Peer Review Mechanism (APRM) created in 2003, establishing the link between human rights, good governance, and development, and aimed at fostering a culture of compliance supported by peer support.[11] Both NEPAD and the APRM are based on an integrated approach, accepting that a variety of factors, including democracy, good governance, and human rights, are essential conditions for sustainable development.[12] In 2002 the OAU was dissolved and effectively succeeded by the African Union (AU).[13] The AU has a rights-based approach to policy-making and, in contrast to the OAU, has explicitly committed itself in its founding principles to promote and protect human rights and democratic values.[14] Under the AU, human rights moved from the margins, so to speak, to a central role. The centrality of human rights is underlined by the role of the Peace and Security Council.[15] The AU consequently set out to expand on the OAU's accomplishments of establishing a treaty regime embodying an African vision of human rights and ridding the continent of colonialism and apartheid. Despite lofty commitments to human rights and democracy, the AU has been beset by problems such as institutional weaknesses, financial dependency, and an apparent unwillingness to address abuses of power by Africa's political elite. Empty promises of human rights protection and enforcement are criticisms often hurled at the AU.

[9] Under Rule 3 the Commission is described as 'an autonomous treaty body working within the framework' of the AU, Rules of Procedure of the African Commission of Human and Peoples' Rights 2010, reprinted in ibid (n 8) 168. Another monitoring body is the African Committee of Experts on the Rights and Welfare of the Child (ACERWC) set up under the African Charter on the Rights and Welfare of the Child (adopted 1 July 1990, entered into force 29 November 1999) (1989) 28 ILM 1456 (Children's Rights Charter) Article 32. The ACERWC has been held to be an AU organ with a quasi-judicial function, *Request for Advisory Opinion by the African Committee of Experts on the Rights and Welfare of the Child on the Standing of the African Committee of Experts on the Rights and Welfare of the Child before the African Court of Human and Peoples' Rights* (Advisory Opinion) (2014) 1 ACtLR 725 paras 56–57, 87.

[10] Grand Bay (Mauritius) Declaration and Plan of Action (adopted April 1999) reprinted in Heyns and Killander (n 8) 149 (Grand Bay Declaration) para 22.

[11] The New Partnership for Africa's Development Declaration (adopted July 2001).

[12] NEPAD para 71.

[13] Constitutive Act of the African Union (adopted 11 July 2000, entered into force 26 May 2001) 2158 UNTS 3 (Constitutive Act).

[14] Constitutive Act Articles 3(g), (h), 4(m). See KD Magliveras and GJ Naldi, 'The African Union – a new dawn for Africa?' (2002) 51 International and Comparative Law Quarterly 415, 416–17.

[15] Protocol Relating to the Establishment of the Peace and Security Council of the African Union (adopted 9 July 2002, entered into force on 26 December 2003) reprinted in (2005) 13 African Journal of International and Comparative Law 96 Articles 3(f) and 4(c) (PSC Protocol).

This chapter will highlight a significant body of jurisprudence by the Commission and the Court to the development of human and peoples' rights pointing to the fact that treaty-based human rights are indeed regarded as binding and enforceable by AU Member States. The questions this chapter seeks to answer are whether it is possible to discern a distinctive African approach to human rights and how this can contribute to an emerging AU law. It is suggested that enforceable human rights are a foundational building block in establishing an AU law.

2. The Imperative of Human Rights in AU Law

Human rights are an essential purpose of the AU. Such ideals are enshrined in the operative sections of the Constitutive Act.[16] The promotion and protection of human rights in accordance with the Charter and other relevant human rights instruments is one of the AU's objectives.[17] Similarly, among its governing principles is respect for, *inter alia*, human rights and the promotion of social justice.[18] The latter necessarily implies an acceptance of socio-economic rights. Although the wording of these provisions is inchoate it is now generally accepted that, as with the UN Charter, they create binding obligations for the AU Member States.[19] This observation is reinforced by the fact that the Court has confirmed jurisdiction over the interpretation and application of the Constitutive Act.[20] It also reflects the primacy of international human rights.[21] But what is truly exceptional is that the Constitutive Act confers upon the AU the right to intervene in the internal affairs of Member States in certain circumstances.[22] In fact, the principle of non-interference in the internal affairs of states applies to other Member States only, not the AU.[23]

[16] Supplemented by the PSC Protocol Articles 3(f), 4(c); African Charter on Democracy, Elections and Governance (adopted 30 January 2007, entered into force 15 February 2012) reprinted in Heyns and Killander (n 8) 125 (African Charter on Democracy) Articles 3(f) and 4(c)6. See also Protocol Establishing the African Economic Community relating to the Pan-African Parliament (adopted 2 March 2001, entered into force 14 December 2003) reprinted in (2005) 13 African Journal of International and Comparative Law 86 Article 3(2).

[17] Constitutive Act Article 3(h). See *Chacha v Tanzania* (Admissibility) (2014) 1 AfCLR 398 para 124; *Alex Thomas v Tanzania* (2015) 1 AfCLR 465 para 52.

[18] Constitutive Act Article 4(m), (n).

[19] H Lauterpacht, *Oppenheim's International Law*, vol I, 8th edn) (Longmans, 1955) 738–43; *Legal Consequences for States of the Continued Presence of South Africa in Namibia* (Advisory Opinion) [1971] ICJ Rep 16, 57.

[20] See *Omary and Others v Tanzania* (Admissibility) (2014) AfCLR 358 para 70.

[21] F Ermacora, 'Human rights and domestic jurisdiction (Article 2, ¶ 7, of the Charter)' (1968) 124 Recueil des Cours de l'Académie de Droit International 371; AP Vijapur, ' The question of domestic jurisdiction and the evolution of United Nations Law of Human Rights' (2010) 47 International Studies 247.

[22] Constitutive Act art 4(h), (p). See further PSC Protocol Article 7(e)–(g). See B Kioko, 'The right of intervention under the African Union's Constitutive Act: from non-interference to non-intervention' (2003) 85 International Review of the Red Cross 807.

[23] Constitutive Act Article 4(g). See further Vienna Declaration and Programme of Action (1993) 32 ILM 1661 Pt I, para 2.

It demonstrates that the AU is committed actively to protect human rights *within* states. The sovereignty of Member States and the principle of non-interference are no longer viewed as sacrosanct or inviolable; humanitarian or other intervention by the AU is considered permissible. It is therefore possible to discern elements of supranationalism in the Constitutive Act and the PSC Protocol.

As expected in such documents the Constitutive Act does not contain concise definitions of human rights, lending itself as a source for future development; the Constitutive Act, unlike the OAU Charter, provides the AU with a clear and explicit mandate to act in this field. But the AU did not start from scratch, it was building on the OAU's endeavours, notably the Charter. The AU has proceeded to reaffirm its commitment to human rights in a number of soft law documents and subject-specific treaties. The former include the Kigali Declaration, which reiterates the pledges undertaken in the Grand Bay Declaration, highlighting the importance of second-generation rights.[24] An important development was Agenda 2063, a bold strategic people-driven plan for Pan-African renewal of an 'integrated, prosperous and peaceful Africa' based on, *inter alia*, peace, human rights, and good governance, building upon NEPAD, among other initiatives.[25] Agenda 2063 reflects deeply held desires for unity and integration, peace and improved human security, progress and development, and a meaningful voice for Africa on the global stage.[26] It covers a number of areas, including for present purposes good governance and peace and security. It seeks to achieve these goals by, *inter alia*, entrenching human rights.

In terms of treaty development a widespread belief existed that the rights of vulnerable and marginalized groups such as children and the aged were insufficiently secured under the Charter. Hence the OAU/AU considered it necessary to adopt dedicated human rights instruments that specifically addressed their needs and concerns from an African perspective. The first of these treaties was the Children's Rights Charter.[27] There followed the Women's Rights Protocol,[28] the African Youth Charter,[29] the Older Persons Protocol,[30] and the Persons with Disabilities Protocol[31].

[24] Kigali Declaration (adopted May 2003) reprinted in Heyns and Killander (n 8) 154.

[25] Assembly, *Decision on the Report of the Commission on Development of the African Union Agenda 2063*, AU Doc Assembly/AU/Dec. 565(XXIV) (adopted 30–31 January 2015).

[26] African Union, Agenda 2063 – The Africa We Want: First Ten-Year Implementation Plan (2015).

[27] See (n 9) above.

[28] Protocol to the African Charter on Human and Peoples' Rights on the Rights of Women in Africa (adopted 11 July 2003, entered into force 25 November 2005) reprinted in Heyns and Killander (n 8) 65 (Women's Rights Protocol).

[29] African Youth Charter (adopted 2 July 2006, entered into force 8 August 2009) reprinted in Heyns and Killander (n 8) 112.

[30] Protocol to the African Charter on Human and Peoples' Rights of Older Persons in Africa (adopted 31 January 2016) (Older Persons Protocol).

[31] Protocol to the African Charter on Human and Peoples' Rights on the Rights of Persons with Disabilities in Africa (adopted 29 January 2018) (Persons with Disabilities Protocol).

In the light of this it is suggested that the OAU and the AU have been at the forefront in advancing the law on human rights in terms of treaty developments. The AU in particular has been much more proactive than the EU or the OAS in legislating to protect vulnerable persons. It is further important to note that the rights embodied in the African treaties often go further than their UN or regional counterparts. In theory, the AU has put in place an impressively comprehensive system that should ensure that the rights of no vulnerable person are overlooked. Impressive as these developments are, however, rights can ultimately be effectively protected only if the treaties are properly implemented and enforced. In large measure they are dependent on states taking their obligations seriously and successfully implementing them.

3. The African Charter on Human and Peoples' Rights: A Unique and Enforceable Instrument?

The discussion here will start by assessing whether there is merit to the claim that the Charter is indeed unique within the field of international and regional human rights protection.[32] Within this context, aspects such as state sovereignty, the right to development, and environmental human rights will be discussed. In addition, the important issue of justiciability of African instruments will be considered.

Launching the era of African human rights, the Charter contains a catalogue of rights and freedoms and is well-known for its inclusion of all three categories, or generations, of rights: civil and political rights; economic, social, and cultural rights; and peoples', or group, rights. The latter is arguably its defining characteristic.[33] It is a reflection of the African viewpoint that human rights are universal, indivisible, interdependent, and inter-related but also that human beings cannot have a dignified life in isolation.[34] The Charter must also be considered in the context of the values of African civilization and historical traditions which emphasizes the nexus between the individual and the wider community.[35] Moreover, it must be assessed against the background of the 'uniqueness' of the African condition,[36] including underdevelopment, poverty, weak states, economic exploitation, and so forth,[37] which obliges international human rights to be responsive to African needs.[38] Second- and third-generation rights are essential elements of the African

[32] For a further discussion of different aspects of African human rights see chapters 11, 15, 16, and 20 of this book.

[33] Mbaye (n 1) 28–9; RM D'Sa, 'Human and peoples' rights: distinctive features of the African Charter' (1985) 29 Journal of African Law 72, 77–9.

[34] Grand Bay Declaration para 2; Kigali Declaration para 1; African Charter on Democracy art 6.

[35] Charter Preamble; Mbaye (n 1) 27; D'Sa (n 33) 73–4.

[36] Mbaye (n 1) 29–30.

[37] ibid 20–1; D'Sa (n 33) 74.

[38] *The Social and Economic Rights Action Center and the Center for Economic and Social Rights (SERAC) v Nigeria* (2001) AHRLR 60 para 68.

concept of rights and have therefore been embedded in later treaties such as the Children's Rights Charter and the Women's Rights Protocol. As will be seen, these are recurring themes. Of course, the Charter is not the first treaty to give prominence to second-generation rights but it is distinctive in providing for all three categories of human rights in a single binding legal instrument.[39]

In the seminal *SERAC* case, the Commission stressed that 'collective rights, environmental rights, and economic and social rights are essential elements of human rights in Africa'.[40] Moreover, the inclusion of third-generation rights constitutes one of the Charter's foremost distinctive features.[41] Nonetheless, all categories of rights are considered of equal validity, none having priority.[42] And significantly, the Commission considers them as justiciable, enforceable, and capable of realization.[43] It has stated that 'there is no right in the African Charter that cannot be made effective' and that it will apply to 'any of the diverse rights contained' therein.[44] A review of the Commission's jurisprudence lends support to these claims.[45] It is also important to note that parties assume obligations in this regard. There appears to be an expectation that the Charter will be incorporated into, or implemented in, municipal law.[46] According to the Court, upon ratification a state 'has an obligation to make laws in line with the intents and purposes of the Charter'.[47] According to the Commission, this should result in its practical implementation producing tangible results.[48] Whether this commitment is backed up by state practice is, however, another question. The Commission's Concluding

[39] The closest example seems to be the EU Charter on Fundamental Rights. The UDHR paved the way but it is not a treaty. However, the Court has expressed the view that the UDHR forms part of customary international law, *Anudo v Tanzania* (Merits) (2018) 2 AfCtLR 248 para 76.

[40] *SERAC* (n 38) para 68.

[41] *Bissangou v Republic of Congo* (2006) AHRLR 80 para 80.

[42] *SERAC* (n 38) para 44.

[43] ibid para 68; C Odinkalu, 'Implementing Economic, Social and Cultural Rights under the African Charter on Human and Peoples' Rights' in M Evans and R Murray (eds), *The African Charter on Human and Peoples' Rights: The System in Practice, 1986–2000* (CUP, 2002) 178–218, 196. A similar conclusion was reached by the ECOWAS Court of Justice, *SERAP v Nigeria* (Judgment) ECW/CCJ/APP/0808 (27 October 2009) para 19.

[44] *SERAC* (n 38) para 68; *International Pen, Constitutional Rights Project, Interights on behalf of Ken Saro-Wiwa Jr and Civil Liberties Organization v Nigeria* (2000) AHRLR 212 para 68.

[45] KD Magliveras and GJ Naldi, *The African Union (AU)*, 2nd edn (Kluwer, 2018) 249–306.

[46] Similar to the International Covenant on Civil and Political Rights (adopted 16 December 1966, entered into force 23 March 1976) 999 UNTS 171 (ICCPR) art 2, UNHCR 'General Comment 3' in 'Note by the Secretariat, Compilation of General Comments and General Recommendations adopted by Human Rights Treaty Bodies' (1997) HRI/GEN/1/Rev.3. Whether a state adheres to the dualist or monist tradition is immaterial, *Good v Botswana* Comm No 306/2005, 28th Activity Report 2009–2010 paras 236–239.

[47] *Tanganyika Law Society et al v Tanzania* (Judgment) (2013) 1 AfCtLR 34 para 109. See also *Jawara v The Gambia* (2000) AHRLR 107 para 46; *Purohit and Moore v The Gambia* (2003) AHRLR 96 para 41. Or as it was put in *Association of Victims of Post Electoral Violence & INTERIGHTS v Cameroon* Comm No 272/2003, 27th Activity Report 2009 para 87, to respect, protect, promote, and implement the rights. The Commission has therefore described it as an obligation of means and of result, *Mbianku v Cameroon* Comm No 389/10 (2015) para 126.

[48] ibid para 108.

Reports on State Reports offers a mixed picture on this issue.[49] Typically, while a state is often commended on the measures it has taken to give domestic effect to the Charter rights, at the same time it will be censured for the lack of specific information on the enactment or implementation of appropriate legislative and policy measures. Additionally, the Commission has no means of domestic enforcement of its decisions and relies on national legal systems to implement them.[50] By contrast, the judgments of the Court appear to be binding in that states undertake to comply with them and guarantee their execution.[51] But a lamentable consequence of this international supervision has been that four states, Benin, Côte d'Ivoire, Rwanda, and Tanzania, have withdrawn their declarations recognizing the right of individual petition under the Charter.[52]

Furthermore, in keeping with fundamental principles of international law, the Court has held that states cannot seek to evade their international obligations by reference to their municipal law.[53] However, the Commission has decided that the effect of Article 1 of the Charter goes further, expressing the view that '[a]ny violation of the provisions of the African Charter automatically means a violation of Article 1 and that goes to the root of the African Charter since the obligations imposed by Article 1 ... are peremptory'.[54] In so doing, the Commission assumes the task of being able to examine the extent to which domestic law complies with the provisions of the Charter.[55]

This promising position on the supremacy of human rights law could potentially be undermined however by the extensive use within the Charter of limitations or restrictions that seemingly make rights subject to municipal law, thereby providing parties with a legitimate loophole to evade their international obligations. This would appear to explain the absence of a derogation clause, because it was considered superfluous.[56] Unlike the ICCPR or the European Convention on

[49] See <https://www.achpr.org/statereportsandconcludingobservations> accessed 16 June 2020. See G Pascale, 'An optimistic perspective on the proliferation of human rights monitoring bodies in Africa' (2018) 12 Diritti Umani e Diritto Internazionale 145, 154–5, who points out that the states are generally not cooperative. It seems that with a few notable exceptions, such as that of South Africa, socio-economic rights are generally overlooked by African states, JC Mubangizi, 'The Constitutional protection of socio-economic rights in selected African countries: a comparative evaluation' (2006) 2 African Journal of Legal Studies 1.

[50] Under Rule of Procedure 112, in instances of a decision against a state the Commission must be informed of the measures taken to implement the decision. Again, it has been noted that states are often unresponsive to the Commission's decisions, Pascale (n 49) 153.

[51] Court Protocol Article 30.

[52] N de Silva and M Plagis, 'A Court in Crisis: African States' Increasing Resistance to Africa's Human Rights Court' (19 May 2020) available at <http://opiniojuris.org/2020/05/19/a-court-in-crisis-african-states-increasing-resistance-to-africas-human-rights-court/> accessed 13 July 2020.

[53] *Tanganyika Law Society* (n 47) paras 108–109.

[54] *Zimbabwe Human Rights NGO Forum v Zimbabwe* (2005) AHRLR 128 para 78. See also *Jawara* (n 47) ibid; *Alex Thomas* (n 17) paras 135–136.

[55] *Purohit and Moore* (n 47) para 43; *Good* (n 46) para 240. The Commission has stated that it can examine a state's compliance with the Charter; 'the point of the exercise is to interpret and apply the African Charter rather than to test the validity of domestic law for its own sake', *Legal Resources Foundation v Zambia* (2001) AHRLR 84 paras 59, 61.

[56] Pascale (n 49) 151.

Human Rights (ECHR), which subject the use of limitations to strict and specific conditions, these limitations are phrased in vague terms which could conceivably make the African rights vulnerable.[57] There are numerous examples, including Article 9(2) which guarantees the freedom of expression 'within the law'.[58] These provisions therefore attracted considerable criticism from scholars.[59] Indeed, the Commission itself shared this disapproval, stating that 'if "law" is interpreted to mean any domestic law regardless of its effect, Parties to the Charter would be able to negate the rights conferred upon individuals by the Charter'.[60] But if it was the intention of states to rely on these restrictions to ensure the primacy of municipal law then the manoeuvre appears to have backfired since the Commission's practice abundantly demonstrates that it will not uphold the legality of a restriction that leaves its precise scope and nature to the whim of the state.[61] It has interpreted such clauses as 'constituting a reference to international law, meaning that only restrictions on rights which are consistent with the Charter and with Parties' international obligations should be enacted by the relevant national authorities'.[62] The applicable standard is therefore that of international human rights law, which prevails over any inconsistent municipal law.[63] Furthermore, according to the Court, a general limitation clause can be found in Article 27(2) of the Charter.[64] While the wording of the Charter with respect to limitations is flawed, it is encouraging to observe that through their jurisprudence the monitoring bodies have interpreted the relevant provisions to conform with international human rights standards.

3.1 The Protection of Second-generation Rights

As noted above, the Charter is not the only African instrument enshrining socio-economic rights, the latter also being guaranteed in a number of treaties for the

[57] See generally A Conte and R Burchill, *Defining Civil and Political Rights: The Jurisprudence of the United Nations Human Rights Committee*, 2nd edn) (Ashgate, 2009) 46–58; DJ Harris, M O'Boyle, and others, *Law of the European Convention on Human Rights*, 2nd edn (OUP, 2009) 344–59.

[58] See *Umuhoza v Rwanda* (Merits) (2017) 2 AfCtLR 165 paras 139–40. Others include Article 8, which guarantees the freedom of conscience and religion, and Article 10(1) on the right of association.

[59] See D'Sa (n 33) 110; EA Ankumah, *The African Charter on Human and Peoples' Rights* (Martinus Nijhoff, 1997) 176; R Gittleman, 'The African Charter on Human and Peoples' Rights: a legal analysis' (1982) 22 Virginia Journal of International Law 667, 692, 694.

[60] *Article 19 v Eritrea* (2007) AHRLR 73 para 91. The Commission has further stated that the rights must not become illusory, *Media Rights Agenda and Constitutional Rights Project v Nigeria* (2000) AHRLR 200 para 70.

[61] See GJ Naldi, 'Limitation of rights under the African Charter on Human and Peoples' Rights: the contribution of the African Commission on Human and Peoples' Rights' (2001) 17 South African Journal on Human Rights 109.

[62] *Article 19* (n 60) para 92; *Media Rights Agenda* (n 60) para 68; *Tanganyika Law Society* (n 47) paras 107–108.

[63] *Media Rights Agenda* (n 60) para 66; *Amnesty International v Mauritania* Comm No 61/91, 13th Activity Report 1999–2000, para 102.

[64] *Tanganyika Law Society* (n 47) para 107; *Umuhoza* (n 58) para 139.

protection of vulnerable and marginalized groups. Some of these rights may differ to a greater or lesser extent from comparable rights in universal or regional documents and may diverge further as a result of their interpretation by the African treaty monitoring bodies.[65] The following sections will draw attention to the distinctive second- and third-generation rights in the African human rights instruments.

Prominent among the second-generation rights secured in the Children's Rights Charter[66] is the right to education.[67] An exceptional feature of this Charter is its elements of cultural variation and civic and patriotic values.[68] Education of the child is thus directed to, *inter alia*, the preservation and strengthening of positive African morals, traditional values, and cultures; the preservation of national independence and territorial integrity; the promotion and achievement of African unity and solidarity; and the promotion of the child's understanding of primary healthcare.[69]

With regard to cultural and associated practices it must be highlighted that any custom, tradition, cultural or religious practice inconsistent with the Children's Rights Charter shall to the extent of the inconsistency be discouraged.[70] More specifically, harmful social and cultural practices are to be eliminated.[71] These are practices that amount to a 'total denial of the dignity and worth of the child'.[72] Begging, specifically prohibited by Article 29(b) of the Children's Rights Charter, is one such pernicious practice[73] while slavery is another.[74] Other practices may include traditional birth practices, which often jeopardize mother and child,[75] *trokosi*, the giving of 'virgin girls to priests as appeasement for past crimes committed by family members',[76] and female genital mutilation (FGM).[77] Child, or

[65] According to the Commission the Charter must be interpreted in a culturally sensitive way permitting 'justifiable modifications', *Constitutional Rights Project and Civil Liberties Organisation v Nigeria* Comm Nos 143/95, 150/96 (2000) AHRLR 235 para 26.

[66] As with the rights protected by the Charter, the rights enshrined in the Children's Rights Charter are considered indivisible, *IHRDA and Open Society Justice Initiative (OSJI) (on behalf of children of Nubian descent in Kenya) v Kenya* Comm No 2/09 (2011) AHRLR 181, para 58.

[67] Children's Rights Charter Article 11. See further Charter Article 17(1); African Youth Charter Articles 13, 23(d), (e), (g), (k); African Charter on Democracy Article 43(1). See *Centre for Human Rights (University of Pretoria) v Senegal* Comm No 001/2012 (2014) para 50; *Michelo Hunsungule and Others (on behalf of Children in Northern Uganda) v Uganda* Comm No 1/2005 (2013) paras 72–73.

[68] B Thompson, 'Africa's Charter on Children's Rights: a normative break with cultural traditionalism' (1992) 41 International and Comparative Law Quarterly 432, 435–6.

[69] Children's Rights Charter Article 11(2)(c), (e), (f), (h).

[70] ibid Article 1(3).

[71] ibid Article 21(1).

[72] *Minority Rights Group and SOS-Esclaves (on behalf of Said Ould Salem and Yarg Ould Salem) v Mauritania* Comm No 007/Com 003/2015 (2017) para 91.

[73] *Centre for Human Rights* (n 67) paras 69–73.

[74] *Minority Rights Group* (n 72) para 91.

[75] UNHCR 'Report by Special Rapporteur Ms Halima Embarek Warzazi' (2005) UN Doc E/CN.4/Sub.2/2005/36 paras 75–76.

[76] ibid para 49. See J Asamoah, 'Cultural rights versus human rights: A critical analysis of the *trokosi* practice in Ghana and the role of civil society' (2015) 15 African Human Rights Law Journal 129.

[77] See also African Youth Charter Article 23(l). This practice has been condemned by the UN Fourth World Conference on Women (Beijing Platform for Action) (1996) 35 ILM 401 para 283(d). See further

early, marriages are expressly prohibited and the fact that 18 years is specified as the minimum age at which marriage can be lawfully entered into is noteworthy.[78] However, forced marriage is not explicitly addressed.[79]

A variety of socio-economic rights for women are enumerated in considerable detail in the Women's Rights Protocol.[80] These include a right to education,[81] a right to health,[82] and a right to adequate housing[83]. The Women's Rights Protocol is especially notable in that it seeks to address deeply rooted cultural prejudices in traditional societies governed by customary or religious laws that confer upon women a hierarchically inferior status, often considered 'junior males' or 'minors'.[84] This is particularly true in relation to various aspects of marriage, its dissolution, and widowhood where the Women's Rights Protocol is much more prescriptive than other instruments which merely require that the issues be regulated by domestic law.[85] Because in many African countries the husband, or other male relative, is considered the custodian of the wife's person and property, and because customary law often adversely affects the woman's inheritance rights,[86] the woman's right to own and administer property is a significant development.[87] Another critical advance is the inclusion of reproductive rights,[88] including termination of pregnancy in certain circumstances.[89] A traditional cultural practice that is prohibited as harmful is FGM.[90]

Under the Older Persons Protocol states are obliged to adopt affirmative measures and allocate resources, for example, in relation to social security.[91] States must make certain that persons who retire have adequate pensions and other social security measures and must additionally ensure some form of universal social

UNGA Res. 67/146 (20 December 2012) para 4. It has been reported that FGM exists in at least 26 countries in Africa, 'Report by Special Rapporteur Ms Halima Embarek Warzazi' (2005) UN Doc E/CN.4/Sub.2/2005/36 para 10.

78 Children's Rights Charter Article 21(2). Note Beijing Platform for Action para 274(e).
79 However, the African Youth Charter art 8(2) states that marriage must be based on free consent.
80 See (n 28) above.
81 Protocol on Women's Rights Article 12.
82 ibid Article 14.
83 ibid Article 16. See further ibid Article 13.
84 See the controversial judgment of the Supreme Court of Zimbabwe in *Magaya v Magaya* [1999] 3 LRC 35.
85 Women's Rights Protocol Articles 6, 7. cf European Convention on Human Rights (ECHR) Article 12.
86 Ankumah (n 59) 153–4. In *Bhe and others v The Magistrate, Khayelitsha and others* 2005 (1) SA 580 (CC) the Constitutional Court of South Africa held that the African customary rule of male primogeniture in relation to the inheritance of property was discriminatory.
87 Women's Rights Protocol Article 6(j). See Beijing Platform for Action para 61(b).
88 ibid Article 14. See also African Youth Charter Article 16(b), (c). And see, for example, Beijing Platform for Action para 106(e).
89 ibid Article 14(2)(c).
90 ibid Article 5(b). See Beijing Platform for Action para 107(a).
91 Older Persons Protocol Article 19 (n 30).

protection is in place for those who may not have contributed to any social security scheme.[92] While the Older Persons Protocol does not in fact provide for a right to health as such, which is guaranteed by the Charter, it does oblige parties to grant older persons access to health services.[93] Parties are under a general obligation to eliminate social and cultural stereotypes.[94] Older women should be protected from harmful traditional practices, including accusations of witchcraft.[95]

The Persons with Disabilities Protocol contains a number of second-generation rights, including the right to education, the right to health, the right to work, and the right to an adequate standard of living.[96] As with the previous treaties, persons with disabilities are to be protected from harmful traditional practices and superstitions which are to be eliminated.[97] This includes witchcraft, abandonment and, shockingly, ritual killings.[98]

It can therefore be seen from the inclusion and prominence of second-generation rights in these human rights instruments that their furtherance is a key characteristic of the African system. But one common feature stands out, that of protection against harmful traditional cultural practices. Such practices are clearly incompatible with notions of human dignity and arguably amount to inhuman treatment. They cannot be justified on grounds of cultural relativity or variation. It is therefore encouraging to note that in recent years the practice of FGM has been, or is being, prohibited by law and made a criminal offence in a number of African countries.[99] Of added significance is that the Commission has been at the forefront in pronouncing on socio-economic rights.[100] It has

[92] ibid Article 7(1)–(2).
[93] ibid Article 15(1)–(2).
[94] ibid Article 3.
[95] ibid Article 8(1), (2). See also Women's Rights Protocol Article 5(b).
[96] Persons with Disabilities Protocol Articles 16–20 (n 31).
[97] ibid Article 11(1).
[98] ibid Articles 4(d), 30(2)(e), 11(1). Ritual killings refer to killings motivated by cultural, religious or superstitious beliefs, mostly associated with albinism, that a body or body parts has medicinal value, supernatural powers, or brings good luck, ibid Preamble.
[99] UNHCR 'Report by Special Rapporteur Ms Radhika Coomaraswamy' (2002) UN Doc E/CN.4/2002/83 para 17. The latest state to do so is Sudan, BBC News, 'Sudan criminalises female genital mutilation (FGM)' (1 May 2020) available at <https://www.bbc.co.uk/news/world-africa-52502489> accessed 14 July 2020.
[100] By adopting a broad view of the combined effect of a number of these provisions the Commission has successfully read implied rights into the Charter, for example, a right to shelter or housing, and food, *SERAC* (n 38) paras 121–123. For in-depth analysis see Odinkalu (n 43); M Ssenyonjo, 'Analysing the economic, social and cultural rights jurisprudence of the African Commission: 30 years since the adoption of the African Charter' (2011) 29 Netherlands Quarterly on Human Rights 358. It should be observed that the UN Committee on Economic, Social and Cultural Rights (CESR) has only been able to hear individual complaints since 2013 and has not been very active in this regard. See <https://ijrcenter.org/un-treaty-bodies/committee-on-economic-social-and-cultural-rights/> accessed 22 June 2020.

thus ruled on the right to work,[101] the right to health,[102] and the right to culture[103]. Its jurisprudence is broadly consistent with the CESR General Comments and hence, although of some consequence, adds little that is ground-breaking jurisprudentially.[104] However, it is not the only such body to perform such a task, the ACERWC possessing a very specific mandate in relation to the rights of children. Significantly, it has held that the rights contained in the Children's Rights Charter are enforceable.[105] It is also important to note that the Court has jurisdiction over disputes concerning all the subject-specific treaties.[106]

3.2 The Protection of Peoples' Rights

It seems fair to assert that the Commission has led the way pronouncing on peoples' rights.[107] Because of their distinctiveness and the dearth of judicial or quasi-judicial scrutiny at the international level the Commission's observations are particularly illuminating. This section will therefore focus only on those peoples' rights that have been considered by the African monitoring bodies rather than on a doctrinal discussion.

One of the rights highly cherished in Africa because of its resonance with Pan-Africanism and the liberation struggle is that of self-determination.[108] The Charter is not the first treaty to recognize self-determination as a human right and the Commission has had the opportunity to elucidate its meaning and ramifications.[109] Self-determination has two dimensions, external and internal, the former relating to the creation of new states and the latter encompassing a variety of features, including the equality of states, sovereignty over natural resources, and good governance for groups and minorities within a state.[110] With regard to the former variant the Commission has held that the exercise of self-determination under Article 20 of the Charter must be compatible with the sovereignty and

[101] *Monim Elgak, Osman Hummeida and Amir Suleiman v Sudan*, Comm No 379/09 (2014) para 129.
[102] *Purohit and Moore* (n 47) para 80; *Egyptian Initiative for Personal Rights and INTERIGHTS v Egypt* (2011) AHRLR 90 para 264.
[103] *Centre for Minority Rights Development (Kenya) and Minority Rights Group International on behalf of Endorois Welfare Council v Kenya* (2009) AHRLR 75 paras 241, 246, 248. See also *African Commission on Human and Peoples' Rights v Kenya* (Merits) (2017) 2 AfCtLR 9 paras 177–179.
[104] See, for example, CESR 'General Comment 13' (8 December 1999) UN Doc E/C.12/1999/10; CESR 'General Comment 14' (11 August 2000) UN Doc E/C.12/2000/4; CESR 'General Comment 18' (6 February 2006) UN Doc E/C.12/GC/18.
[105] *Hunsungule* (n 67) paras 37–38.
[106] Court Protocol Article 3(1).
[107] See C Baldwin and C Morel, 'Group rights' in M Evans and R Murray (eds) *The African Charter on Human and Peoples' Rights: The System in Practice, 1986–2006*, 2nd edn (CUP, 2008) 244–288.
[108] Charter Article 20(1).
[109] Conte and Burchill (n 57) 257–9.
[110] L-C Chen, *An Introduction to Contemporary International Law*, 2nd edn) (Yale University Press, 2000) 31.

territorial integrity of states and that secession is not sanctioned.[111] Accordingly, 'secession is not recognised as a variant of the right of self-determination within the context of the African Charter'.[112] Consequently, self-determination must be exercised in a manner compatible with the sovereignty and territorial integrity of states.[113] This approach mirrors the stance of the AU, and the OAU before it, in upholding the principle of the territorial integrity of states,[114] reflecting in turn the standpoint of African states.[115] A current illustration is that of Cameroon, where an English-speaking minority claim that they have been denied their right to self-determination.[116]

The Commission has invoked the internal dimension of self-determination to uphold democratic values.[117] Interestingly, this pre-dated the adoption of the Constitutive Act which embodies a culture of constitutionalism and democracy.[118] It should be borne in mind that African states were artificially demarcated in response to the whims of colonial rulers and did not reflect the needs, history, and identities of the inhabitants. The result is that modern African states generally have heterogeneous populations comprising different language and cultural groups. In order to reduce separatist sentiments, the Commission has promoted the internal dimension of self-determination that provides for some form of self-government to certain groups or peoples within a state.[119] This approach may not be popular amongst African rulers who tend to centralize power but it should be observed that the African Charter on Democracy contains a commitment to decentralize power to local authorities.[120] It would also be in keeping with good governance. An alternative scenario would be that in extreme cases of oppression and persecution of minorities secession may be justified.[121]

The Charter incorporates the concept of permanent sovereignty over natural resources and must be viewed in the context of the negative legacy of the colonial era.[122] This right vests not only in the state itself[123] but extends to indigenous

[111] *Katangese Peoples' Congress v Zaire* (2000) AHRLR 72; *Gunme et al v Cameroon* (2009) AHRLR 9 paras 190, 200.

[112] ibid para 200.

[113] *Katangese Peoples' Congress* (n 111) ibid; *Gunme* (n 111) paras 190, 200.

[114] Constitutive Act Article 3(b); PSC Protocol 4(e). In relation to the OAU see OAU Charter Articles2(1)(c), 3(3). See further AHG/Res. 51(IV) (1967) whereby the OAU condemned secession in Member States, reaffirmed its support for the principle of territorial integrity, and declared that the right of self-determination did not apply to cases of secession.

[115] See GJ Naldi, 'Secession: The African Experience' in CC Jalloh and O Elias (eds), *Shielding Humanity: Essays in International Law and Policy in Honour of Abdul Koroma* (Martinus Nijhoff Brill, 2015) 680–704.

[116] See V Muguoh Chiatoh, 'Self-Determination and Territorial Integrity: Southern Cameroons and the Republic of Cameroun' (2019) 27 African Journal of International and Comparative Law 629.

[117] *Jawara* (n 47) para 73.

[118] Constitutive Act Articles 3(g), 4(m), and the African Charter on Democracy.

[119] *Katangese Peoples' Congress* (n 111) ibid; *Gunme* (n 111) para 190.

[120] African Charter on Democracy Article 34.

[121] *Katangese Peoples' Congress* (n 111) para 6; *Gunme* (n 111) paras 197, 199.

[122] Charter Article 21; *SERAC* (n 38) para 56.

[123] *Democratic Republic of Congo v Burundi, Rwanda and Uganda* (2004) AHRLR 19 para 94.

peoples.[124] Parties are obliged to eliminate all forms of foreign economic exploitation, particularly that practised by international monopolies.[125] In cases of spoliation, dispossessed people have the right to the lawful recovery of their property and adequate compensation.[126] It is not clear by whom the compensation will be payable, or what appropriate levels of compensation should be, but the Commission has suggested the respondent state pay compensation.[127] This plea has not found favour with African states.

The right to development is another prized right and states are under an individual or collective duty to ensure its exercise under the Charter.[128] While there is doubt as to whether such a right has yet emerged in international law,[129] the support expressed for it in Africa remains strong.

The Charter pioneered a human right to the environment.[130] The right to environment is not defined but coming within its scope is protection of the environment from, *inter alia*, pollution and polluting activities.[131] Thus, in *SERAC* the Commission found a violation of the right of peoples to a clean and safe environment when exploitation of oilfields polluted the environment. It reported that states were under an obligation to take reasonable measures 'to prevent pollution and ecological degradation, to promote conservation, and to secure an ecologically sustainable development and use of natural resources'.[132] Securing a right to a satisfactory environment can be highlighted as one of the Charter's preeminent achievements; it has been included in later human rights instruments.[133]

[124] *Endorois Welfare Council* (n 103) paras 255, 263; *African Commission* (n 103) para 201. In *Case of the Mayagna (Sumo) Community of Awas Tingni v Nicaragua*, Judgment, Series C No 79 (31 August 2001), the IACHR, relying on ACHR art 21, found that international law protects the collective right of indigenous people to land and resources.

[125] Charter Article 21(5). In *SERAC* (n 38) para 58 the Commission found that Nigeria had facilitated the destruction of Ogoniland in league with oil companies.

[126] Charter Article 21(2).

[127] *Endorois Welfare Council* (n 103) para 268.

[128] Charter Article 22. Later treaties enshrine a right to sustainable development, Constitutive Act Article 3(j); PSC Protocol Article 3(a); Protocol on Women's Rights Article 19.

[129] A Aust, *Handbook of International Law*, 2nd edn (CUP, 2010) 218.

[130] Ankumah (n 59) 168–70. The OAS followed this example in the Additional Protocol to the American Convention on Human Rights in the Area of Economic, Social, and Cultural Rights (adopted 17 November 1988, entered into force 16 November 1999) (1989) 28 ILM 156 Article 11. Notwithstanding the absence of any provision on the environment in the ECHR the European Court of Human Rights has read an obligation of environmental protection in Article 8 thereof, Harris, and others (n 57) 390–1.

[131] Charter Article 24. See also Protocol on Women's Rights Article 18(c), (d). Under the African Charter on Democracy Article 42, states commit themselves to implement policies to protect the environment to achieve sustainable development for the benefit of present and future generations.

[132] *SERAC* (n 38) para 52.

[133] See Protocol on Women Rights art 18; African Youth Charter Article 19; African Convention on the Conservation of Nature and Natural Resources (Revised) (adopted 11 July 2003) Article 3(1). The Grand Bay Declaration paras 2, 8(n), reiterated the right to a healthy environment as a human right that was infringed by environmental degradation.

A right to national and international peace and security is also undertaken.[134] While the term 'peace and security'[135] is not explicitly defined reference is made to the principles of solidarity and friendly relations affirmed by the UN and the OAU.[136] In *Congo v Burundi* the Commission established a link between this provision and the principle of the peaceful settlement of disputes set out in the UN and the OAU Charters. It held that the occupation of the DRC by the armed forces of neighbouring states was 'impermissible' and a violation of Article 23 of the Charter.[137]

The Charter is one of the few regional human rights instruments to give prominence to third-generation rights, the Women's Rights Protocol being another. Many of these rights reflect basic principles of international law, such as a right to peace, which are binding on states but in the present context they impose obligations on states not only to realign their internal affairs in conformity with their international obligations but they are also required to pursue particular forms of foreign policy calculated to achieve such ends. By enshrining peoples' rights, the Charter and the Women's Rights Protocol reflect a special conception of human rights.

4. Conclusion

Human rights are an integral component of the AU. The AU particularly has built up over time a regional system for the promotion, protection, and implementation of human rights. It has accordingly adopted a number of treaties and related documents which considered overall constitutes a comprehensive network of protection for different groups of peoples, such as children and the aged. One of the outstanding features of the Charter is the inclusion of all three categories of rights. This facet has been replicated to a greater or lesser extent in the later treaties. This emphasis, on group rights especially, is a particular and prominent characteristic of African human rights which distinguishes it from developments elsewhere. Of added significance is the fact that second- and third-generation rights have not remained as mere abstractions but are being turned into reality by the Commission and the Court which are playing an all-important role regarding their justiciability

[134] Charter Article 23(1). See also Protocol on Women's Rights art 10. The African Charter on Democracy Articles 38, 39, acknowledges the nexus between the realization of human rights and the maintenance of peace and security.

[135] In *Malawi African Association et al v Mauritania* (2000) AHRLR 149 para 140, the Commission held that unprovoked attacks on villages amounted to a denial of the right to live in peace and security.

[136] The UN Declaration on the Principles of International Law Concerning Friendly Relations and Cooperation Among States in Accordance with the UN Charter UNGA Res. 2625 (XXV) (24 October 1970) is directly relevant, *Congo v Burundi* (n 123) para 73.

[137] ibid paras 66, 74–75.

and enforceability. They are making a constructive input into an emerging body of jurisprudence in these areas, specific to Africa perhaps in some instances but also influential more broadly. Africa is making a distinctive contribution to the human rights discourse, that the 'full-belly thesis' is itself worthy of serious consideration. These are notable African achievements. The view that on 'its interpretation of the Charter, the Commission has been mostly positive and sometimes even innovative' seems truer today than ever.[138]

[138] C Odinkalu, 'The individual complaints procedures of the African Commission on Human and Peoples' Rights: a preliminary assessment' (1998) 8 Transnational Law & Contemporary Problems 359, 402.

18

Sustainable Development and the AU Legal Order

Eghosa Ekhator

1. Introduction

Sustainable development has been at the centre of discourse in the African Union (AU) and its Member States in recent times. This is especially relevant in the light of international initiatives in relation to the Sustainable Development Goals (SDGs) and initiatives developed under the auspices of the AU (e.g. Agenda 2063). This chapter critically analyses the emergent AU legal order through a sustainable development lens. This chapter focuses on the AU instruments and initiatives promoting sustainable development and how these initiatives are also contributing to the emergent AU Law. Hence, the question this chapter seeks to answer is whether the AU sustainable development mechanisms are an integral part of the emergent AU legal order.

The chapter is divided into five sections. Section 2 provides a brief discussion of AU Law and its relationship with sustainable development norms on the continent. Section 3 focuses on the evolution of sustainable development in the international sphere. Section 4 focuses on some AU initiatives on sustainable development on the continent. Arguably, these AU sustainable development initiatives have led to the development of standards/norms/laws at the continental level which is part of the emergent AU legal order. Section 5 makes some recommendations and Section 6 concludes. This chapter contends that the AU mechanisms on sustainable development are an essential part of the emergent AU legal order. This chapter also concludes that AU mechanisms on sustainable development will contribute to the development of common standards/norms/laws at the continental level which enhances the emergent continental AU legal order.

2. AU Law and Sustainable Development

Due to the different institutions, norms and frameworks developed under the AU, some scholars have argued that the concept of 'African Union law' is emerging or

Eghosa Ekhator, *Sustainable Development and the AU Legal Order* In: *The Emergent African Union Law*. Edited by: Olufemi Amao, Michèle Olivier and Konstantinos D. Magliveras, Oxford University Press.
DOI: 10.1093/oso/9780198862154.003.0019

evolving.[1] AU law has been defined 'as the bodies of treaties, resolutions and decisions that have direct and indirect application to the member States of the Union'.[2] The concept of an AU law or AU legal order can be traced especially to the creation of the African Union.[3] The AU in contradistinction to its predecessor, the Organisation of African Union (OAU), is said to have kick-started a new continental legal order in Africa with its unique strengths and characteristics.[4] Unlike, the OAU, the AU was created via a Constitutive Act of the AU. Furthermore, it has been argued that the Constitutive Act created a continental social contract and a constitutional tool.[5] Hence, Addaney, and Jegede, and other contributors to their volume argue that this development suggests that Africa currently lays the foundation or basis for a continental-wide legal order.[6] However, the concept of AU law is not yet a generally recognized term in law and practice.[7] A major criticism of AU law points to the fact that the AU law lacks the depth and complexity seen in the European Union (EU) law.[8]

Notwithstanding the criticism against and apparent weaknesses of the AU law or AU legal order, this section posits that AU law is indeed emerging. Magliveras and Naldi suggest that AU law is an important development in the scholarship on the AU and that it should be extensively studied by AU researchers or scholars.[9] Fortunately, there have been recent publications that have based their analysis on the concept of AU law.[10] For example, Addaney and Jegede's edited collection focuses on human rights and environment and relies on AU law as its analytical framework.[11]

The concept of AU law engages with the AU's capacity for norm creation through its institutions and decisions and raises the questions whether it paves the way for an emerging continental legal system with supranational qualities. Also, arguably sustainable development can form part of that body of norms. AU law is more than treaties adopted by AU but refers to capacity of the AU and its institutions to enforce decisions/norms as matter of law/soft law. However, the remit of the AU legal

[1] O Amao, *African Union Law: The Emergence of a Sui Generis Legal Order* (Routledge, 2018); M Olivier, 'The role of African Union law in integrating Africa' (2015) 22(5) South African Journal of International Affairs 513

[2] ibid 22.

[3] ibid.

[4] ibid.

[5] ibid.

[6] M Addaney and A Jegede (eds), *Human Rights and the Environment under African Union Law* (Palgrave Macmillan, 2020)

[7] Generally, see K Magliveras and G Naldi, *The African Union* (Kluwer, 2018) 87

[8] ibid.

[9] ibid 87. Also, Amao (n 1) 17 suggests that the development of AU law has been 'largely gone unnoticed or is under-explored within the academic discourse'.

[10] For example, see Addaney and Jegede (n 6); R Garrido, 'African regional jurisdiction: how African Union is creating an innovative regional jurisdiction for international crimes' (2020) 4(1) Portuguese Law Review 51; N Negm and G-F Ntwari, 'African Union legal drafting: process, mechanisms and challenges' (2019) 8 International Journal of Legislative Drafting and Law Reform 85.

[11] Addaney and Jegede (n 6).

order is still limited especially with respect to the enforcement of sub-regional and regional judiciaries in Africa.[12]

The creation of the AU has led to a 'new era of regional cooperation, which elevated sustainable development to a primary objective of the AU'.[13] In essence, the AU's normative framework encompasses sustainable development.[14] One of the aims of the AU is to promote or enhance sustainable development at the economic, social, and cultural levels including the integration of African economies, and cooperation in all aspects of human activity to improve the living standards of Africans.[15] This is embedded in Article 3(j) of the Constitutive Act. Hence, the Constitutive Act provides a good foundation for the development of laws or norms on sustainable development in Africa.

Furthermore, some AU environmental law conventions and recent mechanisms (including Agenda 2063 and AUDA-NEPAD) promote sustainable development in their provisions. Examples of AU environmental law conventions promoting sustainable development includes the Revised African Convention on the Conservation of Nature and Natural Resources (2017), the African Charter on Human and Peoples' Rights,[16] and the Bamako Convention on the Ban and the Import into Africa and Control of Transboundary Movement and Management of Hazardous Waste within Africa.[17] For example, the African Charter has substantive provisions (e.g. Article 24) that have been interpreted as promoting sustainable development on the continent. Also, the Revised African Convention on the Conservation of Nature and Natural Resources provides for a plethora of environmental principles including the right to satisfactory environment enshrined in Article III of the Convention.[18] A key objective of the Revised Convention (2003) is the promotion of sustainable development in environmental issues in Africa as demonstrated by Article II.[19] This is also reflected in the 2017 version. These conventions encompass diverse normative standards, which according to Maluwa forms an integral part of the corpus of the evolving rules of international law in

[12] Magliveras and Naldi (n 7) 87.

[13] W Scholtz and J Verschuuren, 'Introduction' in W Scholtz and J Verschuuren (eds), *Regional Environmental Law: Transregional Comparative Lessons in Pursuit of Sustainable Development* (Edward Elgar Publishing, 2015) 1–17, 5.

[14] ibid.

[15] Generally, see Constitutive Act of the African Union, adopted July 11, 2000, OAU Doc. CAB/LEG/ 23.15 (entered into force May 26, 2001) (AU Constitutive Act) for the aims and objectives of the AU.

[16] African Charter of Human and Peoples' Rights OAU CAB/LEG/67/3 rev. 5, 21 ILM 58 entered into force 21 October 1986.

[17] Bamako Convention on the Ban of the Import into Africa and the Control of Transboundary Movement and Management of Hazardous Wastes (1991) 30 ILM 773 (1991)

[18] B Erinosho, 'The Revised African Convention on the Conservation of Nature and Natural Resources: prospects for a comprehensive treaty for the management of Africa's Natural Resources' (2013) 21(3) African Journal of International and Comparative Law *378*.

[19] E Ekhator, 'Regulating the activities of multinational corporations in Nigeria: a case for the African Union?' (2018) 20(1) International Community Law Review 30

these spheres.[20] These conventions are expected to be respected and implemented in AU Member States that have signed and ratified them. For example, the African Charter has had a significant but modest impact in many African states.[21] Few countries (e.g. Nigeria) have domesticated the Charter, and it has been enforced in several countries in Africa.[22] Also, the African Charter has been extensively cited by domestic courts in Africa, thereby impacting positively on national laws.[23] By virtue of the various AU environmental conventions, at the continental level in Africa, environmental rights and protection (including sustainable development) are recognized as specific treaty norms or standards and this coheres with other rights and corresponding commitments or obligations.[24] Hence, the main crux of the argument in this chapter is that AU environmental conventions or treaties and regional courts (including sub-regional courts) are key to the evolution of sustainable development norms in the AU legal order.

Furthermore, this chapter focuses on the African Charter and Agenda 2063.[25] The next section discusses the evolution of the sustainable development paradigm in the international sphere.

3. Evolution of Sustainable Development in the International Sphere

Sustainable development has been a recurring theme in the international sphere in different mutations. The Brundtland Commission also known as the World Commission on Environment and Development (WCED) defined sustainable development as 'the development that meets the needs of the present without compromising the ability of future generations to meet their own needs'.[26] The Stockholm Declaration of 1972 embodies a set of principles to guide the people in the protection and preservation of their environment.[27] Hence, this Declaration

[20] T Maluwa, 'International law-making in post-colonial Africa: the role of the Organization of African Unity' (2002) 49(1) Netherlands International Law Review *81*

[21] Generally, see O Okafor, *The African Human Rights System and International Institutions* (CUP, 2007).

[22] V Ayeni, 'The Impact of the African Charter and the Maputo Protocol in Nigeria' in V Ayeni (ed) *The Impact of the African Charter and Women's Protocol in selected African States* (Pretoria University Law Press, 2016) 183–202.

[23] Generally, see ibid.

[24] L Chenwi, 'The Right to a Satisfactory, Healthy, and Sustainable Environment in the African Regional Human Rights System' in J Knox and R Pejan (eds), *The Human Right to a Healthy Environment* (CUP, 2018) 59–85.

[25] This chapter will not discuss AU resolutions on environment and the Agreement for the establishment of the African Continental Free Trade Area (AfCFTA).

[26] WCED (1987) 3. Generally, see I Owosuyi, 'The Pursuit of Sustainable Development through Cultural Law and Governance Frameworks: A South African Perspective' (2015) 18(5) Potchefstroom Electronic Law Journal 2010, 2011.

[27] Report of the UN Conference on the Human Environment UN Doc A/Conf48/14 (1987); Stockholm Declaration of the United Nations Conference on the Human Environment (1972) (hereafter Stockholm Declaration). Also cited in ibid 2012.

'formed the foundation of modern international environmental law and shaped its direction'.[28] The definition by the WCED has become the most commonly accepted definition.[29] Furthermore, the publication of 'Our Common Future' by the WCED in 1987 popularized the sustainable development paradigm and 'researches into the concept in a holistic manner'.[30] This definition is said to promote sustainable development as an environmental concept.[31]

There have been recent UN conferences on sustainable development which include Johannesburg in 2002 and the Rio +20 Conference in 2012.[32] In 2012, countries attending the Rio +20 Conference engaged in the process that would lead to the development of the Sustainable Development Goals (SDGs) to replace the Millennium Development Goals (MDGs) which were due to expire in 2015.[33] The sustainable development paradigm is now fully embedded within the UN system with the development of the SDGs in 2015.[34]

Rich countries (the Global North) are the major recipients of the accruing benefits arising from international economic activity whilst the developing countries (the Global South) are the major victims of its negative environmental consequences.[35] The overarching view in academic literature on global governance norms is that developing countries do not play major roles in the development of global mechanisms or initiatives.[36] Arguably, this is no longer the case with the development of the SDGs and other recent international mechanisms. For example, the Global South (including Africa and other developing countries) played integral roles in the development of the SDGs framework.[37] Fukuda-Parr and Bhumika assert that scholars and stakeholders from the Global South were some of the significant contributors to ideas and concepts that eventually culminated in the emergence and development of the SDGs in 2015.[38] For example, Paula Caballero of the Delegation of Colombia proposed the idea of establishing the SDGs in the preparatory process for Rio +20.[39] Hence, Caballero's (Colombia's) contribution to

[28] S Atapattu, 'From our common future to sustainable development goals: evolution of sustainable development under international law' (2019) 36 Wisconsin International Law Journal 215, 218.

[29] Generally, see P Oniemola and O Tasie, 'Engendering constitutional realization of sustainable development in Nigeria' (2020) 13(1) Law and Development Review 159 for the various criticisms of the definition of sustainable development by the Brundtland Commission.

[30] R Ako, 'Challenges to Sustainable Development in the Niger Delta (Nigeria)' in S Ibaba (ed), *Niger Delta: Constraints and Pathways to Development* (Cambridge Scholars, 2012) 9–28.

[31] Owosuyi (n 26) 2012.

[32] R Scheyvens, G Banks, and others, 'The private sector and the SDGs: The need to move beyond 'business as usual' (2016) 24(6) Sustainable Development 371, 372.

[33] ibid.

[34] Oniemola and Tasie (n 29).

[35] C Gonzalez and S Atapattu 'International environmental law, environmental justice, and the Global South' (2016) 26 Transnational Law and Contemporary Problems 229.

[36] Generally, see S Fukuda-Parr and B Muchhala 'The southern origins of sustainable development goals: Ideas, actors, aspirations' (2020) 126 World Development 104706..

[37] Generally, see ibid.

[38] ibid.

[39] ibid; P Caballero, 'The SDGs: changing how development is understood' (2019) 10 Global Policy 38

the development of the SDGs exemplifies the role of the Global South in the creation of recent global mechanisms.

Furthermore, African states played noteworthy roles in the development of the SDGs.[40] African states and representatives were actively involved in the negotiation process of the development of the SDGs.[41] In 2013, a high-level committee of heads of states and government of African states produced the Common African Position (CAP) on the Post-2015 Development Agenda.[42] The CAP was adopted by the Member States of the AU at the January 2014 AU Summit in Addis Abba.[43] In January 2015, the AU set up a group of African negotiators to help promote the interests of Africa during the negotiations of the SDGs.[44] The CAP on 'the post-2015 development agenda provides an agreed set of specific African priorities, many of which are mirrored by the SDGs and fully aligned with AU Agenda 2063'.[45] The AU is an important stakeholder in the SDGs and the post-2015 international development agenda. Section 4 now focuses on sustainable development under the AU.

4. Sustainable Development Mechanisms as a Source of AU Law

The AU actively promotes sustainable development as part of its legal architecture. This is exemplified in Article 3(j) of the Constitutive Act of the AU and hence one of the major aims of the AU is the promotion of sustainable development on the continent. From an AU law perspective, this chapter argues that sustainable development is an aspirational goal that can be achieved by the development of norms by the AU and its institutions (e.g. regional and sub-regional courts). This is notwithstanding the view that 'there are only a few concrete principles or binding rules that are explicitly aimed at sustainable development within the AU legal system'.[46] This chapter argues that AU has developed a plethora of measures, policies, programmes, and conventions promoting sustainable development on the continent.

[40] K Shettima, 'Achieving the Sustainable Development Goals in Africa: call for a paradigm shift' (2016) 20(3) African Journal of Reproductive Health 19–21.

[41] ibid 19.

[42] S Lawan, 'An African take on the Sustainable Development Goals' (October 2015) available at <https://www.brookings.edu/blog/africa-in-focus/2015/10/13/an-african-take-on-the-sustainable-development-goals>/ accessed 21 July 2020.

[43] ibid.

[44] Office of the Special Adviser on Africa (OSAA) 'The 2020 Agenda for Sustainable Development available at <https://www.un.org/en/africa/osaa/peace/sdgs.shtml> accessed 21 July 2020.

[45] M Ladan, 'Achieving sustainable development goals through effective domestic laws and policies on environment and climate change' (2018) 48(1) Environmental Policy and Law 42, 59.

[46] J Verschuuren, 'The Growing Significance of the Principle of Sustainable Development as a Legal Norm' in D Fisher (ed), *Research Handbook on Fundamental Concepts of Environmental Law* (Edward Elgar Publishing, 2016.)

Furthermore, by virtue of the various AU environmental treaties at the continental level in Africa, environmental rights, and protection (including sustainable development) are recognized as specific treaty norms or standards in tandem with the normative harmony with other allied rights and corresponding commitments or obligations.[47] Hence, the main crux of the argument in this chapter is that AU environmental conventions or treaties are at the centre of the sustainable development norms in the AU legal order.

This chapter adopts the Brundtland Commission's definition of sustainable development which is 'the development that meets the needs of the present without compromising the ability of future generations to meet their own needs.' This section focuses on the contribution of the African Charter and Agenda 2063 to the development of sustainable development norms under the AU's framework. Furthermore, this section adopts the framework developed by Verschuuren on whether the sustainable development is legal norm in international law.[48] Verschuuren states that the following should be considered:

- a description of the emergence of sustainable development in soft law instruments;
- a description of the references to sustainable development in legally binding international instruments as in multilateral conventions;
- a description of the references to sustainable development in decisions by courts and tribunals;
- an analysis of these instruments and decisions whose aim is to determine the status of sustainable development as a legal norm.[49]

Hence, an application of the framework enunciated by Verschuuren to sustainable development norms under the AU system corroborates the notion that sustainable development is an important aspect of the emergent AU legal order. Arguably, this framework on the legal status of sustainable development (developed by Verschuuren) can be the basis for identifying sustainable development norms under the AU legal order. Furthermore, according to Amao, the AU legal order is based on 'several sources of law'.[50] Soft law is one of the sources of AU legal order.[51] Similar to the development of sustainable development in the international

[47] Chenwi (n 24) 59.

[48] Verschuuren (n 46); also see J Viñuales, 'Sustainable Development' in L Rajamani and J Peel (eds, *The Oxford Handbook of International Environmental Law*, 2nd edn (OUP, 2019) available at <SSRN: https://ssrn.com/abstract=3307841>, 3–23, forthcoming who also states that sustainable development is a norm of international law.

[49] Verschuuren (n 46).

[50] Amao (n 1) 25; Negm and Ntwari (n 10).

[51] Amao (n 1) 37–8 defines soft law under AU system as 'instruments that are non-binding but have quasi-legal character. Such instruments are useful in areas in which regulation is desirable but agreements are difficult to reach.'

sphere which can also be traced to international soft law mechanisms (such as the Stockholm Declaration, the Brundtland Report 1987, the Rio Declaration 1992, and Rio+20: 2012, amongst others), the AU also has soft law instruments (Agenda 2063 and AUDA-NEPAD amongst others) promoting sustainable development on the continent.

Subsection 4.1 focuses on Agenda 2063 as an example of a soft law mechanism on sustainable development under the AU legal order.

4.1 Soft Law and AU Legal Order

The AU in May 2013 developed an initiative called Agenda 2063.[52] Agenda 2063 is said to be 'Africa's blueprint and master plan for transforming Africa into the global powerhouse of the future'.[53] Agenda 2063 encompasses the AU's Aspirations for the future, and it also showcases key Flagship Programmes which are expected to enhance the economic growth and development of Africa and lead to the accelerated transformation of the continent.[54] Furthermore, under Agenda 2063, certain crucial activities are expected to be undertaken in its '10 year Implementation Plans which will ensure that Agenda 2063 delivers both quantitative and qualitative Transformational Outcomes for Africa's people'.[55]

A plethora of stakeholders including civil society groups, women, children, private sector, think tanks, Africans in the diaspora, and the regional economic communities (RECs) were involved and consulted during the development of the Agenda 2063.[56] Thus, unlike the development of the MDGs which had little or no input from Africans, Agenda 2063 involved consultation with African people thereby enhancing the legitimacy of the measure.[57]

The AU has developed norms on regional integration, peace, security, governance, and development, amongst other matters.[58] Arguably, Agenda 2063 is a mechanism that could lead to norm creation, for example by establishing norm-creating institutions. Agenda 2063 was adopted by the AU Assembly in 2015 and it is the latest initiative that attempts to provide a supranational direction in

[52] Agenda 2063 website <https://au.int/agenda2063/overview> accessed 25 March 2020.

[53] ibid.

[54] See the Agenda 2063 flagship projects website <https://au.int/en/agenda2063/flagship-projects> accessed 21 July 2020.

[55] Agenda 2063 website (n 52).

[56] Generally, see M Addaney, 'The African Union's Agenda 2063: Education and Its Realization' in A Onuora-Oguno, W Egbewole, and others (eds), *Education Law, Strategic Policy and Sustainable Development in Africa* (Palgrave Macmillan, 2018) 181–97.

[57] O Tella, 'Agenda 2063 and Its Implications for Africa's Soft Power' (2018) 49(7) Journal of Black Studies 714, 716.

[58] T Murithi, 'Briefing: The African Union at ten: an appraisal' (2012) 111(445) African Affairs 662, 663.

African integration.[59] This subsection briefly highlights the roles of two of the AU organs that are essential to the implementation of the Agenda 2063 – the African Union Commission (AUC) and the Pan-African Parliament (PAP).[60] A major objective of the AUC in this regard is to seek technical and financial support from strategic partners and Member States.[61] Thus, according to Fagbayibo, this puts the AUC 'in the driving seat of the implementation matrix' of Agenda 2063.[62] Furthermore, the PAP is expected to provide legislative rules to civil society and sub-regional parliaments on implementation of Agenda 2063 as a strategy for development.[63]Currently, both AUC and PAP suffer from institutional deficits and until they are reformed, Agenda 2063 will not be successful and this will impact negatively on the bourgeoning supranational ambition of the AU. Hence, Fagbayibo avers that Agenda 2063 will not be successful until the AUC and PAP are garnished with the requisite powers of enforcement to ensure its effective implementation.[64]

The implementation of Agenda 2063 requires different actions by countries concomitant to their various levels of development, priorities, and resources.[65] Also, State Parties and the AU and other relevant stakeholders play invaluable roles in the implementation process of Agenda 2063.[66] However, the proposed plan of action under Agenda 2063 has been criticized because it 'does not include steps for working with those member states that may need assistance'.[67] Notwithstanding the weaknesses of Agenda 2063, it constitutes one of the building blocks of the emergent AU legal order on sustainable development and is also tailored towards enhancing the sustainable development norms in Africa.[68]

59 B Fagbayibo, 'Nkrumahism, Agenda 2063, and the role of intergovernmental institutions in fast-tracking continental unity' (2018) 53(4) Journal of Asian and African Studies 629, 630.

60 Other AU organs that play a role in the implementation, monitoring, and evaluation of Agenda 2063 include NEPAD Planning and Coordinating Agency (NPCA) and Economic, Social and Cultural Council (ECOSOCC), amongst others. Generally, see African Union Commission (2015a) Agenda 2063: Popular version available at <https://au.int/Agenda2063/popular_version> accessed 21 July 2020.

61 AU Commission (2013), African Union Agenda 2063: A shared strategic framework for inclusive growth and sustainable development: Background note available at <https://www.au.int/web/sites/default/files/newsevents/workingdocuments/29732-wd-27_08_agenda_2063_background_note_en_0.pdf> accessed 21 July 2020.

62 Fagbayibo (n 59) 630.

63 AU Commission (2015b) Agenda 2063 – The Africa We Want: A shared strategic framework for inclusive growth and sustainable development: First ten-year implementation plan 2014–2023 available at <https://www.tralac.org/documents/resources/african-union/1135-agenda-2063-first-ten-year-implementation-plan-2014-2023/file.html> accessed 21 July 2020. Also see Fagbayibo (n 59) 630.

64 ibid 631.

65 K DeGhetto, J Gray, and others, 'The African Union's Agenda 2063: aspirations, challenges, and opportunities for management research' (2016) 2(91) Africa Journal of Management 93.

66 Generally, see K Muigua, 'Africa's Agenda 2063: What is in it for Kenya?' (2020) 18(1) African Sociological Review/Revue Africaine De Sociologie 59.

67 DeGhetto, Gray, and others (n 65) 99.

68 Generally, see Muigua (n 66).

4.2 AU Instruments and Sustainable Development: The Impact of the African Charter on Human and Peoples' Rights

The AU has a plethora of treaties and conventions promoting sustainable development in their provisions.[69] However, this subsection focuses on the African Charter.

The African Charter is 'often heralded as the first international law instrument to have expressly recognized a generally satisfactory environmental as a human right'.[70] Article 24 of the African Charter states that '[a]ll peoples shall have the right to a generally satisfactory environment favourable to their development'. This right reaffirms the expectation that the AU and its institutions or mechanisms (such as the African Charter and Agenda 2063) will promote sustainable development and protect the environment on the continent.[71] Arguably, due to the expansive wordings of Article 24, the African Charter is said to have fashioned a balance between the environmental and other relevant factors essential for development such as social, cultural, and economic considerations.[72] When discussing the relevance of the African Charter to the promotion of sustainable development on the continent, Article 24 should be read in tandem with Article 22 (right to development).[73] It is contended that the attainment of sustainable development (which is one of the key objectives of the AU) provides a route or framework in reconciling the tension between rights to the environment and development in the African Charter.[74] Scholtz argues that sustainable development 'serves as conceptual and normative bridge between Article 22 and Article 24, and the rights contained therein need to be interpreted as being components of this overarching concept'.[75]

Arguably, the sustainable development concept under the African Charter is unable to resolve the trade-offs between environment and economic concerns in many African countries.[76] Notwithstanding that the language of Article 24 enshrines a normative link between the environment and development, it is somewhat imprecise or vague.[77] Hence, it has been contended that it is difficult to determine the meaning of the words 'satisfactory' and 'favourable to their

[69] Generally, see Ekhator (n 19). Furthermore, Maluwa (n 20) contends that the African Convention on the Conservation of Nature and Natural Resources (1968) was the first international mechanism that expressly recognized the principles of sustainable development.

[70] A du Plessis, 'The Balance of Sustainability Interests from the Perspective of the African Charter on Human and Peoples' Rights' in M Faure and W du Plessis (eds), *The Balancing of Interests in Environmental Law in Africa* (Pretoria University Law Press, 2011) 36.

[71] ibid.

[72] ibid.

[73] W Scholtz, 'Human Rights and the Environment in the African Union Context' in Scholtz and Verschuuren (eds) (n 13) 102–27.

[74] Scholtz (n 73).

[75] Scholtz (n 73) 118.

[76] Scholtz (n 73); Chenwi (n 24).

[77] Chenwi (n 24).

environment' as enshrined in Article 24 of the African Charter.[78] In *SERAC*, it was held that while a state may be permitted to engage in industrial pursuits for socio-economic development, it has to weigh this with protection and promotion of the rights of its peoples.[79] However, Chenwi argues that a major criticism of the *SERAC* case is that the decision did not adequately clarify the link or relationship between right to a satisfactory environment and development.[80] Notwithstanding some of these criticisms, Article 24 of the African Charter has had positive influence on the right to environment jurisprudence in Africa and beyond.

Subsection 4.3 discusses the role of the African Commission on Human and Peoples' Rights (African Commission) and African Court on Human and Peoples' Rights in the promotion of sustainable development norms in Africa.

4.3 The Roles of Courts and Tribunals in Promoting Sustainable Development under the AU Legal Order

The concept of sustainable development has become widespread in international law and this has led to the rise of courts (including domestic, regional, and sub-regional courts) in developed and developing countries referring or alluding to sustainable development in their judgments and decisions.[81] The judiciary plays an indispensable role in the interpretation of sustainable development norms,[82] and the courts and the judiciary help to clarify the legal status of the concept of sustainable development.[83]

The first explicit judicial elucidation by any international law tribunal on the concept of sustainable development was by the International Court of Justice (ICJ) in the case concerning the Gabčíkovo–Nagymaros Project.[84] The ICJ stated that the 'need to reconcile economic development with protection of the environment is aptly expressed in the concept of sustainable development'.[85] The Court of Justice of the European Union (CJEU) arguably possesses the most advanced case law on the standards of environmental law at the regional level.[86] However, sub-regional

[78] M Lumina, 'The Right to a Clean, Safe and Healthy Environment under the African Human Rights System' in Addaney and Jegede (n 6) 36.
[79] Generally, see ibid.
[80] Chenwi (n 24).
[81] Generally, see Verschuuren (n 46).
[82] O Osuji and P Abba, 'Domestic Adjudicative Institutions, Developing Institutions, Developing Countries and Sustainable Development: Linkages and Limitations' in O Osuji, F Ngwu, and others (eds), *Corporate Social Responsibility in Developing and Emerging Markets Institutions, Actors and Sustainable Development* (CUP, 2019) 49–84, 50.
[83] Verschuuren (n 46).
[84] Viñuales (n 48).
[85] *Gabčíkovo–Nagymaros Project (Hungary v Slovakia)*, Judgment, ICJ Reports 1997, p 7, para 140. Also cited in Viñuales (n 48) 8.
[86] Verschuuren (n 46) 292.

and regional courts in Africa function in distinctive legal and political environments from their European counterparts.[87] Hence, Daly suggests that the 'insights provided by scholarship on Europe will have limited relevance to regions outside Europe'.[88]

The judicial organs of the AU have also examined the concept of sustainable development and similar notions in some of their decisions and judgments. This section focuses on the African Commission on Human and Peoples' Rights and the African Court on Human and Peoples' Rights. The African regional human rights system is said to consist of three treaty institutions or bodies (or supervisory mechanisms) that 'may make findings or take decisions in respect of African Union (AU) member states'.[89] The AU institutions are the African Commission, the African Court on Human Rights Court, and the African Committee of Experts on the Rights and Welfare of the Child (African Children's Rights Committee).[90]

The African Commission 'is primarily responsible for monitoring the implementation of the African Charter and the Protocol on the Rights of Women in Africa'.[91] The findings or decisions of the African Commission are referred to as recommendations.[92] There have been debates on whether African Commission's decisions are binding or not.[93] Viljoen suggests that recommendations are final and binding if they are contained in the Activity Reports of the African Commission and are approved by the OAU/AU Assembly or Executive Council.[94] As highlighted earlier, the African Charter is lauded for the indivisibility and justiciability of all generations of human rights (including civil and political and socio-economic rights, among others) enshrined in its provisions. The African Commission in its jurisprudence has expounded on a range of human rights including socio-economic rights, women's rights, group rights, indigenous rights, and individual rights.[95]

[87] J Gathii, 'Introduction' in J Gathii (ed), *The Performance of Africa's International Courts: Using International Litigation for Political, Legal, and Social Change* (OUP, 2020) 1–34.

[88] T Daly, 'The alchemists: courts as democracy-builders in contemporary thought' (2017) 6(1) Global Constitutionalism 101, 123.

[89] F Viljoen, 'The African Human Rights System and Domestic Enforcement' in M Langford, and others (eds), *Social Rights Judgments and the Politics of Compliance: Making it Stick* (CUP, 2017) 351–98, 352.

[90] Generally, see F Viljoen, *International Human Rights Law in Africa*, 2nd edn (OUP, 2012).

[91] M Ssenyonjo (ed), *The African Regional Human Rights System: 30 Years after the African Charter on Human and Peoples' Rights* (Martinus Nijhoff Publishers, 2012) 18. See Article 45 of the African Charter.

[92] F Viljoen and L Louw, 'State compliance with the recommendations of the African Commission on Human and Peoples' Rights, 1994–2004' 101 (2007) American Journal of International Law 1, 2.

[93] R Murray and D Long, *The Implementation of the Findings of the African Commission on Human and Peoples' Rights* (CUP, 2015) 50; Amao (n 1) 39.

[94] Viljoen (n 89) 339; generally, see, Chairman Okoloise 'Circumventing obstacles to the implementation of recommendations by the African Commission on Human and Peoples' Rights' (2018) 18(1) African Human Rights Law Journal 27.

[95] Generally, see Ssenyonjo (n 91).

Sustainable development appears not to be a major part of the case law that emerges from the regional human rights tribunals or instruments such as the European Court of Human Rights and CJEU.[96] Peeters and Eliantonio argue that in the few cases or instances wherein 'the CJEU has considered sustainable development show that this concept may only serve as a point of general reference, but does not have a direct impact on the outcome of a case'.[97] Arguably, this is not the position in Africa and Latin America.[98] Hence, in the *SERAC* case,[99] which concerned the environmental degradation occasioned by the activities of multinational corporations and governmental inertia in Ogoniland in Nigeria, the African Commission held that Article 24 of the African Charter (which promotes right to satisfactory and healthy environment) enjoins African states 'to take reasonable and other measures to prevent pollution and ecological degradation, to promote conservation, and to secure an ecologically sustainable development and use of natural resources'.[100] The African Commission also held that the Nigerian government and its agencies were in violation of the African Charter. The African Commission further held that the Nigerian state had violated a plethora of rights including rights to life (Article 4), non-discrimination, property (Article 14), health (Article 16), family life (Article 18), the right of people to dispose freely of their wealth and resources (Article 21), and the right to a clean and general satisfactory environment (Article 24) as provided in the African Charter. In *SERAC*, the African Commission deepened the applicability of Article 24 and arguably this has not 'only enhanced existing jurisprudence on the fulfilment of environmental rights, but also provided concrete guidelines for state parties on the meaning that can be afforded to environmental rights generally'.[101] These guidelines developed in *SERAC* are said to be obligatory rather than voluntary.[102] Also, the *SERAC* decision confirms the justiciability and enforceability of environmental rights on the continent.[103] Hence, African countries should endeavour to legislate and provide for environmental rights/protection in their countries and these environmental laws or legislation should be enforced and realizable in practice.[104] Also, some African

[96] Verschuuren (n 46).

[97] M Peeters and M Eliantonio, 'On Regulatory Power, Compliance, and the Role of the Court of Justice in EU Environmental Law' in M Peeters and M Eliantonio (eds), *Research Handbook on EU Environmental Law* (Edward Elgar Publishing, 2020) 475–99, 494.

[98] Verschuuren (n 46). The Inter-American human rights system is renowned for its innovation decisions in different areas such as right to environment, socio-economic rights, indigenous rights, and sustainable development amongst others.

[99] *Social and Economic Rights Action Centre & Centre for Economic and Social Rights v. Nigeria (SERAC Case)* 3 Comm No 155/96 (2001).

[100] Ibid, para 52.

[101] Du Plessis (n 70) 43.

[102] ibid.

[103] ibid; generally, see Chenwi (n 24).

[104] R Murray, *The African Charter on Human and Peoples' Rights: A Commentary* (OUP, 2019); J Oloka-Onyango 'Have Economic, Social and Cultural Rights (ESCRs) Come of Age?' (2020) available at <https://papers.ssrn.com/sol3/papers.cfm?abstract_id=3617295> accessed 21 July 2020.

states have explicitly incorporated environmental rights provisions in their constitutions[105] and this 'places the environment within its proper legal framework and shows a commitment to sustainable development' in Africa.[106] Examples of countries that have made the right to environment justiciable in Africa include Kenya, South Africa, Zimbabwe, and Uganda.[107] For example, Article 42 of Constitution of Kenya (2010) expressly provides for right to a healthy and clean environment.[108] The overarching scholarly view is that this constitutional provision has impacted positively on environmental rights and environmental justice (including sustainable development) issues in Kenya.[109]

Notwithstanding that the recommendations or rulings by the African commission are non-binding on states,[110] this section argues that the jurisprudence arising from the *SERAC* case supports the view that there is an emergent AU Law on the continent and *SERAC* adds to the existing blocks of regional sustainable development norms (e.g. Agenda 2063) at the continental level.[111] Furthermore, judicial decisions from sub-regional and regional tribunals or judiciaries are one of the sources of AU law, according to Amao's interpretation.[112] The *SERAC* case exemplifies this assertion.[113]

Due to the weaknesses and criticisms of the African Commission, an African Court on Human and Peoples' Rights was created in 2006.[114] An overarching weakness of the African Commission is said to be the non-binding nature of its findings or decisions. On the other hand, the judgments of the African Court are binding and it has jurisdiction over the African Charter, the African Women's Protocol, and the African Charter on the Rights and Welfare of the Child (African Children's Charter), including other international human rights convention or treaties ratified by the affected states.[115] Currently, 31 AU states have ratified the

[105] ibid.

[106] T Murombo, 'The utility of environmental rights to sustainable development in Zimbabwe: A contribution to the constitutional reform debate' (2011) 11(1) African Human Rights Law Journal 120, 125..

[107] Oloka-Onyango (n 104).

[108] C Soyapi, 'Environmental protection in Kenya's environment and land court' Journal of Environmental Law (2019) 31(1) 151–61.

[109] K Muigua, 'The Role of Courts in Safeguarding Environmental Rights in Kenya: A Critical Appraisal' (January 2019) available at <The-Role-of-Courts-in-Safeguarding-Environmental-Rights-in-Kenya-A-Critical-Appraisal-Kariuki-Muigua-17th-January-2019-1.pdf (kmco.co.ke)> accessed 21 July 2020.

[110] Olivier (n 1) 522.

[111] This theme is thoroughly explored in the section on the impacts of SERAC case in Nigeria and other African states. Generally, see Amao (n 1) 40 wherein he states that 'the Commission's jurisprudence has been a key building block in shaping the AU legal order, especially in human rights sphere and in the development of key underlying principles of the AU legal order'.

[112] Generally, see Amao (n 1).

[113] The SERAC case was extensively analysed in sections 4.3 and 4.4 of this chapter.

[114] Generally, Oloka-Onyago (n 104); Protocol to the African Charter on Human and Peoples' Rights on the Establishment of an African Court on Human and Peoples' Rights, July 10, 1998, in force January 25, 2004, OAU Doc. OAU/LEG/EXP/AFCHPR/PROT (III) (African Court Protocol), cited in Chenwi (n 24) 62.

[115] Article 3 of the Protocol to the African Charter on Human and Peoples' Rights on the Establishment of an African Court on Human and Peoples' Rights; Viljoen (n 89) 354.

African Court, only six of them have deposited the declaration acknowledging the jurisdiction of the African Court to receive cases directly from individuals and NGOs.[116] Also, by virtue of Article 34(6) of the Protocol to the African Court, the jurisdiction is optional, and states may decide whether to recognize direct access to the court.[117] This has led to a restriction of direct access to the court and hence some states now proceed to the African Court via the African Commission.

Furthermore, under the African Court on Human and Peoples' Rights, individuals do not have direct access to the Court. Member States make declarations recognizing the jurisdiction of the Court, thereby allowing direct access to individuals in such countries. However, the African Court may receive complaints or applications from the African Commission, state parties to the Protocol, and African intergovernmental organizations.[118] In addition, non-governmental organizations (NGOs) with observer status before the African Commission and individuals from countries which have made declaration recognizing the jurisdiction of the court can also file or institute cases directly.

By virtue of Article 30 of the Protocol, decisions of the African Court are binding, and states are expected to comply with these decisions. Due to the fact that the African Court has started 'issuing strong merits judgments',[119] Abebe has ambitiously argued that the Court has been effectively acting as a 'constitutional court for Africa'.[120] Arguably, this will lead to hostile reaction from African countries as exemplified by the political backlash from the governments of Tanzania and Rwanda on unfavourable judgments of the African Court against them.[121]

There has been a plethora of cases that have been decided by the African Court.[122] However, according to Chenwi, only one case on alleged violations of the African Charter provisions on environmental protection has been heard by the

[116] African Court of Human and Peoples' Rights website 'Welcome to the African Court' available at <Welcome to the African Court | African Court on Human and Peoples' Rights (african-court.org)/> accessed 21 July 2020.

[117] A Rachovitsa, 'On new "judicial animals": the curious case of an African Court with material jurisdiction of a global scope' (2019) 19(2) Human Rights Law Review 255.

[118] 'African Court in Brief', African Court on Human and Peoples' Rights available at <http://www.african-court.org/en/index.php/about-the-court/brief-history> accessed 21 July 2020.

[119] Daly (n 88) 103.

[120] A Abebe, 'Taming regressive constitutional amendments: The African Court as a continental (super) Constitutional Court' (2019) 17(1) International Journal of Constitutional Law 89. Also, Bado argued that in some respects, the ECOWAS Court of Justice resembles a constitutional court. K Bado, *The Court of Justice of the Economic Community of West African States as a Constitutional Court* (Nomos Verlagsgesellschaft mbH & Co. KG, 2019).

[121] T Daly, 'As Karlsruhe and Luxembourg Feud, are Jo'burg and Arusha growing closer?' (July 2020) I-CONNECT Blog available at <http://www.iconnectblog.com/2020/07/as-karlsruhe-and-luxembourg-feud-are-joburg-and-arusha-growing-closer/> accessed 21 July 2020. In 2020, Benin and Cote d'Ivoire withdrew their declarations allowing NGOs and individuals to petition the African Court. Generally, see P Brett and LE Gissel, *Africa and the Backlash Against International Courts* (Zed Books, 2020).

[122] African Court cases and judgments available at <https://www.african-court.org/en/index.php/cases> accessed 21 July 2020.

African Court and this was the *Ogiek* case.[123] The case was originally brought before the African Commission, but due to the extensive violations of human rights and non-compliance with the Provisional Measures issued by the African Commission to Kenya, the Commission referred the case to the African Court.[124] The *Ogiek* case is said to be the African Court's first significant decision on Indigenous peoples' rights.[125] This case involved the Ogiek Community, an Indigenous community of the Mau forest in Kenya. The Kenyan government made an order to evict the Ogiek community from the Mau forest (which is their ancestral land). The government contended that the eviction was essential for the environmental sustainability or conservation of the area. The African Court held that the Kenyan government had violated seven articles of the African Charter, Articles 1, 2, 8, 14, 17(2) and (3), 21, and 22 of the African Charter, and ruled that the Ogiek community is an Indigenous community.[126] In the *Ogiek* case, the African Court 'made indirect reference to the protection of environmental rights'.[127] Even though it mainly focused on indigenous rights, the case also highlighted the utility of environmental conservation.[128] The African Court held that contrary to the view by the Kenyan government (that the eviction of the Ogiek people was necessary to maintain the environment), the action of the Kenyan government was neither proportionate or necessary to justify its eviction of the people from their land.[129] The Ogiek people have sentimental attachment to their lands and the environmental degradation was exacerbated by the actions and activities of the Kenyan government and its agents such as the 'encroachments upon the land by other groups and government excisions for settlements and ill-advised logging concessions'.[130]

Furthermore, the African Court has also been buffeted by resistance from some states refusing to enforce its judgments.[131] African states and governments should endeavour to respect and implement decisions of regional and sub-regional courts on the continent. This is particularly important, because the African Court is the only functioning judicial organ of the AU.

123 *African Commission on Human and Peoples' Rights v Kenya*, App No 006/2012, Judgment (African Court of Human and Peoples' Rights, 2017) (*Ogiek* case or *ACHPR. Kenya* (Judgment)). Also cited in Chenwi (n 24) 64.

124 ibid 78.

125 Furthermore, the African Commission have provided extensive analysis of people's rights (including indigenous rights) in Southern *Cameroon*, *Darfur*, and *Endorois* cases. Generally, see T Maluwa, 'Reassessing aspects of the contribution of African States to the development of international law through African regional multilateral treaties' (2020) 41(2) Michigan Journal of International Law 327, 364–8.

126 *Ogiek* case (n 123).

127 F Abioye, 'Advancing Human Rights through Environmental Rule of Law in Africa' in Addaney and Jegede (n 6) 81–105, 97. Generally, see L Claridge, 'Litigation as a tool for community empowerment: the case of Kenya's Ogiek' (2018) 11 Erasmus Law Review 57.

128 ibid.

129 *Ogiek* case (n 123) para 130.

130 ibid.

131 Generally, see TG Daly and M Wiebusch, 'The African Court on Human and Peoples' Rights: mapping resistance against a young court' (2018) 14(2) International Journal of Law in Context 294.

4.4 Impact of Judicial Decisions and Treaties on the Evolution of Sustainable Developments Norms in Africa

This subsection focuses on the impacts of the decisions of regional and domestic courts on sustainable development in different parts of Africa. The overarching academic view on the impact of African Commission and African Court jurisprudence on domestic courts and national law is that very few domestic courts in Africa refer to them.[132] Furthermore, notwithstanding that Nigeria has incorporated the African Charter into domestic law, Nigerian courts are yet to refer explicitly to case law of regional courts in Africa.[133] However, in a recent judgment of the Nigerian Supreme Court in *Centre for Oil Pollution Watch v NNPC*, the court expressly relied on the provisions of Article 24 of the African Charter, section 33(1) of the Nigerian Constitution and section 17(4) of the Oil Pipelines Act to hold that the right to environment can be justiciable in Nigeria and hence, these instruments recognized the fundamental rights of Nigerians to a clean and healthy environment.[134]

Arguably, things are changing and some domestic courts in Africa have expressly referred to the case law from the African Commission and African Court. Dinokopila avers that domestic courts that have referred to the African Commission in their jurisprudence includes courts in South Africa, Ghana, Zimbabwe, Gambia, and Kenya.[135] For example, some municipal courts have relied on the African Charter and African Commission's decisions or case law to find breaches of human rights.[136] For example, in 2015, the High Court of Kenya in *Eric Gatari* case relied on provisions (Article 10) of the African Charter and African Commission case law on freedom of association to protect the rights of sexual minorities in Kenya.[137] Furthermore, the Supreme Court of Zimbabwe in *Kachingwe and Others v Minister of Home Affairs and Commissioner of Police* suggested that the decisions of the African Commission were of persuasive authority in the country.[138]

[132] Generally, see O Oluduro, *Oil Exploitation and Human Rights Violations in Nigeria's Oil Producing Communities* (Intersentia, 2014) 454.

[133] Generally, see ibid.

[134] *Centre for Oil Pollution Watch v. Nigerian National Petroleum Corporation* (2019) 5 Nigeria Weekly Law Reports 518. The implications of this case will be further explored in later part of this section.

[135] B Dinokopila 'The Impact of Regional and Sub-regional Courts and Tribunals on Constitutional Adjudication in Africa' in C Fombad (ed), *Constitutional Adjudication in Africa* (OUP, 2017) 225–46, 232.

[136] M Ssenyonjo, 'Responding to human rights violations in Africa: Assessing the role of the African Commission and Court on Human and Peoples' Rights (1987–2018)' (2018) 7(1) International Human Rights Law Review 1, 18–19. The influence or impact of the African Charter, African Commission and African Court will be in focus in a later section of this chapter.

[137] *Eric Gitari v Non-governmental Organisation Coordination Board and 4 Others*, Petition 440 of 2013, [2015] eKLR (High Court of Kenya at Nairobi, 24 April 2015). Cited in ibid 19.

[138] Dinokopila (n 135) 233.

Scholars argue that the impact of the African Charter has been modest but significant on the continent.[139] For example, the Charter has been extensively relied on in Nigeria and South Africa to ventilate the rights of litigants in a plethora of cases.[140] Arguably, a major limitation or barrier to the enforcement of the African Charter is the manner in which international law/ratified treaties are received or implemented in Member States. This is exemplified by the so-called dualist and monist divide. In dualist countries, treaties are not applied domestically unless incorporated via municipal legislation. On the other hand, in monist countries, international law applies directly. However, the dualist–monist dichotomy has been argued to be inappropriate to analyse the reception of international law by African countries.[141] The overarching view is that in Africa, civil law countries are monist and common law countries are dualist in nature. However, this does not always reflect the reality or practice in some of these countries. For example, even though Kenya is a 'dualist' country, it has recently amended its constitution to make ratified treaties directly applicable with or without the need for parliamentary domestication.[142] Furthermore, in monist states such as Côte d'Ivoire, the African Charter and ratified international instruments or treaties are said to have a higher status than its constitution and in Ethiopia, international human rights treaties including the African Charter 'have a status higher than ordinary legislation, and are equal in status to the Constitution'.[143] Despite the criticism of the monist–dualist dichotomy in Africa, once a dualist state incorporates or transforms a treaty into domestic law, it is free to assign which ever status it would give to it. The monist/dualist issues remain relevant because dualist states need a two-step process regarding transforming treaties into domestic law, ratify and incorporate, whilst in monist states only one step is needed. Once ratified in a monist state, the treaty applies automatically, but may still be subject to the national constitution.[144]

Notwithstanding these advances by the African Charter on the continent, some parts of Africa are still mired in gross violations of human rights. Hence, African countries should not just sign and ratify (and in some instances, domesticate) the

[139] Okafor (n 21); Ayeni (n 22).

[140] Ayeni (n 22). Generally, see P Oamen, 'Realisation of the Right to Health in Nigeria: The Prospects of a Dialogic Approach' (13 August 2020) available at <SSRN: https://ssrn.com/abstract=3673480> accessed 21 July 2020.

[141] M Barnard, 'Legal reception in the AU against the backdrop of the monist/dualist dichotomy' (2015) 48(1) Comparative and International Law Journal of Southern Africa 144.

[142] V Ayeni 'Introduction and Preliminary Overview of Findings' in V Ayeni (ed) The Impact of the African Charter and Women's Protocol in selected African States (Pretoria University Press, 2016) 1–15. Also, in Nigeria (which is also a 'dualist' country) in a constitutional amendment (by virtue of section 254(c)(2) of the Constitution (Third Alteration) Act 2010) now makes International Labour Organization (ILO) conventions directly applicable in the National Industrial Court of Nigeria. Generally, see F Onomrerhinor, 'A re-examination of the requirement of domestication of treaties in Nigeria' (2016) 7 Nnamdi Azikiwe University Journal of International Law and Jurisprudence 17, 23.

[143] ibid 14.

[144] Generally, see M Olivier, *International law in South African Municipal Law: Human rights procedure, policy and practice* (PhD Dissertation, 2002).

African Charter, they should endeavour to respect and enforce it. Otherwise, the African Charter will remain a paper tiger.

Notwithstanding that Nigerian courts are yet to cite African Commission and African Court in their judgments expressly, the African Charter has had a significant influence on Nigerian courts and laws.[145] For example, in a recent Supreme Court decision in Nigeria, some of the Justices in *Centre for Oil Pollution Watch v. Nigerian National Petroleum Corporation* explicitly referred to sections 20 and 30 of the Nigerian Constitution, 17(4) Oil Pipelines Act and Article 24 of the African Charter to hold that the right to a clean and healthy environment can be recognized under Nigerian law.[146] This case has liberalized the *locus standi* of NGOs in environmental matters in Nigeria thereby improving access to environmental justice and promoting sustainable development for litigants, victims, and communities in Nigeria.[147] This is the first time that the Nigerian Supreme Court has stated that the right to the environment can be justiciable in Nigeria. This judgment creates a binding judicial precedent in Nigeria and all other (lower) courts in the country are expected to follow it. Under Nigerian law, socio-economic rights are neither justiciable nor enforceable (unlike civil and political rights). This is exemplified by section 20 of the Nigerian Constitution, which seeks to promote and protect the environment, is in Chapter II of the Constitution and therefore neither justiciable nor enforceable.[148] Hence, the decision in the *Centre for Oil Pollution Watch v Nigerian National Petroleum Corporation* has made right to environment (a socio-economic right) justiciable in Nigeria. However, it should be noted these comments by the Supreme Court Justices on the right to environment were made *obiter* and right to environment was not an issue directly before the court. On the other hand, this decision can serve as a launchpad to further develop the evolving jurisprudence around economic and social rights (ESR) in Nigeria.

The Supreme Court in the *Centre for Oil Pollution Watch v Nigerian National Petroleum Corporation* further stated that the being a domesticated treaty, the African Charter is part of Nigerian law and as long as Nigeria remains a signatory to the African Charter and other relevant international treaties on the environment, Nigerian courts would continue to protect and vindicate the human rights entrenched in such international mechanisms.[149] A major criticism of the decision is that the court did not refer to the *SERAC* case or case law of the African

[145] Ayeni (n 22); Okafor (n 21).

[146] *Centre for Oil Pollution Watch v. Nigerian National Petroleum Corporation* (2019) 5 NWLR 518, 587, 597–8.

[147] Also, see A Babalola, 'The right to a clean environment in Nigeria: a fundamental right' (2020) 26 Hastings Environmental Law Journal 3.

[148] E Ekhator, 'Improving access to environmental justice under the African Charter on human and peoples' rights: the roles of NGOs in Nigeria' (2014) 22(1) African Journal of International and Comparative Law 63, 70.

[149] *Centre for Oil Pollution Watch v Nigerian National Petroleum Corporation* (2019) 5 Nigerian Weekly Law Reports 518, 598.

Commission or African Court. Arguably, reference or reliance on the *SERAC* case and the jurisprudence of regional courts (including sub-regional judiciaries) would have added more nuance or clarity to the right to environment analysis in the judgment. Notwithstanding the criticism of the judgment in *Centre for Oil Pollution Watch v Nigerian National Petroleum Corporation*, this case evidences the extent and the positive impact of the African Charter on domestic law in sustainable development in Nigeria. Even though the Supreme Court Justices in the *Oil Pollution Watch* case did not expressly refer to the *SERAC* decision, one of the Justices (Justice Nweze) in a public lecture given in 2017, explicitly mentioned reliance on the *SERAC* case as one of the strategies of extending environmental rights in Nigeria.[150] Justice Nweze delivered the leading judgment in the *Oil Pollution* case. Arguably, the *SERAC* case was a persuasive influence on Justice Nweze, notwithstanding that he (and the other Justices) did not expressly refer to the *SERAC* case and other relevant case law from sub-regional and regional courts in the judgment in *Oil Pollution* case.[151] Also, Justice Nweze in his public lecture avers that the National Assembly in Nigeria 'rise to the occasion and constitutionalise socio-economic rights as other African countries have done. This is the only way of eradicating poverty and illiteracy; confronting diseases and mitigating hunger and hardship in the land etc.'[152]

Many domestic courts in Africa are yet to cite the jurisprudence of the African Court.[153] For example, the South African Constitutional Court is one of the most international law-friendly courts in Africa.[154] However, the Constitutional Court cited the jurisprudence of the African Court for the first time in June 2020.[155] Thus, Dinokopila argues that there is little evidence of the use of the African Court by domestic courts in Africa.[156] This is arguably due to the fact that the African Court

150 Justice Chima Centus Nweze, 'Constitutional Adjudication for Democratic Consolidation in Nigeria: The Role of The Supreme Court' 16th Justice Idigbe Memorial Lecture, which held at the University of Benin (UNIBEN, 2017) 34.

151 However, Justice Chima Centus Nweze has written extensively on the justiciability of environmental rights in Nigeria. Generally, see C Nweze, 'Justiciability or judicialization: circumventing Armageddon through the enforcement of socio-economic rights' (2007) 15(1) African Yearbook of International Law Online/Annuaire Africain de droit international Online 107.

152 Nweze (n 150) 35.

153 T Daly, 'Kindred strangers: why has the Constitutional Court of South Africa never cited the African Court on Human and Peoples' Rights? the limited influence of African moral theory & law on the Constitution' (2019) 9(1) Constitutional Court Review 387.

154 D Tladi, 'Interpretation and international law in South African courts: the Supreme Court of Appeal and the Al Bashir saga' (2016) 16(2) African Human Rights Law Journal 310, 311.

155 The Constitutional Court in *New Nation Movement NPC and Others v President of the Republic of South Africa and Others* (CCT110/19) [2020] ZACC 11 (11 June 2020) made explicit reference to the decision of the African Court in *Mtikila v Tanzania*. Generally, see Daly blog post (n 121).

156 Dinokopila (n 135) 236. However, things are changing for the better. For example, the Lesotho Constitutional Court cited the African Court in *Peta v Minister of Law, Constitutional Affairs and Human Rights* (CC 11/2016) [2018] LSHC 3 (18 May 2018). Furthermore, the ECOWAS Court of Justice referred to the jurisprudence of the African Court in *Umeh and Others v. Nigeria* (ECW/CCJ/APP/48/18) [2020] ECOWASCJ 10 (1 July 2020). Generally, see the AFcite Project, 'Mapping Citation of the African Court on Human and Peoples' Rights Decisions' (Project Summary October 2020) available at <AfCite_Concept_Note.pdf (up.ac.za)> accessed 10 July 2021.

(in comparison with the African Commission) is a recent development. A major problem is the lack of information on the number of domestic courts that have cited the jurisprudence of the African Court. Fortunately, the ACtHPR Monitor has begun a project to map out the influence of the African Court on domestic courts in Africa.[157]

4.5 Impacts of SERAC Case in Nigeria and Other Parts of Africa

The African Commission in the *SERAC* case made five orders or recommendations that the Nigerian government should follow.[158] One of the orders was a directive that the Nigerian government 'stop all attacks on Ogoni communities' and to permit 'citizens and independent investigators free access to the territory'. During the *SERAC* case, the Nigerian government accepted that it had exacerbated the environmental problems in the Niger Delta. The government posited via a *note verbale* delivered to the African Commission that 'there is no denying the fact that a lot of atrocities were and are still being committed by oil companies in Ogoni Land and indeed in the Niger Delta area'.[159] The Nigerian government further averred that it had initiated remedial mechanisms to alleviate the suffering of the Ogoni people. These include the creation of the Federal Ministry of Environment, Niger Delta Development Commission (NDDC), and a Judicial Commission of Inquiry to investigate the issues of human rights violations amongst other measures to ameliorate the impacts of the activities of the oil MNCs on the Niger Delta and the environment.[160] The Nigerian government in recent years has established more interventionist agencies such as the Ministry of Niger Delta Affairs, the National Environmental Standards and Regulations Enforcement Agency (NESREA), and National Oil Spill Detection and Response Agency (NOSDRA), amongst others, and measures (e.g. the Amnesty programme for repentant militants) to ameliorate the suffering in the Niger Delta. However, some of these measures cannot be directly traced to the *SERAC* decision and all the orders or recommendations in the *SERAC* case are yet to be fully implemented in Nigeria.[161] The general consensus in academic literature is that the aforementioned governmental initiatives have been ineffectual.[162] The United Nations Environment Programme (UNEP) environmental assessment on Ogoniland was conducted at the behest of the Nigerian

[157] The ACtHPR Monitor is an independent website dedicated to the African Court on Human and Peoples' Rights available at <http://www.acthprmonitor.org/> accessed 21 July 2020.

[158] *SERAC* case; Viljoen (n 89) 371.

[159] ibid para 42.

[160] ibid para 30.

[161] Viljoen (n 89).

[162] Generally, see N Ojukwu-Ogba, 'Legislating development in Nigeria's oil-producing region: the N.D.D.C. Act seven years on' (2009) 17(1) African Journal of International and Comparative Law 136.

government[163] and two different Nigerian Presidents (Goodluck Jonathan and Mohammadu Buhari) have tried to implement the UNEP report; unfortunately progress has been very slow.[164]

Following the *SERAC* decision, there appears to be some direct engagement by the African Commission to ascertain whether the Nigerian government did fully comply with the decision.[165] For example, the African Commission Concluding Observations in 2008, advised the Nigerian government to establish an 'effective monitoring mechanism for the implementation of decisions of regional and domestic bodies on violations of the rights in the Niger Delta'.[166] However, it is uncertain if the Nigerian government did actually respond to the African Commission on whether it explicitly implemented the *SERAC* decision.[167] Notwithstanding the criticisms of the implementation of the *SERAC* decision in Nigeria, it has positively impacted on sustainable development and environmental protection in the country because the Nigerian government created governmental agencies as a direct response to the *SERAC* case (as highlighted in the *note verbale*).

Furthermore, some domestic courts in Africa have directly referred to the SERAC case in their *jurisprudence*. For example, the South African Constitutional Court in *President of the Republic of South Africa v Modderklip Boerdery (Pty) Ltd* referred to the African Commission's decision in *SERAC*.[168]

Arguably, the Constitutive Act of the AU does not explicitly promote sustainable development as a norm under the AU legal order. However, the position of this section is that an application of Verschuuren's framework on sustainable development as legal norm in international law evidences the notion that the various AU treaties on environment and regional courts have engaged in norm creation on sustainable development in Africa. Thus, sustainable development is a norm which is implicit in the Constitutive Act. The contention of this chapter is that notwithstanding that domestic and regional (including sub-regional) courts have not expressly referred to AU law in their jurisprudence, there is evidence that the case law on sustainable development in domestic, regional, and sub-regional courts can form part of the body of norms under the emergent AU law. It is suggested that this also contributes to the emergent continental legal system with supranational qualities.

[163] UNEP Assessment of Ogoniland Report (2011) available at <https://www.unenvironment.org/explore-topics/disasters-conflicts/where-we-work/nigeria/environmental-assessment-ogoniland-report> accessed 21 July 2020.

[164] Amnesty International 'Nigeria: No Clean-Up, No Justice: An Evaluation of the implementation of UNEP's Environmental Assessment of Ogoniland, Nine Years On' (June 2020) available at <https://www.amnesty.org/en/documents/afr44/2514/2020/en/> accessed 21 July 2020.

[165] Viljoen (n 89) 375.

[166] Concluding Observations and Recommendations on the Third Periodic Report of the Federal Republic of Nigeria, 10–24 November 2008, para 40 available at <https://www.achpr.org/sessions/concludingobservation?id=77> accessed 21 July 2020.

[167] Viljoen (n 89).

[168] Dinokopila (n 135) 230.

5. Recommendations

Contracting states to treaties cannot rely on domestic laws as reasons or justification for not performing its expected obligations under such treaties. This is exemplified in Article 27 of the Vienna Convention on the Law of Treaties which states that a 'party may not invoke the provisions of its internal law as justification for its failure to perform a treaty'. Hence, State Parties to AU treaties or conventions should endeavour to respect and fulfil the obligations arising from such treaties.

The AU should harmonize the various AU environmental law treaties to promote sustainable development on the continent expressly.[169] A major advantage of harmonizing the AU instruments promoting sustainable development is that this will help to clarify the extent of sustainable development norms in the AU legal order.[170] It is understood that institutional barriers such as state sovereignty and the reluctance of some AU Member States to respect and implement AU decisions might negatively impact on harmonization of sustainable development norms in Africa.

The AU Constitutive Act should be amended expressly to provide for sustainable development as a legal norm or in the alternative, an explicit sustainable development treaty should be adopted by AU. Here, allusions can be made to the EU, under which sustainable development became a legal norm through a gradual process.[171] Hence, new AU institutions (or existing institutions such as the Pan-African Parliament and AU Commission) should be mandated to ensure the full implementation of sustainable development norms throughout the continent. This will ensure consistency amongst African states in this sphere. Furthermore, African states should endeavour to respect and implement the decisions of the African Commission, African Court, and relevant domestic courts decisions on sustainable development on the continent.

6. Conclusion

This chapter has focused on the African Charter and Agenda 2063 as AU mechanisms promoting sustainable development on the continent. There have been divergent arguments whether sustainable development is a legal norm in international law. This chapter has relied on Verschuuren's framework on the status of

[169] O Aholu, 'Greening AU environmental law: how can harmonisation help?' (2019). A paper delivered at the South Western Universities Environmental Law Conference held at the Hilary Rodham Clinton School of Law, Swansea University, United Kingdom available at <Greening African Union Environmental Law: How can Harmonization Help? – Charles Aholu> accessed 21 July 2020.

[170] ibid in respect of AU environmental law states that one of the advantages of harmonizing AU treaties on environment is that it will help 'clarify the depth of environmental policy within the AU'.

[171] Generally, see G Bándi, 'Principles of EU Environmental Law Including (the Objective of) Sustainable Development' in Peeters and Eliantonio (eds) (n 97).

sustainable development in international law, and it posits that arguably sustainable development is a legal norm in the AU legal order. This is exemplified by the impacts of the African Charter and decisions of regional (including sub-regional) courts in domestic laws and legislation in Africa. This chapter contends that the AU mechanisms on sustainable development are an essential part of the emergent AU legal order. Furthermore, AU mechanisms on sustainable development will contribute to the development of common standards/norms/laws at the continental level which enhances the emergent continental AU legal order.

PART 5

ENFORCING AFRICAN UNION LAW: PERSPECTIVES

19

The Several Sanctioning Regimes in the AU: Analysis and Synthesis

Konstantinos D Magliveras

I. Introduction

The OAU Charter, concluded in 1963, did not stipulate sanctions or other forms of punitive action to be taken against recalcitrant Member States. This was arguably a deliberate choice of the drafters. On the other hand, in international organizations it may be difficult to ensure that members comply with the obligations and duties stipulated in the constitutive instrument if no sanctions are envisaged. Even in the very closely knitted European Union (EU), sanctions have been considered a necessity in order to address any Member State which fails to observe democratic ideals and the rule of law, two EU cornerstones.[1]

In the 1990s, the OAU could no longer avoid dealing in earnest with the scourge of unconstitutional and often violent regime changes as well as with the developing norm of democratic governance. Indeed, at the time, a number of regional international institutions had adopted what has become known as 'the democratic (or democracy) clause', namely a commitment by the whole membership that democratic principles shall be followed and respected.[2] Moreover, there was external pressure on African states by donor countries and international organizations (e.g. the EU) to address the continent's democratic deficit, sometimes associating it with the continuation of economic aid and other forms of assistance. Making the disbursement of aid on the recipient states' compliance with the triptych

[1] See Article 7 of the Treaty on European Union, Consolidated versions of the Treaty on European Union and the Treaty on the Functioning of the European Union – Consolidated version of the Treaty on European Union – Protocols – Declarations annexed to the Final Act of the Intergovernmental Conference which adopted the Treaty of Lisbon, signed on 13 December 2007, OJ C 326, 26.10.2012, p 13.

[2] GM Genna and T Hiroi, *Regional Integration and Democratic Conditionality. How Democracy Clauses Help Democratic Consolidation and Deepening* (Routledge, 2015); N Woods, 'Good governance in international organizations' (1999) 5 Global Governance 39. For the African continent, see M Olivier, 'The Emergence of a Right to Democracy – An African Perspective' in C Panara and G Wilson (eds), *The Arab Spring – New Patters of Democracy and International Law* (Martinus Nijhoff Publishers, 2013) 29–52.

Konstantinos D Magliveras, *The Several Sanctioning Regimes in the AU: Analysis and Synthesis* In: *The Emergent African Union Law.* Edited by: Olufemi Amao, Michèle Olivier and Konstantinos D. Magliveras, Oxford University Press.
 DOI: 10.1093/oso/9780198862154.003.0020

of democracy/rule of law/human rights is usually referred to as 'aid or political conditionality'.[3]

In July 2000, the Declaration on the Framework for an OAU Response to Unconstitutional Change of Government (Lomé Declaration) was adopted to address these matters coherently and collectively.[4] It laid down common values and principles applying to the entire membership and pertaining to democratic governance as well as measures to respond to unconstitutional changes of government. Importantly, it introduced an implementation mechanism. Finally, an OAU Assembly decision adopted on the same day dealt specifically with coups d'état, the most common form of unconstitutional change of government.[5]

The procedural aspects of these two instruments, which arguably led to the *de facto* amendment of the OAU Charter, were entrusted to the so-called Central Organ operating within the Mechanism for Conflict Prevention, Management and Resolution. The Mechanism, which was introduced in 1992 and constituted another *de facto* Charter amendment,[6] was the culmination of the efforts to revamp the defunct Commission of Mediation, Conciliation and Arbitration, which had been established under Article XIX of the Charter.[7] That these important changes in the OAU's functioning were implemented through *de facto* amendments and not through the ordinary amendment process had advantages and disadvantages: on the one hand, they were applied immediately without having to wait for the lengthy and uncertain amendment process but, on the other hand, the new sanctioning regime did not have a proper legal foundation.

In the area of sanctions, a comparison between the OAU Charter and the AU Constitutive Act is quite striking considering the nakedness of the former and the fullness of the latter. The Member States' move towards punitive measures in the 1990s signified that they were prepared to shift attitudes and accept the infliction of sanctions when agreed norms and obligations were breached. Moreover, there were considerations of pragmatism. For example, when the AU began operating in the summer of 2001, budgetary contributions in arrears had spiralled to almost 45 million USD,[8] an amount exceeding the budget for financial year 2003,

[3] Overseas Development Institute, *Aid and Political Reform*, Briefing Paper (London, 1992) available at <https://www.odi.org/sites/odi.org.uk/files/odi-assets/publications-opinion-files/6774.pdf> accessed 26 June 2021.

[4] OAU Assembly, AHG/Decl.5(XXXVI), 12 July 2000.

[5] OAU Assembly, *Decision on Unconstitutional Changes of Government in Africa*, AHG/Dec.150(XXXVI), 12 July 2000.

[6] OAU Assembly, *Decision on a Mechanism for Conflict Prevention, Management and Resolution*, AHG/Decl.1(XXVIII), 1 July 1992.

[7] It was operationalized through the namesake Protocol signed during the First OAU Assembly Session on 21 July 1964, (1964) 3 ILM 1116. See K Magliveras and G Naldi, *The African Union* (Kluwer Law International, 2009) 46–8.

[8] OAU Council of Minsiters, *Decision Relating to the Sixteenth Ordinary Session of the Committee on Contributions*, CM/Dec.2(LXXIV), 8 July 2001.

which had been set at 35.6 million USD.[9] Therefore, it was only logical that the Constitutive Act would lay down a sanctioning regime for unpaid contributions.

Therefore, the Constitutive Act's provisions on sanctions were a combination of institutionalizing the OAU sanctioning regime,[10] of addressing pressing situations, and of catering for the much augmented, compared to the OAU, powers and functions which were afforded to the AU. But arguably it was overdone because, as will be explained, the content of the sanction clauses is not always clear, and clarity is of fundamental importance in any legal system, including those established in the context of international organizations and *in casu* AU law.

In particular, the Constitutive Act envisages three sanctioning regimes. First, when Member States have defaulted in the payment of assessed budgetary contributions (Article 23(1)). Second, when they have failed to comply with AU decisions and policies (Article 23(2)). Third, when a new regime has come to power through unconstitutional means (Article 30). These provisions have been modified or enlarged under the AU Assembly Rules of Procedure, while Article 30 should be read in conjunction with Article 7 of the Protocol establishing the Peace and Security Council of the AU (PSC Protocol) as well as with Articles 23–26 of the African Charter on Democracy, Elections and Governance (African Charter).

2. Sanctions for Non-payment of Budgetary Contributions

Article 23(1) empowers the Assembly to determine the sanctions to be imposed upon any Member State defaulting in its assessed contributions to the AU budget. At first glance, it is a very strict clause, a fact revealed if compared with the corresponding provision in the Charter of the United Nations (UN), namely Article 19. The latter stipulates that, if the budgetary contributions in arrears equal or exceed the amount due by the Member State in question for the last two financial years, a specific sanction (deprivation of voting rights in the General Assembly) shall be ordered against it. It follows that the UN cannot but endure those states which, for whatever reason, are not diligent in paying up their contributions to the budget even for prolonged periods of time, as long as their arrears do not exceed a given amount.

This is not the case with the AU, where the Assembly is mandated (i.e. it does not enjoy any discretion) to impose an array of punitive measures upon Member States which are in default in paying any amount of budgetary contributions (there is no low ceiling for triggering Article 23(1)). Sanctions include refusing the right

[9] K Magliveras and G Naldi, *The African Union (AU)* (Wolters Kluwer, 2013) 186.

[10] What is meant by this regime are the various decisions and declarations by the OAU Assembly approving the adoption of punitive measures when Member States have violated certain duties as well the various OAU Council of Ministers decisions implementing the former.

of recalcitrant states to speak and vote at AU organs, the right to present candidates for competitive AU positions and professional posts (e.g. the AU Commission Chairperson), and the right to benefit from AU activities, programmes, and commitments. The wording of Article 23(1) would suggest that there is a grading severity: for example, refusing the right to vote at AU organs' sessions is evidently far more important than not being allowed to speak. Equally, to deny participation in AU activities should constitute far more severe 'punishment' than denying the right to present candidates for AU professional posts.

Two observations should be made based on the wording and the apparent aim of Article 23(1). First, there is a general rule of international law, and the law of international organizations in particular, that punitive measures have to be proportional to the severity of the infraction.[11] If a state happens to owe a relatively small amount of budgetary contributions, to refuse it the right to vote should be considered disproportional sanction and, therefore, inappropriate. The second observation is that, depending on which the recalcitrant states are, different sanctions may have different effects and consequences. For example, for Member State X with limited recourses to be banned from enjoying AU benefits may have serious domestic repercussions, while to be denied the right to present candidates for AU posts may be of little importance, especially if it never intended it. Thus, the effectiveness of Article 23(1) sanctions could vary among the membership, a factor to be considered when ensuring that sanctions have the desired effect, *in casu* making recalcitrant states comply in full and promptly with their budgetary obligations.

Some of the above arguments appear to contradict Rule 35 of the Assembly Rules of Procedure (2002), pursuant to which the Assembly's action will not be uniform but varied and will be based on Executive Council and Permanent Representatives Committee (PRC) recommendations as well as on the information provided by the Commission. The determining factor is whether the amount in arrears equals two or more years but does not exceed five years of assessed contributions or whether it exceeds five years. In the former case, the following sanctions will be imposed: (a) suspension of the right to speak, vote, and receive documentation at AU meetings; (b) suspension of the right to offer to host future sessions of the Assembly and of the Executive Council (invariably the take place every six months); and (c) suspension of the right to present candidates for AU positions. In the latter case, the right to have their nationals' contracts of employment with the AU renewed and the right to receive AU funds for new projects in their territory shall be additionally suspended. Finally, Rule 35 envisages the temporary lifting of sanctions when the recalcitrant state has paid at least half of the outstanding amount of arrears and the payment was made 30 days before the next scheduled session of the Executive Council.

[11] K Magliveras, *Exclusion from Participation in International Organisations: The Law and Practice Behind Member States' Expulsion and Suspension of Membership* (Kluwer Law International, 1999) 271.

Thus, the two-year threshold in accumulated arrears for ordering sanctions applies also to the AU, even though it is not laid down in Article 23(1). Moreover, the possibility of provisionally suspending sanctions, when the state in question has deposited only half the amount of contributions in arrears (it could actually correspond to several years of partially unpaid assessed contributions) might question the sanctions' effectiveness and their deterrent role. Since the rule is that Member States must pay contributions promptly and in full, the differing stipulations in the Assembly Rules of Procedure, a secondary legal instrument, raises the question whether it could be said that they have effectively modified the Constitutive Act. While the matter does not appear to have been addressed by commentators,[12] the answer could very well be in the affirmative. After all, as mentioned above, Member States have been accustomed to *de facto* amendments of the constitutive instrument since the OAU days, especially through the adoption of sanctioning regimes by the OAU Assembly. Notwithstanding the validity of this submission, one must be very careful with *de facto* changes in the constitutive instruments of international organizations. However, if most Member States appear to follow them without protest and they do not oppose them over a long period of time, it will be very difficult for a single Member or a small group of Members to dispute them at a later stage.

Another notable issue is that Article 23(1) and Rule 35 fail to appreciate that, at any given moment, several African countries may be facing economic and financial problems, and, therefore, the non-payment of budgetary contributions may arguably be attributed to a force majeure situation and not to a deliberate act of disregarding obligations. That this eventuality has not been addressed in the relevant provisions is difficult to explain, given that the constitutive instruments of the African Economic Community (AEC)[13] as well as of several African Regional Economic Communities (RECs) expressly acknowledge it and sometimes go as far as exonerating affected Member States from the obligation to pay.[14]

In practice, the AU has granted temporary and exceptional exemptions to Member States. Examples include Sierra Leone in July 2003 (no conditions were attached to the dispensation granted) and the Democratic Republic of Congo (DRC) in January 2012 (conditions were attached). But these have been ad hoc arrangements and it is questionable whether Member States may invoke it as precedence to

[12] On the possible *de facto* amendment of the Constitutive Act, see K Magliveras and G Naldi, *The African Union*, 2nd edn (Wolters Kluwer, 2018), paras 85 et seq.

[13] It was established by the namesake Treaty concluded in June 1991. The purpose was to create Africa's first ever regional economic integration organization but it never set off the ground despite having 50 contracting parties. The AEC–AU relationship is regulated in Article 33(2) of the Constitutive Act.

[14] K Magliveras, 'African international organisations: suspension and expulsion of members' (1999) Australian International Law Journal 158, 169–70; cf Article 171(6) of the Common Market of Eastern and Southern Africa (COMESA) Treaty (1994): when public or natural calamities or exceptional circumstances have gravely affected a Member State's economy, the non-payment of budgetary contributions shall not lead to sanctions.

be granted exemption. It is suggested that the AU should have already streamlined these situations. In particular, it should have devised a mechanism setting out specific conditions for suspending, for a certain period of time, the obligation to pay budgetary contributions if Member States were to face economic or political problems[15] or other unforeseen and unforeseeable circumstances, while allowing them to continue enjoying membership rights and privileges. The Assembly moved towards this direction only in late 2018, when it decided that it '[m]ay consider requests from Member States experiencing force majeure circumstances making them temporarily enable to pay their assessed contributions [and] may … take a decision'.[16]

Unpaid budgetary contributions will not be written off or be borne by other Member States. While in the past it was a practice of Colonel Gaddafi's Libya to pay them to the AU on behalf of other Members,[17] presently no state appears willing or able to replicate this practice. The amounts owed by Member States in economic/financial or other kind of distress will continue to be in arrears and, through negotiations with the AU, they will have to work out how to pay them in full. A decisive move towards ensuring that budgetary contributions are paid promptly and in full was made in 2018 when the Assembly decided that a new sanctioning regime for unpaid contributions should be concluded. The new regime, *inter alia*, reduces the period within which a state will be deemed to be in default from two years to six months.[18] While the Commission was mandated to consult Member States on its implementation and submit a report by February 2020,[19] apparently it never did. However, in February 2020 the Assembly operationalized the 2018 decision and ordered sanctions,[20] but, at the same time, avoided dealing with the requests submitted by the Saharawi Arab Democratic Republic, Seychelles, and Burundi, which had been unable to meet their annual contributions. The Assembly asked the Commission to engage with those Member States facing difficulties in the payment of their contributions and with those in arrears for two or more years and to agree on a payment plan for clearing them. While the Commission was meant to report back to the Executive Council in July 2020,[21]

[15] cf Executive Council, *Decision on the Report of Ministerial Committee on Scale of Assessment and Contributions*, EX.CL/Dec.1071(XXXV), 5 July 2019, para 7 withholding the imposition of sanctions against Somalia and Libya because of the domestic security and political situation.

[16] AU Assembly, *Decision on the New African Union Sanctions Regime for the Non-Payment of Contributions*, Ext/Assembly/AU/Dec.3(XI), 18 November 2018, para 4.

[17] S Allison, 'After Gaddafi, who will fund the AU?', *Daily Maverick* (29 September 2011) available at <http://www.dailymaverick.co.za>; B Malone, 'Insight: Africa to miss Gaddafi's money, not his meddling' *Reuters* (11 November 2011) available at <http://www.reuters.com> both accessed 26 June 2021.

[18] AU Assembly (n 16) para 3.

[19] Executive Council (n 15) para 5.

[20] AU Assembly, *Decision of the Joint Sitting Report of the Ministerial Committee on Scale of Assessment and Contributions and the Committee of Fifteen Ministers of Finance (F15)*, Assembly/AU/Dec.752(XXXIII), 10 February 2020, para 12.

[21] ibid para 14.

a Report on AU finances, which it published in June 2020, did not discuss the matter.[22]

As regards those Member States, which deliberately or without good cause fail to pay assessed budgetary contributions, the AU must deal with them in a resolute manner, which must be objective, unbiased, and leave no room for any political considerations. It should be understood that it is the whole AU that suffers when its membership does not pay promptly and in full budgetary contributions. Therefore, the AU should find ways to recuperate any and all (direct and indirect) loss from the non-payment. For example, it could replicate the practice of other international organizations, such as the International Telecommunications Union, which accrues interest on the amount in arrears,[23] or it could set off the arrears against sums owed to recalcitrant Member States or amounts that they are due to receive from AU programmes, activities, etc.

Although Article 23(1) entrusts the power to impose sanctions against Member States in arrears exclusively to the Assembly, in reality sanctions have invariably been ordered by the Executive Council. Given that this power does not appear to have ever been delegated to the latter,[24] the legal basis of all relevant decisions is at least ambiguous. While it is true that the AU, and before it the OAU, have occasionally acted without adhering to the proper legal stipulations, this cannot be condoned when the stipulations are regarded as part and parcel of the AU legal system.

The confines of the present chapter do not allow for a detailed analysis of the Executive Council's practice on sanctions but only an overview. Starting with 2003, it determined that eight states (Guinea-Bissau, Liberia, Central African Republic (CAR), DRC, San Tomé and Principe, Seychelles, Somalia, and the Comoros) will remain under sanctions; that the sanctions on Niger be lifted; and that 'a temporary and exceptional exemption' be granted to Sierra Leone.[25] In early 2006 it imposed sanctions against Member States in arrears even though several of them had been facing internal turmoil and strife of such magnitude that already their involvement in AU activities had been problematic. In particular, sanctions were continued for eight Member States (CAR, DRC, Eritrea, Guinea-Bissau, Sao Tomé and Principe, Somalia, Liberia, and Seychelles); sanctions were imposed on Benin, Cape Verde, Côte d'Ivoire, Guinea, and Mauritania; sanctions were lifted from Niger, Djibouti,

[22] See Financing the Union: Towards the Financial Autonomy of the African Union, Status Report – An Update, Version Four, 16 June 2020 available at <https://au.int/sites/default/files/documents/38739-doc-report_on_financing_of_the_union_jun_2020_002.pdf> accessed 26 June 2021.

[23] See Article 33.3 of the Convention of the International Telecommunications Union (2018): 'The amounts due [by Member States] shall bear interest from the beginning of the fourth month of each financial year of the Union at 3% per annum during the following three months, and at 6% per annum from the beginning of the seventh month'.

[24] See Article 9(2) of the Constitutive Act on delegation of Assembly powers and functions to any other organ.

[25] Executive Council, *Decision on the Report of the Sub-Committee on Contributions*, EX/CL/Dec.25(III), 4 July 2003, while Executive Council, *Decision on the Report of the Sub-Committee on Contributions*, EX/CL/Dec.76(IV), 16 March 2004, maintained them during the following year.

and Gabon (they had already paid their arrears); and it was resolved that Sierra Leone would avoid sanctions if it honoured the agreed payment schedule.[26] Two years later, the situation had not changed considerably and only 29 Member States had paid contributions to the budget.[27] This state of affairs showed that this sanctioning regime might not have had the desired effect.

During the second decade of the 21st century, the number of Member States under sanctions for being in arrears has been drastically reduced. Thus, in January 2013 the Executive Council imposed sanctions only on Guinea-Bissau and Madagascar and decided that Somalia's temporary exemption from sanctions be maintained.[28] However, this reduction has not necessarily been the result of Member States paying assessed contributions promptly and in full. And this because, as this sanctioning regime operates, they are imposed only when a state has been in arrears for more than two years. That in 2016 the Executive Council deplored the membership's non-compliance with paying assessed contributions as and when due as well as its warning that 'the persistent pattern of arrears' has impacted the AU's financial situation most adversely[29] supports this argument. And, in 2018, the Executive Council played the card of threatening to impose sanctions to exert pressure on Member States with accumulated arrears to promptly fulfil their obligations.[30] Finally, during the last (36th) Executive Council Ordinary Session, four Member States were placed under sanctions: Guinea Bissau, Sao Tome & Principe, Liberia, and South Sudan.[31]

3. Sanctions for Not Complying with AU Decisions and Policies

The second paragraph of Article 23 concerns more generally Member States' non-compliance with AU decisions or policies and not specifically with budgetary matters. In particular, they may be subjected to further sanctions (e.g. denial of transport and communications links with the other Member States), while the Assembly is empowered to determine the imposition of additional 'measures of

[26] Executive Council, *Decision of the Eighth Extraordinary Session of the Executive Council on the Contributions by Member States*, Ext/EX.CL/Dec.2 (VIII), 19 January 2006.

[27] Executive Council, *Decision on the Contributions of Member States*, EX.CL/Dec.379(XII), 31 January 2008.

[28] Executive Council, *Decision on Contribution of the African Union Member States towards the 2012 Budget of the African Union*, EX.CL/Dec.731(XXII), 25 January 2013.

[29] Executive Council, *Decision on the Oversight and Accountability Mechanism(s)*, EX.CL/Dec. 931(XXIX), 15 July 2016, para 5.

[30] Executive Council, *Decision on the Scale of Assessment and Contributions*, EX.CL/Dec.1001(XXXII), 26 January 2018, para 4

[31] Executive Council, *Decision on the Report of the Joint Sitting of the Ministerial Committee on Scale of Assessment and Contributions and the Committee of Fifteen Finance Ministers*, EX.CL/Dec. 1089(XXXVI), 7 February 2020, para 12.

a political and economic nature'. Several important issues are raised. The first is to determine whether the Article 23(2) sanctions are additional to those envisaged in Article 23(1) and whether those states defaulting in budgetary obligations may face sanctions pursuant to both paragraphs. Arguably, the answer should be in the negative because Article 23(1) caters solely for a specific infraction. Thus, to inflict Article 23(2) sanctions as well as those under Article 23(1) for the same infraction would violate the aforementioned principle of proportionality.

The second issue is whether the reference in Article 23(2) that the Assembly may determine the infliction of any other 'measures of a political and economic nature' can be interpreted to include the sanctions mentioned in the first paragraph thereof. Notwithstanding that it would depend on the nature of the breach and which AU decision or policy was not observed, arguably to deny the right to speak and to vote could fall into the ambit of other 'measures of a political nature'. And there exist other international organizations which 'punish' recalcitrant Member States by suspending wholly or partly their participation in the organization's operation.[32]

Article 23(2) offers to the Assembly carte blanche to establish additional political and economic punitive measures, without placing any restrictions on this law-making power. It follows that it could potentially violate the principles of the protection of legitimate expectations and of legal certainty, two norms to which international institutions should adhere to.[33] Thus, a third issue arises: could a wide interpretation of this provision justify the Assembly expelling a Member State which has repeatedly breached AU decisions or policies? The Constitutive Act does not contain an expulsion clause, but there may be instances where a Member State's behaviour leaves no other choice but to have it expelled. Presumably, if the Assembly were to take a unanimous vote in favour of expulsion, the recalcitrant state must be expelled, this being the uniform wish of the entire membership. However, in this case it would not be necessary to cite Article 23(2) as the legal basis for expulsion because it is a rule of the law of international organizations that, if all Member States agree, the organization is entitled to act even if the constitutive instrument is silent. On the other hand, it would be rather difficult to legitimize the ultimate sanction of expulsion on the basis of a clause as indistinct as Article 23(2).

32 cf Article 5 of the UN Charter.

33 Both principles derive principally from domestic administrative law, see Venice Commission of the Council of Europe, Rule of Law Checklist, adopted by the Venice Commission at its 106th Plenary Session (Venice, 11–12 March 2016) (Council of Europe, May 2016), but are also applied in the context of international organizations and their action vis-à-vis Member States. The first principle denotes that an international organization, acting through its organs, has given to a Member State exact and accurate pledges, promises, or assurances which have led it to a well-founded belief that it could have specific expectations from the organization in question. The second principle denotes that the prior action of an international organization has validly created to a Member State the certainly that it will not change its action in the future. Both principles are considered to be general principles of EU law and have been applied by the European Court of Justice, see, for example, Case C-537/08 P, *Kahla Thüringen Porzellan GmbH v European Commission*, Judgment of 16 December 2010, *European Court Reports* 2010 I–12917.

Rule 36 of the Assembly Rules of Procedure, the corresponding provision to Article 23(2), does not shed any light on the above issues. Rule 36 lays down a procedure, which is not fully compatible with the spirit of Article 23(2). Thus, the Executive Council will recommend to the Assembly that a Member State has not, without good and reasonable cause, complied with AU decisions or policies, the Assembly will record the infraction and it will then determine the sanctions to be ordered. Rule 36 as well as Article 23(2) would suggest that there is automaticity in the procedure: a Member State does not comply, the Assembly confirms the infraction, and sanctions are subsequently ordered. But Rule 36(3) differs because the recalcitrant state must first be offered the chance to rectify the situation, in which case no sanctions will be imposed even though the Constitutive Act was breached.

More specifically, Rule 36(3) reads as follows: 'When taking any decision in this regard, the Assembly shall stipulate the time frame for compliance and indicate when the failure to comply with that decision will trigger the sanctions regime provided for under Article 23(2) of the Constitutive Act and this Rule'. It goes on to stipulate that recalcitrant Member States are entitled to present their case to the Assembly and presumably they could present mitigating factors. Finally, even though not expressly stipulated in the Rules, Member States under sanctions should be able to request the Assembly to lift or vary them because they have (wholly or partly) complied with the decision/policy they breached.

Until today, Article 23(2) has not been applied. To the best of one's knowledge the Assembly has not deliberated ordering sanctions against any specific Member State and neither has the Executive Council made any recommendations to that effect. The only instance where the Assembly has threatened sanctions has been in relation to Member States failing to comply with its decisions vis-à-vis the arrest warrants which have been issued by the International Criminal Court (ICC) against al-Bashir.[34] As is well known, the latter is the former Sudanese President, who was deposed in April 2019 and is wanted by the ICC for his alleged involvement in genocide and crimes against humanity perpetrated in Darfur. The Assembly has demanded that no Member State cooperate with the ICC in his arrest and surrender.[35] In February 2020, the regime in power in Sudan appeared to be seriously inclined towards handing al-Bashir over to the ICC.[36] However, he is still

[34] AU Assembly, *Decision on the International Criminal Court*, Assembly/AU/Dec.590(XXVI), 31 January 2016, para 4.

[35] AU Assembly, *Decision on the Meeting of African States Parties to the Rome Statute of the International Criminal Court (ICC)*, Assembly/AU/Dec.245(XIII) Rev.1, 3 July 2009, para 10. See NJ Udombana, 'Who Blinks First? The International Criminal Court, the African Union and the Problematic of International Criminal Justice' in T Maluwa (ed), *Law, Politics and Rights – Essays in Memory of Kader Asmal* (Martinus Nijhoff, 2014) 92, 112; K Magliveras, 'The withdrawal of African States from the ICC: good, bad or irrelevant?' (2019) 66 Netherlands International Law Review 419.

[36] See D Walsh and AL Dahir, 'Sudan's Ex-Ruler May Face War Crimes Trial, Official Says' *New York Times* (11 February 2020) available at <https://www.nytimes.com/2020/02/11/world/africa/sudans-ex-ruler-may-face-war-crimes-trial-official-says.html> accessed 26 June 2021.

at large.[37] If and when it happens, it will be interesting to see how the AU will react; until then, the AU organs continue to oppose ICC judgments delivered in the case of al-Bashir.[38]

4. Sanctions against Unconstitutional Regimes and Coups d'État

According to Article 30, governments which came into power through unconstitutional means 'shall not be allowed to participate in the activities of the Union'. Effectively, this clause inserted in the Constitutive Act the gist of the aforementioned Lomé Declaration and related OAU practice. Article 30 sanctions may be retained only until constitutional normalization has been achieved, that is when free and fair elections have been held and/or a new democratic Constitution has been accepted by the population in a free and fair referendum. According to the wording of Article 30, only the regimes that resorted to unconstitutional means shall be barred, not the states themselves; their membership status should not be affected. However, in the international relations among states (including dealings pertaining to their membership in international organizations) it is invariably difficult to distinguish between the regimes in power and the sovereign states per se. Thus, for all intents and purposes, it is the Member State itself which should be considered as having been excluded. If the AU wanted to avoid this, it could accept as the legitimate government another regime (e.g. a government in exile)[39] and allow it to perform the functions associated with membership.

Article 30 refers to an unconstitutional and not to an undemocratic assumption of power as well. Arguably, in Africa the term 'unconstitutional' is now closely associated to 'undemocratic' due to the consolidation of a continental democratic agenda.[40] But for 'constitutional' to mean 'democratic' and for 'unconstitutional' to mean 'undemocratic' and vice versa, Member States' constitutions should (in substance and in nature) be democratic to start with, as the term is understood in the Western liberal thought. Suppose that the constitution of Member State X, which, as in most African countries, subscribes to the executive presidential type of government, stipulates that presidential terms of office last seven years and places no

[37] See <https://www.icc-cpi.int/darfur/albashir> accessed 26 June 2021.

[38] See, for example, Executive Council, *Decision on the International Criminal Court*, EX.CL/Dec. 1091(XXXVI), 7 February 2020, para 7.

[39] Note that the Sahrawi Arab Democratic Republic, which joined the OAU in the early 1980s, has always been represented by a government in exile, which has its seat in Algiers.

[40] cf the Preamble and Articles 3 and 4 of the Constitutive Act. See further the African Charter. Generally, see K Magliveras, 'Extending Presidential Terms in Office beyond what is Acceptable: Non-Interference in Domestic Affairs v. The African Democratic Agenda', revised paper presented at the Association of African Studies in Germany (VAD) Conference, Leipzig, July 2018 available at <http://www.researchgate.net> accessed 26 June 2021.

restrictions on the number of terms of office.[41] If the regime in power were overturned after being in power for, say, 25 or 30 years (not uncommon in Africa) without following the relevant constitutional provisions, should Article 30 be applied and should the new regime be regarded as unconstitutional? Or would the (evidently undemocratic) constitutional clause on unlimited presidential terms of office negate the unconstitutional nature of the regime change? These questions have not been addressed in earnest.

The fact that Article 30 does not mention which organ will order sanctions is not an omission because it is an automatic procedure. Since unconstitutional regimes '*shall* not be allowed' to participate in the AU, political discretion should not come into play. However, Article 30 does not stipulate which organ will determine that a new government has assumed power in an unconstitutional fashion or that a coup d'état has taken place. In practice, it is the Peace and Security Council (PSC) which makes such determinations. Its decisions, like those of the UN Security Council,[42] are deemed to be binding upon all Member States. But the PSC is not a principal AU organ. It was created pursuant to a Protocol to the Constitutive Act concluded in 2002, whose legal basis was Article 5(2) enabling the Assembly to establish, without restrictions, new organs.[43] While the PSC Protocol was meant to incorporate the aforementioned OAU Central Organ into the AU's institutional architecture and augment its role, capacity, and powers, it did not amend the Constitutive Act.[44] However, Member States have accepted PSC decisions (they take the form communiqués published after the conclusion of each session) and have, more often than not, followed them.

The laconic text of Article 30 does not shed much light on the extent of the unconstitutional regime's non-participation in AU activities, which presumably includes barring it from taking part and voting in the meetings of all organs but should not lead to suspending the targeted states' membership. It is rather a punitive measure exerting substantial pressure on the 'illegal regime' to restore constitutional normalcy. Arguably, it comprises the sanctions of Article 23(1) but not those envisaged in the second paragraph thereof, because the latter are measures of a general nature and not directly related to AU activities. Finally, for as long as an unconstitutional government is barred from participation, the Member State in

[41] These states include Gabon (Constitution of 1991, revised in 2011); Togo (Constitution of 1992, revised in 2007); Uganda (Constitution of 1995, revised in 2005); Cameroon (Constitution of 1972, revised in 2008); Chad (Constitution of 1996, revised in 2005); Gambia (Constitution of 1996, revised in 2004); South Sudan (Constitution of 2011, revised in 2013); Djibouti (Constitution of 1992, revised in 2010); and Algeria (Constitution of 1963, revised in 2008).

[42] Article 25 of the UN Charter.

[43] Protocol relating to the Establishment of the Peace and Security Council of the African Union concluded on 9 July 2002 (PSC Protocol). Cape Verde, DRC, and South Sudan have still not ratified it.

[44] The necessary changes were made in a Protocol of Amendments, which was concluded in 2003 but has never entered into force due to lack of ratifications.

question must fulfil all duties, for example pay assessed budgetary contributions, comply with mandatory Assembly decisions, etc.

Rule 37 of the Assembly Rules of Procedure, the provision corresponding to Article 30, has considerably augmented the latter's arguably insufficient content. Some of its provisions appear to run contrary to the submissions made above. More specifically, Rule 37(4) lays down a five-stage procedure for dealing with unconstitutional changes of government. The first stage is to condemn the unconstitutional overthrow of government or the coup d'état immediately on behalf of the entire AU and demand that constitutional order be promptly reinstated. The second stage is to convey a clear and unequivocal warning that the illegal change of government shall neither be tolerated nor recognized by the AU (presumably this binds the whole membership and, consequently, no state is allowed to offer recognition to the new (illegal) regime). The third stage is to ensure consistency in the action to be taken against the unconstitutional regime at bilateral level (i.e. the other Member States towards the illegal regime), at sub-regional level (i.e. the competent REC/s towards the illegal regime) and at international level (i.e. non-African states, other intergovernmental organizations (including the UN and the EU) etc., towards the illegal regime). However, at this third stage it is difficult to ensure control of the action taken or ordered by the different stakeholders. The fourth stage is to request the PSC to convene and discuss the matter as a matter of urgency (in practice the PSC deliberates such incidents on its own initiative). Finally, the fifth stage is to suspend the Member State in question (or as explained above, the illegal regime) from AU activities and prohibit its participating in AU organs at once. Interestingly enough, Rule 37(4) expressly states that the membership status shall not be affected but all obligations towards the AU must continue to be observed.

Rule 37(5) allows the Assembly to order (in a non-exclusive fashion) the following punitive measures against the unconstitutional regime. First, visa denials for the perpetrators (and presumably for their entourage as well). Second, restrictions in the contacts between the illegal regime and the governments of the other Member States (this could be interpreted as partial severance of diplomatic relations). Third, trade restrictions (presumably curtailment of economic relations but not a trade embargo as it would have severe consequences for the population's welfare).[45] Fourth, the sanctions provided for in Article 23(2). Fifth, any additional sanctions to be recommended by the PSC. Finally, Rule 37(6) stipulates that the Commission Chairperson should assist in the peaceful reinstatement of democratic order. In terms of dispute settlement methods, this would entail a mixture of mediation and good offices. Thus, the Chairperson is asked, *inter alia*, to establish

[45] Given that the African Continental Free Trade Agreement (AfCFTA) entered into force on 30 May 2019 and the operational phase of Free Trade Area was launched in July 2019, AU Assembly, *Decision on the Launch of the Operational Phase of the African Continental Free Trade Area*, Ext/Assembly/AU/Dec.1(XII), 7 July 2019, the effects of trade sanctions on the future African single market should be a topic of discussion.

appropriate contacts with the perpetrators without recognizing or legitimizing them and to enlist the contribution of African leaders and personalities as a conduit for securing cooperation between the unconstitutional regime and the AU.

The events in Madagascar in March 2009 offer a good illustration of the procedure and the ambit of the sanctions ordered against a regime which came into power through a coup d'état.[46] Thus, when President Marc Ravalomanana announced that he was handing power over to the military, his arch rival Andry Rajoelina, the Mayor of Antananarivo, the capital city of Madagascar, took the opportunity to form a transitional government and gave a rather vague promise to hold elections. The PSC promptly determined that these events constituted an unconstitutional change of government and suspended Madagascar from participation in AU activities.[47] It also threatened the Rajoelina regime and its supporters with 'appropriate measures, including targeted sanctions', if they failed to implement the so-called 'Maputo Agreements', a roadmap that had in the meantime been agreed between the rival camps to ensure a peaceful and consensual transition to constitutionality.[48] In mid-February 2010, the PSC repeated the threat to impose sanctions, which were to be automatically applied, if by 16 March 2010 'the de facto authorities borne out of the unconstitutional change' had not complied with the Maputo Agreements.[49]

The threatened sanctions were quite severe and included the following. First, a travel ban, subject to exemptions on humanitarian grounds, against the de facto authorities and the followers of the 'Rajoelina camp' whose actions impeded AU and Southern African Development Community (SADC)[50] efforts to restore constitutional order. Second, a freeze, again subject to exemptions, on funds and assets of all individuals and entities contributing to the maintenance of the unconstitutional status quo. Third, the diplomatic isolation of the *de facto* authorities through concerted action by all Member States (they were also mandated to challenge *de facto* authorities' participation in non-African international organizations, including the UN and its Specialized Agencies). The PSC met next on 17 March 2010 and, having concluded that the Rajoelina regime had not complied with the

[46] For the PSC practice on unconstitutional overthrow of government between 2003 and 2015, see Magliveras and Naldi (n 12) 192–215.

[47] PSC/PR/COMM.(CLXXXI), 20 March 2009.

[48] PSC/PR/BR(CCII), 10 September 2009.

[49] PSC/PR/COMM.1(CCXVI), 19 February 2010.

[50] The involvement of SADC is not surprising given that very often the AU seeks the assistance of the REC, in which the recalcitrant state participates, and thereafter they attempt to coordinate their response and take collective measures. The foundation of this joint action is the principle of subsidiarity and comparative advantage, as the PSC stated in the summer of 2019 when it suspended, with immediate effect, Sudan from all AU activities until a civilian-led Transitional Authority was established, PSC/PR/COMM.(DCCCXLIV), 6 June 2019, para 12. In this case, the relevant REC was the Intergovernmental Authority on Development (IGAD), see further PSC/PR/COMM.(DCCCLXXV), 6 September 2019, para 8.

ultimatum, resolved that the sanctions had entered into force on the same day.[51] Interestingly enough, the first time that the Assembly expressly addressed the situation in Madagascar was in June 2011: it called upon SADC and the AU to continue cooperating and find a consensual and sustainable solution to the crisis while complying with the relevant AU instruments.[52] The constitutional crisis in Madagascar dragged on until 2013. The PSC lifted the sanctions in September 2013.[53] However, it allowed the country to participate again in the AU in January 2014, when the new President, who had been elected in free and fair elections, assumed his duties.[54]

It transpires that the PSC's role in unconstitutional changes of government is extremely important. Arguably, the Assembly has left this matter to be handled by the PSC, even though this could not have been the intention of the Constitutive Act's drafters. As will be recalled, the PSC Protocol was concluded after the Constitutive Act was adopted. In particular, Article 7 of the former endows the PSC with multifaceted powers, which form part of the so-called African Security and Peace Architecture (ASPA).[55] Thus, not only may the PSC institute sanctions but it may also (a) authorize the deployment of peace missions; (b) recommend to the Assembly intervention in a Member State in case of grave circumstances;[56] (c) implement the AU common defence policy;[57] and (d) take appropriate action where a Member State's independence and sovereignty is threatened by acts of aggression.[58]

As regards specifically PSC sanctions, presumably the Assembly would have to approve them *ex post facto* (even if it meant rubberstamping them). An analysis of the relevant practice reveals that this has happened in only a few cases.[59] However, given that decisions on sanctions fall into the ambit of AU law (the legal systems of other international organizations also have a system of punitive measures to deal with recalcitrant Member States), a number of pertinent questions arise which should be addressed in the very context of AU law. For example, targeted Member States might want to challenge the legality of PSC decisions ordering sanctions. And, supposing they were held to be null and void or ultra vires, they could demand compensation on account of the PSC's liability. These are of course legal

[51] PSC/PR/BR(CCXXI), 17 March 2010. The sanctions concerned 109 persons whose names appeared in a list attached to the Communiqué.

[52] AU Assembly, *Decision on the Report of the Peace and Security Council on its Activities and the State of Peace and Security in Africa*, Assembly/AU/Dec.369(XVII), 1 July 2011, para 5.

[53] PSC/PR/COMM.(CCCXCIV), 5 September 2013.

[54] PSC/PR/COMM.(CDXV), 27 January 2014.

[55] cf Article 2(2) of the PSC Protocol.

[56] cf Article 4(h) of the Constitutive Act. PSC invoked it for the first time on 17 December 2015 in the case of Burundi, PSC/PR/COMM.(DLXV). Generally, see S Dersso, 'To Intervene or Not to Intervene? An inside view of the AU's decision-making on Article 4(h) and Burundi' (World Peace Foundation, 2016) available at <https://sites.tufts.edu/wpf/files/2017/05/AU-Decision-Making-on-Burundi_Dersso.pdf> accessed 26 June 2021.

[57] cf Article 4(d) of the Constitutive Act (n 56).

[58] cf Article 4(a) and (j) of the Constitutive Act (n 56).

[59] Magliveras and Naldi (n 12).

questions and intricately linked to the AU judicial organ, which should be the bedrock of the whole legal system.

Presently, there is no functionable judicial organ in the AU. The African Court of Justice (ACJ), the organ envisaged in Article 18 of the Constitutive Act, has never been operationalized,[60] while the legal instrument creating the African Court of Justice and Human Rights has been shunned and it is doubtful if it will ever be realized.[61] For the AU law to develop into a proper and self-standing legal system applicable to all Member States without exceptions, the operation of a judicial organ is a prerequisite. This is a priority matter which the AU must address with the utmost urgency.

The AU sanctioning system as regards unconstitutional overthrow of governments has been expanded through the following three instruments, which shall be briefly examined in chronological order. The first is the aforementioned African Charter, concluded on 30 January 2007. Pursuant to Article 24 thereof, contracting parties have entrusted the maintenance of constitutional order to the PSC. Should a situation arise in their territory, which, in the PSC's opinion, 'may affect ... democratic political institutional arrangements or the legitimate exercise of power', the PSC is mandated to exercise its responsibilities. It is open to question if such opinions can be regarded as proper AU acts and, consequently, whether their legality may be challenged before and reviewed by the AU's judicial organ (when of course it becomes operative). The wording of Article 25 thereof clearly suggests that, in such instances, the competent organ to order and to lift sanctions against unconstitutional regimes is the PSC and not the Assembly. The latter is instructed to impose Article 23 sanctions on any Member State which instigated or supported coups d'état in another state and has the discretion to order 'punitive economic measures' and other (undefined) forms of sanctions on the perpetrators of unconstitutional changes of government. Finally, the latter shall not be allowed to participate in elections to be held to restore democratic order or hold any public office in their country and 'may also be tried before the competent court of the [AU]'.

The second instrument is the Ezulwini Framework for the Enhancement of the Implementation of Measures of the African Union in Situations of Unconstitutional Changes of Governments in Africa, which the PSC adopted in December 2009.[62] Its principal purpose was to implement a previous PSC Decision establishing a Committee on Sanctions,[63] in conformity with Article 8(1) of the PSC Protocol. The Committee, whose status is that of a subsidiary organ, is mandated to

[60] The Protocol establishing the ACJ came into force on 11 February 2009.

[61] See Protocol on the Statute of the African Court of Justice and Human Rights, which was concluded on 1 July 2008 and merged the ACJ with the African Court on Human and Peoples' Rights. Of the 33 states which have presently signed it, only eight have ratified it (Angola was last on 21 February 2020).

[62] <http://www.peaceau.org/uploads/ezulwini-framework-english.pdf> accessed 26 June 2021.

[63] PSC/PR/COMM.3 (CLXXVIII), 13 March 2009.

complement AU efforts in preventing unconstitutional changes of government. It is made up of five PSC members appointed on the basis of regional representation, that is one member from each African region and is supposed to monitor and make recommendations on the implementation of already ordered sanctions. Thus, its functioning appears similar to the ad hoc Sanctions Committees, which have been established by the UN Security Council to control compliance by Member States with resolutions ordering mandatory punitive measures pursuant to Chapter VII of the UN Charter. A PSC document which reviewed the implementation of PSC decisions from 2007 to 2016 revealed that the Committee, alongside other subsidiary organs, had fallen to disuse and, therefore, it was decided to reactivate them and ensure that they operate continuously.[64]

The third instrument is Assembly Decision 269(XIV) of February 2010. It contains further measures to enhance the AU's effectiveness when responding to coups d'état.[65] As is invariably the case with Assembly decisions, it did not mention any legal basis. Over and above suspending the participation of the Member State where the coup d'état took place, it envisaged that the Assembly will take the following action: (a) bar perpetrators from taking part in any elections to be held to restore constitutional order in the country; (b) order sanctions against those Member States proven to have supported the coup d'état; and (c) take additional punitive measures, including economic sanctions, if considered appropriate under the circumstances. A comparison between these provisions and Article 25 of the African Charter reveals that their text is almost identical, which raises the question which was the real purpose of adopting the former. The only rational explanation is that, as the scourge of unconstitutional overthrow of governments had continued unabetted and the African Charter had not entered into force at the time (it did so on 15 February 2012), the Assembly wanted to put the Article 25 sanctions into force at once and, therefore, adopted Decision 269(XIV) which had immediate effect. If this suggestion is correct, it is an interesting development how the law-making process in the AU, which is principally carried out through the conclusion of treaties under its auspices, may be substituted with the adoption of Assembly decisions. Even though one commentator writing in 2015 maintained that Decision 269(XIV) was still in force,[66] it should be considered as lapsed following the entry into force of the African Charter.

[64] Conclusions of the Retreat of the Peace and Security Council on the Implementation of the Conclusions of Successive PSC Retreats and the Related Adoptive Decisions from 2007 to 2016, Kigali, Rwanda, PSC/Retreat/10, May 2017; see further PSC/PR/COMM.(DCLXXXVIII), 26 May 2017, para 2.

[65] AU Assembly, *Decision on the Prevention of Unconstitutional Changes of Government and Strengthening the Capacities of the African Union to Manage such Situations*, AU Doc. Assembly/AU/Dec.269(XIV) Rev. 1, 2 February 2010.

[66] SR Ratner, *The Thin Justice of International Law: A Moral Reckoning of the Law of Nations* (OUP, 2015) 128.

The African Charter (and Decision 269(XIV) for that matter) leaves several questions unanswered. For example, how will it be authoritatively determined which Member State have instigated unconstitutional overthrows of legitimate (i.e. truly constitutional and democratic) governments? If the government in the country where the coup d'état took place was not constitutionally elected, as is often the case in Africa, could a third Member State's intervention be condoned if certain circumstances are present? The latter question effectively seeks to determine whether there are exceptions to the AU principle of non-interference in internal affairs.[67] This principle should be associated with the Member States' right to request the AU's intervention to restore peace and security domestically but also with the principle of interdependence among Member States.[68] The former should be interpreted to mean that, unless intervention has been requested, no third state may interfere, unless of course war crimes, genocide, and crimes of humanity have been perpetrated, in which case the AU has an express right to intervene.[69] However, the principle of interdependence, as applied in Africa, a continent fraught with coup d'états, might possibly justify interference by a group of democratic Member States committed to the promotion of constitutional ideals.

5. Conclusion

AU law, as a developing system of norms and rules, which is applied to the relations between this Organization and its Member States and which also regulates the transactions partaking among the membership, cannot but include a sanctioning regime. Its purpose is, *inter alia*, to place the behaviour of Member States under check and balances and to ensure that the Organization will have the competence, the jurisdiction, and the ability to react to infractions efficiently within the shortest possible period of time. The purpose of the punitive measures envisaged in the Constitutive Act is to make the AU neither vindictive against Member States nor to annihilate recalcitrant states. Principally, they aim at protecting it from the latter, exerting, at the same time, pressure upon them to ensure compliance with AU law and the ensuing duties and obligations.

There is considerable practice on imposing sanctions for non-payment of assessed budgetary contributions and for when regimes have come to power through unconstitutional means (today this should be understood through undemocratic means as well). This practice indicates that there is a large degree of automaticity. Thus, when the amount of contributions in arrears has exceeded a certain threshold, sanctions are imposed. Equally, when the PSC has taken the view that

67 Article 4(g) of the Constitutive Act.
68 Respectively, ibid Article 4(j) and 4(a).
69 ibid Article 4(h).

a legitimate regime has been unconstitutionally overturned and/or a coup d'état has taken place, sanctions are ordered against what are considered to be the 'illegal authorities' without requiring the assent of another AU organ. And such sanctions are usually promptly ordered, as revealed by the fact that they are contained in the same communiqué in which the PSC determined the unconstitutional nature of the regime change in the Member State concerned.

In relation to the third sanctioning regime, namely the breach of AU decisions or policies, no sanctions have ever been ordered. This is very interesting because it is the most closely connected to the AU law sanctioning regime. Indeed, Member States have accepted and promised not to violate this legal system, which is based on specific norms and rules forming the legal basis for the AU's operation and including those decisions reached by AU organs which dictate to Member States which behaviour is allowed and which is disallowed. In their turn, these decisions must be implemented and be given effect in their domestic legal systems. The lack of sanctions under Article 30 might be explained by the AU's unwillingness to impose them in situations, which have to do with the Member States' internal sphere and domestic affairs. This policy of non-interference, which during the OAU era was considered sacred and is still very much prevalent, cannot be sustained for much longer if the AU legal system is to develop even further and flourish. This is particularly true today when the AU has embarked, among others, towards creating a common market with free and unhindered trade in goods and services.[70] However, sanctions should not only be understood as a form of punishment and the ensuing shame. They are mainly a tool, a device, to ensure compliance with obligations which are vital for the performance of a legal system (*in casu* AU law) and to act as deterrence against future breaches, thus preventing further violations of the legal system.

It is very important that the AU has in place an adequate and effective sanctioning system. If applied without political manoeuvring, it will allow it to tackle most challenges and problems and, in the process, assist in consolidating AU law. However, until now the lack of any sanctions pursuant to Article 30 is worrisome. Many a Member State might perceive the application of this provision as an attack against their sovereignty. But this kind of mentality belongs to a bygone era. Presently, the existence of AU law as a separate legal system regulating increasingly the relations among 55 states necessitates a completely different mentality, one which will allow the AU to function without hindrances and to reach its lofty goals for the benefit of the African populace.

[70] To date, all Member States, except Eritrea, have signed the AfCFTA and two-thirds have ratified it.

20
Enforcement Mechanisms in AU Human Rights Treaties: Lessons for the Wider AU Law

Michèle Olivier

1. Introduction

Fundamentally, AU law refers to decisions taken by the African Union (AU) that will bind its Members States as a matter of law. A broad interpretation of AU law would include treaties negotiated under the auspices of the Organisation of African Unity (OAU)/AU and open for AU Member States to accede to or ratify. African human rights treaties and the obligations thus created have the potential to complement decisions AU institutions may take on matters such as security, governance, and human rights, and as such form an important component of AU law. In a discussion of AU law it is therefore important to take note of the nature of the obligations created within a specific field such as human rights and access how it may aid an emergent AU law.

For a meaningful discussion of regional human rights and their enforcement status, in Africa and elsewhere, regard to the context is essential. The African value of 'ubuntu' provides a useful backdrop to understand African views on the individual's rights, duties, and position in the community.[1] Ubuntu, which literary means 'I am because you are', reminds us that a person derives humanity and dignity through others. Politicians like Nelson Mandela, theologians like of Archbishop Desmond Tutu,[2] and courts,[3] have referred to this notion to emphasize the fact that individual well-being and prosperity cannot occur where the individual stands in

[1] NN Mabovula, 'The erosion of African communal values: a reappraisal of the African Ubuntu philosophy' (2011) 3(1) Inkanyiso: Journal of Humanities and Social Sciences available at <https://www.ajol.info/index.php/ijhss/article/view/69506> accessed 23 July 2019; N Gianan, 'Valuing the emergence of Ubuntu philosophy' [2010] 7(1) Cultura International Journal of Philosophy of Culture and Axiology 86; E Onyebuchi, 'I am because you are: cosmopolitanism in the age of xenophobia' (2017) 46(1) Philosophical Papers 85–109.

[2] D Tutu, ' Who we are: Human uniqueness and the African spirit of Ubuntu' (2013) available at <https://www.youtube.com/watch?v=0wZtfqZ271w#t=162> accessed 23 July 2019.

[3] For example, *Afri-Forum and Another vs. Malema and others* (The Equality Court, Johannesburg 2011) 23.

Michèle Olivier, *Enforcement Mechanisms in AU Human Rights Treaties: Lessons for the Wider AU Law* In: *The Emergent African Union Law.* Edited by: Olufemi Amao, Michèle Olivier and Konstantinos D. Magliveras, Oxford University Press.
 DOI: 10.1093/oso/9780198862154.003.0021

isolation. Although the content of 'ubuntu' is somewhat opaque and means different things to different people, it is embraced as a value system that is distinctly African. Despite its vagueness, it is suggested that the broad meaning of the notion is well expressed in the African (Banjul) Charter on Human and Peoples' Rights of 1981.[4] In addition to covering universally recognized individual human rights as protected by a range of United Nations (UN) instruments, it introduces the notion that peoples or groups are also worthy of protection and pays special attention to socio-economic rights. Protection of individual rights depends on the protection of those around them. Such interconnectedness of individuals is expressed by the Banjul Charter through the concepts of group rights as well as duties, thereby codifying African values into positive law. The value of codified law lies, *inter alia*, in that it lends itself to clarity, certainty, and better enforcement.

The adoption of the Banjul Charter was followed by a range of treaties adopted by the OAU and the AU. They focus on specific human rights or vulnerable groups, giving rise to a fully fledged African human rights regime.[5] African human rights treaties exist alongside the multilateral human rights regime of the UN and due recognition is given to the fact that the one is not applied to the exclusion of the other.[6] The African regime is however uniquely focused on African challenges and often goes beyond the minimum requirements of the UN counterparts. A further characteristic of this bespoke human rights regime is that the approach to enforcement also follows prevailing African values opting for a rather strict interpretation of state sovereignty over internationalism. As a result, the practice on compliance and enforcement favoured by the AU has traditionally been broad and non-prescriptive, pointing to recommended good practice and consultation instead of punitive measures. This differs from expectations of protection of individual rights prevailing in a Western context, for example through enforcement of regional human rights under the European system.

Against this background, the chapter considers whether mechanisms provided for by AU treaties indeed allow for effective enforcement at both international and domestic levels to support the emergent AU law. In order to get a better understanding of enforcement, means and methods including periodic reports, communications from states, the role of the African Commission on Human and Peoples' Rights, and the African Court, are considered. The second part of the chapter considers a model of transformation of treaty obligations into domestic law using South African law as a case study. The focus is not on how specific rights are interpreted and enforced but rather on the specific legal mechanisms. The research is done through an analysis of a selection of treaty texts and relevant secondary

[4] African Charter on Human and Peoples' Rights adopted 27 June 1981, OAU Doc. CAB/LEG/67/3 rev. 5, 21 ILM 58 (1982), entered into force 21 October 1986.

[5] (*African Union*, July 2019) available at <https://au.int/en/treaty-category-tags/human-rights-treaties> accessed 3 January 2020.

[6] African Charter on Human and Peoples' Rights (n 4) Article 60.

material. The case study is based on an analysis of the South African Constitution's provisions dealing with the status of international law referring to applicable case law of domestic courts.

2. Enforcement Provisions under the Banjul Charter

The enforceability of treaty rights by AU institutions provides an important indicator of the existence of supranational law, set as a benchmark to qualify as AU law.[7] Here the Banjul Charter (the Charter) will be considered as a 'parent treaty' followed by a specific treaty on children's rights which operate under its coverage.

2.1 Safeguarding by the African Commission on Human and Peoples' Rights

As a treaty, the Charter is binding under international law.[8] The human rights provided for are 'safeguarded' through the African Commission on Human and Peoples' Rights (the Commission).[9] The Charter establishes the Commission (not to be confused with the Commission established under Article 20 of the Constitutive Act of the AU) to act as a supervisory mechanism.[10] The Commission is a quasi-judicial body charged with monitoring the implementation of the Charter and promoting and protecting human and peoples' rights in Africa.[11] As part of the African human rights system, the Commission has a broad mandate, ranging from studies on human and peoples' rights to formulating rules and principles aimed at resolving human rights problems.[12] It may receive communications from State Parties about Charter violations by other State Parties, as well as from individuals and non-governmental organizations who are not necessarily aggrieved parties.[13]

[7] For a discussion see Part 1 of this book.

[8] R Murray, *The African Commission on Human and Peoples' Rights and International Law* (Hart Publishing, 2000).

[9] African Charter on Human and Peoples' Rights (n 4) Part II: *Measures of Safeguard.*

[10] G Bekker, 'The African Commission on Human and Peoples' Rights and Remedies for Human Rights Violations' (2013) 13(3) Human Rights Law Review 499–528; UO Umozurike, 'The African Charter on Human and Peoples' Rights: suggestions for more effectiveness' (2007) 13(1) available at <http://digitalcommons.law.ggu.edu/annlsurvey/vol13/iss1/8> accessed 10 January 2020; EA Ankumah, *The African Commission on Human and Peoples' Rights – Practice and Procedures* (Brill Nijhoff, 1996); NS Rembe, *The System of Protection of Human Rights Under The African Charter on Human and Peoples' Rights: Problems and Prospects* (Institute for Southern African Studies, National University of Lesotho, 1991).

[11] African Charter on Human and Peoples' Rights (n 4), *Establishment and Organization of the African Commission on Human and Peoples' Rights* Article 30.

[12] ibid *Mandate of the Commission* Article 45.

[13] ibid *Communication from States* Article 47.

The extent to which resolutions and concluding observations of the Commission are binding on states is contested.[14] Although the powers allocated to the Commission mostly fall into the category of the soft and non-binding, that is, to promote, collect, and disseminate information, cooperate, and interpret, Murray points out that the Commission has consistently described the nature of its decisions as binding[15] and supports this assertion by state practice. However, a textual interpretation of the Charter does not point to an intention to endow the Commission with law-making capacity and clearly underlines the status of the Charter as the supreme enabling source of the Commission's powers.[16] The mandate of the Commission stops short of guaranteeing protection of human rights, but points in the direction of an obligation to 'promote human rights and ensure their protection'.[17] What is meant by 'ensuring protection' remains open to debate.[18] Given the fact that the Charter in general does not engage with law-making, it is doubtful that 'ensuring protection' would actually entail the taking of binding decisions.

The Commission is, however, well placed to act as a human rights watchdog by interpreting Charter provisions, considering interstate and other complaints, and analysing the reports submitted by State Parties on their implementation of the Charter and other African human rights conventions, as discussed in paras 2.2 and 3.[19] By defining Charter provisions, resolutions adopted by the Commission seek to provide an important normative resource.[20] An example includes declaring maternal mortality a violation of women's rights to life, dignity, and equality, including calls on governments to address the issue and to provide access to healthcare.[21] These resolutions are not intended to have binding force as they merely call on states to follow a certain course of action. As such they can be compared with UN General Assembly resolutions which are by nature non-binding but designed to put soft pressure on states to promote and protect human rights.

Individual and state complaints provide an important potential enforcement mechanism. The Charter allows State Parties, through written communication to the AU Secretary-General and to the Chairman of the Commission, to draw the attention to Charter violations of another party, requiring a written explanation within three months from the state in question.[22] The response shall include the

[14] R Murray, *The African Charter on Human and Peoples' Rights A Commentary* (OUP, 2019) 33.
[15] ibid 34.
[16] African Charter on Human and Peoples' Rights (n 4) Article 45(2).
[17] ibid Article 30.
[18] Murray (n 14) 19.
[19] African Charter on Human and Peoples' Rights (n 4) Article 62.
[20] F Viljoen and L Louw, 'State compliance with the recommendations of the African Commission on Human and Peoples' Rights, 1994–2004' (2007) 101(1) American Journal of International Law 1 32.
[21] African Commission Resolution on Maternal Mortality [2008] ACHPR/Res 135 08
[22] African Charter on Human and Peoples' Rights (n 4) Article 47.

redress already given and the course of action available. The matter may be referred directly to the Commission if parties do not wish to settle it bilaterally.[23] The Commission shall then prepare a report sent to the states involved and also communicate it to the heads of state and government. The Commission also entertains complaints from non-State Parties,[24] followed by findings and recommendations. In neither case will complaints by states or non-states result in enforceable action or remedies awarded to complaining parties.

Communications are only admissible once domestic remedies are exhausted.[25] This requirement is criticized by Onoria, who remarks that the qualification endorses the primacy of domestic legal orders over allegations of human rights violations thus respecting the principle of state sovereignty.[26] The Commission takes a wide and objective interpretation of this requirement in rendering communications as inadmissible, as evidenced in the *Dambaya* case.[27] However, on occasion it has declared domestic remedies unavailable or ineffective, pointing to a prevailing reality in many State Parties.[28]

Despite the Commission's assertion to possess binding powers, commentators point to the fact that jurisprudence in relation to remedies leans towards favouring the state and refrains from providing effective redress for victims of human rights abuses. Careful not to alienate states, there is an emphasis on attainment of amicable resolutions.[29] It is surprising that the latter is not covered under the requirement of exhaustion of local remedies. A pro-state approach has been exacerbated by low state compliance. These failures can perhaps be best explained within the context of its treaty mandate, pointing to a need for reform. Okafor regards the outputs of the Commission at best as resources to be mobilized by other actors such as states, non-governmental organizations, sub-state groups, and individuals.[30] Weak state compliance is regarded as the greatest stumbling block rendering individual petitions almost worthless.[31] One may speculate whether the compliance is low because the decisions are non-binding to start with, or whether states are not persuaded because they do not recognize the authority of the Commission to pass judgment on their domestic violations.

[23] ibid Article 49.

[24] ibid Articles 55–59.

[25] ibid Article 50.

[26] H Onoria, 'The African Commission on Human and Peoples' Rights and the exhaustion of local remedies under the African Charter' (2003) 3 African Human Rights Law Journal 1, 3.

[27] Comm No 127/94, Dambaya v The Gambia (Dambaya case) Activity Report, paras 2 and 3.

[28] Onoria (n 26) 5.

[29] Bekker (n 10).

[30] O Okafor, *The African Human Rights System, Activist Forces and International Institutions* (CUP, 2007) 63.

[31] Viljoen and Louw (n 20).

2.2 Reporting on Domestic Implementation

The obligation calling on parties to submit periodic reports on legislative and other measures adopted to implement the Charter provides the Commission with an opportunity to monitor implementation of the Charter in a non-confrontational environment. This mechanism, however, points to an expectation that certain provisions should be given legal effect through incorporation into domestic law. That said, many Charter provisions permit a large measure of leeway for parties to limit the scope of rights through national legislation via so-called claw-back clauses.[32] These claw-back provisions mean that provisions are subject to, and can be amended by, national legislation of a given party. National legislation will in effect enjoy supremacy over Charter obligations. Article 10 of the Charter is a typical example: 'Every individual shall have the right to free association provided that he abides by the law'. The thinking behind claw-back architecture runs contrary to the raison d'être of AU law, namely that the latter should in given circumstances enjoy supremacy over national legislation. Claw-back clauses in effect provide a treaty mechanism to limit application. It undermines the integrity of individual rights. The restrictive outcome can be compared to what is normally achieved by reservations qualifying treaty provisions – it is a mechanism for state sovereignty to prevail over international governance.

Practice shows that many states do not enthusiastically comply with this reporting duty.[33] Reports are often infrequent and inadequate.[34] This tendency is exacerbated by the fact that the Commission adopted a restrained approach when considering the substance of reports that were in fact submitted and that the examination process had serious shortcomings. Commentators identify a variety of reasons for the deplorable state of reporting[35] ranging from lack of expertise, resources, institutional support, and understanding of what is expected to the financial burden it places on states. Reporting is a low priority measured against other demands and competes with overlapping reporting obligations under various AU and UN human rights treaties as well as the African Peer Review Mechanism

32 L Mapuva, 'Negating the promotion of human rights through "claw-back" clauses in the African Charter on Human and People's Rights' (2016) 51 International Affairs and Global Strategy available at <https://iiste.org/Journals/index.php/IAGS/article/viewFile/34503/35504> accessed 19 July 2019.

33 Strategic Plan 2015–2019 of African Commission on Human and Peoples' Rights, 'Delivering Better', identifies inadequate implementation mechanisms of state reporting practices as a one of the Commission's weaknesses. Available at <https://www.achpr.org/public/Document/file/English/achpr_strategic_plan_2015_19.pdf> accessed 20 April 2020.

34 F Viljoen, 'State reporting under the African Charter on Human and Peoples' Rights: a boost from the South' (2000) 44/1 Journal of Africa Law 110,111. Viljoen mentions that up to the Commission's 26th Session held as far back as 1999, only 24 of the 53 states parties have reported at all and there were more than 225 reports overdue.

35 M Evans and R Murray, 'The State of Reporting Mechanism of the African Charter' in M Evans and R Murray (eds), *The African Charter on Human and Peoples' Rights: The System in Practice*, 2nd edn (CUP, 2008) 49–75, 70.

(APRM). An important factor within the present discussion is that African states often enter into treaties without a full appreciation of the legal obligations and consequences it brings. Within a culture of soft obligations and recommendations of good practice instead of directives on core obligations, aspects such as reporting often fall by the wayside when competing with other governance priorities. Moreover, states are generally not keen to be too transparent about problems experienced on the human rights front and regard these as matters falling outside international scrutiny.

3. Enforcement Provisions under the African Charter on the Rights and Welfare of the Child

The African Charter on the Rights and Welfare of the Child (ACRWC)[36] is considered here as an example of African human rights agreements, illustrating the variety of enforcement mechanisms provided. The ACRWC focuses on the critical position of African children and their need for special protection. As of April 2020, the ACRWC was ratified by 50 out of 55 AU members.[37] The Preamble confirms adherence to other OAU/AU and UN conventions aimed at the protection of child rights and welfare.[38]

The ACRWC provides for enforcement at three levels:

i) Article 1 underlines the obligations on state parties to 'recognise the rights, freedoms and duties enshrined in this Charter' and requires the taking of 'necessary steps, in accordance with their constitutional processes ... to adopt such legislation or other measures as may be necessary'. Article 1(3) takes a bold stand and points to custom, traditions, culture and religious practices that violate the rights of many African children, but then cautiously directs state parties that these should only be discouraged. This is another example of a claw back mechanism that is common in the Banjul Charter. The wording, however, reflects the challenge human rights regulation face when dealing with traditional legal systems and the difficulty in challenging culturally engrained ideas on marriage and children.[39]
ii) An African Committee of Experts on the Rights and Welfare of the Child is established[40] to 'promote and protect' the rights of the child.[41] The committee

[36] African Charter on the Rights and Welfare of the Child adopted 11 July 1990, entered into force 29 November 1999.
[37] See <https://www.acerwc.africa/ratifications-table/> accessed 26 April 2020.
[38] BD Memzur, 'The African Children's Charter versus the UN Convention on the Rights of the Child: a zero-sum game?' (2008) 23(1) South African Public Law 1–29.
[39] J Sarich, M Olivier, and others, 'Forced marriage, slavery, and plural legal systems: an African example' (2016) 38(2) Human Rights Quarterly 450–76.
[40] African Charter on the Rights and Welfare of the Child (n 36) part II.
[41] ibid Article 32.

is mandated to assess problems and make recommendations to governments,[42] and to monitor implementation and 'ensure' protection of the child rights in the Charter.[43] The functions replicate that of the Commission under the Charter, with the exception that the mandate of the present committee includes the 'monitoring of implementation' of the ACRWC in addition to the commitment to 'ensure protection' that both committees share. The ACRWC committee has the power to receive and investigate complaints received from parties, the UN, individuals or groups recognised by the OAU relating to a matter covered by the Charter. These are reported to the Assembly of Heads of State and Government every two years.[44]

On paper, the ACRWC committee has a similar, if not somewhat stronger, mandate than that of the Commission. In the case of the present convention, parties are directed to submit reports to the said committee.[45]

iii) The obligation of parties to submit periodic reports to the ACRW committee on measures of implementation adopted provides a third mechanism of enforcement linked to the above. Article 43 of the ACRWC directs parties to submit their Initial State Party Reports within two years of ratification to the ACRWC and Periodic Reports on the implementation of the ACRWC every three years. Thus far, 20 years after entry into force, 34 countries out of the 49 parties have submitted initial reports to the Committee, out of which 6 have also submitted their periodic reports.[46] The picture of late and inadequate reports reflects the experience of reporting under the Charter. Regrettably, there is a paucity of recent scholarship engaging with this trend. It can be assumed that reasons for this are very similar to that offered above in relation to the Charter.

The reporting obligations under the ACRWC can be compared with the enforcement mechanisms provided for under the Protocol on the Rights of Women in Africa.[47] As a more recent human rights treaty, the latter is progressive in that it uses stronger language and emboldened enforcement provisions. Discrimination against women 'shall be' combatted through appropriate legislative and regulatory measures as well as policy.[48] Parties also commit themselves to modify social and cultural patterns of conduct through education with a view to eliminate harmful

[42] ibid Article 42(a).
[43] ibid Article 42(b)
[44] ibid Articles 44, 45
[45] ibid Article 43.
[46] 'ACERWC, 33 Ordinary Session' available at <https://www.acerwc.africa/reporting-table/initial-reports/> accessed January 2020.
[47] Protocol to the African Charter on Human and Peoples' Rights on the Rights of Women in Africa, adopted 11 July 2013 entered into force 25 November 2005.
[48] ibid Article 2.

traditional practices. Parties 'shall ensure the implementation of this Protocol'[49] and make available budgetary and other resources to do so.[50] Parties are directed by Article 25 to provide for appropriate remedies under national law to deal with violations. Again, there is a reporting obligation but no special committee has been established to consider reports. Periodic reports shall be submitted under Article 62 of the African Charter to be considered by the Commission.

4. Lessons Learnt from Enforcement Provisions and Treaty Monitoring Practices

The range of enforcement mechanisms provided for by African human rights treaties as evidenced by the Charter and the ACRWC are ambitious but weak in their attempt to simultaneously submit to strong sovereign states while also protecting human rights. The compulsory reporting reflects an accepted practice under UN treaties but suffers from various shortcomings. The fact that African states are often party to the full range of AU and UN human rights treaties brings a heavy burden of report writing and presenting for which many are, for practical and political reasons, not equipped to deliver on. The treaty monitoring bodies, viz the Commission and the ACRW committee, duplicate functions and suffer from vague and unclear mandates. The Commission does not appear to have binding decision-making powers, although it perceives itself in a different light. Even if they are capable of taking binding enforcement action, it is not worth much if the violators of human rights do not abide by these decisions through actual enforcement action under domestic law. Enforcement bodies apparently try to set non-compliance off against not wanting to step on the toes of sovereign states, hence rendering it ineffective in providing remedies for human rights violations.

Unconcise and ambiguous treaty drafting pose a problem. Protecting both strong sovereign interests and the vulnerable cannot be achieved at the same time. From a practical perspective it might be better to consider a less ambitious structure, limiting treaty monitoring to the Commission under a clear mandate and to follow up on non-enforcement. Success will depend on the status of these treaties under domestic law of parties through relevant constitutional provisions, legislation, and decisions of domestic courts.

[49] ibid Article 26(1).
[50] ibid Article 26(2).

5. The African Court on Human and Peoples' Rights

Given the shortcomings of the Commission and the ongoing human rights abuses in Africa, the Protocol on the Establishment of an African Court on Human and Peoples' Rights (the Protocol)[51] was entered into in 2004, with a view to complement and reinforce the functions of the Commission.[52]

The African Court on Human and Peoples' Rights (the Court) has jurisdiction to deal with all cases and disputes submitted to it regarding the interpretation and application of the Charter and other human rights instruments.[53] The Court may, at the request of the Commission, AU Member States, AU organs, or any African organization recognized by the AU, provide an opinion on any legal matter relating to the Charter or any other relevant human rights instrument, provided that the subject matter of the opinion is not related to a matter under examination by the Commission. A further proviso applies, namely that the state against which the complaint is brought has deposited the Article 34(6) declaration recognizing the jurisdiction of the Court to accept cases from individuals and non-governmental organizations (NGOs).

Of the 30 State Parties to the Protocol,[54] only nine[55] have deposited the declaration accepting the jurisdiction of the Court to receive cases from individuals and NGOs.[56] The low level of ratifications and declarations threatens to limit the Court's role as a human rights watchdog within the AU. The Court has finalized in the order of 58 applications[57] and five advisory opinions[58] since it started functioning in 2006. These deal with a wide range of human rights issues.

In 2008, the AU called for the merger of this Court with the Court of Justice of the African Union to form a single court by adopting the Protocol on the Statute of the African Court of Justice and Human Rights as the main judicial organ of the AU. As of June 2021, the Protocol received 33 signatures and only eight ratifications,[59] falling well short of the 15 ratifications required for entry into force.

[51] Protocol on the Establishment of an African Court on Human and Peoples' Rights, adopted 10 June 1998 entered into force 25 January 2004.

[52] GJ Naldi and K Magliveras, 'Reinforcing the African system of human rights: the protocol on the establishment of a regional Court of Human and Peoples' Rights' (1998) 16(4) Netherlands Quarterly of Human Rights 431

[53] Protocol on the Establishment of an African Court on Human and Peoples' Rights (n 51) Article 3.

[54] African Court on Human and Peoples' Rights available at <http://www.african-court.org/en/> accessed 28 April 2020.

[55] Benin, Burkina Faso, Côte d'Ivoire, Gambia, Ghana, Mali, Malawi, Tanzania, and Republic of Tunisia.

[56] Protocol on the Establishment of an African Court on Human and Peoples' Rights (n 51) Article 5(3).

[57] African Court on Human and Peoples' Rights, June 2019 available at <http://www.african-court.org/en/index.php/cases/2016-10-17-16-18-21> accessed 30 June 2021.

[58] ibid.

[59] African Union Protocol on the Statute of the African Court of Justice and Human Rights, February 2019 available at <https://au.int/sites/default/files/treaties/36396-sl-protocol_on_the_statute_of_the_african_court_of_justice_and_human_rights.pdf> accessed 28 April 2020.

Although practical considerations played a role in bringing the two courts together, the strengthening of AU institutions lacking the necessary powers to carry out their mandate effectively is paramount.

The African Court of Justice and Human Rights will enjoy broad jurisdiction over all cases and all legal disputes submitted to it, which relate to:[60]

(1) the interpretation and application of the Constitutive Act;
(2) the interpretation, application or validity of other treaties and all subsidiary legal instruments adopted within the framework of the OAU/AU;
(3) the interpretation and the application of the Charter, the ACRWC, the Protocol to the African Charter on Human and Peoples' Rights on the Rights of Women in Africa, or any other legal instrument relating to human rights, ratified by the States Parties concerned;
(4) any question of international law;
(5) all acts, decisions, regulations, and directives of the organs of the AU;
(6) all matters specifically provided for in any other agreements that States Parties may conclude among themselves, or with the AU, and which confer jurisdiction on the African Court of Justice and Human Rights;
(7) the existence of any fact which, if established, would constitute a breach of an obligation owed to a State Party or to the AU; and
(8) the nature or extent of the reparation to be made for the breach of an international obligation.

A strongly worded Article 46 specifically provides for the 'Binding Force and Execution of Judgments'. Parties shall comply with the judgment and guarantee its execution. Where a party has failed to comply with a judgment, the court shall refer the matter to the Assembly, which shall decide upon measures to be taken to give effect to that judgment. The Assembly may in turn impose sanctions by virtue of paragraph 2 of Article 23 of the Constitutive Act.

This would potentially remedy what can be described as one of the basic weaknesses of the African human rights system, namely the lack of an authoritative, robust, and effective supervisory and enforcement mechanism.[61] Enforceable judgments will provide a good example of supranational AU law and provide a firm foundation for enforcement of the African human rights treaty regime. The reluctance of AU members to ratify the Protocol may be indicative of their reluctance to achieve just that – robust enforcement of human rights by a supranational African body that might infringe on national sovereignty and the concomitant impunity of

60 ibid Article 28.

61 GJ Naldi, 'Interim measures of protection in the African System for the protection of human and peoples' rights' (2002) 2(1) African Human Rights Law Journal 1, 10.

the political elite. Be that as it may, even a fully functional court cannot be expected to solve all of Africa's human rights problems.

Ultimately, the relationship between international human rights law and national legal systems determines the enforcement of international obligations arising from such treaties. Even where treaties provide for directly enforceable provisions, it ultimately depends on the rules of national constitutions how those rules will be regarded under national law.[62] The South African Constitution is a prime example where the status of international law is determined by a supreme constitution and thus regarded as part of the law of the land.

6. Domestic Application under South African Law

The system of apartheid in South Africa that embodied a range of human rights violations in a society racially divided by law formally came to an end with the adoption of the country's first democratic constitution in 1993.[63] This constitution replaced parliamentary supremacy with constitutional supremacy and established a constitutional court empowered to overlook the constitutionality of governmental actions and legislation. The South African Constitution of 1993 (1993 Constitution) and the Constitution of 1996 (1996 Constitution)[64] which replaced it after the first democratic elections in 1994, contain notable provisions recognizing the important status held by international law in South African domestic law. Section 231 of the 1996 Constitution provides for entry into international agreements and their status in South African law, whilst section 39 recognizes the role of international law when interpreting human rights.

6.1 International Law as Law of the Land

Under section 231, it is the responsibility of parliament to approve entry into international agreements (treaties) that would require incorporation into South African law. These are international agreements that would impose obligations on South Africa as a party to implement or enforce relevant treaty provisions in its domestic legal system. They are typically provisions which set international standards, grant or protect individual rights, or criminalize certain actions. Section 231(4) states that international agreements become law in South African through one of the following ways:

[62] B Kabumba, 'The application of African Union (human rights) law in Uganda: trends and prospects from a comparative review' (2018) 2 African Human Rights Yearbook 89, 90–1.

[63] Constitution of the Republic of South Africa, Act 200 of 1993.

[64] ibid Act 108 of 1996.

- The first alternative restates the classical dualist approach familiar to South Africa and endorsed by legal precedent prior to 1993,[65] namely that international agreements become law in South Africa only when incorporated into national legislation.
- Section 231(4), however introduces a second alternative to South African law: Self-executing provisions of an agreement approved by parliament form part of South African law without the need for legislative incorporation, provided they are consistent with parliamentary legislation and the Constitution. This is in accordance with the monist approach which regard international law and national law as being part of the same legal order. International law can therefore be applied in domestic law without legislative incorporation.

The intention behind the drafting of this provision was that once parliament had agreed that South Africa become party to an international agreement, such agreement should become part of South African law, subject of course to the Constitution. Previously treaty-making was exclusively an executive matter in South Africa and the legislator became involved for the first time when it had to incorporate such treaty obligations into South African law[66] as the executive could not legislate for South African citizens through international agreements. Under the 1993 and 1996 Constitutions the treaty-making capacity was placed in the hands of the legislator. Before approving South Africa's becoming party to an international agreement, parliament is advised and considers the effect such treaty would have on South African law. Only if parliament is satisfied that the limitations a particular treaty would place on South African sovereignty are acceptable would it approve the treaty.

The introduction of a provision for self-execution or direct application of treaties was a bold move by the constitutional drafters. It was aimed at preventing parliament from neglecting to incorporate treaty obligations into law that they have already agreed to or to adopt legislation that does not correctly reflect the treaty. It would counter the caution common amongst African states to incorporate international law directly into their legal systems because it would limit their freedom of auto-interpretation of the applicable international law principles.[67] In practice, however, and given South Africa's historic dualist tradition, this notion has led to uncertainty as to when a treaty can be considered self-executing.[68]

[65] The position is regarded as trite law in *Pan American Airways Incorporated v SA Fire and Accident Insurance Co Ltd* 1965(3) SA 150 (AD) 161.

[66] M Olivier, 'South Africa and international human rights agreements: procedure, policy and practice – Part 1' (2003) 2 Journal of South African Law 293–310.

[67] T Maluwa, 'The incorporation of international law and its interpretational role in municipal legal systems in Africa: an exploratory survey' (1998) 23 South African Yearbook of International Law 57.

[68] N Botha, 'Extradition, self-execution and the South African Constitution: a non-event? South African judicial decisions' (2008) 33(1) South African Yearbook of International Law 253–66.

The self-executing nature of a treaty is usually derived from a characteristic inherent to the treaty provisions that can be directly applied by the national courts and authorities. Strydom, however, points to the anomaly that in practice national constitutional law determines whether provisions can be directly applied.[69] In the case of a supranational AU law, enforcement of provisions capable of direct application would still depend on whether the constitutional law of Member States provides for self-execution, as section 231(4) does.

For purposes of legal certainty, it would be advisable for parliament to state which provisions it regards as self-executing when agreeing that South Africa becomes party to an agreement. In the absence of such a statement, this would be a question for the courts to determine in accordance with relevant international law on self-execution.

6.2 International Law as a Tool to Interpret Human Rights

The South African constitutional Bill of Rights contains a specific interpretation clause that points to the role of international law in interpreting the human rights safeguarded by the 1996 Constitution. Section 39(1) provides that:

> When interpreting the Bill of Rights, a court of law, tribunal or forum-
>
> (a) must promote the values that underlie an open and democratic society based on human dignity, equality and freedom;
> (b) must consider international law; and
> (c) may consider foreign law.

As this provision is substantially similar to section 35 of the 1993 Constitution, interpretative case law and scholarly interpretation of the latter remains relevant. It is clear that the term 'international law' should be used in a broad and general sense to include both international law binding on South Africa, international law not binding on South Africa (treaties to which South Africa is no party and custom not binding on South Africa), and also non-binding or evolving international law.[70] It will therefore, for example, include all treaties whether South Africa is a party or not, other sources named in Article 38(1) of the ICJ Statute and soft law.[71] The term

[69] HA Strydom 'The International Law Openness of the South African Constitution' in G Carpenter (ed), *Suprema Lex: Essays on the Constitution presented to Marinus Wiechers* (Butterworths 1997) 93; JH Jackson, 'The status of treaties in domestic legal systems: a policy analysis' (1992) 86 American Journal of International Law 310; L Henry, 'When is a treaty self-executing?' (1929) XXVII Michigan Law Review 776.

[70] *S v Makwanyane and Another* (1995) 6 BCLR 665 [CC] at 686 D–F.

[71] *S v Williams and Another* (1995) 7 BCLR 861 [CC] para 21 at 869.

'international law' is however qualified in the sense that it must be applicable to the rights entrenched in the Bill of Rights. Thus, courts are directed to apply only those rules of international law dealing with human rights, commonly termed 'international human rights law' which of course includes African human rights law.[72]

It is made clear by use of the word 'must' that courts do not have a choice in having to consider international human rights law. This mandatory tone of 'must' is watered down by the use of the word 'consider' which does not imply an obligation to apply such international law where appropriate. Having regard to comparable to foreign case law is on the other hand, only permitted and not mandated. The application of neither is compulsory.[73]

In a landmark decision of *Makwanyane and Another*, the Constitutional Court dealt with the constitutionality of the death penalty, providing a lucid interpretation of section 35.[74] The 1993 Constitution did not express itself on the matter of capital punishment. The President of the Court, Justice Chaskalson, displayed openness towards international law influences by making extensive use of international law in his judgment. He considered circumstances existing at the time the Constitution was adopted in interpreting the relevant provisions of the Constitution. He points out that *travaux preparatoires* are often used as interpretation aids in states such as the United States, Canada, and India as well as by the European Court of Human Rights and the UN Committee on Human Rights. The judge also refers to the Vienna Convention on the Law of Treaties, which may assist the court in interpretation of the Constitution.[75]

Chaskalson clearly distinguishes between decisions of courts of foreign countries and that of international tribunals, as directed by section 35. As previously indicated, the consideration of the former is discretionary and of the latter obligatory. He holds that the sources of international law can be found in Article 38(1) of the Statute of the International Court of Justice. Both binding and non-binding sources may be used as tools of interpretation. He lists treaties, customary international law, and decisions of international tribunals and reports of specialized agencies as such sources, which may provide guidance in interpretation. The judge stresses that application of none of above listed sources is compulsory.[76]

Mahomed J states that public international law is one of the factors that may be considered in interpreting the Constitution.[77] Makgoro J speculates about the similarities between the spirit of the African concept of 'ubuntu' and the rights to life and dignity as embodied in the International Covenant in Civil and Political

[72] N Botha, 'International law and the South African interim Constitution' (1994) 9(2) South African Public Law 245–56.
[73] *S v Makwanyane and Another* (n 70) para 39 at 688 A.
[74] ibid 665.
[75] ibid 697.
[76] ibid 688 A para 39.
[77] ibid para 266 at 759H.

Rights,[78] prompting Botha to comment that Western ideals and African indigenous law need not differ in spirit.[79]

7. Possible Enforcement of AU Law under the South African Constitution

The international law friendly provisions of the 1996 Constitution recognize the significance of a broad range of sources of international law. These will have an impact on South African law either through direct application, legislative incorporation, or as tool of interpretation subject to the supreme Constitution. Although a continental legal system is not referred to by name, African human rights treaties are accommodated under the wider provisions of sections 231 and 39(1).

Considerations of state sovereignty and constitutional supremacy are normally taken into account before entering into a treaty. Parliament is then advised on the potential impact of treaty obligations on domestic law in order to make a full consideration regarding whether or not to enter into a treaty. In the normal process preceding ratification of treaties, provisions incompatible with South African law are identified. If it is decided to go ahead with becoming party to a treaty, governmental law advisors will advise on statutory amendments to align South African law with the treaty or new legislation required to give domestic effect to the treaty. Treaty provisions that have an impact on South African law will be incorporated either through legislation or through self-execution. Treaties will then be applied as part of the law of the land.

Section 231 provides an enabling framework to give effect to South Africa's human rights treaty obligations. It is suggested for that for binding supranational AU law emanating from AU institutions to enjoy direct application in South Africa, additional legislation will be required to deal with this specific issue. This is because supranational AU law will fall into a separate category of international law and is different from AU treaties that will bind South Africa in accordance with the constitutional provisions dealing with treaty incorporation. However, both South Africa's AU treaty obligations and instruments of soft AU law will be used to interpret the constitutional human rights as directed by section 39(1) of the 1996 Constitution.

[78] ibid para 309 at 772G.

[79] N Botha, 'Incorporation of treaties under the interim constitution: a pattern emerges?' [1995] South African Yearbook of International Law 202, 227.

8. Conclusion

Successful human rights protection relies on the dual elements of international regulation and domestic enforcement. From an international perspective, the African human rights treaty regime provides a good foundation for regional human rights protection embodying uniquely African values and addressing the specific human rights challenges experienced by the continent. The range of enforcement mechanisms and bodies leading the process, however, follow the design of multilateral human rights treaties of the UN. These are complex, come with demanding responsibilities that State Parties are often unable to meet and do not fit in with the current institutional design and ethos of the AU composed of strong sovereign states reluctant to accommodate supranational regional governance. Moreover, the drafting style of AU treaties allowing for rights to be qualified by national law, provides a further difficulty within the enforcement regime. As such, the good intentions embodied in treaties unfortunately do not always translate into effective protection. Enforcement mechanisms need tailoring to accommodate the specific needs and challenges faced, accommodating the realities of good governance deficit in states. In addition, the fact that institutions and bodies tasked with treaty monitoring and implementation suffer from unclear and overlapping mandates yet lack real powers, calls for action.

At an institutional level, weak and ineffective enforcement points to serious shortcomings in continental governance, resulting in a lack of accountability, certainty, justiciability, and democratic governance. These weaknesses shelter states instead of keeping them accountable to provide remedies for human rights transgressions. It is suggested that further work is required to find an African solution to this African problem.

The status international law enjoys in the domestic law of states plays an important part in the justiciability and enforcement of human rights. It is suggested that the South African Constitution provides an enabling and international law friendly framework to support the domestic enforcement of African human rights in addition to other human rights instruments. Human rights treaties that South Africa is party to will form part of South African law once incorporated under section 231. Provisions lending themselves to self-execution will potentially apply without legislative intervention. The only proviso is that international obligations should be subject to the Constitution. Although every effort is made to identify conflicts before entering into treaties, the Constitution as supreme law will prevail in cases of conflict. It can be mentioned that the Vienna Convention on the Law of Treaties, binding on South African law by virtue of its customary status, will prevent acting in bad faith and violating the principle of *pacta sunt servanda*. Binding and non-binding international human rights are used as an interpretative tool of the constitutionally protected human rights contained in the Bill of Rights. These provisions are conducive in absorbing African human rights into South African law and provide additional resources for courts in protecting human rights. The compliance with treaty-based reporting and application of decisions and recommendations of AU institutions on human rights enforcement, on the other hand, fall outside the scope of the Constitution and are hampered by an array of factors. How South African law will react to a supranational AU law remains left to the creative thinking of South African constitutional lawyers.

21
The AU and Issues of Institutional Capacity and Enforcement

Ovo Imoedemhe

1. Introduction

In May 2013, African leaders launched a 50-year programme aimed at achieving an integrated peaceful, progressive, and prosperous Africa of the future in what is known as Agenda 2063. Pursued under Pan-Africanism and African Renaissance, Agenda 2063 is Africa's blueprint for transforming Africa. Therefore, it is imperative to evaluate how Agenda 2063 would reshape Africa from the decays of human and environmental rights abuses, corruption, crises, and conflicts into a continent of inclusivity, peace and security, and economic and sustainable development. This calls for assessment of institutions and enforcement mechanisms of the African Union (AU). Critically, the AU replaced the defunct Organisation of African Unity (OAU) in July 2002 and has since its operational phase enjoyed the support of institutions and courts for the enforcement of its policies. Although the African continent has never been bereft of laws, policies, and institutions, issues of enforcement and compliance remain endemic.

With focus on enforcement mechanisms and institutional capacity, this chapter proceeds in five sections. Section 2 analyses AU institutions. Essentially, there are judicial and quasi-judicial bodies empowered to enforce AU policies. Nevertheless, the report by President Paul Kagame of Rwanda on AU institutional reforms demonstrates that most AU institutions are weak, fragmented and arguably cannot be relied upon as effective enforcement mechanisms. Section 3 discusses Aspiration 3 of Agenda 2063 and it is posited that certain mechanisms should be put in place to achieve institutional capacity within the African region in order to attain the integrated and prosperous Africa of the future.

The Paul Kagame Report on the AU institutional reforms is analysed through the prism of institutional theory in section 4. It is argued that regulatory institutions, which represent formal laws, rules, and policies are relatively easy to change. However, normative and cognitive or cultural institutions, which are informal norms, values, beliefs, and behavioural patterns that shape social interactions, are a lot more difficult to manage. Therefore, using the collective intentionality

Ovo Imoedemhe, *The AU and Issues of Institutional Capacity and Enforcement* In: *The Emergent African Union Law*. Edited by: Olufemi Amao, Michèle Olivier and Konstantinos D. Magliveras, Oxford University Press. © Ovo Imoedemhe 2021. DOI: 10.1093/oso/9780198862154.003.0022

and wilful actor pillars of institutional theory, it is proposed that certain cultural frames, symbolic patterns, and subconscious practices that are prevalent in the African continent should also be the focus for reforms.

Section 5 analyses AU enforcement mechanisms. Arguably, the African Commission and the African Court on Human and Peoples' Rights are AU's operational enforcement mechanisms. The African Court on Human and Peoples' Rights (the Court or African Court) was established to ensure the protection of human and peoples' rights in Africa. The Court has jurisdiction over disputes and cases relating to the interpretation and application of the African Charter on Human and Peoples' Rights (the Charter or African Charter). Attempts to merge the African Court on Human and Peoples' Rights and the Court of Justice of the African Union have been unproductive. Therefore, the strategy to extend the jurisdiction of the African Court of Justice and Human Right to include international crimes in the Malabo Protocol has equally been unsuccessful.

Section 6 proposes that the EU parallel of an African Court of Justice for AU law might be necessary. This might appear superfluous in view of the multiplicity of courts and might result in overlap of function. Nevertheless, it is argued that the emerging AU law, Agenda 2063 and the AU Constitutive Act could provide the foundation upon which a unifying permanent African Court may be established, and other courts and laws could be consolidated in order to achieve an inclusive enforcement mechanism. The chapter concludes that in so far as African leaders are willing to make a shift in the normative, cultural, or cognitive norms within the continent, the evolving AU law has space in the continent and globally, both in the legal and scholarly landscapes, to push for the actualization of Agenda 2063.

2. AU Institutions

Within the AU are institutions and specialized agencies. The principal organs of the AU include the Assembly of the Union, Executive Council, the Peace and Security Council, Pan-African Parliament, Permanent Representative Committee, the African Commission, and the Court of Justice. Thus, the continent has never lacked institutions for its development, and yet issues of institutional capacity are ongoing. The President Paul Kagame of Rwanda Report on AU institutional reforms of 2017 and Aspiration 3 of Agenda 2063, which envisions a continent of good governance, democracy, respect for human rights, justice, and the rule of law, attests to the need for ongoing reforms and initiatives on the continent. Therefore, the place of institutional capacity becomes crucial in attaining these ideals. In subsection 2.1 AU institutions will be discussed through the prism of institutional theory.

2.1 AU Institutions Through the Prism of Institutional Theory

Institutional theory centres around the concept of institutions. Therefore, it is important to understand what institutions are and why they work and do not work. The term 'institution' has been given diverse definitions within different academic disciplines. North defined institution to include all 'rules of the game', formal or written rules, laws, and the constitutions that define formally the way the game is played.[1] According to Hoffman, institutions are 'rules, norms, and beliefs that describe reality for the organisation, explaining what is and is not, what can be acted upon and what cannot'.[2] Similarly, Scott notes that institutions include 'social structures that have attained a high degree of resilience composed of cultural-cognitive, normative, and regulative elements that, together with associated activities and resources, provide stability and meaning to social life'.[3] Furthermore, Hodgson asserts that institution is a relatively stable 'system of established and embedded social rules that structure social interactions'.[4]

Institutional theory holds 'that organisations, and the individuals who populate them are suspended in a web of values, norms, rules, beliefs, and taken-for-granted assumptions, that are at least partially of their own making'.[5] Obviously, institutions influence behaviour. Thus, as proposed by Scott, there are three mutually inclusive pillars that make up the institutional framework.[6] These are regulatory, normative, and cognitive or cultural institutions. Regulatory institutions are formal laws, rules, and regulations that are usually explicit, flexible, and adaptable to changes such as changes in constitutions in domestic settings. Normative institutions are informal rules and consciously shared norms, values, and beliefs and expectations for behaviour and social interactions,[7] while cognitive or cultural institutions include implicit, subconscious, and symbolic interpretative frames.[8] Culture refers to symbolic patterns, social discourses, and narratives of different scope while social

[1] DC North, 'Why some countries are rich and some are poor' (2001) 77 Chicago-Kent Law Review 319–32, 321.

[2] A Hoffman, 'Institutional Evolution and Change: Environmentalism and the US Chemical Industry' (1999) 42(4) The Academy of Management Journal 351–71 cited by O Osuji and P Abba, 'Domestic Adjudicative Institutions, Developing Countries and Sustainable Development: Linkages and Limitations' 49.

[3] W Scott, *Institutions and Organizations* (Sage Publications Inc., 2001); W Scott, 'Approaching Adulthood: The Maturing of Institutional Theory' (2008) 37(5) Theory and Society 427–42; SR Lyons, *X-Marks: Native Signatures of Assent* (University of Minnesota Press, 2010) 6.

[4] GM Hodgson, 'What Are Institutions?' (2006) XL(1) Journal of Economic Issues 18 cited by A Drew and A Kriz, 'Framework for Examining Societal-Level Institutional Change' in LL Tihanyi, TM Devinney, and T Pedersen (eds), *Institutional Theory in International Business and Management* (Emerald Publishing, 2012) 66.

[5] SR Barley and PS Tolbert, 'Institutionalisation and structuration: studying the links between action and institution' (1997) 18(1) Organization Studies 93–117, 93.

[6] Scott (n 3) 73.

[7] Osuji and Abba (n 2) 53.

[8] ibid 54.

structures define interpersonal, interorganizational, or transnational patterns of action and social positions.[9]

Abdelnour, Hasselbladh, and Kallinikos describe institutions as the enduring and central manifestations of culture and social structures, and that the notion of 'institution' signals that individuals are not the building block of society. Rather, they argued that institutions are better seen as rationalized patterns, general principles, and cultural schemes variously manifested across social settings.[10] Furthermore, Kufuor noted that defined as rules that shape human interactions, institutions emerge in response to social, political, or economic change.[11] Thus, as articulated by North,

> We live by informal constraints, conventions, codes of conduct. Informal norms are a lot tougher to deal with because it is hard to define them, hard to measure them, and hard to see how they work. And, particularly, it is hard to change them. You can change formal rules ... But how do you change norms of behavior, or codes of conduct?[12]

These definitions serve as reference points to analyse the AU institutional reforms proposed by Kagame. Arguably, for any constitutional reforms to work it must take into consideration the prevailing institutional circumstances and enforcement mechanisms. This is important because without an enforcement mechanism, it may be difficult to achieve any reforms:

> To the extent that the formal rules and informal norms are not enforced, obviously they are ineffective. If you have a rule on the books that says nobody should steal, but you do not have any enforcement mechanisms, then the rule is ineffective. The consequences of a set of institutions are in the interaction between formal rules, informal norms, and the enforcement characteristics of both.[13]

The AU institutional reforms framework calls for evaluation on how it fits into the concept of institution and institutional theory discussed in this section. This will be examined later but first, a brief overview of AU's Agenda 2063 would be undertaken.

[9] SAbdelnour, H Hasselbladh, and others, 'Agency and institutions in organization studies' (2017) 38(12) Organization Studies 1775–92, 1777.

[10] ibid 1789.

[11] KO Kufuor, *The African Human Rights System: Origin and Evolution* (Palgrave Macmillan, 2010) 36.

[12] North (n 1), 321.

[13] North (n 1), 322.

2.2 Agenda 2063: A 50-Year Journey

At the 50th anniversary celebration of the OAU in 2013,[14] the idea of an Agenda 2063 was mooted and in 2015, at the 24th Ordinary Session of the African Heads of State and Government, the AU adopted the African Union Agenda 2063.[15] Agenda 2063 is both a vision and an action plan to actualize Africa's integration, development, and socio-economic transformation for the next 50 years.[16] It is a vision because it provides a picture of where Africans would like to be in 2063, when Africans will be celebrating the centenary of the OAU. Thus, with Agenda 2063, the AU sought to achieve its vision of an integrated, prosperous, and peaceful Africa, driven by its own citizens and representing a dynamic force in the international arena.[17] The framework draws on the successes of the past with the aim to put Africa on a development path led by Africans. DeGhetto, Gray, and Kiggundu assert that the strategic plan 'is aimed to getting Africa to do things differently (people-centred), bigger (scaling and scoping up) and better'.[18]

Distinctively, Agenda 2063 was not only crafted in Africa and by Africans[19] but it also represents 'a call to action to all Africans and people of African descent, to take personal responsibility for the destiny of the continent and as the primary agents of change and transformation'.[20] Furthermore, Agenda 2063 highlights the need for commitment from citizens, leadership, governments, and institutions at national, regional, and continental levels to act, coordinate, and cooperate for the realization of its vision.[21] Thus, Agenda 2063 presents an opportunity for Africans

[14] African Union, '50th Anniversary Solemn Declaration'. Adopted by the 21st Ordinary Session of the Assembly of Heads of State and Government of the African Union Addis Ababa 26 May 2013 available at <https://www.un.org/en/africa/osaa/pdf/au/50anniv_declaration_2013.pdf> accessed 20 September 2019.

[15] African Union, 'Assembly of the Union Twenty-Fourth Ordinary Session' Addis Ababa Ethiopia, 30–31 January 2015 Assembly/AU/Dec.565(XXIV), 46–8 available at https://au.int/sites/default/files/decisions/9665-assembly_au_dec_546_-_568_xxiv_e.pdf> accessed 20 September 2019). (At the 24th Ordinary Session Agenda 2063 Framework Document; Agenda 2063 Popular Version and the Agenda 2063 First Ten Year Implementation Plan were adopted see 46–8).

[16] African Union, 'Agenda 2063-SDGs' available at <https://au.int/en/ea/statistics/a2063sdgs> accessed 20 September 2019. Noting that Agenda 2063 is a concrete and implementable framework with a clear vision, 7 aspirations, 20 goals and 39 priority areas.

[17] See Directorate of Strategic Policy Planning AUC, 'African Agenda 2063, The Africa We Want' available at <https://www.un.org/en/africa/osaa/pdf/au/agenda2063-presentation.pdf> accessed 20 September 2019. See also AUC, 'Agenda 2063 Framework Document' September 2015 available at <https://www.un.org/en/africa/osaa/pdf/au/agenda2063-framework.pdf> accessed 20 September 2019.

[18] K DeGhetto, J Gray, and others, 'The African Union's Agenda 2063: aspirations, challenges and opportunities for management research' (2016) 2(1) African Journal of Management 94

[19] By contrast, the UN crafted the Millennium Development Goals (MDGs) in 2000. Having reached their expiration date, 15 years later, in 2015, the UN created the Sustainable Development Goals (SDGs) to focus on 17 Goals over the next 15 years until 2030.

[20] The African Union Commission, 'Agenda 2063 the Africa We Want: First Ten-Year Implementation Plan 2013–2023', September 2015, 13.

[21] See Agenda 2063 Article 7(ii) which states that member states of the AU are to accelerate the domestication of Agenda 2063 and integrate it into their respective Development Initiatives and Plans.

to take ownership of their development.[22] Of the seven aspirations of Agenda 2063, Aspiration 3 envisions 'an Africa of good governance, democracy, respect for human rights, justice, and the rule of law'.[23]

2.2.1 Aspiration 3: An Africa of Good Governance, Justice, and the Rule of Law

Aspiration 3 is critical because it stipulates that by 2063 Africa will be

> [a] continent where democratic values, practices, universal principles of human rights, justice and the rule of law are entrenched, and it will fully adhere to and observe the African Human Rights instruments, including the African Charter on Human and Peoples Rights and the Protocols thereto; and Characterized by *institutions capable* of designing and implementing, empowering multisectoral processes and leadership that is transformative at all levels.[24]

To appreciate its full potential, this aspiration needs unpacking. Significantly, it highlights the importance of *capable institutions* as the driving force for its actualization. This suggests that African transformation is in the hands of Africans. Currently, impunity, power of incumbency, lack of transparency, irregularities in electoral processes, corruption, killings, crisis, and conflicts are rife on the continent. Africa's development is tied to a complete overhaul of these endemic vices by Africans and the imbibing of a culture that enthrones good governance, democracy, human rights, justice, and the rule of law that will transform the continent for the better.[25]

Succinctly, Agenda 2063 aspires that 'Africa will be a continent that conducts free, fair and credible elections which includes: (i) multiparty, plural systems; (ii) level, transparent playing field in the political process; (iii) education of the electorate to make informed choices; and (iv) Pan Africanism, equality, diversity excellence and solidarity'.[26] While ambitions as these seem far-fetched, they may be attainable with complete reorientation of the minds of Africans including overhaul of its institutions and ensuring transparent, accountable, and credible leadership. This implies that the importance of efficient institutions cannot be overemphasized. Therefore, institutional reform necessary for the implementation and attainment of Agenda 2063 is critical.

22 O Tella, 'Agenda 2063 and its implication for Africa's soft power' (2018) 48(7) Journal of Black Studies 714–30, 716.

23 Agenda 2063, Aspiration 3. A step towards achieving the aspirations was the launch of the 'First Ten-year Implementation Plan 2014–2023' by the AUC in September 2015 available at <https://www.un.org/en/africa/osaa/pdf/au/agenda2063-first10yearimplementation.pdf> accessed 20 September 2019.

24 Agenda 2063 Framework Document 2015, 12–13 (emphasis mine).

25 ibid.

26 ibid.

2.3 The Kagame Report on AU Institutional Reforms

Driven by the vision of inclusive economic growth and development in Africa, as encapsulated in Agenda 2063, African leaders endorsed the need for institutional reforms. To this end, in July 2016, the Assembly of Heads of State of the AU mandated President Paul Kagame of Rwanda to lead the process to actualizing institutional reforms in the continent.[27] Highlighting some of the areas of weaknesses and challenges within the AU, the Kagame-led team noted as follows:

- The AU is highly fragmented with too many focus areas;
- The AU's complicated structure and limited managerial capacity leads to inefficient working methods, poor decision-making, and a lack of accountability;
- The AU is neither financially independent nor self-sustaining, relying instead on partner funding for much of its financing;
- Coordination between the AU and the Regional Economic Communities (RECs) is limited.[28]

Consequently, the reforms advisory team consulted with AU Member States and concluded that to realize the ambitions of Agenda 2063, the 'AU needed to reposition itself and ensure that it has the requisite institutional capacity and capabilities given the evolving economic, political and social needs of the continent'.[29] In January 2017, the outcome of the consultations – the Kagame Report on AU Institutional Reforms – was published. The report identified five focal areas for improvement:

- The AU needed to focus on fewer priority areas with continental scope;
- There was a need to review the structure and operations of the AU and ensure institutional realignment for better service delivery;
- The AU needs to connect with African citizenry;
- The AU needs to become operationally effective and efficient in the performance of its mandate;
- The AU needs to identify and implement sustainable financing for its programmes and reduce over reliance on development partners.

[27] President Kagame appointed a Pan-African advisory team to assist him and the team consisted of Ms Cristina Duarte (Former Minister of Finance, Cape Verde); Dr Donald Kaberuka (Former President, African Development Bank); Dr Acha Leke (Senior Partner, McKinsey & Company); Dr Carlos Lopes (Former Executive Secretary, United Nations Economic Commission for Africa); Mr Strive Masiywa (Founder, ECONET Wireless); Mr Tito Mboweni (Former Governor, South African Reserve Bank); Ms Amina Mohammed (Minister of Environment, Nigeria); Ms Mariam Mahamat Nour (Minister of Economy and International Cooperation, Chad); Dr Vera Songwe (Regional Director for West and Central Africa, International Finance Corporation).

[28] African Union, 'Overview of Institutional Reforms' (AU Institutional Reforms Overview) available at <https://au.int/en/aureforms/overview> accessed 12 September 2019.

[29] AU Institutional Reforms Overview (n 28) statement by Pierre Moukoko Mbonjou of Cameroon.

2.3.1 The Kagame Report and Agenda 2063 through the Lens of Institutional Theory.

Having adopted Agenda 2063 and set out institutional reforms for the socio-political, economic, and cultural transformation of Africa and Africans, it is important to evaluate how these reforms and transformation will be realized. As mentioned earlier, for institutional reforms to work, the prevailing institutional circumstances and contexts must be taken into consideration. Therefore, it may be asked what is the prevailing institutional context within the continent? What are the institutional circumstances of AU's individual Member States? Identifying these will be useful to determine the actualization of the ideals of Agenda 2063 and the Kagame Report on institutional reforms.

Lounsbury and Crumley posit that for institutional reform to be effective, it has to leave behind its predominant micro-orientation and reconnect with the broader cultural and institutional context in which practice fields are embedded.[30] This indicates that to actualize the institutional reforms, the AU's 55 Member States must be ready and willing to embrace the changes, first at the domestic levels and then within the cultural setting of the broader African continent. It is only when connected to wider institutions that the variation that result from the enactment of rules and routines at micro levels can significantly contribute to understanding innovation and institutional change. Accordingly, the approach expands, revises, and complements the strong individualistic focus and micro-orientation of institutional framework.[31] Without sounding pessimistic, currently, most African states appear distant and disconnected from the reform proposals and efforts of the AU, not least because they prefer it this way but because they have deeply rooted protracted challenges that appear much more immediate and crucial and sometimes with vested interests of the leadership in the status quo. Several African governments are faced with autocratic rule, predatory state behaviour, corruption, and conflicts that have culminated in killings and internal displacements. These challenges, which in the words of Malley, are a 'perilous mix' of 'social unrest' and 'political contestation', have resulted in violent repressions in Sudan, Zimbabwe, Cameroon, Somalia, Nigeria, Mali, and the Central African Republic.[32]

Abdelnour, Hasselbladh, and others analysed four lenses through which agency and institutions could be conceptualized. The lenses are the wilful actor, collective intentionality, patchwork institutions and modular individuals.[33] The scholars noted that the wilful actor unpacks the 'agentic turn' in institutional theory and

[30] M Lounsbury and E Crumley, 'New practice creation: an institutional perspective on innovation' (2007) 28(7) Organisation Studies 993–1012.

[31] Abdelnour, Hasselbladh, and others (n 9) 1782.

[32] Crisis Group, 'Eight Priorities for the African Union in 2019' Introduction by Robert Malley, President & CEO of International Crisis Group 6 February 2019 available at <https://www.crisisgroup.org/africa/eight-priorities-african-union-2019> accessed 20 September 2019.

[33] Abdelnour, Hasselbladh, and others (n 9) 1780.

hold institutions to be malleable to individuals' purposive action and recognizes that institutional contexts shape purpose.[34] In their view, the collective intentionality explores contradictions associated with the assumption that organizations are simple aggregations of individuals and it reinforces the idea that institutions and organizations are more than derivations of individuals,[35] challenging the monolithic and static notions of institutions and exploring the extent to which institutions are inherently fluid and heterogeneous is the focus of patchwork institutions, while modular individuals lens introduces the idea that individuals are clusters of roles enacted in different settings to navigate the complex demands of modern life, and that groups and organizations are assemblages of roles.[36]

Applying the first two lenses to the AU, it is argued that the AU's individual Member States are wilful actors who make choices and decisions based on their specific contexts and divergent interests. Therefore, it may well be that the AU's interests in institutional reforms may not be the immediate concern of Somalia, for example. It is hardly comprehensible that South Africa, Cameroon, Central African Republic, for example, would exhibit identical levels of interests for Aspiration 3 of Agenda 2063. Granted that good governance, democracy, justice, respect for human rights, and the rule of law are considered top priority ideals and aspirations for any government, conflict-torn countries are constrained by multidimensional challenges at varying degrees, and they will always prioritize survival above these aspirations. States like Somalia, Sudan, Nigeria, and Cameroon, for example, may appear interested and willing to participate in the AU's efforts, but in reality, they may be saddled with more imminent problems of insecurity, instability, poverty, corruption, and wanton killings, which would impact on their level of commitment to the AU. Therefore, inabilities of actors to overcome constraints must be addressed.

Similarly, collective intentionality is the socialization of individuals into collectives. Being a collective, the AU needs the active participation of its 55 Member States. Although institutional theory indicates that institutions are not straightforward derivations of individuals,[37] King, Felin, and Whetten postulated that if collective entities are treated as actors, then the characteristics of their collective decision must be more complex than the simple accretion of individuals and their interests.[38] Also, Wijen and Ansari raised concerns regarding the extent to which institutional entrepreneurship can explain complex collective decisions.[39] Indeed

34 ibid.

35 ibid.

36 ibid.

37 ibid 1783.

38 B King, T Felin, and D Whetten, 'Finding the organisation in organisational theory: a meta-theory of the organisation as a social actor' (2010) 21(1) Organisation Science 290–305.

39 F Wijen and S Ansari, 'Overcoming inaction through collective institutional entrepreneurship: insights from regime theory' (2007) 28(7) *Organisation Science* 1079–100.

there are challenges with collective action, particularly under complex conditions that entail diverse interests and dispersed actors, such as those prevalent in the AU.

Certainly, achieving collaboration under such conditions requires overcoming problems of divergent interests and indifference that may result in a state of collective inaction.[40] The 55 countries that make up the collective – the AU – do not only appear distant but they also have divergent interests. Therefore, collaboration, unity and the concentration of authority that the AU assumes in the efforts towards institutional change are conditions that transcend the capacity of the individual Member State.[41] Admittedly, there is a nexus between individuals and collectives; the collective has roots in individuality and it is the contribution of individual AU Member States that aggregate to collective action.[42] Therefore, Aspiration 3 of Agenda 2063 can be truly actualized in the continent only when individual Member States of the AU prioritize the implementation of good governance, justice, human rights, and the rule of law at national levels.

The link between individual actor and collective intentionality is highlighted in the President Kagame report on AU institutional reforms. If collective action does not derive straightforwardly from individual interests then the mechanisms that allow individuals to act on behalf of more inclusive entities need to be unpacked. In the AU's institutional reforms context, the divergent interests of the 55 Member States must align with the interests of the AU. Therefore, awareness of individual and collective interests, and the alignment of Member States' interests with those of the AU are essential prerequisites to actualizing AU's collective intentionality and institutional reforms.

Arguably, collective intentionality could be effective within the AU institutional reforms framework, especially as the Kagame Report proposes the need for the AU to connect with African citizenry and to become operationally effective and efficient in the performance of its mandate. However, collective intentionality entails the calibration and recalibration of expectations held by different actors. Therefore, AU Member States should individually and collectively recalibrate their

[40] See, for example, M Plaut, 'African Union missing in Action in Conflicts from Mali to South Sudan' *The Guardian* (6 January 2014) available at https://www.theguardian.com/global-development/2014/jan/06/african-union-missing-action-conflicts-mali-south-sudan> accessed 21 September 2019 (Noting that '[w]eak leadership and rivalry between states have hampered African efforts to bring security to the conflict-hit continent. From Mali to Somalia, the Continent has been convulsed by an arc of conflict. Noting further that in all the bloodshed in wars in CAR, South Sudan and Mali where hundreds of thousands were killed and more than 785,000 people were displaced, the AU was nowhere to be seen. The much-vaunted African Standby Force ... has also failed to materialise'); M Kimenyi, 'An African Union for an emerging continent: reforms to increase effectiveness' (2015) Foresight Africa The Brookings Institution Africa Growth Initiative 29–35 (noting that '[i]n the case of other African crises during the last several years, the AU has failed to lead or even function as a relevant party in their resolution. At other times, the AU has been willing to act, but has been too slow in taking action.').

[41] Abdelnour, Hasselbladh, and others (n 9) 1782–3.

[42] ibid 1784.

expectations to ensure the effectiveness of the reforms both in their individual domestic settings and in the broader context of the continent.

2.3.2 Regulatory, Normative and Cultural Patterns Within the African Region

Culture refers to symbolic patterns, social discourses, and narratives of different scope.[43] The discourse on the wilful actor and collective intentionality pillars implies that AU Member States need to recalibrate cultural settings and mindsets at the national levels. As analysed earlier, the AU institutional reforms reflect the regulatory institution, which are the formal laws, rules, and policies that are usually explicit, flexible, and adaptable.[44] Therefore, without undermining the herculean tasks that President Kagame and his team of experts have put into the AU institutional reform framework, it is argued that within the field of institutional theory, the formulation, reformulation, and change of formal laws are less cumbersome in comparison with the processes, procedures, and rigour required with change of informal norms, values, beliefs, and expectations for behaviour and social interactions. Even more crucial is cognitive or cultural institution that relate to implicit, subconscious, and symbolic interpretative frames.

Certainly, there are diverse normative and cognitive/cultural institutions prevalent in the African region. They range from insecurity, instability in government, autocratic rule, bad and insensitive leadership, lack of transparency and accountability on the part of leaders, lopsided distribution of resources, poverty, corruption, conflicts, wanton destruction of property, forced disappearances, kidnappings, killings, and internal displacements. It is an open-ended list of vices that have been entrenched as symbolic patterns and narratives of most African countries. Thus, as noted by North, 'you change formal rules, but how do you change norms of behaviour, or codes of conduct?'[45] It is proposed therefore, that for the effective implementation of the AU institutional reforms and to achieve the 'Africa We Want' in Agenda 2063, these normative and cognitive patterns must be tackled.

The principles of 'non-indifference' and 'ubuntu' are values and norms that could promote the advancement of the AU's institutional reforms of effectiveness and efficiency. Non-indifference is a form of active solidarity that approximates the maxim in most African cultures that 'you do not fold your hands and just look on when your neighbour's house is on fire'.[46] The African Peer Review Mechanism (APRM) and the Peace and Security Council (PSC) are AU institutions saddled

[43] ibid.
[44] See Osuji and Abba (n 2).
[45] North (n 1).
[46] O Imoedemhe, *The Complementarity Regime of the International Criminal Court: National Implementation in Africa* (Springer, 2017) 136, (quoting Ben Kioko former Legal Adviser of the AU from 2001 to 2012). The principle of non-indifference represents a departure from the OAU's principle of non-interference. Therefore, Article 4(h) of the Constitutive Act of the AU establishes the right of the AU to intervene in a member state to prevent grave human rights violations.

with the responsibility of ensuring respect for human rights and the mechanism for conflict prevention, management, and resolution in the continent.[47]

Furthermore, 'ubuntu' (I am because we are, therefore how can one be happy when others are sad?) represents the AU's driving force for solidarity and integration. This cultural model is replicated in all 55 African states, albeit in slightly different variations. It is the culture that advocates humanistic values, such as forgiveness, humanness, reciprocity, care, and compassion. Ubuntu highlights the principles of collective intentionality because it places primacy on the community rather than on the individual.[48] Arguably, variants of ubuntu were demonstrated in the post-apartheid Truth and Reconciliation Commission in South Africa and in the *Gacaca* Courts in Rwanda. Consequently, ubuntu could be used to enrich a range of new paradigms and foster the needed solidarity, cooperation, and collaboration for the attainment of AU institutional reforms and the actualization of Agenda 2063.

2.4 Enforcement Mechanisms within the African Region: African Commission

Motivated by the need for institutional realignment for better service delivery and to reconnect with the African citizenry, AU treaties/instruments established enforcement mechanisms. Undoubtedly the African Charter on Human and Peoples Rights (African Charter) is a pioneer enforcement mechanism open to the AU.[49] For compliance and enforcement, the African Charter provides for the establishment of the African Commission on Human and Peoples' Rights (African Commission),[50] a quasi-judicial body charged with the interpretation and implementation of the Charter. Its main function is to promote, protect, and interpret the provisions of the Charter.

Procedurally, the African Commission is authorized to receive communications from State Parties to the African Charter, individuals, non-governmental organizations (NGOs), and non-state actors who perceive that a State Party has violated one or more of the rights contained in the Charter.[51] Cumulatively, at the time of writing, about 658 communications have been received by the African Commission and with the exception of two, all have been filed by NGOs and

[47] ibid.

[48] Tella (n 22) 725.

[49] E Emeseh and O Imoedemhe, 'The African Human Rights System and Access to environmental Justice' (paper yet to be published on file with the author). Analysis within this section is adapted from the paper.

[50] See ACHPR, Article 30.

[51] See ACHPR Articles 47–49 allow communications by one state claiming that another State Party to the Charter has violated one or more of the provisions of the Charter; Article 55 allows individuals and organizations to submit communications alleging violations.

individuals.[52] This implies that victims of human rights abuses who, for one reason or the other could not obtain justice in their home countries after exhausting all available remedies, have successfully approached the African Commission for justice. Despite its powers to adjudicate in cases relating to victims of human rights abuses, the African Commission has been described as a toothless bulldog.[53] This is due to its limited remit to issue non-binding recommendations as it lacked the power to enforce compliance.[54]

2.4.1 The African Court on Human and Peoples' Rights

The Protocol to the African Charter on Human and Peoples' Rights on the Establishment of an African Court (the Protocol),[55] created the African Court on Human and Peoples' Rights (African Court).[56] The establishment of the African Court has been discussed in previous chapters.[57] The African Court has jurisdiction *rationae persona*, that is, personal jurisdiction by which individuals and NGOs can make applications to it. Article 2 of the Protocol delineates the relationship between the African Court on Human and Peoples Right and the African Commission to the effect that the former is to complement the protective mandate of the latter. Thus, the African Commission is empowered to make applications to the African Court.[58] The African Court has handed down some influential decisions in a plethora of cases.[59] For example, on 26 May 2017, in the *African Commission* case,[60] the African Court considered the far-reaching implication of the political, social, and economic survival of the Ogiek Community and the

[52] For a full list of communications see African Commission on Human and People's Rights available at <http://www.achpr.org/communications/> accessed 14 May 2021. The Commission website lists Comm No 658/17 *Shereen Said Hamd Bakhet v Arab Republic of Egypt* as the most recent communication although the case was struck out on 10 June 2019 following the 63rd Extraordinary Session held in October–November 2018.

[53] JIsanga, 'The Constitutive Act of the African Union, African Courts and the protection of human rights: new dimensions?' (2013) 11(2) Santa Clara Journal of International Law 267–300, 278 (noting that the African Charter created an enforcement body – the African Commission – that can bark but not bite).

[54] B Szewczyk, 'The African Human Rights System' in C Giorgetti (ed), *The Rules and Jurisprudence of International Courts and Tribunals* (BRILL, 2014) 393–412, 398.

[55] The Protocol on the Establishment of an African Court on Human and Peoples' Right adopted in Ouagadougou, Burkina Faso on 9 June 1998. Entered into force on 25 January 2004.

[56] See Article 1 of the Protocol.

[57] As of June 2020, 52 out of the 55 African states have signed the Protocol and 30 have ratified it. See Protocol to the African Charter on Human and Peoples' Rights on the Establishment of the African Court on Human and Peoples' Rights Status List available at <https://au.int/en/treaties/protocol-african-charter-human-and-peoples-rights-establishment-african-court-human-and> accessed 20 June 2020. In accordance with its Article 34(3), the Protocol entered into force on 25 January 2004.

[58] ibid Article 5(1)(a).

[59] See for example, *Mulindahabi Fidele v Rpoublic of Rwanda* App Np 008/2017; *Interpretation of Judgment of 20 November 2015-Alex Thomas v United Repulic of Tanzania* App. No 001/2017; *Mamadou Diakite and Diakite Habibata B. Guindo v Republic of Mali* App No 009/2016; *Kennedy Owino Onyachi and Others v United Republic of Tanzania* App No 003/2015.

[60] *African Commission on Human and Peoples' Rights v Republic of Kenya* App No 006/2012. (*African Commission* case).

irreparable harm community members would suffer if they were to be evicted. Consequently, the African Court upheld the decision of the African Commission and declared the eviction notice illegal. Similarly, on 24 November 2017 in the *Ingabire Victoire Umuhoza* case,[61] the African Court unanimously ruled against the government of Rwanda.[62]

Significantly, the *Anudo* case[63] is a landmark decision of the African Court on the right of citizenship.[64] The relevance of this case cannot be overemphasized as it reveals the nuances of the issue of citizenship, which is one of the AU's institutional reforms framework vis to reconnect to African citizenry. Anudo was born in Butiama district in north-west of Tanzania. During the registration of his marriage in 2012, his passport was retained by the Tanzanian authorities on the grounds that there were doubts about his citizenship.[65] In September 2013, he wrote to the Tanzanian Minister of Home Affairs and Immigration protesting the confiscation of his passport.[66] Ultimately, Anudo was compelled to sign a notice of deportation and a document attesting that he was a Kenyan citizen and he was then forcefully deported to Kenya.[67]

On arrival, the Kenyan authorities expelled Anudo from Kenya back to Tanzania on the allegation that he had irregular status, but he was refused re-entry into Tanzania.[68] Anudo was left in limbo, as he lived in 'no man's land'[69] between Kenya and Tanzania for three years.[70] In May 2015, Anudo emailed the African Court directly to seek redress. The issues for determination amongst others were the right to nationality and the right not to be arbitrarily deprived of nationality.[71] Although the African Charter lacked provisions on nationality, the Court filled the gap by drawing on Article 15(2) of the Universal Declaration of Human Rights,[72] stating that no-one should be arbitrarily deprived of his nationality.[73] The Court held that the deprivation of Anudo's Tanzanian nationality was arbitrary and his citizenship was restored.[74]

61 *Ingabire Victoire Umuhoza v Republic of Rwanda* App No 003/2014.

62 *Umuhoza case*, see Ruling on Withdrawal of Declaration 3 June 2016.

63 *Anudo Ochieng Anudo v Tanzania*, Judgment of the African Court on Human and Peoples' Rights, App No 012/2015, 22 March 2018 (*Anudo* case).

64 B Mandy, 'Case Note Anudo Ochieng Anudo v Tanzania (Judgment) African Court on Human and Peoples' Right, App No 012/2015, 22 March 2018)' 170–4 available at <https://statelessnessandcitizenshipreview.com/index.php/journal/article/view/75/25> accessed 21 September 2019.

65 *Anudo* case (n 63), 2 [1] and [4].

66 ibid 3 [5].

67 ibid.

68 ibid 4 [11].

69 Mandy (n 64) 171.

70 *Anudo* case (n 63) 4 [12].

71 Mandy (n 64) 172.

72 Universal Declaration of Human Rights (UDHR) GA Res 217A (III), UN GAOR, UN Doc A/810 10 December 1948.

73 UDHR, Article 15(2). See also Mandy (n 64) 173.

74 *Anudo* case (n 63) 28–9 [132]. See also B Mandy, *Citizenship in Africa: The Law of Belonging* (Hart Publishing, 2018) 126–8.

2.4.2 The Merged and Expanded African Court: The Malabo Protocol

With its seat in Arusha Tanzania, the African Court has handed down landmark decisions. Therefore, it is a significant enforcement mechanism for the AU. However, with the creation of the AU in 2002, and by a Protocol of the Court of Justice of the African Union adopted on 11 July 2003 (Maputo Protocol), the AU established the Court of Justice of the African Union.[75] The Court of Justice of the African Union was intended to be the principal judicial organ of the AU.[76] In accordance with Article 60, the Maputo Protocol entered into force in February 2009.[77] By Article 19, the Court of Justice of the AU was intended to have wide jurisdiction over all disputes including the interpretation of the Constitutive Act, and AU treaties as well as jurisdiction over any dispute as the Assembly may confer on it.[78] Regrettably, the Court of Justice of the AU has never been operational because the AU decided to merge both courts.

In July 2008, the AU adopted the Protocol on the Statute of the African Court of Justice and Human Rights.[79] This Protocol merged the African Court on Human and Peoples' Rights and the Court of Justice of the African Union into a single court – the African Court of Justice and Human Rights.[80] The 2008 Protocol requires 15 ratifications to enter into force. However, as of June 2020, with 33 signatures out of 55 AU Member States, only eight states have ratified it, therefore, it has not entered into force.[81]

In June 2014 the AU adopted another Protocol on the Amendments to the Protocol on the Statute of the African Court of Justice and Human Rights (Malabo Protocol) which sought to extend the jurisdiction of the merged courts now known as the African Court of Justice and Human Rights over international crimes. The Malabo Protocol has been described as a 'crucial legal instrument'[82] and a great step by the AU in the right direction, especially as it expanded the jurisdiction of the court to crimes under international law and transnational crimes.[83] Crucially,

75 Protocol of the Court of Justice of the African Union adopted in Maputo Mozambique 11 July 2003 entered into force on 11 February 2009 (Maputo Protocol) available at <https://au.int/en/treaties/protocol-court-justice-african-union> accessed 20 July 2020.

76 Maputo Protocol. See Article 2(2)

77 ibid Article 60. As of June 2020, the Maputo Protocol has attracted 45 signatures and 19 ratifications. See 'Status List'.

78 ibid Article 19(1) and (2).

79 African Union, Protocol on the Statute of the African Court of Justice and Human Rights, adopted in Sharm ElSheikh, Egypt on 1 July 2008, (hereinafter, 'AU 2008 Protocol') available at <https://www.refworld.org/docid/4937f0ac2.html> accessed 14 September 2019.

80 AU 2008 Protocol, Article 2.

81 The eight African Countries who have deposited their instruments of ratification are Angola, Benin, Burkina Faso, Congo, Gambia, Libya, Liberia, and Mali. See 'List of Countries which have Signed, Ratified/Acceded to the Protocol . . .' <https://au.int/en/treaties/protocol-statute-african-court-justice-and-human-rights> accessed 20 July 2020.

82 See Amnesty International, 'Malabo Protocol: Legal and Institutional Implications of the Merged and Expanded African Court' 2016 7–8 available at <https://www.amnesty.org/download/Documents/AFR0130632016ENGLISH.PDF> accessed 14 September 2019.

83 For a detailed chronological events and historical backgrounds to the adoption of the Malabo Protocol see ibid 9–12.

the African Court on Human and Peoples' Rights had two sections, namely a general affairs section and a human rights section. However, the Malabo Protocol introduced a third section known as the international criminal law section. Therefore, when the merged court becomes operational, it will exercise jurisdiction over international crimes such as genocide, crimes against humanity, and war crimes.[84] In essence, the international criminal law section will make the court a regional criminal court, albeit to function in parallel with the International Criminal Court (ICC).

The Malabo Protocol specifically expanded the jurisdiction of the unborn court to crimes such as unconstitutional change of government, piracy, terrorism, mercenarism, corruption, money laundering, and trafficking in person. While the underlying justification for the expanded jurisdiction created by the Malabo Protocol may be sound, the Malabo Protocol is 'a protocol too many'; it is superfluous and may not count as an addition to the AU enforcement mechanism. Why expand the jurisdiction of a court that is not yet functional? Arguably, the motivation behind the expanded criminal jurisdiction for the court is an attempt by the AU to shield African leaders from ICC prosecution.[85] It is an effort to score political points with the ICC rather than address the need for justice and accountability for international crimes in Africa.[86] As of June 2020, only 15 out of the 55 Member States of the AU have signed the Malabo Protocol and interestingly, Equatorial Guinea, which hosted the 23rd Ordinary Session of the Assembly of Heads of States at which the Protocol was adopted, signed the Protocol only in February 2019, five years after its adoption.[87] The Protocol has attracted no ratifications and

[84] By virtue of Article 28 of the Malabo Protocol, the merged court has expanded jurisdiction over 14 crimes, as follows: genocide, crimes against humanity, war crimes, the crime of unconstitutional change of government, piracy, terrorism, mercenarism, corruption, money laundering, trafficking in persons, trafficking in drugs, trafficking in hazardous wastes, illicit exploitation of natural resources, and the crime of aggression

[85] See, for example, O Abe and A Odor, 'Addressing human rights concerns in the extractive resource industry in Sub-Saharan African using the lens of Article 46(C) of the Malabo Protocol' (2018) Law and Development Review 1–36; B Van Schaack, 'Immunity before the African Court of Justice and Human and Peoples' Rights – The potential outlier' available at <http://www.justsecurity.org/12732/immunity-african-court-justice-human-peoples-rights-the-potential-outlier/> accessed 4 September 2019; GAbraham, 'Africa's Evolving Continental Court Structures: At the Crossroads? SAIIA Occasional Paper 209, January 2015 available at <http://www.saiia.org.za/occasional-papers/africas-evolving-continental-court-structures-at-the-crossroads> accessed 1 September 2019; S Dey, 'Protecting the Powerful: The African Union's Response to Allegations of Human Rights Violations' available at <http://cjicl.org.uk/2015/02/02/protecting-powerful-african-unions-response-allegations-human-rights-violations/> accessed 10 September 2019.

[86] Amnesty International (n 82) 7.

[87] As of June 2020, the 15 African Countries that have signed the Malabo Protocol are Benin, Chad, Comoros, Congo, Equatorial Guinea, Ghana, Guinea-Bissau, Guinea, Kenya, Mozambique, Mauritania, Sierra-Leone, Sao Tome & Principe, Togo, and Uganda. See 'Status List' available at https://au.int/en/treaties/protocol-amendments-protocol-statute-african-court-justice-and-human-rights> accessed 20 July 2020.

therefore, the Malabo Protocol is yet to come into force and the African Court of Justice and Human Rights is not functional.[88]

2.5 AU/EU Comparison

Like EU law, the concept of AU law is gradually emerging. Certainly an emulation of the EU, the AU differs significantly from the EU, though both have been subjected to a strained comparison. First, their historic integration experiences and conditions differ. The EU was formed by supposedly strong democracies and economies of 28 Member States, whereas the AU is made up of not so strong democracies and weak economies of over 50 countries. Second, where the EU integration process aimed at attaining mutually beneficial and stronger economic bases for its Member States, African integration was built on strong impenetrable sovereign states.[89] Thus, beyond the struggle for political independence, African states expressed strong commitment to sovereignty and the principle of non-interference, but failed to build strong national institutions, creating instead national enclaves of failed governance.[90]

2.5.1 Similarities between AU and EU Law

Undoubtedly, AU law copies certain legal principles from EU law. For example, the principles of subsidiarity and proportionality are entrenched in EU law.[91] Subsidiarity requires that decisions should be taken at the local levels, except where continental-level decision-making would be more effective.[92] This principle regulates the division of power between the AU and other regional bodies and its Member States. Closely linked to subsidiarity is proportionality, which prescribes that actions at the continental level should not extend beyond what is necessary to achieve the objectives of the Union.[93] This concept has been borrowed from the EU and applied in judicial decisions of the AU.[94]

88 Article 11 provides 'This Protocol and the Statute annexed to it shall enter into force thirty (30) days after the deposit of instruments of ratification by fifteen (15) Member States'. See Article 11 Malabo Protocol.

89 M Olivier, 'The role of African Union law in integrating Africa' (2015) 22(4) South African Journal of International Affairs 513–33, 515

90 D Geldenhuys, 'Brothers as keepers: Africa's new sovereignty regime' (2006) 28(1) Strategic Review of Southern Africa 1–14.

91 F Amao, 'Could African Union Law Shape a New Legal Order for the Continent?' *Huffpost* (14 July 2018). See also *The Conversation* 9 July 2018.

92 ibid.

93 ibid.

94 IJRI, 'Advocacy before the African Human Rights System: Preventing and Remedying Human Rights Violations Through the International Framework' (Manual for Attorneys and Advocates) October 2017 available at <https://ijrcenter.org/wp-content/uploads/2017/11/2.-African-Human-Rights-System-Manual.pdf> accessed 20 July 2020.

Other areas of similarities include human rights and the gradual integration processes. Human rights are fundamental to the EU legal order. To this end, Member States of the EU are mandated to apply the Charter of Fundamental Rights of the EU. Similarly, the AU Constitutive Act has consolidated and advanced the framework for the promotion and protection of human rights in Africa by making it binding on all AU Member States. Furthermore, the European integration was slow and incremental.[95] Highlighting this point, Monnet asserts that the 'European Coal and Steel Community was integrating Europe by stealth'.[96] This can also be said of the AU which evolved over time. Critically, EU integration has suffered some setbacks such as the Eurozone crisis, the decline in national economies within the EU, and the exit of Britain from the EU (Brexit). While AU law is in its teething stages, the EU provides example and guidance for AU Member States to guide against potential areas of conflicts and pitfalls.

2.5.2 An AU Court Akin to the EU Court?

The Court of Justice of the European Union (CJEU) also known as the European Court of Justice (ECJ) is the judicial organ of the EU.[97] It was established in 1952, with the primary objective of interpretation of EU law, ensuring uniform application in all EU Member States, and to settle legal disputes between national governments and EU institutions. The CJEU has three divisions, namely the Court of Justice, General Court, and the Civil Service Tribunal. The Court of Justice deals with requests for preliminary rulings from national courts. Actions brought by individuals, companies, EU governments, and EU countries are handled by the General Court while the Civil Service Tribunal is responsible for labour disputes raised by EU civil servants against EU institutions. However, since 2016, disputes meant for the Civil Service Tribunal are now being dealt with by the General Court.

In the prospect of AU law is the possibility of an AU Court. Nevertheless, the creation of yet another court for the purpose of interpretation and application of AU law appears premature but may become relevant as a result of current reform initiatives. The AU court system is in flux because the merged African Court of Justice and Human Right is not yet operational. The possible impact of the AU enforcement mechanism on the emerging AU law implies that issues regarding interpretation, application, and enforcement of AU law could be problematic.

[95] Olivier (n 89) 3.
[96] Cited in ibid.
[97] Significantly, the CJEU is different and should not be confused with the European Court of Human Right (ECtHR) in Strasbourg France. The Strasbourg Court was established under the auspices of the Council of Europe in 1959 and it is not part of the EU.

3. Conclusion

Reforms are certainly required to achieve Agenda 2063. Analysis in this chapter suggests that a concrete way to actualize the 'Africa We Want' goes beyond the changes that has been proposed on paper. Thus, in addition to the institutional reforms, the normative and cultural norms, values, and behaviours that shape social interactions should also be focal points for reforms. Arguably, both the Kagame Report and Agenda 2063 can be likened to 'new wine in an old wine skin'. The outcome could be catastrophic if the prevailing cultural paradigm within the continent does not shift towards a complete overhaul and reorientation of the minds of Africans. Issues of insecurity, instability, autocratic rule, power of incumbency, lack of transparency and accountability, corruption, conflicts, and wanton destruction of property and lives are entrenched in most African states and if supporting cultural patterns that support these behaviours are not dealt with, an integrated, peaceful, and prosperous Africa in 2063 might remain a mirage.

The pillars of wilful actors and collective intentionality are proposed for African leaders to first ensure implementation of Aspiration 3 on good governance, democracy, respect for human rights, justice, and the rule of law at national levels. The instrumentality for achieving this rest on not only formal institutions but also on cultural shifts. The principles of 'non-indifference' and ubuntu, which represent AU's driving force for solidarity and integration and which manifest in diverse variations in different African cultural norms could support Africans' collective intentionality towards the attainment of Agenda 2063.

Analysis of enforcement mechanisms within the AU demonstrates significant decisions handed down by the African Commission and the African Court. The *African Commission* and *Anudo* cases are landmark decisions that impact the continent generally and the emerging AU law specifically. However, the shortcoming of highly fragmented institutions within the AU implies that the Malabo Protocol appears superfluous. Whether or not a new court would be required for the implementation of the emerging AU law would depend on how the AU would consolidate these fragmented courts. It is proposed that when the African Court of Justice and Human Rights becomes operational, a Protocol consolidating the Constitutive Act and the Malabo Protocol could constitute founding statutes for AU law. Undoubtedly, the global, continental, legal, and scholarly landscapes have room for the emerging AU law. The foundation for the 50-year journey to actualizing Agenda 2063 has been laid down by the Kagame Report. However, there must be collective intentionality on the part of African leaders and Africans generally to change the normative and cognitive norms within the continent. The time to set the stage for a desired outcome is now.

22

The (Domestic) Enforcement of AU International Economic Law Instruments: Exploring the Desirability of Direct Effect

Regis Yann Simo

1. Introduction

Until the end of the Second World War, with the rise in the international protection of human rights and the creation of international organizations (IOs), international treaty law was premised on the idea that only sovereign states had the capacity to undertake international obligations since they were the only subjects of international law. According to that general principle, a treaty had effects only with regard to the signatory state and not on individuals.[1] Consequently, the direct effect, meaning the effect on individuals, of international agreements remains an exception rather than a rule, even in contemporary international law. Both US constitutional law through the concept of self-executing treaties[2] and the Permanent Court of International Justice (PCIJ) in *Danzig*[3] have been instrumental in shaping the doctrine of direct effect. Indeed, in *Danzig* the PCIJ recognized that, despite the foregoing well-established principle of international law, 'the very object of an international agreement, according to the intention of the contracting Parties, may be the adoption by the Parties of some definite rules creating individual rights and obligations and enforceable by the national courts'.[4]

[1] See, for instance, the International Law Commission (ILC) Draft Articles on Diplomatic Protection with Commentaries, UN Doc. A/CN.4/SER.A/2006/Add.l (Part 2) (2006), Article 1(4).

[2] US law refers to a self-executing treaty as a treaty that, upon ratification, may be enforced in the courts without prior legislation by Congress, while a non-self-executing treaty is a treaty that may not be enforced without prior legislative implementation. On the definition and inherent confusions, see, for example, CM Vazquez, 'The four doctrines of self-executing treaties' (1995) 89 American Journal of International Law 695.

[3] Jurisdiction of the Courts of Danzig (*Pecuniary Claims of Danzig Railway Officials who have Passed into the Polish Service, against the Polish Railways Administration*), (Advisory Opinion) [1928] PCIJ Series B no 15.

[4] ibid 17–18.

Regis Yann Simo, *The (Domestic) Enforcement of AU International Economic Law Instruments: Exploring the Desirability of Direct Effect* In: *The Emergent African Union Law.* Edited by: Olufemi Amao, Michèle Olivier and Konstantinos D. Magliveras, Oxford University Press. © Regis Yann Simo 2021. DOI: 10.1093/oso/9780198862154.003.0023

However, European Union (EU) law, with the seminal case of *Van Gen den Loos*,[5] has taken the direct effect doctrine even further up to a level that is still unmatched by other regional economic integration organizations (REIOs). In that case, the European Court of Justice (ECJ) decided that the European Community Law requirement that Member States eliminate customs duties amongst themselves in light of the formation of a customs union produced direct effect and created individual rights which national courts were bound to protect.[6] These welcomed developments in the EU differ with African Union (AU) economic law instruments, which are framed in a way that leaves little to no room for direct effect.[7] This is unfortunately the case in a context where inter-state disputes, which would have provided opportunities to give life to, and interpretation of, treaty commitments are simply non-existent.

This chapter investigates the desirability or not of direct effect of African regional trade law instruments, notably those setting up the African Continental Free Trade Area (AfCFTA)[8] and related regulations. It argues that, while some international treaties, after domestication, should remain within the prerogatives of the government acting in the interests of the population, others, on the contrary, should have a direct effect and be enforceable directly by the natural and legal persons (e.g. the treaties on free movement of people, goods, etc.).

Having direct effect in this context presupposes two scenarios. The first relates to a situation where international law is applied as such without incorporation into domestic law.[9] In such a case, national courts protect an international right without necessarily waiting for domestic implementation. For instance, in *Re the Estate of Andrew Kamunzyu Musyoka*, the Kenya High Court held that international law is applicable as part of Kenyan law 'even without specific legislation adopting them'.[10] It then proceeded to set aside a customary law which prevented a married daughter

[5] *NV Algemene Transport- en Expeditie Onderneming van Gend & Loos v Netherlands Inland Revenue Administration*, Case 26/62 [1963] ECR 1 .

[6] ibid.

[7] It is, however, worth noting that while today's EU was from the outset formed as a REIO, the AU was designed instead mainly as a regional political organization with a primacy on security issues. On these objectives, see Article 3 of the AU Constitutive Act (adopted 11 July 2000, entered into force 26 May 2001) 2158 UNTS 3. While the AU has as parts of its 14 objectives the acceleration of socio-economic integration and the coordination and harmonisation of Regional Economic Communities' (RECs) policies (Article 3(c) and (l)), this does not necessarily transform it into an REIO as the EU was at its inception. On the AU objectives and principles, see KD Magliveras and G Naldi, 'The African Union – a new dawn for Africa?' (2002) 51(2) International and Comparative Law Quarterly 415.

[8] On a similar proposal to ensure a 'genuine' economic space in the old North America Free Trade Agreement (NAFTA), see A de Mestral and J Winter, 'Giving Direct Effect to NAFTA: Analysis of Issues' in T Courchene, D Savoie, and others (eds), *Thinking North America, the Art of the State*, Vol II (Institute for Research on Public Policy, 2004) 35, 36. The United States–Mexico–Canada Agreement (USMCA), the NAFTA successor, has not revised its interstate DSM meaningfully as to alter the proposal proffered towards NAFTA, which therefore remains valid with the entry into force of the USMCA.

[9] A Nollkaemper, 'The duality of direct effect of international law' (2014) 25(1) European Journal of International Law 105, 110.

[10] *Andrew Kamunzyu Musyoka (Deceased)*, Succession Cause 303 of 1998 [2005] High Court of Kenya at Machakos; [2005] eKLR.

from inheriting her father's estate as it was discriminatory and contrary to the Convention on the Elimination of All forms of Discrimination Against Women (CEDAW) and the African Charter on Human and Peoples' Rights (ACHPR).[11] The second, most common, scenario arises when domestic courts apply international law to protect individual rights against the state, usually the state of which he is a national. The latter could lead a court to admit reliance on international law 'as the exclusive basis for its decision'.[12]

The AfCFTA Agreement[13] together with its Protocol on Trade in Goods (PTG), the Protocol on Trade in Services (PTS), and the Protocol on Rules and Procedures on the Settlement of Disputes, entered into force on 30 May 2019. To give impetus to the aspirations of the African Economic Community (AEC) characterized by not only the free movement of goods, services, and capital but also the free movement of people, AU Member States adopted a Protocol to the AEC Treaty concerning the free movement of persons, and the associated rights of residence and establishment.[14] AfCFTA comes at a very good time for the continent amidst a backlashed multilateral trading system and the UK's exit from the EU (Brexit), which may lead many to question the value of regional integration in the 21st century. Nevertheless, while the AfCFTA is acclaimed to be part of the so-called African solutions to African problems, adherence to the rules and the possibility to challenge violations are key for its effective implementation and ensuing benefits.

Efforts towards Africa's regional integration date back to the formation of the Organization of African Unity (OAU) in 1963. The OAU subsequently gave birth to the AU. The Abuja Treaty (1991), an important milestone that underpins the African Economic Community (AEC), later embraced the steps towards promoting continental economic unity.[15] The AEC intends to rely on RECs as its building blocks.[16] While these RECs have undeniably sustained tremendous progress,[17] particularly in relation to trade liberalization and to some extent the free

[11] Article 18(3) ACHPR (adopted 27 June 1981, entered into force 21 October 1986) 1520 UNTS 217 provides that 'States shall ensure the elimination of every discrimination against women and also ensure the protection of rights of the women and the child as stipulated in international declarations and conventions'.

[12] Nollkaemper (n 9) 110.

[13] See Agreement Establishing the African Continental Free Trade Area (adopted 21 March 2018, entered into force 30 May 2019) (hereinafter AfCFTA Agreement).

[14] Protocol to the Treaty Establishing the African Economic Community Relating to Free Movement of Persons, Right of Residence and Right of Establishment (adopted 29 January 2018, opened for signature 21 March 2018, not yet in force) available at <https://au.int/sites/default/files/treaties/36403-treaty-protocol_on_free_movement_of_persons_in_africa_e.pdf> accessed 19 June 2020 (hereinafter Free Movement of Persons Protocol).

[15] See Treaty Establishing the African Economic Community (adopted 3 June 1991, entered into force 12 May 1994) available at <https://au.int/sites/default/files/treaties/37636-treaty-0016_-_treaty_establishing_the_african_economic_community_e.pdf> accessed 19 June 2020 (hereinafter AEC Treaty or Abuja Treaty).

[16] See Article 88 of the Abuja Treaty.

[17] To address the proliferation of RECs and crisscrossing membership, the AU Assembly adopted the *Decision on the Moratorium on the Recognition of Regional Economic Communities*, AU Doc Assembly/AU/Dec. 112 (VII), 2 July 2006.

movement of persons, continental integration has been quite modest compared to set goals due to a lack of political will as well as of human and economic resources and the reliance on a model focusing merely on eliminating border barriers to trade.[18] To meet the aspiration for an 'integrated continent', a key pillar of Agenda 2063, several issues need addressing, including the elimination of non-tariff barriers to trade, the lifting of obstacles to the free movement of persons, services, and capital, and enforcing treaty commitments.

At the time when Africa is moving forward with its economic integration, to make the continental rules directly effective becomes critical in the realization of state treaty commitments. Given that states seldom litigate trade disputes despite appropriate mechanisms in the RECs,[19] direct effect is imperative to provide clarifications and predictability of these instruments since individuals' claims offer the courts the possibility to interpret them, which will not otherwise happen given states' reluctance. The AfCFTA Dispute Settlement Protocol sets out to settle disputes arising between State Parties concerning their rights and obligations under the provisions of the AfCFTA Agreement.[20] In preserving Member s' rights and obligations under the Agreement, including by clarifying them when they are subject to interpretation, the Dispute Settlement Protocol sits at the centre of the integration process in that it is called to provide 'security and predictability to the regional trading system'.[21] However, in the absence of individuals' standing, the disinclination of the contracting parties to activate the relevant clauses does not augur well with these objectives.

This chapter is structured as follows. Section 3 introduces the notion of direct effect as developed in the context of the European economic integration. It also spells out the requirements that a rule should satisfy to be directly effective. Section 4 explores the application of direct effect in the African situation where inter-state litigious settlement of trade disputes is rather non-existent. Noting the proliferation of adjudicating authorities at the continental level, none of which actually grants access to individuals to uphold their rights under their founding treaties, it is argued that the AfCFTA Agreements' drafters might not have been very careful to exclude such a possibility. Therefore, direct effect could evolve to establish itself

[18] See RY Simo, 'Trade in services in the African Continental Free Trade Area: prospects, challenges and WTO compatibility' (2020) 23(1) Journal of International Economic Law 65.

[19] See, for example, Article 28 of the Treaty Establishing the East African Community (EAC) (adopted 30 November 1999, entered into force 7 July 2000) (hereinafter EAC Treaty), Article 10 of Protocol A/P.l/7/91 of the ECOWAS Community Court of Justice (ECCJ) (adopted 6 July 1991, entered into force 6 July 1991). These provisions, which guarantee access to these respective courts to states, are simply not used.

[20] See AfCFTA Protocol on Rules and Procedures on the Settlement of Disputes (adopted 21 March 2018, entered into force 30 May 2019) available at <https://au.int/sites/default/files/treaties/36437-treaty-consolidated_text_on_cfta_-_en.pdf> accessed 19 June 2020 (hereinafter 'Dispute Settlement Protocol'), Article 3(1).

[21] ibid Article 4(1). See also Recital 6 of the AfCFTA Agreement's Preamble which recognizes the need to establish 'clear, transparent, predictable' rules to govern trade.

as a principle of AU law though these loopholes, thus constituting a welcome development. Section 5 concludes the chapter.

2. The Concept of Direct Effect in Community Law

2.1 Definitions and Some Conceptual Clarifications

African regional economic law treaties are classic international agreements in that they create mutual obligations between State Parties, and rarely, if ever, confer rights and obligations on individuals. Direct effect describes a situation where treaty provisions give rise to rights that individuals can defend in the courts of a country. Accordingly, this chapter adopts, mainly for practical reasons, the definition of direct effect by Cottier and Schefer as meaning that a person (both natural and legal) located or established in a state may base a claim before, and be granted relief from, the domestic courts against another person or the state based on the state's obligations under a ratified international treaty. Individuals can make such claims without a prior transformation of the obligation by national rule-makers. They may equally be made against implementing legislation on grounds that it is not compatible with the provisions of a treaty.[22]

The emancipation of EU law from certain rules of international law took shape in the 1960s when the ECJ made pronouncements in favour of an autonomous legal order. Since it is not so frequent to find 'an express provision in a community's founding treaty that the community constitutes an autonomous and separate legal system', such has sometimes to be inferred by examining that community's 'founding treaty by examining its law-making powers, legal status, modes of the application of its laws and the character of its dispute settlement institutions'.[23] In general, countries make room in their constitution for the rules governing the treaty making power of the state organs, the legal effects of duly ratified treaties and possible conflicts relating thereto. However, through the principles of primacy (or supremacy)[24] and direct effect[25] proclaimed by the judges, EU law began to bypass the constitutional rules of the original six Member States regarding

[22] See T Cottier and KK Nadakavukaren Schefer, 'The relationship of World Trade Organization law, national and regional law' (1998) 1 Journal of International Economic Law 83, 91.

[23] R Frimpong Oppong, *Legal Aspects of Economic Integration in Africa* (CUP, 2011) 41.

[24] See *Flaminio Costa v ENEL*, Case 6/64 [1964]ECR 585 in which the ECJ held that states had transferred their rights and obligations arising under the Treaty 'from their domestic legal system to the Community legal system', and this transfer carried with it 'a permanent limitation of their sovereign rights, against which a subsequent unilateral act incompatible with the concept of the Community [could not] prevail'.

[25] See *Van Gend en Loos* [1963] ECR 12 in which the ECJ held that the EEC constituted 'a new legal order of international law ... the subjects of which comprise not only Member States but also their nationals'. Consequently, Community law 'not only imposes obligations on individuals' but it is 'also intended to confer upon them rights'.

the introduction of standards in their own legal orders, contrary to the rules accompanying the reception of international law instruments. The ECJ has several times recalled these distinctive traits of EU law.[26] For instance in Opinion 2/13, it stated: 'EU law is characterised by the fact that it stems from an *independent* source of law, the Treaties, by its *primacy* over the laws of the Member States . . ., and by the *direct effect* of a whole series of provisions which are applicable to their nationals and to the Member States themselves'.[27]

In Africa, rather than being judge made as in *Costa v Enel*, certain treaties have expressly affirmed their supranational character and their supremacy over domestic laws. The Treaty instituting the Organization for the Harmonization of Business Law in Africa (OHADA) is a good example.[28] OHADA currently comprises 17 contracting parties and the Treaty is opened to signature by any AU Member State. Article 10 states that Uniform Acts (UAs)[29] 'shall be directly applicable to and binding on the States Parties notwithstanding any previous or subsequent conflicting provisions of the national law'. Not only are UAs directly applicable without the need for domestic incorporation but they also supersede and *de facto* abrogate any conflicting (both anterior and posterior) domestic laws.[30] Finally, when national judges are seized of a matter they must apply UAs as such and cannot invoke non-incorporation as an excuse.[31]

Another example of express mention of the supremacy of community law over national laws is found in the EAC region. In effect, while Article 8(4) of the EAC Treaty states that 'Community organs, institutions and laws shall take precedence over similar national ones on matters pertaining to the implementation' of that Treaty, Article 8(5) stipulates that Partner States 'undertake to make the necessary legal instruments to confer [such] precedence'.

[26] See Opinion of the Court of 14 December 1991 (Opinion 1/91), *Draft agreement between the Community, on the one hand, and the countries of the European Free Trade Association, on the other, relating to the creation of the European Economic Area* [1991] ECR I–6079, 6102, referring to direct effect and primacy as 'essential characteristics' of EU law.

[27] Opinion of the Court (Full Court) of 18 December 2014 (Opinion 2/13), *Accession of the European Union to the European Convention for the Protection of Human Rights and Fundamental Freedoms*, ECLI:EU:C:2014:2454, para 166 (emphasis added).

[28] See Treaty on the Harmonisation of Business Law in Africa (adopted 17 October 1993, entered into force 19 September 1995) available at <http://www.ohada.com/traite/10/treaty-on-the-harmonisation-of-business-law-in-africa.html> accessed 19 June 2020. See also Revised OHADA Treaty (adopted 17 October 2008, entered into force 21 March 2010) available at <https://www.droit-afrique.com/uploads/OHADA-Treaty-2008-harmonization-business-law.pdf> accessed 19 June 2020 (which did not amend Article 10 of the original treaty).

[29] Article 5 of the 1993 OHADA Treaty defines them as 'Acts enacted for the adoption of the common rules'.

[30] See OHADA Common Court of Justice and Arbitration (CCJA) Advisory Opinion No. 001/2001/EP of 30 April 2001, in Special Issue of the Case law Collection of the CCJA, January 2003, p 74.

[31] On the OHADA law-making process and its implications, see RY Simo, 'Law and development *à l'Africaine*: evidence from the OHADA's harmonisation process' (2014) 20 African Yearbook of International Law 323, 344–9.

2.2 Requirements for an Agreement to be Directly Effective

With direct effect, EU law ceases 'to be mere intergovernmental agreements' and becomes integrated 'into Member States' legal systems' where national courts, individuals and companies become its 'enforcers'.[32] EU law must satisfy three main criteria to have direct effect, namely be clear and unambiguous, unconditional and self-sufficient, in other words 'not requiring further legislative measures by the authorities of the Community or the Member States'.[33] While subsequent *Van Gend en Loos* cases tried at varying degrees to expand or narrow direct effect, the current position is that an EU instrument 'will be accorded direct effect provided it is intended to confer rights on individuals and that it is sufficiently clear, precise, and unconditional'.[34]

3. African Regional Economic Law Instruments and the Desirability of Direct Effect

3.1 Enforcement of African Economic Law Instruments: A Critique of Inter-State Trade Dispute Settlement

In their current state, the AfCFTA instruments do not guarantee standing for individuals and legal persons. Consequently, the likelihood of inferring direct effect from their interpretation from states' litigation might also be jeopardized. Following the launch of the AfCFTA Agreement's operational phase, contracting parties are required to implement it. Pursuant to Article 8 thereof, AfCFTA is based on the principle of single undertaking, and the settlement of disputes through the Protocol is a compulsory obligation for all contracting parties.[35] Article 20 of the AfCFTA Agreement establishes a dispute settlement mechanism (DSM), which must be not only transparent and objective but also equitable and predictable and conducted pursuant to the AfCFTA Agreement.[36] However, presently it is only accessible to contracting parties, either as litigant parties or as third parties. With the ideal of boosting intra-African trade, AU Member States should be aware that the negotiated rules are not worth much without a system in place responsible to enforce them and to solve issues of interpretation.

However, the AfCFTA DSM is a replica of the World Trade Organization (WTO) mechanism and this poses a range of problems. For instance, it runs

[32] Oppong (n 23) 46.
[33] JH Weiler, 'The transformation of Europe' (1991) 100(8) Yale Law Journal 2403, 2413.
[34] PCraig and G de Búrca, *EU Law: Texts, Cases and Materials*, 4th edn (OUP, 2007) 277.
[35] See AfCFTA Dispute Settlement Protocol Article 3(1) (that the Protocol 'shall apply to disputes arising between State Parties').
[36] ibid Article 2.

against the usual habit of African States not to litigate trade disputes, not only before the WTO but particularly before regional courts of justice. Likewise, a legalized dispute settlement of this kind defeats the tendency of the overwhelming preference of business entities for non-judicial solutions to their trade disputes[37] and consequently their non-use of Africa's regional courts of justice.[38] Nevertheless, some authors see the replication of the WTO DSM in RECs to be a commendable step because their Member States would in such a way familiarize themselves with WTO procedures, which will 'prepare them for effective participation in the multilateral process'.[39]

And yet, until very recently, African WTO Member States have rarely, if ever, made use of its dispute settlement system (DSS),[40] which nevertheless guarantees a de jure equality between litigant parties regardless of their economic weight.[41] Unlike their readiness to litigate before the International Court of Justice (ICJ), notably boundary disputes, and their contribution in shaping international investment disputes,[42] the non-participation of African states in the WTO DSS has not escaped the literature, which has critically addressed the issue rather extensively.[43] Celebrated as the WTO's jewel of the crown and contributing to the global economy's stability, the impressive number of disputes decided by its Dispute Settlement Body (DSB) is simply remarkable in the history of international relations. Even when regional trade agreements (RTAs) provide for independent DSMs, studies show that their parties prefer the WTO partly because of its

[37] While they shun traditional courts, there nevertheless seems to be a rather increasing use of commercial arbitration between business entities as the preferred means of dispute resolution. See, for instance, E Onyema, 'Reimagining the framework for resolving intra-African commercial disputes in the context of the African Continental Free Trade Area Agreement' (2020) 19(3) World Trade Review 446.

[38] See JT Gathii, 'The variation in the use of sub-regional integration courts between business and human rights actors: the case of the East African Court of Justice' (2016) 79 Law and Contemporary Problems 37, 45–9.

[39] See C Ng'ong'ola, 'Replication of WTO Dispute Settlement processes in SADC' (2011) 1 SADC Law Journal 35, 60.

[40] Only recently, did the WTO register the first intra-African trade dispute, see R Simo, 'The Tunisia/Morocco scuffle at the WTO: A Missed Opportunity to Establish a Record of Regional Interstate Trade Disputes or a Chance to Contribute to Shaping WTO Jurisprudence?' (*Afronomicslaw Blog*, 4 April 2019) available at <https://www.afronomicslaw.org/2019/04/03/the-tunisia-morocco-scuffle-at-the-wto-a-missed-opportunity-to-establish-a-record-of-regional-interstate-trade-disputes-or-a-chance-to-contribute-to-shaping-wto-jurisprudence/> accessed 19 June 2020.

[41] That '*right* perseveres over *might*' in the WTO DSM, see J Lacarte-Muro and P Gappah, 'Developing countries and the WTO Legal and Dispute Settlement system: a view from the bench' (2000) 3(3) Journal of International Economic Law 395, 401 (original emphasis).

[42] See P-J Le Cannu, 'Foundation and innovation: the participation of African States in the ICSID Dispute Resolution System' (2018) 33(2) ICSID Review – Foreign Investment Law Journal 456; OD Akinkugbe, 'Reverse contributors? African State Parties, ICSID and the development of international investment law' (2019) 34(2) ICSID Review – Foreign Investment Law Journal 434.

[43] See, for example, V Mosoti, 'Africa in the first decade of WTO Dispute Settlement' (2006) 9(2) Journal of International Economic Law 427; A Alavi, 'African countries and the WTO's Dispute Settlement Mechanism' (2007) 25(1) Development Policy Review 25; J Apecu, 'The level of African engagement at the World Trade Organization from 1995 to 2010' (2013) 4(2) International Development Policy 29.

established experience and its strong enforcement mechanism.[44] The same dynamism cannot be said of the African regional courts, whose taciturnity for some and desuetude for others in trade matters have also not escaped careful scrutiny.[45] Notwithstanding the foregoing, the AfCFTA Dispute Settlement Protocol was nevertheless carefully reproduced from the WTO DSM.

That the AfCFTA has been endowed with a specific DSS is laudable principally because the legal order of the AU is not yet operative. There is therefore a DSS with the potential to contribute to the development of AU law even if that contribution were to be confined in trade matters alone. Nonetheless, considering that none of the AfCFTA States Parties has ever initiated a dispute before the RECs courts of justice regarding trade matters, one is entitled to question the reliance on the WTO mechanism. If one recalls the demise of the Southern African Development Community (SADC) Tribunal,[46] and the fact that most of the RECs' courts with the initial mandate to adjudicate trade disputes have over time morphed into human rights courts sometimes without any explicit treaty basis,[47] one could be pessimistic about the effectiveness of the AfCFTA DSM under the WTO model. In effect, the SADC Tribunal, initially empowered to hear disputes not only amongst Member States but also between natural and legal persons against Member States,[48] suffered from a stinging setback after its first landmark decision in *Mike Campbell (Pvt) Ltd and Others v Republic of Zimbabwe*,[49] resulting in the amputation of its competence to be seized by individuals. This backlash had the effect of disbanding it. In case of a subsequent restoration, its role will be limited to interstate matters.[50]

[44] See RY Simo, 'Mounting uncertainty and power shifting in global economic governance: addressing multilateral stability in the context of rising regionalism' (2015) 16 Journal of World Investment and Trade 173, 177.

[45] See generally JT Gathii, 'The COMESA Court of Justice' in R Howse, H Ruiz-Fabri, and others (eds), *The Legitimacy of International Trade Courts and Tribunals* (CUP, 2018) 314; JT Gathii, 'The under-appreciated jurisprudence of Africa's regional trade judiciaries' (2010) 12 Oregon Review of International Law 245.

[46] See, for example, E de Wet, 'The rise and fall of the Tribunal of the Southern African Development Community: implications for dispute settlement in Southern Africa' (2013) 28 ICSID Review – Foreign Investment Law Journal 45.

[47] See generally Gathii (n 45) 245. See also KJ Alter, JT Gathii, and others, 'Backlash against International Courts in West, East and Southern Africa: causes and consequences' (2016) 27 European Journal of International Law 293.

[48] See Article 15(1) of the SADC Protocol on the Tribunal and Rules Thereof (signed 7 August 2000, entered into force 14 August 2011) available at <https://www.sadc.int/files/1413/5292/8369/Protocol_on_the_Tribunal_and_Rules_thereof2000.pdf> accessed 19 June 2020. This SADC Tribunal Protocol nevertheless conditioned such a standing before the regional court on the exhaustion of local remedies. See ibid Article 15(2).

[49] *Mike Campbell (Pvt) Ltd and Others v Republic of Zimbabwe* [2008] SADCT 2 (28 November 2008).

[50] On 18 August 2014, SADC Summit amended the Tribunal's Protocol to allow access only to State parties; Article 33 of the Protocol on the Tribunal in the SADC available at <https://ijrcenter.org/wp-content/uploads/2016/11/New-SADC-Tribunal-Protocol-Signed.pdf> accessed 19 June 2020. It continues to lack the minimum threshold of ratifications (two-thirds of Member States, namely 10 out of current 15 Member States) for its entry into force (pursuant to Article 53). Although signed by nine Member States in 2014, none of them has ratified it.

Two judgments by the South African Constitutional Court[51] and by the Tanzanian High Court[52] condemning the acts by which their respective governments contributed to stripping the SADC Tribunal of its powers recently raised expectations on its possible revival. Interestingly, in assuming jurisdiction to hear the matter, especially the ability to overturn, change or proclaim the SADC Summit decision that amended the Tribunal Protocol ineffective, the High Court in Tanzania spoke to the topic of this chapter. It invoked the Member States' commitment to 'take all necessary steps to accord th[e] [SADC] Treaty the force of national law',[53] interpreting this undertaking as entailing that the Treaty had direct effect in that it 'creates norms capable of enforcement in the domestic courts of competent jurisdiction'.[54] The High Court also relied on the EU rule in *Francovich*, in which the ECJ held that a Member State's failure to transpose directives into its domestic law was ground for its liability to pay damages to individuals before national courts.[55] It concluded that undermining the Tribunal's operational capacity exposed State Parties to liability to third parties.[56] Indeed, since suspending the Tribunal's operation 'eroded existing rights of parties' who had access to the Tribunal at all times,[57] any aggrieved party was thus founded to resort to a domestic court to seek remedy.[58]

In contrast to the SADC Tribunal's slow death, there is a buoyant dynamism of the Courts of Justice of ECOWAS, COMESA, and EAC (East African Court of Justice (EACJ)) which, in the absence of disputes between states, have positioned themselves as the bulwark of justice in terms of human rights and free movement of goods in their respective regions.[59] Thus, the early 2000s initiative by the EACJ

[51] See *Law Society of South Africa and Others v President of the Republic of South Africa and Others* (CCT67/18) [2018] ZACC 51 (11 December 2018): it held that the South African President's participation in the decision-making and his signature of the 2014 Protocol was 'unconstitutional, unlawful and irrational' because it removes access to individuals. Consequently, it directed the President to withdraw his signature, which he did; see Communiqué of the 39th SADC Summit of Heads of State and Government (17–18 August 2019), para 20 available at <https://www.sadc.int/files/1915/6614/8772/Communique_of_the_39th_SADC_Summit-English.pdf> accessed 19 June 2020.

[52] See *Tanganyika Law Society v Ministry of Foreign Affairs and International Cooperation & Attorney General*, Misc. Civil Cause No 23 of 2014 (4 June 2019) available at <https://africanlii.org/sites/default/files/Judgment.%20TLS%20vs%20Ministry%20of%20Foreign%20Affairs%20and%20International%20Cooperation%20%26%20AG%2C%20Misc%20Civil%20Cause%20No.%2023%20of-%202014._0.pdf> accessed 19 June 2020: it held that the 'suspension of the operations of the SADC Tribunal; and failure or refusal to appoint Judges contrary to the clear Treaty provisions, was inimical to the Rule of law as a foundational principle inherent to the legitimacy of the [SADC] Community'. The Court enjoined the respondents to give effect to the SADC Treaty.

[53] See Article 6(5) of the SADC Treaty. Note that this provision is also a denial of the direct applicability of SADC Treaty at national level. Indeed, it requires Member States to 'take all necessary steps' for its incorporation into their domestic legal system, thus leaving it to States to resort to their respective constitutional procedures to that effect.

[54] *Tanganyika Law Society* (n 52) 8.

[55] *Andrea Francovich and Danila Bonifaci and others v Italian Republic*, Joined Cases C-6/90 and C-9/90 [1991] ECR I-5357.

[56] *Tanganyika Law Society* (n 52) 10 and 46.

[57] ibid 44.

[58] ibid 46.

[59] See Gathii (n 45); Alter, Gathii, and others (n 47).

to embrace human rights without a specific mandate is attributed to judicial activism and fell within the 'new trend in African regional human rights enforcement'.[60] Moreover, the *British American Tobacco* case, where the EACJ held that a Ugandan additional excise duty on imported cigarettes constituted a violation of the Common Market Treaty,[61] testifies to the need to broaden access to natural and legal persons to advance the interpretation and enforcement of regional trade agreements.[62] In that case, British American Tobacco (BAT) Uganda Ltd, a company incorporated under the laws of Uganda, decided to move its cigarette-manufacturing factory from Uganda to Kenya on the understanding that they were parties of the EAC customs territory characterized by the elimination of tariffs and other restrictive regulations of commerce.[63] The applicant contended that the Uganda Revenue Authority's application of the impugned excise duty, which had the effect of reclassifying previous domestically manufactured cigarettes as *imported* goods, amounted to a discrimination between goods originating from Uganda and those from Kenya, and therefore contravened the national treatment provisions of the EAC Treaty and the Customs Union Protocol and of the Common Market Protocol, which prohibit imposition of internal taxes on other states parties' products in excess of that imposed on like domestic products.[64] According to BAT, the excise duty discriminated between imported and locally manufactured goods by attracting higher excise duty rates compared to goods locally manufactured and, therefore, negated the EAC Treaty.[65]

Moreover, it was reported that individuals dragged Uganda and Rwanda before the EACJ over what they saw as the 'arbitrary border closure', claiming that these actions violated the EAC Treaty provisions on free movement of persons and goods and therefore sought compensation for economic losses.[66] While this petition was

[60] JT Gathii, 'Mission creep or a search for relevance: the East African Court of Justice's human rights strategy' (2013) 24 Duke Journal of Comparative & International Law 249, 250.

[61] *British American Tobacco (U) Ltd v The Attorney General of Uganda* [2019], EACJ 4, Reference No 7 of 2017 (26 March 2019) available at <https://africanlii.org/sites/default/files/REFERENCE-NO-7-OF-2017.pdf> accessed 19 June 2020. For the interim order in favour of the applicant, see App No 13 of 2017 (Arising from Reference No 7 of 2017), *British American Tobacco (U) Ltd v The Attorney General of Uganda* [2018], EACJ 86 (25 January 2018) available at <http://eacj.org/wp-content/uploads/2018/01/Applicaiton-No.13-of-2017.pdf> accessed 19 June 2020.

[62] It also showed that regional trade courts are 'most likely to be accessible' to business entities that can afford it, thus excluding those lacking knowledge such as farmers and handicraftsmen who usually trade across borders and are often victims of regional trade laws breaches; see Gathii (n 38) 50–1.

[63] cf Article XXIV GATT.

[64] See Article 75(6) of the EAC Treaty, Articles 15(1)(a) and (2) of the EAC Customs Union Protocol (adopted 2 March 2004, entered into force 1 January 2005), and Article 6 of the EAC Common Market Protocol (adopted 20 November 2009, entered into force 1 July 2010).

[65] See *British American Tobacco (U) Ltd v The Attorney General of Uganda* [2019] (n 61), paras 117 and 120.

[66] See Press Statement on a Public Interest Litigation Case on the Closure of Uganda-Rwanda Border available at <https://www.eassi.org/wp-content/uploads/2019/07/Press-statement-on-a-public-interest-litigation-case-on-the-closure-of-uganda-rwanda-border.pdf> accessed 19 June 2020. See also MT Kahungu, 'Border: Women Traders Sue Uganda, Rwanda' (*Daily Monitor*, 2 July 2019) available at <https://www.monitor.co.ug/News/National/Border-Women-traders-Uganda-Rwanda-Tanzania-/688334-5178970-c303maz/index.html> accessed 19 June 2020.

subsequently withdrawn,[67] these examples demonstrate how offering standing to individuals tends to contribute to guaranteeing justice in RECs, when Member States are reluctant to litigate against one another. From the foregoing, subsection 3.2 assesses the reliance on the WTO DSM centred on inter-state relationships and explores the desirability of the principle of direct effect as developed in EU law.

3.2 Exploring Direct Effect and Standing for Individuals to Enforce AU International Economic Law Treaties

Criticisms of regimes for lack of public participation and their response thereto are not new especially when these call into question their legitimacy. The WTO dispute settlement itself, which the AfCFTA copies so assiduously, has also had over the years to reflect on its modus operandi to respond to mounting criticisms. For instance, accused of meeting 'behind closed doors' in Geneva,[68] the WTO took note some years ago of the crisis of legitimacy it was experiencing and the criticisms of its DSM's transparency. That is why it undertook somehow to *democratize* its procedures, notably through accepting amicus curiae briefs[69] (albeit without being bound to consider them in deciding the cases) and opening panels' and the Appellate Body's hearings to the public.[70] These reforms certainly marked a progress in third-party involvement in the WTO dispute mechanism, even though Member States kept their right to be the only parties to disputes. Therefore, to be effective, and although it is yet to be tested, the AfCFTA's DSS should not be content with its provisions in their present state.

Any criticism of the AfCFTA DSS based on the WTO regime would be incomplete without mentioning African countries' preference for political solutions to legal problems.[71] In effect, states may be reluctant to initiate legal actions if they think that such disputes might disrupt the broader relationship between them. This suggests that rebukes over lack of adjudication amongst African countries may seem improper. If one were to assume that AfCFTA parties would trigger the DSM, it is also very likely that, consistent with their practice for political solutions to legal

[67] See J Kigongo, 'Uganda Law Society Withdraws Border Closure Case against Rwanda' (*Daily Monitor*, 11 November 2019) available at <https://www.monitor.co.ug/News/National/Uganda-Law-society-withdraws-border-closure-case-against-Rwanda/688334-5345688-o78hbpz/index.html> accessed 19 June 2020.

[68] See L Wallach, 'Introduction: It's Not About Trade' in L Wallach and P Woodall (eds), *Whose Trade Organization?: The Comprehensive Guide to the WTO* (New Press, 2004), 15.

[69] See PC Mavroidis, 'Amicus Curiae Briefs before the WTO: Much Ado about Nothing' (2002) Jean Monnet Working Paper 2/01 available at <https://jeanmonnetprogram.org/archive/papers/01/010201.html> accessed 19 June 2020.

[70] See, for example, A Alvarez-Jiménez, 'Public hearings at the WTO Appellate Body: the next step' (2010) 59(4) International and Comparative Law Quarterly 1079.

[71] See T Maluwa, 'The peaceful settlement of disputes among African States, 1963–1983: some conceptual issues and practical trends' (1989) 38(2) International and Comparative Law Quarterly 299.

problems, the matter would not proceed beyond the consultations and good offices stages provided in Articles 7 and 8 of the Dispute Settlement Protocol.[72] In other words, and taking into account the inclination of African states, no case is likely to reach the stage of the panels, let alone that of the Appellate Body. This is simply because mediation is the typical means of settling disputes in Africa.[73] Even though the dockets of the ICJ regularly feature African territorial disputes as mentioned above, it also demonstrates, according to observers, the interest of African states in border issues and their neglect of trade matters.[74]

While the doctrine of direct effect has been efficient in the EU, the AfCFTA's DSM is not built around a court of justice as is the case with the EU Treaties. The reason for this choice is unknown to the present author.[75] One can however speculate that the non-operation of the ACJHR at the date of conclusion of AfCFTA negotiations might have dictated the choice. And yet, this preference contrasts with the AEC Treaty whose dispute settlement clause, drafted prior to the conclusion of the Uruguay Round that gave birth to the WTO, was reliant on the Court of Justice.[76] What is more, the AEC Court of Justice had envisaged a mechanism through which individuals could have access to the Court. In effect, Article 18(4) of the AEC Treaty stipulated that the Assembly of Head of States and Government, the supreme organ of the Community, 'may confer on the Court of Justice the power to assume jurisdiction by virtue of this Treaty over any dispute'. The AfCFTA chosen archetype also runs counter to the tendency of RECs to be modelled after the ECJ where individuals have standing before the relevant Community court.[77]

Indeed, as already alluded to, some RECs currently allow individuals to litigate directly against Member States and the communities' institutions before their courts of justice. For instance, Article 26 of the COMESA Treaty stipulates that its

[72] Akinkugbe argues that consultation offers the 'most realistic chance of engaging with the AfCFTA-DSM' given their culture of non-litigation of trade disputes. See OD Akinkugbe, 'Dispute settlement under the African Continental Free Trade Area Agreement: a preliminary assessment' (2020) 28(Supplement) African Journal of International and Comparative Law 138, 140.

[73] See, for example, Article 3(f) of the Abuja Treaty: in pursuing the AEC objectives, the High Contracting Parties 'solemnly affirm and declare their adherence' to the principle of 'peaceful settlement of disputes among Member States, active cooperation between neighbouring countries and promotion of a peaceful environment as a pre-requisite for economic development'.

[74] See M Forere, 'Revisiting African States participation in the WTO Dispute Settlement through Intra-Africa RTA Dispute Settlement' (2013) 6(2) Law and Development Review 155, 176.

[75] Gathii believes that the 'adoption of a WTO style dispute settlement system … reflects the preferences of a small set of African states and technical experts, favoring [sic] a strong system of dispute settlement as a guarantee of ensuring compliance with the commitments embodied in the AfCFTA'. See JT Gathii, 'Evaluating the Dispute Settlement Mechanism of the African Continental Free Trade Agreement (*Afronomicslaw Blog*, 10 April 2019) available at <https://www.afronomicslaw.org/2019/04/10/evaluating-the-dispute-settlement-mechanism-of-the-african-continental-free-trade-agreement/> accessed 19 June 2020.

[76] See Articles 7(1)(e), 18, and 87 of the Abuja Treaty.

[77] While initially not allowing for individual standing, some courts like the ECOWAS had to wait for an amendment of the founding Treaty to have such jurisdiction. Generally, see ST Ebobrah 'Critical issues in the human rights mandate of the ECOWAS Court of Justice' (2010) 54(1) Journal of African Law 1.

Court of Justice has jurisdiction on matters referred to it by 'any person who is resident in a Member State'. In *Polytor Paints and Adhesive Manufacturers Co. Ltd v The Republic of Mauritius*, the COMESA Court of Justice confirmed that this provision confers direct effect to legal and natural persons when a Member State breaches its Treaty obligations.[78] Likewise, Article 30 of the EAC Treaty provides for the same right for individuals. In both COMESA and EAC this right is not conferred on ground of nationality to any of the REC State Parties but rather by virtue of one being a 'resident' therein. The reason is simply to avoid denying benefit to individuals and business entities established and conducting business in the relevant REC, which may not be owned or controlled by nationals of that region. Therefore, the AfCFTA dispute settlement regime is a setback to the acquired private rights of action under these RECs. This may appear problematic as these same RECs are supposed to be the AfCFTA's building blocks.

Given this inter-state feature of the AfCFTA DSM, there is however a possible silver lining. Unlike the WTO DSM, which is exclusive, the AfCFTA DSM is not. It is true that Article 3(4) of the Dispute Settlement Protocol precludes the use of any other forum to settle the same matter once a State Party has invoked it. This is a choice of forum clause. To guard against forum shopping is not fortuitous in a context where a country's trade measure though compliant with its obligations under a specific treaty, say the WTO, may still be found to violate AfCFTA commitments, or vice versa. The case of *Argentina – Poultry Anti-Dumping Duties*,[79] which proceeded to a WTO panel after adjudication before a Southern Common Market (MERCOSUR) ad hoc tribunal, illustrates this type of scenario. In that case, Brazil brought a dispute against Argentina claiming that Argentina's imposition of anti-dumping charges on imported Brazilian poultry violated its obligations under the WTO Anti-Dumping Agreement (ADA). Although the MERCOSUR tribunal had dismissed Brazil's prior claim, the WTO Panel nevertheless found that Argentina had acted inconsistently with certain provisions of ADA, even though Argentina had invoked estoppel and good faith to try to prevent the WTO Panel from hearing the case. Despite the choice of forum clause, which precluded MERCOSUR countries from pursuing the *same claim* before two different fora, the Panel noted that the clause had not yet entered into force at the time the dispute came before it, thus leaving open the possibility of declining jurisdiction in favour of regional courts.

It follows that African states that are also WTO Members may therefore choose between litigating the matter at the multilateral or the continental level. While practice shows a preference for WTO fora,[80] a forum-shopping rule seeks to avoid

[78] *Polytor Paints and Adhesive Manufacturers Co. Ltd v The Republic of Mauritius* [2013] COMESACJ 14 Reference No 1 of 2012 (31 August 2013) available at <https://africanlii.org/comesa/judgment/comesa-court-justice/2013/14> accessed 19 June 2020.

[79] WTO, *Argentina: Definitive Anti-Dumping Duties on Poultry from Brazil – Report of the Panel*, WT/DS241/R, [2003]DSR:V, 1727.

[80] Simo (n 44) 177.

collision between the AfCFTA DSB and other regimes including the potential of conflicting rulings. Despite this rule, the AfCFTA Protocol is not exclusive. Its Article 3(2) states:

> This Protocol shall apply subject to such special and additional rules and procedures on dispute settlement contained in the Agreement. To the extent that there is a difference between the rules and procedures of this Protocol and the special or additional rules and procedures in the Agreement, the special or additional rules and procedures shall prevail.

Presently, the only special and additional rule in relation to dispute settlement is found in Annex 5 of the PTG dealing with the elimination of non-tariff barriers (NTBs). NTBs are understood here as including, but not limited to, customs and administrative entry procedures, technical barriers to trade, sanitary and phytosanitary measures, charges on imports, etc.[81] While subjecting '[a]ny dispute between the State Parties arising out of or relating to the interpretation or application of any provision' of the Annex to the general rule of dispute settlement under the AfCFTA Dispute Settlement Protocol,[82] Article 12 of Annex 5 provides for a specific 'mechanism for identifying, reporting and monitoring' the elimination of NTBs. It provides, *inter alia*, for the use of facilitators (i.e. independent experts) to resolve NTBs complaints. This is a non-judicial mechanism 'accessible to States Parties' Economic Operators, National Focal Points, REC Secretariats, academic researchers and other Interested Parties'.[83]

The *lex specialis* rule in Article 3(2) of the AfCFTA Dispute Settlement Protocol is interesting in other respects as well. In 2008, the AU adopted a Protocol on the Statute of the African Court of Justice and Human Rights (ACJHR).[84] Upon entering into force, it will replace the Protocol to the African Charter on Human and Peoples' Rights on the establishment of an African Court on Human and Peoples' Rights,[85] and the Protocol of the Court of Justice of the African Union.[86] It will also have three chambers; one dealing with general legal matters, a second in charge of human rights questions,[87] and a third, which was added by the Malabo Protocol, to deal with international criminal law issues.[88] None of these procedural routes envisages the direct participation by individuals,[89] just like the AfCFTA DSM, and

[81] See Annex 5 of the AfCFTA Protocol on Trade in Goods, Article 3.
[82] ibid Article 16.
[83] ibid Article 12(7).
[84] Adopted 1 July 2008, (2009) 48 ILM 317.
[85] Adopted 10 June 1998, entered into force 25 January 2004.
[86] Adopted 11 July 2003, entered into force 11 February 2009.
[87] Article 16 of the Protocol on the Statute of the ACJHR.
[88] See Article (16 New) of the Protocol on Amendments to the Protocol on the Statute of the African Court of Justice and Human Rights (adopted 27 June 2014, not yet in force).
[89] Article 30(f) of the Protocol on the Statute of the ACJHR states that individuals and accredited NGOs can submit cases, but only if the Member State concerned has made a declaration accepting the jurisdiction of the Court to receive such cases.

therefore consists in a retrograde development compared to REC Courts of Justice. One instance that can lead to confusion is when seized for matters relating to free movement of persons.

It is worth noting that the Free Movement of Persons Protocol envisages its own DSM, which considers referral to the ACJHR and not the AfCFTA DSM. In effect, Article 31 of that Protocol stipulates that any dispute arising out of its interpretation, application, and implementation may be referred to the ACJHR when it becomes operational.[90] Pending its operationalization, a Panel of Arbitrators will deal with any disputes.[91] This separate DSM deliberately extricates the free movement of persons from the AfCFTA agenda. Indeed, as its name indicates, it is the 'Protocol to the *Treaty Establishing the African Economic Community* Relating to Free Movement of Persons, Right of Residence and Right of Establishment', and as such under the umbrella of the AU Commission, from which the AfCFTA is supposed to be independent.[92] It also possibly illustrates the recognition by AU Member States that the free movement of persons is so controversial that it is best addressed as either a human right issue or a question falling under the jurisdiction of the ACJHR general affairs chamber. And yet, even as a human rights matter,[93] lack of unqualified direct standing for individuals who are the victims of barriers to free movement is particularly shocking.[94]

However, this exercise of disconnection may not always work as intended. This is because the movement of persons is also relevant for the trade agenda. For instance, under the PTS, 'trade in services' is also defined, amongst others, as the supply of services 'by a service supplier of one State Party, through presence of natural persons of a State Party in the territory of any other State Party'.[95] Given that the realization of the benefits of that mode of supply of services under the AfCFTA PTS rests largely on the progress made under the Free Movement of Persons Protocol, for instance in the lifting of immigration hurdles, these two instruments are interconnected.[96] Likewise, Article 1(p)(iii) of the AfCFTA PTS defines trade in services as the supply of services 'by a service supplier of one State Party, through commercial presence in the territory of any other State Party'. The latter regulates

[90] Free Movement of Persons Protocol, Article 31(2)(b).

[91] ibid Articles 31(2)(a) and 31(4).

[92] In effect, Article 13(3) and (4) of the AfCFTA Agreement states that upon establishment, the AfCFTA Secretariat 'shall be a functionally autonomous institutional body within the African Union system with an independent legal personality' and 'shall be autonomous of the African Union Commission'.

[93] See ACHPR (n 11), Article 12 which consecrates freedom of movement and residence of individuals as a human right.

[94] Article 31 of the Free Movement of Persons Protocol speaks of settling disputes between 'State Parties'. In human rights-related matters, individuals can only bring claims at the ACJHR if a Member State expressly admits such a possibility at the signature, ratification, or accession to the Protocol. See Protocol on the Statute of the ACJHR, Articles 8(3) and 30(f). This is without prejudice to an eventual exercise of diplomatic protection by one contracting party one behalf of its citizens.

[95] AfCFTA Protocol on Trade in Services, Article 1(p)(iv).

[96] See Simo (n 18) 86–7.

'establishment',[97] which describes a situation where a natural person leaves the state of his nationality and takes part 'on a stable and uninterrupted basis in the economic life of another state'.[98] It is therefore possible that a dispute over restrictions to the free movement of persons and obstacles to the freedom of establishment triggers the provisions of these two instruments and consequently capable of falling under the AfCFTA DSM and the ACJHR. While the AfCFTA DSM provides for a choice of forum clause,[99] it does not preclude other fora from hearing matters arising out of AfCFTA violations. Likewise, the ACJHR may in the future have to adjudicate trade matters even though the AU has sought to disentangle the Free Movement of Persons from the AfCFTA.

In the same vein, the Protocol on Investment, currently under negotiations under Phase II of the AfCFTA, could also incorporate the feature of existing international investment agreements (IIAs) which is the investor–state dispute settlement (ISDS), just as the Pan-African Investment Code before it.[100] The problem stems from the fact that the WTO General Agreement on Trade in Services (GATS) allows for two types of investors under an RTA. The regional investor is governed by Article V:3(b) of GATS,[101] while a foreign investor by Article V:6.[102] Should the AfCFTA Investment Protocol embrace ISDS, it is likely that regional investors or foreign investors could have the options to bring a claim either under the Investment Protocol or the PTS (which does not allow private access).

The above-mentioned jurisdictional overlaps in the African international economic law sphere notwithstanding, the question of direct effect remains unaddressed. The ACJHR Statute excluded the previous Article 18(4) of the AEC Treaty, which allowed individuals to take part directly in proceedings before the AEC Court of Justice on matters relating to the interpretation, enforcement, and validity of AEC laws. This neglect makes the current regime 'ill-suited for the level of

[97] See also Free Movement of Persons Protocol, Article 17.

[98] Simo (n 18) 86.

[99] Article 3(4) of the AfCFTA Dispute Settlement Protocol.

[100] See Pan-African Investment Code (PAIC) (31 December 2016) available at <https://au.int/en/documents/20161231/pan-african-investment-code-paic> accessed 19 June 2020. Contrary to experts' recommendations, the AU finally took the political decision to adopt the PAIC as a non-binding model investment treaty. See MM Mbengue and S Schacherer, 'The "Africanization" of international investment law: The Pan-African Investment Code and the reform of the international investment regime' (2017) 18(3) Journal of World Investment and Trade 414, 420. On the challenge of the current ISDS and the disservice done to Africa, see generally F Adeleke, *International Investment Law and Policy in Africa: Exploring a Human Rights Based Approach to Investment Regulation and Dispute Settlement* (Routledge, 2017).

[101] Article V:3(b) of the General Agreement on Trade in Services (GATS) stipulates that 'in the case of an agreement ... involving only developing countries', like the AfCFTA, 'more favourable treatment may be granted to juridical persons owned or controlled by natural persons of the parties to such an agreement'. On the potential legal challenges under bilateral investment agreements should such a clause be activated, see Simo (n 18) 92–4.

[102] Article V:6 GATS provides that a regional trade agreement (RTA) can benefit foreign investors incorporated under the laws of any contracting state if they engage into substantive business operations in one of those states.

integration envisaged' in Africa.[103] If the reforms of the ACJHR to keep up with the pace recorded in RECs courts are undertaken, it could be the gateway for direct effect of the AU international economic law instruments.

In effect, Oppong evokes three scenarios to grant standing to private entities before the ACJHR. The first is to emulate 'the special leave of the court' introduced in the Caribbean Community (CARICOM) in 2001.[104] In effect, Article 222 of the CARICOM Revised Treaty stipulates that natural or juridical persons may be allowed to appear as parties in proceedings before the Caribbean Court of Justice (CCJ) 'with the special leave of the Court' if four cumulative conditions are met.[105] First, the Court has to determine that, in the case at hand, the Treaty intended that a right or benefit conferred under the treaty on a Member State 'enure[s] to the benefit of such persons directly'. Second, the applicants must establish that they have been prejudiced in the enjoyment of that right or benefit. Third, the respondent state has either omitted or declined to bring the claim on behalf of the private entity or 'expressly agreed' that such persons can bring the claim instead of the state. Finally, the Court must find 'that the interest of justice requires that the persons be allowed to espouse the claim'. This is consequently not a direct access to the CCJ per se since it is based on its discretion.[106] Thus, while this avenue will be a step forward for the ACJHR, the four-pronged requirement would however be more stringent than the current scenario under the RECs, where standing is not burdened by any of these conditions.[107] Thus, it would be a step back.[108]

Another alternative would be to grant *locus standi* conditioned upon exhaustion of local remedies.[109] Finally, the third suggestion has been to create procedures to allow national courts to refer cases to the continental court.[110] These three options would be a gateway to introduce direct effect in AU trade instruments. This could also eventually induce the contracting parties to AfCFTA to amend the Dispute Settlement Protocol, or, in a more drastic way, lead to the AfCFTA DSM being subsumed as a 'trade chamber' of the ACJHR.[111]

[103] RF Oppong, 'The African Union, the African Economic Community and Africa's Regional Economic Communities: untangling a complex web' (2010) 18(1) African Journal of International and Comparative Law 92, 101.

[104] ibid.

[105] See Revised Treaty of Chaguaramas Establishing the Caribbean Community including the CARICOM Single Market and Economy (signed 5 July 2001, entered into force 2 February 2002) 2259 UNTS 293, Article 222.

[106] For an assessment of this provision as interpreted by the CCJ, see Adrian D Saunders, 'A Commentary on the Early Decisions of the Caribbean Court of Justice in its Original Jurisdiction' (2010) 59(3) International and Comparative Law Quarterly 761, 766–72.

[107] See Oppong (n 103) 101.

[108] Note however that the generous interpretation of this provision by the CCJ in *Trinidad Cement Ltd v The State of the Co-operative Republic of Guyana*, CCJ App No AR 1 of 2008, [2009] CCJ 1 (OJ), may also mean that the obstacle is not unsurmountable.

[109] Oppong (n 103) 101.

[110] ibid.

[111] See however Gathii (n 75), holding that to adopt the WTO-style DSM was certainly a way to avoid the AfCFTA dispute settlement becoming a trade chamber of the ACJHR leading the AfCFTA to become a 'dead-letter law'.

4. Conclusion

This chapter addresses the enforcement (or lack) of AU international economic law treaties by contracting parties. It explores the raison d'être for the desirability of applying the doctrine of direct effect, which allows individuals to bring complaints directly before regional courts against contracting parties for treaty violations. By not guaranteeing standing for private and legal persons, the AfCFTA Agreement and other AEC treaties take a backward step from these rights acquired under some RECs courts, even though they are building blocks to both AfCFTA and AEC.

While Article 3(2) of the AfCFTA Dispute Settlement Protocol regulates any future conflict between its provisions and any other DSM by relying on the *lex specialis* principle, it also opens the door for the litigation of trade issues before other courts, including the ACJHR. It remains to be seen, like any pessimist would be tempted to think, whether the transplantation of the WTO DSM model in the AfCFTA was a deliberate attempt to nip the project of a supreme trade court in the bud. This is so even though, as some have argued, it might have well been a prudent attempt to save the AfCFTA from being absorbed as a mere chamber of the ACJHR. How the eventual Investment Protocol's ISDS feature would eventually reflect on the AfCFTA DSM and on the doctrine of direct effect also remains to be seen.

23

Propagation and Enforcement of AU Law: Perspectives from the Peace and Security Arena

Rhuks Ako

1. Introduction

Africa's growing youth demographic and its human rights-related issues are matters that have caught the attention of scholars, practitioners, policy-makers, and politicians alike.[1] The role of youth in all spheres of national, regional, and continental activities is considered important but no more so than in the peace and security arena. Increasingly, youth are being recognized as agents of peace and no longer simply as perpetrators and victims of insecure societies.[2] Interestingly, the role of human rights as an underlying factor to threats to peace and security on the continent has been widely acknowledged.[3] Hence, both issues – youth and human rights – are important factors to consider in contemporary discussions on peace and security in Africa. This chapter aims to bring to the fore the role that the

[1] M Ssenyonjo, 'Responding to human rights violations in Africa: assessing the role of the African Commission and Court on Human and Peoples' Rights (1987–2018)' (2018) 7 Immigration and Human Rights Law Review 1; R Murray, D. Long, and others, 'Monitoring implementation of the decisions and judgments of the African Commission and Court on Human and Peoples' Rights' (2017) 1 African Human Rights Yearbook 150; D Owen, and others, 'Preventing conflict through human rights-based early warning in Africa' (4 February 2019) available at <https://blogs.worldbank.org/dev4peace/preventing-conflict-through-human-rights-based-early-warning-africa> accessed 15 December 2019; R Grasa and O Mateos, 'Conflict, peace and security in Africa: An assessment and new questions after 50 years of African independence', ICIP Working Papers: 2010/08, Institut Català Internacional per la Pau Barcelona, December 2010; G Atuhaire, 'African Union's securitization of youth: A milestone for regional coordination of youth programmes in peace and security' (2019) 13(5) IPSS Policy Brief 1; and V-C Browning, P Akanonu, and others, 'Opportunities and pitfalls in practical translation of youth inclusivity for sustainable peacebuilding in Africa', Konrad-Adenauer-Stiftung, March 2019 available at <https://www.kas.de/documents/273004/0/YPS_Paper.pdf/35a7e12a-7148-ef44-989c-1883aa6d46dc?version=1.0&t=1552748162594> accessed 15 December 2019.

[2] M Kujeke, 'Turning Africa's youth into peacebuilders' (*ISS Today*, 18 September 2017) available at <https://issafrica.org/iss-today/turning-africas-youth-into-peacebuilders> accessed 15 December 2019.

[3] G Keng, 'New threats to Africa's peace and security: the role of youth in preventing conflicts and building sustainable peace' (Kujenga Amani, Keng, 9 November 2017) available at <https://kujenga-amani.ssrc.org/2017/11/09/new-threats-to-africas-peace-and-security-the-role-of-youth-in-preventing-conflicts-and-building-sustainable-peace/> accessed 20 December 2019.

Rhuks Ako, *Propagation and Enforcement of AU Law: Perspectives from the Peace and Security Arena* In: *The Emergent African Union Law.* Edited by: Olufemi Amao, Michèle Olivier and Konstantinos D. Magliveras, Oxford University Press.
 DOI: 10.1093/oso/9780198862154.003.0024

African Union (AU) through its African Peace and Security Architecture (APSA) plays in propagating and enforcing norms and practice that contribute to the body of evolving AU law.

The AU established the APSA in 2002 to promote the organization's aspirations towards a peaceful, secure, and stable continent.[4] The wide ambit of the architecture includes (direct and structural) conflict prevention, early warning and preventive diplomacy, peace-making and peace building, the encouragement and promotion of democratic practices as well as intervention and humanitarian action and disaster management.[5] Put simply, the architecture aims to recognize, establish, and promote a holistic approach to peace and security issues in Africa. Technically, the APSA underpins the work of the AUC's Peace and Security Department (PSD). However, before the chapter focuses on the APSA, it is important to note that there is a second architecture within the AU with some overlapping responsibilities.

The African Governance Architecture (AGA) was developed in 2010, formally adopted in 2011 and came into operation in 2012.[6] The architecture was created to ensure the enhancement of the promotion of democracy, human rights, and good governance through improved coordination among various actors. The AGA secretariat, housed in the AUC's Department of Political Affairs (DPA),[7] serves as the focal coordination point for various stakeholders with mandates to promote good governance and strengthen democracy in Africa as envisaged in the African Charter on Democracy, Elections and Governance[8] as well as translating the objectives of the legal and policy pronouncements in the AU Shared Values. In essence, AGA aims to enhance the capacity of AU organs, institutions, and Regional Economic Communities (RECs) to support Member States to strengthen governance and consolidate democracy through implementation of the Shared Values agenda.[9]

[4] JA Appiah, 'Africa peace and security architecture: reflections on over a decade of promoting peace and security in Africa' (2018) 47(4) Africa Insight 29.
See also Article 3(f) of the AU Constitutive Act 2002.

[5] AU Commission / Peace and Security Department, 'African Peace and Security Architecture. APSA Roadmap 2016–2020', December 2015, 12.

[6] Decision of the 15th Ordinary Session of the Assembly of African Union (AU) Heads of State and Government (AU/Dec.304 (XV) held in July 2010. See also, K Kariseb and Chairman Okoloise, 'Reflections on the African Governance Architecture: Trends, Challenges and Opportunities' in M Addaney, MG Nyarko, and others (eds), *Governance, Human Rights, and Political Transformation in Africa* (Palgrave Macmillan, 2020).

[7] Objective 16 of the AGA Framework.

[8] F Aggad and P Apiko, 'The African Union: the African Governance Architecture and the Charter for Democracy, Elections and Good Governance' [2017] European Centre for Development Policy Management Policy Brief available at <https://ecdpm.org/wp-content/uploads/African-Union-Governance-Policy-Brief-PEDRO-Political-Economy-Dynamics-Regional-Organisations-Africa-ECDPM-2017.pdf> accessed 20 December 2019.

[9] African Governance Architecture, Youth Engagement Strategy 2016–2020 (2018) available at <https://au.int/sites/default/files/documents/38528-doc-aga-yes_web_english-2.pdf> accessed 10 August 2020.

These include AU norms related to human rights and the rule of law, democratic governance, respect for the constitution, gender equality, youth empowerment, development, environmental protection, popular participation, democratic elections, and durable solutions to humanitarian crises.[10]

The AGA and APSA have overlapping responsibilities including human rights and youth, the case study themes in this chapter.[11] With regard to the former, there are inextricable links between and among rule of law, democracy, human rights, and good governance as well as peace and security. At the global level, the World Bank and United Nations (UN) Pathways for Peace Report[12] as well as the UN Sustaining Peace Initiative[13] highlight the fact that conflict prevention goes beyond dealing with the symptoms of conflict. The reports stress that to be effective, conflict prevention efforts must identify and address the structural root causes of conflict. In Africa, this often entails engaging with governance-associated risks and human rights deficits. The links are even more clearly outlined in the AU normative documents. For example, the PSC Protocol relating to the Establishment of the Peace and Security Council expressly states that 'the development of strong democratic institutions and culture, observance of human rights and the rule of law' are essential to conflict prevention and promotion of peace, security, and stability in Africa.[14]

With regards to youth issues, Africa's large and still growing youth population has captured the attention of policy-makers at the international and continental levels. At the UN, Security Council Resolutions 2250 (2015) and 2419 (2018) highlight the integral role youth must play in the peace and security agenda and arena to optimize the attainment of sustainable peace in society. At the AU, the AGA-inspired Africa Youth Charter[15] and Youth Engagement Strategy (YES)[16] form the normative basis of youth mainstreaming in governance generally as well as in the peace and security arena. It is noteworthy to point out though that even though the Africa Youth Charter preceded both UN Security Council Resolutions 2250 (2015) and 2419 (2018), the latter's recognition of youth roles in peace and security

[10] See Objectives 5 and 6 of the AGA Framework.

[11] Y Bedzigui, 'Enhancing AU responses to instability: Linking AGA and APSA', (2018) ISS Policy Brief 113 available at <https://issafrica.s3.amazonaws.com/site/uploads/policy-brief-113.pdf> accessed 29 December 2019.

[12] United Nations and World Bank, *Pathways for Peace: Inclusive Approaches to Preventing Violent Conflict* (World Bank, 2018).

[13] United Nations, 'Peacebuilding and sustaining peace: Report of the Secretary-General', A/72/707–S/2018/43 available at <https://www.un.org/peacebuilding/sites/www.un.org.peacebuilding/files/documents/sg_report_on_peacebuilding_and_sustaining_peace.as_issued.a-72-707-s-2018-43.e.pdf> accessed 29 December 2019.

[14] Preamble of the PSC Protocol. See also the AGA Framework document.

[15] Adopted by the Seventh Ordinary Session of the Assembly, held in Banjul, The Gambia, on 2 July 2006.

[16] African Governance Architecture, Youth Engagement Strategy 2016–2020, (2018) available at <https://au.int/sites/default/files/documents/38528-doc-aga-yes_web_english-2.pdf> accessed 10 August 2020.

provided the required momentum to firmly place youth, peace, and security (YPS) on the front burner.

What may be gleaned from this is that both architectures – APSA and AGA – are strategic continental frameworks to tackle the structural challenges to socio-economic development and political stability in Africa. This includes the development, operationalization, and enforcement of norms including those in the spheres of human rights and youth. For instance, Objective 5(h) of the AGA Framework provides that the AGA Secretariat should facilitate joint engagement while deepening synergy with the APSA in strategic interventions including in preventive diplomacy and conflict prevention, amongst others. Thus, while subsequent sections of the chapter will focus on the APSA, it is necessary to acknowledge that there is a complementary architecture in AGA. The complementarity of both architectures has significant implications both normatively and practically. As will be revealed in subsequent discussions, AGA-related efforts underscored the development of normative frameworks that underlie critical interventions from the APSA elements with both ultimately contributing to the evolution of AU law.

However, this chapter specifically interrogates the role of the APSA plays in the evolution of AU law. Specifically, the chapter examines how AU law can evolve through the development of normative principles that set the tone for the initiatives and activities of the AU; that is, including its organs, RECs, and regional mechanisms as well as Member States. Given the wide scope of the peace and security landscape, the chapter highlights the role of the APSA in developing norms in two contemporary themes – youth and human rights – within a peace and security perspective. It reveals how the APSA elements are developing new norms to precipitate a shift in culture from addressing and responding to the symptoms of conflicts rather than their root causes. It argues that the recent development of norms and practice are premised on extant AU treaties – the ACHPR and the African Youth Charter – that are binding on Member States that have signed, ratified, and acceded to them.

With regards the human rights thematic, the PSC expressly noted that its meeting with the African Commission on Human and Peoples' Rights was premised on Article 45 of the ACHPR, a Charter that has been signed – ratified and acceded by all but one of the 55 Member States of the AU – as well as Article 19 of the PSC Protocol and some of its previous pronouncements. Regarding the latter, it includes in particular the PSC Communiqué (PSC/PR/Comm(LXXXV))[17] in which the PSC adopted working methods of the Peace and Security Council as contained in the conclusions of the Dakar Brainstorming Retreat, including holding an annual consultative meeting with the ACHPR on the state of human rights in conflict areas on the continent. While the number of Member States that have signed and

[17] Adopted at its 85th meeting held on 8 August 2007.

ratified the African Youth Charter are fewer, it entered into force just over a decade ago on August 08, 2009.[18] In essence, contemporary norms and practices evolving in both themes are being propagated from legal instruments that have been acceded to by a majority of the Member States.

The thematic sessions at the PSC have significant value in the process of developing norms. These meetings are usually followed by the Chair of the PSC session's statement which highlights the discussions on the subject and more specifically, outlines the official stand of the organ. The latter is captured in the press statement or communiqué with the latter adopted in situations where the PSC deems the issue to be of a serious nature. Resolutions can, in other words, be regarded as building blocks, contributing to the creation of new custom. Voting in favour of a resolution can supply the subjective element (*opinio juris*) as well as state practice (*usus*). The inherent value in the PSC's communiqués cannot be underestimated in the way that they contribute to the evolution of norms and law over time. Regarding the former, Dupuy argues regarding the former:

> Cross references from one institution to another, the recalling of guidelines adopted by other apparently concurrent international authorities, recurrent invocation of the same rules formulated in one way or another at the universal, regional and more restricted levels, all tend progressively to develop and establish a common international understanding. As a result of this process, conduct and behaviour which would have been considered challenges to State sovereignty twenty years ago are now accepted within the mainstream.[19]

Referring specifically to UNGA, Olivier opined that Resolutions may be regarded as building blocks that contribute to the creation of new custom with voting in favour of a resolution supplying the subjective element (*opinio juris*) as well as state practice (*usu*).[20] Similarly, PSC decisions, especially those contained in subsequent communiqués such as those relating to the YPS and human rights, peace, and security, are potential foundations to custom amongst its Member States.

It should be noted that due to the wide ambit of the APSA, the chapter will focus on the roles of the PSC and the Continental Early Warning System (CEWS) that are at the forefront of mainstreaming both youth and human rights into conflict prevention and peace building. Nonetheless it is important to discuss all the elements of the architecture, albeit briefly, specifically to intimate us on how they interact in their contribution to the evolving AU law.

[18] Of the 55 Member States, 43 have signed while 39 have ratified and deposited with the AU.

[19] P-M Dupuy, 'Soft law and the international law of the environment' (1990) 12(2) Michigan Journal of International Law 424.

[20] M Olivier, 'The relevance of "soft law" as a source of international human rights' 2002 35(3) The Comparative and International Law Journal of Southern Africa 289–307.

2. The Africa Peace and Security Architecture: Composition and Roles

The APSA is built around structures, objectives, principles, and values, as well as decision-making processes relating to the prevention, management, and resolution of crises and conflicts, post-conflict reconstruction, and development on the continent.[21] The APSA comprises five elements built around the PSC and contributes to the effective functioning of the said Council to discharge its functions of promoting peace and security in Africa. These are the AU Commission (AUC), the Panel of the Wise (PoW), the Continental Early Warning System (CEWS), the African Standby Force (ASF), and the Peace Fund. Also, integral to the architecture are RECs/RMs and the international community including AU organs as well as the UN and its agencies.[22]

The APSA elements have been broadly categorized along the lines of either being conflict prevention or conflict management tools, or being within or outside the AU.[23] Clearly our discussions refer to the elements within the AU and those in the conflict prevention category. While these have been classified to include the PSC and CEWS elsewhere, the chapter posits that the AUC and the Peace Fund also straddle this categorization. Thus, each pillar of the APSA has an existing or potential role in preventing conflicts.[24] It is also important to note that the AU adopts a human security conceptualization of peace and security thus issues of democracy, human rights, and governance feature prominently.[25] While several Shared Values Instruments draw the links between socio-economic factors and conflicts on the continent,[26] the AU is developing a Human Security Development Index that will take cognizance of the specificities of African countries to strengthen peace and contribute to achieving development agendas.[27] It is within these contexts that the roles of the APSA elements are discussed in this and subsequent sections of this chapter. It focuses on how they contribute to the evolution of norms, facilitate and promote and monitor implementation of these norms.

[21] AU, Protocol Relating to the Establishment of the Peace and Security Council of the African Union, preface, July 2002.

[22] ibid.

[23] AL de Albuquerque, 'The African Peace and Security Architecture (APSA) – Discussing the remaining challenges', FOI-R-4301-SE (2016) available at <https://observatoire-boutros-ghali.org/sites/default/files/APSA.pdf> accessed 28 December 2019.

[24] G de Carvalho, 'Conflict prevention: What's in it for the AU? [2017] ISS Policy Brief 103.

[25] S Dersso, 'The quest for Pax Africana: The case of the African Union's peace and security regime' (2012) 12(2) AJCR 11.

[26] See for examples, the Constitutive Act of the African Union, Preamble, para 9 and the African Union Non-aggression and Common Defence Pact, Preamble, para 9.

[27] African Union, Press Release: AU AND UN Join Efforts towards Developing an African Human Security Index, 5 March 2020 available at <https://au.int/en/pressreleases/20200305/au-and-un-join-efforts-towards-developing-african-human-security-index> accessed 11 August 2020.

The AUC, the secretariat of the AU, led by its Chairperson, plays a significant role in coordinating the activities of its composite departments and reporting to the PSC on issues related to peace and security. It also plays a critical role in contributing to the evolution of AU law. For example, the Chairperson sends election observation monitors to elections in Member States. These missions, which include officers from the DPA and PSD, provide critical information to the Chairperson to understand the intricacies, dynamics, and outcomes of elections in Member States. These are integrated into reports – either directly from the Chairperson of through the DPA/PSD – to the PSC during the Council's sessions related to the issue.[28] This enables the PSC to take stock of elections – and their peace and security implications – on the continent and to make the necessary pronouncements and/or follow-up actions taking into consideration the African Charter on Democracy, Elections and Governance (ACDEG), the AU treaty on the subject matter.

The PoW is composed of five highly respected African individuals appointed by the AU Chairperson from various segments of society who have made outstanding contribution to the cause of peace, security, and development on the continent.[29] The Panel is to support the efforts of the AU Chairperson and the PSC in the prevention of conflicts.[30] The provision of the PSC Protocol above clearly refers to the role of the PoW as a conflict prevention mechanism, which is broader than the common reference to the Panel as a mediation-oriented body. Amongst other things, the PoW is required to regularly brief the PSC on potential threats and crises to enable Council to take timeously appropriate decisions.[31] The Panel also produces reports based on annual thematic issues it takes on to highlight issues that may be considered 'under the radar'.[32] In addition to shedding light on the issue, the report also comes to the attention of the PSC that makes pronouncements and gives policy direction that contribute to the evolution of relative normative framework.

[28] This may be briefings to the PSC on elections, conflict prevention, or the state of peace and security in Africa. See, for example, Communiqué of the 869th meeting of the PSC, held on 19 August 2019, on Elections in Africa for the period January to December 2019 (PSC/PR/COMM.(DCCCLXIX).

[29] Article 11(2) of the PSC Protocol.

[30] ibid Article 11(4).

[31] The 577th meeting of the Peace and Security Council of the AU on early warning. See also communiqué PSC/PR/COMM.(CCCLX) on the Full Use of All Available Tools in Preventive Diplomacy, adopted at its 360th meeting held on 22 March 2013, as well as communiqué PSC/PR/COMM.(CDLXIII) on structural conflict prevention, adopted by Council at its 463rd meeting held on 27 October 2014.

[32] African Union Panel of the Wise, 'Election-related disputes and political violence: strengthening the role of the African Union in preventing, managing, and resolving conflict', Report of the AU Panel of the Wise (New York, International Peace Institute, African Union, 2010); African Union Panel of the Wise, 'Peace, justice, and reconciliation in Africa: opportunities and challenges in the fight against impunity', Report of the AU Panel of the Wise (New York, International Peace Institute, African Union, 2013); African Union Peace and Security Council and Panel of the Wise, 'Expert report on eliminating vulnerabilities of women and children in armed conflicts', Addis Ababa, 2014; and African Union Panel of the Wise, 'Strengthening Political Governance for Peace, Security, and Stability in Africa', Final Report, Addis Ababa, 2012.

The CEWS comprises a Situation Room housed in the CPEWD – the forefront of the AU's approaches to conflict prevention[33] – and adopts a similar structure in the regional organizations with an interphase with the former that enables data and information gathering, analysis, and sharing.[34] CEWS/CPEWD play critical roles in providing the mechanisms for processed analysis reaching the right decision-making bodies, primarily the AUC Chairperson and the PSC.[35] This also includes scheduled progress report briefings on the state of conflict prevention in Africa to the PSC through bi-annual horizon-scanning methods. CEWS continually upgrades its data collection systems to take contemporary conflict indicators into consideration, including human rights, as will be discussed in subsequent sections of this chapter.[36] This is a critical aspect of actualizing normative principles as will be discussed using the mainstreaming of human rights as a case study. Importantly, CEWS trains and conducts refresher training exercises for RECs/RMs, AU organs, and CSOs including youth organizations that either provide information and/or use the systems for early warning at regional and/or country level.

The Peace Fund was established in 1993 to be the principal financing instrument for the (then) Organization for African Unity's (OAU) peace and security activities. In 2016, AU Assembly of Heads of State and Government decided to endow the Peace Fund with $400 million in Member State contributions to be drawn from the 0.2% levy that has been instituted to finance the overall AU budget.[37] Funding from the Peace Fund will be around the three thematic windows of Mediation and Preventive Diplomacy, Institutional Capacity, and Peace Support Operations. While the first two clearly indicate the conflict prevention credentials of the Fund, it remains unclear how the funds will be disbursed in reality. Thus far, administrative procedures are ongoing to institutionalize oversight and operational structures to ensure strong accountability and financial governance for the effective, transparent, and prudent use of resources.

The African Standby Force (ASF) is based on standby arrangements with Africa's five regions. The force, conceptualized as a quick response mechanism for the AU, is to be composed of multidimensional capabilities, including military, police, and civilian, on standby in their countries of origin and ready for rapid deployment. Regional capacities to contribute to make the force a reality remain at different stages, thus delaying its operationalization.[38] Meanwhile there are several ad hoc

[33] de Carvalho (n 24).

[34] Article 21(1) and (2) of the PSC Protocol.

[35] ibid Article 12(5).

[36] Climate change and gender are other contemporary thematic subjects that have received attention recently with CEWS at different stages of the process of including these in the datasets.

[37] L Louw-Vaudran, 'A new financing model for the AU: will it work?' (*ISS Today*, 25 July 2016) available at <https://issafrica.org/iss-today/a-new-financing-model-for-the-au-will-it-work> accessed 29 December 2019.

[38] Assembly of the Union, Twenty-sixth Ordinary Session held in Addis Ababa on 30–31 January 2016, Assembly/AU/Dec.589(XXVI)).

military intervention forces operating across the continent in response to regional security challenges including the Multinational Joint Task Force (MNJTF), Group of Five Sahel Joint Force, and RCILRA (the Regional Co-operation Initiative for the elimination of the Lord's Resistance Army). When effective, the ASF is expected to carry out several kinds of operations including preventive deployment to prevent a dispute or a conflict from escalating, an ongoing violent conflict from spreading to neighbouring areas or states, and the resurgence of violence after parties to conflict have reached an agreement. As conflict prevention broadly covers situation of containing conflicts and preventing them from escalating, the ASF also has conflict prevention mandates.

In addition to the five elements discussed above, there are other essential stakeholders that are integral to the APSA. These include RECs/RMs and Member States,[39] the primary beneficiaries of the APSA. RECs/RMs and Member States are integral to the process of norms developing to become 'law' as their adoption and operationalization of PSC decisions are essential to the evolution process. As will be highlighted subsequently using the examples of mainstreaming human rights and youth into conflict prevention, some decisions of the PSC have implications at the regional and national level that generate new methodologies and practices. These, when operationalized by Member States have the added potential to become customary practice and thereby contribute to the body of laws of the Union.

Other stakeholders to the APSA expressly mentioned in the PSC Protocol include international organizations and other organs of the AU including the Pan-African Parliament and the African Commission on Human and Peoples' Rights as well as CSOs.[40] Collaboration with the UN and its agencies, amongst several other international organizations have contributed to the funding and operationalization of the APSA elements. Recently, as will be discussed in more detail, CEWS has benefitted from collaborations with the UN and its agencies as well as the World Bank. Specifically, the UN Office of the High Commissioner on Human Rights – East Africa Regional Office (OHCHR-EARO) – is the lead technical partner alongside the World Bank in the CEWS project to enhance the latter's collection and analysis of data using a human rights-based approach (HRBA) methodology.

3. APSA Contributions to AU Law: Norms-Setting and Operationalization in the Peace and Security Arena

As noted in the previous section of the chapter, norm-setting and operationalization underlie the development of AU law and the APSA is central to these, at least within the peace and security sphere. This section interrogates the roles played by these

[39] See Articles 16(1) and 13(17) of the PSC Protocol.
[40] ibid Articles 18–20.

APSA elements based on their mandates, competencies, and priorities. It will focus particularly on the roles played by the PSC (the core of the APSA), CEWS, and its administrative host department (PSD) and division (CPEWD), as well as the ACHPR to reflect on how they have influenced developments in the two themes of mainstreaming human rights and youth into peace and security. The discussions in this section reveal the significance of the roles played by the APSA elements to the development of AU law.

Briefly, the PSC as the standing decision-making organ on matters of peace and security plays a vital role in dictating the direction and priorities of the peace and security agenda. These (direction and priorities) sometimes derive from decisions of the Assembly of Heads of State as with the case of the two thematic issues – human rights and youth – discussed in this chapter.[41] The African Charter on Human and Peoples' Rights and the African Youth Charter provide the legal foundations for the evolution of norms to express and expand on the relevance and imperatives of mainstreaming human rights and youth respectively into the peace and security arena. As subsequent discussions will reveal, elements of the APSA – particularly the PSC and the CEWS – have relied on these instruments as the basis for evolving norms and practice in the spheres of human rights and youth mainstreaming into peace and security which have the potential to contribute to AU law.

PSC decisions – either contained in communiqués or press briefings – have two outcomes that are relevant to this discussion. First, PSC decisions signal that a certain issue has received the political blessing of the decision-making organ, a step that is important to drive administrative initiatives and activities the Peace and Security Department. Second, PSC decisions mandate the Commission (often through the PSD as with the case studies in this chapter) to adopt particular methodologies or carry out specific initiatives and activities. In other words, the decisions of the PSC may either contribute to the development of normative principles or initiatives/activities in furtherance of them. Notably, the PSC also plays a role in monitoring and evaluation of adherence to both normative principles and initiatives. The Council via its sessions, particularly the thematic sessions such as those on human rights and youth, enables stock-taking on those specific topics.

The PSD is fundamental to the implementation of norms in the peace and security arena being the department within the AUC primarily responsible for the operationalization of the APSA. Although the department is composed of four divisions, focus will be on the CPEWD. The division hosting CEWS provides immediate administrative direction and supervision for both the Human Rights and

[41] The African Youth Charter was endorsed by the Seventh Ordinary Session of the Assembly of Heads of State and Government on 2 July 2006 in Banjul, The Gambia while the African Charter was prepared following Decision 115 (XVI) of the Assembly of Heads of State and Government at its Sixteenth Ordinary Session held in Monrovia, Liberia, 17–20 July 1979.

Y4P Africa Program clusters with responsibilities to mainstream human rights and youth into conflict prevention, respectively. The Human Rights Cluster's main focus is to promote the adoption of human rights-based approach to the entire spectrum of early warning operations; that is, data collection for analysis, dissemination, and storage. This approach recognizes the role of human rights at conceptual and practical levels; that is to integrate human rights considerations into the working methodologies and to adopt a human rights approach to data management, respectively. The significance of the latter should not be lost especially when underscored by the reality of that the essence of CEWS is to collect, analyse, and disseminate data collected based on the methodologies referred.

The Y4P Africa Program was inaugurated to advance the active and sustained participation of youth in the peace and security arena, both in terms of the continental agenda and that of the AUC. With the growing youth demographic, the essence of integrating them into peace and security endeavours has become necessary as they are not only active in the field – either as those in the forefront of activities that contribute to insecurity but even more so as partners to advance peace and security measures. Although the Program has its origins and administration rooted in the CPEWD, it has a departmental and inter-departmental approach to its functionality. In other words, the Program comprises task force members that are drawn from other divisions of the PSD as well as other departments of the AUC including DPA/AGA Secretariat and the Department of Human Resources, Science and Technology (HRST) – particularly its Youth Division as well as the AUC Chairperson's Special Envoy on Youth (Office of the Youth Envoy).

The following sections will discuss how the APSA elements act and interact in the development and operationalization of norms that underlie AU law. The discussion runs along thematic lines of human rights and youth, respectively.

4. Human Rights, Peace, and Security: Normative Background

The African Charter is often discussed for its contributions to international human rights law due to its express recognition of second- and third-generation rights.[42] More recently, the PSC has referred to the Charter to underscore its decision to adopt a human rights-based approach to conflict prevention. While the African Charter provides the basis for substantive human rights, it also underpins the evolution of norms in the human rights arena. To achieve the main function of the

[42] Justice Nwobike, 'The African Commission on Human and Peoples' Rights and the demystification of second and third generation rights under the African Charter: Social and Economic Rights Action Center (SERAC) and the Center for Economic and Social Rights (CESR) v. Nigeria' (2005) 1(2) African Journal of Legal Studies 129–46. See also, F Coomans, 'The *Ogoni* case before the African Commission on Human and Peoples' Right' (July 2003) 52(3) International and Comparative Law Quarterly 749–60.

ACHPR, which is to promote the operationalization of the Charter, it is mandated to, amongst other things, cooperate with other African and international institutions concerned with the promotion and protection of human and peoples' rights and ensure the protection of human and peoples' rights under conditions laid down by the African Charter.[43] In this regard, the PSC is one of such African institutions that is instrumental in enabling the ACHPR achieve its main objective. Conversely, the PSC is to seek close cooperation with the ACHPR in all matters relevant to the latter's objectives and mandate.[44] In other words, the PSC and the ACHPR must collaborate to ensure the protection and promotion of human rights including towards conflict prevention.

The intrinsic links between human rights and peace and security in Africa is well established in AU normative documents including the AU Constitutive Act,[45] Protocol Relating to the Establishment of the Peace and Security Council of the African Union,[46] and Agenda 2063 amongst others. Agenda 2063 succinctly highlights the link via aspiration 4 which is themed 'A peaceful and secure Africa'. Article 34 states that to achieve a peaceful and secure Africa by 2063, the continent shall have '[a]n entrenched and flourishing culture of human rights, democracy, gender equality, inclusion and peace'. The links are further underscored via Article 35 that lists necessary preconditions for a peaceful and conflict-free continent. It states that good governance, democracy, social inclusion, and respect for human rights, justice, and the rule of law are prerequisites to attaining a prosperous, integrated, and united Africa. There is a salient point to note regarding the reference to 'an entrenched and flourishing culture' in Article 34. This provision may be interpreted broadly to refer to the methodology of achieving human rights rather than a narrow interpretation of adhering to provisions on substantive human rights. This is, as will be highlighted in the subsequent parts of this section, what mainstreaming human rights in conflict prevention seeks to achieve. Of course, this intent captures the essence of Article 35 that recognizes how the respect for human rights (broadly interpreted) is one of the prerequisites for peaceful and secure continent.

While the above and other related provisions may be regarded as aspirational statements, the process of actualizing them entails a process wherein these norms are transformed to standard practice, which over time have the potential to contribute to the 'body of laws' of the AU and its Member States. This section discusses in detail the roles the APSA elements play and how their interaction contributes to the evolution of AU law. Specifically, it highlights the roles played by the PSC, CPEWD-PSD (via the human rights mainstreaming cluster), and the ACHPR to

[43] Article 45 of the African Charter. See also Article 3(f), 4(c), 7(1)(m).
[44] Article 19 of the PSC Protocol.
[45] See particularly Preamble, para 9.
[46] See particularly the Preamble and Articles 3 and 4.

reflect how individual and collaborative efforts of these APSA elements align to contribute to the development of AU law.

5. Operationalizing Norms: APSA Elements

The core theme of the 866th meeting of the PSC in consultation with the ACHPR was the issue of mainstreaming human rights in all phases of the conflict cycle – from prevention to post-conflict situations – in Africa. The PSC made critical decisions that build on the established human rights norms with the intent to operationalize them. Some of these decisions impacts on the work already done within the PSD-CPEWD through its human rights cluster. The work of the latter will be briefly highlighted to provide the background necessary to understand how the PSC/ACHPR session and its outcomes has contributed to the evolving AU law.

The human rights cluster's main objective, as previously noted, is to mainstream human rights into conflict prevention. To achieve this rather broad objective, the cluster prioritized working on a methodology that would ensure that CPEWD's early warning processes would be underpinned by a human rights-based approach. Thus, the first phase entailed two elements: first, to mainstream human rights into CEWS' conflict prevention analytical tools, and second, to adopt a human rights-based approach to data (HRBAD). Imperatives of the HRBAD approach include participation, disaggregation, self-identification, transparency, privacy, and accountability. The HRBAD promotes the informed participation of data providers, protection of their identity and data collected, as well as the disaggregation of data to enable better understanding of inequalities that have been identified as a significant root cause of conflicts in Africa.

The next phase of the project aims to boost the regional capacities and partnerships of AU-CEWS' primary stakeholders (the AU analysts, RECs/RMs, as well as CSOs that feed into and analyse CEWS' datasets) on strengthening the links between conflict prevention and response through a human rights-based approach to data, including collection, analysis, and dissemination. The project integrates a wide range of actors from within and outside the AU[47] in consonance with provisions of the PSC Protocol.[48] Articles 7(j) and (k) particularly envisages the participation of RECs/RMs and CSOs in peace and security matters but also aims to promote close cooperation and partnerships with them. In essence, methodologies to bring to life aspirations of the AU and PSC are systematic and underlined by

[47] From the AU were various departments of the Commission including the DPA, Department of Social Affairs, Office of the Legal Counsel; and organs of the AU including the Committee of Experts on Rights and Welfare of the Child and the African Commission on Human and Peoples' Rights. RECs/RMs, the National Association of National Human Rights Institutions (NAHRI) and networks of Civil Society Organizations (CSOs). Technical partners included the UN OHCHR-EARO and the World Bank Group that also provided resource support through its Global Program for Reintegration Support (GPRS).

[48] See Articles 7(j) and (k) of the PSC Protocol.

existing norms. The point being made here is that the process of norms evolving itself goes through a process that promotes participation and ownership by stakeholders with ramifications including the capacity to influence Member States to recognize and/or be held accountable for the principles that the norms in question enunciate.

Depending on the situation, the stakeholders differ but usually include RECs/RMs and CSOs. The roles these actors play are fundamental in the process of translating norms into practice. First, their active involvement in the process of the evolution of norms ensures they are aware and understand its essence and shape them to take into cognizance regional and national peculiarities. Secondly, these actors play important advocacy roles as they bring the norms to the attention of Member States' institutions to recognize them through practice and/or through the process of legally adopting them. Either way, RECs/RMs and CSOs play fundamental roles in bringing norms closer to the attention and practice of Member States, an important part of laws developing within the AU.

6. Norms Evolution and Operationalization: The Centrality of the PSC

Having considered the role and contributions of the PSD/CPEWD, the role of the PSC is considered here. Focus is on how the PSC interacts with the other APSA elements – including the ACHPR – to advance the evolution and operationalization of norms. Two decisions emanating from the PSC's 866th meeting are noteworthy with regards the evolution of norms and practice on mainstreaming human rights into conflict prevention. They are to have human rights and peace and security as a standing thematic agenda of the PSC, and for the PSC to receive regular briefings from the African Commission. These decisions will promote the requisite flow of information that is critical to making future policy decisions as well as taking stock of the implementation of extant ones. The latter will necessarily include the progress that has been made in implementing extant norms at various levels including the AUC, ACHPR, RECs/RMs, and ultimately Member States. This will include the progress made regarding the mainstreaming of human rights into conflict prevention by the PSD-CPEWD. Furthermore, having the subject matter as a standing thematic agenda of the PSC puts it, and related issues, in the spotlight of the highest decision-making organ of the AU on peace and security matters. Thus, the potential exists not only to mainstream human rights into conflict prevention at institutional level – continental and regional – but also at Member State level.

There is also considerable merit and purpose in the PSC decision that the PSC and ACHPR communicate decisions on peace and security issues with particular focus on human rights, to each other, while ensuring coherence and complementarity in decision-making processes. This suggests that the decisions in the Communiqué of the 866th meeting and future decisions of the PSC will form the basis upon which the ACHPR will consider issues before it. In other words, ACHPR pronouncements on communications before it – including those related to mainstreaming human rights into peace and security – should be influenced by PSC decisions. Conversely, decisions reached by the ACHPR will influence conversations in the Council and have an impact on the pronouncements from the highest decision-making organ in the peace and security arena. With regards to mainstreaming human rights into conflict prevention specifically, it is not wrong to posit that the ground is set to ensure that policy and judicial pronouncements are in tandem and will continually benefit from each other, thereby evolving and operationalizing normative principles.

Indeed, the decisions contained in the Communiqué following the 866th meeting held jointly with the ACHPR has signalled how the collaboration will contribute to the evolution of norms and their operationalization. With regard to the evolution of norms, the PSC necessarily took note of existing normative underpinnings including the PSC Protocol and the African Charter, both of which formed the basis of the decisions that emanated from the meeting. In terms of operationalizing the norms promoting the mainstreaming of human rights into conflict prevention, the PSC requested the AU Commission to ensure the inclusion in its reports and briefing notes to the PSC of a section highlighting human rights issues of concern and in the conflict early warning indicators amongst others. The 'request' to the AUC is in practice a mandate to the latter to carry out a specific decision. There are two requests contained in the communiqué that expressly placed the responsibility on the AUC (via the PSD/CPEWD/CEWS) to ensure that the normative decisions are operationalized.

First, the PSC requested that the early warning reports and other briefings from the PSD/CPEWD/CEWS to it must thereafter include a section that highlights human rights issues in conflict situations. By this request, the PSC has added a new element to the expected contents of reports it is bound to receive in accordance with the PSC Protocol. Article 12(4) of the PSC Protocol that lists the indicators that CEWS should use to underpin their analysis, reports, and recommendations to the PSC include 'clearly defined and accepted political, economic, social, military and humanitarian indicators'. Thus, the decision either adds a new layer or highlights the necessity to expressly include human rights either as a sub-stratum of the social indicator or as a crosscutting one that is present in all the listed indicators. While both options recognize the importance of human rights in conflict analysis, the latter option will ensure that the analyses on all indicators are more nuanced. This option has more potential to achieve the intent of the PSC's request that relevant reports and briefings presented to the PSC from 2020 onwards must include 'human rights of concern in conflict situations'.[49]

[49] Communiqué of the 866th meeting of the PSC held on 8 August 2019 on its consultation with the African Commission on Human and Peoples' Rights (ACHPR) PSC/PR/COMM.(DCCCLXVI). Article 7.

Second is the request from the PSC that CEWS includes human rights as an indicator in its early warning tools. While this is fundamental to CEWS ability to include 'human rights of concern' adequately and effectively in its reports to the PSC, the fact that that it is now a PSC mandate means that progress made in this regard must be reported to the Council. As a matter of fact, the PSC will expect to be provided updates as the occasions arise – including from its next human rights session. Even though, as noted earlier, the PSD/CPEWD/CEWS had initiated the process of integrating human rights indicators into its data collection tools before the 866th Session of the PSC, the impact of this decision is considerable. First, if PSD/CPEWD/CEWS reports to the PSC in a future session (horizon scanning on conflict prevention, for instance) contained progress reports on its human rights thematic group's work regarding mainstreaming human rights into conflict prevention, Council would take cognizance and commend them for taking such an approach. However, the dynamics change with a PSC decision as the Council will now, as of right, require updates with regards the operationalization of decisions contained in the communiqué issued after its 866th meeting. Put differently, the political acknowledgement and pronouncements from the PSC imposes added responsibility on the PSD/CPEWD/CEWS to ensure the operationalization of the mandate as well as the duty to report on progress to Council.

Notably, by the same token the PSC decision has provided the requisite political voice and processes necessary to guide the other APSA elements and stakeholders in the development and operationalization of norms in the human rights, peace, and security arena. The decision provides the requisite motivation to galvanize relevant stakeholders – AU organs, the ACHPR, AUC departments, as well as international and development partners – to play their roles in implementing the normative principles that promote norms development and operationalization. Actions from these stakeholders will have a direct impact on recognition of the mainstreaming of human rights into peace and security, particularly conflict prevention, among Member States.

From the international partners, there are two related outcomes. The partners would be encouraged to provide the requisite resource support to the AU to progress with the mainstreaming of human rights agenda as well as keeping the issue on the agenda. In this regard, the World Bank and OHCHR are keen to provide the necessary support to ensure that progress is made on the agenda with the second phase of the project that is to focus on building RECs/RMs and CSO capacities. The involvement of RECs/RMs and CSOs – integral partners to the functioning of CEWS – has the added advantage of integrating the methodology into the regional systems as well as bringing it even closer to Member States. RECs/RMs and CSOs are integral to the development and operationalization of norms as well as the process of Member States adopting them. Further, CSOs as primary drivers of advocacy processes have the capacity to influence Member States with regards recognizing and adopting the HRBA methodology in the peace and security arena while promoting accountability at both intergovernmental and Member States levels. Hence, over the next few years, the expectation is that Member States will also begin to absorb the methodology into their systems alongside the continental and regional organizations.

However, whether there exist effective mechanisms to ensure, or even measure, compliance with Member States adopting the HRBA methodology in the peace and security field is a different matter entirely. The PSC needs to take stock of what becomes of its decisions, especially, as in this case, those that require action from the secretariat of the AU. While thematic sessions of the Council provide an opportunity to provide feedback, these are not necessarily in-depth and subject to rigorous interrogation and critique. Also, the formality of the sessions may sometimes deprive of critical sentiments that may be necessary to effectively advance the subject matter. In the interim, the annual thematic sessions on human rights and peace and security provide an avenue to highlight relevant issues including developments at continental, regional, and national levels.

Nonetheless, these PSC sessions provide an opportunity for the relevant AU stakeholders including AU organs, Member States, development partners, and CSOs to present statements on their priorities, initiatives, activities, opportunities, and challenges. While these tend to be relatively short political statements, they provide insights into an institution's position on and plans towards a thematic issue presented by the AU. These often enable conversations between the AU and its partners to advance thematic issue, including the operationalization of existing norms and the development of new ones thereby contributing to evolving practices and law.

7. Youth, Peace and Security –Normative Background

The YPS agenda is gaining attention on the continent. This is not to suggest that the role of youth in Africa – and in peace and security particularly – is a novel one. Rather, the point being made is that policy-makers and organs are increasingly recognizing that young people have immense potential, creativity, and energy that must be harnessed to optimize the opportunities they offer in the peace and security arena. Put succinctly, youth roles as viable and active partners are increasingly being recognized on the continent. The recognition of youth roles in peace and security in Africa is well established in normative frameworks, primarily the African Youth Charter (AYC), that was adopted in 2006. Specifically, Article 17 of the AYC encourages the involvement of youth in peace and security efforts. In essence, the AU has, since 2006, recognized its youth as partners in peace and security, even before the UN resolutions that popularized youth roles in peace and security with both Security Council Resolutions (UNSCR) 2250[50] and 2419.[51] While UNSCR 2250 recognizes that young people play an important and positive role in the maintenance and promotion of international peace and security, UNSCR 2419 focuses on increasing the role of youth in negotiating and implementing peace agreements as well as the UN Youth 2030 Strategy.[52]

At the continental level, normative frameworks recognize the role young people have to play in contributing to peace and security in Africa. These include the AU Constitutive Act, the Protocol Relating to the Establishment of the Peace and Security Council of the AU (Article 20), as well as aspirations 4 and 6 of Agenda 2063 that explicitly recognize the agency of youth as drivers of development, peace, and security. In 2017, the adoption of a youth-focused theme of the year – 'Harnessing the Demographic Dividend through Investments in the Youth'[53] – laid the foundation for the mainstreaming of youth in the programmes of the AUC.[54]

8. Operationalizing Norms: APSA Elements

The inauguration of the Youth for Peace (Y4P) Africa Program in September 2018 was the significant milestone in the process to purposefully mainstream youth into the peace and security arena from the AUC. The overarching mandate of the Y4P Africa Program is to 'implement all relevant AU, regional and international instruments relating to the role of the youth in the promotion of peace and security in Africa', while changing the dominant but patently wrong narrative that 'African youth are the harbingers of violence'.[55] The Y4P Africa Programme is both intra- and inter-departmental as well as cross-institutional in its operations, with a task force that draws membership from all the PSD divisions as well as from other departments, including the DPA/AGA Secretariat, HRST (Youth Division), and the AU Chairperson's Youth Envoy. The task force also includes focal points from the RECs/RMs which promotes the integration of youth programming into the regional peace and security arena. Notably, the regional institutions have collaborated with the AU Y4P Program to actualize youth for peace national networks

[50] Adopted by the Security Council at its 7573rd meeting, on 9 December 2015.
[51] Adopted by the Security Council at its 8277th meeting, on 6 June 2018.
[52] The UN launched its strategy 'Youth 2030: Working with and for Young People' on 24 September 2018.
[53] Assembly/AU/Dec.591 (XXVI) – adopted by the 26th Ordinary Session of the AU Assembly held in Addis Ababa, Ethiopia from 30 to 31 January 2016.
[54] Communiqué 807 of the PSC, PSC/PR/COMM. (DCCCVII), 8 November 2018.
[55] ibid.

chapters as is the case with ECOWAS in Nigeria and Cote d'Ivoire[56] and with IGAD in Ethiopia in collaboration with the Ministry of Peace.[57]

In the first year since its operations, the Y4P Africa Program has achieved notable outcomes that have contributed to the recognition of youth as partners in peace and security. Most relevant to our discussion is the Program's successful pursuit of a dedicated PSC session on the theme 'Youth, Peace and Security'. The process to achieve the PSC session is indicative of how the APSA elements at the AUC collaborate to develop and actualize norms. Interaction and collaboration with other APSA stakeholders, particularly RECs/RMs and CSOs, have also influenced the redefinition of the YPS agenda at the continental level and increasingly so, at the regional and national levels as this section reveals.

9. Norms Evolution and Operationalization: The Centrality of the PSC

The first PSC YPS session was held on 8 November 2018 in commemoration of the Africa Youth Day. The PSC took cognizance of the Y4P Africa Program's role in promoting the YPS agenda in Africa and made decisions that are shaping the evolution and operationalization of norms on YPS. Four decisions are highlighted in this regard. They are the Council urging Member States to develop national action plans for the implementation of UNSCR 2250; the Council requesting the Commission to finalize the continental framework on YPS; the Council appointing five regional Africa youth ambassadors for peace (AYAP); and the Council conducting a study on the roles and contributions of youth to peace and security in Africa.[58]

The PSC's call on Member States to develop national action plans for the implementation of UN Resolution 2250 (2015) reveals how international norms permeate the national realm. By encouraging Member States to adopt national plans, the PSC is advocating, even if indirectly, the development of custom with regards YPS. Indeed, some of the continental norms on YPS further enunciate the intent of the UN Resolution 2250 (2015) thus in creating national action plans for the security council resolution, Member States are also doing so for relevant continental norms. The PSC requested the Commission to expedite the finalization of a Framework on YPS for consideration by the relevant AU policy organs as early

[56] ECOWAS, 'ECOWAS, AU Convene Youth Dialogue in Nigeria Towards the Promotion of Peace and Security' available at <https://www.ecowas.int/ecowas-au-convene-youth-dialogue-in-nigeria-towards-the-promotion-of-peace-and-security/> accessed 23 July 2020.

[57] AU, Youth for Peace Ethiopia: Cross-Regional Dialogue and Experience Sharing Workshop available at <https://au.int/en/newsevents/20191126/youth-peace-ethiopia-cross-regional-dialogue-and-experience-sharing-workshop> accessed 23 July 2020.

[58] Communiqué 807 of the PSC, PSC/PR/COMM. (DCCCVII), 8 November 2018.

as possible. The framework has two main objectives. First, to facilitate the meaningful engagement and participation of African youth in all spectrums of peace and security at national, regional, and continental levels. Second, to institutionalize accountability mechanisms for the systematic monitoring and reporting on the implementation of key decisions on YPS agenda in Africa.

In other words, the framework seeks to adopt a uniform methodology to promote the YPS agenda in Africa with a systematic approach to accountability. Again, this aims to promote custom, even if indirectly, by encouraging a uniform methodology for Member States and African inter-governmental organizations to approach the YPS Agenda. Although the framework is an AU-led initiative, RECs/RMs and CSOs (mainly youth representatives) are integral to the process to ensure their ownership. As noted previously, these stakeholders are critical to promote awareness, adoption, and reporting from relevant regional and Member State authorities.

To further highlight the role the PSC plays in the evolution and operationalization of norms, it is pertinent to note that work had already begun in developing the continental framework prior to the PSC's first YPS session. However, as with the discussion on mainstreaming human rights into conflict prevention in the previous section, as soon as the PSC lent their voice to the process, it immediately placed a responsibility on the Commission (working through the Y4P Africa Program) to prioritize it and report back on the progress made. The PSC mandated the AUC to conduct a continental study on the role and contributions of youth to peace and security. Specifically, the PSC requires the study to be empirical document that outlines the roles, vulnerabilities, and opportunities with regards youth participation in Africa's peace and security arena with a view to develop appropriate policy responses. These policy decisions will not only mark progression with regards norms development in YPS but they will also impact their operationalization.

The PSC also decided to institutionalize an annual open session dedicated to the theme of 'Youth, Peace and Security in Africa' and ensure it appears in future sessions.[59] This decision underlies the future of the YPS agenda in Africa especially with regards norms development and operationalization because annual thematic sessions provide the opportunity for the PSC to focus on the progress, challenges, and opportunities on a particular theme. Further, it enables the Council to take stock on the implementation of its decisions as was the case during the second open session on YPS that was held on 15 November 2019.[60] Progress reports were presented on the study and Continental Framework on YPS while the five selected AYAPs were presented to the Council. A significant outcome of the second session

[59] ibid Article 15.

[60] AU Media Advisory: 2nd Open Session of the PSC on YPS in Africa, online: available at <https://www.peaceau.org/uploads/media-advisory-2nd-open-session-of-the-peace-and-security-council-on-youth-peace-and-security-in-africa-.pdf> accessed 23 July 2020.

was the PSC's decision to study both documents closely to ensure that they meet the expected standards as a prerequisite to adopting them. This reveals the collaboration that takes place between APSA elements in the furtherance of the development of norms and their eventual implementation. Equally fundamental to note is how the annual thematic sessions provide an opportunity for the PSC to interrogate outstanding issues and monitor developments with regards the implementation of its decisions. However, as already noted, the adequacy of these formal sessions to serve as effective mechanisms to measure compliance remains questionable.

Notably, the PSC had a third session on YPS on 23 June 2020 wherein it endorsed the study and the continental framework – including the latter's 10-year implementation plan.[61] A few points are particularly noteworthy from this meeting. First, the timing of the meeting – about midway before the next dedicated session in November – is a reflection of the positive inner workings and collaboration among the APSA elements. The meeting was a culmination of constant engagement and collaboration among the PSC, the PSC Committee of Experts, the PSC Secretariat, the Y4P Africa Program, and the RECs/RMs. Indeed, the working relationship as envisaged in the APSA framework was fundamental to maintaining YPS conversations and activities, especially within the AU, overcoming challenges including the change in membership of the PSC, the shift in peace and security priorities occasioned by the COVID-19 pandemic, as well as the consequent change in working methods evidences the APSA's working relationships.

The fundamental importance of the APSA collaboration was highlighted during the session as highlighted in the emanating communiqué wherein the PSC took cognizance of the fact that the continental framework and its 10-year implementation plan was a product of collaboration among the AU, RECs/RMs, and Youth. The PSC further expressed that the continental framework provides the normative guidance for Member States, RECs and RMs on the promotion of meaningful participation of youth in all areas of peace, security and development; the importance of ensuring that the AU takes full ownership of all processes relating to its implementation; and, encouragement to Member States to domesticate and implement the continental framework including the development of National Action Plans (NAPs) in accordance with national youth policies and national development plans with a view to address all challenges to effective youth participation in the promotion of peace and security in the Continent. Finally, the PSC recognized the role of international partners in supporting the AU to achieve the effective implementation of the Africa Youth Charter, as well as UN Resolutions 2250 (2015) and 2419 (2018).

[61] Communiqué 933 of the PSC, PSC/PR/COMM.(CMXXXIII), 23 June 2020.

The highlighted sections above reveal the expectations regarding the roles and responsibilities of actors required to drive and actualize the YPS agenda in Africa. For the AU, there are two fundamental responsibilities. The first, which has been discharged, is the development of the continental framework on YPS containing the guiding principles on the promotion and implementation of YPS in Africa. The second responsibility pertains to driving the implementation process of the continental framework which includes, but is not limited to, activities such as the advocacy to Member States, RECs, and RMs as well as providing requisite technical assistance as required. In essence, the AU will be the primary actor driving the YPS agenda in Africa. The RECs and RMs, in addition to being integral to the development the continental framework and its 10-year implementation plan, are now fundamental to propagating the framework and the plan to Member States to adopt and implement. The RECs and RMs will expectedly continue the collaboration with the AU on YPS to provide requisite support to Member States. The primary responsibility of Member States is to domesticate the documents with a view to promote their implementation, particularly through the adoption of NAPs as envisaged by the PSC.

Finally, the PSC recognized the role that its international partners play in providing support to the AU to promote the YPS agenda. International partners provided support – technical, human, and financial – to the consultation, drafting, and validation processes that culminated in the continental framework. Notably, the PSC referred to both AU and UN normative frameworks on YPS – the African Youth Charter as well as the UN Resolutions 2250 (2015) and 2419 (2018) – as due for implementation. This recognition indicates that the AU considers the normative frameworks on YPS in a holistic manner irrespective of the fact that the African Youth Charter predates both UN resolutions. Nonetheless, the frameworks are almost identical and the adoption of the continental framework is in fact actualizing the intent of the norms from both the AU and UN. It is noteworthy that both institutions – the AU and UN – are increasingly collaborating on the YPS agenda based on recent policy developments.[62]

10. Conclusion

This chapter analysed the interactive roles the APSA elements play in developing and operationalizing norms in the peace and security arena with case studies of two thematic areas, human rights and youth. The chapter revealed the centrality of the PSC, both in terms of being the core of the APSA as well as being fundamental to the evolution and operationalization of norms in the peace and security

[62] D Forti and P Singh, 'Toward a More Effective UN-AU Partnership on Conflict Prevention and Crisis Management', International Peace Institute and Institute for Security Studies, October 2019, 31.

arena. The Council's pronouncements, especially during special thematic sessions, have significant impacts including elevating the issues to gain political and technical traction and establishing new methodologies in furtherance of evolution and operationalization of norms.

The discussion on the two themes – mainstreaming human rights and youth into conflict prevention – illustrated how the PSC outcomes are central to the priorities and activities of the other APSA elements and stakeholders that contribute to norms development and operationalization, which contribute to the evolution of AU law. PSC thematic sessions provide the requisite political environment for the issue at stake to be brought to the fore for discussions among stakeholders including relevant AU organs and authorities, RECs/RMs, Member States, CSOs, as well as international and development partners. The PSC pronouncements that emanate from the meetings provide direction for all the stakeholders on the matter. For the AU PSD that bears the primary responsibility to operationalize decisions from the PSC, it may add new responsibilities. As discussed, it may involve the adoption of new methodologies as exemplified by the human rights cluster or carrying out specific activities as in the case of the Y4P Africa Program on youth mainstreaming into the peace and security arena. In both instances, the PSC decisions to have dedicated annual thematic sessions is a pathway to ensure a continuum with regards the development of normative principles, decisions to implement them as well as an avenue to report, monitor, and evaluate progress.

The interaction between and among APSA elements also makes significant contributions to the evolution and operationalization of norms. First, the PSD through its divisions and thematic clusters can and do play influential roles in bringing issues to the attention of the PSC. As highlighted with the Y4P Africa Program, lobbying for, and achieving, the first PSC open session on YPS has proved extremely instrumental to the evolution and operationalization of relevant norms. Having annual sessions on YPS and completing the framework on YPS to promote uniformity in integrating youth into the peace and security arena across the continent are steps that can propel good practice to custom. With the human rights mainstreaming, the interaction between the PSC and the ACHPR culminated in the joint session that enabled both organs to interrogate the nexus between human rights and peace and security. The decisions emanating from the session placed a bigger responsibility on PSD/CPEWD/CEWS. Not only do they now have to prioritize the adoption and integration of the human rights-based approach methodology but there is also the added responsibility to report back to the PSC on progress and challenges to enable future policy direction from the Council.

24

AU Law and Its Future: Reform and the Kagame Report

Femi Amao and Michèle Olivier

As AU law progresses into the future and takes its place among the legal systems created at the international level by international or supranational organizations, it is envisaged that the ideas and proposals expressed in this book will make significant contributions in several areas of its development. In the short term, the contributions will enhance legal debate amongst scholars and researchers of Africa as regards the evolving continental legal system. They will also influence decision-makers at both the Member States and the regional level. Furthermore, the ideas contained in this book will facilitate and pave the way for the incremental theoretical and systematic understanding of this emergent legal system and make a positive contribution towards achieving the objectives of the AU's Agenda 2063 and beyond. In the long run, key proposals from this book could very well shape decision-making, enhance the rule of law, empower Africa on the international stage, promote an investor-friendly environment with legal certainty and harmonization, and improve political accountability and the human security of ordinary Africans.

A key significance of the study of AU law, as presented in this collection, is that it has established a platform to examine legal developments in Africa from an Afrocentric perspective as opposed to the dominant Eurocentric/Western approach. The emergence of the AU legal system can be seen as a step away from the legal systems in Member States which remain hamstrung by the strong influences of colonialism. Thus, AU law can be seen as an effort to develop a modern legal order that is homegrown on the continent and takes into account the particular needs and aspirations of Africa and Africans. In fact, the legal order stemming from AU law could be regarded as a tangible and direct response to the need to find African solutions to African problems, a mantra that is prominent in the AU and its institutions. The development gives the continent 'ownership' of the legal system which will be an important driver towards greater accountability and legitimacy as it moves forward.

At the heart of the AU legal order is the Constitutive Act. In his contribution, Amao described the Constitutive Act as a social contract and a constitutional instrument governing distribution and allocation of powers within the AU. The

Femi Amao and Michèle Olivier, *AU Law and Its Future: Reform and the Kagame Report* In: *The Emergent African Union Law*. Edited by: Olufemi Amao, Michèle Olivier and Konstantinos D. Magliveras, Oxford University Press. DOI: 10.1093/oso/9780198862154.003.0025

argument in this book is not that an *acquis communautaire* similar to the European Union (EU) has been achieved by the Act but that the AU legal system is gradually moving in that direction. The norms and standards that are developing around the Constitutive Act as explored in this book are evidence of this trajectory. It is acknowledged that the AU and its institutions will need robust support for the legal system to flourish and its success will depend on Member States' political will, as many of the contributors argued.

The contributions to this volume presented some of the notable advancements that have been made to date in relation to normative development and standard setting at the AU level in areas such as human rights, economic integration, harmonization, and democratic governance. Amao noted in his contribution that new and significant norms are emerging under the AU legal order. These norms include non-indifference, intervention in Member States' internal affairs, the rejection of unconstitutional change of government, the protection of human rights and fundamental freedoms, the responsibility to protect, and democratic constitutionalism. With respect to human rights, Naldi argued persuasively in his contribution that human rights agreements adopted by the AU (and the OAU) paved the way for an AU law to emerge and develop an African conceptualization of human rights. Mwankwo in his contribution on the problem of statelessness explored ways in which human rights norms could be used to tackle the issue. Garrido and Balde examined the positive impact of human rights norms on the right to education.

In relation to the rejection of unconstitutional change of government, Omorogbe in her contribution recognized the advancement that the AU has made in relation to the framework to deter coups d'état. These comprise a robust legal framework and a zero-tolerance policy. The framework is reinforced by the creation of a novel regional crime of unconstitutional change of government, which has been brought under the jurisdiction of the African Court of Justice and Human Rights. Omorogbe contended that these measures are building blocks in the progressive development of the AU legal system that could ultimately support decisive and enforceable action, though implementation so far has been weak.

A discourse around AU law would necessarily raise the question of whether there are parallels between AU law and EU law. Though the legal order established by the AU cannot be directly comparable to the well-established EU legal order, however and to a limited extent, it is incrementally exhibiting similar traits. Magliveras observed in his contribution that the AU has not been granted competences which are comparable to the EU. Nonetheless, it could be argued that such competences are inferred from Articles 3 and 4 of the Constitutive Act setting out the AU objectives and principles, as well as from Articles 9 and 13 on the functions of the Assembly and the Executive Council. To remove any ambiguity and to expand the scope of the AU's competences, Magliveras suggested that a revision of the Constitutive Act will be needed. He further argued that the entry into force of the Continental Free Trade Area Agreement (AfCFTA) and the adoption of the

Protocol on the Free Movement of Persons are evidence of this need. Magliveras and Olivier share the view that the AU's constitutive instruments needs clear provisions that define its competence in relation to these instruments.

The suggestion for the revision or reform of the AU Constitutive Act by Magliveras is a theme echoed by many of the chapters in this volume. The quest for legitimacy, the need for institutional reform, and the requirement of financial independence feed into the reform agenda of the AU contained in the Kagame report.[1] The commissioning of the Kagame Report shows that African leaders recognize the need for reform in order to make progress. Law and legal systems are never static because of the constant need to respond to political, moral, social, economic, and technological changes. Therefore, reform or revision is an ever-present theme in the discourse around legal systems. A new and evolving legal system, like the AU, will necessarily undergo constant changes on its way to maturity. African leaders should be prepared for this and accept it as an eventuality.

Keeping in line with the theme of reform that runs throughout this book, Omorogbe called for further revision of the regime governing unconstitutional change of government to address the challenge faced when incumbent heads of state refuse to leave office after their term expires or when they lose elections. Omorogbe persuasively argued for the revision of the AU definition of unconstitutional change of government to specifically include regimes which remain in power through undemocratic means. Such an approach, she contended, would widen the scope of the coverage of the governing framework and also potentially made enforcement easier.

Some of the chapters offered innovative proposals for reform that could possibly impact on the future of AU legal order. For instance, in order to improve dispute resolution and advance AU law in the private arena, Osuji and Taiwo have suggested the need for a viable African alternative dispute resolution (ADR) model that is centred around arbitration for private disputes. The authors argue in favour of a legal framework for arbitration which will take into account the pan-African perspective in the provision of its arbitration processes and ensure adequate institutional support for the recognition and enforcement of arbitral awards across the continent. They argue further that their proposed system fits the African context, has legitimacy, and fosters investment confidence and commercial activities.

Another innovative and unique proposal was made by Otabor-Olubor in his contribution in relation to business registration. Otabor-Olubor made the proposal for the harmonization of business registration procedures through the vehicle of an AU Business Registration Agreement. This is significant and would advance some of the work that has been done at the level of the Organisation for the Harmonisation of Corporate Law in Africa which is applicable in several Member

[1] Summarized in this chapter.

States. What this proposal would do, if implemented, is to create a registration or incorporation mechanism at continental level which could in turn widen market access for businesses. This would be important in the context of the AU development agenda and the implementation of the AfCFTA.

Writing from the perspective of harmonization of tax regulations, Onyejekwe proposed a specially designed Model Law on Taxation for the AU which could be used as a foundation to achieve not only the goals of Agenda 2063 but also to finance the AU itself. This would build on existing policies and successes of several sub-regional and Regional Economic Communities (RECs). According to the author, the Model Law would act as a vehicle to solidify the integration agenda and set the continent towards a path of sustainable growth and development.

In his chapter and in the context of financial regulation, Iglesias-Rodriguez argues that AU law and institutions could play an important role in enhancing the position of Africa in the global financial standard-setting. This would require the operationalization of financial markets and institutions proposed in Agenda 2063. According to the author, this would lead to the establishment of a distinct architecture of AU financial supervision alongside AU Member States' financial supervision. The AU financial architecture would serve as the umbrella for coordinating among and with Member States' financial supervisors thereby having a stronger voice and presence on the global stage.

Dawar and Lipimile argued, in their chapter, that in relation to competition law, the AU is best placed to put in place minimum requirement competition principles advancing regulatory developments at the regional and state levels. The authors noted the need for guidance and coordination to harmonize the diverse approaches that Member States are taking in relation to competition regulation. Given the fact that significant developments are happening at the AU level, especially in relation to the AfCFTA Agreements, the authors contended that there is a need to ensure that competition law is designed by Member States in a manner that is consistent with these developments.

Apart from the theme of reform, another recurring theme that emerges from the contributions to this volume is the need to address the lack of enforcement and effective mechanisms for compliance with AU law. Though it is acknowledged that non-binding norms can, strictly speaking, form part of applicable laws, enforceability is crucial to the effectiveness and robustness of legal systems.

Magliveras and Olivier correctly argued in separate contributions that the lack of or weak enforcement is a glaring weakness in the realization of AU law. Magliveras noted further that in relation to Member States' obligations, the AU has in place an adequate and effective sanctioning system under Article 30 that could be used to compel compliance. However, that power of sanctions has not been used as envisaged. For example, Member States have routinely failed to meet their financial obligations to the AU and have largely ignored orders or judgments from the African Court on Human and Peoples' Rights that have gone against them. He therefore argues that the exercise of the sanctioning powers is necessary to improve compliance, and this would also help to consolidate AU law.

In a similar vein, Home analyses the challenge faced by the African Court on Human and Peoples' Rights in relation to enforcement of its judgments given in the context of land cases. He argued that Member States' compliance has to improve to enhance the prospect of the effectiveness of AU law.

The issue of enforcement is also of critical importance in the private domain. In his chapter, Simo addressed the issue of lack of enforcement of AU international economic law treaties by contracting parties. Simo explored the possibility of using the doctrine of direct effect, a key feature of EU law, to address this gap. The application of the doctrine or a similar provision would guarantee standing for private and legal persons to bring complaints before regional courts against contracting parties for violation of treaty obligations. This is currently absent in the AU economic law framework and in the broader AU legal system. In Simo's view, the failure of AU economic treaties to guarantee legal standing for private and legal persons weakens the AU legal order.

While most of the contributions in the book see harmonization as an important goal in strengthening African integration, other chapters, such as Oke's, suggested alternative methods. In the case of the Pan-African Intellectual Property Organization (PAIPO), because of the differential level of development in Member States he suggested that it might be more prudent to coordinate intellectual property rights among Member States rather than pursuing harmonization of the regulatory regime at a continental level.

Contributions to this volume clearly pointed to the need for further research on AU law and suggested the direction for such endeavours. For instance, Okoye, writing on customary law, suggested the need to embark on further detailed empirical research into traditional justice systems and customary law across Africa. This would facilitate a fuller grasp of commonalities and differences between the systems and laws and assist in efforts to harmonize customary law at the AU level. Further research in this regard would help in understanding better the different contexts in Member States as well as the interrelationship between customary law and AU fundamental principles such as human rights.

As previously noted, the call for AU reform is closely linked to discussion points raised in many of the chapters as it underlines the need to increase the AU's relevance and meet the imperatives of African integration. In furtherance of this objective, the Kagame Report on AU Reform, endorsed by the AU Assembly in January 2017,[2] calls for a more streamlined AU, which will necessitate significant organizational overhaul in the short to medium term. High expectations for a

[2] Report on the Implementation of the Decision on the Institutional Reform of the African Union available at <https://au.int/sites/default/files/documents/33272-doc-au_reform_implementation_report_july_2017_final_v2.pdf> accessed 13 February 2021.

potentially radical reform initiative are evident in AU Commission Chair Moussa Faki Mahamat's hope that it will be a starting point of a 'new African renaissance'.[3] However, given several African leaders' vested interests in maintaining the status quo, expectations are that the institutional reform is likely to be slow and progress incremental rather than revolutionary. Fears are that decisions on reform may remain ideals on the horizon reminiscent of the general reluctance to implement AU decisions that the Kagame Report indicates has become endemic in AU governance. As expected, not all Member States agree that the Kagame Report was produced in accordance with the AU's Constitutive Act. Some commentators suggest that the consensus of all AU Member States is needed for the successful implementation of reform initiatives but this is unlikely in the light of conflicting domestic agendas, the required financial discipline, and the possibility of job losses of AU officials. Member States, the AU Commission, and RECs have complained about a lack of consultation in the reform process. An inclusive process is vital to its success, especially when grappling with technical and financial issues such as the raising of extra resources through a proposed 0.2% import tax across the continent to make the AU more financially self-sufficient.[4]

The Kagame Report makes the following key findings: a chronic failure to implement AU decisions; the AU has limited relevance to African populations; an overdependence on non-African partner funding; the underperformance of some organs and institutions; limited managerial capacity; lack of accountability; unclear division of jurisdiction and functions between the AU Commission and RECs; and inefficient working methods of the AU Commission and the Assembly. It is suggested that the AU's focus be narrowed down to four areas, namely peace and security, political affairs, establishment of a continental free trade area, and a single voice and representation in global affairs. Although not mentioned by name in the report, AU law will facilitate the recommendations made by a Reform Implementation Unit set up by the AU Commission, particularly where elements of supranationalism and legitimacy are implied. These include the following: 'the adoption of a mechanism to ensure the implementation of legally binding decisions'; 'the strengthening and enforcement of a sanctions mechanism'; and 'the adoption of quotas for women and youth among AU staff and measures to ensure private sector participation'.[5]

Touching on aspects of sovereignty and supranationalism, lack of implementation, legitimacy deficit, and cumbersome and ineffective institutions, these recommendations underscore the need for AU law as discussed above. Hence the

[3] Speech of HE Moussa Faki Mahamat, Chairperson of the African Union Commission at the opening of the 29th AU summit in Addis Ababa on 3 July 2017.

[4] L Louw-Vaudran, 'ISS Today: With AU reforms, a 'new African Renaissance' is possible', *Daily Maverick* (11 August 2017).

[5] Seven Priorities for the African Union in 20018, Crisis Group Africa Briefing No135, 17 January 2018, 3.

Kagame Report's reference to the AU as being 'dysfunctional'. To pursue the reforms of the Kagame Report, the AU will indeed need to streamline its structures and governance procedures and to move towards closer economic integration. On the positive side, AfCFTA's emergence on 1 January 2021 presents a significant step forward towards the meeting of integration targets.

The Kagame Report speaks to the present context where the AU's executive structures present a stage for national governments to further their interests and no provision is made for executive scrutiny or any form of accountability. An opportunity for any direct democratic input would go a long way to address legitimacy issues.

The Kagame Report reiterates that the duplication of cumbersome institutions remains a concern. The status of the African Court of Justice and Human Rights and of the Pan-African Parliament (PAP) must be resolved if reforms are to be implemented. With the said Court's jurisdiction over disputes related to the interpretation of the Constitutive Act and other AU treaties, Member States are in no rush to agree to such accountability. Another factor deterring ratifications of the Protocol on the Statute of the African Court of Justice and Human Rights is the provision of Article 46, namely that Court decisions shall be binding on the parties and thus limit national sovereignty.

Suffice it to say that African leaders, who are at the same time members of the Assembly, will be reluctant to agree to grant supranational powers to a legislature and to a judiciary that would enable these bodies to take binding decisions and challenge the AU's executive bodies consisting of themselves. However, a fully operational legislature and a court system will only increase the AU's relevance to the African populations, promote the much-needed legitimacy, and galvanize the evolution of AU law.

The statement by President Kagame made at the 34th African Union Summit on 6 February 2021 presented an important opportunity to take stock of progress on institutional reform four years down the line.[6] Beside noting 'some good progress on the sustainable financing of the Union and the Peace Fund', progress on other tough issues such as reform of judicial organs, the Pan-African Parliament, the Commission structures, and the division of labour with Regional Economic Communities have all stalled. This state of play commands urgent reflection.

Given the recommendations from the Kagame Report and the ideas, perspectives, and reform proposals expressed in this book, it now up to the AU to muster the support needed to make the present reform initiative flourish into a renaissance

[6] Statement by President Paul Kagame Progress Report on the Institutional Reform of the African Union and on Domestic Health Financing 34th African Union Summit 6 February 2021 available at <https://au.int/sites/default/files/speeches/39953-sp-20210206_-_pres_kagame_34th_au_summit_-_as_delivered_1.pdf> 13 February 2021.

instead of flounder as just another expensive bureaucratic exercise whose principal driver might be to secure jobs at the AU's Headquarters.

On a final note, it is acknowledged that it is impossible to cover all aspects of AU law in one single volume, but this collection has provided a solid foundation upon which a second volume examining and analysing other themes within the AU legal system could be built.

Index

For the benefit of digital users, indexed terms that span two pages (e.g., 52–53) may, on occasion, appear on only one of those pages.

Note - Figures and maps are indicated by *f* and *m* following the page number